Microsoft® Visual Basic® 2008: RELOADED

Third Edition

Diane Zak

COURSE TECHNOLOGY
CENGAGE Learning™

Australia • Brazil • Japan • Korea • Mexico • Singapore • Spain • United Kingdom • United States

COURSE TECHNOLOGY
CENGAGE Learning™

Microsoft Visual Basic 2008:
RELOADED, Third Edition

Diane Zak

Executive Editor: Marie Lee

Acquisitions Editor: Amy Jollymore

Managing Editor: Tricia Coia

Editorial Assistant: Patrick Frank

Marketing Manager: Bryant Chrzan

Content Project Manager: Daphne Barbas

Art Directors: Bruce Bond/Marissa Falco

Cover Designer: Cabbage Design Company

Cover Photo: Cabbage Design Company

Manufacturing Coordinator: Julio Esperas

Proofreader: Wendy Benedetto

Indexer: Alexandra Nickerson

Compositor: International Typesetting
    and Composition

Title Editor: Linda Linardos

For product information and technology assistance, contact us at
Cengage Learning Customer & Sales Support, 1-800-354-9706

For permission to use material from this text or product, submit all requests online at **cengage.com/permissions**
Further permissions questions can be emailed to
permissionrequest@cengage.com

ISBN-13: 978-1-4239-0250-8

ISBN-10: 1-4239-0250-5

Course Technology
20 Channel Center Street
Boston, MA 02210
USA

Cengage Learning is a leading provider of customized learning solutions with office locations around the globe, including Singapore, the United Kingdom, Australia, Mexico, Brazil, and Japan. Locate your local office at: **international.cengage.com/region**

Cengage Learning products are represented in Canada by Nelson Education, Ltd.

For your lifelong learning solutions, visit **course.cengage.com**

Purchase any of our products at your local college store or at our preferred online store **www.ichapters.com**

Printed in China
3 4 5 6 7 12 11 10

TABLE OF CONTENTS

CHAPTER 2
CREATING A USER INTERFACE

CHAPTER 3

VARIABLES, CONSTANTS, AND ARITHMETIC OPERATORS 121

CHAPTER 4

MAKING DECISIONS IN A PROGRAM 183

CHAPTER 5

MORE ON THE SELECTION STRUCTURE

CHAPTER 6

CHAPTER 7
THE FOR...NEXT LOOP AND STRING MANIPULATION

CHAPTER 8

SUB AND FUNCTION PROCEDURES   409

CHAPTER 10
STRUCTURES AND SEQUENTIAL ACCESS FILES   527

CHAPTER 11
CREATING CLASSES AND OBJECTS

CHAPTER 12

WORKING WITH ACCESS DATABASES AND LINQ   657

THE FOLLOWING APPENDICES ARE AVAILABLE ELECTRONICALLY AT WWW.COURSE.COM.

PREFACE

Microsoft Visual Basic 2008: RELOADED, Third Edition uses Visual Basic 2008, an object-oriented language, to teach programming concepts. This book is designed for a beginning programming course; however, it assumes students have learned basic Windows skills and file management from one of Course Technology's other books that cover the Microsoft Windows operating system.

ORGANIZATION AND COVERAGE

Microsoft Visual Basic 2008: RELOADED, Third Edition contains 12 chapters and 5 appendices (A through E). Additional appendices covering Web applications, menus, collections, printing, locating syntax and logic errors, and Silverlight can be obtained electronically from the Course Technology Web site (*www.course.com*), and then navigating to the page for this book.

In the chapters, students with no previous programming experience learn how to plan and create their own interactive Windows applications. By the end of the book, students will have learned how to use TOE charts, pseudocode, and flowcharts to plan an application. They also will learn how to work with objects and write Visual Basic statements such as If...Then...Else, Select Case, Do...Loop, For...Next, and For Each...Next. Students also will learn how to create and manipulate variables, constants, strings, sequential access files, structures, classes, and arrays. In addition, they will learn how to connect an application to a Microsoft Access database, and then use Language Integrated Query (LINQ) to query the database. LINQ is the new query language feature built into Visual Studio 2008. The text also introduces students to OOP concepts and terminology.

Appendix A lists the names and locations of the How To boxes included in the chapters. The How To boxes summarize important concepts and provide a quick reference for students. Appendix B lists the most commonly used properties of the objects covered in the text. Appendix C contains the Visual Basic conversion functions, and Appendix D recaps the GUI design rules mentioned in the chapters. Appendix E provides an introduction to LINQ to SQL.

APPROACH

Like the previous editions, *Microsoft Visual Basic 2008: RELOADED, Third Edition* focuses on programming concepts. The concepts are introduced using simple examples, and are then utilized in larger applications. The completed application files are provided to the instructor. A Programming Tutorial appears after the concepts section in each chapter. The Programming Tutorial guides students through the process of creating an application. With the exception of Chapter 1, the applications in the Programming Tutorials are games. Game applications are used because research shows that the fun and exciting nature of games helps motivate students to learn. A Programming Example follows the Programming Tutorial. The Programming Example is a completed program that demonstrates the concepts taught in the chapter. Following the Programming Example are the Quick Review, Key Terms,

Self-Check Questions and Answers, Review Questions, Review Exercises—Short Answer, Computer Exercises, and Case Projects sections. In response to instructor feedback, most of the Case Projects now include a sample interface.

FEATURES

Microsoft Visual Basic 2008: RELOADED, Third Edition is an exceptional textbook because it also includes the following features:

» **Objectives.** Each chapter begins with a list of objectives so you know the topics that will be presented in the chapter. In addition to providing a quick reference to topics covered, this feature provides a useful study aid.

» **How To boxes.** The How To boxes in each chapter summarize important concepts and provide a quick reference for students. For instance, the steps for performing a task (such as starting Microsoft Visual Studio 2008 or adding a control to a form) are listed in a How To box. Likewise, when a new statement or method is introduced, the student will find its syntax in a How To box along with examples of using the syntax.

» **Tip.** Tips provide additional information about a concept, such as an alternate way of performing a task.

» **Programming Tutorials.** A Programming Tutorial follows the concepts section in each chapter. The Programming Tutorial gives students step-by-step instructions on using the chapter's concepts to create and program a game application.

» **Complete Programming Examples.** After the Programming Tutorial in each chapter is an example of a completed program. The Programming Example shows the TOE chart and pseudocode used to plan the program, as well as the user interface, Object/Property/Setting chart, and Visual Basic 2008 code. The Programming Example demonstrates the concepts covered in the chapter.

» **Quick Review.** Following the Programming Example in each chapter is a Quick Review, which recaps the concepts covered in the chapter.

» **Key Terms.** Following the Quick Review in each chapter is a collection of all the key terms found throughout the chapter, along with their definitions.

» **Self-check Questions and Answers.** Following the Key Terms section in each chapter is the Self-check Questions and Answers section. This section helps students determine whether they understand the chapter's concepts.

» **Review Questions, Review Exercises—Short Answer, and Computer Exercises.** Following the Self-check Questions and Answers are the Review Questions and Review Exercises—Short Answer sections. These sections provide meaningful, conceptual questions and exercises that test students' understanding of what they learned in the chapter. The next section contains Computer

Exercises, which provide students with additional practice of the skills and concepts they learned in the chapter.

» **Discovery Exercises.** Discovery Exercises are designated by a "discovery" icon in the margin. These exercises encourage students to challenge and independently develop their own programming skills while exploring the capabilities of Visual Basic 2008.

» **Debugging Exercises.** One of the most important programming skills a student can learn is the ability to find and fix problems in an existing application. The Debugging Exercises are designated by the "debugging" icon in the margin and provide an opportunity for students to detect and correct errors in an existing application.

» **Case Projects.** At the end of each chapter are four Case Projects. The Case Projects give the student the opportunity to independently synthesize and evaluate information, examine potential solutions, and make recommendations. Most of the Case Projects include a sample interface.

» **Think Tank Case Projects.** The last Case Project in each chapter is designated by the "Think Tank" icon. The Think Tank Case Projects are more challenging than the other Case Projects.

» **Glossary.** A glossary is included at the end of the book. The glossary lists all the key terms in alphabetical order, along with definitions.

INSTRUCTOR RESOURCES

All of the resources available with this book are provided to the instructor on a single CD-ROM. Many also can be found at the Course Technology Web site (*www.course.com*).

» **Electronic Instructor's Manual.** The Instructor's Manual that accompanies this textbook includes additional instructional material to assist in class preparation, including items such as Sample Syllabi, Chapter Outlines, Technical Notes, Lecture Notes, Quick Quizzes, Teaching Tips, Discussion Topics, and Additional Case Projects.

» **ExamView®.** This textbook is accompanied by ExamView, a powerful testing software package that allows instructors to create and administer printed, computer (LAN-based), and Internet exams. ExamView includes hundreds of questions that correspond to the topics covered in this text, enabling students to generate detailed study guides that include page references for further review. The computer-based and Internet testing components allow students to take exams at their computers, and also save time for the instructor by grading each exam automatically.

» **PowerPoint Presentations.** This book comes with Microsoft PowerPoint slides for each chapter. These are included as a teaching aid for classroom presentation, to make available to students on the network for chapter review, or to be printed for classroom distribution. Instructors can add their own slides for additional topics they introduce to the class.

» **Data Files.** Data Files are necessary for completing many of the Programming Tutorials and Computer Exercises in the book. The Data Files are provided on the Instructor Resources CD-ROM and may also be found on the Course Technology Web site at *www.course.com*.

» **Solution Files.** Solutions to end-of-chapter Review Questions, Review Exercises—Short Answer, Computer Exercises, and Case Projects are provided on the Instructor Resources CD-ROM and also may be found on the Course Technology Web site at *www.course.com*. The Solution Files also include the applications that appear in the concepts section in each chapter; these applications are used to illustrate the concepts being taught. The solutions are password protected.

» **Distance Learning.** Course Technology offers online WebCT and Blackboard courses for this text to provide the most complete and dynamic learning experience possible. When you add online content to one of your courses, you're adding a lot: automated tests, topic reviews, quick quizzes, and additional case projects with solutions. For more information on how to bring distance learning to your course, contact your local Course Technology sales representative.

ACKNOWLEDGMENTS

Writing a book is a team effort rather than an individual one. I would like to take this opportunity to thank my team, especially Tricia Coia (Managing Editor), Daphne Barbas (Production Editor), and the Quality Assurance testers who carefully test each chapter. Thank you for your support, enthusiasm, patience, and hard work. I could not have completed this project without you. Last, but certainly not least, I want to thank the following reviewers for their invaluable ideas and comments: Rachelle Kristof Hippler, Bowling Green State University Firelands; Susan Mahon, Collin County Community College; Lawrence Eric Meyer Jr, Miami Dade College—Kendall; Joshua Pauli, Dakota State University; Elaine Seeman, East Carolina University.

—*Diane Zak*

READ THIS BEFORE YOU BEGIN

TO THE USER

DATA FILES

You will need data files to complete some of the tutorials and exercises in this book. Your instructor will provide the data files to you. You also can obtain the files electronically from the Course Technology Web site (*www.course.com*), and then navigating to the page for this book.

Each chapter in this book has its own set of data files, which are stored in a separate folder within the VbReloaded2008 folder. The files for Chapter 1 are stored in the VbReloaded2008\Chap01 folder. Similarly, the files for Chapter 2 are stored in the VbReloaded2008\Chap02 folder. Throughout this book, you will be instructed to open files from or save files to these folders.

You can use a computer in your school lab or your own computer to complete the Programming Tutorials, Programming Examples, Computer Exercises, and Case Projects in this book.

USING YOUR OWN COMPUTER

To use your own computer to complete the material in this book, you will need the following:

» A Pentium® 4 processor, 1.6 GHz or higher, personal computer running Microsoft Windows. This book was written using Microsoft Windows Vista. It was Quality Assurance tested using Microsoft Windows Vista and Microsoft Windows XP.

» Microsoft Visual Studio 2008 installed on your computer. This book was written using Microsoft Visual Studio 2008 Professional Edition, and Quality Assurance tested using Microsoft Visual Studio 2008 Express and Professional Editions. If your book came with a copy of Microsoft Visual Studio 2008 (Express or Professional), then you may install that on your computer and use it to complete the material.

FIGURES

The figures in this book reflect how your screen will look if you are using Microsoft Visual Studio 2008 Professional Edition and a Microsoft Windows Vista system. Your screen may appear slightly different in some instances if you are using another version of Microsoft Visual Studio, Microsoft Visual Basic, or Microsoft Windows.

VISIT OUR WORLD WIDE WEB SITE

Additional materials designed for this textbook might be available through the Course Technology Web site, *www.course.com*. Search this site for more details.

TO THE INSTRUCTOR

To complete some of the Programming Tutorials and Computer Exercises in this book, your users must use a set of data files. These files are included on the Instructor's Resource CD. They also may be obtained electronically through the Course Technology Web site at *www.course.com*. Follow the instructions in the Help file to copy the data files to your server or standalone computer. You can view the Help file using a text editor such as WordPad or Notepad. Once the files are copied, you should instruct your users how to copy the files to their own computers or workstations.

The Programming Tutorials, Programming Examples, Computer Exercises, and Case Projects in this book were Quality Assurance tested using Microsoft Visual Studio 2008 (Express and Professional) on a Microsoft Windows (Vista and XP) operating system.

COURSE TECHNOLOGY DATA FILES

You are granted a license to copy the data files to any computer or computer network used by individuals who have purchased this book.

AN INTRODUCTION TO VISUAL BASIC 2008

After studying Chapter 1, you should be able to:

Define the terminology used in programming

Create a Visual Basic 2008 Windows-based application

Manage the windows in the Integrated Development
    Environment (IDE)

Set the properties of an object

Add a control to a form

Use the Label, Button, and PictureBox tools

Enter code in the Code Editor window

Save a solution

Start and end an application

Print an application's code and interface

Write an assignment statement

Close and open an existing solution

Find and correct a syntax error

PROGRAMMERS

Although computers appear to be amazingly intelligent machines, they cannot yet think on their own. Computers still rely on human beings to give them directions. The directions are called **programs**, and the people who write the programs are called **programmers**. Programmers make it possible for us to communicate with our personal computers; without them, we wouldn't be able to use the computer to write a letter or play a game. Typical tasks performed by a computer programmer include analyzing a problem statement or project specification, planning an appropriate solution, and converting the solution to a series of instructions that the computer can follow.

According to the 2006–07 Edition of the Occupational Outlook Handbook (OOH), published by the U.S. Department of Labor's Bureau of Labor Statistics, "When hiring programmers, employers look for people with the necessary programming skills who can think logically and pay close attention to detail. The job calls for patience, persistence, and the ability to work on exacting analytical work, especially under pressure. Ingenuity, creativity, and imagination also are particularly important when programmers design solutions and test their work for potential failures.... Because programmers are expected to work in teams and interact directly with users, employers want programmers who are able to communicate with nontechnical personnel." If this sounds like you, then you probably have what it takes to be a programmer. But if it doesn't sound like you, it's still worth your time to understand the programming process, especially if you are planning a career in business. Knowing even a little bit about the programming process will allow you to better convey your company's needs to a programmer.

But if you are excited about the prospect of working as a computer programmer, here is some information on employment opportunities. According to the Bureau of Labor Statistics, computer programmers held about 455,000 jobs in 2004. Computer programmers are employed in almost every industry. You will find large numbers of programmers working for telecommunications companies, software publishers, financial institutions, insurance carriers, educational institutions, and government agencies. The Bureau of Labor Statistics predicts that employment of programmers will grow up to 8% between 2004 and 2014. "As organizations attempt to control costs and keep up with changing technology, they will need programmers to assist in conversions to new computer languages and systems. In addition, numerous job openings will result from the need to replace programmers who leave the labor force or transfer to other occupations such as manager or systems analyst." However, there will be a great deal of competition for programming jobs, so jobseekers will need to keep up to date with the latest programming languages and technologies. According to the OOH, median annual earnings of computer programmers were $62,890 in May 2004. The OOH also reports that, "According to the National Association of Colleges and Employers, starting salary offers for graduates with a bachelor's degree in computer science averaged $50,820 a year in 2005." You can find more information about computer programmers on the Bureau of Labor Statistics Web site at *www.bls.gov*.

PROGRAMMING LANGUAGES

Just as human beings communicate with each other through the use of languages such as English, Spanish, Hindi, and Chinese, programmers use a variety of special languages, called **programming languages**, to communicate with the computer. Some popular programming languages are Visual Basic, C#, C++, and Java. In this book, you will use the Visual Basic 2008 programming language.

Visual Basic 2008 is an **object-oriented programming language**, which is a language that allows the programmer to use objects to accomplish a program's goal. An **object** is anything that can be seen, touched, or used; in other words, an object is nearly any *thing*. The objects used in an object-oriented program can take on many different forms. For example, programs written for the Windows environment typically use objects such as check boxes, list boxes, and buttons. A payroll program, on the other hand, might utilize objects found in the real world, such as a time card object, an employee object, and a check object. Every object used in an object-oriented program is created from a **class**, which is a pattern or blueprint that the computer uses to create the object. You will learn more about object-oriented programs later in this book.

Visual Basic 2008 is available as a stand-alone product (called Visual Basic 2008 Express Edition) or as part of Visual Studio 2008.

VISUAL STUDIO 2008

Visual Studio 2008 is Microsoft's newest integrated development environment. An **integrated development environment** (**IDE**) is an environment that contains all of the tools and features you need to create, run, and test your programs. Included in Visual Studio 2008 are the Visual Basic 2008, Visual C++ 2008, and Visual C# 2008 programming languages. You can use the languages available in Visual Studio 2008 to create Windows-based or Web-based programs, referred to as **applications**. A **Windows-based application** has a Windows user interface and runs on a desktop computer. A **user interface** is what you see and interact with when using an application. Examples of Windows-based applications include graphics programs, data-entry systems, and games. A **Web-based application**, on the other hand, has a Web user interface and runs on a server. You access a Web-based application using your computer's browser. Examples of Web-based applications include e-commerce applications available on the Internet and employee handbook applications accessible on a company's intranet. In this chapter, you will learn how to create Windows-based applications. Web-based applications are covered in a later chapter.

SOLUTIONS, PROJECTS, AND FILES

Windows-based applications created in Visual Studio 2008 are composed of solutions, projects, and files. A **solution** is a container that stores the projects and files for an entire application. A **project** also is a container, but it stores files associated with only a specific piece of the solution. Although the idea of solutions, projects, and files may sound confusing, the concept of placing things in containers is nothing new to you. Think of a solution as being similar to a drawer in a filing cabinet. A project then is similar to a file folder that you store in the drawer, and a file is similar to a document that you store in the file folder. You can place many file folders in a filing cabinet drawer, just as you can place many projects in a solution. You also can store many documents in a file folder, similar to the way you can store many files in a project. Figure 1-1 illustrates this analogy.

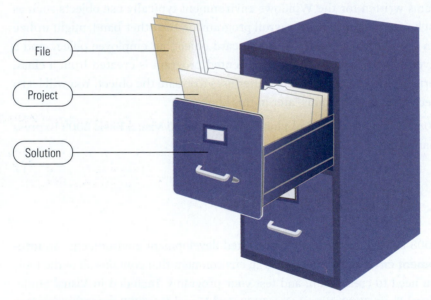

Figure 1-1: Illustration of a solution, project, and file

STARTING MICROSOFT VISUAL STUDIO 2008

Figure 1-2 shows the steps you follow to start Microsoft Visual Studio 2008, which is the version of Visual Studio used in this book. As mentioned in the Read This Before You Begin section of this book, you are not expected to follow the steps listed in the How To boxes right now. The How To boxes provide a quick reference that you can use when completing the Programming Tutorial, Programming Example, Computer Exercises, and Case Projects found at the end of each chapter.

»HOW TO . . .

START MICROSOFT VISUAL STUDIO 2008

1. Click the Start button on the taskbar, then point to All Programs.

2. Click Microsoft Visual Studio 2008, then click Microsoft Visual Studio 2008. (If the Choose Default Environment Settings dialog box appears, choose Visual Basic Development Settings, then click Start Visual Studio.)

Figure 1-2: How to start Microsoft Visual Studio 2008

When you start the Professional Edition of Microsoft Visual Studio 2008, your screen will appear similar to Figure 1-3; however, your Recent Projects list might include the names of projects or solutions with which you have recently worked. If you are using a different edition of Visual Studio, your startup screen might look slightly different than the one shown in Figure 1-3. As Figure 1-3 indicates, the IDE contains three windows: Start Page, Toolbox, and Solution Explorer.

Start Page window

Solution Explorer window

Toolbox window

Figure 1-3: Microsoft Visual Studio 2008 Professional Edition startup screen

»TIP

You also can use the Start Page to open the New Project dialog box. To do so, click Project..., which appears next to Create: in the Recent Projects list.

CREATING A VISUAL BASIC 2008 WINDOWS-BASED APPLICATION

Figure 1-4 shows the steps you follow to create a Visual Basic 2008 Windows-based application, and Figure 1-5 shows an example of a completed New Project dialog box.

»HOW TO . . .

CREATE A VISUAL BASIC 2008 WINDOWS-BASED APPLICATION

1. Start Microsoft Visual Studio 2008.
2. This step is necessary so that your screen agrees with the figures and steps in this book. Click Tools on the menu bar, then click Options to open the Options dialog box. Click Projects and Solutions. Verify that the following three check boxes are selected: Always show Error List if build finishes with errors, Always show solution, and Save new projects when created. Also verify that the Show Output window when build starts check box is not selected. Click the OK button.
3. Click File on the menu bar, then click New Project to open the New Project dialog box.
4. If necessary, expand the Visual Basic node in the Project types list, then click Windows.
5. If necessary, click Windows Forms Application in the Visual Studio installed templates section of the Templates list.
6. Enter an appropriate name and location in the Name and Location boxes, respectively.
7. If necessary, select the Create directory for solution check box.
8. Enter an appropriate name in the Solution Name box.
9. Click the OK button.

Figure 1-4: How to create a Visual Basic 2008 Windows-based application

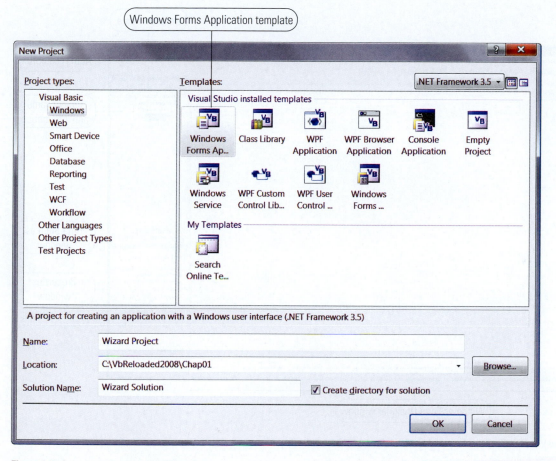

Windows Forms Application template

Figure 1-5: Completed New Project dialog box

A template is a pattern that Visual Studio uses to create solutions and projects. Each template listed in the Templates list includes a set of folders and files appropriate for the solution or project. When you click the OK button in the New Project dialog box, Visual Studio creates a solution and adds a Visual Basic project to the solution. It also records the names of the solution and project, as well as other information pertaining to the project, in the Solution Explorer window, as shown in Figure 1-6.

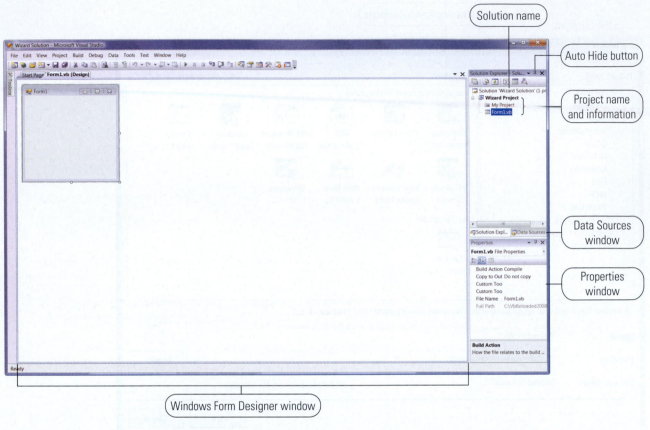

Figure 1-6: Solution and Visual Basic Project created by Visual Studio 2008

Notice that, in addition to the three windows mentioned earlier, three new windows appear in the development environment: the Windows Form Designer window, the Properties window, and the Data Sources window. Having so many windows open at the same time can be confusing, especially when you are first learning the IDE. In most cases, you will find it easier to work in the IDE if you either close or auto-hide the windows you are not currently using. You learn how to auto-hide a window in the next section.

MANAGING THE WINDOWS IN THE IDE

The easiest way to close an open window in the IDE is to click the Close button on the window's title bar. In most cases, the View menu provides an appropriate option for opening a closed window. Rather than closing a window, you also can auto-hide it. You auto-hide a window using the Auto Hide button (shown earlier in Figure 1-6) on the window's title bar. The Auto Hide button is a toggle button: clicking it once activates it, and clicking it again deactivates it. The Toolbox window shown earlier in Figure 1-6 is an example of an auto-hidden window. Figure 1-7 lists various ways of managing the windows in the IDE.

»HOW TO . . .

MANAGE THE WINDOWS IN THE IDE

» To close an open window, click the Close button on its title bar.

» To open a window, use an option on the View menu.

» To auto-hide a window, click the Auto Hide (vertical pushpin) button on its title bar. When you do this, the window is minimized and appears as a tab on the edge of the IDE.

» To temporarily display an auto-hidden window, place your mouse pointer on the window's tab.

» To permanently display an auto-hidden window, click the Auto Hide (horizontal pushpin) button on its title bar.

Figure 1-7: How to manage the windows in the IDE

In the next several sections, you will take a closer look at the Windows Form Designer, Solution Explorer, Properties, and Toolbox windows. You also will look at a new window: the Code Editor window.

THE WINDOWS FORM DESIGNER WINDOW

Figure 1-8 shows the **Windows Form Designer window**, where you create (or design) the graphical user interface, referred to as a **GUI**, for your project. Recall that a user interface is what you see and interact with when using an application.

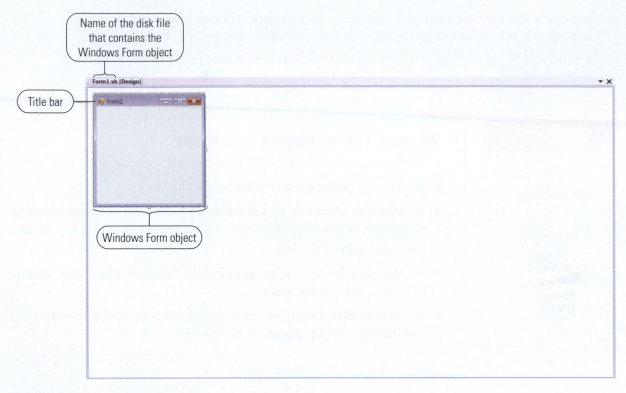

Name of the disk file that contains the Windows Form object

Title bar

Windows Form object

Figure 1-8: Windows Form Designer window

Only a Windows Form object appears in the designer window shown in Figure 1-8. A **Windows Form object**, or **form**, is the foundation for the user interface in a Windows-based application. You create the user interface by adding other objects, such as buttons and text boxes, to the form. Notice that a title bar appears at the top of the Windows Form object. The title bar contains a default caption—in this case, Form1—as well as Minimize, Maximize, and Close buttons.

At the top of the designer window is a tab labeled Form1.vb [Design]. [Design] identifies the window as the designer window. Form1.vb is the name of the file on your computer's hard disk (or on the device designated by your instructor or technical support person) that contains the Visual Basic instructions associated with the Windows Form object.

THE SOLUTION EXPLORER WINDOW

The **Solution Explorer window** displays a list of the projects contained in the current solution, and the items contained in each project. Figure 1-9 shows the Solution Explorer window for the Wizard Solution. The solution contains one project named Wizard Project. Within the Wizard Project is a My Project folder and a file named Form1.vb. The .vb on the filename indicates that the file is a "Visual Basic" source file. A **source file** is a file that contains program instructions, called **code**. The Form1.vb file contains the code associated with the Windows form displayed in the Windows Form Designer window. You can use the Code Editor window, which you will learn about later in this chapter, to view the contents of the Form1.vb file.

Show All Files button

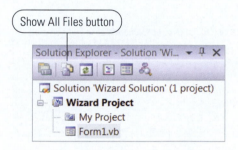

Figure 1-9: Solution Explorer window

TIP

The Wizard Project contains items in addition to the ones shown in Figure 1-9. To display the additional items, which typically are kept hidden, click the Show All Files button in the Solution Explorer window. To hide the items, click the Show All Files button again.

A file that contains the code associated with a Windows form is referred to as a **form file**. The code associated with the first Windows form included in a project is automatically stored in a form file named Form1.vb. The code associated with the second Windows form in the same project is stored in a form file named Form2.vb, and so on. Because a project can contain many Windows forms and, therefore, many form files, it is a good practice to give each form file a more meaningful name. Doing this will help you keep track of the various form files in the project. You can use the Properties window to change the filename.

THE PROPERTIES WINDOW

As is everything in an object-oriented language, a file is considered an object. Each object has a set of attributes that determine its appearance and behavior. The attributes, called **properties**, are listed in the **Properties window**. When an object is created, a default value is assigned to each of its properties. The Properties window shown in Figure 1-10 lists the default values assigned to the properties of the Form1.vb file contained in the Wizard Project.

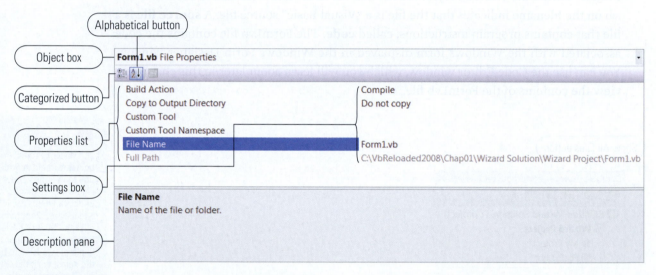

Figure 1-10: Properties window showing the properties of the Form1.vb file

As indicated in Figure 1-10, the Properties window includes an Object box and a Properties list. The **Object box** contains the name of the selected object; in this case, it contains Form1.vb, which is the name of the form file. The **Properties list** has two columns. The left column displays the names of the properties associated with the selected object. You can use the Alphabetical or Categorized buttons, which are located below the Object box, to display the property names either alphabetically or by category. The right column in the Properties list is called the **Settings box** and displays the current value, or setting, of each of the properties. For example, the current value of the File Name property shown in Figure 1-10 is Form1.vb. Notice that a brief description of the selected property appears in the Description pane located at the bottom of the Properties window. Depending on the property, you can change the default value by selecting the property in the Properties list, and then either typing a new value in the Settings box or selecting a predefined value from a list or dialog box. For example, to change the value of the File Name property from Form1.vb to Main Form.vb, you click File Name in the Properties list and then type Main Form.vb in the Settings box.

PROPERTIES OF A WINDOWS FORM

Like a form file, a Windows form also has a set of properties. To display the properties of a form in the Properties window, you first must select the form. You select the form by clicking it in the designer window. The Properties window in Figure 1-11 shows a partial listing of the properties of a Windows form. The vertical scroll bar on the Properties window indicates that there are more properties to view.

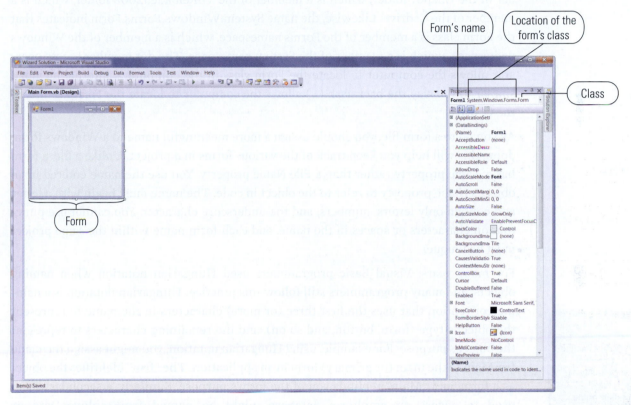

Figure 1-11: Windows form properties listed in the Properties window

Notice that Form1 System.Windows.Forms.Form appears in the Object box in Figure 1-11. Form1 is the name of the form. The name is automatically assigned to the form when the form is created. In System.Windows.Forms.Form, Form is the name of the class used to create the form. System.Windows.Forms is the namespace that contains the Form class definition. A **class definition** is a block of code that specifies (or defines) the appearance and behaviors of an object. All class definitions in Visual Studio 2008 are contained in namespaces, which you can picture as blocks of memory cells inside the computer. Each **namespace** contains the code that defines a group of related classes. The System.Windows.Forms namespace, for instance, contains the definition of the Form class. It also contains the class definitions for objects you add to a form, such as buttons and text boxes.

The period that separates each word in System.Windows.Forms.Form is called the **dot member access operator**. Similar to the backslash (\) in a folder path, the dot member access operator indicates a hierarchy, but of namespaces rather than folders. In other words, the backslash in the path C:\VbReloaded2008\Chap01\Wizard Solution\Wizard Project\Form1.vb indicates that the Form1.vb file is contained in (or is a member of) the Wizard Project folder, which is a member of the Wizard Solution folder, which is a member of the Chap01 folder, which is a member of the VbReloaded2008 folder, which is a member of the C: drive. Likewise, the name System.Windows.Forms.Form indicates that the Form class is a member of the Forms namespace, which is a member of the Windows namespace, which is a member of the System namespace. The dot member access operator allows the computer to locate the Form class in the computer's internal memory, similar to the way the backslash (\) allows the computer to locate the Form1.vb file on the C: drive.

As you do to a form file, you should assign a more meaningful name to a Windows form; doing this will help you keep track of the various forms in a project. Unlike a file, a form has a Name property rather than a File Name property. You use the name entered in an object's Name property to refer to the object in code. The name must begin with a letter and contain only letters, numbers, and the underscore character. You cannot use punctuation characters or spaces in the name, and each form name within the same project must be unique.

For many years, Visual Basic programmers used Hungarian notation when naming objects, and many programmers still follow this practice. Hungarian notation is a naming convention that uses the first three (or more) characters in the name to represent the object's type (form, button, and so on), and the remaining characters to represent the object's purpose. For example, using Hungarian notation, you might assign the name frmMain to the main (or primary) form in an application. The "frm" identifies the object as a form, and "Main" reminds you of the form's purpose. Similarly, a secondary form used to access an employee database might be named frmEmployeeData or frmPersonnel. However, Hungarian notation is not the only naming convention currently used by Visual Basic programmers. Many programmers now assign names that begin with the object's purpose, followed by the object's class; this is the naming convention used in this book. (Your instructor may have a different naming convention you are expected to use.) In addition, form names are entered using **Pascal case**, which means that the first letter in the name, as well as the first letter of each subsequent word in the name, is capitalized. Following this naming convention, you would assign the name MainForm to the main form in an application. "Main" reminds you of the form's purpose, and "Form" indicates the class used to create the form. Similarly, a secondary form used to access an employee database might be named EmployeeDataForm or PersonnelForm.

»TIP

Pascal is a programming language created by Niklaus Wirth in the late 1960s. It was named in honor of the seventeenth-century French mathematician Blaise Pascal, and is used to develop scientific applications.

»TIP

Visit *www.irritatedvowel. com/Programming/ Standards.aspx* for an interesting article on why Hungarian notation has fallen out of favor with many programmers.

In addition to changing the form's Name property, you also should change its Text property, which controls the caption displayed in the form's title bar. The caption also is displayed on the application's button on the taskbar while the application is running. The default caption, Form1, is automatically assigned to the first form in a project. Better, more descriptive captions include "Wizard Viewer", "Commission Calculator", and "Employee Information".

The Name and Text properties of a form always should be changed to more meaningful values. At times, you also may want to change the form's StartPosition property, which controls the location of the form when it first appears on the screen after the application is started. To display a form in the middle of the screen, you change its StartPosition property from WindowsDefaultLocation to CenterScreen.

You can use the form's Font property to change the type, style, and size of the font used to display the text on the form. A **font** is the general shape of the characters in the text. Segoe UI, Tahoma, and Microsoft Sans Serif are examples of font types. Font styles include regular, bold, and italic. The numbers 9, 12, and 18 are examples of font sizes, which typically are measured in points, with one **point** equaling 1/72 of an inch. For applications created for systems running Windows Vista, Microsoft recommends that you use the Segoe UI font, because it offers improved readability. Segoe is pronounced SEE-go, and UI stands for user interface. For most of the elements in the interface, you will use the 9-point size of the font. Applications created for systems running Windows XP typically use the 10- or 12-point Tahoma font.

»»TIP

The Name property is used by the programmer, whereas the Text property is read by the user.

THE TOOLBOX WINDOW

You use the **Toolbox window**, or **toolbox**, to add other objects (such as text boxes and buttons) to a form. The contents of the toolbox vary depending on the designer in use. The toolbox shown in Figure 1-12 appears when you are using the Windows Form designer. Notice that both an icon and a name identify each tool in the toolbox. The toolbox tabs allow you to view the tools by category or in alphabetical order by name. When you rest your mouse pointer on either the tool's name or its icon, the tool's purpose appears in a box, as shown in Figure 1-12.

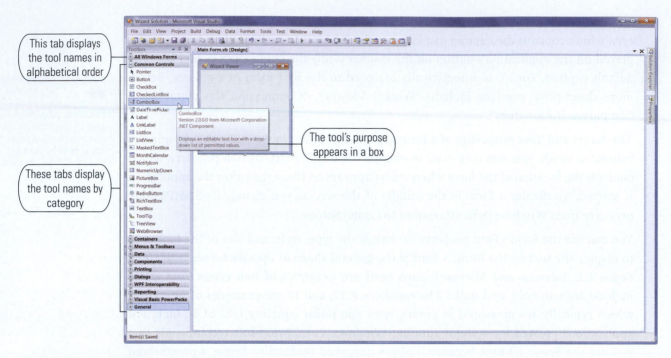

This tab displays the tool names in alphabetical order

These tabs display the tool names by category

The tool's purpose appears in a box

Figure 1-12: Toolbox window

The tools in the toolbox allow you to add objects, called **controls**, to a form. Figure 1-13 lists the steps for adding a control to a form.

»HOW TO . . .

ADD A CONTROL TO A FORM

1. Click a tool in the toolbox, but do not release the mouse button.

2. Hold down the mouse button as you drag the mouse pointer to the form. You will see a solid box, as well as an outline of a rectangle and a plus box, following the mouse pointer.

3. Release the mouse button.

   Additional ways:

   » Click a tool in the toolbox and then click the form.

   » Click a tool in the toolbox, then place the mouse pointer on the form, and then press the left mouse button and drag the mouse pointer until the control is the desired size.

Figure 1-13: How to add a control to a form

Controls on a form can be selected, sized, moved, deleted, locked (which prevents them from being moved inadvertently), and unlocked. When a control is locked, a small lock appears in the upper-left corner of the control. Figure 1-14 summarizes the methods used to manipulate the controls on a form.

MANIPULATE THE CONTROLS ON A FORM

» To select a control, click it in the designer window. You also can use the list arrow button in the Properties window's Object box.

» To size a control, use the sizing handles that appear on the control when it is selected.

» To move a control, drag the control to the desired location.

» To delete a control, select the control in the designer window, then press the Delete key on your keyboard.

» To lock and unlock the controls, right-click the form (or any control on the form), then click Lock Controls on the Context menu. The Lock Controls option is a toggle option: clicking it once activates it, and clicking it again deactivates it. You also can use the Lock Controls command on the Format menu.

Figure 1-14: How to manipulate the controls on a form

In the next three sections, you will learn about the Label control, the Button control, and the Picture box control, all of which appear in the user interface shown in Figure 1-15.

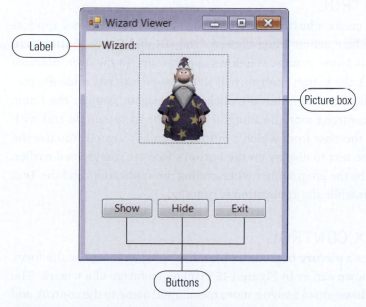

Figure 1-15: Wizard application's user interface

THE LABEL CONTROL

You use the Label tool to add a label control to a form. The purpose of a **label control** is to display text that the user is not allowed to edit while the application is running. Label controls are used in an interface to identify the contents of other controls, such as the contents of text boxes and list boxes. The label control in Figure 1-15 identifies the contents of a picture box control. Label controls also are used to display program output, such as the result of calculations.

You use the Name property to give a label control a more meaningful name. The name should end with the word Label, which is the class used to create a label control. You use the Text property to specify the text to display inside a label control. The Name property is used by the programmer when coding the application, whereas the Text property is read by the user while the application is running.

Some programmers assign meaningful names to all of the label controls in an interface, while others do so only for label controls that display program output; this book follows the latter practice. In the naming convention used in this book, control names are made up of the control's purpose followed by the control's class. Unlike form names, which are entered using Pascal case, control names are entered using **camel case**. This means that you lowercase the first word in the control's name and then uppercase the first letter of each subsequent word in the name, like this: salesTaxLabel. Notice that the uppercase letters, which are taller than the lowercase letters, appear as "humps" in the name.

THE BUTTON CONTROL

You use the Button tool to create a **button control**, which is used in Windows applications to perform an immediate action when clicked. The OK and Cancel buttons are examples of button controls found in most Windows applications. In the user interface shown earlier in Figure 1-15, the button controls will show the picture box, hide the picture box, and exit the application when they are clicked. Here again, you use the Name property to give a button control a more meaningful name. The name should end with the word Button, which is the class from which a button control is created. You use the Text property to specify the text to display on the button's face. As you learned earlier, the Name property is used by the programmer when coding the application, and the Text property is read by the user while the application is running.

THE PICTURE BOX CONTROL

The PictureBox tool creates a **picture box control** for displaying an image on the form. The picture box control shown earlier in Figure 1-15 displays an image of a wizard. The control's Name property allows you to assign a more meaningful name to the control, and its Image property allows you to specify the image to display. The SizeMode property handles how the image will be displayed and can be set to Normal, StretchImage, AutoSize, CenterImage, or Zoom.

THE CODE EDITOR WINDOW

After creating your application's user interface, you then write the Visual Basic instructions to tell the objects how to respond to the user's actions. Those actions—such as clicking, double-clicking, and scrolling—are called **events**. The set of Visual Basic instructions, or code, that tells an object how to respond to an event is called an **event procedure**. You enter an event procedure's code in the **Code Editor window**. Figure 1-16 shows various ways of opening the Code Editor window, and Figure 1-17 shows the Code Editor window opened in the IDE.

»HOW TO . . .

OPEN THE CODE EDITOR WINDOW

» Right-click the form, and then click View Code on the context menu.

» Verify that the designer window is the active window, then click View on the menu bar, and then click Code.

» Verify that the designer window is the active window, then press the F7 key on your keyboard.

» Click the form or a control on the form, then click the Events button ⚡ in the Properties window, and then double-click the desired event.

Figure 1-16: How to open the Code Editor window

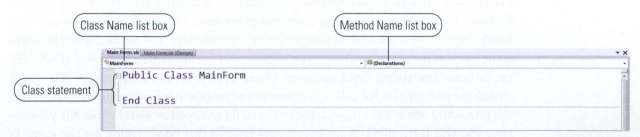

Figure 1-17: Code Editor window opened in the IDE

»TIP

The Public keyword in the Class statement indicates that the class can be used by code defined outside of the class.

»TIP

To display line numbers in the Code Editor window, click Tools, then click Options. Expand the Text Editor node, then click Basic. Select the Show all settings check box, if necessary. Select the Line numbers check box, then click the OK button.

The Code Editor window shown in Figure 1-17 contains the Visual Basic Class statement, which is used to define a class. In this case, the Class statement begins with the Public Class MainForm instruction and ends with the End Class instruction. Within the Class statement you enter the code to tell the form and its objects how to react to the user's actions. The Code Editor window also contains a Class Name list box and a Method Name list box. The **Class Name list box** lists the names of the objects included in the user interface. The **Method Name list box** lists the events to which the selected object is capable of responding. You use the Class Name and Method Name list boxes to select the object and event, respectively, that you want to code. For example, to code the exitButton's Click event, you select exitButton in the Class Name list box and select Click in the Method Name list box. When you do this, a code template for the exitButton's Click event procedure appears in the Code Editor window, as shown in Figure 1-18. The code template helps you follow the rules of the Visual Basic language, called its **syntax**. The first line in the code template is called the **procedure header**, and the last line is called the **procedure footer**.

Figure 1-18: Code template for the exitButton's Click event procedure

The procedure header begins with the two keywords Private Sub. A **keyword** is a word that has a special meaning in a programming language. The Private keyword indicates that the procedure can be used only within the class in which it is defined. In this case, the exitButton's Click event procedure can be used only within the MainForm class. The Sub keyword is an abbreviation of the term **sub procedure**, which, in programming terminology, refers to a block of code that performs a specific task. Following the Sub keyword is the name of the object (exitButton), an underscore (_), the name of the event (Click), and parentheses containing ByVal sender as Object, ByVal e As System.EventArgs. The items within the parentheses are called parameters and represent information that is passed to the procedure when it is invoked. For now, you do not need to worry about the parameters; you will learn more about parameters later in this book. Following the items in parentheses is Handles exitButton.Click. This part of the procedure header indicates that the procedure handles (or is associated with) the exitButton's Click event. In other words, the procedure will be processed when the exitButton is clicked.

The code template ends with the procedure footer, which contains the keywords End Sub. You enter your Visual Basic instructions at the location of the insertion point, which appears between the Private Sub and End Sub lines in Figure 1-18. The Code Editor automatically indents the line between the procedure header and footer. Indenting the lines within a procedure makes the instructions easier to read and is a common programming practice.

Notice that the keywords in the code appear in a different color from the rest of the code. The Code Editor window displays keywords in a different color to help you quickly identify these elements. In this case, the color-coding helps you easily locate the procedure header and footer.

When the user clicks an Exit button on a form, it usually indicates that he or she wants to end the application. You can use the Me.Close() instruction to accomplish this task.

THE ME.CLOSE() INSTRUCTION

The Me.Close() instruction tells the computer to close the current form. If the current form is the main form, closing it terminates the entire application. In the Me.Close() instruction, Me is a keyword that refers to the current form, and Close is one of the methods available in Visual Basic. A **method** is a predefined procedure that you can call (or invoke) when needed. For example, to close the current form when the user clicks the Exit button, you enter the Me.Close() instruction in the exitButton's Click event procedure, as shown in Figure 1-19. Notice the empty set of parentheses after the method's name in the instruction. The parentheses are required when calling some Visual Basic methods. However, depending on the method, the parentheses may or may not be empty.

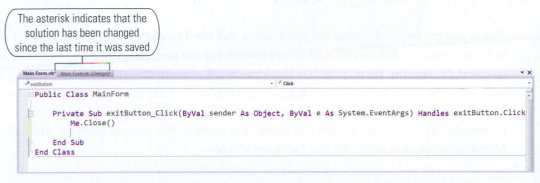

The asterisk indicates that the solution has been changed since the last time it was saved

```
Main Form.vb*   Main Form.vb [Design]*
exitButton                                          ▼  ⚡ Click
  ☐Public Class MainForm

      Private Sub exitButton_Click(ByVal sender As Object, ByVal e As System.EventArgs) Handles exitButton.Click
          Me.Close()

      End Sub
  End Class
```

Figure 1-19: Me.Close() instruction entered in the Click event procedure

When the user clicks the Exit button, the computer processes the instructions shown in the exitButton_Click procedure one after another in the order in which they appear in the procedure. In programming, this is referred to as **sequential processing** or as the **sequence structure**. (You will learn about two other programming structures, called selection and repetition, in later chapters.)

SAVING A SOLUTION

Notice the asterisk (*) that appears on the designer and Code Editor tabs in Figure 1-19. The asterisk indicates that a change was made to the solution since the last time it was saved. It is a good practice to save the current solution every 10 or 15 minutes so that you will not lose a lot of your work if the computer loses power. Figure 1-20 lists two ways to save a solution. When you save a solution, the computer saves any changes made to the files included in the solution. Saving the solution also removes the asterisk that appears on the designer and Code Editor tabs.

»HOW TO . . .

SAVE A SOLUTION
» Click File on the menu bar, and then click Save All.
» Click the Save All button 🖫 on the Standard toolbar.

Figure 1-20: How to save a solution

STARTING AND ENDING AN APPLICATION

When you are finished coding the application, you need to start it to make sure that it is working correctly. Before you start an application for the first time, you should verify the name of the **startup form**, which is the form that the computer automatically displays each time the application is started. You select the name from the Startup form list box in the Project Designer window. Figure 1-21 shows the steps you follow to specify the startup form's name, and Figure 1-22 shows the name of the startup form (in this case, MainForm) selected in the Project Designer window.

» HOW TO . . .

SPECIFY THE STARTUP FORM

1. Open the Project Designer window. You can open the window by right-clicking My Project in the Solution Explorer window, and then clicking Open on the context menu. You also can click Project on the menu bar, and then click *<project name>* Properties on the menu. In addition, you can right-click the project's name in the Solution Explorer window, and then click Properties.

2. Click the Application tab, if necessary, then click the Startup form list arrow in the Application pane. Click the appropriate form name in the list.

3. Click the Close button on the Project Designer window.

Figure 1-21: How to specify the startup form

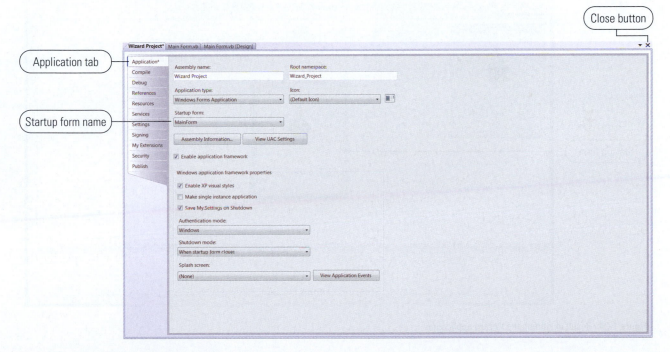

Figure 1-22: Project Designer window

Figure 1-23 shows two ways to start an application, and Figure 1-24 shows the result of starting the Wizard application. The computer automatically displays the startup form, which in this case is the MainForm. (At this point, you do not need to be concerned about any windows that appear at the bottom of the screen.)

»HOW TO . . .

START AN APPLICATION

» Save the solution. Click Debug on the menu bar, then click Start Debugging.

» Save the solution, then press the F5 key on your keyboard.

Figure 1-23: How to start an application

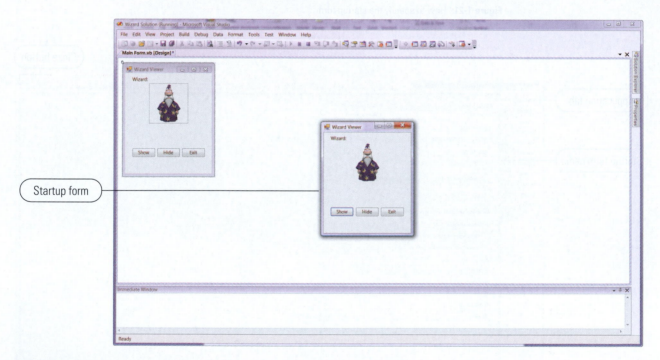

Startup form

Figure 1-24: Result of starting the Wizard application

When you start a Visual Basic application, the computer automatically creates a file that can be run outside of the Visual Studio 2008 IDE. The file, referred to as an **executable file**, has the same name as the project, but with an .exe filename extension. The name of the executable file for the Wizard Project is Wizard Project.exe. The computer stores the executable file in the project's bin\Debug folder. In this case, for example, the Wizard Project.exe file is stored in the VbReloaded2008\Chap01\Wizard Solution\Wizard

Project\bin\Debug folder. In most cases, when you are finished with an application, you will give the user only the executable file, because it does not allow him or her to modify the application's code. To allow someone to modify the code, you will need to provide the entire solution.

The way you end (or close) an application depends on the application's interface. To end the Wizard application shown earlier in Figure 1-24, you can click either the Exit button in the interface or the Close button on the application's title bar. Similarly, you can close Visual Studio 2008 using either the Exit option on the File menu or the Close button on the title bar. Figure 1-25 lists various ways of ending an application.

»HOW TO . . .

END AN APPLICATION
» Click an Exit button in the interface.
» Click File on the application's menu bar, then click Exit.
» Click the Close button on the application's title bar.

Figure 1-25: How to end an application

Next, you learn how to use an assignment statement to change the value of a property while an application is running.

USING AN ASSIGNMENT STATEMENT

As you learned earlier, you can use the Properties window to set an object's properties during design time, which is when you are building the interface. You also can set an object's properties while an application is running; you do this using an assignment statement. An **assignment statement** assigns a value to something, such as the property of an object. The format, or syntax, of an assignment statement that assigns a value to an object's property is *object.property = expression*. *Object* and *property* are the names of the object and property, respectively, to which you want the value of the *expression* assigned. The *expression* can be a number, a **string** (which is zero or more characters enclosed in quotation marks), a calculation, or a keyword. You use a period to separate the object name from the property name, and an equal sign between the *object.property* information and the *expression*. The equal sign (=) in an assignment statement is called the **assignment operator**. For example, to assign the string "Hello" to the Text property of the greetingLabel control, you use the assignment statement greetingLabel.Text = "Hello". As you learned earlier, a control's Text property specifies the text to display inside the control. Likewise, to assign the keyword True to the Visible property of the wizardPictureBox, you use the assignment statement wizardPictureBox.Visible = True. Setting a control's Visible property to True makes the control visible on the form. Similarly, you use the assignment statement wizardPictureBox.Visible = False to assign the keyword False to the control's Visible property. Setting a control's Visible property to False makes the control invisible on the form. Figure 1-26 shows the appropriate assignment statements entered in the Wizard application's Code Editor window.

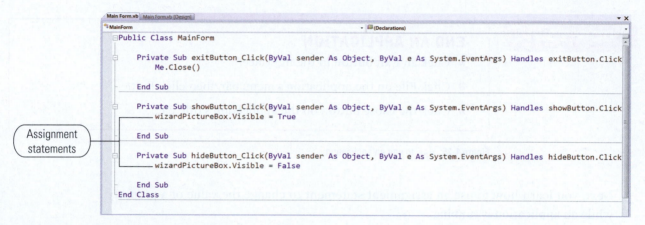

Figure 1-26: Assignment statements entered in the Code Editor window

PRINTING YOUR APPLICATION

You always should print a copy of your application's code, because the printout will help you understand and maintain the application in the future. You also should print a copy of the application's user interface. Figure 1-27 shows the steps you follow to print the code and the user interface.

PRINT AN APPLICATION'S CODE AND USER INTERFACE

1. To print the code, make the Code Editor window the active window, then collapse any code that you do not want to print. You collapse the code by clicking the minus box that appears next to the code.

2. Click File on the menu bar, and then click Print. If you don't want to print the collapsed code, select the Hide collapsed regions check box. To print line numbers, select the Include line numbers check box. Click the OK button to begin printing.

3. To print the interface, make the designer window the active window. Press and hold down the Alt key on your keyboard as you tap the Print Screen (or Prnt Scrn) key, then release the Alt key. Doing this places a picture of the interface on the Clipboard.

4. Start Microsoft Word (or any application that can display a picture) and open a new document (if necessary). Press Control (or Ctrl) + v to paste the contents of the Clipboard in the document. Press Control (or Ctrl) + p to open the Print dialog box, then click the OK button.

Figure 1-27: How to print an application's code and user interface

CLOSING THE CURRENT SOLUTION

When you close a solution, all projects and files contained in the solution also are closed. If unsaved changes were made to the solution, project, or form, a dialog box opens and prompts you to save the appropriate files. Figure 1-28 shows the steps you follow to close a solution. Notice that you use the Close Solution option, rather than the Close option, on the File menu. The Close option does not close the solution; it only closes the open windows, such as the designer and Code Editor windows, in the IDE.

CLOSE A SOLUTION

1. Click File on the menu bar.

2. Click Close Solution.

Figure 1-28: How to close a solution

OPENING AN EXISTING SOLUTION

Figure 1-29 shows the steps you follow to open an existing solution. If a solution is already open in the IDE, it is closed before another solution is opened. In other words, only one solution can be open in the IDE at any one time.

»HOW TO . . .

OPEN AN EXISTING SOLUTION

1. Click File on the menu bar, then click Open Project to open the Open Project dialog box.

2. Locate and then click the solution filename, which is contained in the application's solution folder. The solution filename has an .sln filename extension, which stands for "solution."

3. Click the Open button in the Open Project dialog box.

4. If the Windows Form Designer window is not displayed, click View on the menu bar, and then click Designer.

Figure 1-29: How to open an existing solution

You have completed the concepts section of Chapter 1. The next section is the Programming Tutorial section, which gives you step-by-step instructions on how to apply the chapter's concepts to an application. A Programming Example follows the Programming Tutorial. The Programming Example is a completed program that demonstrates the concepts taught in the chapter. Following the Programming Example are the Quick Review, Key Terms, Self-Check Questions and Answers, Review Questions, Review Exercises—Short Answer, Computer Exercises, and Case Projects sections.

PROGRAMMING TUTORIAL

CREATING A VISUAL BASIC 2008 APPLICATION

In this tutorial, you create an application that contains a label, a picture box, and three buttons. The first button displays the picture box on the form, and the second button hides the picture box. The third button ends the application.

STARTING VISUAL STUDIO 2008

Before you can create a Visual Basic 2008 application, you first must start Visual Studio 2008.

To start Visual Studio 2008:

1. Click the **Start** button on the taskbar, then point to **All Programs**.

2. If you are using Windows Vista, click **Microsoft Visual Studio 2008**, then click **Microsoft Visual Studio 2008**. If you are using Windows XP, point to **Microsoft Visual Studio 2008**, then click **Microsoft Visual Studio 2008**. (If the Choose Default Environment Settings dialog box appears, choose Visual Basic Development Settings, then click Start Visual Studio.) The Microsoft Visual Studio copyright screen appears momentarily, and then the Microsoft Visual Studio window opens.

3. Click **Window** on the menu bar, then click **Reset Window Layout**. When you are asked whether you want to restore the default window layout for the environment, click the **Yes** button. See Figure 1-30. (If you are not using the Professional Edition of Visual Studio 2008, your screen might not look identical to Figure 1-30.)

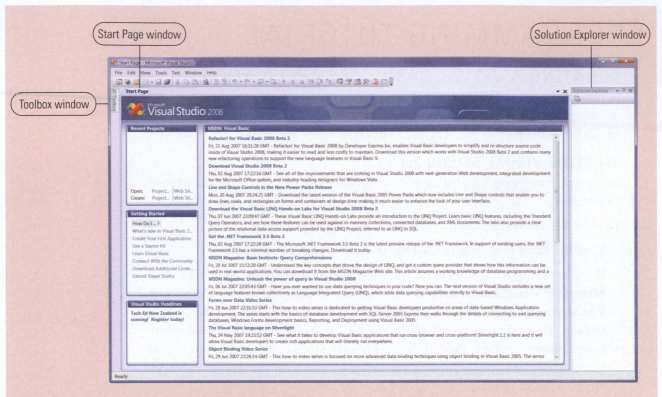

Start Page window

Solution Explorer window

Toolbox window

Figure 1-30: Microsoft Visual Studio 2008 window

CREATING A VISUAL BASIC 2008 WINDOWS-BASED APPLICATION

As you learned in the concepts section of this chapter, Visual Basic 2008 applications are composed of solutions, projects, and files.

To create a Visual Basic 2008 Windows-based application:

1. Click **Tools** on the menu bar, then click **Options**. Click **Projects and Solutions**. If necessary, select the following three check boxes: **Always show Error List if build finishes with errors**, **Always show solution**, and **Save new projects when created**. If necessary, deselect the **Show Output window when build starts** check box. Click the **OK** button.

2. Click **File** on the menu bar, then click **New Project**. The New Project dialog box opens.

3. If necessary, expand the Visual Basic node in the Project types list, then click **Windows**.

4. If necessary, click **Windows Forms Application** in the Visual Studio installed templates section of the Templates list.

5. Type **Wizard Project** in the Name box.

6. Use the Browse button, which appears next to the Location box, to open the Project Location dialog box. Locate and then click the **VbReloaded2008\ Chap01** folder, then click the **Select Folder** (or OK) button.

7. If necessary, select the **Create directory for solution** check box in the New Project dialog box.

8. Type **Wizard Solution** in the Solution Name box. The completed New Project dialog box is shown in Figure 1-31.

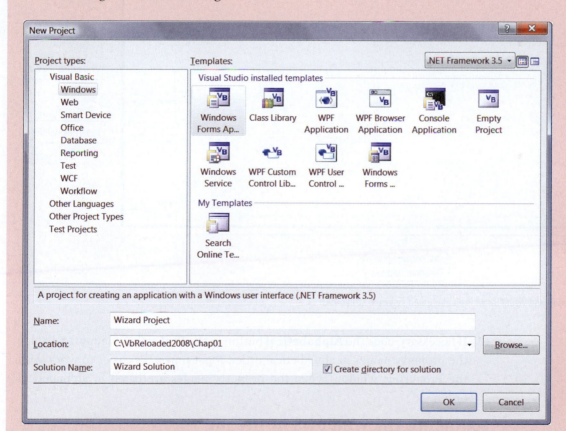

Figure 1-31: Completed New Project dialog box

9. Click the **OK** button to close the New Project dialog box. When you click the OK button, Visual Studio creates a solution and adds a Visual Basic project to the solution, as shown in Figure 1-32.

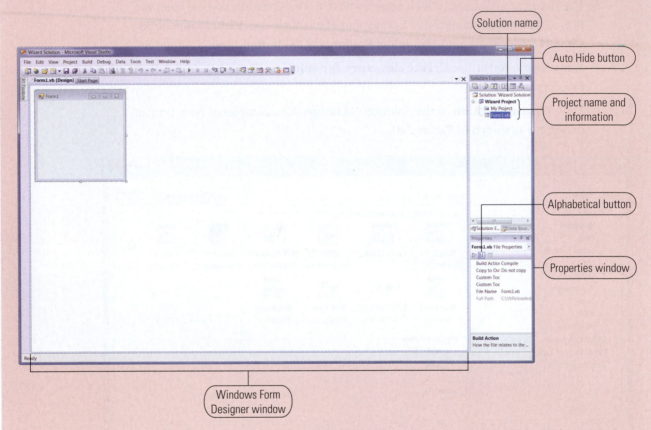

Figure 1-32: Solution and Visual Basic Project created by Visual Studio 2008

10. If necessary, click the **Alphabetical** button in the Properties window to display the property names in alphabetical order. Most times, it's easier to work with the Properties window when the property names are listed in alphabetical order.

MANAGING THE WINDOWS IN THE IDE

In the next set of steps, you practice closing, auto-hiding, and displaying the windows in the IDE.

To close, auto-hide, and display the windows in the IDE:

1. Click the **Start Page** tab to make the Start Page window the active window, and then click its **Close** button.

2. Click the **Data Sources** tab to make the Data Sources window the active window, and then click the **Close** button on its title bar.

3. Next, you will practice auto-hiding a window. Click the **Auto Hide** button (the vertical pushpin) on the Solution Explorer window's title bar. The Solution Explorer window is minimized and appears as a tab on the right edge of the IDE.

4. Now practice temporarily displaying a window. Place your mouse pointer on the Solution Explorer tab. The Solution Explorer window slides into view. Move your mouse pointer away from the Solution Explorer window. The window is minimized and appears as a tab again.

5. Next, you will practice permanently displaying a window. Place your mouse pointer on the Toolbox tab. When the Toolbox window slides into view, click the **Auto Hide** button (the horizontal pushpin) on its title bar. The vertical pushpin button replaces the horizontal pushpin button. If necessary, click the **Common Controls** tab. Figure 1-33 shows the current status of the windows in the development environment.

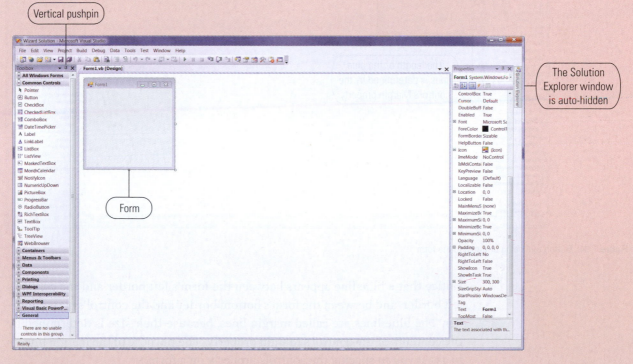

Figure 1-33: Current status of the Windows in the IDE

USING THE TOOLBOX WINDOW TO ADD OBJECTS TO A FORM

The Toolbox window, or toolbox, contains the tools you use when creating your application. You use the tools to add objects, called controls, to a form. In the next set of steps, you will add three button controls, a label control, and a picture box control to the current form. You also practice sizing, moving, deleting, and undeleting a control.

To add controls to the form, and then manipulate the controls:

1. Click the **Button** tool in the toolbox, but do not release the mouse button. Hold down the mouse button as you drag the mouse pointer to the lower-left corner of the form. As you drag the mouse pointer, you will see a solid box, as well as an outline of a rectangle and a plus box, following the mouse pointer. See Figure 1-34.

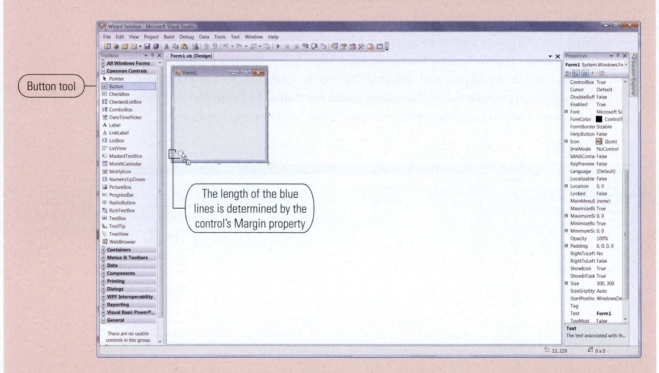

Figure 1-34: Button tool being dragged to the form

Notice that a blue line appears between the form's left border and the control's left border, and between the form's bottom border and the control's bottom border. The blue lines are called margin lines, because their size is determined by the contents of the control's Margin property. The purpose of the margin lines is to assist you in spacing the controls properly on a form.

2. Release the mouse button. A button control appears on the form, as shown in Figure 1-35. The sizing handles on the control indicate that the control is selected. You can use the sizing handles to make a control bigger or smaller.

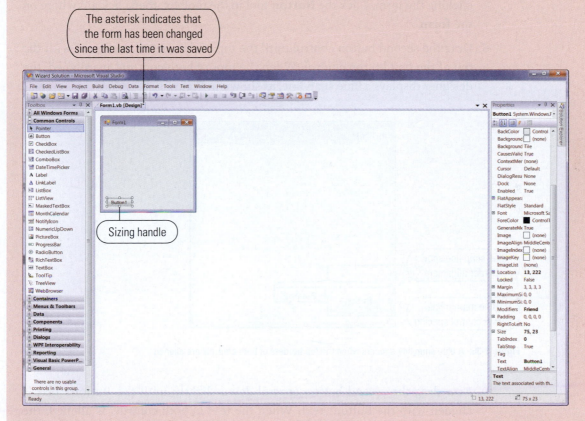

The asterisk indicates that the form has been changed since the last time it was saved

Sizing handle

Figure 1-35: Button control added to the form

Notice that an asterisk (*) appears on the Form1.vb [Design] tab in the designer window. The asterisk indicates that the form has been changed since the last time it was saved.

3. Use the sizing handles to make the button control bigger.

4. Now you will practice repositioning a control on the form. Place your mouse pointer on the center of the button control, then press the left mouse button and drag the control to another area of the form. Release the mouse button.

5. Next, you will practice deleting and then restoring a control. Press the **Delete** key on your keyboard to delete the button control. Click **Edit** on the menu bar, and then click **Undo** to reinstate the button control.

6. Drag the button control back to its original location in the lower-left corner of the form.

7. You also can add a control to a form by clicking the appropriate tool and then clicking the form. Click the **Button** tool in the toolbox, then click anywhere on the **form**.

8. Drag the second button control until the top of the control is aligned with the top of the first button control. When the tops of both controls are aligned, the designer displays a blue snap line, as shown in Figure 1-36.

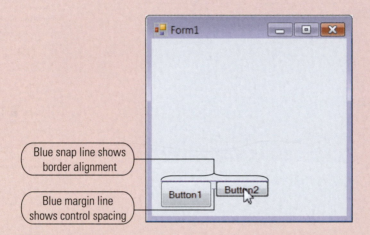

Figure 1-36: A blue snap line appears when the top borders of both controls are aligned

9. Now drag the second button control down slightly, until the Button2 text is aligned with the Button1 text. When the text in both controls is aligned, the designer displays a pink snap line, as shown in Figure 1-37.

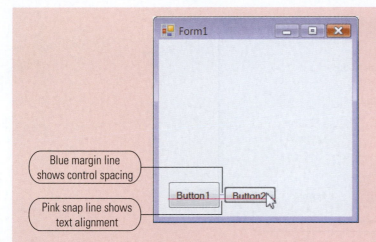

Figure 1-37: A pink snap line appears when the text in both controls is aligned

10. Release the mouse button.

11. Another way to add a control to a form is by clicking the appropriate tool, then placing the mouse pointer on the form, and then pressing the left mouse button and dragging the mouse pointer until the control is the desired size. Click the **Button** tool in the toolbox, then place the mouse pointer on the form. Press the left mouse button and drag the mouse pointer until the control is the desired size, then release the mouse button. (You do not need to worry about the exact location and size of the button.)

12. Drag the third button control until the Button3 text is aligned with the Button2 text, then release the mouse button.

13. Add a label control and a picture box control to the form. Position the controls as shown in Figure 1-38. (You do not need to worry about the exact location and size of the controls in the interface.)

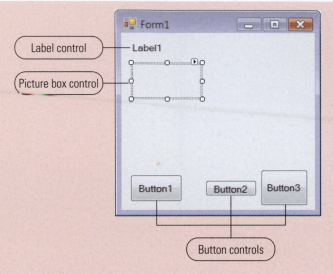

Figure 1-38: Controls added to the form

14. Save the solution by clicking **File** on the menu bar, and then clicking **Save All**.

15. You are finished with the Toolbox window, so you can auto-hide it. Auto-hide the Toolbox window.

USING THE PROPERTIES WINDOW TO CHANGE AN OBJECT'S PROPERTIES

Each object in Visual Basic has a set of properties that determine its appearance and behavior, and each property has a default value assigned to it when the object is created. You can use the Properties window to assign a different value to a property. First, you will change the File Name property of the form file object from Form1.vb to Main Form.vb.

To change the name of the form file object:

1. Temporarily display the Solution Explorer window. Right-click **Form1.vb** in the Solution Explorer window, and then click **Properties**.

2. Click **File Name** in the Properties window, then type **Main Form.vb** and press **Enter**.

In the next set of steps, you will assign values to some of the properties of the form object.

To assign values to some of the properties of the form:

1. Click the **form** (but not a control on the form). Sizing handles appear on the form to indicate that the form is selected, and the form's properties appear in the Properties window, as shown in Figure 1-39. If the property names do not appear in alphabetical order, click the Alphabetical button in the Properties window.

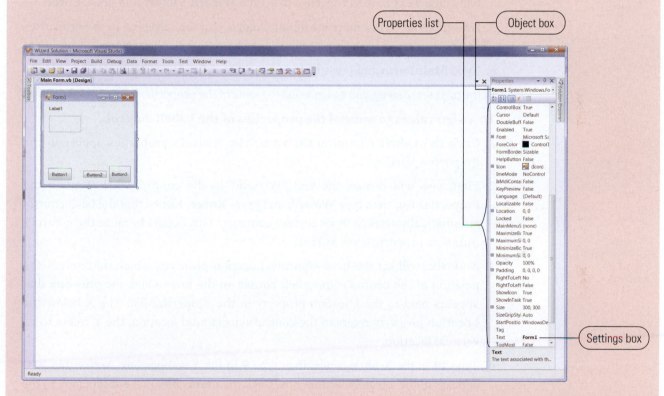

Figure 1-39: Properties window showing the properties of a form

As indicated in Figure 1-39, the Properties window includes an Object box and a Properties list. The Object box contains the name of the selected object. The Properties list has two columns. The left column displays the names of the properties associated with the selected object, and the right column (called the Settings box) displays the current value, or setting, of each of the properties.

2. First, you will change the type and size of the font used to display text on the form. Click **Font** in the Properties list, then click the **...** (ellipsis) button in the Settings box. When the Font dialog box opens, click **Segoe UI** in the Font box and **9** in the Size box, and then click the **OK** button. Notice that this change affects the text displayed in the controls on the form.

3. As you learned earlier, a form's StartPosition property specifies where the form is positioned when the application is started and the form first appears on the screen. Click **StartPosition** in the Properties list. Click the **list arrow** in the Settings box, and then click **CenterScreen**.

4. Recall that a form's Text property specifies the text to display in the form's title bar. Click **Text** in the Properties list. Type **Wizard Viewer** and press **Enter**.

5. Now give the form a more meaningful name. Use the scroll bar in the Properties window to scroll to the top of the Properties list, then click **(Name)**.

6. Type **MainForm** and press **Enter**.

In the next set of steps, you assign values to some of the properties of the Label1 control.

To assign values to some of the properties of the Label1 control:

1. Click the **Label1** control in the form. The control's properties appear in the Properties window.

2. First, you will display the text "Wizard:" in the control. Click **Text** in the Properties list, then type **Wizard:** and press **Enter**. Notice that the label control automatically sizes to fit its current contents. This occurs because the control's AutoSize property is set to True.

3. Now you will set the label control's Location property, which determines the position of the control's upper-left corner on the form. Click the **plus box** that appears next to the Location property in the Properties list. The X below the Location property refers to the control's horizontal location; the Y refers to its vertical location.

4. Type **19** in the X settings box, then type **9** in the Y settings box. Notice that 19, 9 appears in the Location settings box. Click the **minus box** that appears next to the Location property. You also could have set the Location property by typing 19, 9 in the Location property's settings box, or by dragging the control to the desired location.

In the next set of steps, you assign values to some of the properties of the button controls.

To assign values to some of the properties of the button controls:

1. Click the **Button1** control in the form. The control's properties appear in the Properties window. Set the Name property to **showButton**, and set the Text property to **Show**. If necessary, set the Location property to **23, 239**.

2. Click the **Button2** control in the form. Set the Name property to **hideButton**, and set the Text property to **Hide**. If necessary, set the Size property to **75, 29**.

3. Click the **Button3** control in the form. Set the Name property to **exitButton**, and set the Text property to **Exit**.

Now let's say that you want to make the Show and Exit buttons the same size as the Hide button. You can do so by individually setting the Show and Exit buttons' Size properties to the same value as the Hide button's Size property; or, you can use the Format menu.

USING THE FORMAT MENU

The Format menu provides options that you can use to manipulate the controls in the user interface. The Align option, for example, allows you to align two or more controls by their left, right, top, or bottom borders. You can use the Make Same Size option to make two or more controls the same width and/or height. The Format menu also has a Center in Form option that centers one or more controls either horizontally or vertically on the form. Before you can use the Format menu to make the Show, Hide, and Exit button controls the same size, you first must select the controls. The first control you select should always be the one whose size and/or location you want to match. In this case, for example, you want the size of the Show and Exit buttons to match the size of the Hide button; therefore, the Hide button should be the first control you select. The first control selected is referred to as the reference control.

To make the Show and Exit buttons the same size as the Hide button:

1. Click the **Hide** button in the form. Press and hold down the **Control** (**Ctrl**) key as you click the **Show** button and then the **Exit** button, then release the Control key. The three buttons are now selected. Notice that the sizing handles on the reference control (the Hide button) are white, whereas the sizing handles on the Show and Exit buttons are black. See Figure 1-40.

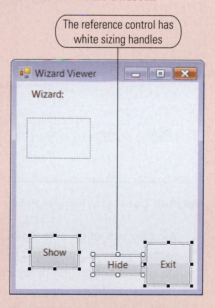

Figure 1-40: Buttons selected on the form

2. Click **Format** on the menu bar. Point to **Make Same Size**, and then click **Both**. The Show and Exit buttons are now the same size as the Hide button.

3. Click the **form** to deselect the buttons.

Next, you will use the Format menu to align the top borders of the Hide and Exit buttons with the top border of the Show button.

To align the top borders of the buttons:

1. Click the **Show** button, which is the reference control, in the form. Press and hold down the **Control** (**Ctrl**) key as you click the other two buttons, then release the Control key.

2. Click **Format** on the menu bar. Point to **Align**, and then click **Tops**. The top borders of the Hide and Exit buttons are now aligned with the top border of the Show button.

3. Click the **form** to deselect the buttons.

4. If necessary, position the buttons to match those shown in Figure 1-41.

Figure 1-41: Location of the buttons on the form

You also can select a group of controls on the form by placing the mouse pointer slightly above and to the left of the first control you want to select, then pressing the left mouse button and dragging. A dotted rectangle appears as you drag. When all of the controls you want to select are within (or at least touched by) the dotted rectangle, release the mouse button. All of the controls surrounded or touched by the dotted rectangle will be selected.

DISPLAYING AN IMAGE IN A PICTURE BOX CONTROL

You can use a picture box control to display an image. The image you will display in the current interface is stored in the Wizard_appears (Wizard_appears.gif) file contained in the VbReloaded2008\Chap01 folder. The Wizard_appears image file was downloaded from the Animation Library site. You can browse and optionally download other free image files at *www.animationlibrary.com.*

To display an image in a picture box control:

1. Click the **PictureBox1** control on the form. The control's properties appear in the Properties window, and a box containing a triangle appears on the control, as shown in Figure 1-42. The box is referred to as the task box because, when you click it, it displays a list of the tasks commonly performed by the control. Each task in the list is associated with one or more properties. You can set the properties using the task list or the Properties window.

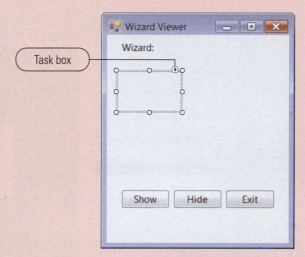

Figure 1-42: Picture box control selected on the form

2. Click the **task box** on the PictureBox1 control. A list of tasks associated with a picture box appears, as shown in Figure 1-43.

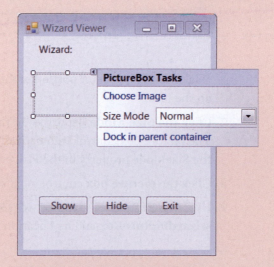

Figure 1-43: Task list for a picure box control

3. Click **Choose Image**. The Select Resource dialog box opens. Verify that the Project resource file radio button is selected in the dialog box.

4. Click the **Import** button. The Open dialog box opens.

5. Open the VbReloaded2008\Chap01 folder, then click **Wizard_appears** (**Wizard_appears.gif**) in the list of filenames. Click the **Open** button. The completed Select Resource dialog box is shown in Figure 1-44.

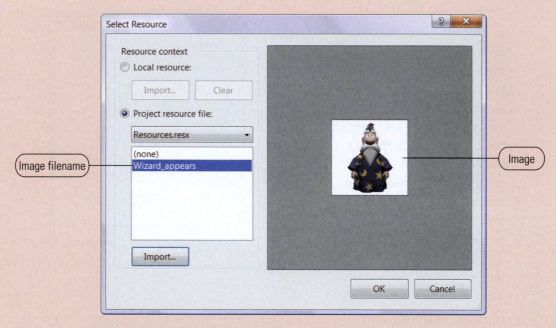

Figure 1-44: Completed Select Resource dialog box

6. Click the **OK** button. A portion of the image appears in the picture box control on the form.

7. Click the **Size Mode** list arrow in the task list box, and then click **AutoSize**. The picture box control automatically sizes to fit its contents. (You also can set the SizeMode property in the Properties window.)

8. Click the **picture box** control to close the task list.

9. Use the Properties window to set the picture box's Name property to **wizardPictureBox** and its Location property to **23, 32**.

10. Use the Format menu to center the picture box horizontally on the form. The completed user interface is shown in Figure 1-45.

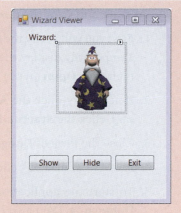

Figure 1-45: Completed user interface

11. Auto-hide the Properties window, then save the solution by clicking **File** on the menu bar, and then clicking **Save All**.

In the next set of steps, you will lock the controls in place on the form. Locking the controls prevents them from being moved inadvertently as you work in the IDE.

To lock the controls:

1. Right-click the **form**, then click **Lock Controls** on the context menu. Notice that a small lock appears in the upper-left corner of the form. (You also can lock the controls by clicking Format on the menu bar, and then clicking Lock Controls.)

2. Click the **Show** button. Here again, notice that a small lock appears in the upper-left corner of the control.

3. Try dragging one of the controls to a different location on the form. You will not be able to do so.

If you need to move a control after you have locked the controls in place, you can change the control's Location property setting in the Properties window. You also can unlock the control by changing its Locked property to False. Or, you can unlock all of the controls by clicking Format on the menu bar, and then clicking Lock Controls. The Lock Controls option is a toggle option: clicking it once activates it, and clicking it again deactivates it.

STARTING AND ENDING AN APPLICATION

Now that the user interface is complete, you can start the application to see how it will look to the user. You can start an application by clicking Debug on the menu bar, and then clicking Start Debugging; or you can simply press the F5 key on your keyboard.

To start and stop the current application:

1. First you will verify the name of the startup form in the Project Designer window. Temporarily display the Solution Explorer window. Right-click **My Project**, and then click **Open** on the context menu. The Project Designer window opens.

2. If necessary, click the **Application** tab to display the Application pane. If necessary, click the **Startup form** list arrow, then click **MainForm** in the list.

3. Close the Project Designer window.

4. Save the solution by clicking the **Save All** button 🖫 on the Standard toolbar.

5. To start the application, click **Debug** on the menu bar, and then click **Start Debugging**. (You also can press the F5 key on your keyboard.) See Figure 1-46.

(Do not be concerned about any windows that appear at the bottom of the screen.)

The form's
Close button

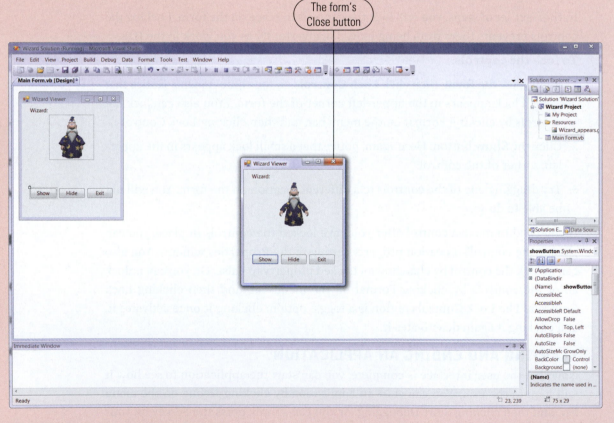

Figure 1-46: Result of starting the Wizard application

6. Click the **Hide** button, then click the **Show** button, and then click the **Exit** button. Currently, the buttons do not perform any tasks when clicked. This is because you have not yet entered the instructions that tell them the tasks to perform.

   At this point, you can stop the application by clicking the Close button on the form's title bar. You also can click the designer window to make it the active window, then click Debug on the menu bar, and then click Stop Debugging.

7. Click the **Close** button on the form's title bar. When the application ends, you are returned to the IDE.

WRITING VISUAL BASIC 2008 CODE

At this point, the buttons in the interface do not know the tasks they should perform when they are clicked by the user. You tell a button what to do by writing an event procedure for it. You write the event procedure in the Code Editor window.

To open the Code Editor window, and then code the Exit button's Click event:

1. Right-click the **form**, then click **View Code**. The Code Editor window opens in the IDE. The Code Editor window contains a Class Name list box and a Method Name list box. You use the list boxes to select the object and event that you want to code.

2. Click the **Class Name** list arrow, then click **exitButton** in the list. Click the **Method Name** list arrow, then click **Click** in the list. When you select an object and event, a code template for the appropriate event procedure appears in the Code Editor window. The Code Editor provides the code template to help you follow the rules of the Visual Basic 2008 programming language. As you learned earlier, the rules of a programming language are called its syntax. Figure 1-47 shows the code template for the exitButton's Click event procedure.

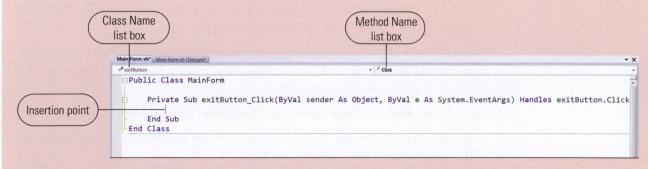

Figure 1-47: Code template for the exitButton's Click event procedure

The insertion point located in the event procedure indicates where you enter your code for the object. In this case, you want to instruct the Exit button to end the application when the button is clicked. As you learned earlier, you use the Me.Close() instruction to accomplish the task. You can type the instruction on your own; or you can use the IntelliSense feature that is built into the Code Editor. In this set of steps, you will use the IntelliSense feature.

3. Type **me.** (but don't press Enter). When you type the period, the IntelliSense feature displays a list of properties, methods, and so on from which you can select. If necessary, click the **Common** tab. The Common tab displays the most commonly used items, whereas the All tab displays all of the items. Type **cl** (but don't press Enter). The IntelliSense feature highlights the Close method in the list, as shown in Figure 1-48.

Important note: If the list of choices does not appear, the IntelliSense feature may have been turned off on your computer system. To turn it on, click Tools on the menu bar, and then click Options. Expand the Text Editor node in the Options dialog box, and then click Basic. If necessary, select the Show all settings check box, then select the Auto list members check box. Click the OK button to close the Options dialog box.

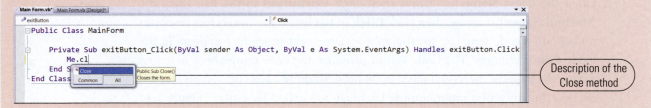

Figure 1-48: Close method highlighted in the list

4. Press the **Enter** key on your keyboard to select the Close method. The Code Editor enters the Me.Close() instruction in the procedure.

When the user clicks the Show and Hide buttons, the buttons' Click event procedures should display and hide, respectively, the picture box control. You can use assignment statements to accomplish both tasks.

To code the Show and Hide buttons' Click event procedures:

1. Use the Class Name and Method Name list boxes to open the code template for the showButton's Click event procedure.

2. To display the picture box, which is named wizardPictureBox, you need to set the control's Visible property to True. You do this using the assignment statement wizardPictureBox.Visible = True. Type **wiz** and then click **wizardPictureBox** in the list.

3. Now you can either press the Tab key to enter wizardPictureBox in the procedure, or you can press the character that follows wizardPictureBox in the assignment statement. In this case, the next character is the period. Type **.** (a period), then type the letter **v**. The IntelliSense feature highlights Visible in the list.

4. Here again, you can either press the Tab key or type the next character in the assignment statement. In this case, the next character is the equal sign. Type **=** (an equal sign), then type **t** to select the True keyword from the list, and then press **Enter**. The Code Editor enters the wizardPictureBox.Visible = True statement in the procedure.

5. Open the code template for the hideButton's Click event procedure. Enter the following assignment statement into the procedure: wizardPictureBox.Visible = False. Figure 1-49 shows the code entered in the Code Editor window.

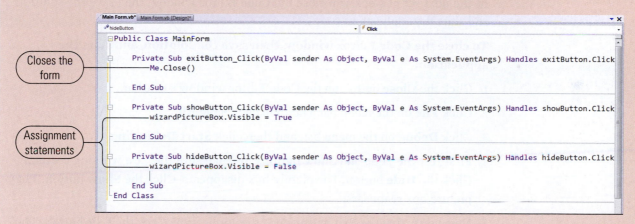

Figure 1-49: Code entered in the Code Editor window

At times, you may want to display line numbers in the Code Editor window.

To display line numbers in the Code Editor window:

1. Click **Tools** on the menu bar, and then click **Options**.

2. Expand the Text Editor node in the Options dialog box, and then click **Basic**. If necessary, select the **Show all settings** check box, then select the **Line numbers** check box.

3. At this point, you can either deselect the Show all settings check box or leave it selected. Click the **OK** button to close the Options dialog box. See Figure 1-50.

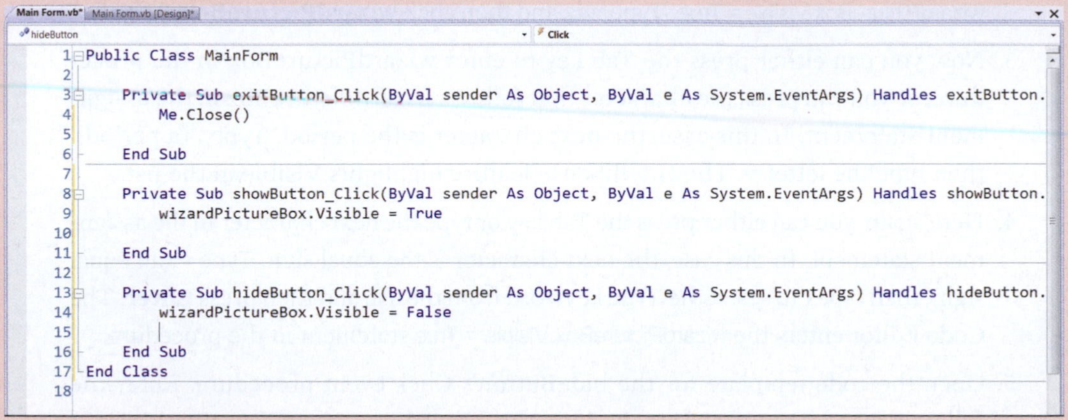

```vb
Main Form.vb*  Main Form.vb (Design)*

hideButton                                                             Click

1  Public Class MainForm
2
3      Private Sub exitButton_Click(ByVal sender As Object, ByVal e As System.EventArgs) Handles exitButton.
4          Me.Close()
5
6      End Sub
7
8      Private Sub showButton_Click(ByVal sender As Object, ByVal e As System.EventArgs) Handles showButton.
9          wizardPictureBox.Visible = True
10
11     End Sub
12
13     Private Sub hideButton_Click(ByVal sender As Object, ByVal e As System.EventArgs) Handles hideButton.
14         wizardPictureBox.Visible = False
15
16     End Sub
17  End Class
18
```

Figure 1-50: Line numbers shown in the Code Editor window

In the next set of steps, you close the Code Editor window, then save the solution and start the application.

To close the Code Editor window, then save the solution, and start the application:

1. Click the **Close** button on the Code Editor window's title bar.

2. Click **File** on the menu bar, and then click **Save All**.

3. Click **Debug** on the menu bar, and then click **Start Debugging**.

4. First test the Hide and Show buttons to make sure they are working correctly. Click the **Hide** button. The picture box disappears. Click the **Show** button. The picture box reappears.

5. Now verify that the Exit button ends the application. Click the **Exit** button. The application ends and you are returned to the designer window.

CLOSING THE CURRENT SOLUTION

When you are finished working with a solution, you should close the solution. You close a solution using the Close Solution option on the File menu. When you close a solution, all projects and files contained in the solution also are closed.

To close the current solution:

1. Click **File** on the menu bar, then click **Close Solution**.

2. Temporarily display the Solution Explorer window to verify that no solutions are open in the IDE.

OPENING AN EXISTING SOLUTION

You can use the File menu or the Start Page to open an existing solution. If a solution is already open in the IDE, it is closed before another solution is opened.

To open the Wizard Solution:

1. Click **File** on the menu bar, then click **Open Project**. The Open Project dialog box opens.

2. Locate and then open the **VbReloaded2008\Chap01\Wizard Solution** folder.

3. If necessary, click **Wizard Solution** (**Wizard Solution.sln**) in the list of filenames, and then click the **Open** button.

4. If the Windows Form Designer window is not open, click **View** on the menu bar, and then click **Designer**.

5. Temporarily display the Solution Explorer window to verify that the solution is open.

PRINTING THE APPLICATION'S CODE

You always should print a copy of the code entered in the Code Editor window, because the printout will help you understand and maintain the application in the future. To print the code, the Code Editor window must be the active, or current, window.

To print the current application's code:

1. Right-click the **form**, then click **View Code** to open the Code Editor window.

2. Click **File** on the menu bar, then click **Print**. The Print dialog box opens.

   Notice that you can include line numbers in the printout. If you select the Include line numbers check box, the line numbers will be printed even if they do not appear in the Code Editor window. If the Include line numbers check box is not selected, no line numbers will appear on the printout, even though they may appear in the Code Editor window.

3. Select the **Include line numbers** check box.

4. If your computer is connected to a printer, click the **OK** button to begin printing; otherwise, click the **Cancel** button. If you clicked the OK button, your printer prints the code.

PRINTING THE APPLICATION'S INTERFACE

To print the application's interface, the Windows Form designer window must be the active, or current, window.

To print the current application's interface:

1. If necessary, click the **Main Form.vb [Design]** tab to make the designer window the active window, then press **Alt + Print Screen** (Prnt Scrn) to place a picture of the interface on the Clipboard.

2. Start an application that can display a picture, such as the Microsoft Word application, and open a new document (if necessary). Press **Control** (Ctrl) + **v** to paste the contents of the Clipboard in the document. Press **Control** (Ctrl) + **p** to open the Print dialog box.

3. If your computer is connected to a printer, click the **OK** button; otherwise, click the **Cancel** button. If you clicked the OK button, your printer prints the document.

4. Close the Microsoft Word (or other) application without saving the changes to the document.

SYNTAX ERRORS IN CODE

In this section, you intentionally introduce a syntax error in the code. Doing this will allow you to observe how syntax errors are treated in Visual Basic, and how you can correct them. You create a syntax error when you enter an instruction that does not follow the rules of the programming language. Most syntax errors are typing errors—for example, typing Flse rather than False.

To introduce a syntax error in the current application:

1. In the hideButton's Click event procedure, change the word False in the assignment statement to Flse, then click the blank line below the assignment statement. Notice that a jagged blue line appears below the mistyped word, Flse. The jagged blue line indicates that the code contains a syntax error.

2. Position your mouse pointer on the mistyped word, Flse. The Code Editor displays a box that contains an appropriate error message, as shown in Figure 1-51. In this case, the message indicates that the Code Editor does not recognize Flse.

```
13      Private Sub hideButton_Click(By Name 'Flse' is not declared. Object, ByVal e As System.EventArgs) Handles hideButton.
14          wizardPictureBox.Visible = Flse
15
16      End Sub
17  End Class
18
```

Figure 1-51: Jagged blue line and box indicate a syntax error

3. At this point, you should correct the error before starting the application. However, observe what happens when you start an application without correcting a syntax error. Save the solution, then start the application. The computer displays the message box shown in Figure 1-52.

Figure 1-52: The message box indicates that the code contains errors

4. Click the **No** button. The Error List window shown in Figure 1-53 opens. Notice that the Error List window indicates that the code has one error, which occurs on Line 14: Name 'Flse' is not declared.

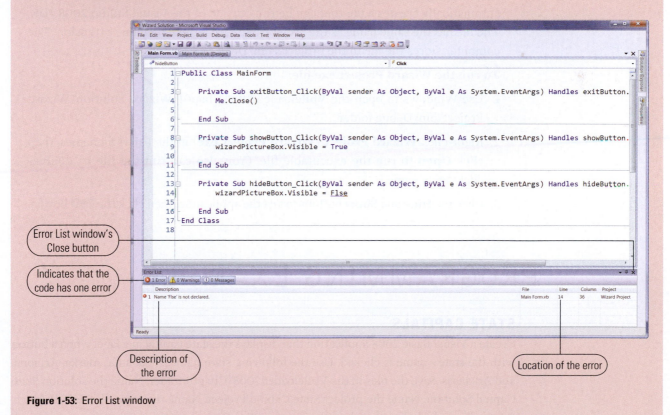

Error List window's Close button

Indicates that the code has one error

Description of the error

Location of the error

Figure 1-53: Error List window

5. Correct the syntax error by changing Flse in Line 14's assignment statement to False, then click the blank line below the assignment statement. Notice that the Error List window shows that the code is error-free.

6. Close the Error List window. Save the solution, then start the application. Test the Hide button to verify that it is working correctly.

7. Click the **Exit** button to end the application, then close the Code Editor window.

EXITING VISUAL STUDIO 2008

You can exit Visual Studio using either the Close button on its title bar, or the Exit option on the File menu.

To exit Visual Studio 2008:

1. Click **File** on the menu bar.

2. Click **Exit** on the menu.

RUNNING THE APPLICATION'S EXECUTABLE FILE

As you learned earlier, when you start a Visual Basic application, the computer automatically creates a file that can be run outside of the Visual Studio 2008 IDE. The file has the same name as the project, but with an .exe filename extension. The computer stores the file in the project's bin\Debug folder.

To run the Wizard Project.exe file:

1. Use Windows to open the VbReloaded2008\Chap01\Wizard Solution\Wizard Project\bin\Debug folder.

2. Right-click **Wizard Project** (**Wizard Project.exe**) in the list of filenames, then click **Open** to run the executable file. (You also can run the file by double-clicking its name.)

3. Click the **Hide** and **Show** buttons to test the application, then click the **Exit** button.

PROGRAMMING EXAMPLE

STATE CAPITALS

Create a Visual Basic 2008 application that displays the state capital in a label when a button with the state's name is clicked. Use the following state names: Alabama, Alaska, Arizona, and Arkansas. Save the files in the VbReloaded2008\Chap01 folder. Name the solution State Capital Solution. Name the project State Capital Project. Name the form file Main Form.vb. Remember to lock the controls in the interface. See Figures 1-54 through 1-56.

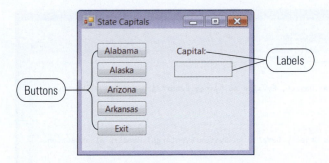

Figure 1-54: User interface

Object	Property	Setting
Form1	Name	MainForm
	Font	Segoe UI
	Size	310, 256
	StartPosition	CenterScreen
	Text	State Capitals
Button1	Name	alabamaButton
	Text	Alabama
Button2	Name	alaskaButton
	Text	Alaska
Button3	Name	arizonaButton
	Text	Arizona
Button4	Name	arkansasButton
	Text	Arkansas
Button5	Name	exitButton
	Text	Exit
Label1	Text	Capital:
Label2	Name	capitalLabel
	AutoSize	False
	BorderStyle	FixedSingle
	Size	100, 27
	Text	(empty) (*Hint*: Delete the text that appears in the Settings box in the Properties window.)
	TextAlign	MiddleCenter (centers the Text property)

Figure 1-55: Objects, properties, and settings

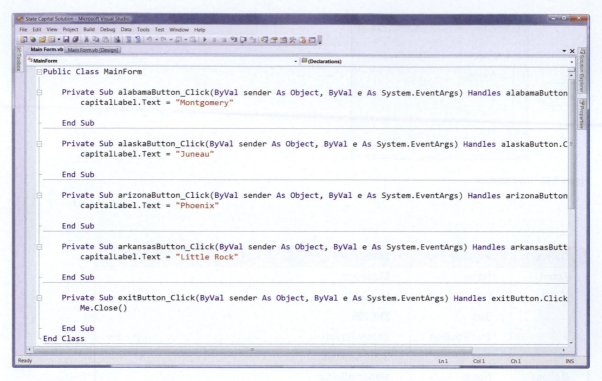

Figure 1-56: Code

QUICK REVIEW

» The directions given to a computer are called programs and are written by programmers using a variety of programming languages.

» Object-oriented programs focus on the objects needed to accomplish a task.

» An object is anything that can be seen, touched, or used. Every object has attributes that control its appearance and behavior.

» A class is a pattern from which an object can be created.

» Applications created in Visual Studio 2008 are composed of solutions, projects, and files.

» You create your application's GUI in the Windows Form Designer window.

» A form is the foundation for the user interface in a Windows-based application.

» A Windows Form object is created from the Windows Form class.

» The Solution Explorer window displays the names of projects and files contained in the current solution.

» The Properties window lists the selected object's properties.

» All class definitions are contained in namespaces.

» The System.Windows.Forms namespace contains the definition of the Windows Form class, as well as the class definitions for objects you add to a form.

» The dot member access operator indicates a hierarchy of namespaces.

» You use the value stored in an object's Name property to refer to the object in code.

» The value stored in the form's Text property displays in the form's title bar and on the taskbar when the application is running.

» The form's StartPosition property determines the position of the form when it first appears on the screen when the application is started.

» Applications created for the Windows Vista environment should use the 9-point size of the Segoe UI font.

» The Toolbox window contains the tools you use when creating your application's GUI.

» The value stored in a control's Text property displays inside the control.

» Controls on a form can be selected, sized, moved, deleted, or locked and unlocked.

» A label control displays text that the user is not allowed to edit while the application is running.

» You use a button control to perform an immediate action when clicked.

» You use a picture box control to display an image on the form.

» You tell an object how to respond to an event by coding an event procedure. You enter the code in the Code Editor window.

» You use the Class Name and Method Name list boxes in the Code Editor window to select the object and event that you want to code.

» The Code Editor provides a code template for each of an object's event procedures. The code template begins with the Private Sub line and ends with the End Sub line. You enter your Visual Basic instructions between those lines.

» You can display line numbers in the Code Editor window.

» You can use the Me.Close() instruction to terminate an application.

» You should save the solution every 10 or 15 minutes.

» When you start a Visual Basic application, the computer automatically creates an executable file. This is the file typically given to the user.

» You can use an assignment statement to assign a value to a property while an application is running.

» You should print an application's code, because the printout will help you understand and maintain the application in the future. You also should print its interface.

» You can print line numbers next to the lines of code entered in the Code Editor window.

» Closing a solution closes all projects and files contained in the solution.

» Only one solution can be open in the IDE at any one time.

KEY TERMS

Application—another name for a program

Assignment operator—the equal sign in an assignment statement

Assignment statement—an instruction that assigns a value to something, such as a property of an object

Button control—the control used to perform an immediate action when clicked

Camel case—the practice of lowercasing the first word in an object's name, and then uppercasing the first letter of each subsequent word in the name

Class—a pattern or blueprint that the computer uses to create an object

Class definition—a block of code that specifies (or defines) the appearance and behaviors of an object

Class Name list box—appears in the Code Editor window and lists the names of the objects included in the user interface

Code—program instructions

Code Editor window—the window in which you enter your application's code

Control—an object (such as a text box or a button) displayed on a form

Dot member access operator—a period; used to indicate a hierarchy of namespaces

Event procedure—a set of Visual Basic instructions that tells an object how to respond to an event

Events—actions to which an object can respond; examples include clicking, double-clicking, and scrolling

Executable file—a file that can be run outside of the Visual Studio 2008 IDE

Font—the general shape of the characters used to display text

Form (Windows Form object)—the foundation for the user interface in a Windows-based application

Form file—a file that contains the code associated with a Windows form

GUI—graphical user interface

IDE—integrated development environment

Integrated development environment (IDE)—an environment that contains all of the tools and features you need to create, run, and test your programs

Keyword—a word that has a special meaning in a programming language

Label control—the control used to display text that the user is not allowed to edit while the application is running

Method—a predefined Visual Basic procedure that you can call (or invoke) when needed

Method Name list box—appears in the Code Editor window and lists the events to which the selected object is capable of responding

Namespace—a block of memory cells inside the computer; contains the code that defines a group of related classes.

Object—in object-oriented programming, anything that can be seen, touched, or used

Object box—the section of the Properties window that contains the name of the selected object

Object-oriented programming language—a language that allows the programmer to use objects to accomplish a program's goal

Pascal case—the practice of uppercasing the first letter in a form's name, as well as the first letter of each subsequent word in the name

Picture box control—the control used to display an image on a form

Point—used to measure font size; 1/72 of an inch

Procedure footer—the last line in a code template

Procedure header—the first line in a code template

Programmers—the people who write programs

Programming languages—the languages that programmers use to communicate with the computer

Programs—the directions given to computers

Project—a container that stores files associated with only a specific piece of a solution

Properties—the attributes of an object that control the object's appearance and behavior

Properties list—the section of the Properties window that lists the names of the properties associated with the selected object, as well as each property's value

Properties window—the window that lists an object's attributes (properties)

Sequence structure (**sequential processing**)—refers to the fact that the computer processes a procedure's instructions one after another in the order in which they appear in the procedure

Sequential processing (**sequence structure**)—refers to the fact that the computer processes a procedure's instructions one after another in the order in which they appear in the procedure

Settings box—the right column of the Properties list; displays the current value (setting) of each of the properties

Solution—a container that stores the projects and files for an entire application

Solution Explorer window—the window that displays a list of the projects contained in the current solution, and the items contained in each project

Source file—a file that contains code

Startup form—the form that appears automatically when an application is started

String—zero or more characters enclosed in quotation marks

Sub procedure—a block of code that performs a specific task

Syntax—the rules of a programming language

Toolbox—Toolbox window

Toolbox window (**toolbox**)—the window that contains the tools used when creating an interface; each tool represents a class

User interface—what you see and interact with when using an application

Web-based application—an application that has a Web user interface and runs on a server

Windows-based application—an application that has a Windows user interface and runs on a desktop computer

Windows Form Designer window—the window in which you create your application's GUI

Windows Form object (**form**)—the foundation for the user interface in a Windows-based application

SELF-CHECK QUESTIONS AND ANSWERS

1. A form contains a button control named exitButton. When the button is selected in the interface, _____ will appear in the Object box in the Properties window.

   a. Button System.Windows.Forms.exitButton

   b. Button System.Windows.Button.exitButton

   c. exitButton System.Windows.Button

   d. exitButton System.Windows.Forms.Button

2. You use _____ case for control names.

   a. camel   b. control

   c. Hungarian   d. Pascal

3. An application calculates and displays a sales tax amount. The application should display the calculated amount in a _____ control.

   a. button   b. form

   c. label   d. text

4. To end an application when a button is clicked, you enter the _____ instruction in the button's Click event procedure.

   a. Close.Me()   b. Me.Close()

   c. Me.End()   d. None of the above.

5. Which of the following assigns the string "Las Vegas" to the cityLabel control?

   a. cityLabel.Label = "Las Vegas"   b. cityLabel.String = "Las Vegas"

   c. cityLabel.Text = "Las Vegas"   d. None of the above.

   Answers: 1) d, 2) a, 3) c, 4) b, 5) c

REVIEW QUESTIONS

1. The set of directions given to a computer is called _____.

   a. computerese   b. commands

   c. instructions   d. a program

2. When a form has been modified since the last time it was saved, _____ appears on its tab in the designer window.

   a. an ampersand (&)   b. a percent sign (%)

   c. a plus sign (+)   d. None of the above.

3. Which of the following assigns the string "785.23" to the amountTextBox control?

   a. amountTextBox = "785.23"

   b. amountTextBox.Label = "785.23"

   c. amountTextBox.String = "785.23"

   d. amountTextBox.Text = "785.23"

4. _____ is a pattern or blueprint for creating an object.

   a. An attribute   b. A behavior

   c. A class   d. An instance

5. A _____ is a container that stores the projects and files for an entire application.

   a. form file   b. profile

   c. solution   d. template

6. The _____ window lists the projects and files included in a solution.

   a. Object   b. Project

   c. Properties   d. Solution Explorer

7. You use the _____ window to set the characteristics that control an object's appearance and behavior.

   a. Characteristics   b. Object

   c. Properties   d. Toolbox

8. Which of the following instructions displays the text "Sales:" in the Label1 control?

   a. Label1.Caption = "Sales:"   b. Label1.Text = "Sales:"

   c. Label1.Name = "Sales:"   d. Label1.Label = "Sales:"

9. The text that appears on the face of a button control is stored in the control's _____ property.

a. Caption   b. Command

c. Label   d. Text

10. Actions such as clicking and double-clicking are called _____.

a. actionEvents   b. events

c. happenings   d. procedures

REVIEW EXERCISES— SHORT ANSWER

1. Explain the difference between a Windows-based application and a Web-based application.

2. Explain the difference between a form's Text property and its Name property.

3. Explain the difference between a form file object and a Windows Form object.

4. What does the dot member access operator indicate in the text System.Windows.Forms.Label?

5. What property determines whether the value stored in the form's Text property appears on the Windows taskbar when the application is running? (*Hint*: Use the Description pane in the Properties window.)

6. What property determines whether an icon is displayed in the form's title bar?

COMPUTER EXERCISES

1. In this exercise, you modify the application from this chapter's Programming Example.

a. If necessary, create the State Capitals application shown in this chapter's Programming Example.

b. Add another label control to the form. Assign the name signingOrderLabel to the control. Modify the application so that it displays a message that indicates the state's U.S. Constitution signing order. For example, when the user clicks the Alabama button, the button's Click event procedure should display the message "Alabama was the 22nd state to sign the U.S. Constitution." (Alaska was the 49th state to sign the Constitution, Arizona was the 48th state, and Arkansas was the 25th state.)

    c. Save the solution, then start and test the application. Close the solution.

    d. Locate the application's .exe file. Run the file from the Run dialog box in Windows.

2. In this exercise, you add label and button controls to a form. You also change the properties of the form and its controls.

    a. Open the Mechanics Solution (Mechanics Solution.sln) file, which is contained in the VbReloaded2008\Chap01\Mechanics Solution folder.

    b. Assign the filename Main Form.vb to the form file object.

    c. Assign the name MainForm to the Windows Form object.

    d. The form's title bar should say IMA. Set the appropriate property.

    e. The form should be centered on the screen when it first appears. Set the appropriate property.

    f. Change the form's Font property to Segoe UI, 9 point.

    g. Add a label control to the form. Change the label control's name to companyLabel.

    h. The label control should display the caption "International Mechanics Association" (without the quotation marks). Set the appropriate property.

    i. Display the label control's text in italics. Change the size of the text to 12 points.

    j. Center the label control horizontally and vertically on the form.

    k. Add a button control to the form. Change the button control's name to exitButton.

    l. The button control should display the caption "Exit" (without the quotation marks). Set the appropriate property.

    m. Lock the controls on the form.

    n. The Exit button should terminate the application when clicked. Enter the appropriate code in the Code Editor window.

    o. Verify that the MainForm is the project's startup form.

    p. Save the solution, then start and test the application. Close the solution.

3. In this exercise, you add label and button controls to a form. You also change the properties of the form and its controls.

    a. Create the user interface shown in Figure 1-57. Name the solution Costello Solution. Name the project Costello Project. Name the form file object Main Form.vb. Save the application in the VbReloaded2008\Chap01 folder.

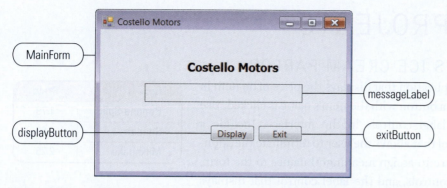

Figure 1-57

b. The Exit button should terminate the application when it is clicked. Enter the appropriate code in the Code Editor window.

c. When the Display button is clicked, it should display the message "We have the best deals in town!" in the messageLabel control. Enter the appropriate code in the Code Editor window.

d. Save the solution. Start and then test the application. Close the solution.

 4. In this exercise, you find and correct an error in an application. The process of finding and correcting errors is called debugging.

a. Open the Debug Solution (Debug Solution.sln) file, which is contained in the VbReloaded2008\Chap01\Debug Solution folder.

b. Start the application. Click the Exit button. Notice that the Exit button does not end the application.

c. Click the Close button on the form's title bar to end the application.

d. Open the Code Editor window. Locate and then correct the error.

e. Save the solution, then start and test the application. Close the solution.

CASE PROJECTS

CASTLE'S ICE CREAM PARLOR

Create an application that displays the price of an item in a label when a button with the item's name is clicked. Use button and label controls in the interface. Include a button control that allows the user to terminate the application. Be sure to assign meaningful names to the form, the button controls, and the label control that displays the price. Name the solution, project, and form file Castle Solution, Castle Project, and Main Form.vb, respectively. Save the application in the VbReloaded2008\Chap01 folder.

Item	Price
Banana Split	1.79
Sundae	.99
Milkshake	2.25

ALLEN SCHOOL DISTRICT

Create an application that displays the name of the principal and the school's phone number in labels when a button with the school's name is clicked. Use button and label controls in the interface. Include a button control that allows the user to terminate the application. Be sure to assign meaningful names to the form, the button controls, and the label controls that display the name and phone number. Name the solution, project, and form file Allen Solution, Allen Project, and Main Form.vb, respectively. Save the application in the VbReloaded2008\Chap01 folder.

School	Principal	Phone number
Primary Center	June Davis	111-9999
Lewis Middle School	Matt Hayes	111-8888
Kaufman Junior High	Sandy Jenkins	111-8978
Allen High School	Perry Thomas	111-2222

ELVIRA LEARNING CENTER

Create an application that displays the equivalent Spanish word in a label when a button with an English word is clicked. Use button and label controls in the interface. Include a button control that allows the user to terminate the application. Be sure to assign meaningful names to the form, the button controls, and the label control that displays the Spanish word. Name the

English	Spanish
Hello	Hola
Good-bye	Adios
Love	Amor
Cat	Gato
Dog	Perro

solution, project, and form file Elvira Solution, Elvira Project, and Main Form.vb, respectively. Save the application in the VbReloaded2008\Chap01 folder.

MARY GOLDS FLOWER SHOP

Create an eye-catching splash screen for the flower shop. A splash screen is the first image that appears when an application is started. It is used to introduce the application and to hold the user's attention while the application is being read into the computer's memory. You can use the tools you learned about in this chapter, or you can experiment with other tools from the toolbox. (For example, the Timer tool creates a timer control, which you can use to close the splash screen after a specified period of time. You can look ahead to Chapter 8 to learn how to use a timer control.) Name the solution, project, and form file Mary Golds Solution, Mary Golds Project, and Main Form.vb, respectively. Save the application in the VbReloaded2008\Chap01 folder.

2

CREATING A USER INTERFACE

After studying Chapter 2, you should be able to:

Plan an application

Complete a TOE chart

Use a text box and table layout panel

Explain the difference between a primary window and a dialog box

Follow the Windows standards regarding the layout and labeling of controls

Follow the Windows standards regarding the use of graphics, fonts, and color

Assign access keys to controls

Set the tab order

Designate a default button and a cancel button

Add a splash screen to a project

PLANNING AN APPLICATION

Before you can create the user interface for your application, you need to plan the application. The plan should be developed jointly with the user to ensure that the application meets the user's needs. It cannot be stressed enough that the only way to guarantee the success of an application is to actively involve the user in the planning phase. Figure 2-1 lists the steps you follow when planning an application.

»HOW TO . . .

PLAN AN APPLICATION
1. Identify the tasks the application needs to perform.
2. Identify the objects to which you will assign those tasks.
3. Identify the events required to trigger an object into performing its assigned tasks.
4. Design the user interface.

Figure 2-1: How to plan an application

You can use a TOE (Task, Object, Event) chart to record the application's tasks, objects, and events, which are identified in the first three steps of the planning phase. In the next several sections, you will complete a TOE chart for the Sunshine Cellular Company.

SUNSHINE CELLULAR COMPANY

The Sunshine Cellular Company takes orders for cell phones by phone. The cell phones are priced at $100 each and are available in two colors: silver and blue. The company employs 10 salespeople to answer the phones. The salespeople record each order on a form that contains the customer's name, address, and the number of silver and blue phones ordered. The salespeople then calculate the total number of phones ordered and the total price of the phones, including a 5% sales tax. The company's sales manager, Sylvia Jacobs, feels that having the salespeople manually perform the necessary calculations is much too time-consuming and prone to errors. She wants you to create a computerized application that will solve the problems of the current order-taking system. The first step in planning this application is to identify the application's tasks.

IDENTIFYING THE APPLICATION'S TASKS

Realizing that it is essential to involve the user when planning the application, you meet with the sales manager of Sunshine Cellular, Ms. Jacobs, to determine her requirements. You ask Ms. Jacobs to bring the form the salespeople currently use to record the orders. Viewing the current forms and procedures will help you gain a better understanding of the application. You also can use the current form as a guide when designing the user interface. Figure 2-2 shows the current order form used by Sunshine Cellular.

Sunshine Cellular Order Form			
Customer name: _____			
Address: _____			
City: _____ State: _____ ZIP: _____			

Number of silver phones ordered	Number of blue phones ordered	Total number of phones ordered	Total price

Figure 2-2: Current order form used by Sunshine Cellular

When identifying the tasks an application needs to perform, it is helpful to ask the following questions:

» What information will the application need to display on the screen and/or print on the printer?

» What information will the user need to enter into the user interface to display and/or print the desired information?

» What information will the application need to calculate to display and/or print the desired information?

» How will the user end the application?

» Will previous information need to be cleared from the screen before new information is entered?

The answers to these questions will help you identify the application's major tasks. The answers for each question for the Sunshine Cellular application are as follows.

What information will the application need to display on the screen and/or print on the printer? (Notice that "display" refers to the screen, and "print" refers to the printer.) The Sunshine Cellular application should display the customer's name, street address, city, state, ZIP code, the number of silver phones ordered, the number of blue phones ordered, the total number of phones ordered, and the total price of the order. In this case, the application does not need to print anything on the printer.

What information will the user need to enter into the user interface to display and/or print the desired information? In the Sunshine Cellular application, the salesperson (the user) must enter the customer's name, street address, city, state, ZIP code, and the number of silver and blue phones ordered.

What information will the application need to calculate to display and/or print the desired information? The Sunshine Cellular application needs to calculate the total number of phones ordered and the total price of the order.

How will the user end the application? All applications should provide a way for the user to end the application. The Sunshine Cellular application will use an Exit button for this task.

Will previous information need to be cleared from the screen before new information is entered? After the salesperson enters and calculates an order, he or she will need to clear the order's information from the screen before entering the next order.

Figure 2-3 shows the Sunshine Cellular application's tasks listed in a TOE chart. The tasks in a TOE chart do not need to be listed in any particular order. In this case, the data entry tasks are listed first, followed by the calculation tasks, display tasks, application ending task, and screen clearing task.

>>TIP

You can draw a TOE chart by hand, or you can use the table feature in a word processor (such as Microsoft Word) to draw one.

Task	Object	Event
Get the following order information from the user:		
Customer's name		
Street address		
City		
State		
ZIP code		
Number of silver phones ordered		
Number of blue phones ordered		
Calculate the total phones ordered and the total price		

Figure 2-3: Tasks entered in a TOE chart (*continued on next page*)

Task	Object	Event
Display the following information:		
Customer's name		
Street address		
City		
State		
ZIP code		
Number of silver phones ordered		
Number of blue phones ordered		
Total phones ordered		
Total price		
End the application		
Clear the screen for the next order		

Figure 2-3: Tasks entered in a TOE chart (*continued from previous page*)

IDENTIFYING THE OBJECTS

After completing the Task column of the TOE chart, you then assign each task to an object in the user interface. For this application, the only objects you will use to handle the tasks are the button, label, and text box controls. As you learned in Chapter 1, you use a label control to display information that you do not want the user to change while your application is running, and you use a button control to perform an action immediately after the user clicks it. You use a **text box** to give the user an area in which to enter data. You create a text box using the TextBox tool in the toolbox.

The first task listed in Figure 2-3 is to get the order information from the user. For each order, the salesperson will need to enter the customer's name, address, city, state, and ZIP code, as well as the number of silver phones ordered and the number of blue phones ordered. Because you need to provide the salesperson with areas in which to enter the information, you will assign the first task to seven text boxes—one for each item of information. The names of the text boxes will be nameTextBox, addressTextBox, cityTextBox, stateTextBox, zipTextBox, silverTextBox, and blueTextBox.

The second task listed in the TOE chart is to calculate both the total number of phones ordered and the total price. So that the salesperson can calculate these amounts at any time, you will assign the task to a button named calcButton.

The third task listed in the TOE chart is to display the order information, the total number of phones ordered, and the total price. The order information will be displayed automatically when the user enters that information in the seven text boxes. The total phones ordered and the total price, however, are not entered by the user; rather, those amounts are calculated by the calcButton. Because the user should not be allowed to change the calculated results, you will have the calcButton display the total phones ordered and the total price in two label controls named totalPhonesLabel and totalPriceLabel. Notice that the task of displaying the total phones ordered involves two objects (calcButton and totalPhonesLabel). The task of displaying the total price also involves two objects (calcButton and totalPriceLabel).

The last two tasks listed in the TOE chart are "End the application" and "Clear the screen for the next order." You will assign the tasks to buttons so that the user has control over when the tasks are performed. You will name the buttons exitButton and clearButton. Figure 2-4 shows the TOE chart with the Task and Object columns completed.

Task	Object	Event
Get the following order information from the user:		
Customer's name	nameTextBox	
Street address	addressTextBox	
City	cityTextBox	
State	stateTextBox	
ZIP code	zipTextBox	
Number of silver phones ordered	silverTextBox	
Number of blue phones ordered	blueTextBox	
Calculate the total phones ordered and the total price	calcButton	
Display the following information:		
Customer's name	nameTextBox	
Street address	addressTextBox	
City	cityTextBox	
State	stateTextBox	
ZIP code	zipTextBox	
Number of silver phones ordered	silverTextBox	
Number of blue phones ordered	blueTextBox	
Total phones ordered	calcButton, totalPhonesLabel	
Total price	calcButton, totalPriceLabel	
End the application	exitButton	
Clear the screen for the next order	clearButton	

Figure 2-4: Tasks and objects entered in a TOE chart

IDENTIFYING THE EVENTS

After defining the application's tasks and assigning those tasks to objects in the user interface, you then determine which objects need an event (such as clicking) to occur for the object to perform its assigned task. The seven text boxes listed in the TOE chart in Figure 2-4 are assigned the task of getting and displaying the order information. Text boxes accept and display information automatically, so no special event is necessary for them to do their assigned task. The two label controls are assigned the task of displaying the total number of phones ordered and the total price of the order. Label controls automatically display their contents; so, here again, no special event needs to occur. (Recall that the two label controls will get their values from the calcButton.) You will have the three buttons listed in the TOE chart perform their assigned tasks when the user clicks them. Figure 2-5 shows the TOE chart with the tasks, objects, and events necessary for the Sunshine Cellular application.

»TIP

Not all objects in a user interface will need an event to occur in order for the object to perform its assigned tasks.

Task	Object	Event
Get the following order information from the user:		
Customer's name	nameTextBox	None
Street address	addressTextBox	None
City	cityTextBox	None
State	stateTextBox	None
ZIP code	zipTextBox	None
Number of silver phones ordered	silverTextBox	None
Number of blue phones ordered	blueTextBox	None
Calculate the total phones ordered and the total price	calcButton	Click
Display the following information:		
Customer's name	nameTextBox	None
Street address	addressTextBox	None
City	cityTextBox	None
State	stateTextBox	None
ZIP code	zipTextBox	None
Number of silver phones ordered	silverTextBox	None
Number of blue phones ordered	blueTextBox	None
Total phones ordered	calcButton, totalPhonesLabel	Click, None
Total price	calcButton, totalPriceLabel	Click, None
End the application	exitButton	Click
Clear the screen for the next order	clearButton	Click

Figure 2-5: Completed TOE chart ordered by task

If the application you are creating is small, as is the Sunshine Cellular application, you can use the TOE chart in its current form to help you write the Visual Basic code. When the application you are creating is large, however, it is often helpful to rearrange the TOE chart so that it is ordered by object instead of by task. To do so, you list the name of each unique object in the Object column. Then list the tasks you have assigned to each object in the Task column, and list the events in the Event column. Figure 2-6 shows the rearranged TOE chart, ordered by object rather than by task.

Task	Object	Event
1. Calculate the total phones ordered and the total price 2. Display the total phones ordered and the total price in totalPhonesLabel and totalPriceLabel	calcButton	Click
Clear the screen for the next order	clearButton	Click
End the application	exitButton	Click
Display the total phones ordered (from calcButton)	totalPhonesLabel	None
Display the total price (from calcButton)	totalPriceLabel	None
Get and display the order information	nameTextBox, addressTextBox, cityTextBox, stateTextBox, zipTextBox, silverTextBox, blueTextBox	None

Figure 2-6: Completed TOE chart ordered by object

DESIGNING THE USER INTERFACE

After completing the TOE chart, the next step is to design the user interface. Although the TOE chart lists the objects you need to include in the application's user interface, it does not tell you *where* to place those objects in the interface. While the design of an interface is open to creativity, there are some guidelines to which you should adhere so that your application is consistent with the Windows standards. This consistency will make your application easier to both learn and use, because the user interface will have a familiar look to it. The guidelines are referred to as GUI guidelines, because they pertain to Graphical User Interfaces.

The first GUI guideline you learn in this chapter relates to the form itself. Most Windows applications consist of a main window, possibly some other primary windows, and one or more secondary windows, called dialog boxes. The primary viewing and editing of your application's data take place in a **primary window**. The primary window shown in Figure 2-7, for example, allows you to view and edit documents created using the Notepad application. **Dialog boxes**, on the other hand, support and supplement a user's activities in the primary windows. The Font dialog box shown in Figure 2-7, for instance, allows you to specify the font of the text selected in the primary window.

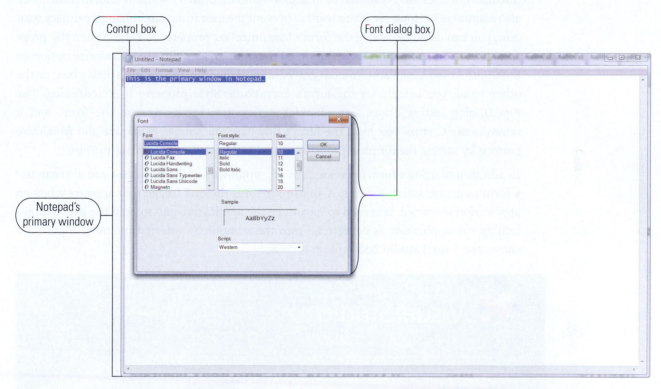

Figure 2-7: Primary window and Font dialog box in Notepad

Primary windows can be resized, minimized, maximized, and closed by the user. To resize a primary window, the user simply drags the window's border. To minimize, maximize, or close a primary window, the user clicks the Minimize, Maximize, or Close buttons that appear on the window's title bar. The user also can click the Control box to display the Control menu, which contains Minimize, Maximize, and Close options. Unlike primary windows, dialog boxes can be closed only. They cannot be resized, minimized, or maximized by the user. The only buttons that appear in a dialog box's title bar are the Close button and, in some cases, the Help button. In addition, a dialog box does not contain a Control box.

In a Visual Basic Windows-based application, you use a form to create both primary windows and dialog boxes. You specify the border style of the window or dialog box using the form's FormBorderStyle property. If the form represents a primary window, you typically leave the form's FormBorderStyle property at its default setting, Sizable. When the FormBorderStyle property is set to Sizable, the user can drag the form's borders to change the form's size while the application is running. You also leave the form's MinimizeBox property and MaximizeBox property set at the default setting, True. This allows the user to minimize and maximize the form using the Minimize and Maximize buttons on the form's title bar. The user always should be able to minimize a primary window and, in most cases, also maximize it. However, if you want to prevent the user from maximizing a primary window, you can do so by setting the form's MaximizeBox property to False. When the property is set to False, the Maximize button on the title bar, as well as the Maximize option on the Control menu, appears dimmed (grayed-out). If the form represents a dialog box, on the other hand, you usually set the form's FormBorderStyle property to FixedDialog. The FixedDialog setting draws a fixed, thick dialog-style border around the form, and it removes the Control box from the form's title bar. You remove Minimize and Maximize buttons by setting the form's MinimizeBox and MaximizeBox properties to False.

In addition to using a form to create primary windows and dialog boxes, you also can use a form to create splash screens. A splash screen is the first image that appears when an application is started. It is used to introduce the application and to hold the user's attention as the application is being read into the computer's internal memory. Figure 2-8 shows the Visual Studio 2008 splash screen.

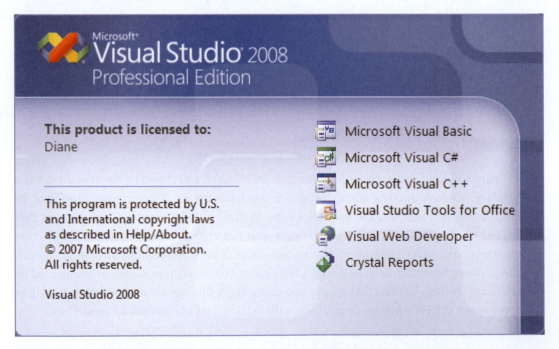

Figure 2-8: Visual Studio 2008 splash screen

If a form represents a splash screen, you typically set the form's FormBorderStyle property to FixedSingle. You also set the form's ControlBox property to False; doing this removes the Control box, as well as the Minimize, Maximize, and Close buttons, from the title bar. You can remove the entire title bar from the form by setting the ControlBox property to False, and then deleting the text that appears in the form's Text property.

ARRANGING THE CONTROLS

In Western countries, you should organize the user interface so that the information flows either vertically or horizontally, with the most important information always located in the upper-left corner of the screen. In a vertical arrangement the information flows from top to bottom; the essential information is located in the first column of the screen, while secondary information is placed in subsequent columns. In a horizontal arrangement, on the other hand, the information flows from left to right; the essential information is placed in the first row of the screen, with secondary information placed in subsequent rows. You can group together related controls using either white (empty) space or one of the tools located in the Containers section of the toolbox. Examples of tools found in the Containers section include the GroupBox, Panel, and TableLayoutPanel tools.

Figures 2-9 and 2-10 show two different interfaces for the Sunshine Cellular application. In Figure 2-9, the information is arranged vertically, and white space is used to group related controls together. In Figure 2-10, the information is arranged horizontally. Related controls in Figure 2-10 are grouped together using a **group box control**, a **panel control**, and a **table layout panel control**. The difference between a panel and a group box is that, unlike a group box, a panel can have scroll bars. However, unlike a panel, a group box has a Text property that you can use to indicate the contents of the control. Unlike the panel and group box controls, the table layout panel control provides a table structure in which you place other controls.

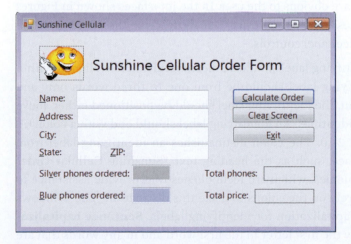

Figure 2-9: Vertical arrangement of the Sunshine Cellular interface

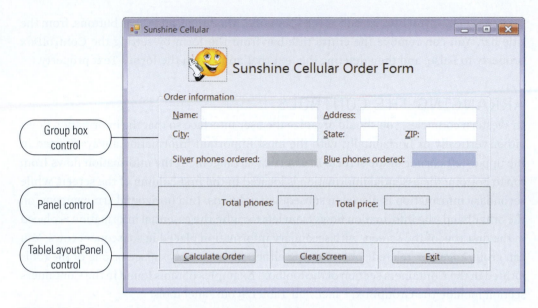

Figure 2-10: Horizontal arrangement of the Sunshine Cellular interface

Each text box and button in the interfaces shown in Figures 2-9 and 2-10 is labeled so the user knows the control's purpose. For example, the "Name:" label that identifies the nameTextBox tells the user the type of information to enter in the text box. Similarly, the "Calculate Order" caption on the calcButton indicates the action the button will perform when it is clicked.

In many applications, program output (such as the result of calculations) is displayed in a label control in the interface. Label controls that display program output should be labeled so that their contents are obvious to the user. In the interfaces shown in Figures 2-9 and 2-10, the "Total phones:" and "Total price:" labels describe the contents of the totalPhonesLabel and totalPriceLabel controls.

The text contained in an identifying label should be meaningful and left-aligned within the label control. The identifying label should be from one to three words only and appear on one line. In addition, the identifying label should be positioned either above or to the left of the control it identifies. An identifying label should end with a colon (:), as shown in Figures 2-9 and 2-10. The colon distinguishes an identifying label from other text in the user interface, such as the heading text "Sunshine Cellular Order Form". Some assistive technologies, which are technologies that provide assistance to individuals with disabilities, rely on the colons to make this distinction. The Windows standard is to use sentence capitalization for identifying labels. **Sentence capitalization** means you capitalize only the first letter in the first word and in any words that are customarily capitalized.

As you learned in Chapter 1, buttons are identified by a caption that appears on the button's face. The caption should be meaningful. In addition, it should be from one to three words only and appear on one line. The Windows standard for button captions is to use book title capitalization. When using **book title capitalization**, you capitalize the first letter in each word, except for articles, conjunctions, and prepositions that do not occur at either the beginning or the end of the caption.

Always size the buttons in the interface relative to each other. When the buttons are positioned horizontally, as they are in Figure 2-10, all the buttons should be the same height; their widths, however, may vary if necessary. If the buttons are stacked vertically, as they are in Figure 2-9, all the buttons should be the same height and the same width. In a group of buttons, always place the most commonly used button first. If the buttons are positioned horizontally, the most commonly used button should be the leftmost button in the group, as shown in Figure 2-10. If the buttons are stacked vertically, the most commonly used button should be at the top of the button group, as shown in Figure 2-9.

When positioning the controls in the interface, be sure to maintain a consistent margin from the edge of the form. Related controls should be placed close to each other on the form. Typically, controls that are not part of any logical grouping are positioned farther away from other controls. Try to minimize the number of different margins used in the interface so that the user can more easily scan the information. You can do this by aligning the borders of the controls wherever possible. You can align the borders using the snap lines that appear as you are building the interface. Or, you can use the Format menu to align (and also size) the controls.

>> TIP

You learned how to use the Format menu in the Programming Tutorial section of Chapter 1.

When designing the user interface, keep in mind that you want to create a screen that no one notices. Snazzy interfaces may get "oohs" and "aahs" during their initial use, but they become tiresome after a while. The most important point to remember is that the interface should not distract the user from doing his or her work. So that you do not overload your user interfaces with too much color, too many fonts, and too many graphics, the next three sections provide some guidelines to follow regarding these elements.

>> TIP

The graphics, font, and color guidelines do not pertain to game applications.

INCLUDING GRAPHICS IN THE USER INTERFACE

The human eye is attracted to pictures before text, so include a graphic in an interface only if you have a good reason for doing so. Graphics typically are used to either emphasize or clarify a portion of the screen. You also can use a graphic for aesthetic purposes, as long as the graphic is small and placed in a location that does not distract the user. The small graphic in the Sunshine Cellular interfaces (shown earlier in Figures 2-9 and 2-10) is included for aesthetics only. The graphic is purposely located in the upper-left corner of the interface, which is where you want the user's eye to be drawn first anyway. The graphic adds a personal touch to the order form without being distracting to the user.

INCLUDING DIFFERENT FONTS IN THE USER INTERFACE

As you learned in Chapter 1, you can use an object's Font property to change the type, style, and size of the font used for the object's text. You should use only one font type for all of the text in the interface. In addition, be sure to limit the number of font sizes used to either one or two. The Sunshine Cellular interfaces (shown earlier in Figures 2-9 and 2-10) employ the Segoe UI font in two font sizes: 14 point for the heading at the top of the interface, and 9 point for everything else. Recall that the 9-point size of the Segoe UI font is recommended for applications created for the Windows Vista environment. Avoid using italics and underlining in an interface, because both make text difficult to read. In addition, limit the use of bold text to titles, headings, and key items that you want to emphasize.

When you add a control to the form, the value stored in the form's Font property is automatically assigned to the control's Font property. Therefore, one way to change the font used in an interface is to change the form's Font property *before* adding the controls to the form. By doing this, you will not need to set each control's Font property separately. You also can change the form's Font property *after* adding the controls. An existing control whose Font property has not been set individually will assume the form's setting.

INCLUDING COLOR IN THE USER INTERFACE

Just as the human eye is attracted to graphics before text, it also is attracted to color before black and white, so use color sparingly. It is a good practice to build the interface using black, white, and gray first, then add color only if you have a good reason to do so. Keep the following three points in mind when deciding whether to include color in an interface:

1. Many people have some form of either color-blindness or color confusion, so they will have trouble distinguishing colors.

2. Color is very subjective; a pretty color to you may be hideous to someone else.

3. A color may have a different meaning in a different culture.

Usually, it is best to use black text on a white, off-white, or light gray background. This is because dark text on a light background is the easiest to read. You should never use a dark color for the background or a light color for the text, because a dark background is hard on the eyes, and light-colored text can appear blurry. If you are going to include color in the interface, limit the number of colors to three, not including white, black, and gray. Be sure that the colors you choose complement each other. Although color can be used to identify an important element in the interface, you should never use it as the only means of identification. In the Sunshine Cellular interfaces, for example, the silver and blue text boxes help the salesperson quickly identify where to enter the order for silver and blue phones, respectively. However, color is not the only means of identifying those areas in the interfaces: the labels to the left of the text boxes also tell the user where to enter the orders for silver and blue phones.

»TIP

If the Segoe UI font is not available, use the Tahoma, Microsoft Sans Serif, or Arial font.

ASSIGNING ACCESS KEYS

Looking closely at the Sunshine Cellular interface shown in Figure 2-11, you will notice that the text in many of the controls contains an underlined letter, called an access key. An **access key** allows the user to select an object using the Alt key in combination with a letter or number. For example, you can select the File menu in Visual Studio by pressing Alt+F, because the letter "F" is the File menu's access key. Access keys are not case sensitive; in other words, you can select the File menu by pressing either Alt+F or Alt+f. Similarly, you can select the Calculate Order button in the interface shown in Figure 2-11 by pressing either Alt+C or Alt+c.

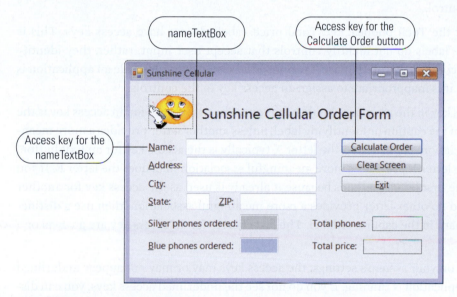

Figure 2-11: Sunshine Cellular interface

You should assign access keys to each of the controls (in the interface) that can accept user input. Examples of such controls include text boxes and buttons, because the user can enter information in a text box and he or she can click a button. The only exceptions to this rule are the OK and Cancel buttons, which do not have access keys in Windows applications. It is important to assign access keys to controls for the following three reasons:

1. Access keys allow a user to work with the application even when the mouse becomes inoperative.

2. Access keys allow users who are fast typists to keep their hands on the keyboard.

3. Access keys allow people with disabilities, which may prevent them from working with a mouse, to use the application.

You assign an access key by including an ampersand (&) in the control's caption or identifying label. For example, to assign an access key to a button, you include the ampersand in the button's Text property, which is where a button's caption is stored. To assign an access key to a text box, on the other hand, you include the ampersand in the Text property of the label control that identifies the text box. (As you will learn later in this chapter, you also must set the identifying label's TabIndex property to a value that is one number less than the value stored in the text box's TabIndex property.) You enter the ampersand to the immediate left of the character you want to designate as the access key. For example, to assign the letter C as the access key for the Calculate Order button, you enter &Calculate Order in the button's Text property. To assign the letter N as the access key for the nameTextBox control, you enter &Name: in the Text property of its identifying label control.

Notice that the Total phones: and Total price: labels do not have access keys. This is because the labels do not identify controls that accept user input; rather, they identify other label controls. Recall that users cannot access label controls while an application is running, so it is inappropriate to assign an access key to the controls.

Each access key in the interface should be unique. The first choice for an access key is the first letter of the caption or identifying label, unless another letter provides a more meaningful association. For example, the letter X typically is the access key for an Exit button, because the letter X provides a more meaningful association than does the letter E. If you can't use the first letter (perhaps because it already is used as the access key for another control) and no other letter provides a more meaningful association, then use a distinctive consonant in the caption or label. The last choices for an access key are a vowel or a number.

Depending on your system's settings, the access keys may or may not appear underlined while an application is running. If you do not see the underlined access keys, you can display them temporarily by pressing the Alt key. You can subsequently hide them by pressing the Alt key again. To always display access keys, click Start on the Windows Vista taskbar, click Control Panel, then click Appearance and Personalization. In the Ease of Access Center section, click Underline keyboard shortcuts and access keys, then select the Underline keyboard shortcuts and access keys check box. Click the Save button, then close the Ease of Access dialog box.

»TIP

To display access keys when using the Classic View in Windows Vista, click Start, double-click Ease of Access Center, click Make the keyboard easier to use, select the Underline keyboard shortcuts and access keys check box, click the Save button, then close the dialog box.

SETTING THE TABINDEX PROPERTY

Most times, the order in which controls are added to a form does not represent the desired tab order, which is the order that each control should receive the focus when the user presses the Tab key. When a control has the **focus**, it can accept user input. You specify the desired order using the TabIndex property of each control. A control's TabIndex property determines the order in which the control receives the focus when the user presses either the Tab key or an access key while the application is running. A control having a TabIndex of 2 will receive the focus immediately after the control whose TabIndex is 1. Likewise, a control with a TabIndex of 18 will receive the focus immediately after the control whose TabIndex is 17.

When you add to a form a control that has a TabIndex property, the computer sets the control's TabIndex property to a number that represents the order in which the control was added to the form. The TabIndex property for the first control added to a form is 0 (zero), the TabIndex property for the second control is 1, and so on. To determine the appropriate TabIndex settings for an interface, you first make a list of the controls that can accept user input. The list should reflect the order in which the user will want to access the controls. In the Sunshine Cellular interface shown earlier in Figure 2-11, the user typically will want to access the nameTextBox first, then the addressTextBox, the cityTextBox, and so on. If a control that accepts user input is identified by a label control, you also include the label control in the list. A text box is an example of a control that accepts user input and is identified by a label control. You place the name of the label control immediately above the name of the control it identifies in the list. In the Sunshine Cellular interface, the Label1 control (which displays Name:) identifies the nameTextBox; therefore, Label1 should appear immediately above nameTextBox in the list. The names of controls that do not accept user input, and those that do not identify controls that accept user input, should be placed at the bottom of the list; these names do not need to appear in any specific order. After listing the controls, you then assign each control in the list a TabIndex value, beginning with the number 0. Figure 2-12 shows the list of controls for the Sunshine Cellular interface along with the appropriate TabIndex values.

»TIP

When a text box has the focus, an insertion point appears inside it. When a button has the focus, it has a darkened border, and a dotted rectangle appears around its caption.

»TIP

If a control does not have a TabIndex property, you do not assign it a TabIndex value. You can tell if a control has a TabIndex property by viewing its Properties list.

Controls that accept user input, along with their identifying label controls	TabIndex setting
Label1 (Name:)	0
nameTextBox	1
Label2 (Address:)	2
addressTextBox	3
Label3 (City:)	4
cityTextBox	5
Label4 (State:)	6
stateTextBox	7
Label5 (ZIP:)	8
zipTextBox	9
Label6 (Silver phones ordered:)	10
silverTextBox	11
Label7 (Blue phones ordered:)	12
blueTextBox	13
calcButton	14
clearButton	15
exitButton	16
Other controls	**TabIndex setting**
Label10 (Sunshine Cellular Order Form)	17
Label8 (Total phones:)	18
Label9 (Total price:)	19
totalPhonesLabel	20
totalPriceLabel	21
PictureBox1	This control does not have a TabIndex property.

Figure 2-12: List of controls and TabIndex settings for the Sunshine Cellular interface

The first column in Figure 2-12 contains two sections. The first section is titled "Controls that accept user input, along with their identifying label controls." This section contains the names of the seven text boxes and three buttons in the interface, because those controls can accept user input. Each text box in the list is associated with an identifying label control, whose name appears immediately above the text box name in the list. Notice that the TabIndex value assigned to each text box's identifying label control is one number less than the value assigned to the text box itself. For example, the Label1 control has a TabIndex value of 0, and its corresponding text box (nameTextBox) has a TabIndex value of 1. Likewise, the Label2 control and its corresponding text box have TabIndex values of 2 and 3, respectively. For a text box's access key (which is defined in the identifying label) to work appropriately, you must be sure to set the identifying label control's TabIndex property to a value that is one number less than the value stored in the text box's TabIndex property. The second section in the list shown in Figure 2-12 is titled "Other controls." In this section you list the names of controls that neither accept user input nor identify controls that accept user input.

You can use the Properties window to set the TabIndex property of each control; or, you can use the Tab Order option on the View menu. The Tab Order option is available only when the designer window is the active window. When you use the Tab Order option, the current TabIndex value for each control (except controls that do not have a TabIndex property) appears in blue boxes on the form. You begin specifying the desired tab order by placing the mouse pointer on the first control you want in the tab order. In this case, you would place the mouse pointer on the Label1 control, which contains the text &Name:. A rectangle surrounds the control and the mouse pointer becomes a crosshair, as shown in Figure 2-13.

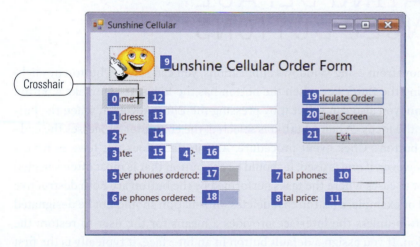

Figure 2-13: Crosshair positioned on Label1 control

You then click the control; when you do this, the number 0 appears in the blue box, and the color of the box changes from blue to white to indicate that you have set the TabIndex value for that control. You then click the next control you want in the tab order, and so on. When you have finished setting all of the TabIndex values, the color of the boxes will automatically change from white to blue, as shown in Figure 2-14. Pressing the Esc key will remove the boxes from the form. You also can click View on the menu bar, and then click Tab Order to remove the boxes.

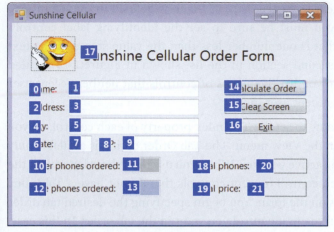

Figure 2-14: Correct TabIndex values shown in the form

DESIGNATING DEFAULT AND CANCEL BUTTONS

As you already know from using Windows applications, you can select a button by clicking it or by pressing the Enter key when the button has the focus. If you make a button the **default button**, you also can select it by pressing the Enter key even when the button does not have the focus. When a button is selected, the computer processes the code contained in the button's Click event procedure. An interface does not have to have a default button. However, if one is used, it should be the button that is most often selected by the user, except in cases where the tasks performed by the button are both destructive and irreversible. For example, a button that deletes information should not be designated as the default button unless the interface provides a means for the user to restore the deleted information. If you assign a default button in an interface, it typically is the first button, which means that it is on the left when the buttons are positioned horizontally on the screen, and on the top when the buttons are stacked vertically. You specify the default button (if any) by setting the form's AcceptButton property to the name of the button. To make the Calculate Order button the default button in the Sunshine Cellular interface, you set the form's AcceptButton property to calcButton. A form can have only one default button. The default button has a darkened border, as shown in Figure 2-15.

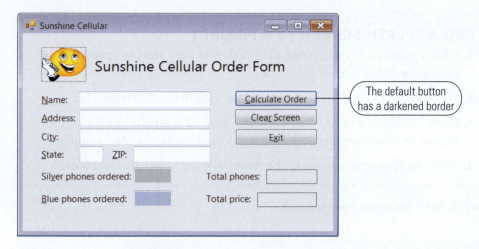

Figure 2-15: Default button shown in the interface

You also can designate a cancel button in an interface. Unlike the default button, the
cancel button is automatically selected when the user presses the Esc key. You specify the cancel button (if any) by setting the form's CancelButton property to the name
of the button. To make the Exit button the cancel button in the Sunshine Cellular
interface, you set the form's CancelButton property to exitButton. A form can have
only one cancel button.

ADDING A SPLASH SCREEN
TO A PROJECT

Figure 2-16 shows the steps you follow to add a new splash screen to a project, and Figure
2-17 shows an example of a completed Add New Item dialog box. You can use the templates listed in the Add New Item dialog box to add many different items to a project. The
Splash Screen template adds a form that is already configured for use as a splash screen.
If you prefer to create your splash screen from scratch, you can use the Windows Form
template to add a blank Windows form to the project.

»HOW TO . . .

ADD A SPLASH SCREEN TO A PROJECT

1. Click Project on the menu bar, then click Add New Item to open the Add New Item dialog box.

2. If necessary, expand the Common Items node in the Categories list.

3. Click Windows Forms, then click the desired template (either Splash Screen or Windows Form) in the list of Visual Studio installed templates.

4. Enter an appropriate name in the Name box, then click the Add button.

Figure 2-16: How to add a splash screen to a project

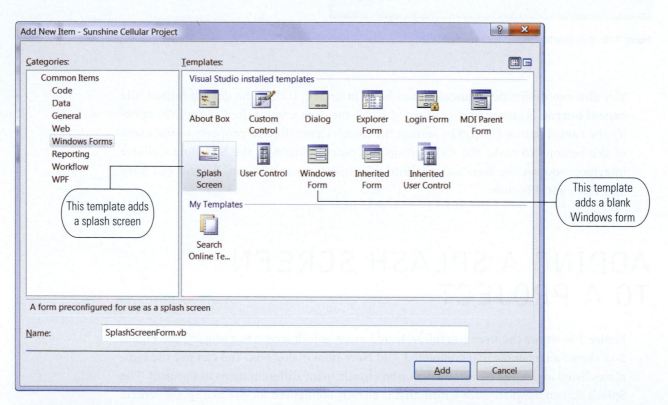

Figure 2-17: Completed Add New Item dialog box

»TIP

To add an existing form to a project, click Project, then click Add Existing Item.

In Chapter 1 you learned that the computer automatically displays an application's startup form each time the application is started. It also automatically displays an application's splash screen form; however, you first must specify the form's name in the Project Designer window. Figure 2-18 shows the steps you follow to indicate the name of the splash screen form, and Figure 2-19 shows the name (in this case, SplashScreenForm) selected in the Project Designer window. When the application is started, the splash screen will appear first. After a few seconds, the splash screen will disappear automatically and the startup form will appear. (You will include a splash screen in this chapter's Programming Tutorial application.)

»HOW TO . . .

SPECIFY THE SPLASH SCREEN FORM

1. Open the Project Designer window. You can open the window by right-clicking My Project in the Solution Explorer window, and then clicking Open on the context menu. You also can click Project on the menu bar, and then click *<project name>* Properties on the menu. In addition, you can right-click the project's name in the Solution Explorer window, and then click Properties.

2. Click the Application tab, if necessary, then click the Splash screen list arrow in the Application pane. Click the appropriate form name in the list.

3. Click the Close button on the Project Designer window.

Figure 2-18: How to specify the splash screen form

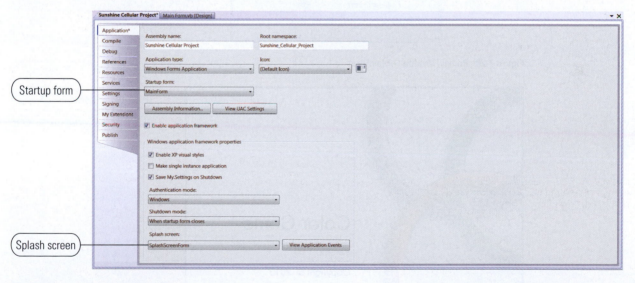

Figure 2-19: Project Designer window

You have completed the concepts section of Chapter 2. The next section is the Programming Tutorial section, which gives you step-by-step instructions on how to apply the chapter's concepts to an application. A Programming Example follows the Programming Tutorial. The Programming Example is a completed program that demonstrates the concepts taught in the chapter. Following the Programming Example are the Quick Review, Key Terms, Self-Check Questions and Answers, Review Questions, Review Exercises—Short Answer, Computer Exercises, and Case Projects sections.

PROGRAMMING TUTORIAL

CREATING THE COLOR GAME APPLICATION

In this tutorial, you create an application that can be used to teach a child the names of nine different colors. The application contains the primary window and splash screen shown in Figures 2-20 and 2-21.

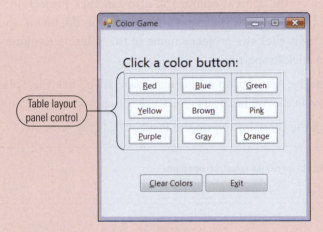

Figure 2-20: Primary window—MainForm

Figure 2-21: Splash screen—SplashScreenForm

COMPLETING THE MAINFORM'S INTERFACE

Included in the data files for this book is a partially completed Color Game application. Before you begin coding the application, you will need to complete the MainForm's interface. Missing from the interface is a table layout panel control.

To complete the MainForm's user interface:

1. Start Visual Studio. If necessary, close the Start Page window.

2. Open the **Color Game Solution** (**Color Game Solution.sln**) file, which is contained in the VbReloaded2008\Chap02\Color Game Solution folder. If necessary, open the designer window. The partially completed MainForm appears on the screen.

3. If necessary, auto-hide the Toolbox window and display the Solution Explorer and Properties windows. If the access keys are not underlined on your screen, press the Alt key.

4. Set the MainForm's StartPosition property to **CenterScreen**.

5. In this application, you will not allow the user to maximize the MainForm. Set the MainForm's MaximizeBox property to **False**.

6. Use the TableLayoutPanel tool, which is located in the Containers section of the toolbox, to add a table layout panel control to the form. The table layout panel control contains a move box, which you can use to move the control to another area of the form. You move the control by placing your mouse pointer on the move box, and then dragging the control to the desired location. If necessary, click the **task box** to open the task list. See Figure 2-22.

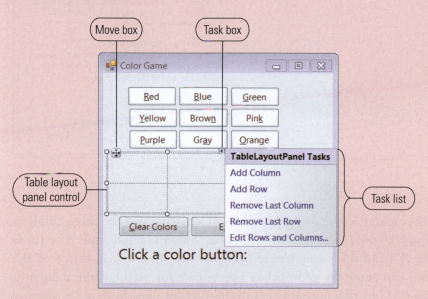

Figure 2-22: Table layout panel control added to the form

7. Currently, the table layout panel control contains two rows and two columns. You will add another column and row to the control. Click **Add Column** on the task list, then click **Add Row**. The table layout panel control now contains three rows and three columns.

8. Now you will make each column the same size. Click **Edit Rows and Columns** on the task list. The Column and Row Styles dialog box opens. Click **Column3** in the Member list, then click the **Percent** radio button in the Size Type section of the dialog box, as shown in Figure 2-23.

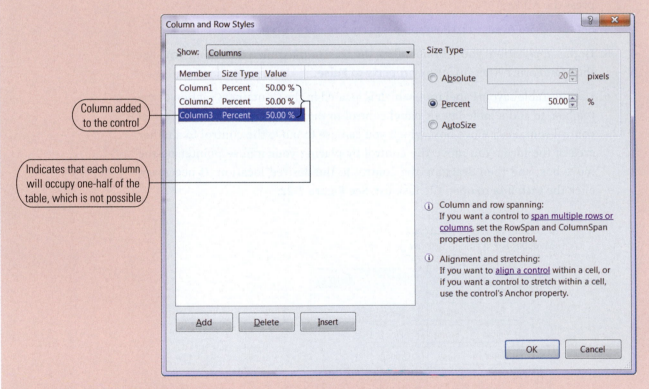

Figure 2-23: Column and Row Styles dialog box

The Value column in the dialog box indicates that each of the three columns will occupy 50.00% (one-half) of the table, which is impossible. The three columns, if sized the same, would each occupy 33.33% (one-third) of the table. You can enter the appropriate percentage for each column manually, using the text box that appears next to the Percent radio button. Or, you can let the computer change the percentages for you; to do so, you simply click the OK button.

9. Click the **OK** button. The Column and Row Styles dialog box closes. Now verify that the computer changed the percentages to 33.33%. Click **Edit Rows and Columns** on the task list to open the Column and Row Styles dialog box. The dialog box now contains the correct percentages, as shown in Figure 2-24.

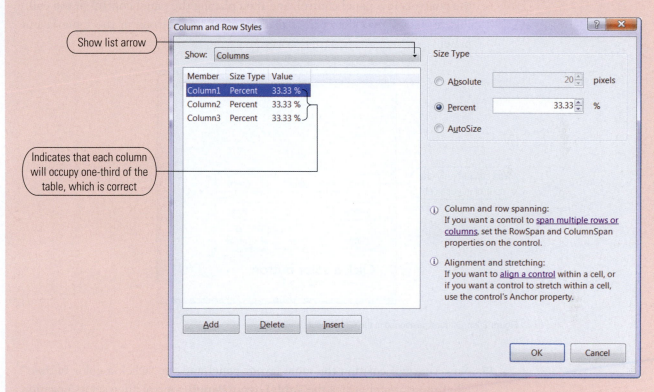

Figure 2-24: Correct percentages shown in the Column and Row Styles dialog box

10. Next, you will make the rows the same size. Click the **list arrow** in the Show box, then click **Rows**. Click **Row3** in the Member list, then click the **Percent** radio button in the Size Type section of the dialog box. Click the **OK** button.

11. On your own, verify that the computer changed each row's percentage to 33.33% in the Column and Row Styles dialog box, then close the dialog box.

12. Now you will put a border around each cell in the table layout panel control. A cell is an intersection of a row and a column. The table layout panel control contains nine cells. Click the **CellBorderStyle** list arrow in the Properties window, then click **OutsetDouble**.

13. Now make the table layout panel control larger. Click **Size** in the Properties window, then type **300, 146** and press **Enter**.

14. Now drag each of the nine color buttons into its own cell in the table layout panel. As you drag the buttons, try placing more than one button in the same cell. You will find that each cell in the table layout panel accepts only one control. (If you need to put several controls in a cell, you can do so by first putting the controls in a panel control, and then placing the panel control in the cell.) Figure 2-25 shows the correct placement of the buttons in the table layout panel.

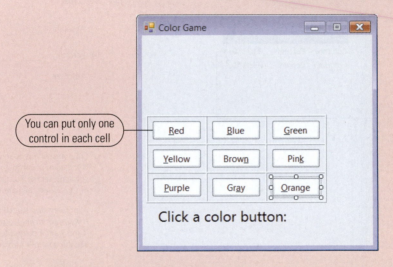

Figure 2-25: Buttons positioned in the table layout panel

15. Now you will position the table layout panel and the "Click a color button:" label appropriately. Click the **TableLayoutPanel1** control, then set its Location property to **41, 78**. Click the **Label1** control (which contains the text "Click a color button:"), then set its Location property to **35, 43**.

16. Click the **Clear Colors** button, then set its Location property to **72, 269**. Click the **Exit** button, then set its Location property to **193, 269**.

17. Now lock the controls in place on the form. Right-click the **MainForm**, then click **Lock Controls**.

18. Now set the TabIndex property for the controls. Click **View** on the menu bar, then click **Tab Order**. Use the information shown in Figure 2-26 to set the tab order.

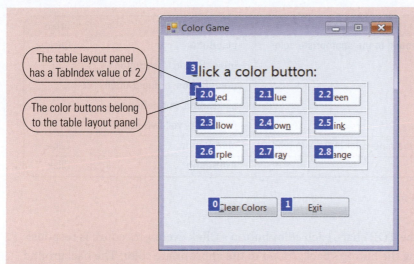

The table layout panel has a TabIndex value of 2

The color buttons belong to the table layout panel

Figure 2-26: Tab order for the controls in the interface

Notice that the TabIndex values of the color buttons begin with the number 2, which is the TabIndex value of the table layout panel. The number 2 indicates that the buttons belong to the table layout panel rather than to the form. If you move or delete the table layout panel, the controls that belong to it also will be moved or deleted. The numbers that appear after the period in the color buttons' TabIndex values indicate the order in which each button will receive the focus within the table layout panel.

19. Press the **Esc** key to remove the tab order boxes from the form. The MainForm's interface is now complete.

20. Save the solution by clicking **File** on the menu bar, and then clicking **Save All**.

CODING THE MAINFORM

When the user clicks one of the color buttons on the MainForm, the button's Click event procedure will change the button's background to the appropriate color. Similarly, when the user clicks the Clear Colors button, the button's Click event procedure will change each color button's background to white. The user can click the Exit button to end the application. Figure 2-27 shows the TOE chart for the MainForm.

Task	Object	Event
Change the button's background to the appropriate color	blueButton, brownButton, grayButton, greenButton, orangeButton, pinkButton, purpleButton, redButton, yellowButton	Click
Change the background of the nine color buttons to white	clearButton	Click
End the application	exitButton	Click

Figure 2-27: TOE chart for the MainForm

According to the TOE chart, each color button's Click event procedure is responsible for changing the button's background to the appropriate color. The background color of a control is specified in the control's BackColor property. To change the value stored in the BackColor property while an application is running, you use an assignment statement in the following format: *controlname*.**BackColor** = *color*.

To code the color buttons' Click event procedures:

1. Open the Code Editor window. Notice that the exitButton's Click event procedure already contains the Me.Close() instruction.

2. Open the code template for the blueButton's Click event, then type **bluebutton. backcolor = color.blue** and press **Enter**.

3. On your own, code the Click event procedures for the remaining eight color buttons. You should assign the following colors to the buttons' BackColor properties: Color.Brown, Color.Gray, Color.Green, Color.Orange, Color.Pink, Color.Purple, Color.Red, and Color.Yellow.

4. Save the solution, then start the application. Click **each of the color buttons** to verify that the code you entered is working correctly. Figure 2-28 shows the MainForm after all of the color buttons are clicked. If the access keys do not appear in the interface, press the **Alt** key on your keyboard.

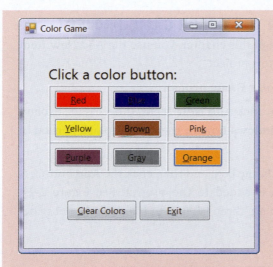

Figure 2-28: Result of clicking the color buttons

5. Click the **Exit** button to end the application.

According to the TOE chart, the Clear Colors button should change the background of each color button to white.

To code the clearButton's Click event procedure:

1. Open the code template for the clearButton's Click event procedure.

2. Type **bluebutton.backcolor = color.white** and press **Enter**.

3. On your own, assign Color.White to the BackColor property of the remaining eight color buttons.

4. Save the solution, then start the application. Click **each of the color buttons**, then click the **Clear Colors** button. The background of each color button should be white.

5. Click the **Exit** button to end the application.

ADDING A SPLASH SCREEN TO THE COLOR GAME PROJECT

As you learned in the concepts section of this chapter, you use the Add New Item dialog box to add a new splash screen to a project.

To add a new splash screen to the Color Game project:

1. Click **Project** on the menu bar, then click **Add New Item**. If necessary, expand the **Common Items** node. Click **Windows Forms**, then click **Splash Screen** in the list of templates.

2. Type **SplashScreenForm.vb** in the Name box, and then click the **Add** button. A form representing a splash screen is added to the project. See Figure 2-29. Automatically included on the form are three labels and two table layout panel controls.

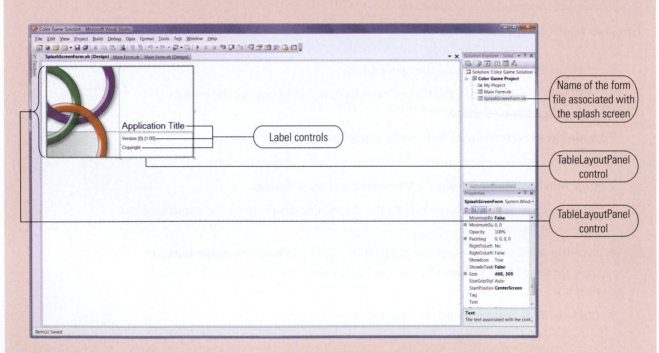

Figure 2-29: Splash screen added to the project

3. Click the **ApplicationTitle** label control, then set its Font property to **Segoe UI, 18pt**.

4. Click the **Version** label control, then set its Font property to **Segoe UI, 9pt**.

5. Click the **Copyright** label control, then set its Font property to **Segoe UI, 9pt**.

6. Right-click **My Project** in the Solution Explorer window, then click **Open**. Click the **Splash screen** list arrow on the Application pane, then click **SplashScreenForm** in the list.

7. Click the **Assembly Information** button on the Application pane. The Assembly Information dialog box opens. Change the Title box's text to **Color Game**. If necessary, change the year number in the Copyright box to **2010**. See Figure 2-30.

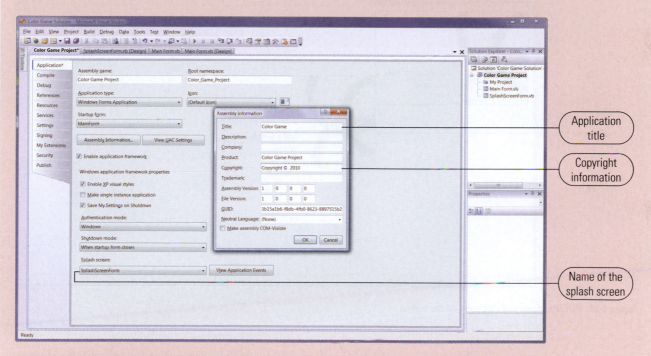

Figure 2-30: Project Designer and Assembly Information dialog box

8. Click the **OK** button to close the Assembly Information dialog box. Save the solution, then close the Project Designer window.

TESTING THE APPLICATION

In the next set of steps, you will test the application to verify that it is working correctly.

To test the application:

1. Start the application. The splash screen appears first. See Figure 2-31.

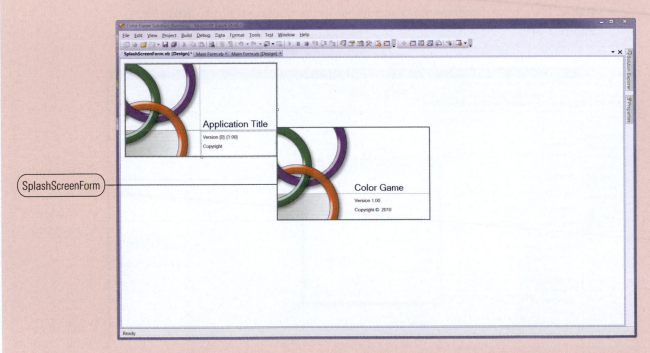

Figure 2-31: SplashScreenForm displayed on the screen

After a few seconds have elapsed, the splash screen disappears and the startup form (the MainForm) appears.

2. Click **each of the color buttons**, then click the **Clear Colors** button.

3. Click the **Exit** button to end the application. Click **File** on the menu bar, and then click **Close Solution**. Figure 2-32 shows the Color Game application's code.

```
Public Class MainForm

    Private Sub exitButton_Click(ByVal sender As Object, _
        ByVal e As System.EventArgs) Handles exitButton.Click
        Me.Close()
    End Sub

    Private Sub blueButton_Click(ByVal sender As Object, _
        ByVal e As System.EventArgs) Handles blueButton.Click
        blueButton.BackColor = Color.Blue
    End Sub

    Private Sub brownButton_Click(ByVal sender As Object, _
        ByVal e As System.EventArgs) Handles brownButton.Click
        brownButton.BackColor = Color.Brown
    End Sub

    Private Sub grayButton_Click(ByVal sender As Object, _
        ByVal e As System.EventArgs) Handles grayButton.Click
        grayButton.BackColor = Color.Gray
    End Sub

    Private Sub greenButton_Click(ByVal sender As Object, _
        ByVal e As System.EventArgs) Handles greenButton.Click
        greenButton.BackColor = Color.Green
    End Sub

    Private Sub orangeButton_Click(ByVal sender As Object, _
        ByVal e As System.EventArgs) Handles orangeButton.Click
        orangeButton.BackColor = Color.Orange
    End Sub

    Private Sub pinkButton_Click(ByVal sender As Object, _
        ByVal e As System.EventArgs) Handles pinkButton.Click
        pinkButton.BackColor = Color.Pink
    End Sub

    Private Sub purpleButton_Click(ByVal sender As Object, _
        ByVal e As System.EventArgs) Handles purpleButton.Click
        purpleButton.BackColor = Color.Purple
    End Sub

    Private Sub redButton_Click(ByVal sender As Object, _
        ByVal e As System.EventArgs) Handles redButton.Click
        redButton.BackColor = Color.Red
    End Sub
```

Figure 2-32: Color Game application's code (*continued on next page*)

```
        Private Sub yellowButton_Click(ByVal sender As Object, _
             ByVal e As System.EventArgs) Handles yellowButton.Click
          yellowButton.BackColor = Color.Yellow
        End Sub

        Private Sub clearButton_Click(ByVal sender As Object, _
             ByVal e As System.EventArgs) Handles clearButton.Click
          blueButton.BackColor = Color.White
          brownButton.BackColor = Color.White
          grayButton.BackColor = Color.White
          greenButton.BackColor = Color.White
          orangeButton.BackColor = Color.White
          pinkButton.BackColor = Color.White
          purpleButton.BackColor = Color.White
          redButton.BackColor = Color.White
          yellowButton.BackColor = Color.White
        End Sub
    End Class
```

Figure 2-32: Color Game application's code (*continued from previous page*)

PROGRAMMING EXAMPLE

MOONBUCKS COFFEE

Create an interface that allows the user to enter the following customer information: name, address, city, state, ZIP code, the number of pounds of regular coffee ordered, and the number of pounds of decaffeinated coffee ordered. The interface will need to display the total number of pounds of coffee ordered and the total price of the order. Name the solution Moonbucks Solution. Name the project Moonbucks Project. Name the form file Main Form.vb. Save the files in the VbReloaded2008\Chap02 folder. In this chapter, you will code only the Exit button's Click event procedure. You will code the Click event procedures for the Calculate Order and Clear Order buttons in Chapter 3. See Figures 2-33 through 2-37.

Task	Object	Event
1. Calculate the total pounds of coffee ordered and the total price of the order 2. Display the total pounds of coffee ordered and the total price of the order in totalPoundsLabel and totalPriceLabel	calcButton	Click
Clear the screen for the next order	clearButton	Click
End the application	exitButton	Click
Display the total pounds of coffee ordered (from calcButton)	totalPoundsLabel	None
Display the total price of the order (from calcButton)	totalPriceLabel	None
Get and display the order information	nameTextBox, addressTextBox, cityTextBox, stateTextBox, zipTextBox, regularTextBox, decafTextBox	None

Figure 2-33: TOE chart

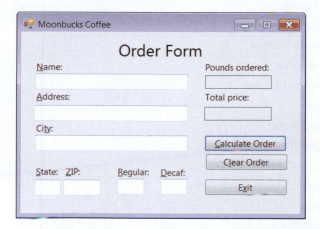

Figure 2-34: User interface

Object	Property	Setting
Form1	Name	MainForm
	AcceptButton	calcButton
	CancelButton	exitButton
	Font	Segoe UI, 9 point
	MaximizeButton	False
	Size	496, 353
	StartPosition	CenterScreen
	Text	Moonbucks Coffee
Label1	Font	Segoe UI, 16 point
	Text	Order Form
		Use the Format menu to center this label horizontally
Label2	Text	&Name:
Label3	Text	&Address:
Label4	Text	Ci&ty:
Label5	Text	&State:
Label6	Text	&ZIP:
Label7	Text	&Regular:
Label8	Text	&Decaf:
Label9	Text	Pounds ordered:
Label10	Text	Total price:
Label11	Name	totalPoundsLabel
	AutoSize	False
	BorderStyle	FixedSingle
	Text	(empty)
	TextAlign	MiddleCenter
Label12	Name	totalPriceLabel
	AutoSize	False
	BorderStyle	FixedSingle
	Text	(empty)
	TextAlign	MiddleCenter
TextBox1	Name	nameTextBox
TextBox2	Name	addressTextBox
TextBox3	Name	cityTextBox

Figure 2-35: Objects, Properties, and Settings (*continued on next page*)

Object	Property	Setting
TextBox4	Name	stateTextBox
	CharacterCasing	Upper (changes entry to uppercase)
	MaxLength	2 (allows the user to enter a maximum of 2 characters)
TextBox5	Name	zipTextBox
TextBox6	Name	regularTextBox
TextBox7	Name	decafTextBox
Button1	Name	calcButton
	Text	&Calculate Order
Button2	Name	clearButton
	Text	C&lear Order
Button3	Name	exitButton
	Text	E&xit

Figure 2-35: Objects, Properties, and Settings (*continued from previous page*)

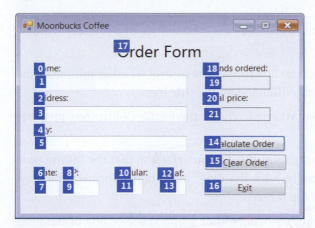

Figure 2-36: Tab order

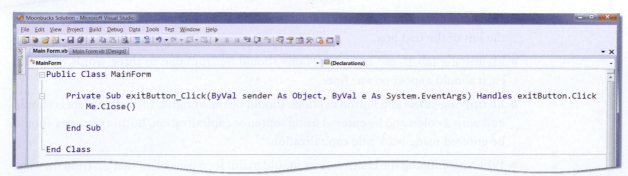

Figure 2-37: Code

QUICK REVIEW

» You should plan an application jointly with the user to ensure that the application meets the user's needs.

» Planning an application requires that you identify the tasks, objects, and events. You then build the interface.

» You can use a TOE chart to record an application's tasks, objects, and events.

» You use a text box control to give the user an area in which to enter data.

» The primary viewing and editing of your application's data takes place in a primary window.

» Dialog boxes are used to support and supplement a user's activities in a primary window.

» Primary windows can be resized, minimized, maximized, and closed by the user. Dialog boxes can be closed only.

» The form's FormBorderStyle property specifies the border style of a primary window or dialog box.

» The form's MinimizeBox and MaximizeBox properties control whether minimize and maximize buttons appear darkened or dimmed on the title bar.

» If a form represents a splash screen, you typically set the form's ControlBox property to False.

» In Western countries, you should organize the user interface so that the information flows either vertically or horizontally, with the most important information always located in the upper-left corner of the screen.

» You can group related controls together using either white space or one of the tools located in the Containers section of the toolbox.

» Labels that identify text boxes should be left-aligned and positioned either above or to the left of the text box.

» Identifying labels and button captions should be from one to three words only, and each should appear on one line.

» Identifying labels and button captions should be meaningful. Identifying labels should end with a colon and be entered using sentence capitalization. Button captions should be entered using book title capitalization.

» When positioning the controls, you should maintain a consistent margin from the edge of the form.

» Related controls typically are placed close together in the interface. Controls that are not part of any logical grouping may be positioned farther away from other controls.

» When buttons are positioned horizontally on the screen, all the buttons should be the same height; their widths, however, may vary if necessary. When buttons are stacked vertically on the screen, all the buttons should be the same height and the same width.

» Align the borders of the controls wherever possible to minimize the number of different margins used in the interface.

» Graphics and color should be used sparingly in an interface.

» You can use an object's Font property to change the type, style, and size of the font used to display the text in the object. It is recommended that you use the Segoe UI (9 point) font for applications that will run on systems running Windows Vista.

» Avoid using italics and underlining in an interface, and limit the use of bold text to titles, headings, and key items that you want to emphasize.

» You should assign access keys to each of the controls that can accept user input—such as text boxes and buttons. You assign an access key by including an ampersand (&) in the control's caption or identifying label.

» The TabIndex property determines the order in which a control receives the focus when the user presses either the Tab key or an access key. The TabIndex property of a text box should be set to a value that is one number more than the value stored in the TabIndex property of its identifying label.

» You use the form's AcceptButton property to designate a default button, and its CancelButton property to designate a cancel button.

» You can use the Add New Item dialog box to add a splash screen to an application.

» You can specify the name of an application's splash screen in the Project Designer window.

KEY TERMS

Access key—the underlined character in an object's identifying label or caption; allows the user to select the object using the Alt key in combination with the underlined character

Book title capitalization—refers to capitalizing the first letter in each word, except for articles, conjunctions, and prepositions that do not occur at either the beginning or the end of the caption; button captions use this capitalization

Cancel button—the button that can be selected by pressing the Esc key

Default button—the button that can be selected by pressing the Enter key even when it does not have the focus

Dialog box—a window that supports and supplements a user's activities in a primary window

Focus—when a control has the focus, it can accept user input

Group box control—used to group together related controls

Panel control—used to group together related controls

Primary window—the window in which the primary viewing and editing of your application's data takes place

Sentence capitalization—refers to capitalizing only the first letter in the first word and in any words that are customarily capitalized; identifying labels use this capitalization

Table layout panel control—used to group together related controls

Text box control—gives the user an area in which to enter data

SELF-CHECK QUESTIONS AND ANSWERS

1. The default button on a form can be selected by _____.

    a. clicking it

    b. pressing the Enter key when the button has the focus

    c. pressing the Enter key when the button does not have the focus

    d. All of the above.

2. TabIndex values begin with the number _____.

    a. 0   b. 1

3. When planning an application, you first identify the necessary _____.

    a. code   b. events

    c. objects   d. tasks

4. Every object in a user interface needs an event to occur in order for it to perform its assigned task.

    a. True   b. False

5. The recommended font type for applications created for the Windows Vista environment is _____.

   a. Arial

   b. Microsoft Sans Serif

   c. Segoe UI

   d. Tahoma

Answers: 1) d, 2) a, 3) d, 4) b, 5) c

REVIEW QUESTIONS

1. Which of the following statements is false?

   a. A button's caption should appear on one line.

   b. A button's caption should be from one to three words only.

   c. A button's caption should be entered using book title capitalization.

   d. A button's caption should end with a colon (:).

2. Which of the following statements is false?

   a. The text that identifies a text box should be aligned on the left in a label control.

   b. An identifying label should be positioned either above or to the left of the control it identifies.

   c. Labels that identify controls should be entered using book title capitalization.

   d. Labels that identify text boxes should end with a colon (:).

3. The _____ property determines the order in which a control receives the focus when the user presses the Tab key or an access key.

   a. OrderTab   b. SetOrder

   c. TabIndex   d. TabOrder

4. If the buttons are stacked vertically on the screen, then each button should be _____.

   a. the same height

   b. the same width

   c. the same height and the same width

5. You use the _____ character to assign an access key to a control.

    a. &   b. *

    c. @   d. ˆ

6. You assign an access key using a control's _____ property.

    a. Access

    b. Caption

    c. KeyAccess

    d. Text

7. You use the _____ property to designate a default button in the interface.

    a. button's AcceptButton

    b. button's DefaultButton

    c. form's AcceptButton

    d. form's DefaultButton

8. If a text box has a TabIndex value of 7, its identifying label should have a TabIndex value of _____.

    a. 6   b. 7

    c. 8   d. 9

9. Which of the following statements is false?

    a. The human eye is attracted to text before graphics.

    b. The human eye is attracted to color before black and white.

    c. Italics make text more difficult to read.

    d. None of the above.

10. Which of the following changes the background color of the blueTextBox to blue?

    a. blueTextBox.BackGround = Color.Blue

    b. blueTextBox.BackGroundColor = Color.Blue

    c. blueTextBox.Color = Color.Blue

    d. None of the above.

REVIEW EXERCISES— SHORT ANSWER

1. Define the following terms:

   a. book title capitalization   b. sentence capitalization

2. List the four steps you should follow when planning a Visual Basic application.

3. Explain the procedure for choosing a control's access key.

4. Explain how you give users keyboard access to a text box.

5. Explain the difference between a primary window and a dialog box.

6. Write the Visual Basic instruction to change the color of the text in the redTextBox to red.

COMPUTER EXERCISES

1. In this exercise, you modify the application from this chapter's Programming Example.

   a. If necessary, create the Moonbucks Coffee application shown in this chapter's Programming Example.

   b. Close the Moonbucks Coffee application, then use Windows to make a copy of the Moonbucks Solution folder. Rename the folder Moonbucks Solution—Modified.

   c. Open the Moonbucks Solution (Moonbucks Solution.sln) file contained in the VbReloaded2008\Chap02\Moonbucks Solution—Modified folder.

   d. Modify the user interface so that it displays the total number of pounds of coffee ordered, the price of the order without any sales tax, the sales tax amount, and the total price of the order. Place the calculated amounts, along with their identifying labels, in a table layout panel control. Be sure to reset the tab order.

   e. Modify the TOE chart shown in Figure 2-33 and the OPS (Object, Property, Setting) chart shown in Figure 2-35.

   f. Save the solution, then start the application. Click the Exit button, then close the solution.

2. In this exercise, you modify an existing application's user interface so that the interface follows the design guidelines you learned in this chapter.

   a. Open the Time Solution (Time Solution.sln) file contained in the VbReloaded2008\Chap02\Time Solution folder.

   b. Lay out and organize the interface so that it follows all of the design guidelines specified in this chapter.

   c. Save the solution, then start the application. Click the Exit button, then close the solution.

3. In this exercise, you prepare a TOE chart and build an interface.

   Scenario: The salespeople at Paper Products are paid a commission, which is a percentage of the sales they make. For example, if your sales are $2,000 and your commission rate is 10%, then your commission is $200. Create an application that will compute the commission after the user enters the salesperson's name, sales, and commission rate.

   a. Prepare a TOE chart ordered by object.

   b. Build an appropriate interface. Name the solution, project, and form file Paper Solution, Paper Project, and Main Form.vb, respectively. Save the solution in the VbReloaded2008\Chap02 folder. Code the Exit button.

   c. Add a splash screen to the application.

   d. Save the solution, then start and test the application. When you are finished testing the application, close it and then close the solution.

4. In this exercise, you prepare a TOE chart and build an interface.

   Scenario: RM Sales divides its sales territory into four regions: North, South, East, and West. The sales manager wants an application in which he can enter the current year's sales for each region and the projected increase (expressed as a percentage) in sales for each region. He then wants the application to compute the following year's projected sales for each region. For example, if Robert enters 10000 as the current sales for the South region, and then enters a 10% projected increase, the application should display 11000 as next year's projected sales.

   a. Prepare a TOE chart ordered by object.

   b. Build an appropriate interface. Name the solution, project, and form file RMSales Solution, RMSales Project, and Main Form.vb, respectively. Save the solution in the VbReloaded2008\Chap02 folder. Code the Exit button.

   c. Save the solution, then start and test the application. When you are finished testing the application, close it and then close the solution.

5. In this exercise, you learn how to bypass a control in the tab order when the user is tabbing.

    a. Open the Johnson Solution (Johnson Solution.sln) file, which is contained in the VbReloaded2008\Chap02\Johnson Solution folder.

    b. Start the application. Press the Tab key several times and notice where the focus is placed each time. Click the Exit button.

    c. Most of Johnson's customers are located in California. Enter CA in the stateTextBox control's Text property.

    d. Find a way to bypass (skip over) the stateTextBox control when the user is tabbing. If the user needs to place the focus in the stateTextBox control—perhaps to change the control's contents—he or she will need to click or double-click the control, or use its access key.

    e. Save the solution, then start and test the application. Click the Exit button, then close the solution.

6. In this exercise, you learn about the group box and panel controls.

    a. Open the GroupPanel Solution (GroupPanel Solution.sln) file, which is contained in the VbReloaded2008\Chap02\GroupPanel Solution folder.

    b. Use the GroupBox tool to add a group box control to the form. Change the group box control's Text property to Shirts. Change its Size property to 200, 136, and its Location property to 40, 24.

    c. Drag four label controls and two text boxes into the group box. Change the Text property of three of the label controls as follows: &Red:, &Green:, Total:. The remaining label control should have a fixed border and be empty. Name the empty label control totalLabel, and set its AutoSize property to False. Name the text boxes redTextBox and greenTextBox. Align and size the label and text box controls appropriately within the group box control.

    d. Use the Panel tool to add a panel control to the form. Change the panel control's BorderStyle property to FixedSingle. Change its Size property to 200, 64, and its Location property to 40, 168.

    e. Drag two button controls into the panel control. Name the buttons calcButton and exitButton. Change the Text property of the buttons as follows: &Calculate and E&xit. Align and size the buttons appropriately within the panel control. Lock the controls.

    f. Click View on the menu bar, and then click Tab Order. Click the group box control, and then click the Red: label, the redTextBox control, the Green: label, the greenTextBox control, the Total: label, and the totalLabel control. What values appear in the tab order boxes for these controls?

    g. Click the panel control, the calcButton control, and the exitButton control. What values appear in the tab order boxes for these controls?

    h. Press the Esc key on your keyboard.

    i. Code the Exit button so that it ends the application.

    j. Save the solution, then start the application. Verify that the tab order and access keys work correctly.

    k. Click the Exit button, then close the solution.

7. In this exercise, you include a dialog box in the Color Game application created in the chapter's Programming Tutorial. You also learn about the Show and ShowDialog methods.

    a. Use Windows to make a copy of the Color Game Solution folder, which is contained in the VbReloaded2008\Chap02 folder. Rename the folder Color Game Solution—Discovery.

    b. Open the Color Game Solution (Color Game Solution.sln) file contained in the VbReloaded2008\Chap02\Color Game Solution—Discovery folder.

    c. Use the Add New Item dialog box to add a dialog box form to the project. Name the dialog box form file Dialog Form.vb.

    d. Change the dialog box form's name to DialogForm, and change its Font property to Segoe UI, 9 pt.

    e. Scan the DialogForm's Properties list. What value is assigned to the FormBorderStyle property? What value is assigned to the MaximizeBox property? What value is assigned to the MinimizeBox property?

    f. Change the DialogForm's Size property to 275, 103. Change its Text property to Options. Set both its AcceptButton and CancelButton properties to (none).

    g. Change the TableLayoutPanel1's Location property to 21, 14. Change its Size property to 226, 45.

    h. Change the OK button's Name property to maroonButton. Change its Size property to 105, 35. Change its Text property to &Maroon Text.

    i. Change the Cancel button's Name property to blackButton. Change its Size property to 105, 35. Change its Text property to &Black Text. Change its DialogResult property to None.

    j. Lock the controls on the DialogForm.

    k. When the user clicks the Maroon Text button in the DialogForm, the button's Click event procedure should change the color of the MainForm's text to maroon. Similarly, when the user clicks the Black Text button, the button's Click event procedure should change the MainForm's text to black. Open the DialogForm's Code Editor window, then delete the text that appears between the Public Class and End Class statements. Enter the appropriate code in the Click event procedures for the maroonButton and blackButton, then save the solution and close the Code Editor window.

l. Add another button to the MainForm. Change the button's name to optionsButton, and change its Text property to Op&tions. Position the button between the Clear Colors and Exit buttons.

m. The optionsButton's Click event procedure should display the DialogForm on the screen. You can display a form using either the Show method or the ShowDialog method. The method you choose depends on whether you want the form to be modal (ShowDialog) or modeless (Show). A modeless form can remain on the screen while the user completes other actions in the application, such as accessing the controls located on another form. The user closes a modeless form by clicking the Close button on its title bar, or by clicking a button designated for this purpose on the form. Several modeless forms can be displayed at the same time in an application, and the user can switch the focus from one form to another. The Windows Form Designer, Solution Explorer, and Properties windows in Visual Basic are examples of modeless forms. The Find and Replace dialog box in Visual Basic is another example of a modeless form. (To open the Find and Replace dialog box in Visual Basic 2008, click Edit on the menu bar, then click Quick Replace.) A modal form, on the other hand, requires the user to take some action in the form before he or she can continue working in the application. The Font dialog box shown earlier in Figure 2-7 is an example of a modal form. When a modal form is displayed, no input from the keyboard or mouse can occur in the application until the form is closed. Although you cannot access other forms in your application when a modal form is open, you can access other applications. You do so by clicking the application's button on the taskbar. The syntax of the Show method is *formname*.**Show()**, where *formname* is the name of the form you want to display. The syntax of the ShowDialog method is *formname*.**ShowDialog()**. Open the code template for the optionsButton's Click event procedure. Enter the appropriate instruction using the ShowDialog method.

n. Save the solution, then start the application. Click the Options button to open the DialogForm. Click the Maroon Text button. The color of the text on the MainForm changes from black to maroon. Try to click the Pink button on the MainForm. Can you click it? Close the Options dialog box, then stop the application.

o. Change the ShowDialog method in the optionsButton's Click event procedure to the Show method. Save the solution, then start the application. Click the Options button to open the DialogForm. Click the Maroon Text button. The color of the text on the MainForm changes from black to maroon. Try to click the Pink button on the MainForm. Can you click it? Close the Options dialog box, then stop the application.

    p. What difference did you observe between using the ShowDialog method and using the Show method?

    q. Close the solution.

8. In this exercise, you find and correct an error in an application. The process of finding and correcting errors is called debugging.

    a. Open the Debug Solution (Debug Solution.sln) file, which is contained in the VbReloaded2008\Chap02\Debug Solution folder.

    b. Start the application. Test all of the access keys in the interface. So that you can test its access key, the Calculate Total button's Click event procedure contains a line of code. Notice that not all of the access keys are working. Stop the application. Locate and then correct any errors.

    c. Save the solution, then start the application and test the access keys again. Click the Exit button, then close the solution.

CASE PROJECTS

CRISPIES BAGELS AND BITES

Create a TOE chart and a user interface for an application that allows the user to enter the number of bagels, donuts, and cups of coffee a customer orders. You can either create your own user interface or create the one shown in Figure 2-38. The application should display the total price of the order. Include a button control that allows the user to terminate the application. Be sure to assign meaningful names to the form, the button controls, the text boxes, and the label control that displays the total price. Name the solution, project, and form file Crispies Solution, Crispies Project, and Main Form.vb, respectively. Save the solution in the VbReloaded2008\Chap02 folder.

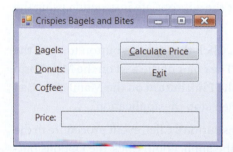

Figure 2-38: Sample interface for Crispies Bagels and Bites

PERRY PRIMARY SCHOOL

Create a TOE chart and a user interface for an application that allows the user to enter two numbers. You can either create your own user interface or create the one shown in Figure 2-39. The application should display the sum of and difference between both numbers. Include a button control that allows the user to terminate the application. Be sure to assign meaningful names to the form, the button controls, the text boxes, and the label controls that display the sum and difference. Name the solution, project, and form file Perry Solution, Perry Project, and Main Form.vb, respectively. Save the solution in the VbReloaded2008\Chap02 folder. Include a splash screen in the application.

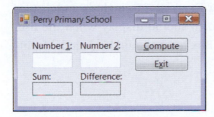

Figure 2-39: Sample interface for Perry Primary School

JASPER HEALTH FOODS

Create a TOE chart and a user interface for an application that allows the user to enter the sales amounts for four states: Illinois, Indiana, Kentucky, and Ohio. You can either create your own user interface or create the one shown in Figure 2-40. The application should display the total sales and the sales commission earned. Include a button control that allows the user to terminate the application. Be sure to assign meaningful names to the form, the button controls, the text boxes, and the label controls that display the total sales and commission. Name the solution, project, and form file Jasper Solution, Jasper Project, and Main Form.vb, respectively. Save the solution in the VbReloaded2008\Chap02 folder. Include a splash screen in the application.

Figure 2-40: Sample interface for Jasper Health Foods

SOPHIA'S ITALIAN DELI

Sophia's offers the following items on its lunch menu: Italian sub, meatball sandwich, slice of pizza, sausage sandwich, meatball/sausage combo, chicken fingers, ravioli plate, lasagna plate, bowl of soup, Caesar salad, calamari, spumoni, and cheesecake. Create a TOE chart and a user interface for an application that allows the user to enter a customer's lunch order. The application should display the price of the order without sales tax, the sales tax amount, and the total price of the order. Name the solution, project, and form file Sophia Solution, Sophia Project, and Main Form.vb, respectively. Save the solution in the VbReloaded2008\Chap02 folder. For an additional challenge, first complete Computer Exercise 7, which shows you how to add a Dialog form to a project and also display the form. Use the information from Computer Exercise 7 to include and display an About Box form in the Sophia application. The form should display when the user clicks an About button on the MainForm. The About Box form should be a modal form.

3

VARIABLES, CONSTANTS, AND ARITHMETIC OPERATORS

After studying Chapter 3, you should be able to:

Declare variables and named constants

Assign data to an existing variable

Convert data to the appropriate type using the TryParse method and the
   Convert class methods

Write arithmetic expressions

Understand the scope and lifetime of variables and named constants

Understand the purpose of the Option statements

Use a TOE chart, pseudocode, and a flowchart to code an application

Clear the contents of a control's Text property while an application is running

Send the focus to a control while the application is running

Explain the difference between syntax errors and logic errors

Format an application's numeric output

VARIABLES

Variables are computer memory locations where programmers can temporarily store data while an application is running. The user at the keyboard may enter the data; or the data may be read from a file or be the result of a calculation made by the computer. The memory locations are called variables because their contents can change as the application is running. Each variable used in a Visual Basic application must be assigned a name by the programmer. The name should be descriptive in that it should help you remember the variable's purpose. In other words, it should help you remember the meaning of the value stored inside the variable. The variable names length and width, for example, are much more meaningful than are the names x and y, because length and width remind you that the amounts stored in the variables represent a length and width measurement, respectively. Although not required by the Visual Basic language, most programmers enter variable names using camel case, which means you lowercase the first word in the variable's name and then uppercase the first letter of each subsequent word in the name. Following this convention, a programmer might assign either the name sales or the name salesAmount to a variable that stores a sales amount. Besides being descriptive, a variable name must follow the rules listed in Figure 3-1. The figure also includes examples of valid and invalid variable names.

» HOW TO . . .

NAME A VARIABLE

<u>Rules</u>

1. The name must begin with a letter or an underscore.

2. The name can contain only letters, numbers, and the underscore character. No punctuation characters or spaces are allowed in the name.

3. Although the name can contain thousands of characters, 32 characters is the recommended maximum number of characters to use.

4. The name cannot be a reserved word, such as Date.

<u>Examples</u>

Valid variable names	Invalid variable names	
reportDate	Date	(the name cannot be a reserved word)
sales2010	2010Sales	(the name must begin with a letter)
westRegion	west Region	(the name cannot contain a space)
firstName	first.Name	(the name cannot contain punctuation)

Figure 3-1: How to name a variable

In addition to assigning a name to each variable used in an application, the programmer also must assign a data type. The **data type** determines the type of data the variable can store. Figure 3-2 describes most of the basic data types available in Visual Basic. Each data type listed in the figure is a class, which means that each data type is a pattern from which objects—in this case, variables—are created.

Data type	Stores	Memory required
Boolean	a logical value (True, False)	2 bytes
Char	one Unicode character	2 bytes
Date	date and time information Date range: January 1, 0001 to December 31, 9999 Time range: 0:00:00 (midnight) to 23:59:59	8 bytes
Decimal	a number with a decimal place Range with no decimal place: +/-79,228,162,514,264,337,593,543,950,335 Range with a decimal place: +/-7.9228162514264337593543950335	16 bytes
Double	a number with a decimal place Range: +/- 4.94065645841247 X 10^{-324} to +/-1.79769313486231 X 10^{308}	8 bytes
Integer	integer Range: -2,147,483,648 to 2,147,483,647	4 bytes
Long	integer Range: -9,223,372,036,854,775,808 to 9,223,372,036,854,775,807	8 bytes
Object	data of any type	4 bytes
Short	integer Range: -32,768 to 32,767	2 bytes
Single	a number with a decimal place Range: +-1.401298 X 10^{-45} to +/-3.402823 X 10^{38}	4 bytes
String	text; 0 to approximately 2 billion characters	

Figure 3-2: Basic data types in Visual Basic

As Figure 3-2 indicates, variables assigned the Integer, Long, or Short data type can store integers, which are whole numbers—positive or negative numbers without any decimal places. The differences among these three data types are in the range of integers each type can store and the amount of memory each type needs to store the integer. Decimal, Double, and Single variables, on the other hand, can store numbers containing a decimal place. Here again, the differences among these three data types are in the range of numbers each type can store and the amount of memory each type needs to store the numbers.

However, calculations involving Decimal variables are not subject to the small rounding errors that may occur when using Double or Single variables. In most cases, the small rounding errors do not create any problems in an application. One exception, however, is when the application contains complex equations dealing with money, where you need accuracy to the penny. In those cases, the Decimal data type is the best type to use.

Also listed in Figure 3-2 are the Char, String, Boolean, Date, and Object data types. The Char data type can store one Unicode character, while the String data type can store from zero to approximately two billion Unicode characters. **Unicode** is the universal coding scheme for characters. It assigns a unique numeric value to each character used in the written languages of the world. (For more information, see The Unicode Standard at *www.unicode.org*.) You use a Boolean variable to store a Boolean value (either True or False), and a Date variable to store date and time information. The Object data type can store any type of data. However, your application will pay a price for this flexibility: it will run more slowly, because the computer has to determine the type of data currently stored in an Object variable. It is best to avoid using the Object data type.

DECLARING A VARIABLE IN CODE

You use a declaration statement to create, or declare, a variable. Declaring a variable tells the computer to set aside a small section of its internal memory. Figure 3-3 shows the syntax of a declaration statement. The {**Dim** | **Private** | **Static**} portion indicates that you can select only one of the keywords appearing within the braces. In this case, you can select Dim, Private, or Static. In most instances, you declare a variable using the keyword Dim. (You will learn about the Private and Static keywords later in this chapter.) *VariableName* is the variable's name, and *dataType* is the variable's data type. *InitialValue* is the value you want stored in the variable when it is created in the computer's internal memory. The square brackets in the syntax indicate that the "= *initialValue*" part of a declaration statement is optional. If you do not assign an initial value to a variable when it is declared, the computer stores a default value in the variable; the default value depends on the variable's data type. A variable declared using one of the numeric data types is automatically initialized to—in other words, given a beginning value of—the number 0. The computer automatically initializes a Boolean variable using the keyword False, and String variables using the keyword Nothing. A variable initialized to Nothing does not actually contain the word "Nothing"; rather, it contains no value at all. However, because some Visual Basic instructions cannot process a variable that does not contain a value, it's a good programming practice to assign a value to a String variable when it is created. In most cases, you will initialize String variables to the empty string using either the value String.Empty or two quotation marks with nothing between, like this: "". In addition to showing the syntax of a declaration statement, Figure 3-3 also shows several examples of declaring variables.

»HOW TO . . .

DECLARE A VARIABLE

Syntax

{**Dim** | **Private** | **Static**} *variableName* **As** *dataType* [= *initialValue*]

Example 1

Dim hours As Integer

Dim payRate As Double

declares an Integer variable named hours and a Double variable named payRate; the variables are automatically initialized to the number 0

Example 2

Dim isDataOk As Boolean = True

declares a Boolean variable named isDataOk and initializes it using the keyword True

Example 3

Dim studentName As String = String.Empty

Dim age As Integer = 4

declares a String variable named studentName and an Integer variable named age; the String variable is initialized to the empty string and the Integer variable is initialized to the number 4

Figure 3-3: How to declare a variable

»TIP

Dim comes from the word "dimension", which is how programmers in the 1960s referred to the process of allocating the computer's memory. "Dimension" refers to the "size" of something.

»TIP

The empty string is also referred to as a zero-length string.

After a variable is declared, you can use an assignment statement to store other data in the variable.

ASSIGNING DATA TO AN EXISTING VARIABLE

In the previous chapters, you used assignment statements to assign values to the properties of controls while an application is running. You also use assignment statements to assign values to variables while an application is running. Figure 3-4 shows the syntax of an assignment statement that assigns a value to a variable. The figure also includes several examples of such assignment statements. In the examples, firstName and zipCode are

String variables, quantity is an Integer variable, and discountRate is a Double variable. The numbers 500 and .03 used in the examples, as well as the string "Mary", are called literal constants. A **literal constant** is an item of data whose value does not change while the application is running. The numbers 500 and .03 are numeric literal constants; the string "Mary" is a string literal constant. String literal constants are enclosed in quotation marks, but numeric literal constants and variable names are not. The quotation marks differentiate a string from both a number and a variable name. In other words, "500" is a string, but 500 is a number. Similarly, "Mary" is a string, but Mary (without the quotation marks) would be interpreted by the computer as the name of a variable. As the examples in Figure 3-4 indicate, you can store literal constants in variables.

» HOW TO . . .

ASSIGN A VALUE TO A VARIABLE

Syntax

variableName = value

Example 1

firstName = "Mary"

assigns the string "Mary" (without the quotes) to a String variable named firstName

Example 2

zipCode = zipTextBox.Text

assigns the string contained in the zipTextBox's Text property to a String variable named zipCode

Example 3

quantity = 500

assigns the integer 500 to an Integer variable named quantity

Example 4

discountRate = .03

assigns the Double number .03 to a Double variable named discountRate

Figure 3-4: How to assign a value to a variable

When the computer processes an assignment statement, it assigns the value that appears on the right side of the assignment operator (=) to the variable whose name appears on the left side of the assignment operator. In other words, the computer stores the value inside the variable (memory location). The value's data type should be the same as the variable's data type. When assigning the value, keep in mind that a value enclosed in quotation marks is considered a string, and so is the value stored in the Text property of an object. Because of this, the first two examples in Figure 3-4 assign strings—"Mary" and the Text property of the zipTextBox—to the String variables named firstName and zipCode. A number without a decimal place is treated as an integer in Visual Basic. Therefore, Example 3 tells the computer to store the integer 500 in the Integer quantity variable. A number with a decimal place, on the other hand, is treated as a Double number. Because of this, the data type of the number .03 in Example 4 matches the variable's data type, which is Double.

At times, the data type of the value you need to assign to a variable is different from the data type of the variable itself. You can change the value's data type to match the variable's data type using either the TryParse method or one of the methods in the Convert class. You learn about the TryParse method first.

USING THE TRYPARSE METHOD

As you learned earlier, each data type in Visual Basic is a class. Most classes have one or more methods. A **method** is a specific portion of the class instructions, and its purpose is to perform a task for the class. Every numeric data type in Visual Basic has a **TryParse method** that can be used to convert a string to that numeric data type. The basic syntax of the TryParse method is *dataType*.**TryParse(***string*, *variable***)**. In the syntax, *dataType* is one of the numeric data types available in Visual Basic, such as Double, Decimal, or Integer. You use a period to separate the class name (*dataType*) from the method name. Recall from Chapter 1 that the period is called the dot member access operator, and it indicates that what appears to the right of the operator is a member of what appears to the left of the operator. In this case, the dot member access operator indicates that the TryParse method is a member of the *dataType* class. The items within the parentheses in the syntax are called **arguments** and represent information the programmer provides to the method. In this case, the *string* argument represents the string you want converted to a number of the *dataType* type; the *string* argument typically is the Text property of a control. The *variable* argument is the name of a numeric variable where the TryParse method can store the number. The numeric variable must have the same data type as specified in the *dataType* portion of the syntax. In other words, when using the TryParse method to convert a string to a Double number, you need to provide the method with the name of a Double variable in which to store the number. The TryParse method parses the string, which means it looks at each character in the string, to determine whether the string can be converted to a number of the specified data type. If the string can be converted, the TryParse method converts the string to a number and stores the number in the variable specified in the *variable* argument. However, if the TryParse method determines that the string cannot be converted to the appropriate data type, the method assigns the number 0 to the variable specified in the *variable* argument. Figure 3-5 shows the basic syntax of the TryParse method and includes examples of using the method.

» HOW TO . . .

USE THE BASIC SYNTAX OF THE TRYPARSE METHOD

Syntax

dataType.**TryParse**(*string, variable*)

Example 1

Dim sales As Double

Double.TryParse(salesTextBox.Text, sales)

If the string entered in the salesTextBox can be converted to a Double number, the TryParse method converts the string and stores the result in the sales variable; otherwise, it stores the number 0 in the sales variable. Examples of strings that the method can convert to Double include "34", "12.55", "-4.23", "1,457.99", and " 33 " (notice the space before and after the 33). The strings will be converted to the numbers 34, 12.55, -4.23, 1457.99, and 33, respectively. Examples of strings that the method cannot convert to Double include "$5.67", "(4.23)", "7.88-", "7%", "122o", "1 345", and "" (the empty string).

Example 2

Dim num As Integer

Integer.TryParse(numTextBox.Text, num)

If the string entered in the numTextBox can be converted to an Integer number, the TryParse method converts the string and stores the result in the num variable; otherwise, it stores the number 0 in the num variable. Examples of strings that the method can convert to Integer include "6", " 7 " (notice the space before and after the 7), and "-896". The strings will be converted to 6, 7, and –896, respectively. Examples of strings that the method cannot convert to Integer include "5,889", "$78", "(11)", "4-", "7.5", and "" (the empty string).

Figure 3-5: How to use the basic syntax of the TryParse method

The TryParse method in Example 1 tries to convert the string stored in the salesTextBox to a Double number. If the conversion is successful, the method stores the Double number in the Double sales variable; otherwise, it stores the number 0 in the sales variable. As indicated in Figure 3-5, the TryParse method can convert (to Double) a string that contains only numbers, as well as one that also contains a decimal point, a leading sign, a comma, or leading and/or trailing spaces. It cannot, however, convert a string that contains a dollar sign, parentheses, a trailing sign, a percent sign, a letter, a space within the string, or the empty string.

The TryParse method in Example 2 tries to convert the string stored in the numTextBox to an Integer. If the string can be converted, the method stores the result in an Integer variable named num; otherwise, it stores the number 0 in the num variable. The TryParse method in this example can convert (to Integer) strings containing numbers, as well as strings that also contain a leading sign, leading spaces, or trailing spaces. It cannot, however, convert a string that contains a comma, a dollar sign, parentheses, a trailing sign, a decimal point, or the empty string.

USING THE CONVERT CLASS

At times, you may need to convert a number, rather than a string, from one data type to another. Visual Basic provides several ways of accomplishing this task. One way is to use the Visual Basic conversion functions, which are listed in Appendix C in this book. You also can use one of the methods defined in the **Convert class**. In this book you will use the Convert class methods, because they have an advantage over the conversion functions: the methods can be used in any of the languages built into Visual Studio, whereas the conversion functions can be used only in the Visual Basic language. The more commonly used methods in the Convert class are the ToDouble, ToDecimal, ToInt32, and ToString methods. The methods are used to convert a value to the Double, Decimal, Integer, and String data types, respectively. Figure 3-6 shows the syntax of the Convert class methods. In the syntax, *value* is the value you want to convert to a different data type. In most cases, *value* will be a numeric value that you want to convert either to the String data type or to a different numeric data type (for example, from Double to Decimal). Although you can use the Convert methods to convert a string to a numeric data type, the TryParse method is the recommended method to use for that task. This is because, unlike the Convert methods, the TryParse method does not produce an error when it tries to convert the empty string; instead, it assigns the number 0 to its *variable* argument. In addition to showing the syntax of the Convert class methods, Figure 3-6 also shows examples of using the methods.

»HOW TO . . .

USE THE CONVERT CLASS METHODS

Syntax

Convert.*method*(*value*)

Example 1

Dim rate As Decimal = Convert.ToDecimal(.05)

converts the Double number .05 to Decimal before storing it in a Decimal
variable named rate

Example 2

Dim testScore As Integer = 98

totalLabel.Text = Convert.ToString(testScore)

converts the contents of an Integer variable named testScore to String, and
then assigns the result to the totalLabel's Text property

»TIP

The dot member access
operator in Figure 3-6
indicates that the
method is a member of
the Convert class.

Figure 3-6: How to use the Convert class methods

Example 1 in Figure 3-6 converts the Double number .05 to Decimal, storing the result in
the rate variable. (Recall that a number with a decimal place is automatically treated as a
Double number in Visual Basic.) Example 2 converts the contents of the Integer testScore
variable to String before assigning it to the totalLabel's Text property.

OPTION EXPLICIT, OPTION INFER, AND OPTION STRICT

It is important to declare the variables used in an application, because doing so allows
you to control their data type. It also makes the application more self-documenting,
which means it will be clearer and easier to understand by anyone reading your code.
Unfortunately, in Visual Basic you can create variables "on the fly," which means that if
your code contains the name of an undeclared variable, Visual Basic creates the variable
for you and assigns the Object data type to it. (An undeclared variable is a variable that
does not appear in a declaration statement, such as a Dim statement.) As you learned earlier, the Object data type is not a very efficient data type and its use should be limited.
Because it is so easy to forget to declare a variable—and so easy to misspell a variable's
name while coding, thereby inadvertently creating an undeclared variable—Visual Basic

provides a way that prevents you from using undeclared variables in your code. You simply enter the statement Option Explicit On in the General Declarations section of the Code Editor window. The General Declarations section is located above the Public Class line. (You can look ahead to Figure 3-8 to see the location of the General Declarations section.) Then if your code contains the name of an undeclared variable, the Code Editor informs you of the error. When you also enter the Option Infer Off statement in the General Declarations section, the Code Editor ensures that every variable is declared with a data type.

In this chapter you also learned that the data type of the value assigned to a variable should be the same as the data type of the variable itself. If the value's data type does not match the memory location's data type, the computer uses a process called **implicit type conversion** to convert the value to fit the memory location. For example, if you assign the integer 9000 to a Double variable—as does the statement Dim sales As Double = 9000— the computer converts the integer to a Double number before storing the value in the variable. It does this by appending a decimal point and the number 0 to the end of the integer. In this case, for example, the integer 9000 is converted to the Double number 9000.0, and it is the Double number 9000.0 that is assigned to the Double sales variable. When a value is converted from one data type to another data type that can store larger numbers, the value is said to be **promoted**. If the Double sales variable is used subsequently in a calculation, the results of the calculation will not be adversely affected by the implicit promotion of the number 9000 to the number 9000.0. However, if you inadvertently assign a Double number to a variable that can store only integers—as does the statement Dim score As Integer = 3.2—the computer converts the Double number to an integer before storing the value in the variable. It does this by rounding the number to the nearest whole number and then truncating (dropping off) the decimal portion of the number. In this case, the computer converts the Double number 3.2 to the integer 3. As a result, the number 3, rather than the number 3.2, is assigned to the score variable. When a value is converted from one data type to another data type that can store only smaller numbers, the value is said to be **demoted**. If the score variable is used subsequently in a calculation, the results of the calculation probably will be adversely affected by the implicit demotion of the number 3.2 to the number 3. More than likely, the demotion will cause the calculated results to be incorrect.

With implicit type conversions, data loss can occur when a value is converted from one data type to a narrower data type, which is a data type with less precision or smaller capacity. You can eliminate the problems that occur as a result of implicit type conversions by entering the Option Strict On statement in the General Declarations section of the Code Editor window (shown later in Figure 3-8). When the Option Strict On statement appears in an application's code, the computer uses the type conversion rules listed in Figure 3-7. The figure also includes examples of these rules.

> **»TIP**
> Option Infer On tells Visual Basic to infer (or assume) a variable's data type based on the value assigned to it. Option Infer Off prevents Visual Basic from making any assumptions about data type.

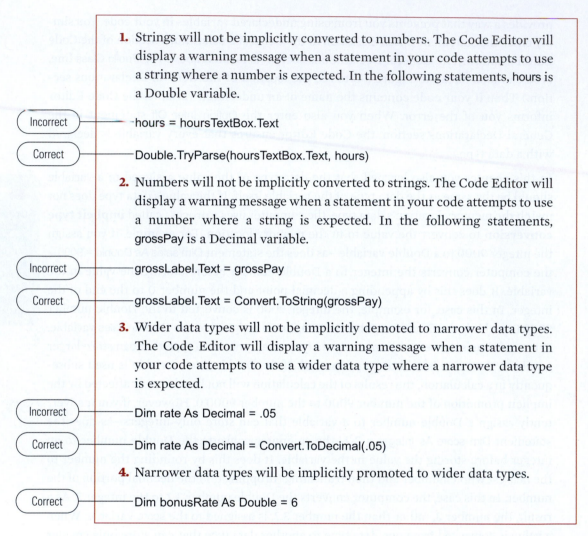

1. Strings will not be implicitly converted to numbers. The Code Editor will display a warning message when a statement in your code attempts to use a string where a number is expected. In the following statements, hours is a Double variable.

Incorrect — hours = hoursTextBox.Text

Correct — Double.TryParse(hoursTextBox.Text, hours)

2. Numbers will not be implicitly converted to strings. The Code Editor will display a warning message when a statement in your code attempts to use a number where a string is expected. In the following statements, grossPay is a Decimal variable.

Incorrect — grossLabel.Text = grossPay

Correct — grossLabel.Text = Convert.ToString(grossPay)

3. Wider data types will not be implicitly demoted to narrower data types. The Code Editor will display a warning message when a statement in your code attempts to use a wider data type where a narrower data type is expected.

Incorrect — Dim rate As Decimal = .05

Correct — Dim rate As Decimal = Convert.ToDecimal(.05)

4. Narrower data types will be implicitly promoted to wider data types.

Correct — Dim bonusRate As Double = 6

Figure 3-7: Rules and examples of type conversions

According to the first rule listed in Figure 3-7, the computer will not implicitly convert a string to a number. As a result, the Code Editor will issue the warning "Option Strict On disallows implicit conversions from 'String' to 'Double'" when your code contains the hours = hoursTextBox.Text statement, because the statement tells the computer to store a string in a Double variable. As you learned earlier, you should use the TryParse method to explicitly convert a string to the Double data type before assigning it to a Double variable. In this case, the appropriate statement to use is Double.TryParse(hoursTextBox.Text, hours).

According to the second rule, the computer will not implicitly convert a number to a string. Therefore, the Code Editor will issue the warning "Option Strict On disallows implicit conversions from 'Decimal' to 'String' when your code contains the grossLabel.Text = grossPay statement, because the statement assigns a number to a string. Recall that you can use the Convert class methods to explicitly convert a number to the String data type. The appropriate statement to use here is grossLabel.Text = Convert.ToString(grossPay).

The third rule states that wider data types will not be implicitly demoted to narrower data types. A data type is wider than another data type if it can store larger numbers, or store numbers with greater precision. Because of this rule, a Double number will not be implicitly demoted to the Decimal or Integer data types. If your code contains the statement Dim rate As Decimal = .05, the Code Editor will issue the "Option Strict On disallows implicit conversions from 'Double' to 'Decimal'" warning, because the statement assigns a Double number to a Decimal variable. The correct statement to use in this case is Dim rate As Decimal = Convert.ToDecimal(.05).

According to the last rule listed in Figure 3-7, the computer will implicitly convert narrower data types to wider data types. For example, when processing the Dim bonusRate As Double = 6 statement, the computer will implicitly promote the integer 6 to the Double number 6.0 before assigning it to the bonusRate variable.

Figure 3-8 shows the three Option statements entered in the General Declarations section of the Code Editor window.

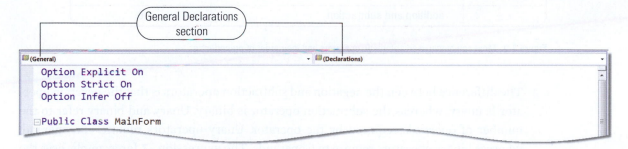

Figure 3-8: Option statements entered in the General Declarations section

USING A VARIABLE IN AN ARITHMETIC EXPRESSION

Most applications require the computer to perform one or more calculations. You instruct the computer to perform a calculation by writing an arithmetic expression that contains one or more arithmetic operators, as well as one or more variables or literal constants. Figure 3-9 lists the most commonly used arithmetic operators available in Visual Basic, along with their precedence numbers. The precedence numbers indicate the order in which the computer performs the operation in an expression. Operations with a precedence number of 1 are performed before operations with a precedence number of 2, which are performed before operations with a precedence number of 3, and so on. However, you can use parentheses to override the order of precedence, because operations within parentheses always are performed before operations outside of parentheses.

Operator	Operation	Precedence number
^	exponentiation (raises a number to a power)	1
–	negation	2
*, /	multiplication and division	3
\	integer division	4
Mod	modulus	5
+, –	addition and subtraction	6

Figure 3-9: Most commonly used arithmetic operators and their order of precedence

The difference between the negation and subtraction operators is that the negation operator is unary, whereas the subtraction operator is binary. Unary and binary refer to the number of operands required by the operator. Unary operators require one operand, whereas binary operators require two operands. The expression –7, for example, uses the negation operator to turn the positive number 7 into a negative number. The expression 9 – 4, on the other hand, uses the subtraction operator to subtract the number 4 from the number 9.

Notice that some operators shown in Figure 3-9 have the same precedence number. For example, both the addition and subtraction operators have a precedence number of 6. If an expression contains more than one operator having the same priority, those operators are evaluated from left to right. In the expression 5 + 12 / 3 – 1, for instance, the division (/) is performed first, then the addition (+), and then the subtraction (–). In other words, the computer first divides 12 by 3, giving 4. It then adds the result of the division to 5, giving 9. Lastly, it subtracts 1 from the result of the addition, giving 8. You can use parentheses to change the order in which the operators in an expression are evaluated. For example, the expression 5 + 12 / (3 – 1) evaluates to 11, not 8. This is because the parentheses tell the computer to subtract 1 from 3 first, then divide the difference (2) into 12, and then add the quotient (6) to 5, giving 11.

Two of the arithmetic operators listed in Figure 3-9 might be less familiar to you: the integer division operator (\\) and the modulus operator (Mod). You use the **integer division operator** (\\) to divide two integers, and then return the result as an integer. For instance, the expression 211\\4 results in 52, which is the integer result of dividing 211 by 4. (If you use the standard division operator [/] to divide 211 by 4, the result is 52.75 rather than 52.) You might use the integer division operator in a program that determines the number of quarters, dimes, and nickels to return as change to a customer. For example, if a customer should receive 53 cents in change, you could use the expression 53 \\ 25 to determine the number of quarters to return; the expression evaluates to 2.

The modulus operator also is used to divide two numbers, but the numbers do not have to be integers. After dividing the numbers, the **modulus operator** returns the remainder of the division. For instance, 211 Mod 4 equals 3, which is the remainder of 211 divided by 4. You can use the modulus operator to determine whether a number is even or odd. If you divide the number by 2 and the remainder is 0, the number is even; if the remainder is 1, however, the number is odd.

When entering an arithmetic expression in code, you do not enter the dollar sign ($) or the percent sign (%) in the numeric literal constants in the expression. If you want to enter a percentage amount in an arithmetic expression, you first must change the percentage amount to its decimal equivalent; for example, you would change 5% to .05. Alternatively, you can use 5/100 to represent 5% in an expression. Figure 3-10 shows examples of including arithmetic expressions in assignment statements. The expressions contain arithmetic operators, literal constants, and variables. When an expression contains a variable, the computer uses the value stored inside the variable to process the expression. The variables and literal constants in Examples 1 and 2 have the Integer data type. The variables and literal constants in Example 3 have the Double data type. Example 4 shows how to include a Decimal variable and a Double literal constant in an arithmetic expression. Example 5 shows how to assign the Double result of a calculation to the Text property of a control. Notice that the variables and literal constants in each example have the same data type.

»HOW TO ...

INCLUDE ARITHMETIC EXPRESSIONS IN ASSIGNMENT STATEMENTS

Example 1

age = age + 1

adds the integer 1 to the contents of the Integer age variable, then assigns the result to the age variable

Example 2

quarters = change \ 25

uses the integer division operator to divide the contents of the Integer change variable by the integer 25, then assigns the result to the Integer quarters variable

Example 3

bonus = sales *.05

multiplies the contents of the Double sales variable by the Double number .05, then assigns the result to the Double bonus variable

Example 4

price = price * Convert.ToDecimal(1.04)

converts the Double number 1.04 to Decimal, then multiplies the result by the contents of the Decimal price variable, then assigns the result to the price variable

Example 5

bonusTextBox.Text = _
    Convert.ToString(sales * .05)

multiplies the contents of the Double sales variable by the Double number .05, then converts the result (a Double number) to the String data type before assigning it to the bonusTextBox

Line continuation character

Figure 3-10: How to include arithmetic expressions in assignment statements

The underscore (_) that appears at the end of the first line in Example 5 is called the line continuation character. You use the **line continuation character** to break up a long instruction into two or more physical lines in the Code Editor window. Breaking up a long instruction in this manner makes the instruction easier to read and understand. The line continuation character must be immediately preceded by a space, and it must appear at the end of a physical line of code.

Keep in mind that a variable can store only one value at any one time. When you use an assignment statement to assign another value to the variable, the new value replaces the existing value. To illustrate this point, assume that a button's Click event procedure contains the following two lines of code: Dim number As Integer = 500 and number = number * 2. When you run the application and click the button, the two lines of code are processed as follows:

» The Dim statement creates the number variable in memory and initializes it to the number 500.

» The number = number * 2 assignment statement first multiplies the contents of the number variable by the number 2, giving 1000. The assignment statement then replaces the current contents of the number variable (500) with 1000. Notice that the calculation appearing on the right side of the assignment operator is performed first, and then the result is assigned to the variable whose name appears on the left side of the assignment operator.

THE SCOPE AND LIFETIME OF A VARIABLE

Besides a name, data type, and initial value, every variable also has both a scope and a lifetime. A variable's **scope** indicates where in the application's code the variable can be used, and its **lifetime** indicates how long the variable remains in the computer's internal memory. Variables can have module scope, procedure scope, or block scope. However, most of the variables used in an application will have procedure scope. This is because fewer unintentional errors occur in applications when the variables are declared using the minimum scope needed, which usually is procedure scope. A variable's scope and lifetime are determined by where you declare the variable—in other words, where you enter the variable's declaration statement. Typically, you enter the declaration statement either in a procedure, such as an event procedure, or in the Declarations section of a form. A form's Declarations section is not the same as the General Declarations section (shown earlier in Figure 3-8). The General Declarations section is located above the Public Class line in the Code Editor window, whereas the form's Declarations section is located within the Public Class statement. (You can look ahead to Figure 3-13 to view the location of both sections.)

Variables declared in a procedure have either procedure scope or block scope, depending on where in the procedure they are declared. Variables declared in a form's Declarations section have module scope. In the following two sections, you will learn about procedure scope variables and module scope variables. Variables having block scope are covered in Chapter 4.

> **» TIP**
>
> Variables also can have namespace scope; these variables are referred to as namespace variables, global variables, or public variables. Using namespace variables can lead to unintentional errors in a program and should be avoided, if possible. For this reason, they are not covered in this book.

USING VARIABLES HAVING PROCEDURE-SCOPE

When you declare a variable in a procedure, the variable is called a **procedure-level variable** and it has **procedure scope**, because only that procedure can use the variable. For example, if you enter the Dim number As Integer statement in the calcButton's Click event procedure, only the calcButton's Click event procedure can use the number variable. No other procedures in the application are allowed to use the variable. As a matter of fact, no other procedures in the application will even be aware of the number variable's existence. Procedure-level variables remain in the computer's internal memory only while the procedure in which they are declared is running; they are removed from memory when the procedure ends. In other words, a procedure-level variable has the same lifetime as the procedure that declares it. As indicated earlier, most of the variables in your applications will be procedure-level variables.

The Sales Tax application that you view next illustrates the use of procedure-level variables. Figure 3-11 shows the MainForm in the application, and Figure 3-12 shows the Click event procedures for the Calculate 2% Tax and Calculate 5% Tax buttons. As the MainForm indicates, the application allows the user to enter a sales amount. It then calculates and displays either a 2% sales tax or a 5% sales tax, depending on the button selected by the user.

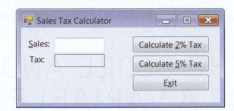

Figure 3-11: The MainForm in the Sales Tax application

Comment

Procedure-level variables declared in the calcTax2Button's Click event procedure

Procedure-level variables declared in the calcTax5Button's Click event procedure

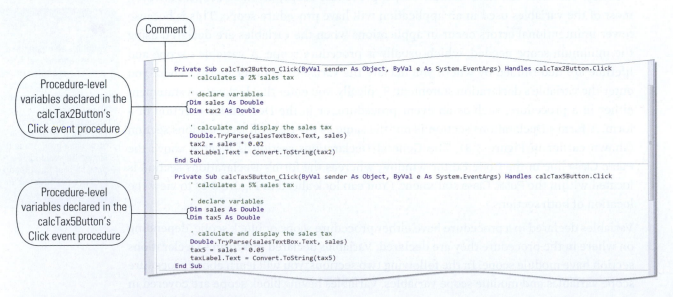

```
Private Sub calcTax2Button_Click(ByVal sender As Object, ByVal e As System.EventArgs) Handles calcTax2Button.Click
    ' calculates a 2% sales tax

    ' declare variables
    Dim sales As Double
    Dim tax2 As Double

    ' calculate and display the sales tax
    Double.TryParse(salesTextBox.Text, sales)
    tax2 = sales * 0.02
    taxLabel.Text = Convert.ToString(tax2)
End Sub

Private Sub calcTax5Button_Click(ByVal sender As Object, ByVal e As System.EventArgs) Handles calcTax5Button.Click
    ' calculates a 5% sales tax

    ' declare variables
    Dim sales As Double
    Dim tax5 As Double

    ' calculate and display the sales tax
    Double.TryParse(salesTextBox.Text, sales)
    tax5 = sales * 0.05
    taxLabel.Text = Convert.ToString(tax5)
End Sub
```

Figure 3-12: Examples of using procedure-level variables

Both procedures shown in Figure 3-12 declare two procedure-level variables. It is customary to enter the variable declaration statements at the beginning of the procedure, as shown in the figure. Each procedure also contains three lines of green text. The lines, called **comments**, are used to internally document the procedure. You create a comment in Visual Basic by placing an apostrophe (') before the text that represents the comment. The computer ignores everything that appears after the apostrophe on that line. Although it is not required, some programmers use a space to separate the apostrophe from the comment, as shown in the figure. Many programmers use comments to document a procedure's purpose. Such comments are entered below the Private Sub line in the procedure. Here again, although it is not required, many programmers follow the comments with a blank line. It is a good programming practice also to include comments that explain various sections of the procedure's code, because comments make the code more readable and easier to understand by anyone viewing it.

When the user enters a sales amount and then clicks the Calculate 2% Tax button, the calcTax2Button's Click event procedure creates and initializes the sales and tax2 variables; only the calcTax2Button's Click event procedure can use the variables. The procedure then converts the sales amount to Double and stores the result in the sales variable. Then the procedure multiplies the contents of the sales variable by .02 and stores the result in the tax2 variable. Finally, the procedure assigns the contents of the tax2 variable, converted to String, to the taxLabel's Text property. When the procedure ends, the computer removes the sales and tax2 procedure-level variables from memory. The variables will be created again the next time the user clicks the Calculate 2% Tax button. A similar process is followed when the user clicks the Calculate 5% Tax button, except the variable that stores the tax amount is named tax5, and the tax is calculated using a rate of .05 rather than .02.

Both procedures in Figure 3-12 declare a variable using the same name, sales. When you use the same name to declare a variable in more than one procedure, each procedure creates its own variable when the procedure is invoked. Each procedure also destroys its own variable when the procedure ends. In other words, although the sales variables in both procedures have the same name, they are not the same variable. Rather, each refers to a different section in the computer's internal memory, and each is created and destroyed independently from the other.

USING A VARIABLE HAVING MODULE-SCOPE

Besides declaring a variable in a procedure, you also can declare a variable in the form's Declarations section, which begins with the Public Class line and ends with the End Class line. When you declare a variable in the form's Declarations section, the variable is called a **module-level variable** and it has **module scope**. You typically use a module-level variable when you need more than one procedure in the same form to use the same variable, because a module-level variable can be used by all of the procedures in the form, including the procedures associated with the controls contained on the form. Unlike a procedure-level variable, which you declare using the Dim keyword, you declare a module-level variable using the Private keyword. For example, when the statement Private number As Integer is entered in the form's Declarations section, it creates a module-level variable named number. Because the variable has module scope, it can be used by every procedure in the form. Module-level variables retain their values and remain in the computer's internal memory until the application ends. In other words, a module-level variable has the same lifetime as the application itself. You can write the Sales Tax application (which you viewed in the previous section) a different way, using a module-level variable (rather than procedure-level variables) to store the sales amount. Figure 3-13 shows the appropriate code.

General Declarations
section

Comment and module-level
variable declaration
entered in the MainForm's
Declarations section

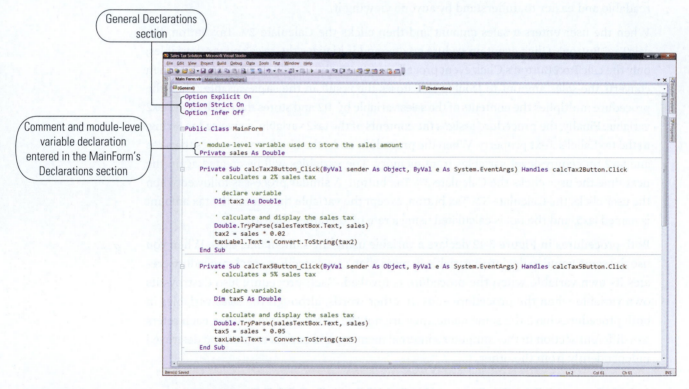

Figure 3-13: Example of using a module-level variable

In this case, when the Sales Tax application is started, the Private sales As Double statement contained in the MainForm's Declarations section is processed first. The statement creates and initializes (to the number 0) a Double variable named sales. The variable is created and initialized only once, when the application is first started. It remains in the computer's internal memory until the application ends. When the user enters a sales amount and then clicks the Calculate 2% Tax button, the button's Click event procedure creates and initializes a procedure-level variable named tax2. The procedure then converts the sales amount entered by the user to Double and stores the result in the module-level sales variable. Then the procedure multiplies the contents of the sales variable by .02 and stores the result in the tax2 variable. Finally, the procedure displays the contents of the tax2 variable, converted to String, in the taxLabel. When the procedure ends, the computer removes only the procedure-level variable (tax2) from its memory; it does not remove the module-level variable (sales). A similar process is followed when the user clicks the Calculate 5% Tax button, except the procedure-level variable is named tax5 and the tax rate is .05. The module-level sales variable is removed from the computer's memory only when the application ends. Although you can code the Sales Tax application using procedure-level variables only, or a combination of a module-level and procedure-level variables, many programmers would argue that you should use module-level variables only when you can't code the program using procedure-level variables. As you learned earlier, fewer unintentional errors occur in applications when the variables are declared using the minimum scope needed.

As the syntax shown earlier in Figure 3-3 indicates, you can declare a variable using the Dim, Private, or Static keywords. You already know how to use the Dim keyword to declare a procedure-level variable, and how to use the Private keyword to declare a module-level variable. In the next section, you learn how to use the Static keyword to declare a special type of procedure-level variable, called a static variable.

STATIC VARIABLES

A **static variable** is a procedure-level variable that remains in memory and also retains its value even when the procedure in which it is declared ends. You declare a static variable using the Static keyword rather than the Dim keyword. Similar to a module-level variable, a static variable is not removed from the computer's internal memory until the application ends. However, a module-level variable can be used by all of the procedures in a form, whereas a static variable can be used only by the procedure in which it is declared. In other words, a static variable has a narrower scope than does a module-level variable. As you learned earlier, you can prevent many unintentional errors from occurring in an application by declaring the variables using the minimum scope needed. The Total Sales application that you view next illustrates the use of a static variable. Figure 3-14 shows the MainForm in the application, and

> **》TIP**
> The Static keyword can be used only in a procedure.

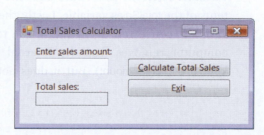

Figure 3-14: The MainForm in the Total Sales application

Figure 3-15 shows the MainForm's code. The application uses a static variable named totalSales to accumulate (add together) the sales amounts entered by the user. Notice that the General Declarations section in Figure 3-15 contains comments that document the project's name and purpose, as well as the programmer's name and the date the code was either created or modified. The section also contains the Option statements discussed earlier.

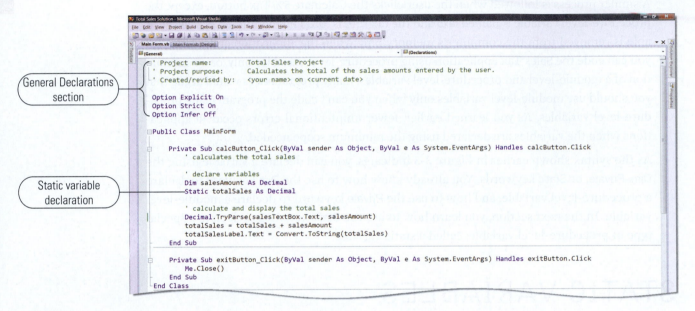

Figure 3-15: Example of using a static variable

The first time the user clicks the Calculate Total Sales button, the button's Click event procedure creates and initializes (to the number 0) a procedure-level variable named salesAmount and a static variable named totalSales. The procedure then converts the sales amount entered by the user to Decimal, and stores the result in the salesAmount variable. Then the procedure adds the contents of the salesAmount variable to the contents of the totalSales variable. Lastly, the procedure displays the contents of the totalSales variable, converted to String, in the totalSalesLabel. When the procedure ends, the computer removes from its internal memory the variable declared using the Dim keyword (salesAmount). But it does not remove the variable declared using the Static keyword (totalSales). Each subsequent time the user clicks the Calculate Total Sales button, the computer re-creates and re-initializes the salesAmount variable declared in the button's Click event procedure. However, it does not re-create or re-initialize the totalSales variable because that variable, as well as its current value, is still in the computer's memory. After re-creating and re-initializing the salesAmount variable, the computer processes the remaining instructions contained in the button's Click event procedure. Here again, each time the procedure ends, the salesAmount variable is removed from the computer's internal memory. The totalSales variable is removed only when the application ends.

NAMED CONSTANTS

In addition to using literal constants and variables in your code, you also can use named constants. Like a variable, a **named constant** is a memory location inside the computer. However, unlike a variable, the contents of a named constant cannot be changed while the application is running. You create a named constant using the **Const statement**. Figure 3-16 shows the syntax of the Const statement. In the syntax, *constantName* is the name of the named constant. Many programmers use Pascal case for the names of named constants; using this convention helps them distinguish the constants from the variables used in a program. (Recall that variable names are entered using camel case.) As you learned in Chapter 1, Pascal case means that you capitalize the first letter in the name, as well as the first letter of each subsequent word in the name. *DataType* in the syntax is the named constant's data type, and *expression* is the value you want stored in the named constant. The *expression* must have the same data type as the named constant. The *expression* can contain a literal constant, another named constant, or an arithmetic operator; however, it cannot contain a variable or a method. In addition to showing the Const statement's syntax, Figure 3-16 also shows examples of declaring named constants. The Const statements in the first three examples can be used to create procedure-level named constants; you do this by entering the statements in the appropriate procedure. You can use the Const statement in Example 4 to create a module-level named constant. Notice that you precede the Const keyword with the Private keyword when creating a module-level constant. In addition, you need to enter the statement in the form's Declarations section.

» TIP
Recall that Pascal case is also used for the names of forms.

»HOW TO . . .

DECLARE A NAMED CONSTANT

Syntax

Const *constantName* **As** *dataType* = *expression*

Example 1

Const Pi As Double = 3.141593

declares Pi as a Double named constant and initializes it to the Double number 3.141593

Example 2

Const MaxHours As Integer = 40

declares MaxHours as an Integer named constant and initializes it to the integer 40

Example 3

Const TaxRate As Decimal = .05D

declares TaxRate as a Decimal named constant and initializes it to the Decimal number .05

Example 4

Private Const Heading As String = "ABC Company"

declares Heading as a String named constant and initializes it to the string "ABC Company"

Use the D literal type character to change the number to Decimal

Figure 3-16: How to declare a named constant

Notice the letter D that appears after the number .05 in Example 3. The letter D is one of the literal type characters in Visual Basic. A **literal type character** forces a literal constant to assume a data type other than the one its form indicates. In this case, the letter D forces the Double number .05 to assume the Decimal data type. At this point, you may be wondering why the Convert.ToDecimal method was not used to convert the Double number .05 to the Decimal data type, like this: Const TaxRate As Decimal = Convert.ToDecimal(.05). As you learned earlier, the *expression* assigned to a named constant cannot contain a method.

Named constants make code more self-documenting and easier to modify, because they allow you to use meaningful words in place of values that are less clear. The named constant Pi, for example, is much more meaningful than is the number 3.141593, which is the value of pi rounded to six decimal places. Once you create a named constant, you then can use the constant's name (rather than its value) in the application's code. Unlike the value stored in a variable, the value stored in a named constant cannot be inadvertently changed while the application is running. Using a named constant to represent a value has another advantage: if the value changes in the future, you will need to modify only the Const statement in the program, rather than all of the program statements that use the value.

The Area Calculator application that you view next illustrates the use of a named constant. Figure 3-17 shows the MainForm in the application, and Figure 3-18 shows the code for the Calculate Area button's Click event procedure. As the MainForm indicates, the application allows the user to enter the radius of a circle. It then calculates and displays the area of the circle. The

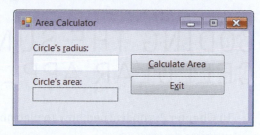

Figure 3-17: The MainForm in the Area Calculator application

formula for calculating the area of a circle is πr^2, where π stands for pi (3.141593).

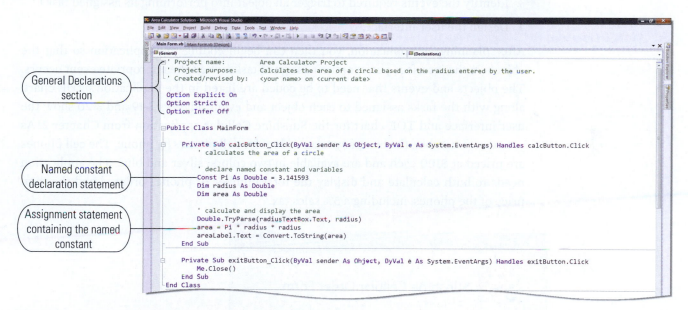

Figure 3-18: Example of using a named constant

The calcButton's Click event procedure declares and initializes a named constant (Pi) and two variables (radius and area). It then converts (to Double) the radius value entered by the user, storing the converted value in the radius variable. The area = Pi * radius * radius statement calculates the circle's area using the values stored in the Pi named constant and radius variable, and then assigns the result to the area variable. Lastly, the procedure displays the contents of the area variable (converted to String) in the areaLabel. When the procedure ends, the computer removes the named constant and the two variables from its internal memory.

Next, you will use what you learned about variables, constants, and calculations to code the Sunshine Cellular application from Chapter 2. You also will learn how programmers plan a procedure's code.

CODING THE SUNSHINE CELLULAR APPLICATION

In Chapter 2, you learned how to plan an application. Recall that planning an application requires you to:

1. Identify the tasks the application needs to perform.

2. Identify the objects to which you will assign those tasks.

3. Identify the events required to trigger an object into performing its assigned tasks.

4. Design the user interface.

After planning an application, you then can begin coding the application so that the objects in the interface perform their assigned tasks when the appropriate event occurs. The objects and events that need to be coded are listed in the application's TOE chart, along with the tasks assigned to each object and event. Figures 3-19 and 3-20 show the user interface and TOE chart for the Sunshine Cellular application from Chapter 2. As you may remember, the company takes orders for cell phones by phone. The cell phones are priced at $100 each and are available in two colors: silver and blue. The application needs to both calculate and display the total number of phones ordered and the total price of the phones, including a 5% sales tax.

Figure 3-19: Sunshine Cellular interface

Task	Object	Event
1. Calculate the total phones ordered and the total price 2. Display the total phones ordered and the total price in totalPhonesLabel and totalPriceLabel	calcButton	Click
Clear the screen for the next order	clearButton	Click
End the application	exitButton	Click
Display the total phones ordered (from calcButton)	totalPhonesLabel	None
Display the total price (from calcButton)	totalPriceLabel	None
Get and display the order information	nameTextBox, addressTextBox, cityTextBox, stateTextBox, zipTextBox, silverTextBox, blueTextBox	None

Figure 3-20: Sunshine Cellular TOE chart

According to the TOE chart, only the three buttons require coding, as they are the only objects with an event—in this case, the Click event—listed in the third column of the chart. Before you begin coding an object's event procedure, you should plan the procedure. Programmers frequently use either pseudocode or a flowchart when planning a procedure's code.

USING PSEUDOCODE TO PLAN A PROCEDURE

Pseudocode uses short phrases to describe the steps a procedure needs to take to accomplish its goal. Figure 3-21 shows the pseudocode for the procedures that need to be coded in the Sunshine Cellular application. As the pseudocode indicates, the calcButton's Click event procedure is responsible for calculating the total phones ordered and the total price, and then displaying the calculated results in the appropriate label controls in the interface. The clearButton's Click event procedure will prepare the screen for the next order by removing the contents of the text boxes and two label controls, and then sending the focus to the nameTextBox. The exitButton's Click event procedure will simply end the application.

---

calcButton Click Event Procedure (pseudocode)
1. assign user input to variables
2. total phones ordered = silver phones ordered + blue phones ordered
3. subtotal = total phones ordered * phone price
4. sales tax = subtotal * sales tax rate
5. total price = subtotal + sales tax
6. display total phones ordered and total price in totalPhonesLabel and totalPriceLabel

clearButton Click Event Procedure (pseudocode)
1. clear the Text property of the 7 text boxes
2. clear the Text property of the totalPhonesLabel and totalPriceLabel
3. send the focus to the nameTextBox so the user can begin entering the next order

exitButton Click Event Procedure (pseudocode)
1. end the application

Figure 3-21: Pseudocode for the Sunshine Cellular application

USING A FLOWCHART TO PLAN A PROCEDURE

Unlike pseudocode, which consists of short phrases, a **flowchart** uses standardized symbols to show the steps a procedure must follow to reach its goal. Figure 3-22 shows the flowcharts for the procedures that need to be coded in the Sunshine Cellular application. The flowcharts contain three different symbols: an oval, a rectangle, and a parallelogram. The symbols are connected with lines, called **flowlines**. The oval symbol is called the **start/stop symbol**. The start oval indicates the beginning of the flowchart, and the stop oval indicates end of the flowchart. The rectangles that appear between the start and stop ovals are called process symbols. You use the **process symbol** to represent such tasks as making assignments and calculations. The parallelogram in a flowchart is called the **input/output symbol** and is used to represent input tasks (such as getting information from the user) and output tasks (such as displaying information). The parallelogram shown in Figure 3-22 represents an output task. Notice that the logic depicted in the flowcharts is the same as the logic shown in the pseudocode.

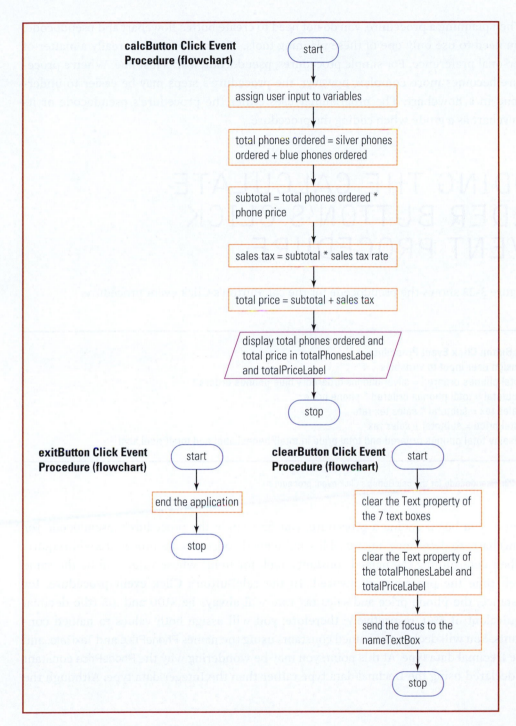

calcButton Click Event Procedure (flowchart)

start

↓

assign user input to variables

↓

total phones ordered = silver phones ordered + blue phones ordered

↓

subtotal = total phones ordered * phone price

↓

sales tax = subtotal * sales tax rate

↓

total price = subtotal + sales tax

↓

display total phones ordered and total price in totalPhonesLabel and totalPriceLabel

↓

stop

exitButton Click Event Procedure (flowchart)

start

↓

end the application

↓

stop

clearButton Click Event Procedure (flowchart)

start

↓

clear the Text property of the 7 text boxes

↓

clear the Text property of the totalPhonesLabel and totalPriceLabel

↓

send the focus to the nameTextBox

↓

stop

Figure 3-22: Flowcharts for the Sunshine Cellular application

When planning a procedure, you do not need to create both a flowchart and pseudocode; you need to use only one of these planning tools. The tool you use is really a matter of personal preference. For simple procedures, pseudocode works just fine. When a procedure becomes more complex, however, the procedure's steps may be easier to understand in a flowchart. The programmer uses either the procedure's pseudocode or its flowchart as a guide when coding the procedure.

CODING THE CALCULATE ORDER BUTTON'S CLICK EVENT PROCEDURE

Figure 3-23 shows the pseudocode for the calcButton's Click event procedure.

---

calcButton Click Event Procedure
1. assign user input to variables
2. total phones ordered = silver phones ordered + blue phones ordered
3. subtotal = total phones ordered * phone price
4. sales tax = subtotal * sales tax rate
5. total price = subtotal + sales tax
6. display total phones ordered and total price in totalPhonesLabel and totalPriceLabel

---

Figure 3-23: Pseudocode for the calcButton's Click event procedure

Before you begin coding a procedure, you first study the procedure's pseudocode (or flowchart) to determine any variables and named constants the procedure will require. When determining the named constants, look for items whose value will be the same each time the procedure is invoked. In the calcButton's Click event procedure, for instance, the phone price and sales tax rate will always be $100 and .05 (the decimal equivalent of 5%), respectively; therefore, you will assign both values to named constants. You will declare the named constants using the names PhonePrice and TaxRate, and the Decimal data type. At this point, you may be wondering why the PhonePrice constant is declared using the Decimal data type rather than the Integer data type. Although the price of a phone does not currently contain any decimal places, it is possible that the price may include a decimal place in the future. By using the Decimal data type now, you can change the constant's value to include a decimal place without having to remember to also change its data type.

When determining the variables a procedure will use, look in the pseudocode (or flow-chart) for items whose value probably will change each time the procedure is processed. In the calcButton's Click event procedure, the numbers of silver and blue phones ordered, as well as the total number of phones ordered, the subtotal, the sales tax, and the total price, probably will be different each time the procedure is processed; therefore, you will use variables to store the values. You will use Integer variables to store the number of silver phones ordered, the number of blue phones ordered, and the total number of phones ordered, because those values can be whole numbers only. You will use Decimal variables to store the subtotal, sales tax, and total price of the order, because those amounts may contain a decimal place. Figure 3-24 lists the names, data types, and values of the two named constants. It also lists the names and data types of the six variables, as well as the source of their values.

Named constants	Data type	Value
PhonePrice	Decimal	100
TaxRate	Decimal	.05
Variables	Data type	Value source
silverPhones	Integer	user input (silverTextBox)
bluePhones	Integer	user input (blueTextBox)
totalPhones	Integer	procedure calculation
subtotal	Decimal	procedure calculation
salesTax	Decimal	procedure calculation
totalPrice	Decimal	procedure calculation

Figure 3-24: Named constants and variables for the calcButton's Click event procedure

Figure 3-25 shows the named constant and variable declaration statements entered in the calcButton's Click event procedure. The green jagged lines indicate that the named constants and variables have been declared, but they do not appear in any other statement in the code.

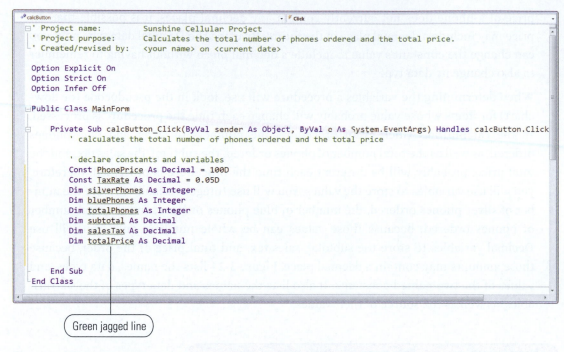

Green jagged line

Figure 3-25: Declaration statements entered in the calcButton's Click event procedure

The first step listed in the pseudocode shown in Figure 3-23 is to assign the user input to the appropriate variables. In this case, the user input is the number of silver phones ordered and the number of blue phones ordered. The user enters those values in the silverTextBox and blueTextBox in the interface. You will assign the Text properties of those two text boxes to the **silverPhones** and **bluePhones** variables, using the TryParse method to convert the Text property values to the Integer data type, as shown in Figure 3-26.

```
      Private Sub calcButton_Click(ByVal sender As Object, ByVal e As System.EventArgs) Handles calcButton.Click
          ' calculates the total number of phones ordered and the total price

          ' declare constants and variables
          Const PhonePrice As Decimal = 100D
          Const TaxRate As Decimal = 0.05D
          Dim silverPhones As Integer
          Dim bluePhones As Integer
          Dim totalPhones As Integer
          Dim subtotal As Decimal
          Dim salesTax As Decimal
          Dim totalPrice As Decimal

          ' assign user input to variables
          Integer.TryParse(silverTextBox.Text, silverPhones)
          Integer.TryParse(blueTextBox.Text, bluePhones)

      End Sub
```

Figure 3-26: User input assigned to variables

Step 2 in the pseudocode is to calculate the total number of phones ordered by adding together the number of silver phones ordered and the number of blue phones ordered. You can perform this task using the statement totalPhones = silverPhones + bluePhones. Step 3 is to calculate the subtotal by multiplying the total number of phones ordered by the phone price. The correct statement to use here is subtotal = totalPhones * PhonePrice. Step 4 is to calculate the sales tax; this step is accomplished with the statement salesTax = subtotal * TaxRate. Step 5 is to calculate the total price of the order. You do this with the statement totalPrice = subtotal + salesTax. The last step in the pseudocode is to display the total number of phones ordered and the total price of the order in the appropriate label controls. Figure 3-27 shows the completed Click event procedure for the calcButton.

```vb
Private Sub calcButton_Click(ByVal sender As Object, ByVal e As System.EventArgs) Handles calcButton.Click
    ' calculates the total number of phones ordered and the total price

    ' declare constants and variables
    Const PhonePrice As Decimal = 100D
    Const TaxRate As Decimal = 0.05D
    Dim silverPhones As Integer
    Dim bluePhones As Integer
    Dim totalPhones As Integer
    Dim subtotal As Decimal
    Dim salesTax As Decimal
    Dim totalPrice As Decimal

    ' assign user input to variables
    Integer.TryParse(silverTextBox.Text, silverPhones)
    Integer.TryParse(blueTextBox.Text, bluePhones)

    ' perform calculations
    totalPhones = silverPhones + bluePhones
    subtotal = totalPhones * PhonePrice
    salesTax = subtotal * TaxRate
    totalPrice = subtotal + salesTax

    ' display calculated amounts
    totalPhonesLabel.Text = Convert.ToString(totalPhones)
    totalPricelabel.text = Convert.ToString(totalPrice)

End Sub
```

Figure 3-27: Completed calcButton's Click event procedure

COMPLETING THE SUNSHINE CELLULAR APPLICATION

To complete the Sunshine Cellular application, you still need to code the Click event procedures for the exitButton and clearButton. According to the application's TOE chart (shown earlier in Figure 3-20), the exitButton's Click event procedure is assigned the task of ending the application. You accomplish that task using the Me.Close() statement. The clearButton's Click event procedure is assigned the task of clearing the screen for the next order. The procedure's pseudocode is shown in Figure 3-28. The procedure does not perform any tasks that require user input or calculations; therefore, the procedure will not need any named constants or variables.

```
clearButton Click Event Procedure
1. clear the Text property of the 7 text boxes
2. clear the Text property of the totalPhonesLabel and totalPriceLabel
3. send the focus to the nameTextBox so the user can begin entering the next order
```

Figure 3-28: Pseudocode for the clearButton's Click event procedure

The pseudocode indicates that the procedure should clear the Text property of the text boxes and two of the labels in the interface, and then send the focus to the nameTextBox. You can clear the Text property by assigning the String.Empty value to the property. (Or, you can assign the empty string [""].) To move the focus to a specified control while an application is running, you use the **Focus method**. As you learned in Chapter 2, a control that has the focus can accept user input. The Focus method's syntax is *object*.**Focus()**, where *object* is the name of the object to which you want the focus sent. Figure 3-29 shows the completed code for the Sunshine Cellular application.

```vb
' Project name:        Sunshine Cellular Project
' Project purpose:     Calculates the total number of phones ordered and the total price.
' Created/revised by:  <your name> on <current date>

Option Explicit On
Option Strict On
Option Infer Off

Public Class MainForm

    Private Sub calcButton_Click(ByVal sender As Object, _
        ByVal e As System.EventArgs) Handles calcButton.Click
        ' calculates the total number of phones ordered and the total price

        ' declare constants and variables
        Const PhonePrice As Decimal = 100D
        Const TaxRate As Decimal = 0.05D
        Dim silverPhones As Integer
        Dim bluePhones As Integer
        Dim totalPhones As Integer
        Dim subtotal As Decimal
        Dim salesTax As Decimal
        Dim totalPrice As Decimal

        ' assign user input to variables
        Integer.TryParse(silverTextBox.Text, silverPhones)
        Integer.TryParse(blueTextBox.Text, bluePhones)
```

Figure 3-29: The Sunshine Cellular application's code (*continued on next page*)

```
        ' perform calculations
        totalPhones = silverPhones + bluePhones
        subtotal = totalPhones * PhonePrice
        salesTax = subtotal * TaxRate
        totalPrice = subtotal + salesTax

        ' display calculated amounts
        totalPhonesLabel.Text = Convert.ToString(totalPhones)
        totalPricelabel.text = Convert.ToString(totalPrice)

    End Sub

    Private Sub exitButton_Click(ByVal sender As Object, _
        ByVal e As System.EventArgs) Handles exitButton.Click
        Me.Close()

    End Sub

    Private Sub clearButton_Click(ByVal sender As Object, _
        ByVal e As System.EventArgs) Handles clearButton.Click
        ' prepares the screen for the next order

        nameTextBox.Text = String.Empty
        addressTextBox.Text = String.Empty
        cityTextBox.Text = String.Empty
        stateTextBox.Text = String.Empty
        zipTextBox.Text = String.Empty
        silverTextBox.Text = String.Empty
        blueTextBox.Text = String.Empty
        totalPhonesLabel.Text = String.Empty
        totalPriceLabel.Text = String.Empty
        nameTextBox.Focus()

    End Sub
End Class
```

Figure 3-29: The Sunshine Cellular application's code (*continued from previous page*)

TESTING AND DEBUGGING THE APPLICATION

After coding an application, you then test it to verify that the code works correctly. If the code contains an error, called a **bug**, you need to correct the error before giving the application to the user. You test an application by starting it and entering some sample data. You should use both valid and invalid test data. **Valid data** is data that the application is expecting the user to enter. For example, the Sunshine Cellular application is expecting the user to enter a numeric value as the number of silver phones ordered. **Invalid data**, on the other hand, is data that the application is not expecting the user to enter. It's a good programming practice to test the application with invalid data because users sometimes make mistakes when entering data. The Sunshine Cellular application, for instance, is not expecting the user to enter a letter for the number of either silver or blue phones ordered. You should test the application as thoroughly as possible, because you don't want to give the user an application that ends abruptly when invalid data is entered.

Debugging refers to the process of locating and correcting any errors (bugs) in a program. Program errors can be either syntax errors or logic errors. A **syntax error** is an error that violates the programming language's syntax (rules). Most syntax errors are simply typing errors that occur when entering instructions, such as typing Me.Clse() instead of Me.Close(). The Code Editor detects most syntax errors as you enter the instructions. An example of a much more difficult type of error to find, and one that the Code Editor cannot detect, is a logic error. You create a **logic error** when you enter an instruction that does not give you the expected results, or when you neglect to enter an instruction, or enter the instructions in the wrong order. An example of a logic error is the instruction average = num1 + num2 / 2, which is supposed to calculate the average of two numbers. Although the instruction is syntactically correct, it is logically incorrect. The instruction to calculate the average of two numbers, written correctly, is average = (num1 + num2) / 2. Because division has a higher precedence number than does addition, you must place parentheses around the num1 + num2 part of the expression.

First, you will test the Sunshine Cellular application using valid data. After entering the data and then clicking the Calculate Order button, the interface will appear as shown in Figure 3-30. The interface indicates that a total of 15 phones were ordered at a cost of 1575.00; both amounts are correct.

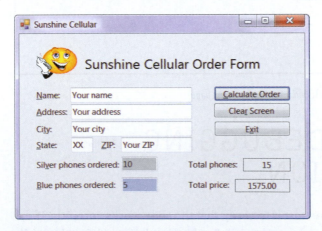

Figure 3-30: Result of testing the application using valid data

Now you will test the Sunshine Cellular application using invalid data. More specifically, you will use the letter t as the number of blue phones ordered. After entering the data and then clicking the Calculate Order button, the interface will appear as shown in Figure 3-31. In this case, the interface indicates that a total of 5 phones were ordered at a cost of 525.00. Notice that the application ignores the letter t entered as the number of blue phones ordered. Although the invalid data did not cause the application to end abruptly, you should check with the person for whom you wrote the application to verify that this is the way he wants the application to work. The person might want the application to remove the invalid data from the interface to avoid any confusion. Or, he might want the application to display a message prompting the user to re-enter the number of blue phones ordered.

Figure 3-31: Result of testing the application using invalid data

The last topic covered in this chapter is how to format an application's numeric output.

FORMATTING NUMERIC OUTPUT

Numbers representing monetary amounts typically are displayed with either zero or two decimal places and usually include a dollar sign and a thousands separator. Similarly, numbers representing percentage amounts usually are displayed with zero or more decimal places and a percent sign. Specifying the number of decimal places and the special characters to display in a number is called **formatting**. You can format a number using the syntax *variableName*.**ToString**(*formatString*). In the syntax, *variableName* is the name of a numeric variable, and ToString is a method that can be used with any of the numeric data types. The ToString method converts the contents of the numeric variable to a string. The *formatString* argument in the syntax is a string that specifies the format you want to use. The *formatString* argument must be enclosed in double quotation marks and it must take the form *Axx*, where *A* is an alphabetic character called the format specifier, and *xx* is a sequence of digits called the precision specifier. The format specifier must be one of the built-in format characters. The most commonly used format characters are listed in Figure 3-32; notice that you can use either an uppercase letter or a lowercase letter as the format specifier. The precision specifier controls the number of digits in the formatted number. Also included in Figure 3-32 are several examples of using the ToString method.

» HOW TO . . .

FORMAT A NUMBER

<u>Syntax</u>

variableName.**ToString(***formatString***)**

<u>Format specifier (Name)</u>	<u>Description</u>
C or c (Currency)	displays the string with a dollar sign; if appropriate, includes a thousands separator; negative values are enclosed in parentheses
N or n (Number)	similar to the Currency format, but does not include a dollar sign, and negative values are preceded by a minus sign
F or f (Fixed-point)	same as the Number format, but does not include a thousands separator
P or p (Percent)	multiplies the value by 100 and displays the result with a percent sign; negative values are preceded by a minus sign

<u>Example 1</u>

commissionLabel.Text = commission.ToString("C2")

if the commission variable contains the number 1250, the statement assigns the string "$1,250.00" to the Text property of the commissionLabel

<u>Example 2</u>

totalLabel.Text = total.ToString("N2")

if the total variable contains the number 123.675, the statement assigns the string "123.68" to the Text property of the totalLabel

<u>Example 3</u>

rateLabel.Text = rate.ToString("P0")

if the rate variable contains the number .06, the statement assigns the string "6 %" to the Text property of the rateLabel

Figure 3-32: How to format a number

In the Sunshine Cellular application, the calcButton's Click event procedure displays the total price of the order in the totalPriceLabel. You can include a dollar sign, thousands separator, and two decimal places when displaying the total price by changing the totalPriceLabel.Text = Convert.ToString(totalPrice) statement in the procedure to totalPriceLabel.Text = totalPrice.ToString("C2"). Figure 3-33 shows the calcButton's modified Click event procedure, and Figure 3-34 shows the formatted output in the interface.

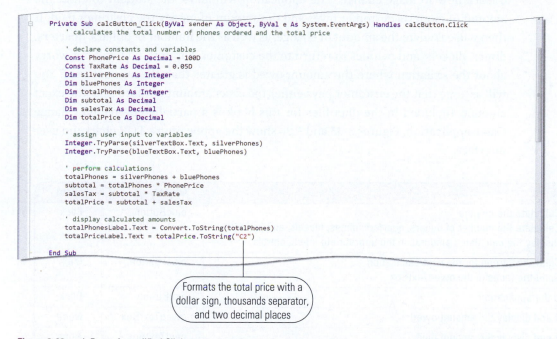

```
Private Sub calcButton_Click(ByVal sender As Object, ByVal e As System.EventArgs) Handles calcButton.Click
    ' calculates the total number of phones ordered and the total price

    ' declare constants and variables
    Const PhonePrice As Decimal = 100D
    Const TaxRate As Decimal = 0.05D
    Dim silverPhones As Integer
    Dim bluePhones As Integer
    Dim totalPhones As Integer
    Dim subtotal As Decimal
    Dim salesTax As Decimal
    Dim totalPrice As Decimal

    ' assign user input to variables
    Integer.TryParse(silverTextBox.Text, silverPhones)
    Integer.TryParse(blueTextBox.Text, bluePhones)

    ' perform calculations
    totalPhones = silverPhones + bluePhones
    subtotal = totalPhones * PhonePrice
    salesTax = subtotal * TaxRate
    totalPrice = subtotal + salesTax

    ' display calculated amounts
    totalPhonesLabel.Text = Convert.ToString(totalPhones)
    totalPriceLabel.Text = totalPrice.ToString("C2")

End Sub
```

Formats the total price with a dollar sign, thousands separator, and two decimal places

Figure 3-33: calcButton's modified Click event procedure

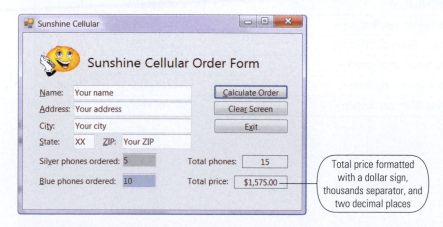

Total price formatted with a dollar sign, thousands separator, and two decimal places

Figure 3-34: Formatted output shown in the interface

You have completed the concepts section of Chapter 3.

PROGRAMMING TUTORIAL

CREATING THE CHANGE GAME APPLICATION

In this tutorial, you create an application that can help students in grades 1 through 6 learn how to make change. The application will allow the student to enter the amount of money a customer owes and the amount of money the customer paid. It then will calculate the amount of change, as well as the number of dollars, quarters, dimes, nickels, and pennies to return to the customer. For now, you will not worry about the situation where the amount owed is greater than the amount paid. You will assume that the customer pays either the exact amount or more than the exact amount. Included in the data files for this book is a partially completed Change Game application. Figures 3-35 and 3-36 show the application's TOE chart and user interface.

Task	Object	Event
1. Calculate the change 2. Calculate the number of dollars, quarters, dimes, nickels, and pennies 3. Display the calculated amounts in the appropriate label controls	calcButton	Click
1. Clear the screen for the next calculation 2. Send the focus to the owedTextBox	clearButton	Click
End the application	exitButton	Click
Get and display the amount owed	owedTextBox	None
Get and display the amount paid	paidTextBox	None
Display the change (from calcButton)	changeLabel	None
Display the number of dollars (from calcButton)	dollarLabel	None
Display the number of quarters (from calcButton)	quarterLabel	None
Display the number of dimes (from calcButton)	dimeLabel	None
Display the number of nickels (from calcButton)	nickelLabel	None
Display the number of pennies (from calcButton)	pennyLabel	None

Figure 3-35: TOE chart

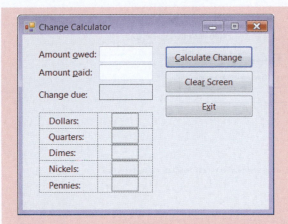

Figure 3-36: User interface

COMPLETING THE CHANGE GAME APPLICATION

As the application's TOE chart indicates, only three Click event procedures need to be coded.

To begin coding the application:

1. Start Visual Studio. If necessary, close the Start Page window.

2. Open the **Change Solution** (**Change Solution.sln**) file, which is contained in the VbReloaded2008\Chap03\Change Solution folder. If necessary, open the designer window. The MainForm appears on the screen.

3. Open the Code Editor window. Notice that the exitButton's Click event procedure has already been coded for you. In the comments that appear in the General Declarations section, replace the <your name> and <current date> text with your name and the current date.

4. The application will use variables, so you should enter the appropriate Option statements in the General Declarations section. Enter the Option statements shown in Figure 3-37.

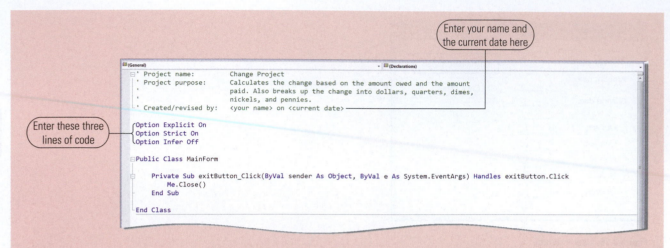

Figure 3-37: Option statements entered in the General Declarations section

According to the application's TOE chart, you need to code the Click event procedures for the calcButton and the clearButton. The calcButton's Click event procedure is responsible for both calculating and displaying the amount of change to give the customer. It also must both calculate and display the number of dollars, quarters, dimes, nickels, and pennies to return. Figure 3-38 shows the procedure's pseudocode.

---

calcButton Click Event Procedure
1. assign user input to variables
2. change = amount paid − amount owed
3. pennies = change * 100
4. dollars = pennies \ 100
5. pennies = pennies − (dollars * 100)
6. quarters = pennies \ 25
7. pennies = pennies − (quarters * 25)
8. dimes = pennies \ 10
9. pennies = pennies − (dimes * 10)
10. nickels = pennies \ 5
11. pennies = pennies − (nickels * 5)
12. display the calculated amounts in the appropriate label controls

---

Figure 3-38: Pseudocode for the calcButton's Click event procedure

The procedure will use eight variables: three Decimal variables and five Integer variables. The Decimal variables will store the amount owed, amount paid, and change, because those values might have a decimal place. The Integer variables will store the number of dollars, quarters, dimes, nickels, and pennies, because those values will be whole numbers. Figure 3-39 lists the names and data types of the variables, along with the source of their values.

Variables	Data type	Value source
owed	Decimal	user input (owedTextBox)
paid	Decimal	user input (paidTextBox)
change	Decimal	procedure calculation
dollars	Integer	procedure calculation
quarters	Integer	procedure calculation
dimes	Integer	procedure calculation
nickels	Integer	procedure calculation
pennies	Integer	procedure calculation

Figure 3-39: Variables for the calcButton's Click event procedure

To code the calcButton's Click event procedure:

1. Open the code template for the calcButton's Click event procedure. Enter the comments and variable declaration statements shown in Figure 3-40. Then position the insertion point as shown in the figure. Do not worry about the green jagged lines below the variable names. Recall that the lines indicate that the declared variable does not appear in any other statement in the code.

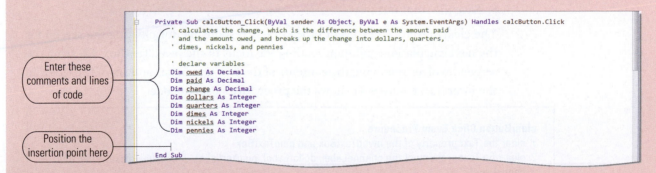

```
Private Sub calcButton_Click(ByVal sender As Object, ByVal e As System.EventArgs) Handles calcButton.Click
    ' calculates the change, which is the difference between the amount paid
    ' and the amount owed, and breaks up the change into dollars, quarters,
    ' dimes, nickels, and pennies

    ' declare variables
    Dim owed As Decimal
    Dim paid As Decimal
    Dim change As Decimal
    Dim dollars As Integer
    Dim quarters As Integer
    Dim dimes As Integer
    Dim nickels As Integer
    Dim pennies As Integer

End Sub
```

Enter these comments and lines of code

Position the insertion point here

Figure 3-40: Comments and declaration statements entered in the calcButton's Click event procedure

2. The first step in the pseudocode is to assign the user input to variables. Type **' assign input to variables** and press **Enter**. Type **decimal.tryparse (owedtextbox.text, owed)** and press **Enter**, then type **decimal.tryparse (paidtextbox.text, paid)** and press **Enter** twice. Notice that the jagged lines no longer appear below the owed and paid names in the declaration statements; this is because the names appear in the two assignment statements.

3. The next 10 steps pertain to calculating the change, as well as calculating the number of dollars, quarters, dimes, nickels, and pennies. Enter the following comment and code. Press **Enter** twice after typing the last assignment statement.

```
' perform calculations
change = paid - owed
pennies = Convert.ToInt32(change * 100)
dollars = pennies \ 100
pennies = pennies - (dollars * 100)
quarters = pennies \ 25
pennies = pennies - (quarters * 25)
dimes = pennies \ 10
pennies = pennies - (dimes * 10)
nickels = pennies \ 5
pennies = pennies - (nickels * 5)
```

4. The last step in the pseudocode is to display the calculated amounts. Enter the following comment and code.

```
' display calculated results
changeLabel.Text = Convert.ToString(change)
dollarLabel.Text = Convert.ToString(dollars)
quarterLabel.Text = Convert.ToString(quarters)
dimeLabel.Text = Convert.ToString(dimes)
nickelLabel.Text = Convert.ToString(nickels)
pennyLabel.Text = Convert.ToString(pennies)
```

5. Save the solution.

The clearButton's Click event procedure is responsible for clearing the screen for the next calculation, and then sending the focus to the owedTextBox. Clearing the screen involves removing the contents of the two text boxes and six of the labels in the interface. Figure 3-41 shows the procedure's pseudocode.

---

clearButton Click Event Procedure
1. clear the Text property of the owedTextBox and paidTextBox
2. clear the Text property of the changeLabel, dollarLabel, quarterLabel, dimeLabel, nickelLabel, and pennyLabel
3. send the focus to the owedTextBox

Figure 3-41: Pseudocode for the clearButton's Click event procedure

To code the clearButton's Click event procedure:

1. Open the code template for the clearButton's Click event procedure, then enter the following comment and code:

   ' prepares the screen for the next calculation

   ```
   owedTextBox.Text = String.Empty
   paidTextBox.Text = String.Empty
   changeLabel.Text = String.Empty
   dollarLabel.Text = String.Empty
   quarterLabel.Text = String.Empty
   dimeLabel.Text = String.Empty
   nickelLabel.Text = String.Empty
   pennyLabel.Text = String.Empty
   owedTextBox.Focus
   ```

2. Save the solution. Figure 3-42 shows the application's code.

```
' Project name:        Change Project
' Project purpose:     Calculates the change based on the amount owed and the amount
'                      paid. Also breaks up the change into dollars, quarters, dimes,
'                      nickels, and pennies.
' Created/revised by:  <your name> on <current date>

Option Explicit On
Option Strict On
Option Infer Off

Public Class MainForm

    Private Sub exitButton_Click(ByVal sender As Object, _
        ByVal e As System.EventArgs) Handles exitButton.Click
        Me.Close()
    End Sub

    Private Sub calcButton_Click(ByVal sender As Object, _
        ByVal e As System.EventArgs) Handles calcButton.Click
        ' calculates the change, which is the difference between the amount paid
        ' and the amount owed, and breaks up the change into dollars, quarters,
        ' dimes, nickels, and pennies

        ' declare variables
        Dim owed As Decimal
        Dim paid As Decimal
        Dim change As Decimal
        Dim dollars As Integer
```

Figure 3-42: Sunshine Cellular application's code (*continued on next page*)

```
        Dim quarters As Integer
        Dim dimes As Integer
        Dim nickels As Integer
        Dim pennies As Integer

        ' assign input to variables
        Decimal.TryParse(owedTextBox.Text, owed)
        Decimal.TryParse(paidTextBox.Text, paid)

        ' perform calculations
        change = paid - owed
        pennies = Convert.ToInt32(change * 100)
        dollars = pennies \ 100
        pennies = pennies - (dollars * 100)
        quarters = pennies \ 25
        pennies = pennies - (quarters * 25)
        dimes = pennies \ 10
        pennies = pennies - (dimes * 10)
        nickels = pennies \ 5
        pennies = pennies - (nickels * 5)

        ' display calculated results
        changeLabel.Text = Convert.ToString(change)
        dollarLabel.Text = Convert.ToString(dollars)
        quarterLabel.Text = Convert.ToString(quarters)
        dimeLabel.Text = Convert.ToString(dimes)
        nickelLabel.Text = Convert.ToString(nickels)
        pennyLabel.Text = Convert.ToString(pennies)
    End Sub

    Private Sub clearButton_Click(ByVal sender As Object, _
        ByVal e As System.EventArgs) Handles clearButton.Click
        ' prepares the screen for the next calculation

        owedTextBox.Text = String.Empty
        paidTextBox.Text = String.Empty
        changeLabel.Text = String.Empty
        dollarLabel.Text = String.Empty
        quarterLabel.Text = String.Empty
        dimeLabel.Text = String.Empty
        nickelLabel.Text = String.Empty
        pennyLabel.Text = String.Empty
        owedTextBox.Focus()
    End Sub
End Class
```

Figure 3-42: Sunshine Cellular application's code (*continued from previous page and on next page*)

Now test the application to verify that it is working correctly.

To test the application:

1. Start the application. Type **39.67** as the amount owed, and **50.00** as the amount paid. Click the **Calculate Change** button. The button's Click event procedure calculates the change, as well as the number of dollars, quarters, dimes, nickels, and pennies. It then displays the calculated results in the interface, as shown in Figure 3-43.

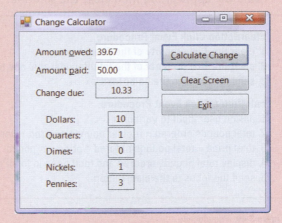

Figure 3-43: Calculated results shown in the interface

2. Click the **Clear Screen** button.

3. Test the application several more times using your own values for the amount owed and amount paid.

4. Click the **Exit** button to end the application, then close the solution.

PROGRAMMING EXAMPLE

COMPLETING THE MOONBUCKS COFFEE APPLICATION

In this chapter's Programming Example, you will complete the Moonbucks Coffee application from Chapter 2's Programming Example. The application's TOE chart and user interface are shown in Figures 2-33 and 2-34 in Chapter 2. According to the TOE chart, the Click event procedures for the calcButton, clearButton, and exitButton need to be coded. You coded the exitButton's Click event procedure in Chapter 2. You will code the remaining two procedures in this chapter. The pseudocode for both procedures is shown in Figure 3-44. Figure 3-45 shows the information pertaining to the named constant and variables used in the calcButton's Click event procedure. First, use Windows to copy the Moonbucks Solution folder from the VbReloaded2008\Chap02 folder to the VbReloaded2008\Chap03 folder. Name the copied folder Moonbucks Solution-Chap3. Next, open the Moonbucks Solution (Moonbucks Solution.sln) file contained in the VbReloaded2008\Chap03\Moonbucks Solution-Chap3 folder. Open the designer window, then open the Code Editor window and enter the code shown in Figure 3-46. Moonbucks charges $11.15 for a pound of coffee. Save the solution, then start and test the application. End the application, then close the solution.

---

clearButton Click Event Procedure
1. clear the Text property of the 7 text boxes
2. clear the Text property of the totalPoundsLabel and totalPriceLabel
3. send the focus to the nameTextBox

calcButton Click Event Procedure
1. assign user input to variables
2. total pounds ordered = regular pounds ordered + decaffeinated pounds ordered
3. total price = total pounds ordered * price per pound
4. display total pounds ordered and total price in totalPoundsLabel and totalPriceLabel
5. send the focus to the clearButton

Figure 3-44: Pseudocode

Named constant	Data type	Value
PricePerPound	Double	11.15
Variables	**Data type**	**Value source**
regularCoffee	Integer	user input (regularTextBox)
decafCoffee	Integer	user input (decafTextBox)
totalPounds	Integer	procedure calculation
totalPrice	Double	procedure calculation

Figure 3-45: Named constant and variables for the calcButton's Click event procedure

---

```
' Project name:        Moonbucks Project
' Project purpose:     Calculates the total pounds of coffee ordered
'                      and the total price
' Created/revised by:  <your name> on <current date>

Option Explicit On
Option Strict On
Option Infer Off

Public Class MainForm

    Private Sub exitButton_Click(ByVal sender As Object, _
        ByVal e As System.EventArgs) Handles exitButton.Click
        Me.Close()
    End Sub
```

Figure 3-46: Code (*continued on next page*)

```
    Private Sub clearButton_Click(ByVal sender As Object, _
        ByVal e As System.EventArgs) Handles clearButton.Click
        ' prepares the screen for the next order

        nameTextBox.Text = String.Empty
        addressTextBox.Text = String.Empty
        cityTextBox.Text = String.Empty
        stateTextBox.Text = String.Empty
        zipTextBox.Text = String.Empty
        regularTextBox.Text = String.Empty
        decafTextBox.Text = String.Empty
        totalPoundsLabel.Text = String.Empty
        totalPriceLabel.Text = String.Empty
        nameTextBox.Focus()
    End Sub

    Private Sub calcButton_Click(ByVal sender As Object, _
        ByVal e As System.EventArgs) Handles calcButton.Click
        ' calculates total pounds ordered and total price

        ' declare constant and variables
        Const PricePerPound As Double = 11.15
        Dim regularCoffee As Integer
        Dim decafCoffee As Integer
        Dim totalPounds As Integer
        Dim totalPrice As Double

        ' assign input to variables
        Integer.TryParse(regularTextBox.Text, regularCoffee)
        Integer.TryParse(decafTextBox.Text, decafCoffee)

        ' perform calculations
        totalPounds = regularCoffee + decafCoffee
        totalPrice = totalPounds * PricePerPound

        ' display calculated results
        totalPoundsLabel.Text = Convert.ToString(totalPounds)
        totalPriceLabel.Text = totalPrice.ToString("C2")

        ' set the focus
        clearButton.Focus()
    End Sub
End Class
```

Figure 3-46: Code (*continued from previous page*)

QUICK REVIEW

» Variables and named constants are computer memory locations that store data. The contents of a variable can change while the application is running. The contents of a named constant, however, cannot change while the application is running.

» All variables and named constants have a name, data type, initial value, scope, and lifetime.

» The name assigned to a variable or named constant should help you remember the memory location's purpose.

» You use a declaration statement to declare a variable. If the variable has procedure scope, you begin the declaration statement with either the keyword Dim or the keyword Static. If the variable has module scope, you begin the declaration statement with the keyword Private.

» You can use an assignment statement to assign a value to an existing variable while the application is running. The data type of the value should be the same as the data type of the variable.

» Unlike variables and named constants, which are computer memory locations, a literal constant is an item of data. The value of a literal constant does not change while the application is running.

» String literal constants are enclosed in quotation marks (""), whereas numeric literal constants are not enclosed in quotation marks.

» You can use the TryParse method to convert a string to a number.

» The Convert class contains methods that convert values to a specified data type.

» The Option Explicit On statement tells the Code Editor to warn you if your code contains the name of an undeclared variable.

» The Option Infer Off statement tells the Code Editor to warn you if you fail to include a data type in a variable declaration statement.

» The Option Strict On statement tells the computer not to perform any implicit type conversions that may lead to a loss of data.

» The integer division operator divides two integers, and then returns the result.

» The modulus operator divides two numbers, and then returns the remainder.

» A variable can store only one item of data at any one time.

» A procedure-level memory location can be used only by the procedure in which it is declared. A module-level memory location can be used by all of the procedures in the form.

» It is a good programming practice to use comments to internally document your application's code. Comments begin with the apostrophe.

» A static variable is a procedure-level variable that retains its value even when the procedure ends.

» You use the Const statement to declare a named constant.

» Programmers commonly use either pseudocode (short phrases) or a flowchart (standardized symbols) when planning a procedure's code.

» While an application is running, you can remove the contents of text box and label controls by assigning either the empty string ("") or the String.Empty value to the control's Text property.

» You can use the Focus method to move the focus to a control while the application is running.

» After coding an application, you should test the application, using both valid and invalid data, to verify that the code works correctly.

» You can format an application's numeric output so that it displays special characters (such as dollar signs and percent signs) and a specified number of decimal places.

KEY TERMS

Arguments—the items within parentheses following a method's name; represent information that the programmer provides to the method

Bug—an error in a program

Comments—used to document a program internally; created by placing an apostrophe (') before the text you want to treat as a comment

Const statement—the statement used to create a named constant

Convert class—contains methods that return the result of converting a value to a specified data type

Data type—determines the type of data a memory location can store

Debugging—refers to the process of locating and correcting any errors in a program

Demoted—the process of converting a value from one data type to another data type that can store only smaller numbers.

Flowchart—uses standardized symbols to show the steps a procedure needs to take to accomplish its goal

Flowlines—the lines connecting the symbols in a flowchart

Focus method—used to move the focus to a control while an application is running

Formatting—specifying the number of decimal places and the special characters to display in a number

Implicit type conversion—the process by which a value is automatically converted to fit the memory location to which it is assigned

Input/output symbol—the parallelogram in a flowchart; used to represent input and output tasks

Integer division operator—represented by a backslash (\); divides two integers, and then returns the quotient as an integer

Invalid data—data that the application is not expecting the user to enter

Lifetime—indicates how long a variable or named constant remains in the computer's internal memory

Line continuation character—the underscore (_); used to break up a long instruction into two or more physical lines in the Code Editor window

Literal constant—an item of data whose value does not change while an application is running

Literal type character—a character (such as the letter D) appended to a literal constant for the purpose of forcing the literal constant to assume a different data type (such as Decimal)

Logic error—occurs when you enter an instruction that is syntactically correct, but does not give you the expected results, or when you neglect to enter an instruction or enter the instructions in the wrong order

Method—performs a task for the class in which it is defined

Module scope—the scope of a module-level variable; refers to the fact that the variable can be used by any procedure in the form

Module-level variable—a variable that is declared in the form's Declarations section; the variable has module scope

Modulus operator—represented by the keyword Mod; divides two numbers and then returns the remainder

Named constant—a computer memory location whose contents cannot be changed while the application is running; created using the Const statement

Procedure scope—the scope of a procedure-level variable; refers to the fact that the variable can be used only by the procedure in which it is declared

Procedure-level variable—a variable that is declared in a procedure; the variable has procedure scope

Process symbol—the rectangle symbol in a flowchart; used to represent assignment and calculation tasks

Promoted—the process of converting a value from one data type to another data type that can store larger numbers

Pseudocode—uses phrases to describe the steps a procedure needs to take to accomplish its goal

Scope—indicates where in the application's code a variable or named constant can be used

Start/stop symbol—the oval symbol in a flowchart; used to mark the beginning and end of the flowchart

Static variable—a special type of procedure-level variable that remains in memory and retains its value even when the procedure ends

Syntax error—occurs when an instruction violates a programming language's syntax; usually a result of typing errors that occur when entering instructions

TryParse method—used to convert a string to a number

Unicode—the universal coding scheme that assigns a unique number to each character in the written languages of the world

Valid data—data that the application is expecting the user to enter

Variables—computer memory locations where programmers can temporarily store data, and also change the data, while an application is running

SELF-CHECK QUESTIONS AND ANSWERS

1. Every variable and named constant has _____.

   a. a data type   b. a lifetime

   c. a scope   d. All of the above.

2. Which of the following statements stores the string contained in the inputValue variable in a Double variable named number?

   a. Double.TryParse(inputValue, number)

   b. Double.TryParse(number, inputValue)

   c. number = Double.TryParse(inputValue)

   d. number = TryParse.Double(inputValue)

3. Which of the following is the line continuation character?

    a. & (ampersand)   b. - (hyphen)

    c. _ (underscore)   d. None of the above.

4. What will be assigned to the Integer answer variable when the answer = 45 Mod 6 statement is processed?

    a. 3   b. 7

    c. 7.5   d. None of the above.

5. Static variables can be declared in _____.

    a. the form's Declarations section

    b. the General Declarations section

    c. a procedure

    d. All of the above.

Answers: 1) d, 2) a, 3) c, 4) a, 5) c

REVIEW QUESTIONS

1. Which of the following is a valid variable name?

    a. income94   b. inc_94

    c. incomeTax   d. All of the above.

2. _____ variable is known only to the procedure in which it is declared.

    a. A localized   b. A module-level

    c. A procedure-level   d. An open-level

3. A _____ is a data item whose value does not change while an application is running.

    a. literal constant   b. literal variable

    c. named constant   d. variable

4. A _____ is a memory location whose value can change while an application is running.

    a. literal constant   b. literal variable

    c. named constant   d. variable

5. Which of the following assigns the sum of two Integer variables, named score1 and score2, to the Text property of the answerTextBox? (The application contains the Option Strict On statement.)

   a. answerTextBox.Text = Convert.ToString(score1 + score2)

   b. answerTextBox.Text = Convert.ToString(score1) + Convert.ToString(score2)

   c. answerTextBox.Text = score1 + score2

   d. All of the above.

6. Which of the following can be used to initialize a String variable to the empty string?

   a. Dim name As String = "Empty"

   b. Dim name As String = String.Empty

   c. Dim name As String.Empty

   d. All of the above.

7. Which of the following declares a Decimal named constant? (The application contains the Option Strict On statement.)

   a. Const Rate As Decimal = .09

   b. Const Rate As Decimal = Convert.ToDecimal(.09)

   c. Const Rate As Decimal = .09D

   d. All of the above.

8. Which of the following assigns the sum of two Integer variables to the Text property of the totalLabel? (The application contains the Option Strict On statement.)

   a. totalLabel.Text = Convert.ToInteger(num1 + num2)

   b. totalLabel.Text = Convert.ToInt32(num1 + num2)

   c. totalLabel.Text = Convert.ToString(num1 + num2)

   d. None of the above.

9. Most of the variables used in an application are _____.

   a. block-level   b. module-level

   c. procedure-level   d. variable-level

10. Which of the following sends the focus to the numberTextBox?

   a. numberTextBox.Focus()   b. numberTextBox.SendFocus()

   c. numberTextBox.SetFocus()   d. SetFocus(numberTextBox)

REVIEW EXERCISES— SHORT ANSWER

1. A procedure needs to store the name of an item in inventory and its height and weight. The height may have decimal places; the weight will be whole numbers only. Write the Dim statements to create the necessary procedure-level variables.

2. Write an assignment statement that adds the contents of the sales1 variable to the contents of the sales2 variable, and then assigns the sum to an existing variable named totalSales. All of the variables have the Decimal data type.

3. Write an assignment statement that multiplies the contents of the salary variable by the number 1.5, and then assigns the result to the salary variable. The salary variable has the Decimal data type.

4. A form contains two buttons named salaryButton and bonusButton. Both buttons' Click event procedures need to use the same variable: a String variable named employeeName. Write the statement to declare the employeeName variable. Also specify where you will need to enter the statement and whether the variable is a procedure-level or module-level variable.

5. Write the statement to declare a procedure-level named constant named Tax_Rate whose value is .05. The named constant should have the Double data type.

6. Write the statement to declare a module-level named constant named Tax_Rate whose value is .05. The named constant should have the Decimal data type.

7. Write the statement to convert the contents of the unitsTextBox to an integer. Store the integer in an Integer variable named numberOfUnits.

8. Write the statement to assign, to the unitsLabel, the contents of an Integer variable named numberOfUnits.

9. Write the statement to assign, to a String variable named totalSales, the sum of the values stored in two Decimal variables named westSales and eastSales.

10. Write the statement to assign, to the payLabel, the value stored in a Decimal variable named grossPay. The value should be displayed with a dollar sign and two decimal places.

COMPUTER EXERCISES

1. In this exercise, you modify the application from this chapter's Programming Example.

   a. Use Windows to make a copy of the Moonbucks Solution-Chap3 folder. Rename the folder Moonbucks Solution-Chap3-Modified.

   b. Open the Moonbucks Solution (Moonbucks Solution.sln) file contained in the VbReloaded2008\Chap03\Moonbucks Solution-Chap3-Modified folder.

   c. Modify the application so that it adds a 2% sales tax and a $5 shipping charge to the total price.

   d. Save the solution, then start and test the application. End the application, then close the solution.

2. In this exercise, you code and then modify the Total Sales application that you viewed in this chapter.

   a. Open the Total Sales Solution (Total Sales Solution.sln) file, which is contained in the VbReloaded2008\Chap03\Total Sales Solution folder.

   b. Enter the code shown earlier in Figure 3-15. Save the solution, then start and test the application. End the application.

   c. Modify the application so that it uses a module-level variable rather than a static variable. Save the solution, then start and test the application. End the application, then close the solution.

3. In this exercise, you modify the Sunshine Cellular application that you viewed in this chapter.

   a. Open the Sunshine Cellular Solution (Sunshine Cellular Solution.sln) file, which is contained in the VbReloaded2008\Chap03\Sunshine Cellular Solution folder.

   b. Enter the code shown earlier in Figure 3-29. Save the solution, then start and test the application. End the application.

   c. Remove any references to the subtotal and salesTax variables in the calcButton's Click event procedure. Then make the appropriate modifications to the statement that calculates the total price. Save the solution, then start and test the application. End the application, then close the solution.

4. In this exercise, you complete the application from Chapter 2's Computer Exercise 2.

   a. Copy the Time Solution folder from the VbReloaded2008\Chap02 folder to the VbReloaded2008\Chap03 folder.

   b. Open the Time Solution (Time Solution.sln) file contained in the VbReloaded2008\Chap03\Time Solution folder.

   c. Open the Code Editor window and enter the appropriate comments at the beginning of the code. Also enter the Option Explicit On, Option Strict On, and Option Infer Off statements.

   d. The application should calculate and display the total number of weekday hours and the total number of weekend hours. Write the appropriate pseudocode, then code the application. Use variables to temporarily store the input and calculated values.

   e. Save the solution, then start and test the application. End the application, then close the solution.

5. In this exercise, you complete the application from Chapter 2's Computer Exercise 3.

   a. Copy the Paper Solution folder from the VbReloaded2008\Chap02 folder to the VbReloaded2008\Chap03 folder.

   b. Open the Paper Solution (Paper Solution.sln) file contained in the VbReloaded2008\Chap03\Paper Solution folder.

   c. Open the Code Editor window and enter the appropriate comments at the beginning of the code. Also enter the appropriate Option statements.

   d. Use the TOE chart you created in Chapter 2 to write the necessary pseudocode, then code the application. Use variables to temporarily store the sales amount, commission rate, and commission amount. Display the commission amount with a dollar sign and two decimal places.

   e. Save the solution, then start the application. Test the application using your name, 2000 as the sales amount, and 10 as the commission rate. The commission should be $200.00. End the application, then close the solution.

6. In this exercise, you complete the application from Chapter 2's Computer Exercise 4.

   a. Copy the RMSales Solution folder from the VbReloaded2008\Chap02 folder to the VbReloaded2008\Chap03 folder.

   b. Open the RMSales Solution (RMSales Solution.sln) file contained in the VbReloaded2008\Chap03\RMSales Solution folder.

c. Open the Code Editor window and enter the appropriate comments at the beginning of the code. Also enter the appropriate Option statements.

d. Use the TOE chart you created in Chapter 2 to write the necessary pseudocode, then code the application. Use variables to temporarily store the sales amounts, projected increase rates, and projected sales amounts. Display the projected sales amounts with a dollar sign and zero decimal places.

e. Save the solution, then start the application. Test the application by entering the following sales amounts and rates:

Region	Sales	Projected Increase (%)
North	25000	5
South	30000	7
East	10000	4
West	15000	11

f. End the application, then close the solution.

7. **Scenario:** Colfax Industries needs an application that allows the shipping clerk to enter the quantity of an item in inventory and the number of the items that can be packed in a box for shipping. When the shipping clerk clicks a button, the application should compute and display the number of full boxes that can be packed and the number of items that are left over.

a. Prepare a TOE chart ordered by object.

b. Build an appropriate interface. Name the solution Colfax Solution. Name the project Colfax Project. Save the application in the VbReloaded2008\Chap03 folder.

c. Write the pseudocode, then code the application.

d. Test the application using the following information. Colfax has 45 skateboards in inventory. If six skateboards can fit into a box for shipping, how many full boxes could the company ship, and how many skateboards will remain in inventory?

e. End the application, then close the solution.

8. **Scenario:** Management USA, a small training center, plans to run two full-day seminars on December 1. The seminars are called "How to Be an Effective Manager" and "How to Run a Small Business." Each seminar costs $200. Registration for the seminars will be done by phone. When a company calls to register its employees, the phone representative will ask for the following information: the company's name, address

(including city, state, and ZIP code), the number of employees registering for the "How to Be an Effective Manager" seminar, and the number of employees registering for the "How to Run a Small Business" seminar. Claire Jenkowski, the owner of Management USA, wants the application to calculate the total number of employees the company is registering and the total cost.

a. Prepare a TOE chart ordered by object.

b. Build an appropriate interface. Name the solution Management Solution. Name the project Management Project. Save the application in the VbReloaded2008\ Chap03 folder. The state entry should contain a maximum of two characters and should always appear in uppercase.

c. Write the pseudocode, then code the application.

d. Test the application using the following data.

Company Name: ABC Company

Address: 345 Main St.

City, State, ZIP: Glen, tx 70122

Registrants for "How to Be an Effective Manager": 10

Registrants for "How to Run a Small Business": 5

e. End the application, then close the solution.

9. In this exercise, you experiment with a static variable.

a. Open the Static Solution (Static Solution.sln) file contained in the VbReloaded2008\ Chap03\Static Solution folder.

b. Start the application. Click the Count button. The message indicates that you have pressed the Count button once, which is correct.

c. Click the Count button several more times. Each time you click the Count button, the message changes to indicate the number of times the button was clicked.

d. Click the Exit button to end the application.

e. Open the Code Editor window and study the code. Notice that the code uses a module-level variable to keep track of the number of times the Count button is clicked. Modify the code so that it uses a static variable rather than a module-level variable.

f. Save the solution, then start the application. Click the Count button several times. Each time you click the Count button, the message should change to indicate the number of times the button was clicked.

g. Click the Exit button to end the application, then close the solution.

10. In this exercise, you experiment with the Visual Basic conversion functions listed in Appendix C.

    a. Open the Conversion Functions Solution (Conversion Functions Solution.sln) file contained in the VbReloaded2008\Chap03\Conversion Functions Solution folder.

    b. Modify the code so that it uses the Visual Basic conversion functions listed in Appendix C. *Hint:* To convert the item price to Decimal, use price = CDec(priceTextBox.Text).

    c. Save the solution, then start and test the application.

    d. Click the Exit button to end the application, then close the solution.

11. In this exercise, you practice debugging an application.

    a. Open the Debug Solution (Debug Solution.sln) file contained in the VbReloaded2008\Chap03\Debug Solution folder. Start the application, then test the application. Locate and then correct any errors. When the application is working correctly, close the solution.

CASE PROJECTS

WILLOW POOLS

Create an application that allows the user to enter the length, width, and height of a rectangle. The application should calculate and display the volume of the rectangle. You can either create your own user interface or create the one shown in Figure 3-47. Name the solution Willow Solution. Name the project Willow Project. Test the application using the following data: the swimming pool at a health club is 100 feet long, 30 feet wide, and 4 feet deep. How many cubic feet of water will the pool contain?

Figure 3-47: Sample interface for Willow Pools

CURRENCY TRADERS

Create an application that converts American dollars to British pounds, Mexican pesos, Canadian dollars, and Japanese yen. The application should make the appropriate calculations and then display the results on the screen. You can either create your own user interface or create the one shown in Figure 3-48. Name the solution, project, and form file Currency Calculator Solution, Currency Calculator Project, and Main Form.vb, respectively. Save the solution in the VbReloaded2008\Chap03 folder. Use the following conversion rates for one American dollar: 0.571505 British pounds, 10.7956 Mexican pesos, 1.23679 Canadian dollars, and 112.212 Japanese yen.

Figure 3-48: Sample interface for Currency Traders

TILE LIMITED

Create an application that allows the user to enter the length and width (in feet) of a rectangle, and the price of a square foot of tile. The application should calculate and display the area of the rectangle and the total price of the tile. You can either create your own user interface or create the one shown in Figure 3-49. Name the solution and project Tile Limited Solution and Tile Limited Project. Test the application using

Figure 3-49: Sample interface for Tile Limited

the following data. Susan Caper, one of Tile Limited's customers, is tiling a floor in her home. The floor is 12 feet long and 14 feet wide. The price of a square foot of tile is $1.59. What is the area of the floor and how much will the tile cost?

QUICK LOANS

Create an application that allows the user to enter the amount of a loan, the interest rate, and the term of the loan (in years). The application should calculate and display the total amount of interest and the total amount to be repaid. (*Hint:* Research Visual Basic's Financial.Pmt method.) Name the solution and project Quick Loans Solution and Quick Loans Project. Test the application using the following data. You visit Quick Loans because you want to borrow $9000 to buy a new car. The loan is for three years at an annual interest rate of 12%. How much will you pay in interest over the three years, and what is the total amount you will repay?

4

MAKING DECISIONS IN A PROGRAM

After studying Chapter 4, you should be able to:

Include the selection structure in pseudocode and in a flowchart

Write an If...Then...Else statement

Write code that uses comparison operators and logical operators

Create a variable having block scope

Concatenate strings

Use the ControlChars.NewLine constant

Change the case of a string

Generate random numbers

THE SELECTION STRUCTURE

The applications you created in the previous three chapters used the sequence programming structure only, where a procedure's instructions are processed one after another in the order in which each appears in the procedure. In many applications, however, the next instruction processed depends on the result of a decision or comparison that the program must make. For example, a payroll program typically compares the number of hours the employee worked with the number 40 to determine whether the employee should receive overtime pay in addition to regular pay. Based on the result of that comparison, the program then selects either an instruction that computes regular pay only or an instruction that computes regular pay plus overtime pay. You use the **selection structure**, also called the decision structure, when you want a program to make a decision or comparison and then select the appropriate path, depending on the result of that decision or comparison. Although the idea of using the selection structure in a program is new, the concept of the selection structure is already familiar to you, because you use it each day to make hundreds of decisions. For example, every morning you have to decide whether you are hungry and, if you are, what you are going to eat. Figure 4-1 shows other examples of selection structures you might use today. The portion in italics in the examples is called the **condition**, and it specifies the decision you are making. The condition must be phrased so that it results in either a true or false answer only. For example, either it is raining (true) or it is not raining (false). Either you have a test tomorrow (true) or you do not have a test tomorrow (false). If the condition is true, you perform a specific set of tasks. If the condition is false, on the other hand, you might or might not need to perform a different set of tasks.

▶▶TIP

As you may remember from Chapter 1, the sequence and selection structures are two of the three programming structures. The third programming structure, repetition, is covered in Chapters 6 and 7.

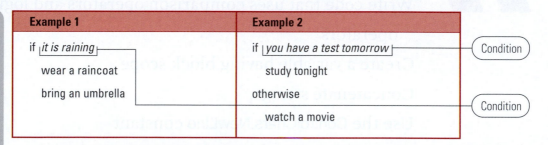

Example 1	Example 2	
if *it is raining*	if *you have a test tomorrow*	Condition
wear a raincoat	study tonight	
bring an umbrella	otherwise	Condition
	watch a movie	

Figure 4-1: Selection structures you might use today

Like you, the computer also can evaluate a condition and then select the appropriate tasks to perform based on that evaluation. When using the selection structure in a program, the programmer must be sure to phrase the condition so that it results in either a true or a false answer only. The programmer also must specify the tasks to be performed when the condition is true and, if necessary, the tasks to be performed when the condition is false. Visual Basic provides four forms of the selection structure: If, If/Else,

WRITING PSEUDOCODE FOR THE IF AND IF/ELSE SELECTION STRUCTURES

An **If selection structure** contains only one set of instructions, which are processed when the condition is true. An **If/Else selection structure**, on the other hand, contains two sets of instructions: one set is processed when the condition is true and the other set is processed when the condition is false. Figure 4-2 shows examples of both selection structures written in pseudocode. Although pseudocode is not standardized—every programmer has his or her own version—you will find some similarities among the various versions. For example, many programmers begin the selection structure with the word "if" and end the structure with the two words "end if". They also use the word "else" to designate the instructions to be performed when the condition is false.

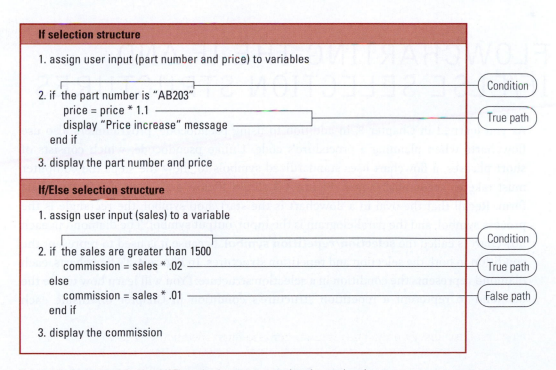

Figure 4-2: Examples of the If and If/Else selection structures written in pseudocode

Notice that each example's condition results in either a true or a false answer only. When the condition is true, the set of instructions following the condition is selected for processing. The instructions following the condition are referred to as the **true path**—the path you follow when the condition is true. The true path ends when you come to the "else" or, if there is no "else", when you come to the end of the selection structure (the "end if"). After the true path instructions are processed, the instruction following the "end if" is processed. In the examples shown in Figure 4-2, the display instructions are processed after the instructions in the true path.

The instructions processed when the condition is false depend on whether the selection structure contains an "else". When there is no "else", the selection structure ends when its condition is false, and processing continues with the instruction following the "end if". In Example 1, for instance, the "display the part number and price" instruction is processed when the part number is not "AB203". In cases where the selection structure contains an "else", the instructions between the "else" and the "end if" are processed before the instruction after the "end if" is processed. In Example 2, the "commission = sales * .01" instruction is processed first, followed by the "display the commission" instruction. The instructions between the "else" and "end if" are referred to as the **false path**—the path you follow when the condition is false.

FLOWCHARTING THE IF AND IF/ELSE SELECTION STRUCTURES

As you learned in Chapter 3, in addition to using pseudocode, programmers also use flowcharts when planning a procedure's code. Unlike pseudocode, which consists of short phrases, a flowchart uses standardized symbols to show the steps the computer must take to accomplish a task. Figure 4-3 shows Figure 4-2's examples in flowchart form. Recall that the oval in a flowchart is the start/stop symbol, the rectangle is the process symbol, and the parallelogram is the input/output symbol. The diamond in each flowchart is called the **selection/repetition symbol**, because it is used to represent the condition in both the selection and repetition structures. In Figure 4-3's flowcharts, each diamond represents the condition in a selection structure. (You will learn how to use the diamond to represent a repetition structure's condition in Chapter 6.) Inside each diamond is a comparison that evaluates to either true or false only. Each diamond also has one flowline entering the symbol and two flowlines leaving the symbol. The two flowlines leading out of the diamond should be marked so that anyone reading the flowchart can distinguish the true path from the false path. You mark the flowline leading to the true path with a "T" (for true), and you mark the flowline leading to the false path with an "F" (for false). You also can mark the flowlines leading out of the diamond with a "Y" and an "N" (for yes and no).

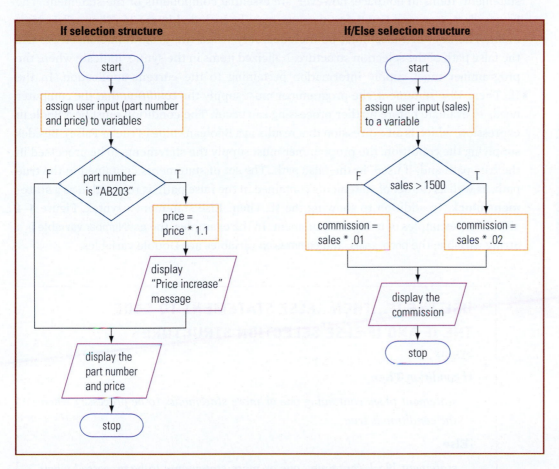

Figure 4-3: Examples of the If and If/Else selection structures drawn in flowchart form

CODING THE IF AND IF/ELSE SELECTION STRUCTURES

You use the **If...Then...Else statement** to code the If and If/Else selection structures in Visual Basic. Figure 4-4 shows the syntax of the If...Then...Else statement. The items in square brackets in the syntax are optional. In other words, you do not always need to include the Else portion of the syntax, referred to as the Else clause, in an If...Then...Else statement. Items in boldface, however, are essential components of the statement. The keywords If, Then, and End If, for instance, must be included in the If...Then...Else statement. The keyword Else must be included only when the programmer needs to use the false path of the selection structure. Italicized items in the syntax indicate where the programmer must supply information pertaining to the current application. In the If...Then...Else statement, the programmer must supply the *condition* that the computer needs to evaluate before further processing can occur. The condition must be a Boolean expression, which is an expression that results in a Boolean value (True or False). Besides supplying the condition, the programmer must supply the statements to be processed in the true path and, if used, in the false path. The set of statements contained in the true path, as well as the set of statements contained in the false path, is referred to as a **statement block**. In addition to showing the If...Then...Else statement's syntax, Figure 4-4 also shows examples of using the statement. In the examples, the partNumber variable is a String variable; the price, sales, and commission variables are Double variables.

»TIP

In Visual Basic, a statement block is a set of statements terminated by an Else, End If, Loop, or Next clause. You will learn about the Loop and Next clauses in Chapters 6 and 7.

»HOW TO . . .

USE THE IF...THEN...ELSE STATEMENT TO CODE THE IF AND IF/ELSE SELECTION STRUCTURES

Syntax

If *condition* **Then**

   statement block containing one or more statements to be processed when the condition is true

[**Else**

   statement block containing one or more statements to be processed when the condition is false]

End If

Figure 4-4: How to use the If...Then...Else statement to code the If and If/Else selection structures (*continued on next page*)

Example 1

```
If partNumber = "AB203" Then
    price = price * 1.1
    messageLabel.Text = "Price increase"
End If
```

If the partNumber variable contains the string "AB203", the computer processes the two instructions in the true path; otherwise, the instructions are skipped over.

Example 2

```
If sales > 1500 Then
    commission = sales * .02
Else
    commission = sales * .01
End If
```

If the sales variable contains a number that is greater than 1500, the instruction in the true path calculates a 2% commission; otherwise, the instruction in the false path calculates a 1% commission.

Figure 4-4: How to use the If...Then...Else statement to code the If and If/Else selection structures (*continued from previous page*)

The If...Then...Else statement's condition can contain variables, literal constants, named constants, properties, methods, arithmetic operators, comparison operators, and logical operators. You already know about variables, literal constants, named constants, properties, methods, and arithmetic operators from previous chapters. You will learn about comparison operators and logical operators in the following sections.

COMPARISON OPERATORS

Figure 4-5 lists the most commonly used comparison operators available in Visual Basic. You use **comparison operators**, also referred to as **relational operators**, to make comparisons in a program. Also included in the figure are examples of using comparison operators in the If...Then...Else statement's condition. Notice that the expression contained in each example's condition evaluates to one of two Boolean values—either True or False. All expressions containing a comparison operator will result in an answer of either True or False only.

»HOW TO . . .

USE THE MOST COMMONLY USED COMPARISON OPERATORS

Operator	Operation
=	equal to
>	greater than
>=	greater than or equal to
<	less than
<=	less than or equal to
<>	not equal to

Example 1

If weight > 190 Then
The condition evaluates to True when the Integer weight variable contains a number that is greater than 190; otherwise, it evaluates to False.

Example 2

If price <= Convert.ToDecimal(45.75) Then
The condition evaluates to True when the Decimal price variable contains a number that is less than or equal to 45.75 (converted to Decimal); otherwise, it evaluates to False. You also could write the condition as price <= 45.75D.

Example 3

If state <> "KY" Then
The condition evaluates to True when the String state variable does not contain the string "KY"; otherwise, it evaluates to False.

Figure 4-5: How to use the most commonly used comparison operators

Unlike arithmetic operators, comparison operators do not have an order of precedence. If an expression contains more than one comparison operator, the computer evaluates the comparison operators from left to right in the expression. Keep in mind, however, that comparison operators are evaluated after any arithmetic operators in the expression. In other words, in the expression 12 / 2 * 3 < 7 + 4, the three arithmetic operators (/, *, +) are evaluated before the comparison operator (<) is evaluated. The result of the expression is the Boolean value False, as shown in Figure 4-6.

Evaluation steps	Result
Original expression	12 / 2 * 3 < 7 + 4
12 / 2 is evaluated first	6 * 3 < 7 + 4
6 * 3 is evaluated second	18 < 7 + 4
7 + 4 is evaluated third	18 < 11
18 < 11 is evaluated last	False

Figure 4-6: Evaluation steps for an expression containing arithmetic and comparison operators

In the next two sections, you view examples of procedures that contain a comparison operator in an If...Then...Else statement. The first procedure uses the If selection structure, and the second procedure uses the If/Else selection structure.

USING COMPARISON OPERATORS—SWAPPING NUMERIC VALUES

Figure 4-7 shows a sample run of an application that displays the lowest and highest of two numbers entered by the user. Figures 4-8, 4-9, and 4-10 show the pseudocode, flowchart, and code for the displayButton's Click event procedure.

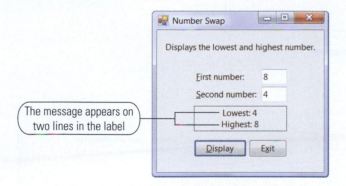

The message appears on two lines in the label

Figure 4-7: Sample run of the Number Swap application

Pseudocode
1. store the text box values in the num1 and num2 variables
2. if the number contained in the num1 variable is greater than the number contained in the num2 variable
    swap the numbers so that the num1 variable contains the smaller number
   end if
3. display (in the messageLabel) a message stating the lowest number and the highest number

---

Figure 4-8: Pseudocode showing the If selection structure

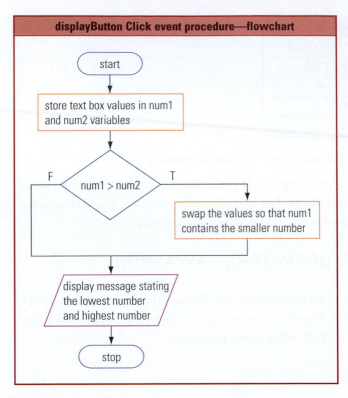

Figure 4-9: Flowchart showing the If selection structure

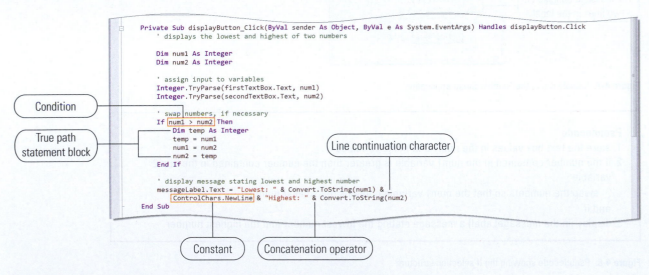

Figure 4-10: The If selection structure shown in the displayButton's Click event procedure

The procedure shown in Figure 4-10 first declares two procedure-level Integer variables named num1 and num2. It then converts the contents of two text boxes to integers and assigns the integers to the num1 and num2 variables. The num1 > num2 condition in the If...Then...Else statement compares the contents of the num1 variable with the contents of the num2 variable. If the condition evaluates to True, it means that the value in the num1 variable is greater than the value in the num2 variable. In that case, the four instructions contained in the statement's true path swap the values contained in those variables. Swapping the values places the smaller number in the num1 variable, and places the larger number in the num2 variable. If the num1 > num2 condition evaluates to False, on the other hand, the true path instructions are skipped over. The instructions do not need to be processed because the num1 variable already contains a number that is smaller than (or possibly equal to) the one stored in the num2 variable. The last statement in the procedure displays a message that indicates the lowest number (which is contained in the num1 variable) and the highest number (which is contained in the num2 variable).

Study closely the instructions used to swap the values stored in the num1 and num2 variables. The first instruction, Dim temp As Integer, declares a variable named temp. Like the variables declared at the beginning of a procedure, variables declared within a statement block remain in memory until the procedure ends. However, unlike variables declared at the beginning of a procedure, variables declared within a statement block have block scope rather than procedure scope. A variable that has procedure scope can be used anywhere within the procedure, whereas a variable that has **block scope** can be used only within the statement block in which it is declared. In this case, for example, the num1 and num2 variables can be used anywhere within the displayButton's Click event procedure, but the temp variable can be used only within the If...Then...Else statement's true path. You may be wondering why the temp variable was not declared at the beginning of the procedure, along with the num1 and num2 variables. Although there is nothing wrong with declaring all variables at the beginning of a procedure, the temp variable is not needed unless a swap is necessary, so there is no reason to create the variable until it is needed.

The second instruction in the If...Then...Else statement's true path, temp = num1, assigns the value in the num1 variable to the temp variable. The temp variable is necessary to store the contents of the num1 variable temporarily so that the swap can be made. If you did not store the num1 variable's value in the temp variable, the value would be lost when the computer processes the next statement, num1 = num2, which replaces the contents of the num1 variable with the contents of the num2 variable. Finally, the num2 = temp instruction assigns the value in the temp variable to the num2 variable. Figure 4-11 illustrates the concept of swapping, assuming the user enters the numbers 8 and 4 in the firstTextBox and secondTextBox, respectively.

	temp	num1	num2
values stored in the variables immediately before the temp = num1 instruction is processed	0	8	4
result of the temp = num1 instruction	8	8	4
result of the num1 = num2 instruction	8	4	4
result of the num2 = temp instruction, which completes the swapping process	8	4	8

Values were swapped

Figure 4-11: Illustration of the swapping concept

»TIP

You also can use the plus sign (+) to concatenate strings. To avoid confusion, however, you should use the plus sign for addition and the ampersand for concatenation.

The code shown earlier in Figure 4-10 contains two items that were not covered in the previous three chapters: the concatenation operator and the ControlChars.NewLine constant. You use the **concatenation operator**, which is the ampersand (&), to concatenate (connect or link) strings together. When concatenating strings, you must be sure to include a space before and after the ampersand; otherwise, the Code Editor will not recognize the ampersand as the concatenation operator. Figure 4-12 shows examples of string concatenation.

»HOW TO . . .

CONCATENATE STRINGS

Variables	Data type	Contents
firstName	String	Sue
lastName	String	Chen
age	Integer	21

Concatenated string	Result
firstName & lastName	SueChen
firstName & " " & lastName	Sue Chen
lastName & ", " & firstName	Chen, Sue
"She is " & Convert.ToString(age) & "!"	She is 21!

Figure 4-12: How to concatenate strings

The concatenation operator appears four times in the messageLabel.Text = "Lowest: " & Convert.ToString(num1) & ControlChars.NewLine & "Highest: " & Convert.ToString(num2) statement. The statement concatenates five strings: the string "Lowest: ", the contents of the num1 variable converted to a string, the ControlChars.NewLine constant, the string "Highest: ", and the contents of the num2 variable converted to a string. The **ControlChars.NewLine constant** advances the insertion point to the next line in the messageLabel and is the reason that the "Highest: 8" text appears on the second line in the label, as shown earlier in Figure 4-7.

USING COMPARISON OPERATORS—EXAMPLE 2

Figure 4-13 shows a sample run of an application that displays either the sum of or the difference between two numbers entered by the user. Figures 4-14, 4-15, and 4-16 show the pseudocode, flowchart, and code for the calcButton's Click event procedure.

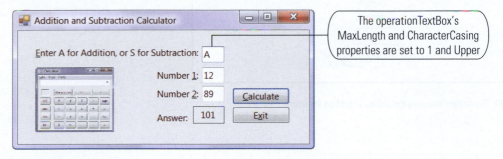

Figure 4-13: Sample run of the Addition and Subtraction Calculator application

Pseudocode
1. store text box values in operation, num1, and num2 variables
2. if the operation variable contains "A"
    answer = num1 + num2
   else
    answer = num1 − num2
   end if
3. display answer in answerLabel

Figure 4-14: Pseudocode showing the If/Else selection structure

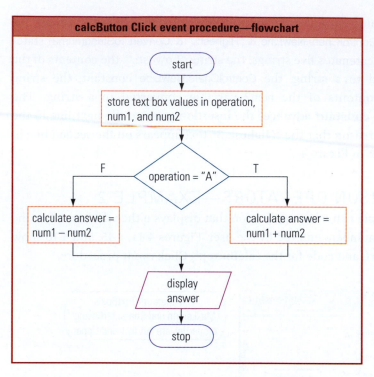

Figure 4-15: Flowchart showing the If/Else selection structure

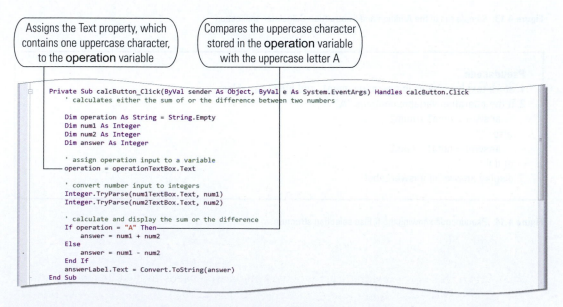

Figure 4-16: The If/Else selection structure shown in the calcButton's Click event procedure

The procedure shown in Figure 4-16 declares four procedure-level variables: a String variable named operation and three Integer variables named num1, num2, and answer. The operation = operationTextBox.Text statement assigns the contents of the operationTextBox's Text property to the operation variable. In this case, the Text property contains one uppercase character; this is because the operationTextBox's MaxLength and CharacterCasing properties are set to 1 and Upper, respectively, in the Properties window. A text box's **MaxLength property** specifies the maximum number of characters that can be entered in the text box, and its **CharacterCasing property** indicates whether the text should remain as typed or be converted to uppercase or lowercase. The procedure uses the TryParse method to convert the contents of both the num1TextBox and num2TextBox to integers. The condition in the If...Then...Else statement then compares the contents of the operation variable with the uppercase letter A. If the condition is true, the procedure calculates and displays the sum of the two numbers entered by the user, as shown earlier in Figure 4-13. If the condition is false, on the other hand, the procedure calculates and displays the difference between the two numbers.

Now assume that the operationTextBox's CharacterCasing property is not set to Upper, but is left at its default value, Normal. If the user enters an uppercase letter A in the text box, the operation = operationTextBox.Text statement assigns an uppercase letter A to the operation variable, and the operation = "A" condition in the selection structure evaluates to True. As a result, the selection structure's true path calculates and displays the sum of the numbers entered by the user, which is correct. However, if the user enters a lowercase letter a in the text box, the operation = operationTextBox.Text statement assigns a lowercase letter a to the operation variable, and the operation = "A" condition in the selection structure evaluates to False; this is because string comparisons in Visual Basic are case-sensitive. As a result, the selection structure's false path calculates and displays the difference between the numbers entered by the user, which is incorrect. Visual Basic provides two methods that you can use to solve the case problems that occur when comparing strings: ToUpper and ToLower.

> **» TIP**
>
> The uppercase letter A has a Unicode value of 41, whereas the lowercase letter a has a Unicode value of 61. Therefore, as far as the computer is concerned, both characters are not the same.

USING THE TOUPPER AND TOLOWER METHODS

As is true in most programming languages, string comparisons in Visual Basic are case-sensitive, which means that the string "Yes" is not the same as either the string "YES" or the string "yes". A problem occurs when a comparison needs to include a string that is either entered by the user or read from a file, because you cannot always control the case of the string. Although you can set a text box's CharacterCasing property to Upper or

Lower, you may not want to change the case of the user's entry as he or she is typing it. And it's entirely possible that you may not be aware of the case of strings that are read from a file. Before using a string in a comparison, you can convert it to either uppercase or lowercase, and then use the converted string in the comparison. You use the **ToUpper method** to convert a string to uppercase, and the **ToLower method** to convert a string to lowercase. Figure 4-17 shows the syntax of both methods and includes several examples of using the methods. In each syntax, *string* typically is the name of a String variable; however, as Example 3 shows, *string* also can be the property of an object. Both methods temporarily convert the *string* to the specified case. You also can use the methods to permanently convert the contents of a String variable to uppercase or lowercase; the same is true for the value stored in a control's Text property. You do this using an assignment statement, as illustrated in Example 5. When using the ToUpper method in a comparison, be sure that everything you are comparing is uppercase. In other words, the clause If letter.ToUpper = "p" Then will not work correctly: the condition will always evaluate to False, because the uppercase version of a letter will never be equal to its lowercase counterpart. Likewise, when using the ToLower method in a comparison, be sure that everything you are comparing is lowercase.

»HOW TO . . .

USE THE TOUPPER AND TOLOWER METHODS

Syntax

string.**ToUpper**

string.**ToLower**

Example 1

If letter.ToUpper <> "P" Then

compares the uppercase version of the string stored in the letter variable with the uppercase letter "P"

Example 2

If item1.ToUpper = item2.ToUpper Then

compares the uppercase version of the string stored in the item1 variable with the uppercase version of the string stored in the item2 variable

Example 3

If "reno" = cityTextBox.Text.ToLower Then

compares the lowercase letters "reno" to the lowercase version of the string stored in the cityTextBox

Figure 4-17: How to use the ToUpper and ToLower methods (*continued on next page*)

Example 4

nameLabel.Text = customer.ToUpper

assigns the uppercase version of the string stored in the customer variable to the Text property of the nameLabel

Example 5

newName = newName.ToUpper
stateTextBox.Text = stateTextBox.Text.ToLower

changes the contents of the newName variable to uppercase, and changes the contents of the stateTextBox to lowercase

---

Figure 4-17: How to use the ToUpper and ToLower methods (*continued from previous page*)

As mentioned earlier, if the CharacterCasing property of the operationTextBox in Figure 4-13 was left at its default value, Normal, the code shown in Figure 4-16 will not work correctly when the user enters a lowercase letter a in the text box. Recall that the code will calculate and display the difference between, rather than the sum of, the two numbers entered by the user. Figures 4-18 and 4-19 show two different ways of using the ToUpper method to fix this problem. In Figure 4-18, the ToUpper method is included in the statement that assigns the text box value to the operation variable. After the statement is processed, the variable will contain an uppercase letter (assuming the user entered a letter). In Figure 4-19, the ToUpper method is included in the If...Then...Else statement's condition. The operation.ToUpper portion of the condition will change the operation variable's value to uppercase only temporarily. In this instance, neither way is better than the other; both simply represent two different ways of performing the same task.

```vb
Private Sub calcButton_Click(ByVal sender As Object, ByVal e As System.EventArgs) Handles calcButton.Click
    ' calculates either the sum of or the difference between two numbers

    Dim operation As String = String.Empty
    Dim num1 As Integer
    Dim num2 As Integer
    Dim answer As Integer

    ' assign operation input to a variable
    operation = operationTextBox.Text.ToUpper

    ' convert number input to integers
    Integer.TryParse(num1TextBox.Text, num1)
    Integer.TryParse(num2TextBox.Text, num2)

    ' calculate and display the sum or the difference
    If operation = "A" Then
        answer = num1 + num2
    Else
        answer = num1 - num2
    End If
    answerLabel.Text = Convert.ToString(answer)
End Sub
```

ToUpper method

Figure 4-18: Code showing the ToUpper method in the assignment statement

```
Private Sub calcButton_Click(ByVal sender As Object, ByVal e As System.EventArgs) Handles calcButton.Click
    ' calculates either the sum of or the difference between two numbers

    Dim operation As String = String.Empty
    Dim num1 As Integer
    Dim num2 As Integer
    Dim answer As Integer

    ' assign operation input to a variable
    operation = operationTextBox.Text

    ' convert number input to integers
    Integer.TryParse(num1TextBox.Text, num1)
    Integer.TryParse(num2TextBox.Text, num2)

    ' calculate and display the sum or the difference
    If operation.ToUpper = "A" Then
        answer = num1 + num2
    Else
        answer = num1 - num2
    End If
    answerLabel.Text = Convert.ToString(answer)
End Sub
```

ToUpper method

Figure 4-19: Code showing the ToUpper method in the If...Then...Else statement's condition

LOGICAL OPERATORS

You also can use logical operators in an If...Then...Else statement's *condition*. **Logical operators** are often referred to as **Boolean operators**, and they allow you to combine two or more conditions into one compound condition. Figure 4-20 lists three of the logical operators available in Visual Basic, along with their order of precedence. The figure also contains examples of using logical operators in the If...Then...Else statement's condition. Like expressions containing comparison operators, expressions containing logical operators always evaluate to a Boolean value.

»HOW TO . . .

»TIP
Visual Basic also provides the And and Or logical operators.

USE THE LOGICAL OPERATORS

Operator	Operation	Precedence number
Not	reverses the truth-value of the condition; True becomes False, and False becomes True	1
AndAlso	all conditions must be true for the compound condition to be true	2
OrElse	only one of the conditions must be true for the compound condition to be true	3

Figure 4-20: How to use the logical operators (*continued on next page*)

Example 1

If Not isInsured Then

The condition evaluates to True when the Boolean isInsured variable contains the Boolean value False; otherwise, it evaluates to False. The clause also could be written as If Not isInsured = True Then. (Or, more clearly as If isInsured = True Then.)

Example 2

If hours > 0 AndAlso hours <= 40 Then

The compound condition evaluates to True when the Integer hours variable contains a number that is greater than zero but less than or equal to 40; otherwise, it evaluates to False.

Example 3

If state = "TN" AndAlso sales > 2299.99 Then

The compound condition evaluates to True when the String state variable contains the letters "TN" and, at the same time, the Double sales variable contains a number that is greater than 2299.99; otherwise, it evaluates to False.

Example 4

If state = "TN" OrElse sales > 2299.99 Then

The compound condition evaluates to True when the String state variable contains the letters "TN" or when the Double sales variable contains a number that is greater than 2299.99; otherwise, it evaluates to False.

Figure 4-20: How to use the logical operators (*continued from previous page*)

The tables shown in Figure 4-21, called **truth tables**, summarize how the computer evaluates the logical operators in an expression. As indicated in the figure, the Not operator reverses the truth-value of the *condition*. If the value of the *condition* is True, then the value of Not *condition* is False. Likewise, if the value of the *condition* is False, then the value of Not *condition* is True. Now compare the AndAlso operator's truth table with the OrElse operator's truth table. When you use the AndAlso operator to combine two conditions, the resulting compound condition is True only when both conditions are True. If either condition is False or if both conditions are False, then the compound condition is False. When you combine conditions using the OrElse operator, on the other hand, the compound condition is False only when both conditions are False. If either condition is True or if both conditions are True, then the compound condition is True.

» TIP

Recall that all expressions containing logical operators always evaluate to a Boolean value.

Truth table for the Not operator

value of *condition*	value of Not *condition*
True	False
False	True

Truth table for the AndAlso operator

value of *condition1*	value of *condition2*	value of *condition1* AndAlso *condition2*
True	True	True
True	False	False
False	(not evaluated)	False

Truth table for the OrElse operator

value of *condition1*	value of *condition2*	value of *condition1* OrElse *condition2*
True	(not evaluated)	True
False	True	True
False	False	False

Figure 4-21: Truth tables

Notice that the computer does not always evaluate both conditions when using the AndAlso or OrElse operators. For example, when you use the AndAlso operator to combine two conditions, the computer does not evaluate the second condition when the first condition is False. Because both conditions combined with the AndAlso operator need to be True for the compound condition to be True, there is no need to evaluate *condition2* when *condition1* is False. On the other hand, when you use the OrElse operator to combine two conditions, the computer does not evaluate the second condition when the first condition is True. Because only one of the conditions combined with the OrElse operator needs to be True for the compound condition to be True, there is no need to evaluate *condition2* when *condition1* is True. The concept of evaluating *condition2* based on the result of *condition1* is referred to as **short-circuit evaluation**. In the next section, you learn how to use the truth tables to determine the appropriate logical operator for a compound condition.

USING THE TRUTH TABLES

A procedure needs to calculate a bonus for each A-rated salesperson whose monthly sales total more than $10,000. The procedure uses the String rating variable to store the salesperson's rating, and the Integer sales variable to store the sales amount. Therefore, you can phrase *condition1* as rating = "A", and phrase *condition2* as sales > 10000. Which logical operator should you use to combine both conditions into one compound condition? You can use the truth tables from Figure 4-21 to answer this question. For a salesperson to receive a bonus, both *condition1* (rating = "A") and *condition2* (sales > 10000) must be True at the same time. If either condition is False, or if both conditions are False, then the compound condition should be False and the salesperson should not receive a bonus. According to the truth tables, the AndAlso and OrElse operators evaluate the compound condition as

True when both conditions are True. However, only the AndAlso operator evaluates the compound condition as False when either one or both of the conditions is False. The OrElse operator evaluates the compound condition as False only when *both* conditions are False. Therefore, the correct compound condition to use is rating = "A" AndAlso sales > 10000.

Now assume that you want to send a letter to all A-rated salespeople and all B-rated salespeople. If the rating is stored in the String rating variable, you can phrase *condition1* as rating = "A", and phrase *condition2* as rating = "B". Now which logical operator should you use to combine both conditions? At first it might appear that the AndAlso operator is the correct one to use, because the example says to send the letter to "all A-rated salespeople and all B-rated salespeople." In everyday conversations, you will find that people sometimes use the word *and* when what they really mean is *or*. Although both words do not mean the same thing, using *and* instead of *or* generally does not cause a problem, because we are able to infer what another person means. Computers, however, cannot infer anything; they simply process the directions you give them, word for word. In this case, you actually want to send a letter to all salespeople having either an A rating or a B rating (a salesperson cannot have both ratings), so you will need to use the OrElse operator. As the truth tables indicate, the OrElse operator is the only operator that evaluates the compound condition as True when one or more of the conditions is True. Therefore, the correct compound condition to use here is rating = "A" OrElse rating = "B".

Figure 4-22 shows the order of precedence for the arithmetic, comparison, and logical operators you have learned so far.

Operator	Operation	Precedence number
^	exponentiation	1
−	negation	2
*, /	multiplication and division	3
\	integer division	4
Mod	modulus arithmetic	5
+, −	addition and subtraction	6
&	concatenation	7
=, >, >=, <, <=, <>	equal to, greater than, greater than or equal to, less than, less than or equal to, not equal to	8
Not	reverses the truth value of a condition	9
AndAlso	all conditions must be true for the compound condition to be true	10
OrElse	only one condition needs to be true for the compound condition to be true	11

Figure 4-22: Order of precedence for arithmetic, comparison, and logical operators

Notice that logical operators are evaluated after any arithmetic operators or comparison operators in an expression. As a result, when the computer processes the expression 12 > 0 AndAlso 12 < 10 * 2, it evaluates the arithmetic operator (*) first, followed by the two comparison operators (> and <), followed by the logical operator (AndAlso). The expression evaluates to True, as shown in Figure 4-23.

Evaluation steps	Result
Original expression	12 > 0 AndAlso 12 < 10 * 2
10 * 2 is evaluated first	12 > 0 AndAlso 12 < 20
12 > 0 is evaluated second	True AndAlso 12 < 20
12 < 20 is evaluated third	True AndAlso True
True AndAlso True is evaluated last	True

Figure 4-23: Evaluation steps for an expression containing arithmetic, comparison, and logical operators

USING LOGICAL OPERATORS IN AN IF . . . THEN . . . ELSE STATEMENT

A procedure needs to calculate and display an employee's gross pay. To keep this example simple, assume that no one at the company works more than 40 hours per week, and everyone earns the same hourly rate, $10.65. Before making the gross pay calculation, the procedure should verify that the number of hours entered by the user is greater than or equal to zero, but less than or equal to 40. Programmers refer to the process of verifying that the input data is within the expected range as **data validation**. In this case, if the number of hours is valid, the procedure should calculate and display the gross pay; otherwise, it should display an error message alerting the user that the input data is incorrect. Figure 4-24 shows two ways of writing the Visual Basic code for the procedure. Notice that the If...Then...Else statement in the first example uses the AndAlso logical operator, whereas the If...Then...Else statement in the second example uses the OrElse logical operator. Both examples produce the same results and simply represent two different ways of performing the same task. Figure 4-25 shows a sample run of the application that contains either of the calcButton Click event procedures shown in Figure 4-24.

Example 1: using the AndAlso operator

```
Private Sub calcButton_Click(ByVal sender As Object, _
    ByVal e As System.EventArgs) Handles calcButton.Click
    ' calculates and displays a gross pay amount

    Dim hoursWorked As Double
    Dim grossPay As Double
```

Figure 4-24: AndAlso and OrElse logical operators in the If...Then...Else statement (*continued on next page*)

```
        ' calculate and display gross pay, or display an error message
        Double.TryParse(hoursTextBox.Text, hoursWorked)
        If  hoursWorked >= 0.0 AndAlso hoursWorked <= 40.0 Then
            grossPay = hoursWorked * 10.65
            grossLabel.Text = grossPay.ToString("C2")
        Else
            grossLabel.Text = "Error"
        End If
    End Sub
```

Example 2: using the OrElse operator

```
Private Sub calcButton_Click(ByVal sender As Object, _
    ByVal e As System.EventArgs) Handles calcButton.Click
    ' calculates and displays a gross pay amount

    Dim hoursWorked As Double
    Dim grossPay As Double

    ' calculate and display gross pay, or display an error message
    Double.TryParse(hoursTextBox.Text, hoursWorked)
    If hoursWorked < 0.0 OrElse hoursWorked > 40.0 Then
        grossLabel.Text = "Error"
    Else
        grossPay = hoursWorked * 10.65
        grossLabel.Text = grossPay.ToString("C2")
    End If
End Sub
```

Figure 4-24: AndAlso and OrElse logical operators in the If…Then…Else statement (*continued from previous page*)

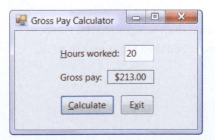

Figure 4-25: Sample run of the application that contains the calcButton's Click event procedure

The last concept you learn in this chapter is how to generate random integers. You will use random integers in the Find The Mouse game that you code in the Programming Tutorial section of this chapter.

GENERATING RANDOM INTEGERS

Visual Basic provides a **pseudo-random number generator**, which is a device that produces a sequence of numbers that meet certain statistical requirements for randomness. Pseudo-random numbers are chosen with equal probability from a finite set of numbers. The chosen numbers are not completely random because a definite mathematical algorithm is used to select them, but they are sufficiently random for practical purposes. Figure 4-26 shows the syntax you use to generate random integers, and it includes examples of using the syntax. As the figure indicates, you first create a Random object to represent the pseudo-random number generator. You create the Random object by declaring it in a Dim statement. You enter the Dim statement in the procedure that will use the number generator. After the Random object is created, you can use the object's Random.Next method to generate random integers. In the method's syntax (shown in Figure 4-26), *randomObjectName* is the name of the Random object. The *minValue* and *maxValue* arguments in the syntax must be integers, and *minValue* must be less than *maxValue*. The **Random.Next method** returns an integer that is greater than or equal to *minValue*, but less than *maxValue*.

» HOW TO . . .

GENERATE RANDOM NUMBERS

<u>Syntax</u>

Dim *randomObjectName* **As New Random**

*randomObjectName***.Next(***minValue***,** *maxValue***)**

<u>Example 1</u>

```
Dim number As Integer
Dim randomGenerator As New Random
number = randomGenerator.Next(1, 51)
```
Creates a Random object named randomGenerator, then assigns (to the number variable) a random integer that is greater than or equal to 1, but less than 51.

<u>Example 2</u>

```
Dim number As Integer
Dim randomGenerator As New Random
number = randomGenerator.Next(-10, 0)
```
Creates a Random object named randomGenerator, then assigns (to the number variable) a random integer that is greater than or equal to -10, but less than 0.

Figure 4-26: How to generate random numbers

Figure 4-27 shows a sample run of the Random Integers application, and Figure 4-28 shows the code for the application's generateButton. The button's Click event procedure generates and displays random numbers from 1 through 10.

Figure 4-27: Sample run of the Random Integers application

Visual Basic code

```
Private Sub generateButton_Click(ByVal sender As Object, _
    ByVal e As System.EventArgs) Handles generateButton.Click
    ' displays random numbers between 1 and 10, inclusive

    Dim number As Integer
    Dim randomGenerator As New Random

    ' generate and display random number
    number = randomGenerator.Next(1, 11)
    randomLabel.Text = Convert.ToString(number)
End Sub
```

Figure 4-28: The generateButton's Click event procedure

> **» TIP**
>
> In Computer Exercise 10, you learn how to use the Random.NextDouble method to generate a random floating-point number.

You have completed the concepts section of Chapter 4.

PROGRAMMING TUTORIAL

CREATING THE FIND THE MOUSE GAME

In this tutorial, you create an application that simulates a game called Find The Mouse. At the start of the game, the player is shown five picture boxes; each picture box contains the "Is the mouse here?" message. The application uses a random number from 1 through 5 to keep track of the picture box that contains the picture of a mouse. For example, if the random number is 1, the first picture box contains the mouse picture. If the random number is 2, the second picture box contains the mouse picture, and so on. The player's task is to find the mouse picture, using as few guesses as possible. Included in the data files for this book is a partially completed Find The Mouse Game application. Figures 4-29 and 4-30 show the application's TOE chart and user interface. (The mouse image was contributed by the photographer, Jean Scheijen. You can browse Jean's other images at *www.vierdrie.nl*.)

Task	Object	Event
1. Generate a random number from 1 through 5 2. Display the "Is the mouse here?" image in PictureBox1, PictureBox2, PictureBox3, PictureBox4, and PictureBox5	startButton	Click
Use the random number generated by the startButton to display either the mouse image or the "Not Here!" image	PictureBox1, PictureBox2, PictureBox3, PictureBox4, PictureBox5	Click
End the application	exitButton	Click
Store the "Is the mouse here?" image	questionPictureBox	None
Store the "Not Here!" image	notHerePictureBox	None
Store the mouse image	mousePictureBox	None

Figure 4-29: TOE chart

Figure 4-30: User interface

COMPLETING THE FIND THE MOUSE GAME APPLICATION

As the application's TOE chart indicates, the Click event procedures for the startButton, exitButton, and five picture boxes need to be coded.

To begin coding the application:

1. Start Visual Studio. If necessary, close the Start Page window.

2. Open the **Mouse Game Solution** (**Mouse Game Solution.sln**) file, which is contained in the VbReloaded2008\Chap04\Mouse Game Solution folder. If necessary, open the designer window. The MainForm appears on the screen.

3. Open the Code Editor window. Notice that the exitButton's Click event procedure has already been coded for you. In the comments that appear in the General Declarations section, replace the <your name> and <current date> text with your name and the current date.

4. The application will use variables, so you should enter the appropriate Option statements in the General Declarations section. Enter the Option statements shown in Figure 4-31.

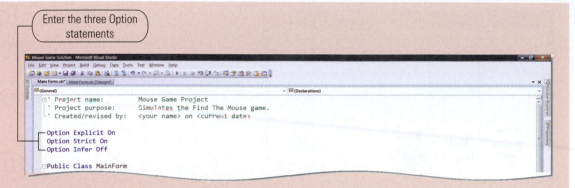

Figure 4-31: Option statements entered in the General Declarations section

The startButton's Click event procedure is responsible for generating a random number from 1 through 5. It also must display the "Is the mouse here?" image in five picture boxes. Figure 4-32 shows the procedure's pseudocode.

---

startButton Click Event Procedure
1. assign a random number from 1 through 5 to a form-level variable
2. assign the "Is the mouse here?" image, which is contained in the questionPictureBox, to PictureBox1, PictureBox2, PictureBox3, PictureBox4, and PictureBox5

Figure 4-32: Pseudocode for the startButton's Click event procedure

The procedure will use two variables: a Random variable to represent the pseudo-random number generator, and an Integer variable to store the random integer. You will name the Random variable randomGenerator, and name the Integer variable randomNumber. The randomGenerator variable will be a procedure-level variable, because it will be used only within the startButton's Click event procedure. The randomNumber variable, however, will be a form-level variable, because it will be used by the Click event procedures for the startButton and the five picture boxes.

To declare the form-level variable, and then code the startButton's Click event procedure:

1. In the blank line below the ' form-level variable for storing a random number comment, type **private randomNumber as integer** and press **Enter**.

2. Open the code template for the startButton's Click event procedure. Type the comment **' prepares the interface for a new game** and press **Enter** twice. Type **dim randomGenerator as new random** and press **Enter** twice.

3. The first step in the pseudocode is to assign a random number from 1 through 5 to the randomNumber variable. Type **' generate random number from 1 through 5** and press **Enter**. Type **randomNumber = randomGenerator.next(1, 6)** and press **Enter** twice.

4. Step 2 in the pseudocode is to assign the image contained in the questionPictureBox to five picture boxes. Enter the following comment and code.

' display the "Is the mouse here?" image
PictureBox1.image = questionPictureBox.image
PictureBox2.image = questionPictureBox.image
PictureBox3.image = questionPictureBox.image
PictureBox4.image = questionPictureBox.image
PictureBox5.image = questionPictureBox.image

5. Save the solution.

According to the TOE chart in Figure 4-29, the PictureBox1's Click event procedure will use the random number generated by the startButton to display either the mouse image or the "Not Here!" image in the picture box. The pseudocode for the PictureBox1's Click event procedure is shown in Figure 4-33.

```
PictureBox1 Click Event Procedure
1. if the random number is 1
      display the mouse image
   else
      display the "Not Here!" image
   end if
```

Figure 4-33: Pseudocode for the PictureBox1's Click event procedure

To code the PictureBox1's Click event procedure:

1. Open the code template for the PictureBox1's Click event procedure, then enter the following comments and code:

' displays either the mouse image or
' the "Not Here!" image

If randomNumber = 1 Then
    PictureBox1.Image = mousePictureBox.Image
Else
    PictureBox1.Image = notHerePictureBox.Image
End If

2. Save the solution.

The Click event procedures for the other four picture boxes are almost identical to the PictureBox1's Click event procedure. The only exception is that the PictureBox2's Click event procedure will display the mouse image in the PictureBox2 control when the random number is 2 (rather than 1). Similarly, the PictureBox3's Click event procedure will display the mouse image in the PictureBox3 control when the random number is 3, and so on.

To finish coding the application:

1. Open the code template for the PictureBox2's Click event procedure. Copy the comments and code from the PictureBox1's Click event procedure to the PictureBox2's Click event procedure.

2. In the PictureBox2's Click event procedure, change the number 1 in the If...Then...Else statement's condition to **2**. Also change PictureBox1 in both the true path and false path to **PictureBox2**.

3. On your own, enter the appropriate code in the PictureBox3, PictureBox4, and PictureBox5 Click event procedures.

4. Save the solution.

Figure 4-34 shows the application's code.

```
' Project name:        Mouse Game Project
' Project purpose:     Simulates the Find The Mouse game.
' Created/revised by:  <your name> on <current date>

Option Explicit On
Option Strict On
Option Infer Off

Public Class MainForm

    ' form-level variable for storing a random number
    Private randomNumber As Integer

    Private Sub exitButton_Click(ByVal sender As Object, _
        ByVal e As System.EventArgs) Handles exitButton.Click
        Me.Close()

    End Sub
```

Figure 4-34: Find The Mouse Game application's code (*continued on next page*)

```vb
Private Sub startButton_Click(ByVal sender As Object, _
    ByVal e As System.EventArgs) Handles startButton.Click
    ' prepares the interface for a new game

    Dim randomGenerator As New Random

    ' generate random number from 1 through 5
    randomNumber = randomGenerator.Next(1, 6)

    ' display the "Is the mouse here?" image
    PictureBox1.Image = questionPictureBox.Image
    PictureBox2.Image = questionPictureBox.Image
    PictureBox3.Image = questionPictureBox.Image
    PictureBox4.Image = questionPictureBox.Image
    PictureBox5.Image = questionPictureBox.Image
End Sub

Private Sub PictureBox1_Click(ByVal sender As Object, _
    ByVal e As System.EventArgs) Handles PictureBox1.Click
    ' displays either the mouse image or
    ' the "Not Here" image

    If randomNumber = 1 Then
        PictureBox1.Image = mousePictureBox.Image
    Else
        PictureBox1.Image = notHerePictureBox.Image
    End If
End Sub

Private Sub PictureBox2_Click(ByVal sender As Object, _
    ByVal e As System.EventArgs) Handles PictureBox2.Click
    ' displays either the mouse image or
    ' the "Not Here" image

    If randomNumber = 2 Then
        PictureBox2.Image = mousePictureBox.Image
    Else
        PictureBox2.Image = notHerePictureBox.Image
    End If
End Sub

Private Sub PictureBox3_Click(ByVal sender As Object, _
    ByVal e As System.EventArgs) Handles PictureBox3.Click
    ' displays either the mouse image or
    ' the "Not Here" image
```

Figure 4-34: Find The Mouse Game application's code (*continued from previous page and on next page*)

```
        If randomNumber = 3 Then
            PictureBox3.Image = mousePictureBox.Image
        Else
            PictureBox3.Image = notHerePictureBox.Image
        End If
    End Sub

    Private Sub PictureBox4_Click(ByVal sender As Object, _
        ByVal e As System.EventArgs) Handles PictureBox4.Click
        ' displays either the mouse image or
        ' the "Not Here" image

        If randomNumber = 4 Then
            PictureBox4.Image = mousePictureBox.Image
        Else
            PictureBox4.Image = notHerePictureBox.Image
        End If
    End Sub

    Private Sub PictureBox5_Click(ByVal sender As Object, _
        ByVal e As System.EventArgs) Handles PictureBox5.Click
        ' displays either the mouse image or
        ' the "Not Here" image

        If randomNumber = 5 Then
            PictureBox5.Image = mousePictureBox.Image
        Else
            PictureBox5.Image = notHerePictureBox.Image
        End If
    End Sub
End Class
```

Figure 4-34: Find The Mouse Game application's code (*continued from previous page*)

Now test the application to verify that it is working correctly.

To test the application:

1. Close the Code Editor window, then start the application.

2. Click the **Start Game** button. The "Is the mouse here?" image appears in the five picture boxes in the interface, as shown in Figure 4-35.

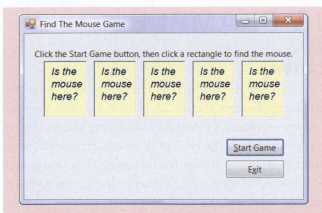

Figure 4-35: Result of clicking the Start Game button

3. Click **one of the "Is the mouse here?" rectangles**. One of two images appears: either the "Not Here!" image or the mouse image. If you found the mouse, the game is over.

4. Click **each of the remaining four rectangles**. Figure 4-36 shows a sample run of the application. Because the application uses a random number, the mouse image may be in a different rectangle on your screen.

Figure 4-36: Find The Mouse application

5. Click the **Start Game** button, then play the game again.

6. Click the **Exit** button to end the application, then close the solution.

PROGRAMMING EXAMPLE

FAT CALCULATOR APPLICATION

Create an application that allows the user to enter the total number of calories and grams of fat contained in a specific food. The application should calculate and display two values: the food's fat calories and its fat percentage. A food's fat calories are the number of calories attributed to fat, and its fat percentage is the ratio of the food's fat calories to its total calories. In addition, the application should display the message "This food is high in fat." when the fat percentage is over 30%; otherwise, it should display the message "This food is not high in fat." Name the solution Fat Calculator Solution. Name the project Fat Calculator Project. Name the form file Main Form.vb. Save the application in the VbReloaded2008\Chap04 folder. See Figures 4-37 through 4-42. Test the application using 150 and 6 as the number of calories and grams of fat, respectively. The fat calories should be 54 and the fat percentage should be 36.0 %. In addition, the "This food is high in fat." message should appear. End the application, then close the solution.

Task	Object	Event
1. Calculate the fat calories 2. Calculate the fat percentage 3. Display the fat calories and fat percentage in fatCalsLabel and fatPercentLabel 4. Display appropriate message in messageLabel	calcButton	Click
End the application	exitButton	Click
Display the fat calories (from calcButton)	fatCalsLabel	None
Display the fat percentage (from calcButton)	fatPercentLabel	None
Get and display the calories and fat grams	caloriesTextBox, fatGramsTextBox	None

Figure 4-37: TOE chart

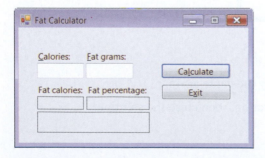

Figure 4-38: User interface

Object	Property	Setting
Form1	Name AcceptButton Font StartPosition Text	MainForm calcButton Segoe UI, 9 point CenterScreen Fat Calculator
Label1	Text	&Calories:
Label2	Text	&Fat grams:
Label3	Text	Fat calories:
Label4	Text	Fat percentage:
Label5	Name AutoSize BorderStyle Text TextAlign	fatCalsLabel False FixedSingle (empty) MiddleCenter
Label6	Name AutoSize BorderStyle Text TextAlign	fatPercentLabel False FixedSingle (empty) MiddleCenter
Label7	Name AutoSize BorderStyle Text TextAlign	messageLabel False FixedSingle (empty) MiddleCenter
TextBox1	Name	caloriesTextBox
TextBox2	Name	fatGramsTextBox
Button1	Name Text	calcButton Ca&lculate
Button2	Name Text	exitButton E&xit

Figure 4-39: Objects, Properties, and Settings

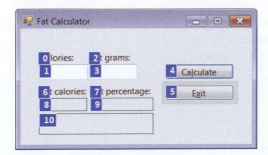

Figure 4-40: Tab Order

exitButton Click Event Procedure
1. close the application

calcButton Click Event Procedure
1. assign user input to variables
2. fat calories = fat grams * 9
3. fat percentage = fat calories / total calories
4. display fat calories and fat percentage in fatCalsLabel and fatPercentLabel
5. if fat percentage is over 30%
    display "This food is high in fat." message in messageLabel
  else
    display "This food is not high in fat." message in messageLabel
  end if
6. send focus to caloriesTextBox

Figure 4-41: Pseudocode

```
' Project name:        Fat Calculator Project
' Project purpose:     Allows the user to enter a food's
'                      calories and grams of fat. It
'                      then calculates the food's fat
'                      calories and fat percentage.
' Created/revised by:  <your name> on <current date>

Option Explicit On
Option Strict On
Option Infer Off

Public Class MainForm

    Private Sub exitButton_Click(ByVal sender As Object, _
        ByVal e As System.EventArgs) Handles exitButton.Click
        Me.Close()
    End Sub

    Private Sub calcButton_Click(ByVal sender As Object, _
        ByVal e As System.EventArgs) Handles calcButton.Click
        ' calculates a food's fat calories and its fat percentage

        Dim calories As Integer
        Dim fatGrams As Integer
        Dim fatCalories As Integer
        Dim fatPercent As Double
```

Figure 4-42: Code (*continued on next page*)

```
        ' assign user input to variables
        Integer.TryParse(caloriesTextBox.Text, calories)
        Integer.TryParse(fatGramsTextBox.Text, fatGrams)

        ' calculate and display fat calories and
        ' fat percentage
        fatCalories = fatGrams * 9
        fatPercent = Convert.ToDouble(fatCalories) / _
            Convert.ToDouble(calories)
        fatCalsLabel.Text = Convert.ToString(fatCalories)
        fatPercentLabel.Text = fatPercent.ToString("P1")

        ' display message indicating whether the food is
        ' or is not high in fat
        If fatPercent > 0.3 Then
            messageLabel.Text = "This food is high in fat."
        Else
            messageLabel.Text = "This food is not high in fat."
        End If

        caloriesTextBox.Focus()
    End Sub
End Class
```

Figure 4-42: Code (*continued from previous page*)

QUICK REVIEW

» The selection structure allows a program to make a decision or comparison and then select one of two paths, depending on the result of that decision or comparison.

» Visual Basic provides four forms of the selection structure: If, If/Else, If/ElseIf/Else, and Case.

» In a flowchart, you use the diamond, called the selection/repetition symbol, to represent the selection structure's condition.

» In Visual Basic, you use the If...Then...Else statement to code the If and If/Else forms of the selection structure.

» All expressions containing a comparison operator will result in an answer of either True or False only.

» Comparison operators do not have an order of precedence in Visual Basic. Rather, they are evaluated from left to right in an expression, and are evaluated after any arithmetic operators in the expression.

» Variables declared in either the true or false path of a selection structure have block scope.

» You connect (or link) strings together using the concatenation operator, which is the ampersand (&).

» The ControlChars.NewLine constant advances the insertion point to the next line in a control.

» String comparisons in Visual Basic are case-sensitive. When comparing strings, you can use either the ToUpper method or the ToLower method to temporarily convert the strings to uppercase or lowercase, respectively.

» You use logical operators to create compound conditions. All expressions containing a logical operator will result in an answer of either True or False only.

» Like arithmetic operators, logical operators have an order of precedence and are evaluated after any arithmetic and comparison operators in an expression.

» You use the pseudo-random number generator in Visual Basic to generate random numbers.

KEY TERMS

Block scope—the scope of a variable declared within a statement block; a variable with block scope can be used only within the statement block in which it is declared

Boolean operators—another term for logical operators

CharacterCasing property—the text box property that indicates whether the case of the text should remain as typed or be converted to uppercase or lowercase

Comparison operators—operators used to compare values in a selection structure's condition; also called relational operators

Concatenation operator—the ampersand (&); used to concatenate strings together; must be preceded and followed by a space character

Condition—specifies the decision you are making and must be phrased so that it results in an answer of either True or False only

ControlChars.NewLine constant—used to advance the insertion point to the next line in a control

Data validation—the process of verifying that a program's input data is within the expected range

False path—contains the instructions that are processed when the selection structure's condition evaluates to False

If/Else selection structure—contains two sets of instructions: one set is processed when the selection structure's condition is true and the other set is processed when the condition is false

If selection structure—contains only one set of instructions, which are processed when the selection structure's condition is true

If...Then...Else statement—used to code the If and If/Else forms of the selection structure in Visual Basic

Logical operators—the operators used to combine two or more conditions into one compound condition; also called Boolean operators

MaxLength property—the text box property that specifies the maximum number of characters that can be entered in a text box

Pseudo-random number generator—used to generate random numbers in Visual Basic

Random.Next method—used to generate a random integer that is greater than or equal to a minimum value, but less than a maximum value

Relational operators—another term for comparison operators

Selection structure—one of the three programming structures; tells the computer to make a decision or comparison, and then select the appropriate path based on the result; also called the decision structure

Selection/repetition symbol—the diamond in a flowchart

Short-circuit evaluation—refers to the fact that the AndAlso and OrElse operators do not always evaluate the second condition in a compound condition

Statement block—in a selection structure, the set of statements terminated by an Else or End If clause

ToLower method—temporarily converts a string to lowercase

ToUpper method—temporarily converts a string to uppercase

True path—contains the instructions that are processed when the selection structure's condition evaluates to True

Truth tables—summarize how the computer evaluates the logical operators in an expression

SELF-CHECK QUESTIONS AND ANSWERS

1. What is the scope of variables declared in an If...Then...Else statement's false path?

   a. the entire application

   b. the procedure in which the If...Then...Else statement appears

   c. the entire If...Then...Else statement

   d. only the false path in the If...Then...Else statement

2. Which of the following concatenates the "Do they live in " message, the contents of the String state variable, and a question mark?

   a. "Do they live in " & state & "?"

   b. "Do they live in & state & ?"

   c. "Do they live in _ " state _ "?"

   d. "Do they live in " # state # "?"

3. Which of the following methods temporarily converts the string stored in the item variable to lowercase?

   a. item.Lower
   b. item.ToLower

   c. LowerCase(item)
   d. Lower(item)

4. If the value of *condition1* is True and the value of *condition2* is False, then the value of *condition1* OrElse *condition2* is _____.

   a. True
   b. False

5. Which of the following declares an object that represents the pseudo-random number generator?

   a. Dim randomGenerator As New Generator

   b. Dim randomGenerator As New Random

   c. Dim randomGenerator As New RandomGenerator

   d. Dim randomGenerator As New RandomObject

Answers: 1) d, 2) a, 3) b, 4) a, 5) b

REVIEW QUESTIONS

1. Which of the following is a valid condition for an If...Then...Else statement?

    a. priceLabel.Text > 0 AndAlso priceLabel.Text < 10

    b. age > 30 OrElse < 50

    c. number > 100 AndAlso number <= 1000

    d. state.ToUpper = "Alaska" OrElse state.ToUpper = "Hawaii"

2. Which of the following conditions should you use to compare the string contained in the firstNameTextBox's Text property with the name Bob? (Be sure the condition will handle Bob, BOB, bob, and so on.)

    a. firstNameTextBox.Text = ToUpper("BOB")

    b. firstNameTextBox.Text.ToUpper = "Bob"

    c. firstNameTextBox.Text.ToUpper = "BOB"

    d. ToUpper(firstName.Text) = "BOB"

3. The expression 3 > 6 AndAlso 7 > 4 evaluates to _____.

    a. True   b. False

4. The expression 4 > 6 OrElse 10 < 2 * 6 evaluates to _____.

    a. True   b. False

5. The expression 7 >= 3 + 4 OrElse 6 < 4 AndAlso 2 < 5 evaluates to _____.

    a. True   b. False

6. Which of the following constants can be used to advance the insertion point to the next line in the answerLabel?

    a. Advance.NewLine   b. ControlChars.NewLine

    c. NewLine.Advance   d. None of the above.

7. Which of the following generates a random integer from 10 to 55, inclusive? (The Random object is named randomGenerator.)

    a. randomGenerator.Next(10, 56)   b. randomGenerator.Next(10, 55)

    c. randomGenerator.Next(9, 55)   d. None of the above.

8. The city variable contains the string "Boston" and the state variable contains the string "MA". Which of the following will display the string "Boston, MA" (the city, a comma, a space, and the state) in the addressLabel?

a. addressLabel.Text = "city" & ", " & "state"

b. addressLabel.Text = city $ ", " $ state

c. addressLabel.Text = city & ", " & state

d. addressLabel.Text = "city," & "state"

REVIEW EXERCISES— SHORT ANSWER

1. Listed below are the logical operators covered in this chapter. Indicate their order of precedence by placing a number (1, 2, and 3) on the line to the left of the operator.

_____ AndAlso

_____ Not

_____ OrElse

2. An expression can contain arithmetic, comparison, and logical operators. Indicate the order of precedence for the three types of operators by placing a number (1, 2, and 3) on the line to the left of the operator type.

_____ Arithmetic

_____ Logical

_____ Comparison

Use the following selection structure to answer Questions 3 and 4:

```
If number <= 100 Then
    number = number * 2
Else
    number = number * 3
End If
```

3. If the number variable contains the number 90, what value will be in the number variable after the above selection structure is processed?

4. If the number variable contains the number 1000, what value will be in the number variable after the above selection structure is processed?

5. Draw the flowchart that corresponds to the following pseudocode:

```
if hours are greater than 40
    display "Overtime pay"
else
    display "Regular pay"
end if
```

6. Write an If...Then...Else statement that displays the string "Pontiac" in the carMakeLabel when the carTextBox contains the string "Grand Am" (in any case).

7. Write an If...Then...Else statement that displays the string "Entry error" in the messageLabel when the units variable contains a number that is less than 0; otherwise, display the string "Valid Number".

8. Write an If...Then...Else statement that displays the string "Reorder" in the messageLabel when the quantity variable contains a number that is less than 10; otherwise, display the string "OK".

9. Write an If...Then...Else statement that assigns the number 10 to the bonus variable when the sales variable contains a number that is less than or equal to $250; otherwise, assign the number 15.

10. Write an If...Then...Else statement that displays the number 25 in the shippingLabel when the state variable contains the string "Hawaii" (in any case); otherwise, display the number 50.

11. You need to calculate a 3% sales tax when the state variable contains the string "Colorado" (in any case); otherwise, you want to calculate a 4% sales tax. You can calculate the sales tax by multiplying the tax rate by the contents of a Decimal variable named sales. Display the sales tax in the salesTaxLabel. Draw the flowchart, then write the Visual Basic code.

12. You need to calculate an employee's gross pay. Employees working more than 40 hours should receive overtime pay (time and one-half) for the hours over 40. Use the variables hours, hourRate, and gross. Display the contents of the gross variable in the grossLabel. Write the pseudocode, then write the Visual Basic code.

13. Write the If...Then...Else statement that displays the string "Dog" in the animalLabel when the animal variable contains the letter "D" (in any case); otherwise, display the string "Cat". Draw the flowchart, then write the Visual Basic code.

14. You need to calculate a 10% discount on desks sold to customers in Colorado. Use the variables item, state, sales, and discount. Format the discount using the "C2" format and display it in the discountLabel. Write the pseudocode, then write the Visual Basic code.

15. You need to calculate a 2% price increase on all red shirts, but a 1% price increase on all other items. In addition to calculating the price increase, you also need to calculate the new price. You can use the variables itemColor, item, origPrice, increase, and newPrice. Format the original price, price increase, and new price using the "N2" format. Display the original price, price increase, and new price in the originalLabel, increaseLabel, and newLabel, respectively. Write the Visual Basic code.

16. Write the Visual Basic code that swaps the values stored in the marySales and jeffSales variables, but only if the value stored in the marySales variable is less than the value stored in the jeffSales variable.

17. In the chapter, you learned about the ControlChars.NewLine constant. Technically, NewLine is the constant, and ControlChars is the class that contains the definition for the constant. Use the Help screens to research the ControlChars class. What other constants (called members) are contained in the class?

COMPUTER EXERCISES

1. In this exercise, you code an application that swaps two values entered by the user.

   a. Open the Number Swap Solution (Number Swap Solution.sln) file, which is contained in the VbReloaded2008\Chap04\Number Swap Solution folder.

   b. Open the Code Editor window and enter the appropriate comments at the beginning of the code. Also enter the appropriate Option statements.

   c. Code the exitButton's Click event procedure so that it ends the application.

   d. Enter the code for the displayButton's Click event procedure, which is shown in Figure 4-10 in the chapter.

   e. Save the solution, then start the application. Test the application by entering the two values 8 and 4, and then clicking the Display button. The user interface should appear as shown in Figure 4-7 in the chapter.

   f. Now test the application by entering the two values 5 and 9, and then clicking the Display button.

   g. Click the Exit button to end the application, then close the solution.

2. In this exercise, you code an application that calculates either the sum of or the difference between two numbers.

   a. Open the AddSub Solution (AddSub Solution.sln) file, which is contained in the VbReloaded2008\Chap04\AddSub Solution folder.

b. Open the Code Editor window and enter the appropriate comments at the beginning of the code. Also enter the appropriate Option statements.

c. Code the exitButton's Click event procedure so that it ends the application.

d. Enter the code for the calcButton's Click event procedure, which is shown in Figure 4-16 in the chapter.

e. Save the solution, then start the application. Test the application by entering the letter a and the two numbers 12 and 89, and then clicking the Calculate button. The interface should appear as shown in Figure 4-13 in the chapter.

f. Now test the application by entering the letter S and the two values 5 and 9, and then clicking the Calculate button.

g. Click the Exit button to end the application, then close the solution.

3. In this exercise, you code an application that calculates a bonus.

a. Open the Bonus Solution (Bonus Solution.sln) file, which is contained in the VbReloaded2008\Chap04\Bonus Solution folder.

b. The user will enter the sales amount in the salesTextBox. The sales amount will always be an integer. Code the calcButton's Click event procedure so that it calculates the salesperson's bonus. A salesperson selling more than $3500 in product receives a 5% bonus; otherwise, he receives a 4% bonus. Display the bonus, formatted with a dollar sign and two decimal places, in the bonusLabel.

c. Save the solution, then start and test the application. End the application, then close the solution.

4. In this exercise, you complete a procedure that calculates and displays the total amount owed by a company.

a. Open the Seminar Solution (Seminar Solution.sln) file, which is contained in the VbReloaded2008\Chap04\Seminar Solution folder.

b. You offer programming seminars to companies. Your price per person depends on the number of people the company registers, as shown in the chart below. (For example, if the company registers seven people, then the total amount owed is $560, which is calculated by multiplying the number 7 by the number 80.) Display the total amount owed in the totalLabel.

Number of registrants	Charge per person
1–10	$80
Over 10	$70

c. Save the solution, then start and test the application. End the application, then close the solution.

5. Jacques Cousard has been playing the lottery for four years; unfortunately, he has yet to win any money. He wants an application that will select the six lottery numbers for him. Each lottery number can range from 1 to 54 only. (An example of six lottery numbers would be: 4, 8, 35, 15, 20, 3.)

   a. Build an appropriate interface. Name the solution, project, and form file Lottery Solution, Lottery Project, and Main Form.vb, respectively. Save the application in the VbReloaded2008\Chap04 folder.

   b. Code the application. For now, do not worry if the lottery numbers are not unique. You learn how to display unique numbers in Chapter 9 in this book.

   c. Save the solution, then start and test the application. End the application, then close the solution.

6. In this exercise, you modify the application from Chapter 3's Programming Example.

   a. Use Windows to copy the Moonbucks Solution-Chap3 folder from the VbReloaded2008\Chap03 folder to the VbReloaded2008\Chap04 folder. Name the copied folder Moonbucks Solution-Chap4.

   b. Open the Moonbucks Solution (Moonbucks Solution.sln) file contained in the VbReloaded2008\Chap04\Moonbucks Solution-Chap4 folder. Open the designer window.

   c. Modify the application so that it gives customers a 2% discount when the total pounds ordered exceeds 3.

   d. Save the solution, then start and test the application. End the application, then close the solution.

7. In this exercise, you modify the application from Chapter 3's Programming Tutorial.

   a. Use Windows to copy the Change Solution folder from the VbReloaded2008\Chap03 folder to the VbReloaded2008\Chap04 folder. Name the copied folder Change Solution-Chap4.

   b. Open the Change Solution (Change Solution.sln) file contained in the VbReloaded2008\Chap04\Change Solution-Chap4 folder. Open the designer window.

   c. Modify the application so that it performs the calculations only when the amount paid is greater than or equal to the amount owed.

   d. Save the solution, then start and test the application. End the application, then close the solution.

8. In this exercise, you code an application that displays a shipping charge.

   a. Open the Shipping Solution (Shipping Solution.sln) file, which is contained in the VbReloaded2008\Chap04\Shipping Solution folder.

   b. The user will enter the customer's ZIP code in the zipTextBox. Use the following information to display the appropriate shipping charge in the zipLabel.

ZIP code	Shipping charge
60618	32.00
60620	32.00
60632	32.00
All other ZIP codes	37.75

   c. Save the solution, then start and test the application. End the application, then close the solution.

9. In this exercise, you create an application that can help the user learn the Spanish words for the following colors: red, blue, and green.

   a. You can either create your own user interface or create the one shown in Figure 4-43 (which contains three text boxes, five buttons, and one label). Name the solution, project, and form file Spanish Colors Solution, Spanish Colors Project, and Main Form.vb, respectively. Save the application in the VbReloaded2008\Chap04 folder.

Figure 4-43: Sample interface for the Spanish Colors application

b. If you are using the interface shown in Figure 4-43, the user should be able to enter (in the appropriate text box) the Spanish word corresponding to the button's color. After entering the Spanish word, the user will need to click the corresponding button to verify her entry. If the Spanish word is correct, the button's Click event procedure should change the color of the text box to match the button's color. The Clear button should change each text box's background color to white.

c. Save the solution, then start and test the application. End the application, then close the solution.

10. In this exercise, you generate and display random floating-point numbers.

a. Open the Random Float Solution (Random Float Solution.sln) file, which is contained in the VbReloaded2008\Chap04\Random Float Solution folder.

b. You can use the Random.NextDouble method to return a floating-point random number that is greater than or equal to 0.0, but less than 1.0. The syntax of the Random.NextDouble method is *randomObjectName***.NextDouble**. Code the Display Random Number button's Click event procedure so that it displays a random floating-point number in the numberLabel.

c. Save the solution, then start the application. Click the Display Random Number button several times. Each time you click the button, a random number that is greater than or equal to 0.0, but less than 1.0, appears in the numberLabel.

d. Click the Exit button to end the application.

e. You can use the following formula to generate random floating-point numbers within a specified range: **(***maxValue* – *minValue* + **1.0)** * *randomObjectName***.NextDouble** + *minValue*. For example, the formula (10.0 – 1.0 + 1.0) * randomGenerator.NextDouble + 1.0 generates floating-point numbers that are greater than or equal to 1.0, but less than 11.0. Modify the Display Random Number button's Click event procedure so that it displays a random floating-point number that is greater than or equal to 25.0, but less than 51.0. Display two decimal places in the floating-point number.

f. Save the solution, then start the application. Click the Display Random Number button several times to verify that the code you entered is working correctly. End the application, then close the solution.

11. In this exercise, you practice debugging an application.

a. Open the Debug Solution (Debug Solution.sln) file, which is contained in the VbReloaded2008\Chap04\Debug Solution folder.

b. Open the Code Editor window. Review the existing code. The calcButton's Click event procedure should calculate a 10% bonus when the code entered by the user is either 1 or 2 and, at the same time, the sales amount is greater than $10,000. Otherwise, the bonus rate is 5%.

c. Start the application. Type the number 1 in the Code text box. Type 200 in the Sales amount text box, then click the Calculate Bonus button. The interface shows that the bonus amount is $20.00 (10% of $200), which is incorrect; it should be $10.00 (5% of $200). Click the Exit button to end the application.

d. Make the appropriate change to the calcButton's Click event procedure. Save the solution, then start the application. Type the number 1 in the Code text box. Type 200 in the Sales amount text box, then click the Calculate Bonus button. The interface should show that the bonus amount is $10.00. End the application, then close the solution.

CASE PROJECTS

ALLENTON WATER DEPARTMENT

Create an application that calculates a customer's water bill. The user will enter the current meter reading and the previous meter reading. The application should calculate and display the number of gallons of water used and the total charge for the water. The charge for water is $1.75 per 1000 gallons, or .00175 per gallon. Make the calculations only when the current meter reading is greater than or equal to the previous meter reading; otherwise, display an appropriate error message. You can either create your own user interface or create the one shown in Figure 4-44. Name the solution, project, and form file Allenton Solution, Allenton Project, and Main Form.vb, respectively. Save the solution in the VbReloaded2008\Chap04 folder.

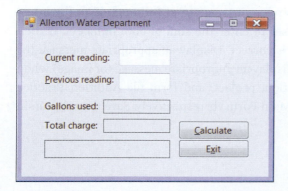

Figure 4-44: Sample interface for the Allenton Water Department

NOVELTY WAREHOUSE

Novelty Warehouse needs an application that allows the user to enter an item's price. When the user clicks a button in the interface, the button's Click event procedure should add the price to the total of the prices already entered; this amount represents the subtotal owed by the customer. The application should display the subtotal on the screen. It also should display a 3% sales tax, the shipping charge, and the grand total owed by the customer. The grand total is calculated by adding together the subtotal, the 3% sales tax, and a $15 shipping charge. For example, if the user enters 26.75 as the price and then clicks the button, the button's Click event procedure should display 26.75 as the subtotal, .80 as the sales tax, 15.00 as the shipping charge, and 42.55 as the grand total. If the user subsequently enters 30.00 as the price and then clicks the button, the button's Click event procedure should display 56.75 as the subtotal, 1.70 as the sales tax, 15.00 as the shipping charge, and 73.45 as the grand total. However, when the subtotal is at least $100, the shipping charge is 0 (zero). Name the solution, project, and form file Novelty Solution, Novelty Project, and Main Form.vb, respectively. Save the solution in the VbReloaded2008\Chap04 folder.

MARCY'S DEPARTMENT STORE

Marcy's is having a BoGoHo (Buy One, Get One Half Off) sale. Create an application that allows the user to enter the prices of two items. The application should calculate the total owed. The half-off should always be taken on the item having the lowest price. For example, if one item costs $24.99 and the second item costs $12.50, the half-off would be taken on the $12.50 item. (In other words, the item would cost $6.25.) Name the solution, project, and form file Marcy Solution, Marcy Project, and Main Form.vb, respectively. Save the solution in the VbReloaded2008\Chap04 folder.

ADDITION PRACTICE

Create an application that displays two random integers from 1 through 10 in the interface. The application should allow the user to enter the sum of both numbers. It then should check whether the user's answer is correct. Display an appropriate message (or image) when the answer is correct. Also display an appropriate message (or image) when the answer is incorrect. Name the solution, project, and form file Addition Practice Solution, Addition Practice Project, and Main Form.vb, respectively. Save the solution in the VbReloaded2008\Chap04 folder.

5

MORE ON THE SELECTION STRUCTURE

After studying Chapter 5, you should be able to:

Include a nested selection structure in pseudocode and in a flowchart

Code an If/ElseIf/Else selection structure

Include a Case selection structure in pseudocode and in a flowchart

Code a Case selection structure

Include radio buttons in an interface

Display a message in a message box

Prevent the entry of unwanted characters in a text box

NESTED SELECTION STRUCTURES

As you learned in Chapter 4, you use the selection structure to make a decision or comparison and then select the appropriate path—either the true path or the false path—based on the result. Both paths in a selection structure can include instructions that declare variables, perform calculations, and so on. Both paths also can include other selection structures. When either a selection structure's true path or its false path contains another selection structure, the inner selection structure is referred to as a **nested selection structure**, because it is contained (nested) within the outer selection structure. You use a nested selection structure when more than one decision must be made before the appropriate action can be taken. An example of this would be a selection structure that displays one of three messages based on a person's voter eligibility. The messages and the criteria for displaying each message are shown in the following chart:

Message	Criteria
You are too young to vote.	person is younger than 18 years old
You can vote.	person is at least 18 years old and is registered to vote
You need to register before you can vote.	person is at least 18 years old but is not registered to vote

As the chart indicates, the person's age and voter registration status determine the appropriate message to display. If the person is younger than 18 years old, the selection structure should display the message "You are too young to vote." However, if the person is at least 18 years old, the selection structure should display one of two different messages. The correct message to display is determined by the person's voter registration status. If the person is registered, then the appropriate message is "You can vote."; otherwise, it is "You need to register before you can vote." Notice that determining the person's voter registration status is important only after his or her age is determined. You can think of the decision regarding the age as being the **primary decision**, and the decision regarding the registration status as being the **secondary decision**, because whether the registration decision needs to be made depends on the result of the age decision. The primary decision is always made by the outer selection structure, while the secondary decision is always made by the inner (nested) selection structure. Figure 5-1 shows a sample run of the Voter Eligibility application. Figures 5-2 and 5-3 show the pseudocode, code, and flowchart

Figure 5-1: Sample run of the Voter Eligibility application

for the displayButton's Click event procedure. In the procedure, the outer selection structure determines the age (the primary decision), and the nested selection structure determines the voter registration status (the secondary decision). Notice that the nested selection structure appears in the outer selection structure's true path in the procedure.

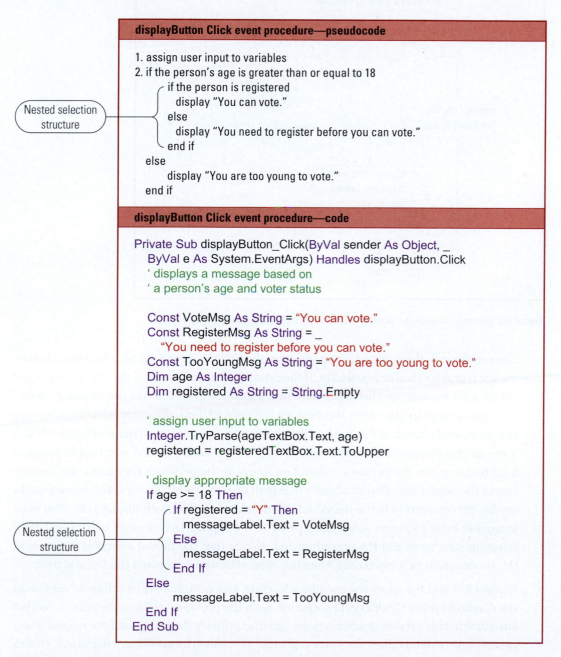

displayButton Click event procedure—pseudocode

1. assign user input to variables
2. if the person's age is greater than or equal to 18
    if the person is registered
      display "You can vote."
    else
      display "You need to register before you can vote."
    end if
else
    display "You are too young to vote."
end if

Nested selection structure

displayButton Click event procedure—code

```
Private Sub displayButton_Click(ByVal sender As Object, _
    ByVal e As System.EventArgs) Handles displayButton.Click
    ' displays a message based on
    ' a person's age and voter status

    Const VoteMsg As String = "You can vote."
    Const RegisterMsg As String = _
        "You need to register before you can vote."
    Const TooYoungMsg As String = "You are too young to vote."
    Dim age As Integer
    Dim registered As String = String.Empty

    ' assign user input to variables
    Integer.TryParse(ageTextBox.Text, age)
    registered = registeredTextBox.Text.ToUpper

    ' display appropriate message
    If age >= 18 Then
        If registered = "Y" Then
            messageLabel.Text = VoteMsg
        Else
            messageLabel.Text = RegisterMsg
        End If
    Else
        messageLabel.Text = TooYoungMsg
    End If
End Sub
```

Nested selection structure

Figure 5-2: Pseudocode and code showing the nested selection structure in the true path

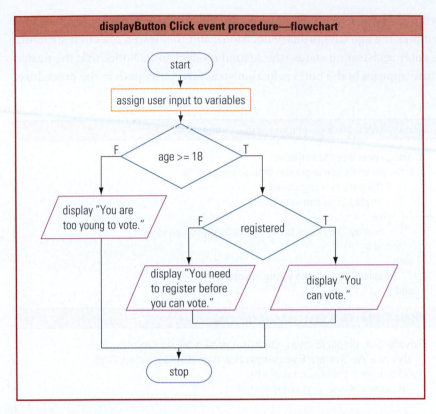

Figure 5-3: Flowchart showing the nested selection structure in the true path

The condition in the outer selection structure shown in Figures 5-2 and 5-3 checks whether the age is greater than or equal to 18. If the condition is false, it means that the person is not old enough to vote. In that case, only one message—the "You are too young to vote." message—is appropriate. After the message is displayed, both the outer selection structure and the procedure end. If the outer selection structure's condition is true, on the other hand, it means that the person *is* old enough to vote. In that case, a nested selection structure is used to determine the person's registration status. If the person is registered, the instruction in the nested selection structure's true path displays the "You can vote." message; otherwise, the instruction in the nested selection structure's false path displays the "You need to register before you can vote." message. After the appropriate message is displayed, both selection structures and the procedure end. Notice that the nested selection structure in this procedure is processed only when the outer selection structure's condition is true.

Figures 5-4 and 5-5 show the pseudocode, code, and flowchart for a different version of the displayButton's Click event procedure. As in the previous version, the outer selection structure in this version determines the age (the primary decision), and the nested selection structure determines the voter registration status (the secondary decision). In this version of the procedure, however, the nested selection structure appears in the false path of the outer selection structure. Both versions of the displayButton's Click event procedure produce the same results. Neither version is better than the other; each simply represents a different way of solving the same problem.

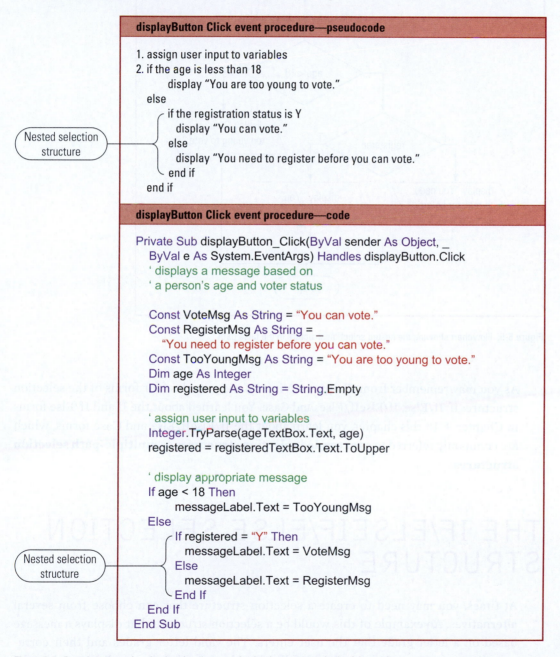

displayButton Click event procedure—pseudocode

```
1. assign user input to variables
2. if the age is less than 18
        display "You are too young to vote."
    else
        if the registration status is Y
          display "You can vote."
        else
          display "You need to register before you can vote."
        end if
    end if
```

Nested selection structure

displayButton Click event procedure—code

```
Private Sub displayButton_Click(ByVal sender As Object, _
    ByVal e As System.EventArgs) Handles displayButton.Click
    ' displays a message based on
    ' a person's age and voter status

    Const VoteMsg As String = "You can vote."
    Const RegisterMsg As String = _
      "You need to register before you can vote."
    Const TooYoungMsg As String = "You are too young to vote."
    Dim age As Integer
    Dim registered As String = String.Empty

    ' assign user input to variables
    Integer.TryParse(ageTextBox.Text, age)
    registered = registeredTextBox.Text.ToUpper

    ' display appropriate message
    If age < 18 Then
        messageLabel.Text = TooYoungMsg
    Else
        If registered = "Y" Then
          messageLabel.Text = VoteMsg
        Else
          messageLabel.Text = RegisterMsg
        End If
    End If
End Sub
```

Nested selection structure

Figure 5-4: Pseudocode and code showing the nested selection structure in the false path

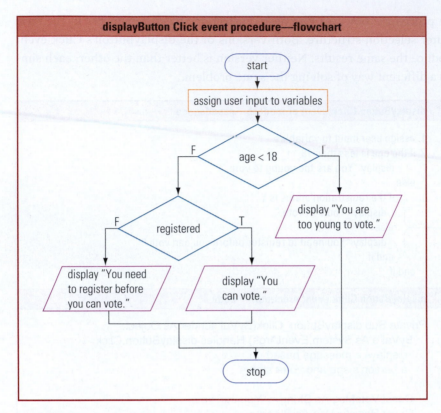

displayButton Click event procedure—flowchart

start

assign user input to variables

age < 18

display "You are too young to vote."

registered

display "You need to register before you can vote."

display "You can vote."

stop

Figure 5-5: Flowchart showing the nested selection structure in the false path

As you may remember from Chapter 4, Visual Basic provides four forms of the selection structure: If, If/Else, If/ElseIf/Else, and Case. You learned about the If and If/Else forms in Chapter 4. In this chapter, you learn about the If/ElseIf/Else and Case forms, which are commonly referred to as **extended selection structures** or **multiple-path selection structures**.

THE IF/ELSEIF/ELSE SELECTION STRUCTURE

At times, you may need to create a selection structure that can choose from several alternatives. An example of this would be a selection structure that displays a message based on a letter grade that the user enters. The valid letter grades and their corresponding messages are shown in the following chart. As the chart indicates, when the letter grade is an A, the selection structure should display the message "Excellent." When the letter grade is a B, the selection structure should display the message "Above Average," and so on.

Letter grade	Message
A	Excellent
B	Above Average
C	Average
D	Below Average
F	Below Average

Figure 5-6 shows a sample run of the Grade Message application, and Figure 5-7 shows two versions of the code for the messageButton's Click event procedure. The first version uses nested If/Else structures to display the appropriate message, while the second version uses the If/ElseIf/Else structure. Although you can write the procedure using the code shown in either version, the If/ElseIf/ Else structure provides a much more convenient way of writing a multiple-path selection structure.

Figure 5-6: Sample run of the Grade Message application

Version 1—nested If/Else structures

```
Private Sub messageButton_Click(ByVal sender As Object, _
    ByVal e As System.EventArgs) Handles messageButton.Click
    ' displays a message corresponding to a grade

    Dim grade As String = String.Empty

    ' display appropriate message
    grade = gradeTextBox.Text.ToUpper
    If grade = "A" Then
        msgLabel.Text = "Excellent"
```

Figure 5-7: Two versions of the messageButton's Click event procedure (*continued on next page*)

```
        Else
            If grade = "B" Then
                msgLabel.Text = "Above Average"
            Else
                If grade = "C" Then
                    msgLabel.Text = "Average"
                Else
                    If grade = "D" OrElse grade = "F" Then
                        msgLabel.Text = "Below Average"
                    Else
                        msgLabel.Text = "Error"
                    End If
                End If
            End If
        End If
End Sub
```

Requires four End If clauses (connected to the four End If lines above)

Version 2—If/ElseIf/Else structure

```
Private Sub messageButton_Click(ByVal sender As Object, _
    ByVal e As System.EventArgs) Handles messageButton.Click
    ' displays a message corresponding to a grade

    Dim grade As String = String.Empty

    ' display appropriate message
    grade = gradeTextBox.Text.ToUpper
    If grade = "A" Then
        msgLabel.Text = "Excellent"
    ElseIf grade = "B" Then
        msgLabel.Text = "Above Average"
    ElseIf grade = "C" Then
        msgLabel.Text = "Average"
    ElseIf grade = "D" OrElse grade = "F" Then
        msgLabel.Text = "Below Average"
    Else
        msgLabel.Text = "Error"
    End If
End Sub
```

Requires only one End If clause (connected to the End If line above)

Figure 5-7: Two versions of the messageButton's Click event procedure (*continued from previous page*)

THE CASE SELECTION STRUCTURE

In situations where the selection structure has many paths from which to choose, it is often simpler and clearer to use the Case form of the selection structure rather than the If/ElseIf/Else form. Figures 5-8 and 5-9 show the pseudocode and flowchart for the messageButton's Click event procedure, using the Case selection structure. The flowchart symbol for the Case form of the selection structure is the same as the flowchart symbol for the If, If/Else, and If/ElseIf/Else forms: a diamond. However, unlike the diamonds used in the other selection structures, the Case diamond does not contain a condition requiring a true or false answer. Instead, the Case diamond contains an expression whose value determines which path is chosen. In Figure 5-9, the expression is *grade*. Like the If, If/Else, and If/ElseIf/Else diamonds, the Case diamond has one flowline leading into the symbol. Unlike the other diamonds, however, the Case diamond has many flowlines leading out of the symbol. Each flowline represents a possible path for the selection structure. The flowlines must be marked appropriately, indicating which value(s) are necessary for each path to be chosen.

messageButton Click event procedure—pseudocode
1. assign user input to variables
2. grade value:

A	display "Excellent"
B	display "Above Average"
C	display "Average"
D, F	display "Below Average"
Other	display "Error"

Figure 5-8: Pseudocode showing the Case selection structure

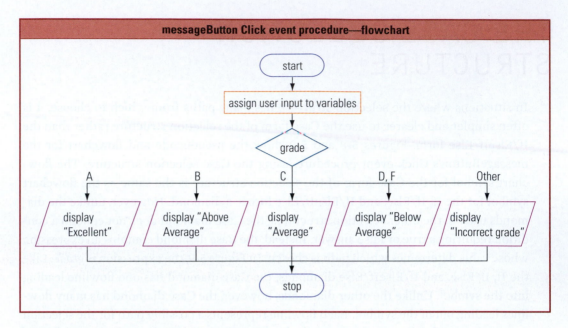

Figure 5-9: Flowchart showing the Case selection structure

You use the **Select Case statement** to code the Case selection structure in Visual Basic. Figure 5-10 shows the statement's syntax. It also shows how to use the statement to code the messageButton's Click event procedure. As the figure indicates, the Select Case statement begins with the keywords Select Case, followed by a *selectorExpression*. The *selectorExpression* can contain any combination of variables, constants, methods, operators, and properties. In the procedure shown in Figure 5-10, the *selectorExpression* is a String variable named grade. The Select Case statement ends with the End Select clause. Between the Select Case and End Select clauses are the individual Case clauses. Each Case clause represents a different path that the computer can follow. It is customary to indent each Case clause, as well as the instructions within each Case clause, as shown in the figure. You can have as many Case clauses as necessary in a Select Case statement. However, if the Select Case statement includes a Case Else clause, the Case Else clause must be the last clause in the statement. Each of the individual Case clauses, except the Case Else clause, must contain an *expressionList*, which can include one or more expressions. To include more than one expression in an *expressionList*, you separate each expression with a comma, as in the *expressionList* Case "D", "F". The *selectorExpression* needs to match only one of the expressions listed in an *expressionList*. The data type of the expressions must be compatible with the data type of the *selectorExpression*. In other words, if the *selectorExpression* is numeric, the expressions in the Case clauses should be numeric. Likewise, if the *selectorExpression* is a string, the expressions should be strings. In the procedure shown in Figure 5-10, the *selectorExpression* (grade) is a string, and so are the expressions—"A", "B", "C", "D", and "F".

USE THE SELECT CASE STATEMENT

Syntax

Select Case *selectorExpression*
    Case *expressionList1*
        [*instructions for the first Case*]
    [**Case** *expressionList2*
        [*instructions for the second Case*]]
    [**Case** *expressionListn*]
        [*instructions for the nth case*]]
    [**Case Else**
        [*instructions for when the selectorExpression does not match any of the expressionLists*]]
End Select

Example

```
Private Sub messageButton_Click(ByVal sender As Object, _
    ByVal e As System.EventArgs) Handles messageButton.Click
    ' displays a message corresponding to a grade

    Dim grade As String = String.Empty

    ' display appropriate message
    grade = gradeTextBox.Text.ToUpper
    Select Case grade
        Case "A"
            msgLabel.Text = "Excellent"
        Case "B"
            msgLabel.Text = "Above Average"
        Case "C"
            msgLabel.Text = "Average"
        Case "D", "F"
            msgLabel.Text = "Below Average"
        Case Else
            msgLabel.Text = "Error"
    End Select
End Sub
```

Figure 5-10: How to use the Select Case statement

When processing the Select Case statement, the computer first compares the value of the *selectorExpression* with the values listed in *expressionList1*. If a match is found, the computer processes the instructions for the first Case, stopping when it reaches either another Case clause or the End Select clause. It then skips to the instruction following the End Select clause. If a match is not found in *expressionList1*, the computer skips to the second Case clause, where it compares the *selectorExpression* with the values listed in *expressionList2*. If a match is found, the computer processes the instructions for the second Case clause and then skips to the instruction following the End Select clause. If a match is not found, the computer skips to the third Case clause, and so on. If the *selectorExpression* does not match any of the values listed in any of the *expressionLists*, the computer processes the instructions listed in the Case Else clause or, if there is no Case Else clause, it processes the instruction following the End Select clause. Keep in mind that if the *selectorExpression* matches a value in more than one Case clause, only the instructions in the first match are processed.

SPECIFYING A RANGE OF VALUES IN AN EXPRESSIONLIST

You also can specify a range of values in an *expressionList*, such as the values 1 through 4 or values greater than 10. You do this using either the keyword To or the keyword Is. You use the To keyword when you know both the upper and lower bounds of the range, and you use the Is keyword when you know only one end of the range (either the upper or lower end). To illustrate this concept, the price of an item sold by ABC Corporation depends on the number of items ordered, as shown in Figure 5-11. The figure also shows the code for the displayPriceButton's Click event procedure, which displays the appropriate price per item. According to the price chart, the price for 1 to 5 items is $25 each. Therefore, you could have written the first Case clause in the procedure as Case 1, 2, 3, 4, 5. However, a more convenient way of writing that range of numbers is to use the keyword To, but you must follow this syntax to do so: **Case** *smallest value in the range* **To** *largest value in the range*. For instance, the expression 1 To 5 in the first Case clause specifies the range of numbers from 1 to 5, inclusive. The expression 6 To 10 in the second Case clause specifies the range of numbers from 6 to 10, inclusive. Notice that both Case clauses state both the lower (1 and 6) and upper (5 and 10) ends of each range. The third Case clause in the procedure, Case Is > 10, contains the Is keyword rather than the To keyword. Recall that you use the Is keyword when you know only one end of the range of values—either the upper end or the lower end. In this case you know only the lower end of the range, 10. You always use the Is keyword in combination with one of the following comparison (relational) operators: =, <, <=, >, >=, <>. The Case Is > 10 clause specifies all numbers greater than the number 10. Because numberOrdered is an Integer variable, you also can write this Case clause as Case Is >= 11. The Case Else clause in the procedure is processed only when the numberOrdered variable contains a value that is not included in any of the previous Case clauses—more specifically, a zero or a negative number.

ABC Corporation price chart	
<u>Number of items ordered</u>	<u>Price per item</u>
1–5	$ 25
6–10	$ 23
More than 10	$ 20

displayPriceButton Click event procedure—code

```
Private Sub displayPriceButton_Click(ByVal sender As Object,_
    ByVal e As System.EventArgs) Handles displayPriceButton.Click
    ' displays the price per item

    Dim numberOrdered As Integer
    Dim itemPrice As Integer

    ' assign user input to a variable
    Integer.TryParse(numberTextBox.Text, numberOrdered)

    ' determine the price per item
    Select Case numberOrdered
        Case 1 To 5
            itemPrice = 25
        Case 6 To 10
            itemPrice = 23
        Case Is > 10
            itemPrice = 20
        Case Else
            itemPrice = 0
    End Select

    ' display the price per item, then set the focus
    priceLabel.Text = itemPrice.ToString("C2")
    numberTextBox.Focus()
End Sub
```

Figure 5-11: Example of using the To and Is keywords in a Select Case statement

> **» TIP**
>
> No error message appears when the value preceding the To in a Case clause is greater than the value following the To. Instead, the Case clause will not work correctly. This is another example of the importance of testing your code thoroughly.

USING RADIO BUTTONS

The If/ElseIf/Else and Case forms of the selection structure are often used when coding interfaces that contain radio buttons. A **radio button** is created using the RadioButton tool in the toolbox, and it allows you to limit the user to only one choice in a group of two or more related but mutually exclusive choices. Figure 5-12 shows a sample run of the Gentry Supplies application, which uses radio buttons in its interface. Notice that each radio button is labeled so that the user knows its purpose. You enter the label using sentence capitalization in the radio button's Text property. Each radio button also has a unique access key that allows the user to select the button using the keyboard.

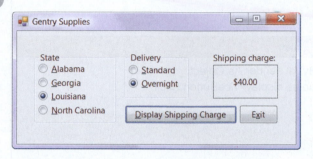

Figure 5-12: Sample run of the Gentry Supplies application

Two groups of radio buttons appear in the Gentry Supplies interface: one group contains the four state radio buttons, and the other contains the two delivery radio buttons. To include two groups of radio buttons in an interface, at least one of the groups must be placed within a container, such as a group box, panel, or table layout panel. Otherwise, the radio buttons are considered to be in the same group and only one can be selected at any one time. In this case, the radio buttons pertaining to the state choice are contained in the GroupBox1 control, and the radio buttons pertaining to the delivery choice are contained in the GroupBox2 control. You create a group box using the GroupBox tool in the toolbox. Placing each group of radio buttons in a separate group box allows the user to select one button from each group. Keep in mind that the minimum number of radio buttons in a group is two, because the only way to deselect a radio button is to select another radio button. The recommended maximum number of radio buttons in a group is seven. It is customary in Windows applications to have one of the radio buttons in each group already selected when the user interface first appears. The selected button is called the **default radio button** and is either the radio button that represents the user's most likely choice or the first radio button in the group. You designate a radio button as the default radio button by setting the button's Checked property to the Boolean value True. When you set the Checked property to True in the Properties window, a black dot appears inside the button's circle to indicate that the button is selected.

When the user clicks the Display Shipping Charge button in the Gentry Supplies interface, the button's Click event procedure should calculate and display the appropriate shipping charge, using the information shown in the following chart. Figure 5-13 shows two versions of the code that will accomplish this task. Notice that the code uses the Checked property to determine the radio button selected in the State group, as well as the radio button selected in the Delivery group.

State	Standard delivery charge
Alabama	20
Georgia	35
Louisiana	30
North Carolina	28
Overnight delivery	add $10 to the standard delivery charge

Version 1—using the If/ElseIf/Else structure

```
Private Sub displayButton_Click(ByVal sender As Object, _
    ByVal e As System.EventArgs) Handles displayButton.Click
    ' displays the appropriate shipping charge

    Dim shipCharge As Integer

    ' determine state shipping charge
    If alabamaRadioButton.Checked Then
        shipCharge = 20
    ElseIf georgiaRadioButton.Checked Then
        shipCharge = 35
    ElseIf louisianaRadioButton.Checked Then
        shipCharge = 30
    Else
        shipCharge = 28
    End If

    ' add $10 for overnight delivery
    If overnightRadioButton.Checked Then
        shipCharge = shipCharge + 10
    End If

    ' display shipping charge
    shipLabel.Text = shipCharge.ToString("C2")
End Sub
```

Figure 5-13: The displayButton's Click event procedure (*continued on next page*)

```
Version 2—using the Case structure

Private Sub displayButton_Click(ByVal sender As Object, _
    ByVal e As System.EventArgs) Handles displayButton.Click
    ' displays the appropriate shipping charge

    Dim shipCharge As Integer

    ' determine state shipping charge
    Select Case True
        Case alabamaRadioButton.Checked
            shipCharge = 20
        Case georgiaRadioButton.Checked
            shipCharge = 35
        Case louisianaRadioButton.Checked
            shipCharge = 30
        Case Else
            shipCharge = 28
    End Select

    ' add $10 for overnight delivery
    If overnightRadioButton.Checked Then
        shipCharge = shipCharge + 10
    End If

    ' display shipping charge
    shipLabel.Text = shipCharge.ToString("C2")
End Sub
```

Figure 5-13: The displayButton's Click event procedure (*continued from previous page*)

THE MESSAGEBOX.SHOW METHOD

At times, an application may need to communicate with the user while it is running. For instance, before calculating an employee's gross pay, the application should alert the user when the hoursTextBox does not contain any data. One means of communicating with the user is through a message box. You display the message box using the **MessageBox.Show method**. The message box contains text, one or more buttons, and an icon. Figure 5-14 shows the syntax of the MessageBox.Show method. It also lists the meaning of each argument used by the method, and includes two examples of using the method to create a message box. Figures 5-15 and 5-16 show the message boxes created by the two examples.

USE THE MESSAGEBOX.SHOW METHOD

Syntax

MessageBox.Show(*text*, *caption*, *buttons*, *icon*[, *defaultButton*]**)**

Argument	Meaning
text	text to display in the message box; use sentence capitalization
caption	text (usually the application's name) to display in the title bar of the message box; use book title capitalization
buttons	buttons to display in the message box; can be one of the following constants:

MessageBoxButtons.AbortRetryIgnore
MessageBoxButtons.OK   (default setting)
MessageBoxButtons.OKCancel
MessageBoxButtons.RetryCancel
MessageBoxButtons.YesNo
MessageBoxButtons.YesNoCancel

icon	icon to display in the message box; typically, one of the following constants:

MessageBoxIcon.Exclamation ⚠
MessageBoxIcon.Information ⓘ
MessageBoxIcon.Question ❓
MessageBoxIcon.Stop ⊗

defaultButton	button automatically selected when the user presses Enter; can be one of the following constants:

MessageBoxDefaultButton.Button1 (default setting)
MessageBoxDefaultButton.Button2
MessageBoxDefaultButton.Button3

Example 1

MessageBox.Show("Record deleted.", "Payroll", _
    MessageBoxButtons.OK, MessageBoxIcon.Information)

displays an informational message box that contains the message "Record deleted."

Example 2

MessageBox.Show("Delete this record?", "Payroll", _
    MessageBoxButtons.YesNo, MessageBoxIcon.Exclamation, _
    MessageBoxDefaultButton.Button2)

displays a warning message box that contains the message "Delete this record?"

Figure 5-14: How to use the MessageBox.Show method

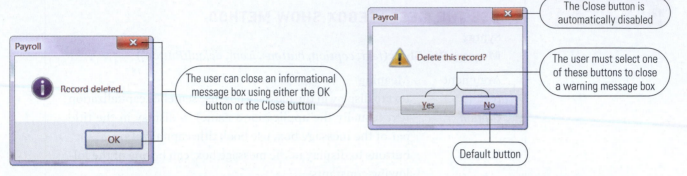

Figure 5-15: Message box displayed by Example 1 in Figure 5-14

Figure 5-16: Message box displayed by Example 2 in Figure 5-14

After displaying the message box, the MessageBox.Show method waits for the user to choose one of the buttons. It then closes the message box and returns an integer that indicates the button chosen by the user. Sometimes you are not interested in the value returned by the MessageBox.Show method. This is the case when the message box is for informational purposes only, like the message box shown in Figure 5-15. Many times, however, the button selected by the user determines the next task performed by an application. For example, selecting the Yes button in the message box shown in Figure 5-16 tells the application to delete the record, whereas selecting the No button tells the application not to delete the record. Figure 5-17 lists the integer values returned by the MessageBox.Show method. Each value is associated with a button that can appear in a message box. The figure also lists the DialogResult values assigned to each integer, and the meaning of the integers and DialogResult values. As the figure indicates, the MessageBox.Show method returns the integer 6 when the user selects the Yes button. The integer 6 is represented by the DialogResult value, Windows.Forms.DialogResult.Yes. When referring to the method's return value in code, you should use the DialogResult values rather than the integers, because the values make the code easier to understand. Figure 5-17 also contains two examples of using the value returned by the MessageBox.Show method. In the first example, the return value is assigned to a DialogResult variable named button. The selection structure in the example compares the contents of the button variable to the Windows.Forms.DialogResult.Yes value. In the second example, the method's return value is not stored in a variable. Instead, the method appears in the selection structure's condition, where its return value is compared to the Windows.Forms.DialogResult.Yes value. The selection structure in the second example performs one set of tasks when the user selects the Yes button in the message box, and another set of tasks when the user selects the No button. It is a good programming practice to document the Else portion of the selection structure as shown in the figure, because it makes it clear that the Else portion is processed only when the user selects the No button.

USE THE VALUE RETURNED BY THE MESSAGEBOX.SHOW METHOD

Number	DialogResult Value	Meaning
1	Windows.Forms.DialogResult.OK	user chose the OK button
2	Windows.Forms.DialogResult.Cancel	user chose the Cancel button
3	Windows.Forms.DialogResult.Abort	user chose the Abort button
4	Windows.Forms.DialogResult.Retry	user chose the Retry button
5	Windows.Forms.DialogResult.Ignore	user chose the Ignore button
6	Windows.Forms.DialogResult.Yes	user chose the Yes button
7	Windows.Forms.DialogResult.No	user chose the No button

Example 1

```
Dim button As DialogResult
button = MessageBox.Show("Delete this record?", _
    "Payroll", MessageBoxButtons.YesNo, _
    MessageBoxIcon.Exclamation, _
    MessageBoxDefaultButton.Button2)
If button = Windows.Forms.DialogResult.Yes Then
    instructions to delete the record
End If
```

Example 2

```
If MessageBox.Show("Play another game?", _
    "Math Monster", MessageBoxButtons.YesNo, _
    MessageBoxIcon.Exclamation) = _
    Windows.Forms.DialogResult.Yes Then
    instructions to start another game
Else    ' No button
    instructions to close the game application
End If
```

Figure 5-17: How to use the value returned by the MessageBox.Show method

The last topic covered in this chapter is the KeyPress event, which you can use to prevent a text box from accepting an inappropriate character. You will use the KeyPress event in this chapter's Programming Example.

CODING THE KEYPRESS EVENT

Earlier, in Figure 5-1, you viewed a sample run of the Voter Eligibility application, which provides text boxes for the user to enter a person's age and whether he or she is registered to vote. The user should enter the age as an integer. The age should not contain any letters, punctuation marks, or special characters. For the registration information, the user should enter only the letter Y (in either uppercase or lowercase) or the letter N (in either uppercase or lowercase). Unfortunately, you can't stop the user from trying to enter an inappropriate character into a text box. However, you can prevent the text box from accepting the character; you do this by coding the text box's KeyPress event procedure. A control's **KeyPress event** occurs each time the user presses a key while the control has the focus. When the KeyPress event occurs, a character corresponding to the pressed key is sent to the KeyPress event's e parameter, which appears between the parentheses in the event's procedure header. For example, when the user presses the period while entering data into a text box, the text box's KeyPress event occurs and a period is sent to the event's e parameter. Similarly, when the Shift key along with a letter is pressed, the uppercase version of the letter is sent to the e parameter. To prevent a text box from accepting an inappropriate character, you first use the e parameter's **KeyChar property** to determine the pressed key. (KeyChar stands for "key character.") You then use the e parameter's **Handled property** to cancel the key if it is an inappropriate one. You cancel the key by setting the Handled property to True, like this: e.Handled = True. Figure 5-18 shows examples of using the KeyChar and Handled properties in the KeyPress event procedure. Notice that you refer to the Backspace key on your keyboard using the ControlChars.Back constant.

»HOW TO . . .

USE THE KEYPRESS EVENT

<u>Example 1</u>
```
Private Sub ageTextBox_KeyPress(ByVal sender As Object, _
    ByVal e As System.Windows.Forms.KeyPressEventArgs) _
    Handles ageTextBox.KeyPress
    ' allows the text box to accept only numbers
    ' and the Backspace key for editing

    If (e.KeyChar < "0" OrElse e.KeyChar > "9") _
        AndAlso e.KeyChar <> ControlChars.Back Then
            e.Handled = True
    End If
End Sub
```

<u>Example 2</u>
```
Private Sub registeredTextBox_KeyPress(ByVal sender As Object, _
    ByVal e As System.Windows.Forms.KeyPressEventArgs) _
    Handles registeredTextBox.KeyPress
    ' allows the text box to accept only the letters
    ' Y, y, N, or n and the Backspace key for editing

    If e.KeyChar <> "Y" AndAlso e.KeyChar <> "y" _
        AndAlso e.KeyChar <> "N" AndAlso e.KeyChar <> "n" _
        AndAlso e.KeyChar <> ControlChars.Back Then
            e.Handled = True
    End If
End Sub
```

Figure 5-18: How to use the KeyPress event

You have completed the concepts section of Chapter 5.

PROGRAMMING TUTORIAL

CREATING THE ROCK, PAPER, SCISSORS GAME

In this tutorial, you create an application that simulates a game called Rock, Paper, Scissors. Typically, two people play the game. However, you will program the game so that one person can play against the computer. "Rock, Paper, Scissors" refers to the three choices each player can indicate using hand gestures. To play the game, the players face each other, call out "Rock, paper, scissors, shoot," and then make the hand gesture corresponding to their choice: a fist (rock), a flat hand (paper), or two fingers forming a V shape (scissors). The rules for determining a win are shown in the chart below. Figures 5-19 and 5-20 show the application's TOE chart and user interface.

» Rock breaks scissors, so rock wins

» Paper covers rock, so paper wins

» Scissors cut paper, so scissors wins

Task	Object	Event
1. Display the appropriate image in the playerPictureBox 2. Generate a random number from 1 to 3, inclusive 3. Use the random number to display the rock, paper, or scissors image in the computerPictureBox 4. Determine whether there is a winner and display an appropriate message in the winnerLabel	rockPictureBox, paperPictureBox, scissorsPictureBox	Click
End the application	exitButton	Click
Display a message that indicates either the winner or a tie game	winnerLabel	None
Display the image corresponding to the player's choice	playerPictureBox	None
Display the image corresponding to the computer's choice	computerPictureBox	None

Figure 5-19: TOE Chart

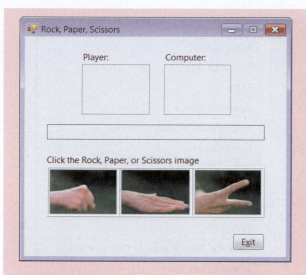

Figure 5-20: User interface

CREATING THE ROCK, PAPER, SCISSORS GAME INTERFACE

Before you can code the Rock, Paper, Scissors game, you need to create the user interface.

To create the user interface:

1. Start Visual Studio. If necessary, close the Start Page window. Create a Visual Basic Windows-based application. Name the solution, project, and form file RockPaperScissorsGame Solution, RockPaperScissorsGame Project, and Main Form.vb, respectively. Save the application in the VbReloaded2008\Chap05 folder.

2. Use the chart shown in Figure 5-21 as a guide when creating the user interface from Figure 5-20. The Rock.jpg, Paper.jpg, and Scissors.jpg image files are contained in the VbReloaded2008\Chap05 folder. The three image files were downloaded from the stock.XCHNG site and were contributed by the photographer, Laura Kennedy. You can browse and optionally download other free images at *www.sxc.hu*. Use the Edit Rows and Columns option in the TableLayoutPanel Tasks box to change the size of each column in the TableLayoutPanel1 control to 33.33%.

Object	Property	Setting
Form1	Name	MainForm
	Font	Segoe UI, 9 pt
	MaximizeBox	False
	StartPosition	CenterScreen
	Text	Rock, Paper, Scissors
TableLayoutPanel1	CellBorderStyle	OutsetDouble
	ColumnCount	3
	RowCount	1
Label1	Text	Player:
Label2	Text	Computer:
Label3	Text	Click the Rock, Paper, or Scissors image
Label4	Name	winnerLabel
	AutoSize	False
	BorderStyle	FixedSingle
	Text	(empty)
	TextAlign	MiddleCenter
PictureBox1	Name	playerPictureBox
	SizeMode	AutoSize
PictureBox2	Name	computerPictureBox
	SizeMode	AutoSize
PictureBox3	Name	rockPictureBox
	Image	Rock.jpg
	SizeMode	AutoSize
PictureBox4	Name	paperPictureBox
	Image	Paper.jpg
	SizeMode	AutoSize
PictureBox5	Name	scissorsPictureBox
	Image	Scissors.jpg
	SizeMode	AutoSize
Button1	Name	exitButton
	Text	E&xit

Figure 5-21: Objects, Properties, and Settings

3. Verify that MainForm appears as the name of the startup form in the Project Designer window, then save the solution.

CODING THE ROCK, PAPER, SCISSORS GAME

As the application's TOE chart indicates, the Click event procedures for the rockPictureBox, paperPictureBox, scissorsPictureBox, and exitButton need to be coded.

To begin coding the application:

1. Open the Code Editor window. The application will use variables, so you should enter the appropriate Option statements in the General Declarations section. Enter the comments and Option statements shown in Figure 5-22. Replace the <your name> and <current date> text with your name and the current date.

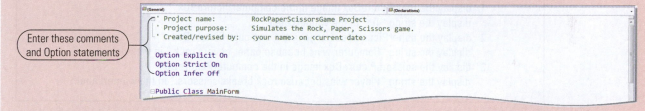

Enter these comments and Option statements

```
(General)                                                          (Declarations)
' Project name:       RockPaperScissorsGame Project
' Project purpose:    Simulates the Rock, Paper, Scissors game.
' Created/revised by: <your name> on <current date>

Option Explicit On
Option Strict On
Option Infer Off

Public Class MainForm
```

Figure 5-22: Comments and Option statements entered in the Code Editor window

2. Open the code template for the exitButton's Click event procedure. Type **me.close()** and press **Enter**.

3. Save the solution, then start the application. Now test the Exit button's code. Click the **Exit** button to end the application.

Before coding the Click event procedures for the picture boxes, study closely the chart shown in Figure 5-23. The chart indicates the combinations that can occur when playing the game, and the corresponding outcome of each combination.

Player's choice	Computer's choice	Outcome
Rock	Rock	Tie
	Paper	Computer wins because paper covers rock
	Scissors	Player wins because rock breaks scissors
Paper	Rock	Player wins because paper covers rock
	Paper	Tie
	Scissors	Computer wins because scissors cut paper
Scissors	Rock	Computer wins because rock breaks scissors
	Paper	Player wins because scissors cut paper
	Scissors	Tie

Figure 5-23: Chart showing combinations and outcomes

Now study the pseudocode shown in Figure 5-24. The pseudocode indicates the tasks to be performed by the rockPictureBox's Click event procedure.

---

rockPictureBox Click Event Procedure
1. display the player's choice, which is represented by the rockPictureBox image, in the playerPictureBox
2. generate a random number from 1 to 3, inclusive
3. use the random number to display (in the computerPictureBox) the image that represents the computer's choice, and to display the appropriate message in the winnerLabel

   random number
   1   display the rockPictureBox image in the computerPictureBox
       display the string "Tie" in the winnerLabel
   2   display the paperPictureBox image in the computerPictureBox
       display the string "Computer wins because paper covers rock." in the winnerLabel
   3   display the scissorsPictureBox image in the computerPictureBox
       display the string "Player wins because rock breaks scissors." in the winnerLabel

---

Figure 5-24: Pseudocode for the rockPictureBox's Click event procedure

To code the rockPictureBox's Click event procedure, then test the procedure's code:

1. Open the code template for the rockPictureBox's Click event procedure. Type **' displays a message indicating a "Tie" or the winner** and press **Enter** twice.

2. The procedure will use a Random object to represent the pseudo-random number generator, and an Integer variable to store the random number. Type **dim randomGenerator as new random** and press **Enter**, then type **dim computerChoice as integer** and press **Enter** twice.

3. The first step in the pseudocode is to display the rockPictureBox image, which represents the player's choice, in the playerPictureBox. Type **' display the image corresponding to the player's choice** and press **Enter**, then type **playerPictureBox.image = rockPictureBox.image** and press **Enter** twice.

4. The next step is to generate a random number from 1 to 3, inclusive. You will assign the random number to the computerChoice variable. Type the following three lines of comments:

> **' generate a random number from 1 to 3, inclusive**
>
> **' use the random number to display the image**
>
> **' corresponding to the computer's choice**

5. Press **Enter**, then type **computerChoice = randomGenerator.next(1, 4)** and press **Enter**.

6. The last step in the pseudocode is to use the random number to display the appropriate image and message in the computerPictureBox and winnerLabel, respectively. Enter the additional code shown in Figure 5-25.

```
rockPictureBox                                    ▾  ⚡ Click

    Private Sub rockPictureBox_Click(ByVal sender As Object, ByVal e As System.EventArgs) Handles rockPictureBox.Click
        ' displays a message indicating a "Tie" or the winner

        Dim randomGenerator As New Random
        Dim computerChoice As Integer

        ' display the image corresponding to the player's choice
        playerPictureBox.Image = rockPictureBox.Image

        ' generate a random number from 1 to 3, inclusive
        ' use the random number to display the image
        ' corresponding to the computer's choice
        computerChoice = randomGenerator.Next(1, 4)
        Select Case computerChoice
            Case 1
                computerPictureBox.Image = rockPictureBox.Image
                winnerLabel.Text = "Tie"
            Case 2
                computerPictureBox.Image = paperPictureBox.Image
                winnerLabel.Text = "Computer wins because paper covers rock."
            Case 3
                computerPictureBox.Image = scissorsPictureBox.Image
                winnerLabel.Text = "Player wins because rock breaks scissors."
        End Select

    End Sub
```

Enter the Select Case statement

Figure 5-25: Completed rockPictureBox's Click event procedure

7. Save the solution, then start the application. Click the **rockPictureBox** several times to verify that its Click event procedure is working properly. Figure 5-26 shows a sample run of the application. Because the procedure generates a random number for the computer's choice, your application might display a different image and message.

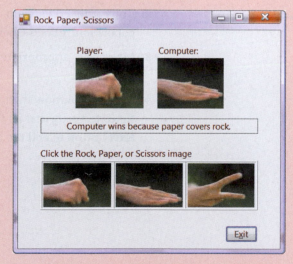

Figure 5-26: Sample run of the Rock, Paper, Scissors application

8. Click the **Exit** button to end the application.

Next, you will code the Click event procedure for the paperPictureBox. The procedure's pseudocode is shown in Figure 5-27.

---

paperPictureBox Click Event Procedure
1. display the player's choice, which is represented by the paperPictureBox image, in the playerPictureBox
2. generate a random number from 1 to 3, inclusive
3. use the random number to display (in the computerPictureBox) the image that represents the computer's choice, and to display the appropriate message in the winnerLabel

    random number
    1   display the rockPictureBox image in the computerPictureBox
        display the string "Player wins because paper covers rock." in the winnerLabel
    2   display the paperPictureBox image in the computerPictureBox
        display the string "Tie" in the winnerLabel
    3   display the scissorsPictureBox image in the computerPictureBox
        display the string "Computer wins because scissors cut paper." in the winnerLabel

---

Figure 5-27: Pseudocode for the paperPictureBox's Click event procedure

To code the paperPictureBox's Click event procedure, then test the procedure's code:

1. Open the code template for the paperPictureBox's Click event procedure.

2. Copy the code from the rockPictureBox's Click event procedure to the paperPictureBox's Click event procedure.

3. Make the appropriate modifications to the paperPictureBox's Click event procedure.

4. Save the solution, then start the application. Click the **paperPictureBox** several times to verify that its Click event procedure is working properly, then click the **Exit** button to end the application.

Finally, you will code the Click event procedure for the scissorsPictureBox. The procedure's pseudocode is shown in Figure 5-28.

---

scissorsPictureBox Click Event Procedure
1. display the player's choice, which is represented by the scissorsPictureBox image, in the playerPictureBox
2. generate a random number from 1 to 3, inclusive
3. use the random number to display (in the computerPictureBox) the image that represents the computer's choice, and to display the appropriate message in the winnerLabel

      random number
     1   display the rockPictureBox image in the computerPictureBox
         display the string "Computer wins because rock breaks scissors." in the winnerLabel
     2   display the paperPictureBox image in the computerPictureBox
         display the string "Player wins because scissors cut paper." in the winnerLabel
     3   display the scissorsPictureBox image in the computerPictureBox
         display the string "Tie" in the winnerLabel

Figure 5-28: Pseudocode for the scissorsPictureBox's Click event procedure

To code the scissorsPictureBox's Click event procedure, then test the procedure's code:

1. Open the code template for the scissorsPictureBox's Click event procedure.

2. Copy the code from the rockPictureBox's Click event procedure to the scissorsPictureBox's Click event procedure.

3. Make the appropriate modifications to the scissorsPictureBox's Click event procedure.

4. Save the solution, then start the application. Click the **scissorsPictureBox** several times to verify that its Click event procedure is working properly, then click the **Exit** button to end the application.

5. Close the Code Editor window, then close the solution. Figure 5-29 shows the application's code.

```vb
' Project name:        RockPaperScissorsGame Project
' Project purpose:     Simulates the Rock, Paper, Scissors game.
' Created/revised by:  <your name> on <current date>

Option Explicit On
Option Strict On
Option Infer Off

Public Class MainForm

    Private Sub exitButton_Click(ByVal sender As Object, _
        ByVal e As System.EventArgs) Handles exitButton.Click
        Me.Close()
    End Sub

    Private Sub rockPictureBox_Click(ByVal sender As Object, _
        ByVal e As System.EventArgs) Handles rockPictureBox.Click
        ' displays a message indicating a "Tie" or the winner

        Dim randomGenerator As New Random
        Dim computerChoice As Integer

        ' display the image corresponding to the player's choice
        playerPictureBox.Image = rockPictureBox.Image

        ' generate a random number from 1 to 3, inclusive
        ' use the random number to display the image
        ' corresponding to the computer's choice
        computerChoice = randomGenerator.Next(1, 4)
        Select Case computerChoice
            Case 1
                computerPictureBox.Image = rockPictureBox.Image
                winnerLabel.Text = "Tie"
            Case 2
                computerPictureBox.Image = paperPictureBox.Image
                winnerLabel.Text = "Computer wins because paper covers rock."
            Case 3
                computerPictureBox.Image = scissorsPictureBox.Image
                winnerLabel.Text = "Player wins because rock breaks scissors."
        End Select

    End Sub
```

Figure 5-29: Rock, Paper, Scissors application's code (*continued on next page*)

```
Private Sub paperPictureBox_Click(ByVal sender As Object, _
    ByVal e As System.EventArgs) Handles paperPictureBox.Click
    ' displays a message indicating a "Tie" or the winner

    Dim randomGenerator As New Random
    Dim computerChoice As Integer

    ' display the image corresponding to the player's choice
    playerPictureBox.Image = paperPictureBox.Image

    ' generate a random number from 1 to 3, inclusive
    ' use the random number to display the image
    ' corresponding to the computer's choice
    computerChoice = randomGenerator.Next(1, 4)
    Select Case computerChoice
        Case 1
            computerPictureBox.Image = rockPictureBox.Image
            winnerLabel.Text = "Player wins because paper covers rock."
        Case 2
            computerPictureBox.Image = paperPictureBox.Image
            winnerLabel.Text = "Tie"
        Case 3
            computerPictureBox.Image = scissorsPictureBox.Image
            winnerLabel.Text = "Computer wins because scissors cut paper."
    End Select

End Sub

Private Sub scissorsPictureBox_Click(ByVal sender As Object, _
    ByVal e As System.EventArgs) Handles scissorsPictureBox.Click
    ' displays a message indicating a "Tie" or the winner

    Dim randomGenerator As New Random
    Dim computerChoice As Integer

    ' display the image corresponding to the player's choice
    playerPictureBox.Image = scissorsPictureBox.Image

    ' generate a random number from 1 to 3, inclusive
    ' use the random number to display the image
    ' corresponding to the computer's choice
    computerChoice = randomGenerator.Next(1, 4)
```

Figure 5-29: Rock, Paper, Scissors application's code (*continued from previous page and on next page*)

```
        Select Case computerChoice
            Case 1
                computerPictureBox.Image = rockPictureBox.Image
                winnerLabel.Text = "Computer wins because rock breaks scissors."
            Case 2
                computerPictureBox.Image = paperPictureBox.Image
                winnerLabel.Text = "Player wins because scissors cut paper."
            Case 3
                computerPictureBox.Image = scissorsPictureBox.Image
                winnerLabel.Text = "Tie"
        End Select

    End Sub
End Class
```

Figure 5-29: Rock, Paper, Scissors application's code (*continued from previous page*)

PROGRAMMING EXAMPLE

CD EMPORIUM APPLICATION

Each CD at CD Emporium costs $11.99. If a customer is entitled to a discount, the discount rate is determined by the number of CDs purchased. If the customer purchases more than 3 CDs, the discount rate is 10%; otherwise, it is 5%. Create an application that allows the sales clerk to enter (in a text box) the number of CDs purchased. The text box should accept only numbers and the Backspace key. The application should use a message box to ask the sales clerk whether the customer gets a discount. The application should calculate and display the total price for the purchased CDs, as well as the discount amount. Display the total price in a label on the form. Display the discount amount in a message box. Name the solution CD Emporium Solution. Name the project CD Emporium Project. Name the form file Main Form.vb. Save the application in the VbReloaded2008\Chap05 folder. See Figures 5-30 through 5-34. Test the application using the data shown in Figure 5-30. Using the first set of test data, the application should show $0.00 and $23.98 as the discount and total price, respectively. Using the second set of test data, the application should show $1.20 and $22.78 as the discount and total price. Using the third set of test data, the application should show $4.80 and $43.16 as the discount and total price. When you are finished testing the application, stop the application and then close the solution.

Number of CDs purchased	Discount?
2	No
2	Yes
4	Yes

Task	Object	Event
1. Determine whether the customer gets a discount 2. If necessary, calculate the discount using the appropriate discount rate 3. Calculate the total price 4. Display the total price in the totalPriceLabel 5. Display the discount in a message box	calcButton	Click
End the application	exitButton	Click
Display the total price (from calcButton)	totalPriceLabel	None
Get and display the number of CDs purchased	cdsTextBox	None
Allow the text box to accept only numbers and the Backspace key		KeyPress

Figure 5-30: Test data and TOE chart

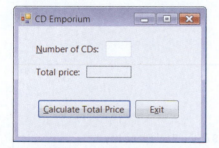

Figure 5-31: User interface

Object	Property	Setting
Form1	Name	MainForm
	AcceptButton	calcButton
	Font	Segoe UI, 9 point
	StartPosition	CenterScreen
	Text	CD Emporium
Label1	TabIndex	0
	Text	&Number of CDs:
Label2	TabIndex	4
	Text	Total price:

Figure 5-32: Objects, Properties, and Settings (*continued on next page*)

Object	Property	Setting
Label3	Name	totalPriceLabel
	AutoSize	False
	BorderStyle	FixedSingle
	TabIndex	5
	Text	(empty)
	TextAlign	MiddleCenter
TextBox1	Name	cdsTextBox
	TabIndex	1
Button1	Name	calcButton
	TabIndex	2
	Text	&Calculate Total Price
Button2	Name	exitButton
	TabIndex	3
	Text	E&xit

Figure 5-32: Objects, Properties, and Settings (*continued from previous page*)

exitButton Click Event Procedure
1. close the application

cdsTextBox KeyPress Event Procedure
1. if the user pressed a key that is not a number from 0 through 9 or the Backspace key
     cancel the key
   end if

calcButton Click Event Procedure
1. assign user input to a variable
2. subtotal = number of CDs purchased * CD price
3. ask the user whether the customer gets a discount
4. if the customer gets a discount
        if the number of CDs purchased > 3
           discount = subtotal * 10%
        else
           discount = subtotal * 5%
        end if
   end if
5. total price = subtotal − discount
6. display the total price in the totalPriceLabel
7. display the discount in a message box

Figure 5-33: Pseudocode

```
' Project name:        CD Emporium Project
' Project purpose:     Displays the discount and total price.
' Created/revised by:  <your name> on <current date>

Option Explicit On
Option Strict On
Option Infer Off

Public Class MainForm

    Private Sub exitButton_Click(ByVal sender As Object, _
        ByVal e As System.EventArgs) Handles exitButton.Click
        Me.Close()
    End Sub

    Private Sub cdsTextBox_KeyPress(ByVal sender As Object, _
        ByVal e As System.Windows.Forms.KeyPressEventArgs) _
        Handles cdsTextBox.KeyPress
        ' allows the text box to accept only numbers
        ' and the Backspace key for editing

        If (e.KeyChar < "0" OrElse e.KeyChar > "9") _
            AndAlso e.KeyChar <> ControlChars.Back Then
            e.Handled = True
        End If

    End Sub

    Private Sub calcButton_Click(ByVal sender As Object, _
        ByVal e As System.EventArgs) Handles calcButton.Click
        ' calculates and displays the
        ' discount and total price

        Const CdPrice As Double = 11.99
        Const MessageBoxTitle As String = "CD Emporium"
        Const DiscountQuestion As String = "Discount?"
        Const DiscountMessage As String = _
            "Total price includes a discount of "
        Const DiscountRate1 As Double = 0.1
        Const DiscountRate2 As Double = 0.05
```

Figure 5-34: Code (*continued on next page*)

```
        Dim numCds As Integer
        Dim subTotal As Double
        Dim discount As Double
        Dim totalPrice As Double
        Dim button As DialogResult

        ' convert user input to integer
        Integer.TryParse(cdsTextBox.Text, numCds)

        ' calculate the total before any discount
        subTotal = Convert.ToDouble(numCds) * CdPrice

        ' ask whether the customer gets a discount
        button = MessageBox.Show(DiscountQuestion, _
              MessageBoxTitle, _
              MessageBoxButtons.YesNo, _
              MessageBoxIcon.Exclamation)

        ' if the customer gets a discount, use the
        ' appropriate rate to calculate the discount
        If button = Windows.Forms.DialogResult.Yes Then
            If numCds > 3 Then
                discount = subTotal * DiscountRate1
            Else
                discount = subTotal * DiscountRate2
            End If
        End If

        ' calculate and display the total price
        totalPrice = subTotal - discount
        totalPriceLabel.Text = totalPrice.ToString("C2")

        ' display the discount
        MessageBox.Show(DiscountMessage & _
              discount.ToString("C2") & ".", _
              MessageBoxTitle, _
              MessageBoxButtons.OK, _
              MessageBoxIcon.Information)
    End Sub
End Class
```

Figure 5-34: Code (*continued from previous page*)

QUICK REVIEW

» You can nest selection structures, which means you can place one selection structure in either the true or false path of another selection structure.

» The primary decision is always made by the outer selection structure. The secondary decision is always made by the inner (nested) selection structure.

» Typically, you use the If/ElseIf/Else and Case forms of the selection structure when the structure must choose from several alternatives.

» In Visual Basic, you use the Select Case statement to code the Case form of the selection structure.

» You use the keyword To in a Case clause's *expressionList* when you know both the upper and lower bounds of the range you want to specify. You use the keyword Is when you know only one end of the range.

» You can use a radio button to limit the user to one choice from a group of two or more related but mutually exclusive choices.

» It is customary to have one radio button in each group of radio buttons selected when the user interface first appears.

» The MessageBox.Show method allows an application to communicate with the user while the application is running.

» The MessageBox.Show method displays a message box. It then returns an integer that indicates the message box button chosen by the user. You should use the DialogResult value associated with the button when referring to the integer in code.

» Use sentence capitalization for the *text* argument in the MessageBox.Show method, but book title capitalization for the *caption* argument. The name of the application typically appears in the *caption* argument.

» You can code a text box's KeyPress event procedure to prevent the text box from accepting an inappropriate character. The pressed key is stored in the event procedure's e.KeyChar property. To cancel an inappropriate character, you set the e.Handled property to False.

» In code, you refer to the Backspace key on your keyboard using the ControlChars.Back constant.

KEY TERMS

Default radio button—the radio button that is automatically selected when an interface first appears

Extended selection structures—refers to the If/ElseIf/Else and Case forms of the selection structure, because they have several alternatives from which to choose; also called multiple-path selection structures

Handled property—a property of the KeyPress event procedure's e parameter; used to cancel the key pressed by the user

KeyChar property—a property of the KeyPress event procedure's e parameter; stores the character associated with the key pressed by the user

KeyPress event—occurs each time the user presses a key while the control has the focus

MessageBox.Show method—displays a message box that contains text, one or more buttons, and an icon; allows the application to communicate with the user as it is running

Multiple-path selection structures—another term for extended selection structures

Nested selection structure—a selection structure contained in either the true or false path of another selection structure

Primary decision—when a selection structure is nested within another selection structure, the primary decision is made by the outer selection structure and determines whether the nested selection structure is processed

Radio button—used in an interface to limit the user to one choice from a group of related but mutually exclusive choices

Secondary decision—when a selection structure is nested within another selection structure, the secondary decision is made by the inner selection structure

Select Case statement—used in Visual Basic to code the Case selection structure

SELF-CHECK QUESTIONS AND ANSWERS

1. The manager of a golf club wants an application that displays the appropriate fee to charge a golfer. The club uses the fee schedule shown in the following chart. In this application, which is the primary decision and which is the secondary decision?

Fee	Criteria
0	Club members
15	Non-members golfing on Monday through Thursday
20	Non-members golfing on Friday through Sunday

2. The _____ constant refers to the Backspace key on your keyboard.

   a. Control.Back
   b. Control.Backspace

   c. ControlKey.Back
   d. None of the above.

3. A Select Case statement's *selectorExpression* is an Integer variable named colorCode. Which of the following Case clauses can be used to process the same instructions for color codes of 10 to 15, inclusive?

   a. Case 10, 11, 12, 13, 14, 15

   b. Case 15 To 10

   c. Case Is >= 10 AndAlso <= 15

   d. All of the above.

4. Which of the following statements can be used in a text box's KeyPress event to cancel the key pressed by the user?

   a. e.Cancel = True
   b. e.Handled = True

   c. e.KeyChar = True
   d. None of the above.

5. If the user clicks the Abort button in a message box, the MessageBox.Show method returns the integer 3, which is equivalent to the _____ value?

   a. Forms.DialogResult.AbortButton

   b. Windows.DialogResult.Abort

   c. Windows.Forms.Dialog.Abort

   d. Windows.Forms.DialogResult.Abort

Answers: 1) The primary decision is whether the golfer is a member. The secondary decision is the day of the week. 2) d, 3) a, 4) b, 5) d

REVIEW QUESTIONS

1. When a selection structure is nested inside another selection structure, the primary decision is always made by the _____ selection structure, while the secondary decision is always made by the _____ selection structure.

   a. inner, outer   b. outer, inner

Use the following code to answer Questions 2 through 5.

```
If num = 1 Then
    nameLabel.Text = "Janet"
ElseIf num = 2 OrElse num = 3 Then
    nameLabel.Text = "George"
ElseIf num = 4 Then
    nameLabel.Text = "Jerry"
Else
    nameLabel.Text = "Sue"
End If
```

2. What will the preceding code display when the num variable contains the number 2?

   a. Janet   b. Jerry

   c. George   d. Sue

3. What will the preceding code display when the num variable contains the number 4?

   a. Janet   b. Jerry

   c. George   d. Sue

4. What will the preceding code display when the num variable contains the number 3?

   a. Janet   b. Jerry

   c. George   d. Sue

5. What will the preceding code display when the num variable contains the number 8?

   a. Janet   b. Jerry

   c. George   d. Sue

6. A nested selection structure can appear in _____ of another selection structure.

   a. only the true path

   b. only the false path

   c. either the true path or the false path

7. If a Select Case statement's *selectorExpression* is an Integer variable named code, which of the following Case clauses is valid?

   a. Case Is > 7   b. Case 3, 5

   c. Case 1 To 4   d. All of the above.

Use the following Select Case statement to answer Questions 8 through 10.

```
Select Case num
    Case 1
        nameLabel.Text = "Janet"
    Case 2 To 4
        nameLabel.Text = "George"
    Case 5, 7
        nameLabel.Text = "Jerry"
    Case Else
        nameLabel.Text = "Sue"
End Select
```

8. What will the preceding Select Case statement display when the num variable contains the number 2?

   a. Janet   b. Jerry

   c. George   d. Sue

9. What will the preceding Select Case statement display when the num variable contains the number 3?

   a. Janet   b. Jerry

   c. George   d. Sue

10. What will the preceding Select Case statement display when the num variable contains the number 6?

    a. Janet   b. Jerry

    c. George   d. Sue

11. If the user clicks the OK button in a message box, the MessageBox.Show method returns the number 1, which is equivalent to which value?

    a. Windows.Forms.DialogResult.OK

    b. Windows.Forms.DialogResult.OKButton

    c. MessageBox.OK

    d. MessageResult.OK

12. A Select Case statement's *selectorExpression* is an Integer variable. Which of the following Case clauses tells the computer to process the instructions when the Integer variable contains one of the following numbers: 1, 2, 3, 4, or 5?

    a. Case 1, 2, 3, 4, And 5   b. Case 1 To 5

    c. Case 5 To 1   d. Both b and c.

13. A text box's _____ event occurs when a user presses a key while the text box has the focus.

    a. Key   b. KeyPress

    c. Press   d. PressKey

14. Which of the following determines whether the user pressed the $ (dollar sign) key?

    a. If ControlChars.DollarSign = True Then

    b. If e.KeyChar = "$" Then

    c. If e.KeyChar = Chars.DollarSign Then

    d. If KeyChar.ControlChars = "$" Then

REVIEW EXERCISES— SHORT ANSWER

1. Write the code to display the message "Highest honors" when a student's test score is 90 or above. When the test score is 70 through 89, display the message "Good job". For all other test scores, display the message "Retake the test". Use the If/ElseIf/Else selection structure. The test score is stored in the score variable. Display the appropriate message in the msgLabel.

2. Write the code to compare the contents of the quantity variable with the number 10. When the quantity variable contains a number that is equal to 10, display the string "Equal" in the msgLabel. When the quantity variable contains a number that is greater than 10, display the string "Over 10". When the quantity variable contains a number that is less than 10, display the string "Not over 10". Use the If/ElseIf/Else selection structure.

3. Write the code that corresponds to the flowchart shown in Figure 5-35. Store the sales-person's code, which is entered in the codeTextBox, in an Integer variable named code. Store the sales amount, which is entered in the salesTextBox, in a Double variable named sales. Display the result of the calculation, or the error message, in the msgLabel.

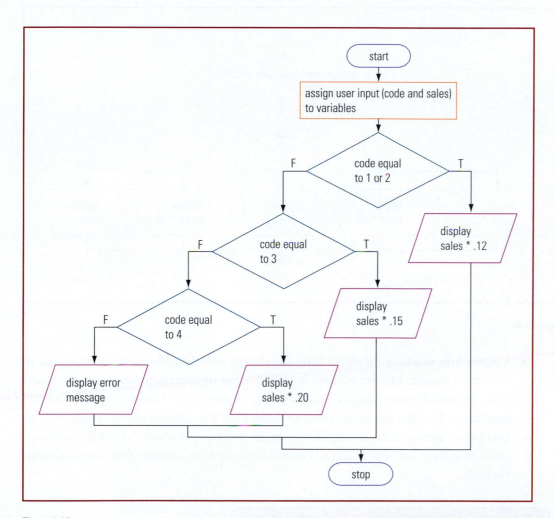

Figure 5-35

4. Write the code that corresponds to the flowchart shown in Figure 5-36. Store the salesperson's code, which is entered in the codeTextBox, in an Integer variable named code. Store the sales amount, which is entered in the salesTextBox, in a Double variable named sales. Display the result of the calculation, or the error message, in the msgLabel.

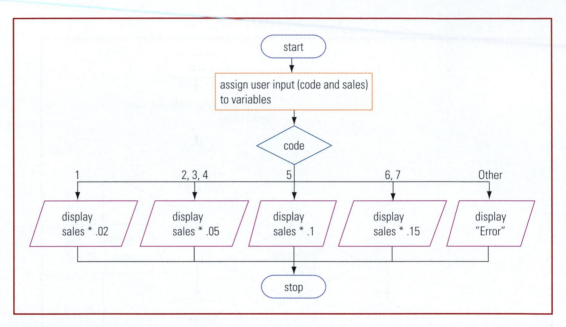

Figure 5-36

5. A procedure needs to display a shipping charge based on the state name stored in the state variable. The state name is stored using uppercase letters. Write a Select Case statement that assigns the shipping charge to a Double variable named shipCharge. Use the following chart to determine the appropriate shipping charge. Display an appropriate message in the msgLabel when the state variable contains a value that does not appear in the chart. Also assign the number 0 to the shipCharge variable.

State entered in the state variable	Shipping charge
HAWAII	$25.00
OREGON	$30.00
CALIFORNIA	$32.50

6. Rewrite the code from Review Exercise 5 using an If...Then...Else statement.

7. The price of a concert ticket depends on the seat location stored in the seatLoc variable. The seat location is stored using uppercase letters. Write a Select Case statement that displays the price in the priceLabel. Use the chart shown here to determine the appropriate price. Display an appropriate message in the priceLabel when the seatLoc variable contains a value that does not appear in the chart.

Seat location	Concert ticket price
BOX	$75.00
PAVILION	$30.00
LAWN	$21.00

8. Rewrite the code from Review Exercise 7 using an If...Then...Else statement.

COMPUTER EXERCISES

1. In this exercise, you modify the Rock, Paper, Scissors Game application from this chapter's Programming Tutorial.

   a. Use Windows to make a copy of the RockPaperScissorsGame Solution folder, which is contained in the VbReloaded2008\Chap05 folder. Rename the folder RockPaperScissorsGame Solution-Modified.

   b. Open the RockPaperScissorsGame Solution (RockPaperScissorsGame Solution.sln) file contained in the RockPaperScissorsGame Solution-Modified folder. Change the Select Case statements to If...Then...Else statements.

   c. Save the solution, then start and test the application. End the application, then close the solution.

2. In this exercise, you code an application that calculates either the sum of or the difference between two numbers.

   a. Open the AddSub Solution (AddSub Solution.sln) file, which is contained in the VbReloaded2008\Chap05\AddSub Solution folder. Set the operationTextBox's MaxLength property to 1.

   b. Open the Code Editor window and enter the appropriate comments at the beginning of the code. Also enter the appropriate Option statements.

   c. Code the exitButton's Click event procedure so that it ends the application.

   d. The operationTextBox should accept only the letters S, s, A, or a, and the Backspace key. Code the appropriate event procedure.

   e. Code the calcButton's Click event procedure.

   f. Save the solution, then start and test the application. End the application, then close the solution.

3. In this exercise, you modify the application created in Computer Exercise 2.

    a. Use Windows to make a copy of the AddSub Solution folder, which is contained in the VbReloaded2008\Chap05 folder. Rename the folder AddSub Solution-Modified.

    b. Provide the user with radio buttons, rather than a text box, for entering the mathematical operation. Make the appropriate modifications to the code.

    c. Save the solution, then start and test the application. End the application, then close the solution.

4. In this exercise, you code an application that calculates a bonus.

    a. Open the Bonus Solution (Bonus Solution.sln) file, which is contained in the VbReloaded2008\Chap05\Bonus Solution folder.

    b. The user will enter the sales amount in the salesTextBox. The sales amount will always be an integer. The salesTextBox should accept only numbers and the Backspace key. Code the appropriate event procedure.

    c. Code the calcButton's Click event procedure so that it calculates the salesperson's bonus. A salesperson selling from 0 through $3500 in product receives a 1% bonus. A salesperson selling from 3501 through 10000 in product receives a 5% bonus. A salesperson selling more than 10000 in product receives a 10% bonus. Display the bonus, formatted with a dollar sign and two decimal places, in the bonusLabel. No calculations should be made when the salesTextBox is empty; rather, display an appropriate message.

    d. Save the solution, then start and test the application. End the application, then close the solution.

5. In this exercise, you complete a procedure that calculates and displays the total amount owed by a company.

    a. Open the Seminar Solution (Seminar Solution.sln) file, which is contained in the VbReloaded2008\Chap05\Seminar Solution folder.

    b. You offer programming seminars to companies. Your price per person depends on the number of people the company registers, as shown in the chart below. (For example, if the company registers seven people, then the total amount owed is $560, which is calculated by multiplying the number 7 by the number 80.) Display the total amount owed in the totalLabel. The numberTextBox should accept only numbers and the Backspace key. No calculations should be made when the numberTextBox is empty; rather, display an appropriate message.

Number of registrants	Charge per person
1–10	$80
11–25	$70
Over 25	$65

c. Save the solution, then start and test the application. End the application, then close the solution.

6. In this exercise, you create an application for Golf Pro, a U.S. company that sells golf equipment both domestically and abroad. Each of Golf Pro's salespeople receives a commission based on the total of his or her domestic and international sales. The application you create should allow the user to enter the amount of domestic sales and the amount of international sales. It then should calculate and display the commission. Use the following information to code the application:

Sales	Commission
0–100,000	2% * sales
100,000.99–400,000	2,000 + 5% * sales over 100,000
Over 400,000	17,000 + 10% * sales over 400,000

a. Build an appropriate interface. Name the solution, project, and form file Golf Pro Solution, Golf Pro Project, and Main Form.vb. Save the application in the VbReloaded2008\Chap05 folder.

b. Code the application. Keep in mind that the sales amounts may contain decimal places.

c. Save the solution, then start and test the application. End the application, then close the solution.

7. In this exercise, you create an application for the JK Department Store. The store has five departments as shown in the following chart. Create an application that allows the user to display a department's telephone extension. Name the solution, project, and form file JK Department Store Solution, JK Department

Department	Extension
Apparel	582
Electronics	340
Small Appliances	168
Pharmacy	456
Toys	233

Store Project, and Main Form.vb. Save the application in the VbReloaded2008\Chap05 folder. Provide the user with radio buttons for selecting the department. Save the solution, then start and test the application. End the application, then close the solution.

8. In this exercise, you learn about the SelectAll method and a text box control's Enter event.

a. Open the Name Solution (Name Solution.sln) file, which is contained in the VbReloaded2008\Chap05\Name Solution folder.

b. Start the application. Type your first name in the First text box, then press Tab. Type your last name in the Last text box, then click the Concatenate Names button. Your full name appears in the fullNameLabel.

c. Press Tab twice to move the focus to the First text box. Notice that the insertion point appears after your first name in the text box. It is customary in Windows applications to have a text box's existing text selected (highlighted) when the text box receives the focus. You can select a text box's existing text by entering the text box's SelectAll method in the text box's Enter event.

d. Click the Exit button to end the application. Open the Code Editor window. Enter the SelectAll method in the Enter event procedures for the firstTextBox and lastTextBox controls. The method's syntax is *object*.**SelectAll**.

e. Save the solution, then start the application. Type your first name in the First text box, then press Tab. Enter your last name in the Last text box, then click the Concatenate Names button. Your full name appears in the fullNameLabel.

f. Press Tab twice to move the focus to the First text box. Notice that your first name is selected in the text box. Press Tab to move the focus to the Last text box. Notice that your last name is selected in the text box. End the application, then close the solution.

9. In this exercise, you practice debugging an application.

a. Open the Debug Solution (Debug Solution.sln) file, which is contained in the VbReloaded2008\Chap05\Debug Solution folder. The application should display the total amount a customer owes; however, it does not always work correctly. Open the Code Editor window and review the existing code. Start and then test the application. Make the necessary modifications to the code. When the application is working correctly, stop the application, then close the solution.

CASE PROJECTS

BARREN COMMUNITY CENTER

Create an application that displays a seminar fee, which is based on the membership status and age entered by the user. Non-members pay $20. Members who are at least 65 years old pay $5. All other members pay $10. You can either create your own user interface or create the one shown in Figure 5-37. Name the solution, project, and form file Barren Solution, Barren Project, and Main Form.vb. Save the solution in the VbReloaded2008\Chap05 folder.

Figure 5-37: Sample interface for the Barren Community Center

WILLOW HEALTH CLUB

Create an application that displays the number of daily calories needed to maintain your current weight. Name the solution, project, and form file Willow Solution, Willow Project, and Main Form.vb, respectively. Save the solution in the VbReloaded2008\ Chap05 folder. Use the following information to code the application.

Moderately active female: total daily calories = weight * 12 calories per pound

Relatively inactive female: total daily calories = weight * 10 calories per pound

Moderately active male: total daily calories = weight * 15 calories per pound

Relatively inactive male: total daily calories = weight * 13 calories per pound

JOHNSON SUPPLY

Create an application that displays the price of an order, based on the number of units ordered and the customer's status (either wholesaler or retailer). The price per unit is shown in the following chart. Name the solution, project, and form file Johnson Solution, Johnson Project, and Main Form.vb, respectively. Save the solution in the VbReloaded2008\ Chap05 folder.

Wholesaler		Retailer	
Number of units	Price per unit ($)	Number of units	Price per unit ($)
1–4	10	1–3	15
5 and over	9	4–8	14
		9 and over	12

JASON'S COFFEE SHOP

Jason's Coffee Shop sells coffee by the pound. Each pound of coffee costs $12. The coffee comes in the following flavors: Hazelnut, French Vanilla, Breakfast Blend, Mocha, and Amaretto. Create an application that displays the total pounds of coffee a customer orders, the sales tax, and the total price of the order. The user will need to enter the number of pounds of each flavor ordered by the customer. He or she will also need to specify whether the customer should be charged any sales tax and, if so, whether the tax rate should be 5% or 6%. Name the solution, project, and form file Jason Coffee Solution, Jason Coffee Project, and Main Form.vb, respectively. Save the solution in the VbReloaded2008\Chap05 folder.

6

THE DO LOOP
AND LIST BOXES

After studying Chapter 6, you should be able to:

Include the Do loop in both pseudocode and a flowchart

Write a Do...Loop statement

Initialize counters and accumulators

Display a dialog box using the InputBox function

Utilize a list box in an interface

Refresh the screen

Delay program execution

Enable and disable a control

THE REPETITION STRUCTURE

As you learned in Chapter 1, the three programming structures are sequence, selection, and repetition. Every procedure in a Visual Basic program contains the sequence structure, where the procedure instructions are processed one after another in the order they appear in the procedure. Most procedures also contain the selection structure, which you learned about in Chapters 4 and 5. Programmers use the selection structure when they need the computer to make a decision and then take the appropriate action based on the result of the decision. In addition to including the sequence and selection structures, many procedures also include the repetition structure. Programmers use the **repetition structure**, referred to more simply as a **loop**, when they need the computer to repeatedly process one or more program instructions until some condition is met, at which time the repetition structure ends. As an example, you may want to process a set of instructions—such as the instructions to calculate net pay—for each employee in a company. Or, you may want to process a set of instructions until the user enters a negative sales amount, which indicates that he or she has no more sales amounts to enter. As with the sequence and selection structures, you already are familiar with the repetition structure. An example of the repetition structure can be found on most shampoo bottles. The bottles typically direct you to repeat the "apply shampoo to hair," "lather," and "rinse" steps until your hair is clean.

A repetition structure can be either a pretest loop or a posttest loop. In both types of loops, the condition is evaluated with each repetition, or iteration, of the loop. In a **pretest loop**, the evaluation occurs *before* the instructions within the loop are processed. In a **posttest loop**, the evaluation occurs *after* the instructions within the loop are processed. Depending on the result of the evaluation, the instructions in a pretest loop may never be processed. The instructions in a posttest loop, however, always will be processed at least once. Of the two types of loops, the pretest loop is the most commonly used. You code a loop (repetition structure) in Visual Basic using one of the following statements: Do...Loop, For...Next, or For Each...Next. You learn about the Do...Loop statement in this chapter. The For...Next statement is covered in Chapter 7, and the For Each...Next statement is covered in Chapter 9.

»TIP

Pretest and posttest loops also are called top-driven and bottom-driven loops, respectively.

THE DO...LOOP STATEMENT

The **Do...Loop statement** can be used to code both a pretest loop and a posttest loop. Figure 6-1 shows two slightly different versions of the statement's syntax, along with an example of using each version to display the numbers 1, 2, and 3 in message boxes.

You use Version 1 of the syntax to code a pretest loop, and Version 2 to code a posttest loop. In both versions of the syntax, the statement begins with the Do clause and ends with the Loop clause. Between both clauses, you enter the instructions you want the computer to repeat. The {**While** | **Until**} portion of each syntax indicates that you can select only one of the keywords appearing within the braces. In this case, you can choose either the keyword While or the keyword Until. You do not type the braces ({}) or the pipe symbol (|) when entering the Do...Loop statement. You follow the While or Until keyword with a *condition*, which can contain variables, constants, properties, methods, and operators. Like the condition used in the If...Then...Else statement, the condition used in the Do...Loop statement must evaluate to a Boolean value—either True or False. The condition determines whether the computer processes the loop instructions. The keyword While indicates that the loop instructions should be processed *while* the condition is true. The keyword Until, on the other hand, indicates that the loop instructions should be processed *until* the condition becomes true. Notice that the keyword (either While or Until) and the condition appear in the Do clause in a pretest loop, but they appear in the Loop clause in a posttest loop.

» HOW TO . . .

USE THE DO...LOOP STATEMENT

Do...Loop syntax (pretest loop)

Do {While | Until} *condition*

[*instructions to be processed either while the condition is true or until the condition becomes true*]

Loop

Pretest loop example

```
Dim number As Integer = 1
Do While number <= 3
    MessageBox.Show(number.ToString)
    number = number + 1
Loop
```

Figure 6-1: How to use the Do...Loop statement (*continued on next page*)

»TIP

You can use the Exit Do statement to exit the Do...Loop statement prematurely, which means to exit it before the loop has finished processing. You may need to do this if the loop encounters an error when processing its instructions.

»TIP

You can nest Do...Loop statements, which means you can place one Do...Loop statement within another Do...Loop statement.

Do...Loop syntax (posttest loop)

Do

   [*instructions to be processed either while the condition is true or until the*
      condition becomes true]

Loop {**While** | **Until**} *condition*

Posttest loop example

Dim number As Integer = 1
Do
      MessageBox.Show(number.ToString)
      number = number + 1
Loop Until number > 3

Figure 6-1: How to use the Do...Loop statement (*continued from previous page*)

Figures 6-2 and 6-3 describe the way the computer processes the code shown in the examples in Figure 6-1.

Processing steps for the pretest loop example

1. The computer creates the number variable and initializes it to 1.
2. The computer processes the Do clause, which checks whether the value in the number variable is less than or equal to 3. It is.
3. The MessageBox.Show method displays 1 (the contents of the number variable).
4. The number = number + 1 statement adds 1 to the contents of the number variable, giving 2.
5. The computer processes the Loop clause, which returns processing to the Do clause (the beginning of the loop).
6. The computer processes the Do clause, which checks whether the value in the number variable is less than or equal to 3. It is.
7. The MessageBox.Show method displays 2 (the contents of the number variable).
8. The number = number + 1 statement adds 1 to the contents of the number variable, giving 3.
9. The computer processes the Loop clause, which returns processing to the Do clause (the beginning of the loop).
10. The computer processes the Do clause, which checks whether the value in the number variable is less than or equal to 3. It is.
11. The MessageBox.Show method displays 3 (the contents of the number variable).
12. The number = number + 1 statement adds 1 to the contents of the number variable, giving 4.
13. The computer processes the Loop clause, which returns processing to the Do clause (the beginning of the loop).
14. The computer processes the Do clause, which checks whether the value in the number variable is less than or equal to 3. It isn't, so the computer stops processing the Do...Loop statement. Processing continues with the statement following the Loop clause.

Figure 6-2: Processing steps for the pretest loop example shown in Figure 6-1

Processing steps for the posttest loop example

1. The computer creates the number variable and initializes it to 1.
2. The computer processes the Do clause, which marks the beginning of the loop.
3. The MessageBox.Show method displays 1 (the contents of the number variable).
4. The number = number + 1 statement adds 1 to the contents of the number variable, giving 2.
5. The computer processes the Loop clause, which checks whether the value in the number variable is greater than 3. It isn't, so processing returns to the Do clause (the beginning of the loop).
6. The MessageBox.Show method displays 2 (the contents of the number variable).
7. The number = number + 1 statement adds 1 to the contents of the number variable, giving 3.
8. The computer processes the Loop clause, which checks whether the value in the number variable is greater than 3. It isn't, so processing returns to the Do clause (the beginning of the loop).
9. The MessageBox.Show method displays 3 (the contents of the number variable).
10. The number = number + 1 statement adds 1 to the contents of the number variable, giving 4.
11. The computer processes the Loop clause, which checks whether the value in the number variable is greater than 3. It is, so the computer stops processing the Do…Loop statement. Processing continues with the statement following the Loop clause.

Figure 6-3: Processing steps for the posttest loop example shown in Figure 6-1

Figure 6-4 shows the flowchart and pseudocode associated with the pretest loop example in Figure 6-1. Figure 6-5 shows the flowchart and pseudocode for the posttest loop example.

Pretest loop's pseudocode and flowchart

1. assign 1 to the number variable
2. repeat while the value in the number variable is less than or equal to 3
       display the contents of the number variable
       add 1 to the number variable
   end repeat

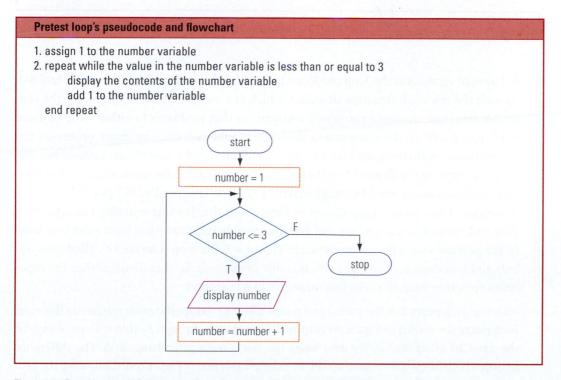

Figure 6-4: Pseudocode and flowchart for the pretest loop example shown in Figure 6-1

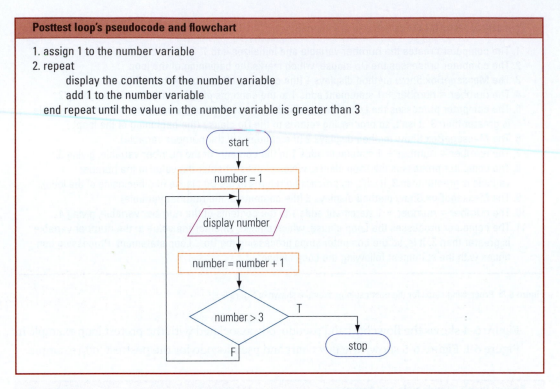

Posttest loop's pseudocode and flowchart

1. assign 1 to the number variable
2. repeat
      display the contents of the number variable
      add 1 to the number variable
    end repeat until the value in the number variable is greater than 3

Figure 6-5: Pseudocode and flowchart for the posttest loop example shown in Figure 6-1

A diamond represents the loop condition in the flowcharts shown in Figures 6-4 and 6-5. As with the selection structure diamond, which you learned about in Chapter 4, the repetition structure diamond contains a comparison that evaluates to either True or False only. The result of the comparison determines whether the computer processes the instructions within the loop. Like the selection diamond, the repetition diamond has one flowline entering the diamond and two flowlines leaving the diamond. The two flowlines leaving the diamond should be marked with a "T" (for True) and an "F" (for False). In the flowchart of the pretest loop shown in Figure 6-4, the flowline entering the repetition diamond, as well as the symbols and flowlines within the True path, form a circle or loop. In the posttest loop's flowchart shown in Figure 6-5, the loop is formed by all of the symbols and flowlines in the False path. It is this loop, or circle, that distinguishes the repetition structure from the selection structure in a flowchart.

Although it appears that the pretest and posttest loops produce the same results—in this case, both examples shown in Figure 6-1 display the numbers 1 through 3—that will not always be the case. In other words, the two loops are not always interchangeable. The difference between both loops is demonstrated in the examples shown in Figure 6-6. Comparing the processing steps listed in both examples, you will notice that the instructions in the pretest loop are not processed. The instructions aren't processed because the number <= 3 condition, which is evaluated *before* the instructions are processed, evaluates to False. The instructions in the posttest loop, on the other hand, are processed once; this is because the number > 3 condition is evaluated *after* (rather than before) the loop instructions are processed.

Pretest loop example and processing steps

```
Dim number As Integer = 10
Do While number <= 3
      MessageBox.Show(number.ToString)
      number = number + 1
Loop
```

1. The computer creates the number variable and initializes it to 10.
2. The computer processes the Do clause, which checks whether the value in the number variable is less than or equal to 3. It isn't, so the computer stops processing the Do…Loop statement. Processing continues with the statement following the Loop clause.

Posttest loop example and processing steps

```
Dim number As Integer = 10
Do
      MessageBox.Show(number.ToString)
      number = number + 1
Loop Until number > 3
```

1. The computer creates the number variable and initializes it to 10.
2. The computer processes the Do clause, which marks the beginning of the loop.
3. The MessageBox.Show method displays 10 (the contents of the number variable).
4. The number = number + 1 statement adds 1 to the contents of the number variable, giving 11.
5. The computer processes the Loop clause, which checks whether the value in the number variable is greater than 3. It is, so the computer stops processing the Do…Loop statement. Processing continues with the statement following the Loop clause.

Figure 6-6: Examples showing that the pretest and posttest loops do not always produce the same results

USING COUNTERS AND ACCUMULATORS

Many times an application will need to display a subtotal, a total, or an average. You calculate this information using a repetition structure that includes a counter, or an accumulator, or both. A **counter** is a numeric variable used for counting something—such as the number of employees paid in a week. An **accumulator** is a numeric variable used for accumulating (adding together) something—such as the total dollar amount of a week's payroll. Two tasks

» TIP

Counters are used to answer the question, "How many?"—for example, "How many salespeople live in Virginia?" Accumulators are used to answer the question, "How much?"—for example, "How much did the salespeople sell this quarter?"

are associated with counters and accumulators: initializing and updating. **Initializing** means assigning a beginning value to the counter or accumulator. Typically, counters and accumulators are initialized to zero; however, they can be initialized to any number, depending on the value required by the application. The initialization task is performed before the loop is processed, because it needs to be performed only once. **Updating**, also called **incrementing**, means adding a number to the value stored in the counter or accumulator. The number can be either positive or negative, integer or non-integer. A counter is always incremented by a constant value—typically the number 1—whereas an accumulator is incremented by a value that varies. The assignment statement that updates a counter or an accumulator is placed within the loop in a procedure, because the update task must be performed each time the loop instructions are processed. You use a counter and an accumulator, as well as a repetition structure, in the Sales Express application, which you view later in the chapter. You also use the InputBox function, which you learn about next.

THE INPUTBOX FUNCTION

A **function** is a procedure that performs a specific task and then returns a value after completing the task. The task performed by the **InputBox function** is to display one of the standard dialog boxes available in Visual Basic. An example of a dialog box displayed by the InputBox function is shown in Figure 6-7. The dialog box contains a message, along with an OK button, a Cancel button, and an input area where the user can enter information. The value returned by the InputBox function depends on whether the user clicks the OK button, Cancel button, or Close button. If the user clicks the OK button, the InputBox function returns the value contained in the input area of the dialog box; this value is always treated as a string. However, if the user clicks either the Cancel button in the dialog box or the Close button on the dialog box's title bar, the InputBox function returns an empty (or zero-length) string.

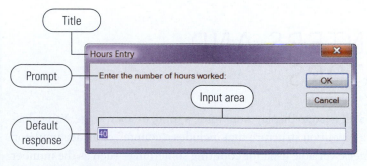

Figure 6-7: Example of a dialog box created by the InputBox function

The message that you display in the dialog box should prompt the user to enter the appropriate information in the input area of the dialog box. The user then needs to click either the OK button or the Cancel button to continue working in the application. Figure 6-8 shows the syntax of the InputBox function and includes several examples of using the function. In the syntax, *prompt* is the message to display inside the dialog box, *title* is the text to display in the dialog box's title bar, and *defaultResponse* is the text you want displayed in the input area of the dialog box. In the dialog box shown in Figure 6-7, "Enter the number of hours worked:" is the *prompt*, "Hours Entry" is the *title*, and "40" is the *defaultResponse*. When entering the InputBox function in the Code Editor window, the *prompt*, *title*, and *defaultResponse* arguments must be enclosed in quotation marks, unless that information is stored in a String named constant or String variable. The Windows standard is to use sentence capitalization for the *prompt*, but book title capitalization for the *title*. The capitalization (if any) you use for the *defaultResponse* depends on the text itself. The *title* and *defaultResponse* arguments are optional, as indicated by the square brackets in the syntax. If you omit the *title*, the project name appears in the title bar. If you omit the *defaultResponse* argument, a blank input area appears when the dialog box opens.

» TIP

You learned about both sentence and book title capitalization in Chapter 2.

» HOW TO . . .

» TIP

The InputBox function's syntax also includes XPos and YPos arguments, which allow you to specify the horizontal and vertical position of the dialog box on the screen. Both arguments are optional; if omitted, the dialog box appears centered on the screen.

USE THE INPUTBOX FUNCTION

Syntax

InputBox(prompt[, title][, defaultResponse]**)**

Example 1

firstName = InputBox("Enter your first name:")

Displays a dialog box that shows "Enter your first name:" as the prompt, the project's name as the title, and an empty input area. Assigns the user's response to a String variable named firstName.

Example 2

city = InputBox("City name:", "City")
Displays a dialog box that shows "City name:" as the prompt, "City" as the title, and an empty input area. Assigns the user's response to a String variable named city.

Figure 6-8: How to use the InputBox function (*continued on next page*)

Example 3

state = InputBox("State name:", "State", "Alaska")
Displays a dialog box that shows "State name:" as the prompt, "State" as the title, and "Alaska" in the input area. Assigns the user's response to a String variable named state.

Example 4

state = InputBox("State name:",, "Alaska")
Displays a dialog box that shows "State name:" as the prompt, the project's name as the title, and "Alaska" in the input area. Assigns the user's response to a String variable named state.

Example 5

Const InputPrompt As String = "Enter the rate:"
Const InputTitle As String = "Rate Entry"
rate = InputBox(InputPrompt, InputTitle, "0.0")
Displays a dialog box that shows the contents of the InputPrompt constant as the prompt, the contents of the InputTitle constant as the title, and "0.0" in the input area. Assigns the user's response to a String variable named rate.

Figure 6-8: How to use the InputBox function (*continued from previous page*)

Next, you view the Sales Express application, which uses the InputBox function, a pretest loop, a counter, and an accumulator.

THE SALES EXPRESS APPLICATION

Sales Express wants an application that the sales manager can use to display the average amount the company sold during the prior year. The sales manager will enter the amount of each salesperson's sales. The application will use a counter to keep track of the number of sales amounts entered by the sales manager, and an accumulator to total the sales amounts. After all of the sales amounts are entered, the application will calculate the average sales amount by dividing the value stored in the accumulator by the value stored in the counter; it then will display the average sales amount on the screen. Figure 6-9 shows the pseudocode for one possible solution to the Sales Express problem.

Pseudocode for the Sales Express application

Priming read — 1. get a sales amount from the user
2. repeat while the user entered a sales amount
        add 1 to the counter variable
        add the sales amount to the accumulator variable
        get a sales amount from the user
    end repeat
3. if the counter variable contains a value that is greater than zero
        average sales amount = accumulator variable divided by counter variable
        display the average sales amount in the averageLabel
    else
        display the number 0 in the averageLabel
    end if

Figure 6-9: Pseudocode for the Sales Express application

Step 1 in the pseudocode is to get a sales amount from the user. Step 2 is a pretest loop whose instructions are processed as long as the user enters a sales amount. The first two instructions in the loop increment the counter variable by one and increment the accumulator variable by the sales amount. The next instruction in the loop requests another sales amount from the user. The loop then checks whether a sales amount was entered; this is necessary to determine whether the loop instructions should be processed again. When the user has finished entering sales amounts, the loop ends and processing continues with Step 3 in the pseudocode. Step 3 is a selection structure that checks whether the counter variable contains a value that is greater than zero. Before using a variable as the divisor in an expression, you always should verify that the variable does not contain the number zero because, as in math, division by zero is not mathematically possible. Dividing by zero in a program will cause the program to end abruptly with an error. As Step 3 indicates, if the counter variable contains a value that is greater than zero, the average sales amount is calculated and then displayed in the averageLabel. Otherwise, the number zero is displayed in the averageLabel. Notice that "get a sales amount from the user" appears twice in the pseudocode shown in Figure 6-9: immediately above the loop and also within the loop. The "get a sales amount from the user" entry that appears above the loop is referred to as the priming read, because it is used to prime (prepare or set up) the loop. In this case, the **priming read** gets only the first salesperson's sales amount from the user. Because the loop in Figure 6-9 is a pretest loop, the first value determines whether the loop instructions are processed at all. The "get a sales amount from the user" entry that appears within the loop gets the sales amounts for the remaining salespeople (if any) from the user. Figure 6-10 shows the Sales Entry dialog box in the Sales Express application, and Figure 6-11 shows the interface after the user enters 7000, 3000, and 2000 in the dialog box and then clicks the Cancel button. Figure 6-12 shows the code entered in the calcButton's Click event procedure.

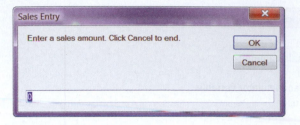

Figure 6-10: Sales Entry dialog box

Figure 6-11: Average sales amount displayed in the interface

```
Private Sub calcButton_Click(ByVal sender As Object, _
    ByVal e As System.EventArgs) Handles calcButton.Click
    ' calculates and displays the average sales amount

    Const Prompt As String = "Enter a sales amount. Click Cancel to end."
    Const Title As String = "Sales Entry"
    Dim inputSales As String = String.Empty
    Dim sales As Decimal
    Dim salesCounter As Integer
    Dim salesAccumulator As Decimal
    Dim salesAverage As Decimal

    ' get first sales amount
    inputSales = InputBox(Prompt, Title, "0")

    ' repeat as long as the user enters a sales amount
    Do While inputSales <> String.Empty
        ' convert the sales amount to a number
        Decimal.TryParse(inputSales, sales)

        ' update the counter and accumulator
        salesCounter = salesCounter + 1
        salesAccumulator = salesAccumulator + sales

        ' get the next sales amount
        inputSales = InputBox(Prompt, Title, "0")
    Loop

    ' verify that the salesCounter is greater than 0
    If salesCounter > 0 Then
        salesAverage = salesAccumulator / Convert.ToDecimal(salesCounter)
        averageLabel.Text = salesAverage.ToString("C2")
    Else
        averageLabel.Text = "$0.00"
    End If
End Sub
```

Figure 6-12: Code for the calcButton in the Sales Express application

USING A LIST BOX IN AN INTERFACE

»TIP

You can learn more about list boxes by completing Computer Exercises 14 and 15 at the end of the chapter.

The Do...Loop statement is often used to assign values to a list box control. You add a list box to an interface using the ListBox tool in the toolbox. A **list box** displays a list of choices from which the user can select zero choices, one choice, or more than one choice. The number of choices the user can select is controlled by the list box's SelectionMode property. The default value for the property is One, which allows the user to select only one choice at a time. You can make a list box any size you want. However, the Windows standard for list boxes is to display a minimum of three selections and a maximum of eight selections at a time. If you have more items than fit into the list box, the control automatically displays a scroll bar that you can use to view the complete list of items. You should use a label control to provide keyboard access to the list box. For the access key to work correctly, you must set the label's TabIndex property to a value that is one less than the list box's TabIndex value.

»TIP

If you have only two options to offer the user, you should use two radio buttons instead of a list box.

ADDING ITEMS TO A LIST BOX

The items in a list box belong to a collection called the **Items collection**. A **collection** is a group of one or more individual objects treated as one unit. The first item in the Items collection appears as the first item in the list box, the second item in the collection appears as the second item in the list box, and so on. You specify each item to display in a list box using the Items collection's **Add method**. The Add method's syntax is shown in Figure 6-13. In the syntax, *object* is the name of the control to which you want the item added, and *item* is the text you want displayed in the control. Figure 6-13 also includes two examples of using the Add method to add items to a list box. In Example 1, the Add methods add the strings "Dog", "Cat", and "Horse" to the animalListBox. In Example 2, the Add method contained in the Do...Loop statement displays the integers from 100 through 105 in the codeListBox. Notice that the ToString method is used to convert each number to the String data type before adding it to the list box. (You also could use the Convert.ToString method to convert the numbers to strings.)

» **HOW TO . . .**

ADD ITEMS TO A LIST BOX

<u>Syntax</u>

object.**Items.Add**(*item*)

<u>Example 1</u>

```
animalListBox.Items.Add("Dog")
animalListBox.Items.Add("Cat")
animalListBox.Items.Add("Horse")
```
displays Dog, Cat, and Horse in the animalListBox

<u>Example 2</u>

```
Dim code As Integer = 100
Do While code <= 105
    codeListBox.Items.Add(code.ToString)
    code = code + 1
Loop
```
displays 100, 101, 102, 103, 104, and 105 in the codeListBox

Figure 6-13: How to add items to a list box

» **TIP**

In Computer Exercise 16, you learn how to use the String Collection Editor dialog box to add items to a list box.

You typically enter a list box's Add methods in the form's Load event procedure. A form's **Load event** occurs when an application is started and the form is displayed the first time. In the Load event procedure, you enter the code you want processed before the form appears on the screen, such as the code to fill a list box with values. Figure 6-14 shows the Add methods from Figure 6-13 entered in the form's Load event procedure, and Figure 6-15 shows the animalListBox and codeListBox after the computer processes the Add methods.

```
Private Sub MainForm_Load(ByVal sender As Object, _
                ByVal e As System.EventArgs) Handles Me.Load

    ' add items to the animalListBox
    animalListBox.Items.Add("Dog")
    animalListBox.Items.Add("Cat")
    animalListBox.Items.Add("Horse")

    ' add items to the codeListBox
    Dim code As Integer = 100
    Do While code <= 105
        codeListBox.Items.Add(code.ToString)
        code = code + 1
    Loop
End Sub
```

Figure 6-14: Add methods entered in the form's Load event procedure

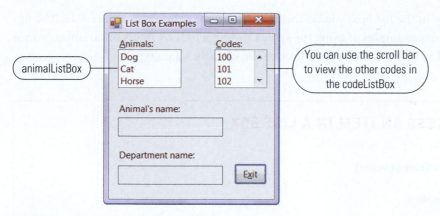

Figure 6-15: Items added to the animalListBox and codeListBox

The position of an item in the list depends on the value stored in the list box's Sorted property. When the Sorted property is set to False (the default value), the item is added at the end of the list. The Sorted property of both list boxes shown in Figure 6-15 is set to False. When the Sorted property is set to True, the item is sorted along with the existing items and then placed in its proper position in the list. The items in the animalListBox will appear in the following order when the list box's Sorted property is set to True: Cat, Dog, Horse. Visual Basic sorts the list box items in dictionary order, which means that numbers are sorted before letters, and a lowercase letter is sorted before its uppercase equivalent. The items in a list box are sorted based on the leftmost characters in each item. As a result, the items "Personnel", "Inventory", and "Payroll" will appear in the following order when the list box's Sorted property is set to True: Inventory, Payroll, Personnel. Likewise, the items 1, 2, 3, and 10 will appear in the following order: 1, 10, 2, 3. The application determines whether you display the list box items in either sorted order or the order in which they are added to the list box. If several list items are selected much more frequently than other items, you typically leave the list box's Sorted property set to False, and then add the frequently used items first so that the items appear at the beginning of the list. However, if the list box items are selected fairly equally, you typically set the list box's Sorted property to True, because it is easier to locate items when they appear in a sorted order.

ACCESSING ITEMS IN A LIST BOX

A unique number called an **index** identifies each item in a list box's Items collection. The first item in the Items collection (which also is the first item in the list box) has an index of zero. The second item has an index of one, and so on. The index allows you to access a specific item in the list box; you do this using the syntax shown in Figure 6-16. The figure also includes examples of using the syntax to assign list box items to variables. Notice that you need to convert the list box item to the variable's data type.

»HOW TO . . .

ACCESS AN ITEM IN A LIST BOX

Syntax

object.**Items**(*index*)

Example 1

Dim animalType As String = String.Empty
animalType = Convert.ToString(animalListBox.Items(0))

assigns the first item in the animalListBox to a String variable; you also can use the statement animalType = animalListBox.Items(0).ToString

Example 2

Dim code As Integer
code = Convert.ToInt32(codeListBox.Items(2))

assigns the third item in the codeListBox to an Integer variable; you also can use the statement Integer.TryParse(codeListBox.Items(2).ToString, code)

Figure 6-16: How to access an item in a list box

DETERMINING THE NUMBER OF ITEMS IN A LIST BOX

At times, you may need to determine the number of items contained in a list box. For example, you would need to know the number of items in order to search the list box, from top to bottom, looking for a specific item. The number of items in a list box is stored in the list box's Items.Count property. The property's value is always one number more than the last index in the list box; this is because the first index in a list box is zero. For example, the highest index in the animalListBox is 2, but the list box's Items.Count property contains 3. Figure 6-17 shows the syntax of the Items.Count property and includes examples of using the property. Notice that the loop instructions in Example 2 will be processed as long as the index variable contains a value that is less than the number of items in the codeListBox. This is because the codeListBox's highest index is 4, but its Items.Count property contains 5.

»HOW TO . . .

DETERMINE THE NUMBER OF ITEMS IN A LIST BOX

Syntax

object.**Items.Count**

Example 1

Dim numberOfAnimals As Integer
numberOfAnimals = animalListBox.Items.Count

assigns the number of items contained in the animalListBox to an Integer variable

Example 2

Dim numCodes As Integer
Dim index As Integer
numCodes = codeListBox.Items.Count
Do While index < numCodes
    MessageBox.Show(Convert.ToString(codeListBox.Items(index)))
    index = index + 1
Loop

displays the items contained in the codeListBox in message boxes; you also can use the statement MessageBox.Show(codeListBox.Items(index).ToString)

Figure 6-17: How to determine the number of items in a list box

THE SELECTEDITEM AND SELECTEDINDEX PROPERTIES

When you select an item in a list box, the item appears highlighted in the list, as shown in Figure 6-18. In addition, the computer stores the item's value (Dog) in the list box's SelectedItem property, and stores the item's index (0) in the list box's SelectedIndex property.

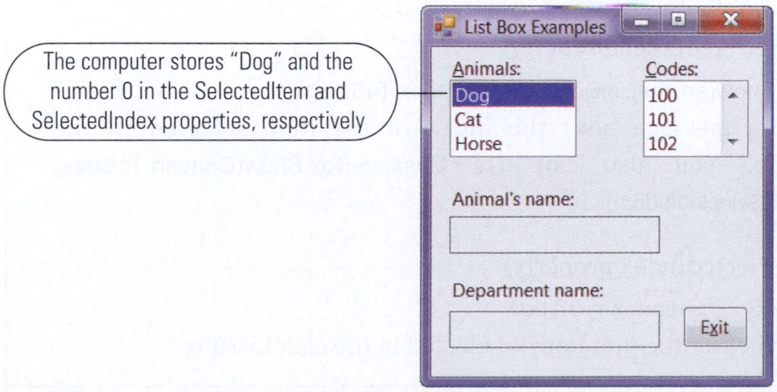

The computer stores "Dog" and the number 0 in the SelectedItem and SelectedIndex properties, respectively

Figure 6-18: Item selected in the animalListBox

You can use either the SelectedItem or SelectedIndex property to determine whether an item is selected in a list box. When no item is selected, the SelectedItem property contains the empty string, while the SelectedIndex property contains the number –1 (negative 1). Otherwise, the SelectedItem and SelectedIndex properties contain the value of the selected item and the item's index, respectively. Figure 6-19 shows examples of using the SelectedItem and SelectedIndex properties.

»HOW TO . . .

USE THE SELECTEDITEM AND SELECTEDINDEX PROPERTIES

Example 1 (SelectedItem property)

animalLabel.Text = Convert.ToString(animalListBox.SelectedItem)
converts the item selected in the animalListBox to String, and then assigns the result to the animalLabel

Example 2 (SelectedItem property)

If Convert.ToInt32(codeListBox.SelectedItem) = 103 Then
converts the item selected in the codeListBox to Integer, and then compares the result with the integer 103; you also can convert the item to String and then compare the result with "103" as follows: Convert.ToString(codeListBox.SelectedItem) = "103"

Example 3 (SelectedItem property)

If Convert.ToString(codeListBox.SelectedItem) <> String.Empty Then
the condition evaluates to True when an item is selected in the codeListBox; otherwise, it evaluates to False

Example 4 (SelectedIndex property)

MessageBox.Show(animalListBox.SelectedIndex.ToString)
displays (in a message box) the index of the item selected in the animalListBox; you also can use MessageBox.Show(Convert.ToString (animalListBox.SelectedIndex))

Example 5 (SelectedIndex property)

If codeListBox.SelectedIndex = 0 Then
determines whether the first item is selected in the codeListBox

Figure 6-19: How to use the SelectedItem and SelectedIndex properties

If a list box allows the user to make only one selection, it is customary in Windows applications to have one of the list box items already selected when the interface appears. The selected item, called the default list box item, should be either the item selected most frequently or, if all of the items are selected fairly equally, the first item in the list. You can use either the SelectedItem property or the SelectedIndex property to select the default list box item from code, as shown in Figure 6-20. In most cases, you enter the appropriate code in the form's Load event procedure, as shown in Figure 6-21.

» HOW TO . . .

SELECT THE DEFAULT LIST BOX ITEM

Example 1 (SelectedItem property)

animalListBox.SelectedItem = "Cat"

selects the Cat item in the animalListBox

Example 2 (SelectedItem property)

codeListBox.SelectedItem = "101"

selects the 101 item in the codeListBox

Example 3 (SelectedIndex property)

codeListBox.SelectedIndex = 2

selects the third item in the codeListBox

Figure 6-20: How to select the default list box item

```vb
Private Sub MainForm_Load(ByVal sender As Object, _
                    ByVal e As System.EventArgs) Handles Me.load

    ' add items to the animalListBox
    animalListBox.Items.Add("Dog")
    animalListBox.Items.Add("Cat")
    animalListBox.Items.Add("Horse")

    ' add items to the codeListBox
    Dim code As Integer = 100
    Do While code <= 105
        codeListBox.Items.Add(code.ToString)
        code = code + 1
    Loop

    ' select default list box item
    animalListBox.SelectedItem = "Dog"
    codeListBox.SelectedIndex = 0
End Sub
```

Selects the default item in each list box

Figure 6-21: Code to select the default item in each list box

THE SELECTEDVALUECHANGED AND SELECTEDINDEXCHANGED EVENTS

Each time either the user or a statement selects an item in a list box, both the list box's **SelectedValueChanged event** and its **SelectedIndexChanged event** occur. You can use the procedures associated with these events to perform one or more tasks when the selected item has changed. Figure 6-22 shows the code entered in both the animalListBox's SelectedValueChanged and codeListBox's SelectedIndexChanged procedures. Each time an item is selected in the animalListBox, the SelectedValueChanged procedure displays the animal's name in the nameLabel. Each time an item is selected in the codeListBox, the SelectedIndexChanged procedure displays (in the departmentLabel) the name of the department associated with the selected code.

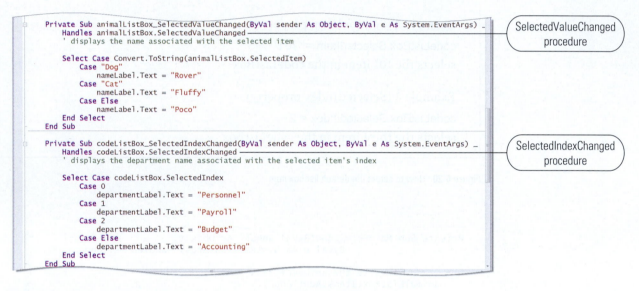

```
Private Sub animalListBox_SelectedValueChanged(ByVal sender As Object, ByVal e As System.EventArgs) _          SelectedValueChanged
    Handles animalListBox.SelectedValueChanged                                                                 procedure
    ' displays the name associated with the selected item

    Select Case Convert.ToString(animalListBox.SelectedItem)
        Case "Dog"
            nameLabel.Text = "Rover"
        Case "Cat"
            nameLabel.Text = "Fluffy"
        Case Else
            nameLabel.Text = "Poco"
    End Select
End Sub

Private Sub codeListBox_SelectedIndexChanged(ByVal sender As Object, ByVal e As System.EventArgs) _           SelectedIndexChanged
    Handles codeListBox.SelectedIndexChanged                                                                  procedure
    ' displays the department name associated with the selected item's index

    Select Case codeListBox.SelectedIndex
        Case 0
            departmentLabel.Text = "Personnel"
        Case 1
            departmentLabel.Text = "Payroll"
        Case 2
            departmentLabel.Text = "Budget"
        Case Else
            departmentLabel.Text = "Accounting"
    End Select
End Sub
```

Figure 6-22: SelectedValueChanged and SelectedIndexChanged event procedures

When the application is started, the animalListBox.SelectedItem = "Dog" and codeListBox.SelectedIndex = 0 statements in the form's Load event procedure invoke the animalListBox's SelectedValueChanged and codeListBox's SelectedIndexChanged event procedures. As a result, "Rover" and "Personnel" appear in the nameLabel and departmentLabel, as shown in Figure 6-23.

Figure 6-23: Result of processing the SelectedValueChanged and SelectedIndexChanged event procedures

THE PRODUCT FINDER APPLICATION

The Product Finder application demonstrates most of what you learned about list boxes; it also provides another example of using a repetition structure. The application allows the user to enter a product ID. It then searches for the ID in a list box that contains the valid product IDs. If the product ID is included in the list box, the application highlights (selects) the ID in the list. If the product ID is not in the list box, the application ensures that no ID is highlighted in the list box, and it displays a message indicating that the ID was not found. Figure 6-24 shows the pseudocode for one possible solution to the Product Finder problem.

Pseudocode for the Product Finder application

1. assign the product ID entered by the user to a variable
2. repeat while the list box item's index is less than the number of items in the list and, at the same time, the product ID has not been found
    if the product ID entered by the user is the same as the current item in the list box
        indicate that the product ID was found
    else
        continue the search by adding 1 to the list box index
    end if
  end repeat
3. if the product ID was found
    select the product ID in the list box
  else
    clear any selection in the list box
    display the "Not found" message
  end if

Figure 6-24: Pseudocode for the Product Finder application

Figures 6-25 and 6-26 show sample runs of the Product Finder application, and Figure 6-27 shows the code entered in the form's Load event and findButton's Click event procedures.

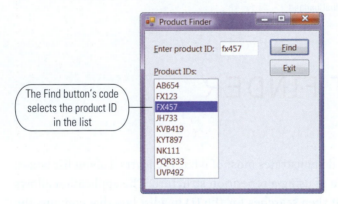

The Find button's code selects the product ID in the list

Figure 6-25: Sample run of the application when the product ID is found

A message is displayed in a message box

No product ID is selected in the list

Figure 6-26: Sample run of the application when the product ID is not found

```
Private Sub MainForm_Load(ByVal sender As Object, _
    ByVal e As System.EventArgs) Handles Me.Load
    ' fills the list box with IDs

    idListBox.Items.Add("FX123")
    idListBox.Items.Add("AB654")
    idListBox.Items.Add("JH733")
    idListBox.Items.Add("FX457")
    idListBox.Items.Add("NK111")
    idListBox.Items.Add("KYT897")
    idListBox.Items.Add("KVB419")
    idListBox.Items.Add("PQR333")
    idListBox.Items.Add("UVP492")
End Sub

Private Sub findButton_Click(ByVal sender As Object, _
    ByVal e As System.EventArgs) Handles findButton.Click
    ' determines whether a list box contains a specific ID

    Dim isFound As Boolean
    Dim index As Integer
    Dim numberOfItems As Integer
    Dim id As String = String.Empty

    ' assign ID and number of list box items to variables
    id = idTextBox.Text.ToUpper
    numberOfItems = idListBox.Items.Count

    ' search the list box, stopping either after the
    ' last item or when the item is found
    Do While index < numberOfItems AndAlso isFound = False
        If id = idListBox.Items(index).ToString.ToUpper Then
            isFound = True
        Else
            index = index + 1
        End If
    Loop

    If isFound = True Then
        idListBox.SelectedIndex = index
    Else
        idListBox.SelectedIndex = -1
        MessageBox.Show("Not found", "Product Finder", _
            MessageBoxButtons.OK, MessageBoxIcon.Information)
    End If
End Sub
```

Figure 6-27: Code for the form's Load event and findButton's Click event procedures

You have completed the concepts section of Chapter 6.

PROGRAMMING TUTORIAL

CREATING THE ROLL 'EM GAME

In this tutorial, you create an application that simulates a dice game called Roll 'Em. The game is played using two dice. Each player takes a turn at rolling the dice. The first player that rolls the same number on both dice wins the game. Figures 6-28 and 6-29 show the application's TOE chart and user interface. The images at the bottom of the user interface represent the six sides of a die. The application will use random numbers to display the appropriate image in the firstDiePictureBox and secondDiePictureBox controls. For example, if the random numbers are 6 and 3, the application will display the image containing 6 dots in the firstDiePictureBox, and display the image containing 3 dots in the secondDiePictureBox. The images in the firstDiePictureBox and secondDiePictureBox controls will correspond to a roll of the dice.

Task	Object	Event
1. Keep track of the current player 2. Display the current player's number in the messageLabel 3. Generate two random numbers from 1 to 6, inclusive 4. Use the random number to display the appropriate image in the firstDiePictureBox and secondDiePictureBox 5. Determine whether the current player won and display an appropriate message in the messageLabel	rollButton	Click
End the application	exitButton	Click
Display a message that indicates either the current player or the winner	messageLabel	None
Display the image corresponding to the first die	firstDiePictureBox	None
Display the image corresponding to the second die	secondDiePictureBox	None

Figure 6-28: TOE Chart

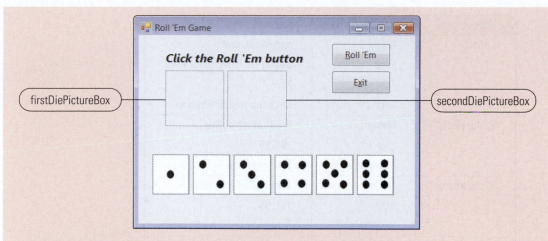

Figure 6-29: User interface

CREATING THE ROLL 'EM GAME INTERFACE

Before you can code the Roll 'Em game, you need to create the user interface.

To create the user interface:

1. Start Visual Studio. If necessary, close the Start Page window. Create a Visual Basic Windows-based application. Name the solution, project, and form file Roll Em Game Solution, Roll Em Game Project, and Main Form.vb, respectively. Save the application in the VbReloaded2008\Chap06 folder.

2. Use the chart shown in Figure 6-30 as a guide when creating the user interface from Figure 6-29. The six image files are contained in the VbReloaded2008\ Chap06 folder.

Object	Property	Setting
Form1	Name	MainForm
	Font	Segoe UI, 9 pt
	MaximizeBox	False
	Size	493, 364
	StartPosition	CenterScreen
	Text	Roll 'Em Game

Figure 6-30: Objects, Properties, and Settings (*continued on next page*)

Object	Property	Setting
Label1	Name	messageLabel
	Font	Segoe UI, Bold Italic, 12 pt
	TabIndex	2
	Text	Click the Roll 'Em button
PictureBox1	Name	firstDiePictureBox
	Size	101, 95
	SizeMode	StretchImage
PictureBox2	Name	secondDiePictureBox
	Size	101, 95
	SizeMode	StretchImage
PictureBox3	Name	dot1PictureBox
	Image	Dot1.jpg
	Size	64, 68
	SizeMode	StretchImage
PictureBox4	Name	dot2PictureBox
	Image	Dot2.jpg
	Size	64, 68
	SizeMode	StretchImage
PictureBox5	Name	dot3PictureBox
	Image	Dot3.jpg
	Size	64, 68
	SizeMode	StretchImage
PictureBox6	Name	dot4PictureBox
	Image	Dot4.jpg
	Size	64, 68
	SizeMode	StretchImage
PictureBox7	Name	dot5PictureBox
	Image	Dot5.jpg
	Size	64, 68
	SizeMode	StretchImage

Figure 6-30: Objects, Properties, and Settings (*continued from previous page and on next page*)

Object	Property	Setting
PictureBox8	Name	dot6PictureBox
	Image	Dot6.jpg
	Size	64, 68
	SizeMode	StretchImage
Button1	Name	rollButton
	TabIndex	0
	Text	&Roll 'Em
Button2	Name	exitButton
	TabIndex	1
	Text	E&xit

Figure 6-30: Objects, Properties, and Settings (*continued from previous page*)

3. Lock the controls, then save the solution.

CODING THE ROLL 'EM GAME

As the application's TOE chart indicates, the Click event procedures for the rollButton and exitButton need to be coded.

To begin coding the application:

1. Open the Code Editor window. The application will use variables, so you should enter the appropriate Option statements in the General Declarations section. Enter the comments and Option statements shown in Figure 6-31. Replace the <your name> and <current date> text with your name and the current date.

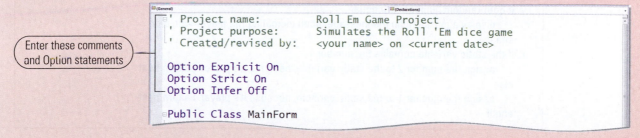

Enter these comments and Option statements

```
' Project name:        Roll Em Game Project
' Project purpose:     Simulates the Roll 'Em dice game
' Created/revised by:  <your name> on <current date>

Option Explicit On
Option Strict On
Option Infer Off

Public Class MainForm
```

Figure 6-31: Comments and Option statements entered in the Code Editor window

2. Open the code template for the exitButton's Click event procedure. Type **me.close()** and press **Enter**.

3. Save the solution, then start the application to test the Exit button's code. Click the **Exit** button to end the application.

Study the pseudocode shown in Figure 6-32, which indicates the tasks to be performed by the rollButton's Click event procedure. As the pseudocode indicates, the procedure will use a static variable to keep track of the player number (either 1 or 2). In addition, it will use two random numbers to display the appropriate images in the firstDiePictureBox and secondDiePictureBox.

---

rollButton's Click Event Procedure

1. initialize a static variable to 1, because player 1 rolls first
2. remove any existing images from the firstDiePictureBox and secondDiePictureBox
3. display a message (in the messageLabel) indicating the current player
4. generate two random numbers from 1 to 6, inclusive
5. use the first random number to display the appropriate image in the firstDiePictureBox
    first random number
      1 display the dot1PictureBox image in the firstDiePictureBox
      2 display the dot2PictureBox image in the firstDiePictureBox
      3 display the dot3PictureBox image in the firstDiePictureBox
      4 display the dot4PictureBox image in the firstDiePictureBox
      5 display the dot5PictureBox image in the firstDiePictureBox
      6 display the dot6PictureBox image in the firstDiePictureBox
6. use the second random number to display the appropriate image in the secondDiePictureBox
    second random number
      1 display the dot1PictureBox image in the secondDiePictureBox
      2 display the dot2PictureBox image in the secondDiePictureBox
      3 display the dot3PictureBox image in the secondDiePictureBox
      4 display the dot4PictureBox image in the secondDiePictureBox
      5 display the dot5PictureBox image in the secondDiePictureBox
      6 display the dot6PictureBox image in the secondDiePictureBox
7. if both random numbers are equal
    display a message (in the messageLabel) indicating the player who won
  end if
8. if the static variable contains the number 1
    assign the number 2 to the static variable, because it's player 2's turn next
  else
    assign the number 1 to the static variable, because it's player 1's turn next
  end if

Figure 6-32: Pseudocode for the rollButton's Click event procedure

To code the rollButton's Click event procedure, then test the procedure's code:

1. Open the code template for the rollButton's Click event procedure. Type **' simulates the Roll 'Em dice game** and press **Enter** twice.

2. The procedure will use a Random object to represent the pseudo-random number generator, and two Integer variables to store the two random numbers. Type **dim randomGenerator as new random** and press **Enter**. Type **dim random1 as integer** and press **Enter**, then type **dim random2 as integer** and press **Enter**.

3. Step 1 in the pseudocode is to initialize a static variable to 1. Type **static player as integer = 1** and press **Enter** twice.

4. Steps 2 and 3 are to remove any existing images from the firstDiePictureBox and secondDiePictureBox controls, and then display a message that indicates the current player. Type **' clear images and display message** and press **Enter**.

5. You can remove an image from a picture box control by assigning the keyword Nothing to the control's Image property. Type **firstDiePictureBox.image = nothing** and press **Enter**, then type **secondDiePictureBox.image = nothing** and press **Enter**.

6. Type **messageLabel.text = "Player " & player.tostring & " rolled:"** and press **Enter** twice.

7. The next step is to generate two random numbers from 1 to 6, inclusive. You will assign the random numbers to the random1 and random2 variables. Type **' generate two random numbers from 1 to 6, inclusive** and press **Enter**. Type **random1 = randomGenerator.next(1, 7)** and press **Enter**, then type **random2 = randomGenerator.next(1, 7)** and press **Enter** twice. See Figure 6-33.

```
rollButton                                              ▼ ⚡ Click

    Private Sub rollButton_Click(ByVal sender As Object, ByVal e As System
        ' simulates the Roll 'Em dice game

        Dim randomGenerator As New Random
        Dim random1 As Integer
        Dim random2 As Integer
        Static player As Integer = 1

        ' clear images and display message
        firstDiePictureBox.Image = Nothing
        secondDiePictureBox.Image = Nothing
        messageLabel.Text = "Player " & player.ToString & " rolled:"

        ' generate two random numbers from 1 to 6, inclusive
        random1 = randomGenerator.Next(1, 7)
        random2 = randomGenerator.Next(1, 7)

        |
    End Sub
```

Insertion point

Figure 6-33: Code entered in the rollButton's Click event procedure

8. Step 5 in the pseudocode is a selection structure that uses the first random number to display the appropriate image in the firstDiePictureBox. Enter the additional comment and code shown in Figure 6-34, then position your insertion point as indicated in the figure.

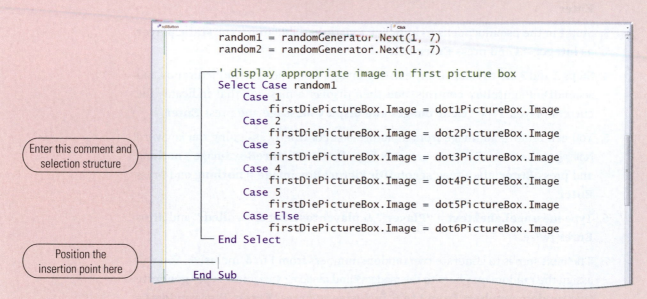

Enter this comment and selection structure

Position the insertion point here

Figure 6-34: First selection structure entered in the procedure

9. Step 6 is a selection structure that uses the second random number to display the appropriate image in the secondDiePictureBox. Enter the additional comment and code shown in Figure 6-35, then position your insertion point as indicated in the figure.

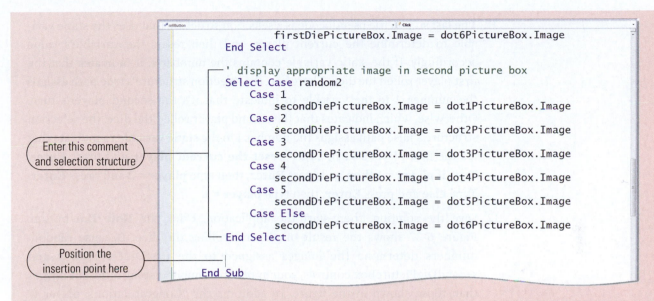

Enter this comment and selection structure

Position the insertion point here

Figure 6-35: Second selection structure entered in the procedure

10. Step 7 is another selection structure. This selection structure compares both random numbers for equality. If both numbers are equal, the procedure should display a message that indicates the winning player. Enter the additional comment and selection structure shown in Figure 6-36, then position the insertion point as indicated in the figure.

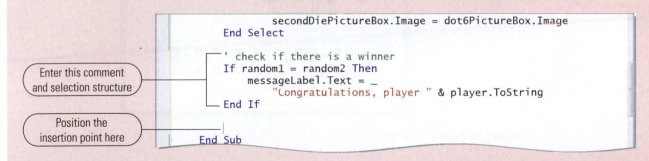

Enter this comment and selection structure

Position the insertion point here

Figure 6-36: Third selection structure entered in the procedure

11. The last step in the pseudocode is a selection structure that uses the static variable to determine the current player, and then resets the variable's value accordingly. If the static variable contains the number 1, it indicates that the first player rolled the dice. Therefore, the selection structure's true path assigns the number 2 to the variable to indicate that it's the second player's turn. Otherwise, which indicates that the second player rolled the dice, the selection structure's false path assigns the number 1 to the static variable to indicate that it's the first player's turn. Type **' reset the current player** and press **Enter**. Type **if player = 1 then** and press **Enter**, then type **player = 2** and press **Enter**. Type **else** and press **Enter**, then type **player = 1**.

12. Save the solution, then start the application. Click the **Roll 'Em** button. Figure 6-37 shows the result of player 1 rolling the dice. Because random numbers determine the images assigned to the firstDiePictureBox and secondDiePictureBox controls, your application might display different images than those shown in the figure. In addition, the "Congratulations, player 1" message, rather than the "Player 1 rolled:" message, may appear on your screen.

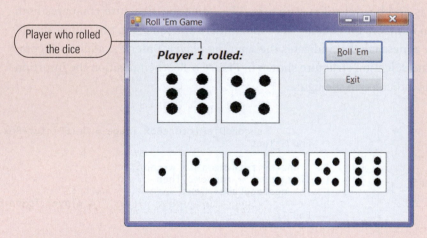

Player who rolled the dice

Figure 6-37: Player 1's roll of the dice

13. Click the **Roll 'Em** button again. Notice that the message—either "Player 2 rolled:" or "Congratulations, player 2"—refers to player 2.

14. Click the **Roll 'Em** button several times until there is a winner. Figure 6-38 shows a sample of the interface when player 2 wins.

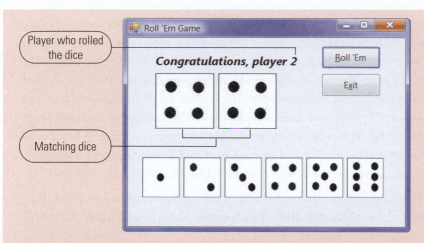

Figure 6-38: Result of player 2 winning

15. Click the **Exit** button to end the application.

16. There is no need to display the six images at the bottom of the form. Change the form's Size property to **493, 240**, then save the solution.

MODIFYING THE APPLICATION

Now you are going to modify the rollButton's Click event procedure to make the application a bit more exciting. First, you will have the computer delay program execution for a short time after the "Player x rolled:" message appears in the messageLabel, but before the dice images appear in the picture boxes. The delay will give the player a short time to anticipate the roll. You can delay program execution using the **Sleep method** in the following syntax: **System.Threading.Thread.Sleep(**_milliseconds_**)**. The _milliseconds_ argument is the number of milliseconds to suspend the program. A millisecond is 1/1000 of a second; in other words, there are 1000 milliseconds in a second. Before delaying the program's execution, you will use the form's **Refresh method** to refresh the interface. The Refresh method will ensure that any code appearing before it that affects the interface's appearance is processed. The Refresh method's syntax is **Me.Refresh()**, where Me refers to the current form.

To modify the rollButton's code, then test the code:

1. Click the blank line above the ' generate two random numbers from 1 to 6, inclusive comment, then press **Enter** to insert a new blank line. Type **' refresh form, then delay execution** and press **Enter**.

2. Type **me.refresh()** and press **Enter**. You'll delay program execution for one second, which is 1000 milliseconds. Type **system.threading.thread.sleep(1000)** and press **Enter**.

3. Save the solution, then start the application. Click the **Roll 'Em** button. Notice that there is a slight delay from when the message appears to when the dice appear. This delay may cause the user to click the Roll 'Em button before the dice images appear. You can fix this problem by disabling the Roll 'Em button after it has been clicked, and then enabling it after all of the code in its Click event procedure is processed. You enable a control by setting its Enabled property to True, and disable it by setting its Enabled property to False. When a control is disabled, it appears dimmed (grayed-out) and does not accept user input. A disabled button, for example, will not react when it is clicked.

4. Click the blank line above the ' refresh form, then delay execution comment, then press **Enter**. Type **' disable Roll 'Em button** and press **Enter**, then type **rollButton.enabled** = **false** and press **Enter**.

5. Click **after the letter f** in the last End If line in the procedure, then press **Enter** twice. Type **' enable Roll 'Em button** and press **Enter**, then type **rollButton.enabled** = **true** and press **Enter**.

6. Save the solution, then start the application. Click the **Roll 'Em** button. Notice that the Roll 'Em button is disabled until after the dice images appear. Click the **Exit** button to end the application.

You will make one final modification to the rollButton's Click event procedure. Specifically, you will use a repetition structure to make the Congratulations message blink several times when a player wins the game. You can make a control blink by switching its Visible property from True to False and then back again several times. However, switching the Visible property isn't all that is needed. Because the computer will process the switching instructions so rapidly, you won't even notice that the control is blinking. To actually see the control blink, you will need to refresh the form and then delay program execution each time you switch the Visible property's setting. Figure 6-39 shows two ways of writing the code to make the Congratulations message blink five times. Notice that Version 2 uses the Not logical operator, which you learned about in Chapter 4. In this case, the Not operator reverses the truth value of the messageLabel's Visible property. If the Visible property contains True when the messageLabel.Visible = Not messageLabel.Visible statement is processed, the Not messageLabel.Visible expression evaluates to False; as a result, the statement assigns False to the Visible property. On the other hand, if the Visible property contains False when the statement is processed, the Not messageLabel.Visible expression evaluates to True and the statement assigns True to the Visible property.

Version 1

```
Dim count As Integer = 1
Do While count <= 10
    If messageLabel.Visible = True Then
        messageLabel.Visible = False
    Else
        messageLabel.Visible = True
    End If
    Me.Refresh()
    System.Threading.Thread.Sleep(100)
    count = count + 1
Loop
```

Version 2

```
Dim count As Integer = 1
Do While count <= 10
    messageLabel.Visible = Not messageLabel.Visible
    Me.Refresh()
    System.Threading.Thread.Sleep(100)
    count = count + 1
Loop
```

Figure 6-39: Two ways of writing the blinking code

To complete the rollButton's Click event procedure, then test the procedure's code:

1. Enter the code shown in Figure 6-40.

```
        ' check if there is a winner
    If random1 = random2 Then
        messageLabel.Text = _
            "Congratulations, player " & player.ToString
        Dim count As Integer = 1
        Do While count <= 10
            messageLabel.Visible = Not messageLabel.Visible
            Me.Refresh()
            System.Threading.Thread.Sleep(100)
            count = count + 1
        Loop
    End If
```

Enter these seven lines of code

Figure 6-40: Blinking code entered in the procedure

2. Save the solution, then start the application. Click the **Roll 'Em** button several times until one player wins, which causes the messageLabel to blink.

3. Click the **Exit** button to end the application. Figure 6-41 shows the completed code.

```
' Project name:          Roll Em Game Project
' Project purpose:       Simulates the Roll 'Em dice game
' Created/revised by:    <your name> on <current date>

Option Explicit On
Option Strict On
Option Infer Off

Public Class MainForm

    Private Sub exitButton_Click(ByVal sender As Object, _
        ByVal e As System.EventArgs) Handles exitButton.Click
        Me.Close()
    End Sub

    Private Sub rollButton_Click(ByVal sender As Object, _
        ByVal e As System.EventArgs) Handles rollButton.Click
        ' simulates the Roll 'Em dice game

        Dim randomGenerator As New Random
        Dim random1 As Integer
        Dim random2 As Integer
        Static player As Integer = 1

        ' clear images and display message
        firstDiePictureBox.Image = Nothing
        secondDiePictureBox.Image = Nothing
        messageLabel.Text = "Player " & player.ToString & " rolled:"

        ' disable Roll 'Em button
        rollButton.Enabled = False

        ' refresh form, then delay execution
        Me.Refresh()
        System.Threading.Thread.Sleep(1000)

        ' generate two random numbers from 1 to 6, inclusive
        random1 = randomGenerator.Next(1, 7)
        random2 = randomGenerator.Next(1, 7)

        ' display appropriate image in first picture box
```

Figure 6-41: Roll 'Em application's code (*continued on next page*)

```vb
Select Case random1
    Case 1
        firstDiePictureBox.Image = dot1PictureBox.Image
    Case 2
        firstDiePictureBox.Image = dot2PictureBox.Image
    Case 3
        firstDiePictureBox.Image = dot3PictureBox.Image
    Case 4
        firstDiePictureBox.Image = dot4PictureBox.Image
    Case 5
        firstDiePictureBox.Image = dot5PictureBox.Image
    Case Else
        firstDiePictureBox.Image = dot6PictureBox.Image
End Select

' display appropriate image in second picture box
Select Case random2
    Case 1
        secondDiePictureBox.Image = dot1PictureBox.Image
    Case 2
        secondDiePictureBox.Image = dot2PictureBox.Image
    Case 3
        secondDiePictureBox.Image = dot3PictureBox.Image
    Case 4
        secondDiePictureBox.Image = dot4PictureBox.Image
    Case 5
        secondDiePictureBox.Image = dot5PictureBox.Image
    Case Else
        secondDiePictureBox.Image = dot6PictureBox.Image
End Select

' check if there is a winner
If random1 = random2 Then
    messageLabel.Text = _
        "Congratulations, player " & player.ToString
    Dim count As Integer = 1
    Do While count <= 10
        messageLabel.Visible = Not messageLabel.Visible
        Me.Refresh()
        System.Threading.Thread.Sleep(100)
        count = count + 1
    Loop
End If
```

Figure 6-41: Roll 'Em application's code (*continued from previous page and on next page*)

```
        ' reset the current player
    If player = 1 Then
        player = 2
    Else
        player = 1
    End If

        ' enable Roll 'Em button
    rollButton.Enabled = True
End Sub
End Class
```

Figure 6-41: Roll 'Em application's code (*continued from previous page*)

PROGRAMMING EXAMPLE

GRADE CALCULATOR

Create a Visual Basic application that allows the user to enter the points a student earns on four projects and two tests. Each project is worth 50 points, and each test is worth 100 points. The application should total the points earned and then assign the appropriate grade using the information shown in the chart below. After assigning the grade, the application should display the total points earned and the grade. Name the solution, project, and form file Grade Calculator Solution, Grade Calculator Project, and Main Form.vb, respectively. Save the application in the VbReloaded2008\Chap06 folder. See Figures 6-42 through 6-46.

Total points earned	Grade
360–400	A
320–359	B
280–319	C
240–279	D
below 240	F

Task	Object	Event
1. Get points earned on four projects and two tests 2. Calculate the total points earned 3. Display the total points earned in the totalPointsLabel 4. Display the grade in the gradeLabel	assignButton	Click
End the application	exitButton	Click
Display the total points earned (from assignButton)	totalPointsLabel	None
Display the grade (from assignButton)	gradeLabel	None

Figure 6-42: TOE chart

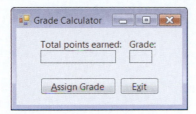

Figure 6-43: User interface

Object	Property	Setting
Form1	Name	MainForm
	Font	Segoe UI, 9 point
	StartPosition	CenterScreen
	Text	Grade Calculator
Label1	TabIndex	2
	Text	Total points earned:
Label2	TabIndex	4
	Text	Grade:
Label3	Name	totalPointsLabel
	AutoSize	False
	BorderStyle	FixedSingle
	TabIndex	3
	Text	(empty)
	TextAlign	MiddleCenter

Figure 6-44: Objects, Properties, and Settings (*continued on next page*)

Object	Property	Setting
Label4	Name	gradeLabel
	AutoSize	False
	BorderStyle	FixedSingle
	TabIndex	5
	Text	(empty)
	TextAlign	MiddleCenter
Button1	Name	assignButton
	TabIndex	0
	Text	&Assign Grade
Button2	Name	exitButton
	TabIndex	1
	Text	E&xit

Figure 6-44: Objects, Properties, and Settings (*continued from previous page*)

exitButton Click Event Procedure
1. close the application

assignButton Click Event Procedure
1. repeat while the number of projects counter is less than 5
      get the points earned on the project
      add 1 to the number of projects counter
      add the project points to the total points accumulator
   end repeat
2. repeat while the number of tests counter is less than 3
      get the points earned on the test
      add 1 to the number of tests counter
      add the test points to the total points accumulator
   end repeat
3. assign the grade based on the value in the total points accumulator:
      >= 360 assign A as the grade
      >= 320 assign B as the grade
      >= 280 assign C as the grade
      >= 240 assign D as the grade
      < 240 assign F as the grade
4. display the total points accumulator's value in the totalPointsLabel
5. display the grade in the gradeLabel

Figure 6-45: Pseudocode

```
' Project name:        Grade Calculator Project
' Project purpose:     Displays the total points earned and the grade
' Created/revised by:  <your name> on <current date>

Option Explicit On
Option Strict On
Option Infer Off

Public Class MainForm

    Private Sub exitButton_Click(ByVal sender As Object, _
        ByVal e As System.EventArgs) Handles exitButton.Click
        Me.Close()
    End Sub

    Private Sub assignButton_Click(ByVal sender As Object, _
        ByVal e As System.EventArgs) Handles assignButton.Click
        ' calculates the total points earned, then displays the total points
        ' earned and the appropriate grade

        Dim inputProjectPoints As String = String.Empty
        Dim inputTestPoints As String = String.Empty
        Dim grade As String = String.Empty
        Dim projectPoints As Integer
        Dim testPoints As Integer
        Dim totalPointsAccumulator As Integer
        Dim projectCounter As Integer = 1
        Dim testCounter As Integer = 1

        ' get and accumulate the project points
        Do While projectCounter < 5
            inputProjectPoints = InputBox("Enter the points earned on project " _
                & projectCounter, "Grade Calculator", "0")
            Integer.TryParse(inputProjectPoints, projectPoints)
            projectCounter = projectCounter + 1
            totalPointsAccumulator = totalPointsAccumulator + projectPoints
        Loop

        ' get and accumulate the test points
        Do While testCounter < 3
            inputTestPoints = InputBox("Enter the points earned on test " _
                & testCounter, "Grade Calculator", "0")
            Integer.TryParse(inputTestPoints, testPoints)
            testCounter = testCounter + 1
            totalPointsAccumulator = totalPointsAccumulator + testPoints
        Loop
```

Figure 6-46: Code (*continued on next page*)

```
         ' assign grade
         Select Case totalPointsAccumulator
             Case Is >= 360
                 grade = "A"
             Case Is >= 320
                 grade = "B"
             Case Is >= 280
                 grade = "C"
             Case Is >= 240
                 grade = "D"
             Case Else
                 grade = "F"
         End Select

         'display the total points earned and the grade
         totalPointsLabel.Text = totalPointsAccumulator.ToString
         gradeLabel.Text = grade
     End Sub
 End Class
```

Figure 6-46: Code (*continued from previous page*)

QUICK REVIEW

- » The three programming structures are sequence, selection, and repetition.

- » You use the repetition structure, also called a loop, to repeatedly process one or more program instructions.

- » A repetition structure can be either a pretest loop or a posttest loop. Depending on the loop condition, the instructions in a pretest loop may never be processed. The instructions in a posttest loop are always processed at least once.

- » You can use the Do...Loop statement to code either a pretest loop or a posttest loop. The condition used in the Do...Loop statement must evaluate to a Boolean value.

- » When used in the Do...Loop statement, the keyword While indicates that the loop instructions should be processed *while* the condition is true. The keyword Until, on the other hand, indicates that the loop instructions should be processed *until* the condition becomes true.

- » A diamond is used in a flowchart to represent the condition in a Do...Loop statement.

» You use a counter and/or an accumulator to calculate subtotals, totals, and averages.

» Counters and accumulators must be initialized and updated. The initialization is done outside of the loop that uses the counter or accumulator, and the updating is done within the loop.

» The InputBox function displays a dialog box that contains a message, an OK button, a Cancel button, and an input area. The function returns a string.

» In the InputBox function, you should use sentence capitalization for the prompt, and book title capitalization for the title.

» Before using a variable as the divisor in an expression, you first should verify that the variable does not contain the number zero. Dividing by zero is mathematically impossible and will cause the program to end with an error.

» A list box should contain a minimum of three selections. A list box should display a minimum of three selections and a maximum of eight selections at a time.

» Use a label control to provide keyboard access to a list box. Set the label's TabIndex property to a value that is one number less than the list box's TabIndex value.

» You use the Items collection's Add method to add an item to a list box.

» The code contained in a form's Load event procedure will be processed before the form appears on the screen.

» List box items are either arranged by use, with the most used entries appearing first in the list, or sorted in ascending order.

» You use a list box item's index to access the item. The index of the first item in a list box is zero.

» The number of items in a list box control is contained in the control's Items.Count property.

» When an item is selected in a list box, the item appears highlighted in the list. The item's value is stored in the list box's SelectedItem property, and the item's index is stored in the list box's SelectedIndex property.

» If a list box allows the user to make only one selection at a time, then a default item should be selected in the list box when the interface first appears. The default item should be either the item selected most frequently or the first item in the list.

» A list box's SelectedItem property and its SelectedIndex property can be used both to determine the item selected in the list box and to select a list box item from code.

» When you select an item in a list box, the list box's SelectedValueChanged and SelectedIndexChanged events occur.

» You can use the Sleep method to delay program execution. The method's syntax is **System.Threading.Thread.Sleep(***milliseconds***)**.

» You use the Refresh method to refresh (redraw) the form. The method's syntax is **Me.Refresh()**.

» You use a control's Enabled property to enable or disable the control.

KEY TERMS

Accumulator—a numeric variable used for accumulating (adding together) something

Add method—the Items collection's method used to add items to a list box

Collection—a group of one or more individual objects treated as one unit

Counter—a numeric variable used for counting something

Do...Loop statement—a Visual Basic statement that can be used to code both a pretest loop and a posttest loop

Function—a procedure that performs a specific task and then returns a value after completing the task

Incrementing—another term for updating

Index—the unique number that identifies each item in a collection; used to access an item in a list box

Initializing—assign a beginning value to a variable, such as a counter variable or an accumulator variable

InputBox function—a Visual Basic function that displays a dialog box containing a message, OK and Cancel buttons, and an input area

Items collection—the collection composed of the items in a list box

List box—a control used to display a list of choices from which the user can select zero choices, one choice, or more than one choice

Load event—the event that occurs when an application is started and the form is displayed the first time

Loop—another term for the repetition structure

Posttest loop—a loop whose condition is evaluated *after* the instructions within the loop are processed

Pretest loop—a loop whose condition is evaluated *before* the instructions within the loop are processed

Priming read—the input instruction that appears above the loop that it controls; determines whether the loop instructions will be processed the first time

Refresh method—used to refresh (redraw) a form

Repetition structure—one of the three programming structures; used to repeatedly process one or more program instructions until some condition is met, at which time the repetition structure ends; also called a loop

SelectedIndexChanged event—an event that occurs when an item is selected in a list box

SelectedValueChanged event—an event that occurs when an item is selected in a list box

Sleep method—used to delay program execution

Updating—adding a number to the value stored in a counter or accumulator variable; also called incrementing

SELF-CHECK QUESTIONS AND ANSWERS

1. Which of the following clauses stops the loop when the value in the **age** variable is less than the number zero?

   a. Do While age >= 0

   b. Do Until age < 0

   c. Loop While age >= 0

   d. All of the above.

2. Which of the following statements prompts the user for the name of a city, and then assigns the user's response to a String variable named cityName?

   a. InputBox("Enter the city name:", "City", cityName)

   b. InputBox("Enter the city name:", cityName)

   c. cityName = InputBox("Enter the city name:", "City")

   d. None of the above.

3. You use the _____ method to add items to a list box.

   a. Add   b. AddList

   c. Item   d. ItemAdd

4. The items in a list box belong to the _____ collection.

   a. Items   b. List

   c. ListItems   d. Values

5. You can use the _____ method to delay program execution.

   a. Delay   b. Pause

   c. Sleep   d. Stop

Answers: 1) d, 2) c, 3) a, 4) a, 5) c

REVIEW QUESTIONS

1. Which of the following flowchart symbols represents the condition in a Do...Loop statement?

   a. diamond

   b. hexagon

   c. parallelogram

   d. rectangle

2. How many times will the MessageBox.Show method in the following code be processed?

```
Dim counter As Integer
Do While counter > 3
    MessageBox.Show("Hello")
    counter = counter + 1
Loop
```

   a. 0   b. 1

   c. 3   d. 4

3. How many times will the MessageBox.Show method in the following code be processed?

```
Dim counter As Integer
Do
    MessageBox.Show("Hello")
    counter = counter + 1
Loop While counter > 3
```

   a. 0   b. 1

   c. 3   d. 4

Refer to Figure 6-47 to answer Questions 4 through 7.

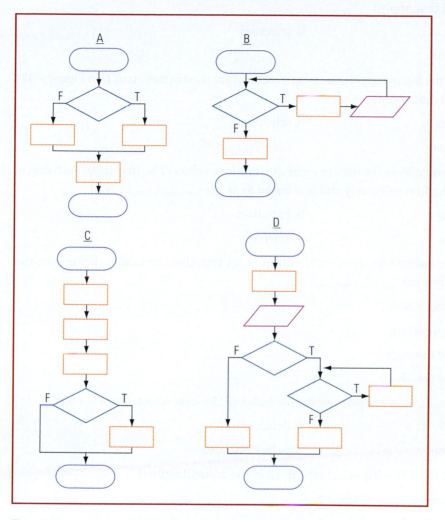

Figure 6-47

4. Which of the following programming structures are used in flowchart A in Figure 6-47? (Select all that apply.)

   a. sequence
   b. selection
   c. repetition

5. Which of the following programming structures are used in flowchart B in Figure 6-47? (Select all that apply.)

   a. sequence
   b. selection
   c. repetition

6. Which of the following programming structures are used in flowchart C in Figure 6-47? (Select all that apply.)

   a. sequence   b. selection

   c. repetition

7. Which of the following programming structures are used in flowchart D in Figure 6-47? (Select all that apply.)

   a. sequence   b. selection

   c. repetition

8. A procedure allows the user to enter one or more values. The first input instruction will get the first value only and is referred to as the _____ read.

   a. entering   b. initializer

   c. priming   d. starter

9. When the user clicks the Cancel button in an InputBox function's dialog box, the function returns _____.

   a. the number zero

   b. the empty string

   c. an error message

   d. None of the above.

10. The _____ property stores the index of the item selected in a list box.

    a. Index   b. SelectedIndex

    c. Selection   d. SelectionIndex

11. Which of the following selects the third in the animalListBox?

    a. animalListBox.SelectedIndex = 2

    b. animalListBox.SelectedIndex = 3

    c. animalListBox.SelectedItem = 2

    d. animalListBox.SelectedItem = 3

12. The _____ event occurs when the user selects an item in a list box.

    a. SelectionChanged

    b. SelectedItemChanged

    c. SelectedValueChanged

    d. None of the above.

REVIEW EXERCISES— SHORT ANSWER

1. Write a Visual Basic Do clause that processes the loop instructions as long as the value in the quantity variable is greater than the number 0. Use the While keyword.

2. Rewrite the Do clause from Review Exercise 1 using the Until keyword.

3. Write a Visual Basic Do clause that stops the loop when the value in the inStock variable is less than or equal to the value in the reorder variable. Use the Until keyword.

4. Rewrite the Do clause from Review Exercise 3 using the While keyword.

5. Write a Visual Basic Loop clause that processes the loop instructions as long as the value in the letter variable is either Y or y. Use the While keyword.

6. Rewrite the Loop clause from Review Exercise 5 using the Until keyword.

7. Write a Visual Basic Do clause that processes the loop instructions as long as the value in the empName variable is not "Done" (in any case). Use the While keyword.

8. Rewrite the Do clause from Review Exercise 7 using the Until keyword.

9. Write a Visual Basic assignment statement that updates the quantity variable by 2.

10. Write a Visual Basic assignment statement that updates the total variable by –3.

11. Write a Visual Basic assignment statement that updates the totalPurchases variable by the value stored in the purchases variable.

12. Write a Visual Basic assignment statement that subtracts the contents of the salesReturns variable from the sales variable.

13. What will the following code display in message boxes?

```
Dim x As Integer
Do While x < 5
    MessageBox.Show(Convert.ToString(x))
    x = x + 1
Loop
```

14. What will the following code display in message boxes?

```
Dim x As Integer
Do
    MessageBox.Show(Convert.ToString(x))
    x = x + 1
Loop Until x > 5
```

15. An instruction is missing from the following code. What is the missing instruction and where does it belong in the code?

```
Dim number As Integer = 1
Do While number < 5
    MessageBox.Show(number.ToString)
Loop
```

16. An instruction is missing from the following code. What is the missing instruction and where does it belong in the code?

```
Dim number As Integer = 10
Do
    MessageBox.Show(number.ToString)
Loop Until number = 0
```

17. What will the following code display in message boxes?

```
Dim totalEmp As Integer
Do While totalEmp <= 5
    MessageBox.Show(totalEmp.ToString)
    totalEmp = totalEmp + 2
Loop
```

18. What will the following code display in message boxes?

```
Dim totalEmp As Integer = 1
Do
    MessageBox.Show(totalEmp.ToString)
    totalEmp = totalEmp + 2
Loop Until totalEmp >= 3
```

19. Write the Visual Basic code that corresponds to the flowchart shown in Figure 6-48. Display the calculated results on separate lines in the resultsLabel control.

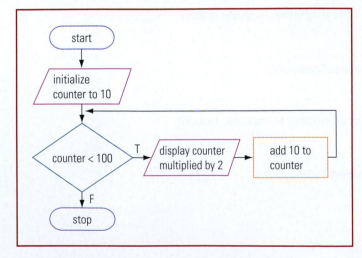

Figure 6-48

20. Write two different statements that you can use to select the fifth item in the departmentListBox. The fifth item is Accounting.

COMPUTER EXERCISES

1. In this exercise, you modify the Roll 'Em application from this chapter's Programming Tutorial. The application will now allow three people to play the game.

    a. Use Windows to make a copy of the Roll Em Game Solution folder, which is contained in the VbReloaded2008\Chap06 folder. Rename the copy Roll Em Game Solution-Modified.

    b. Open the Roll Em Game Solution (Roll Em Game Solution.sln) file contained in the Roll Em Game Solution-Modified folder.

    c. Modify the code to allow three people to play the game. Save the solution, then start and test the application. Click the Exit button to end the application, then close the solution.

2. In this exercise, you code two procedures that display the even integers between 1 and 9 in a label control.

    a. Open the Even Number Solution (Even Number Solution.sln) file, which is contained in the VbReloaded2008\Chap06\Even Number Solution folder.

    b. Code the Do...Loop Pretest button's Click event procedure so that it displays the even integers between 1 and 9 in the evenNumsLabel control. Display each even integer on a separate line in the control. Use the Do...Loop statement.

    c. Code the Do...Loop Posttest button's Click event procedure so that it displays the even integers between 1 and 9 in the evenNumsLabel control. Display each even integer on a separate line in the control. Use the Do...Loop statement.

    d. Save the solution, then start and test the application. End the application, then close the solution.

3. In this exercise, you code a procedure that displays the squares of the even integers from 2 through 12 in a label control.

    a. Open the Even Squares Solution (Even Squares Solution.sln) file, which is contained in the VbReloaded2008\Chap06\Even Squares Solution folder.

    b. Code the Display button's Click event procedure so that it displays the squares of the even integers from 2 through 12 in the squaresLabel control. Display each square on a separate line in the control. Use the Do...Loop statement.

    c. Save the solution. Start and then test the application. End the application, then close the solution.

4. In this exercise, you code an application for Gwen Industries. The application calculates and displays the total sales and bonus amounts.

   a. Open the Gwen Solution (Gwen Solution.sln) file, which is contained in the VbReloaded2008\Chap06\Gwen Solution folder.

   b. Code the Calculate button's Click event procedure so that it allows the user to enter as many sales amounts as he or she wants to enter. Use the InputBox function to get the sales amounts. When the user has completed entering the sales amounts, the procedure should display the total sales in the totalSalesLabel control. It also should display a 10% bonus in the bonusLabel control.

   c. Save the solution, then start the application. Test the application using the following six sales amounts: 600.50, 4500.75, 3500, 2000, 1000, and 6500. Then test it again using the following four sales amounts: 75, 67, 88, and 30. End the application, then close the solution.

5. In this exercise, you code an application for Colfax Industries. The application calculates and displays the total company sales.

   a. Open the Colfax Solution (Colfax Solution.sln) file, which is contained in the VbReloaded2008\Chap06\Colfax Solution folder.

   b. Code the Add button's Click event procedure so that it adds the amount entered in the salesTextBox control to an accumulator variable, and then displays the contents of the accumulator variable in the totalSalesLabel control. Display the total sales with a dollar sign and two decimal places.

   c. Save the solution, then start the application. Test the application using the following sales amounts: 1000, 2000, 3000, and 4000. End the application, then close the solution.

6. In this exercise, you create an application for Premium Paper. The application allows the sales manager to enter the company's income and expense amounts. The number of income and expense amounts may vary each time the application is started. For example, the user may enter five income amounts and three expense amounts. Or, he or she may enter 20 income amounts and 30 expense amounts. The application should calculate and display the company's total income, total expense, and profit (or loss). Use the InputBox function to get the individual income and expense amounts.

   a. Name the solution, project, and form file Premium Solution, Premium Project, and Main Form.vb, respectively. Save the application in the VbReloaded2008\Chap06 folder.

   b. Design an appropriate interface. Use label controls to display the total income, total expenses, and profit (loss). Display the calculated amounts with a dollar sign and two decimal places. If the company experienced a loss, display the amount of the loss using a red font; otherwise, display the profit using a black font.

   c. Code the application. Keep in mind that the income and expense amounts may contain decimal places.

   d. Save the solution, then start the application. Test the application twice, using the following data:

     First test: Income amounts: 57.75, 83.23

              Expense amounts: 200

     Second test: Income amounts: 5000, 6000, 35000, 78000

              Expense amounts: 1000, 2000, 600

   e. End the application, then close the solution.

7. In this exercise, you create an application that allows the user to enter a series of integers. The application then displays the sum of the odd integers and the sum of the even integers.

   a. Open the SumOddEven Solution (SumOddEven Solution.sln) file, which is contained in the VbReloaded2008\Chap06\SumOddEven Solution folder. Code the application.

   b. Save the solution, then start the application. Test the application using the following integers: 45, 2, 34, 7, 55, 90, and 32. The sum of the odd integers should be 107, and the sum of the even integers should be 158. Now test it again using the following integers: 5, 7, and 33. End the application, then close the solution.

8. In this exercise, you create an application that displays a shipping charge based on the state name selected in a list box.

   a. Create an appropriate interface, using a list box to display the following state names: Alabama, Georgia, Louisiana, and North Carolina. Name the solution, project, and form file Gentry Supplies Solution, Gentry Supplies Project, and Main Form.vb, respectively. Save the application in the VbReloaded2008\Chap06 folder.

   b. Code the application using the following information:

State name	Shipping charge
Alabama	$20
Georgia	$35
Louisiana	$30
North Carolina	$28

   c. Save the solution, then start and test the application. End the application, then close the solution.

9. In this exercise, you create an application that displays the telephone extension corresponding to the name selected in a list box. The names and extensions are shown here in the chart.

Name	Extension
Smith, Joe	3388
Jones, Mary	3356
Adkari, Joel	2487
Lin, Sue	1111
Li, Vicky	2222

   a. Open the Phone Solution (Phone Solution.sln) file, which is contained in the VbReloaded2008\Chap06\Phone Solution folder.

   b. The items in the list box should be sorted. Set the appropriate property.

   c. Code the form's Load event procedure so that it adds the five names to the nameListBox. Select the first name in the list.

   d. Code the list box's SelectedValueChanged event procedure so that it assigns the item selected in the nameListBox to a variable. The procedure then should use the Select Case statement to determine the telephone extension corresponding to the name stored in the variable.

   e. Save the solution, then start and test the application. End the application, then close the solution.

10. In this exercise, you modify the application from Computer Exercise 9. The application will now assign the index of the selected item, rather than the selected item itself, to a variable.

   a. Use Windows to make a copy of the Phone Solution folder, which is contained in the VbReloaded2008\Chap06 folder. Rename the copy Modified Phone Solution.

   b. Open the Phone Solution (Phone Solution.sln) file contained in the Modified Phone Solution folder.

   c. Modify the list box's SelectedValueChanged event procedure so that it assigns the index of the item selected in the nameListBox to a variable. Modify the Select Case statement so that it determines the telephone extension corresponding to the index stored in the variable.

   d. Save the solution, then start and test the application. Click the Exit button to end the application, then close the solution.

11. In this exercise, you create an application that displays the first 10 Fibonacci numbers (1, 1, 2, 3, 5, 8, 13, 21, 34, and 55). Notice that, beginning with the third number in the series, each Fibonacci number is the sum of the prior two numbers. In other words, 2 is the sum of 1 plus 1, 3 is the sum of 1 plus 2, 5 is the sum of 2 plus 3, and so on.

a. Open the Fibonacci Solution (Fibonacci Solution.sln) file, which is contained in the VbReloaded2008\Chap06\Fibonacci Solution folder. Code the application. Display the numbers in a label control.

b. Save the solution, then start and test the application. End the application, then close the solution.

12. In this exercise, you create an application that displays a multiplication table similar to the one shown in Figure 6-49, where *x* is a number entered by the user and *y* is the result of multiplying *x* by the numbers 1 through 9.

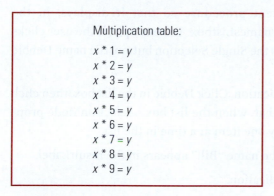

Multiplication table:
$x * 1 = y$
$x * 2 = y$
$x * 3 = y$
$x * 4 = y$
$x * 5 = y$
$x * 6 = y$
$x * 7 = y$
$x * 8 = y$
$x * 9 = y$

Figure 6-49

a. Open the Multiplication Solution (Multiplication Solution.sln) file, which is contained in the VbReloaded2008\Chap06\Multiplication Solution folder. Code the application.

b. Save the solution, then start and test the application. End the application, then close the solution.

13. In this exercise, you create an application that allows the user to enter the gender (either F or M) and GPA for any number of students. The application should calculate the average GPA for all students, the average GPA for male students, and the average GPA for female students.

a. Name the solution, project, and form file GPA Solution, GPA Project, and Main Form.vb, respectively. Save the files in the VbReloaded2008\Chap06 folder.

b. Create an appropriate interface, then code the application. Do not use the InputBox function in the code.

c. Save the solution, then start and test the application. End the application, then close the solution.

14. In this exercise, you learn how to create a list box that allows the user to select more than one item at a time.

   a. Open the Multi Solution (Multi Solution.sln) file, which is contained in the VbReloaded2008\Chap06\Multi Solution folder. The interface contains a list box named namesListBox. The list box's Sorted property is set to True, and its SelectionMode property is set to One.

   b. Open the Code Editor window. Notice that the form's Load event procedure adds five names to the namesListBox.

   c. Code the singleButton's Click event procedure so that it displays, in the resultLabel, the item selected in the namesListbox. For example, if the user clicks Debbie in the list box and then clicks the Single Selection button, the name Debbie should appear in the resultLabel.

   d. Save the solution, then start the application. Click Debbie in the list box, then click Ahmad, and then click Bill. Notice that, when the list box's SelectionMode property is set to One, you can select only one item at a time in the list.

   e. Click the Single Selection button. The name "Bill" appears in the resultLabel.

   f. Click the Exit button to end the application.

   g. Change the list box's SelectionMode property to MultiSimple. Save the solution, then start the application. Click Debbie in the list box, then click Ahmad, then click Bill, and then click Ahmad. Notice that, when the list box's SelectionMode property is set to MultiSimple, you can select more than one item at a time in the list. Also notice that you click to both select and deselect an item. (You also can use Ctrl+click and Shift+click, as well as press the Spacebar, to select and deselect items when the list box's SelectionMode property is set to MultiSimple.)

   h. Click the Exit button to end the application.

   i. Change the list box's SelectionMode property to MultiExtended. Save the solution, then start the application.

   j. Click Debbie in the list, then click Jim. Notice that, in this case, clicking Jim deselects Debbie. When a list box's SelectionMode property is set to MultiExtended, you use Ctrl+click to select multiple items in the list. You also use Ctrl+click to deselect items in the list. Click Debbie in the list, then Ctrl+click Ahmad, and then Ctrl+click Debbie.

   k. Next, click Bill in the list, then Shift+click Jim; this selects all of the names from Bill through Jim.

l. Click the Exit button to end the application.

As you know, when a list box's SelectionMode property is set to One, the item selected in the list box is stored in the SelectedItem property, and the item's index is stored in the SelectedIndex property. However, when a list box's SelectionMode property is set to either MultiSimple or MultiExtended, the items selected in the list box are stored (as strings) in the SelectedItems property, and the indices of the items are stored (as integers) in the SelectedIndices property.

m. Code the multiButton's Click event procedure so that it first clears the contents of the resultLabel. The procedure should then display the selected names (which are stored in the SelectedItems property) on separate lines in the resultLabel.

n. Save the solution, then start the application.

o. Click Ahmad in the list box, then Shift+click Jim. Click the Multi-Selection button. The five names should appear on separate lines in the resultLabel.

p. End the application, then close the solution.

15. In this exercise, you learn how to use the Items collection's Insert, Remove, RemoveAt, and Clear methods.

a. Open the Items Solution (Items Solution.sln) file, which is contained in the VbReloaded2008\Chap06\Items Solution folder.

b. The Items collection's Insert method allows you to add an item at a desired position in a list box while an application is running. The Insert method's syntax is *object*.**Items.Insert(***position*, *item***)**, where *position* is the index of the item. Code the Insert button's Click event procedure so it adds your name as the fourth item in the list box.

c. The Items collection's Remove method allows you to remove an item from a list box while an application is running. The Remove method's syntax is *object*.**Items.Remove(***item***)**, where *item* is the item's value. Code the Remove button's Click event procedure so it removes your name from the list box.

d. Like the Remove method, the Items collection's RemoveAt method also allows you to remove an item from a list box while an application is running. However, in the RemoveAt method you specify the item's index rather than its value. The RemoveAt method's syntax is *object*.**Items.RemoveAt(***index***)**, where *index* is the item's index. Code the Remove At button's Click event procedure so it removes the second name from the list box.

e. The Items collection's Clear method allows you to remove, or clear, all items from a list box while an application is running. The Clear method's syntax is *object*.**Items.Clear()**. Code the Clear button's Click event procedure so it clears the items from the list box.

f. Code the Count button's Click event procedure so it displays (in a message box) the number of items in the list box.

g. Save the solution, then start and test the application. Click the Exit button to end the application, then close the solution.

16. In this exercise, you learn how to use the String Collection Editor dialog box to fill a list box with values.

a. Open the String Collection Solution (String Collection Solution.sln) file, which is contained in the VbReloaded2008\Chap06\String Collection Solution folder.

b. Open the Code Editor window. Remove the four Add methods from the MainForm's Load event procedure, then close the Code Editor window.

c. Click the namesListBox on the form. Click the Items property in the Properties list, then click the ellipsis (...) button in the Settings box. The String Collection Editor dialog box opens. Type any four names, pressing Enter after typing each one.

d. Click the OK button to close the dialog box. The four names appear in the list box. Save the solution, then start the application. End the application, then close the solution.

17. In this exercise, you practice debugging an application.

a. Open the Debug Solution (Debug Solution.sln) file, which is contained in the VbReloaded2008\Chap06\Debug Solution folder. Open the Code Editor window. Review the existing code.

b. Start and then test the application. Click the Exit button to end the application.

c. Correct any errors in the code. Save the solution, then start and test the application again. End the application, then close the solution.

CASE PROJECTS

SONHEIM MANUFACTURING COMPANY

Create an application that the company's accountant can use to calculate an asset's annual depreciation. Name the solution, project, and form file Sonheim Solution, Sonheim Project, and Main Form.vb, respectively. Save the solution in the VbReloaded2008\ Chap06 folder. You can either create your own interface or create the one shown in Figure 6-50. The figure shows a sample depreciation schedule for an asset with a cost of $1,000, a useful life of four years, and a salvage value of $100. The accountant will enter the asset's cost, useful life (in years), and salvage value (which is the value of the asset at the end of its useful life). Use a list box to allow the user to select the useful life.

Display the numbers from 3 through 20 in the list box. The application should use the double-declining balance method to calculate the annual depreciation amounts, and then display the amounts in the interface. You can use the Financial.DDB method to calculate the depreciation. The method's syntax is **Financial.DDB(**cost, salvage, life, period**)**. In the syntax, the cost, salvage, and life arguments are the asset's cost, salvage value, and useful life, respectively. The period argument is the period for which you want the depreciation amount calculated. The method returns the depreciation amount as a Double number. The Asset cost and Salvage value text boxes shown in Figure 6-50 should accept only numbers, the period, and the Backspace key.

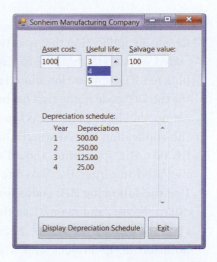

Figure 6-50: Sample interface and depreciation schedule for the Sonheim Manufacturing Company

Below the Depreciation schedule label is a text box whose Multiline and ReadOnly properties are set to True, and whose ScrollBars property is set to Vertical.

COOK COLLEGE

Create an application that displays the total credit hours and GPA for a student during one semester. Name the solution, project, and form file Cook Solution, Cook Project, and Main Form.vb, respectively. Save the solution in the VbReloaded2008\ Chap06 folder. You can either create your own interface or create the one shown in Figure 6-51. The figure, which shows a sample run of the application, uses three labels for the output: one for the total credit hours, one for the GPA, and one for the number of grades entered. When the user clicks the Enter Data button, two input boxes should appear in succession: one for the number of credit hours (such as 3) and the next for the

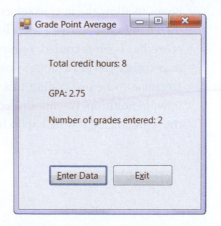

Figure 6-51: Sample interface and output for Cook College

corresponding letter grade (such as A). One credit hour of A is worth 4 grade points, an hour of B is worth 3 grade points, and so on. The Enter Data button's Click event procedure should allow the user to enter as many sets of credit hours and grades as desired. The labels on the form should be updated after the user enters the letter grade.

SHIP WITH US

Create an application that uses two list boxes to store ZIP codes: one for ZIP codes associated with a $15 shipping fee, and the other for ZIP codes associated with a $20 shipping fee. The application should allow the user to enter a ZIP code. It then should search for the ZIP code in the first list box. If it finds the ZIP code in the first list box, the application should display $15 as the shipping fee. If the ZIP code is not in the first list box, the application should search the second list box. If it finds the ZIP code in the second list box, the application should display $20 as the shipping fee. If the ZIP code is not included in either list box, the application should display an appropriate message. Use the following ZIP codes for the first list box: 60611, 60234, 56789, 23467, 60543, 60561, 55905, and 89567. Use the following ZIP codes for the second list box: 50978, 78432, 98432, 97654, and 20245. Name the solution, project, and form file Ship Solution, Ship Project, and Main Form.vb, respectively. Save the application in the VbReloaded2008\Chap06 folder.

POWDER SKATING RINK

Powder Skating Rink holds a weekly ice-skating competition. Competing skaters must perform a two-minute program in front of a panel of six judges. At the end of a skater's program, each judge assigns a score of zero through 10 to the skater. The manager of the ice rink wants an application that calculates and displays a skater's average score. Use list boxes to allow the user to select the names of the judges. (You will need to make up your own names to use.) Also use a list box to allow the user to select the score. After a judge's score has been recorded, remove his/her name from the list box. This will prevent the user from entering a judge's score more than once. (It might help to complete Computer Exercise 15 before coding this application.) Name the solution, project, and form file Powder Solution, Powder Project, and Main Form.vb, respectively. Save the application in the VbReloaded2008\Chap06 folder.

7

THE FOR...NEXT LOOP AND STRING MANIPULATION

After studying Chapter 7, you should be able to:

Include the For...Next loop in both pseudocode and a flowchart

Write a For...Next statement

Calculate a periodic payment using the Financial.Pmt method

Select the existing text in a text box

Code the TextChanged event procedure

Include a combo box in an interface

Manipulate strings

THE FOR...NEXT STATEMENT

As you learned in Chapter 6, you code a loop (repetition structure) in Visual Basic using one of the following statements: Do...Loop, For...Next, or For Each...Next. You already know how to use the Do...Loop statement. You will learn how to use the For...Next statement in this chapter. The For Each...Next statement is covered in Chapter 9. The **For...Next statement** provides a convenient way to code a loop whose instructions you want processed a precise number of times. (You also can use the Do...Loop statement to code this type of loop.) The loop created by the For...Next statement is a pretest loop, because the loop's condition is evaluated *before* the instructions in the loop are processed. Figure 7-1 shows the syntax of the For...Next statement and includes examples of using the statement. The For...Next statement begins with the For clause and ends with the Next clause. Between the two clauses, you enter the instructions you want the loop to repeat. In the syntax, *counter* represents the name of a numeric variable that the computer can use to keep track of the number of times it processes the loop instructions. Notice that *counter* appears in both the For clause and the Next clause. Although, technically, you do not need to specify the name of the *counter* variable in the Next clause, doing so is highly recommended because it makes your code more self-documenting. You can use the As *datatype* portion of the For clause to declare the *counter* variable, as shown in the first two examples in Figure 7-1. When you declare a variable in the For clause, the variable has block scope and can be used only within the For...Next loop. Alternatively, you can declare the *counter* variable in a Dim statement, as shown in Example 3 in Figure 7-1. As you know, when a variable is declared in a Dim statement at the beginning of a procedure, it has procedure scope and can be used by the entire procedure. When deciding where to declare the *counter* variable, keep in mind that if the variable is needed only by the For...Next loop, then it is a better programming practice to declare the variable in the For clause. As you learned in Chapter 3, fewer unintentional errors occur in applications when the variables are declared using the minimum scope needed. Block variables have the smallest scope, followed by procedure-level variables, followed by module-level variables. You should declare the *counter* variable in a Dim statement only when statements outside the loop in the procedure need to use its value.

The *startvalue*, *endvalue*, and *stepvalue* items in the For...Next statement's syntax control the number of times the loop instructions are processed. The *startvalue* tells the computer where to begin counting, and the *endvalue* tells the computer when to stop counting. The *stepvalue* tells the computer how much to count by—in other words, how much to add to the *counter* variable each time the loop is processed. If you omit the *stepvalue*, a *stepvalue* of positive 1 is used. In Example 1 in Figure 7-1, the *startvalue* is 10, the *endvalue* is 13, and the *stepvalue* (which is omitted) is 1. Those values tell the computer to start counting at 10 and, counting by 1s, stop at 13—in other words, count 10, 11, 12, and 13. The computer will process Example 1's loop instructions four times. The For clause's *startvalue*, *endvalue*, and *stepvalue* must be numeric and can be either positive or negative, integer or non-integer. If the *stepvalue* is positive, the *startvalue* must be less than or equal to the *endvalue* for the loop instructions to be processed. For instance, the instruction For price = 10 To 13 is correct, but the instruction For price = 13 To 10 is not correct because you cannot count from 13 (the *startvalue*) to 10 (the *endvalue*) by adding increments of 1 (the *stepvalue*). If, on the other hand, the *stepvalue* is negative, then the *startvalue* must be greater than or equal to the *endvalue* for the loop instructions to be processed. As a result, the instruction For price = 13 To 10 Step -1 is correct, but the instruction For price = 10 To 13 Step -1 is not correct because you cannot count from 10 to 13 by adding increments of negative 1. Notice that you can use either the Convert.ToString method (Example 1) or a numeric data type's ToString method (Examples 2 and 3) to convert the contents of a numeric variable to a string.

»HOW TO . . .

USE THE FOR...NEXT STATEMENT

Syntax

For *counter* [**As** *datatype*] = *startvalue* **To** *endvalue* [**Step** *stepvalue*]

    [*statements*]

Next *counter*

Example 1

```
For price As Integer = 10 To 13
    priceLabel.Text = priceLabel.Text & Convert.ToString(price) _
        & ControlChars.NewLine
Next price
```
displays the numbers 10, 11, 12, and 13 in the priceLabel

Example 2

```
For price As Integer = 13 To 10 Step -1
    priceLabel.Text = priceLabel.Text & price.ToString _
        & ControlChars.NewLine
Next price
```
displays the numbers 13, 12, 11, and 10 in the priceLabel

Example 3

```
Dim x As Decimal
For x = .05D To .1D Step .01D
    rateLabel.Text = rateLabel.Text & x.ToString("P0") _
        & ControlChars.NewLine
Next x
```
displays the values 5 %, 6 %, 7 %, 8 %, 9 %, and 10 % in the rateLabel

Figure 7-1: How to use the For...Next statement

When processing the For...Next statement, the computer performs the three tasks listed in Figure 7-2.

Tasks performed when processing the For...Next statement
1. If the *counter* variable is declared in the For clause, the computer creates the variable and initializes it to the *startvalue*; otherwise, it just performs the initialization task. This is done only once, at the beginning of the loop.
2. If the *stepvalue* is positive, the computer checks whether the value in the *counter* variable is greater than the *endvalue*. (Or, if the *stepvalue* is negative, the computer checks whether the value in the *counter* variable is less than the *endvalue*.) If it is, the computer stops processing the loop, and processing continues with the statement following the Next clause. If it is not, the computer processes the instructions within the loop, and then the next task, task 3, is performed. Notice that the computer evaluates the loop condition before processing the instructions within the loop.
3. The computer adds the *stepvalue* to the contents of the *counter* variable. It then repeats tasks 2 and 3 until the *counter* variable's value is greater than (or less than, if the *stepvalue* is negative) the *endvalue*.

Figure 7-2: Processing tasks for the For...Next statement

Figure 7-3 describes how the computer processes the code shown in Example 1 in Figure 7-1. Notice that when the For...Next statement in the example ends, the value stored in the price variable is 14.

Processing steps for Example 1 in Figure 7-1
1. The computer creates the price (*counter*) variable and initializes it to 10 (*startvalue*).
2. The computer checks whether the value in the price variable is greater than 13 (*endvalue*). It's not.
3. The assignment statement in the loop displays the number 10 on the first line in the priceLabel.
4. The computer processes the Next clause, which adds 1 (*stepvalue*) to the contents of the price variable, giving 11.
5. The computer checks whether the value in the price variable is greater than 13 (*endvalue*). It's not.
6. The assignment statement in the loop displays the number 11 on the next line in the priceLabel.
7. The computer processes the Next clause, which adds 1 (*stepvalue*) to the contents of the price variable, giving 12.
8. The computer checks whether the value in the price variable is greater than 13 (*endvalue*). It's not.
9. The assignment statement in the loop displays the number 12 on the next line in the priceLabel.
10. The computer processes the Next clause, which adds 1 (*stepvalue*) to the contents of the price variable, giving 13.
11. The computer checks whether the value in the price variable is greater than 13 (*endvalue*). It's not.
12. The assignment statement in the loop displays the number 13 on the next line in the priceLabel.
13. The computer processes the Next clause, which adds 1 (*stepvalue*) to the contents of the price variable, giving 14.
14. The computer checks whether the value in the price variable is greater than 13 (*endvalue*). It is, so the computer stops processing the For...Next loop. Processing continues with the statement following the Next clause.

Figure 7-3: Processing steps for the code shown in Example 1 in Figure 7-1

Figure 7-4 shows the pseudocode and flowchart corresponding to Example 1 in Figure 7-1. Many programmers use a hexagon, which is a six-sided figure, to represent the For clause in a flowchart. Four values are recorded inside the hexagon: the name of the *counter* variable, the *startvalue*, the *stepvalue*, and the *endvalue*. Notice that a greater-than sign (>) precedes the *endvalue* in the hexagon shown in Figure 7-4. The greater-than sign reminds you that the loop stops when the value in the *counter* variable is greater than the *endvalue*. When the *stepvalue* is a negative number, a less-than sign (<) should precede the *endvalue* in the hexagon, because a loop with a negative *stepvalue* stops when the value in the *counter* variable is less than the *endvalue*.

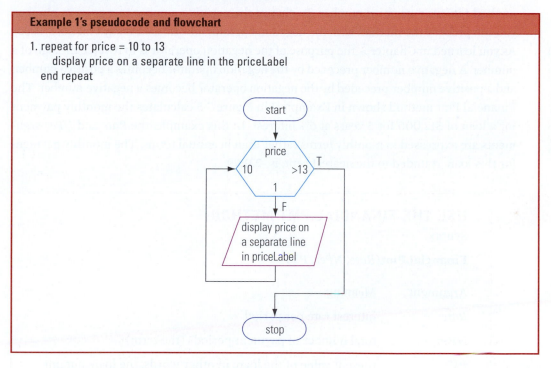

Example 1's pseudocode and flowchart

1. repeat for price = 10 to 13
       display price on a separate line in the priceLabel
   end repeat

Figure 7-4: Pseudocode and flowchart for Example 1 in Figure 7-1

Before viewing the Payment Calculator application, which uses the For...Next statement, you learn about the Financial.Pmt method. The application uses the method to calculate the monthly payments on a loan amount.

THE FINANCIAL.PMT METHOD

You can use the **Financial.Pmt method** to calculate a periodic payment on a loan. ("Pmt" stands for "Payment.") The method returns the periodic payment as a Double type number. Figure 7-5 shows the basic syntax of the Financial.Pmt method and lists the meaning of each of the three arguments included in the method. The *Rate* and *NPer* (number of periods) arguments must be expressed using the same units. If *Rate* is a monthly interest rate, then *NPer* must specify the number of monthly payments. Likewise, if *Rate* is an annual interest rate, then *NPer* must specify the number of annual payments. Figure 7-5 also includes examples of using the Financial.Pmt method. Example 1 calculates the annual payment for a loan of $9,000 for 3 years at 5% interest. As the example indicates, the annual payment returned by the Financial.Pmt method and rounded to the nearest cent is -3,304.88. This means that if you borrow $9,000 for 3 years at 5% interest, you will need to make three annual payments of $3,304.88 to pay off the loan. Notice that the Financial.Pmt method returns a negative number. To change the negative number to a positive number, you can precede the method with the negation operator, like this: -Financial.Pmt(.05, 3, 9000). As you learned in Chapter 3, the purpose of the negation operator is to reverse the sign of a number. A negative number preceded by the negation operator becomes a positive number, and a positive number preceded by the negation operator becomes a negative number. The Financial.Pmt method shown in Example 2 in Figure 7-5 calculates the monthly payment for a loan of $12,000 for 5 years at 6% interest. In this example, the *Rate* and *NPer* arguments are expressed in monthly terms rather than in annual terms. The monthly payment for this loan, rounded to the nearest cent, is -231.99.

»TIP

To learn how to use the Financial.Pmt method to calculate a periodic payment on an investment (rather than on a loan), complete Computer Exercise 13.

»HOW TO . . .

USE THE FINANCIAL.PMT METHOD

Syntax

Financial.Pmt(*Rate*, *NPer*, *PV*)

Argument	Meaning
Rate	interest rate per period
NPer	total number of payment periods (the term)
PV	present value of the loan; in other words, the loan amount

Example 1—Calculates the annual payment for a loan of $9,000 for 3 years at 5% interest. *Rate* is .05, *NPer* is 3, and *PV* is 9000.

Method: Financial.Pmt(.05, 3, 9000)

Annual payment (rounded to the nearest cent):   -3,304.88

Example 2—Calculates the monthly payment for a loan of $12,000 for 5 years at 6% interest. *Rate* is .06/12, *NPer* is 5 * 12, and *PV* is 12000.

Method: Financial.Pmt(.06/12, 5 * 12, 12000)

Monthly payment (rounded to the nearest cent):   -231.99

Figure 7-5: How to use the Financial.Pmt method

THE MONTHLY PAYMENT CALCULATOR APPLICATION

Herman Juarez has been shopping for a new car and has asked you to create an application that calculates and displays his monthly car payment, using terms of 2, 3, 4, and 5 years and annual interest rates of 5%, 6%, 7%, 8%, 9%, and 10%. Figure 7-6 shows a sample run of the Monthly Payment Calculator application, and Figure 7-7 shows the code entered in the form's Load event procedure and in the calcButton's Click event procedure. The Load event procedure fills the termListBox with values and then selects the four-year term in the list. The calcButton's Click event procedure declares three variables to store the principal, term, and payment amounts. The procedure assigns the principal and term entered by the user to two of the variables. It then clears the contents of the paymentsLabel. The For...Next statement is processed next. The For clause tells the computer to create a Double *counter* variable named rate and initialize it to .05. It also tells the computer to repeat the instructions in the For...Next loop six times, using annual interest rates of .05, .06, .07, .08, .09, and .1. The first instruction in the For...Next loop uses the Financial.Pmt method to calculate the monthly payment, using the negation operator to change the negative number returned by the method to a positive number. Notice that the For...Next statement's *counter* variable (rate), which keeps track of the annual interest rates, appears in the Financial.Pmt method's *Rate* argument, where it is divided by 12. It is necessary to divide the annual interest rate by 12 to get a monthly rate, because you want to display monthly payments rather than an annual payment. The term variable, on the other hand, appears in the method's *NPer* argument, where it is multiplied by 12 to get the number of monthly payments. Lastly, the principal variable, which stores the principal entered by the user, is used as the method's *PV* argument. The second instruction in the For...Next loop is an assignment statement that concatenates the current contents of the paymentsLabel with the following items: the annual interest rate converted to a string and formatted to a percentage with zero decimal places, the string " -> " (a space, a hyphen, a greater than sign, and a space), the monthly payment amount converted to a string and formatted with a dollar sign and two decimal places, and the ControlChars.NewLine constant. As you learned in Chapter 4, the ControlChars.NewLine constant advances the insertion point to the next line in a control. The concatenated string is then assigned to the paymentsLabel's Text property. The last instruction in the calcButton's Click event procedure sends the focus to the principalTextBox.

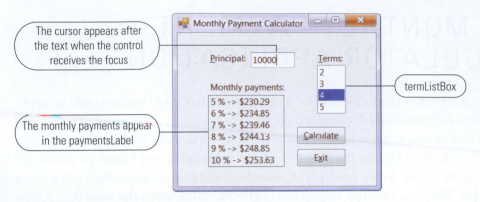

The cursor appears after the text when the control receives the focus

The monthly payments appear in the paymentsLabel

termListBox

Figure 7-6: Sample run of the Monthly Payment Calculator application

```
Private Sub MainForm_Load(ByVal sender As Object, _
    ByVal e As System.EventArgs) Handles Me.Load
    ' fills the termListBox with terms of 2, 3, 4, and 5 years

    For term As Integer = 2 To 5
        termListBox.Items.Add(term.ToString)
    Next term

    ' select the 4-year term
    termListBox.SelectedItem = "4"
End Sub

Private Sub calcButton_Click(ByVal sender As Object, _
    ByVal e As System.EventArgs) Handles calcButton.Click
    ' calculates the monthly payments on a loan using interest rates of
    ' 5% through 10%, and terms of 2, 3, 4, or 5 years

    Dim term As Double
    Dim principal As Double
    Dim monthlyPayment As Double

    ' assign input to variables
    Double.TryParse(principalTextBox.Text, principal)
    Double.TryParse(Convert.ToString(termListBox.SelectedItem), term)

    ' clear contents of the paymentsLabel
    paymentsLabel.Text = String.Empty
```

Figure 7-7: Two of the procedures in the Monthly Payment Calculator application (*continued on next page*)

```
    ' calculate and display monthly payments
    For rate As Double = 0.05 To 0.1 Step 0.01
        monthlyPayment = -Financial.Pmt(rate / 12, term * 12, principal)
        paymentsLabel.Text = paymentsLabel.Text _
            & rate.ToString("P0") & " -> " & monthlyPayment.ToString("C2") _
            & ControlChars.NewLine
    Next rate

    principalTextBox.Focus()
End Sub
```

Figure 7-7: Two of the procedures in the Monthly Payment Calculator application (*continued from previous page*)

SELECTING THE EXISTING TEXT IN A TEXT BOX

Before the calcButton's Click event procedure ends, it sends the focus to the principalTextBox. As you observed earlier in Figure 7-6, this places the cursor after the existing text in the text box. However, it is customary in Windows applications to select (highlight) the existing text when a text box receives the focus. When the text is selected in a text box, the user can remove the text simply by pressing a key—for example, the letter "n" on the keyboard. The key that is pressed—in this case, the letter "n"—replaces the selected text. You use the **SelectAll method** to select all of the text contained in a text box. Figure 7-8 shows the syntax of the SelectAll method and includes an example of using the method. In the syntax, *textbox* is the name of the text box whose contents you want to select.

»HOW TO . . .

SELECT THE EXISTING TEXT IN A TEXT BOX

<u>Syntax</u>

textbox.**SelectAll()**

<u>Example</u>

nameTextBox.SelectAll()
selects (highlights) the contents of the nameTextBox

Figure 7-8: How to select the existing text in a text box

You can use the SelectAll method to select the contents of the principalTextBox when the text box receives the focus. You do this by entering the SelectAll method in the text box's Enter event procedure. A text box's **Enter event** occurs when the text box receives the focus, which can happen as a result of the user tabbing to the control or using the control's access key. It also occurs when the Focus method is used in code to send the focus to the control. Figure 7-9 shows the principalTextBox's Enter event procedure, and Figure 7-10 shows the result of the computer processing the procedure's code.

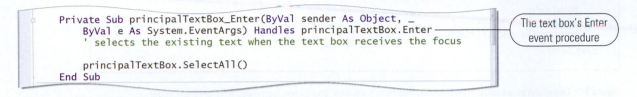

```
Private Sub principalTextBox_Enter(ByVal sender As Object, _
    ByVal e As System.EventArgs) Handles principalTextBox.Enter
    ' selects the existing text when the text box receives the focus

    principalTextBox.SelectAll()
End Sub
```

The text box's Enter event procedure

Figure 7-9: The principalTextBox's Enter event procedure

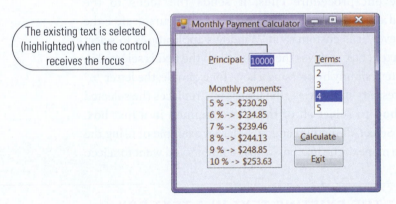

The existing text is selected (highlighted) when the control receives the focus

Figure 7-10: Result of processing the Enter event procedure

CLEARING THE PAYMENTSLABEL CONTROL

Consider what happens when, after calculating the monthly payments on a $10,000 loan, the user enters the number 25000 as the principal, as shown in Figure 7-11. The information that appears in the interface could be misleading, because even though the principal amount has changed, the paymentsLabel still lists the monthly payments for a $10,000 loan. The monthly payments for a $25,000 loan will not appear in the paymentsLabel until the user clicks the Calculate button. To prevent any confusion, it would be better to clear the contents of the paymentsLabel when the principal amount has changed. You can clear the contents by coding the principalTextBox's TextChanged event procedure. A control's **TextChanged event** occurs when a change is made to the contents of the control's Text property. This can happen as a result of the user entering data into the control, or the application's code assigning data to the control's Text property.

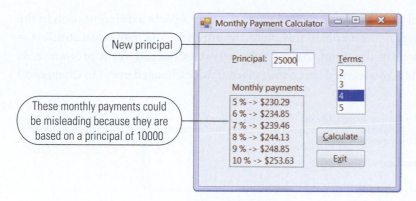

Figure 7-11: New principal entered in the Principal text box

In the Monthly Payment Calculator application, the principalTextBox's TextChanged event procedure should clear the contents of the paymentsLabel when the user changes the principal. Figure 7-12 shows the procedure's code, and Figure 7-13 shows a sample run of the application. In the sample run, the user enters the number 2 in the principalTextBox after calculating the monthly payments for a $10,000 loan. Notice that the monthly payments no longer appear in the paymentsLabel.

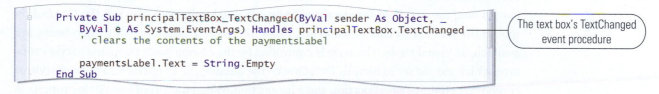

```
Private Sub principalTextBox_TextChanged(ByVal sender As Object, _
    ByVal e As System.EventArgs) Handles principalTextBox.TextChanged
    ' clears the contents of the paymentsLabel

    paymentsLabel.Text = String.Empty
End Sub
```

The text box's TextChanged event procedure

Figure 7-12: The principalTextBox's TextChanged event procedure

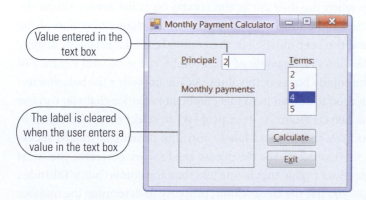

Figure 7-13: Status of the paymentsLabel after entering a value in the text box

The paymentsLabel also should be cleared when the user selects a different term in the termListBox. You can accomplish this task by entering the paymentsLabel.Text = String.Empty statement in the termListBox's SelectedValueChanged event procedure, as shown in Figure 7-14. (You learned about the SelectedValueChanged event in Chapter 6.)

```
Private Sub termListBox_SelectedValueChanged(ByVal sender As Object, _
    ByVal e As System.EventArgs) Handles termListBox.SelectedValueChanged
    ' clears the contents of the paymentsLabel

    paymentsLabel.Text = String.Empty
End Sub
```

The list box's SelectedValueChanged event procedure

Figure 7-14: The termListBox's SelectedValueChanged event procedure

USING A COMBO BOX IN AN INTERFACE

In many interfaces, combo boxes are used in place of list boxes. A **combo box** is similar to a list box in that it allows the user to select from a list of choices. However, unlike a list box, the full list of choices in a combo box can be hidden, allowing you to save space on the form. Also unlike a list box, a combo box contains a text field. Depending on the style of the combo box, the text field may or may not be editable by the user. You use the ComboBox tool in the toolbox to add a combo box to an interface. Three styles of combo boxes are available in Visual Basic. The style is controlled by the combo box's DropDownStyle property, which can be set to Simple, DropDown (the default), or DropDownList. Each style of combo box contains a text portion and a list portion. When the DropDownStyle property is set to either Simple or DropDown, the text portion of the combo box is editable. However, in a Simple combo box the list portion is always displayed, while in a DropDown combo box the list portion appears only when the user clicks the combo box's list arrow. When the DropDownStyle property is set to the third style, DropDownList, the text portion of the combo box is not editable and the user must click the combo box's list arrow to display the list of choices. Figure 7-15 shows an example of each combo box style, and Figure 7-16 shows the code used to fill the combo boxes with values. As you do with a list box, you use the Items collection's Add method to add an item to a combo box. Notice that you can use a combo box's SelectedIndex, SelectedItem, or Text property to select the default item in the list portion of the control. You should use a label control to provide keyboard access to the combo box, as shown in Figure 7-15. For the access key to work correctly, you must set the label's TabIndex property to a value that is one less than the combo box's TabIndex value. As is true with a list box, you use the Items.Count property to determine the number of items in the combo box, and use its Sorted property to sort the items in the list.

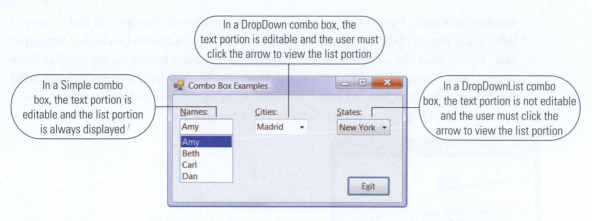

In a Simple combo box, the text portion is editable and the list portion is always displayed

In a DropDown combo box, the text portion is editable and the user must click the arrow to view the list portion

In a DropDownList combo box, the text portion is not editable and the user must click the arrow to view the list portion

Figure 7-15: Examples of the combo box styles

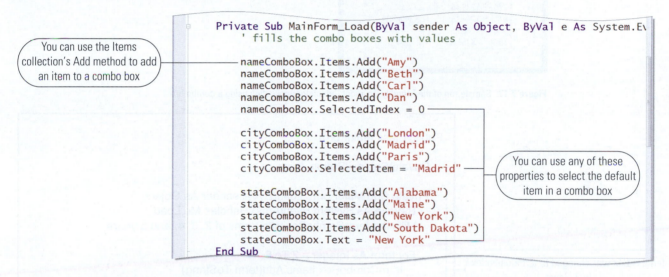

You can use the Items collection's Add method to add an item to a combo box

You can use any of these properties to select the default item in a combo box

```
Private Sub MainForm_Load(ByVal sender As Object, ByVal e As System.Ev
    ' fills the combo boxes with values

    nameComboBox.Items.Add("Amy")
    nameComboBox.Items.Add("Beth")
    nameComboBox.Items.Add("Carl")
    nameComboBox.Items.Add("Dan")
    nameComboBox.SelectedIndex = 0

    cityComboBox.Items.Add("London")
    cityComboBox.Items.Add("Madrid")
    cityComboBox.Items.Add("Paris")
    cityComboBox.SelectedItem = "Madrid"

    stateComboBox.Items.Add("Alabama")
    stateComboBox.Items.Add("Maine")
    stateComboBox.Items.Add("New York")
    stateComboBox.Items.Add("South Dakota")
    stateComboBox.Text = "New York"
End Sub
```

Figure 7-16: Code used to fill the combo boxes in Figure 7-15 with values

It is easy to confuse a combo box's SelectedItem property with its Text property. The SelectedItem property contains the value of the item selected in the list portion of the combo box, whereas the Text property contains the value that appears in the text portion. A value can appear in the text portion as a result of the user either selecting an item in the list portion of the control or typing an entry in the text portion itself. If the combo box is a DropDownList style, where the text portion is not editable, you can use the SelectedItem and Text properties interchangeably. However, if the combo box is either a Simple or DropDown style, where the user can type an entry in the text portion, you should use the Text property because it contains the value either selected or entered by the user. Figure 7-17 shows a sample run of the Monthly Payment Calculator application using a DropDown combo box rather than a list box, and Figure 7-18 shows most of the application's code. Figure 7-18 indicates the changes made to the original code (most of which was shown earlier in Figure 7-7) as a result of using a combo box rather than a list box. Notice that the contents of the paymentsLabel are cleared in the combo box's TextChanged event procedure rather than in the list box's SelectedValueChanged event procedure. The TextChanged event of a combo box occurs when the user either selects an item in the list portion or types a value in the text portion.

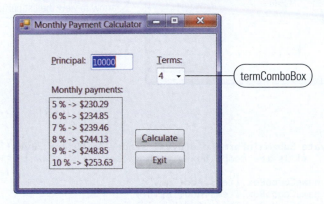

Figure 7-17: Sample run of the Monthly Payment Calculator application using a combo box

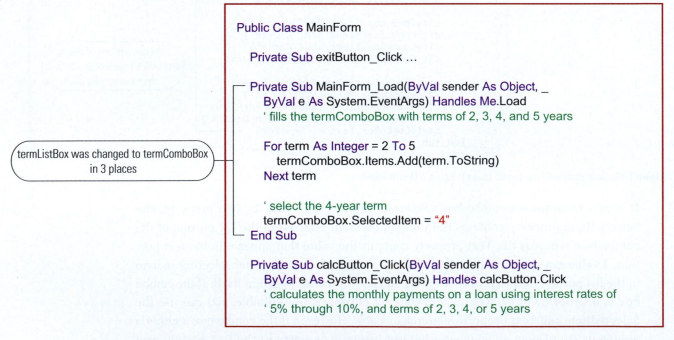

```
Public Class MainForm

    Private Sub exitButton_Click …

    Private Sub MainForm_Load(ByVal sender As Object, _
        ByVal e As System.EventArgs) Handles Me.Load
        ' fills the termComboBox with terms of 2, 3, 4, and 5 years

        For term As Integer = 2 To 5
            termComboBox.Items.Add(term.ToString)
        Next term

        ' select the 4-year term
        termComboBox.SelectedItem = "4"
    End Sub

    Private Sub calcButton_Click(ByVal sender As Object, _
        ByVal e As System.EventArgs) Handles calcButton.Click
        ' calculates the monthly payments on a loan using interest rates of
        ' 5% through 10%, and terms of 2, 3, 4, or 5 years
```

termListBox was changed to termComboBox in 3 places

Figure 7-18: Code for the Monthly Payment Calculator application using a combo box (*continued on next page*)

```
                    Dim term As Double
                    Dim principal As Double
                    Dim monthlyPayment As Double

                    ' assign input to variables
                    Double.TryParse(principalTextBox.Text, principal)
                    Double.TryParse(termComboBox.Text, term)

                    ' clear contents of the paymentsLabel
                    paymentsLabel.Text = String.Empty

                    ' calculate and display monthly payments
                    For rate As Double = 0.05 To 0.1 Step 0.01
                        monthlyPayment = -Financial.Pmt(rate / 12, term * 12, principal)
                        paymentsLabel.Text = paymentsLabel.Text _
                            & rate.ToString("P0") & " -> " & monthlyPayment.ToString("C2") _
                            & ControlChars.NewLine
                    Next rate

                    principalTextBox.Focus()
                End Sub

                Private Sub principalTextBox_Enter(ByVal sender As Object, _
                    ByVal e As System.EventArgs) Handles principalTextBox.Enter
                    ' selects the existing text when the text box receives the focus

                    principalTextBox.SelectAll()
                End Sub

                Private Sub principalTextBox_TextChanged(ByVal sender As Object, _
                    ByVal e As System.EventArgs) Handles principalTextBox.TextChanged
                    ' clears the contents of the paymentsLabel

                    paymentsLabel.Text = String.Empty
                End Sub

                Private Sub termComboBox_TextChanged(ByVal sender As Object, _
                    ByVal e As System.EventArgs) Handles termComboBox.TextChanged
                    ' clears the contents of the paymentsLabel

                    paymentsLabel.Text = String.Empty
                End Sub
            End Class
```

Callout: Convert.ToString(termListBox.SelectedItem) was changed to termComboBox.Text

Callout: This procedure replaces the termListBox's SelectedValueChanged procedure

Figure 7-18: Code for the Monthly Payment Calculator application using a combo box (*continued from previous page*)

STRING MANIPULATION

Many times, an application will need to manipulate (process) string data in some way. For example, an application may need to look at the first character in an inventory part number to determine the part's location in the warehouse. Or, it may need to search an address to determine the street name. In the remainder of this chapter's concepts section, you learn several ways of manipulating strings in Visual Basic. Sample applications that demonstrate each of the **string manipulation** techniques covered in this chapter can be found in the VbReloaded2008\Chap07\String folder. The first string manipulation technique you will learn is how to determine the number of characters in a string.

DETERMINING THE NUMBER OF CHARACTERS CONTAINED IN A STRING

If your application expects the user to enter a 10-digit phone number or a 5-digit ZIP code, you should verify that the user entered the required number of characters. The number of characters contained in a string is stored in the string's **Length property**. Not surprisingly, the value stored in the property is an integer. Figure 7-19 shows the syntax of the Length property and includes examples of using the property. (The Length property is used in the Zip Codes application, which is contained in the VbReloaded2008\Chap07\String\Zip Codes Solution folder.)

»HOW TO . . .

USE THE LENGTH PROPERTY

Syntax	Purpose
string.**Length**	stores the number of characters contained in a string

Example 1
```
Dim numChars As Integer
Dim fullName As String = "Paul Blackfeather"
numChars = fullName.Length
```
assigns the number 17 to the numChars variable

Figure 7-19: How to use the Length property (*continued on next page*)

Example 2

```
Dim phone As String = String.Empty
phone = InputBox("10-digit phone number", "Phone")
Do Until phone.Length = 10
    phone = InputBox("10-digit phone number", "Phone")
Loop
```

gets a phone number from the user until the phone number contains exactly 10 characters

Figure 7-19: How to use the Length property (*continued from previous page*)

REMOVING CHARACTERS FROM A STRING

In some applications, it may be necessary to remove one or more characters from an item of data entered by the user. For example, you may need to remove a percent sign from the end of a tax rate so that you can use the tax rate in a calculation. You can use the **TrimStart method** to remove one or more characters from the beginning of a string, and the **TrimEnd method** to remove one or more characters from the end of a string. To remove one or more characters from both the beginning and end of a string, you use the **Trim method**. Each method returns a string with the appropriate characters removed (trimmed). Figure 7-20 shows the syntax of the TrimStart, TrimEnd, and Trim methods. In each syntax, *trimChars* is a comma-separated list of characters that you want removed. The *trimChars* argument and its surrounding parentheses are optional in each syntax. If you omit the *trimChars* argument, the method removes one or more spaces from the beginning and/or end of the string. In other words, the default value for the *trimChars* argument is the space character (" "). When the computer processes the TrimStart, TrimEnd, and Trim methods, it makes a temporary copy of the *string* in memory, and then performs the necessary trimming on the copy only. The methods do not remove any characters from the original *string*. Figure 7-20 includes examples of using each method. (The Trim method is used in the City Names application, which is contained in the VbReloaded2008\Chap07\String\City Names Solution folder.)

USE THE TRIMSTART, TRIMEND, AND TRIM METHODS

Syntax	Purpose
string.**TrimStart**[(*trimChars*)]	removes characters from the beginning of a string
string.**TrimEnd**[(*trimChars*)]	removes characters from the end of a string
string.**Trim**[(*trimChars*)]	removes characters from both the beginning and end of a string

Example 1

```
Dim fullName As String
fullName = nameTextBox.Text.TrimStart
```
assigns the contents of the nameTextBox's Text property, excluding any leading spaces, to the fullName variable

Example 2

```
Dim rate As Decimal
Decimal.TryParse(rateTextBox.Text.TrimEnd("%"c), rate)
```
converts the contents of the rateTextBox, excluding any trailing percent signs, to Decimal and then assigns the result to the rate variable

Example 3

```
Dim fullName As String = String.Empty
fullName = nameTextBox.Text.Trim
```
assigns the contents of the nameTextBox, excluding any leading and trailing spaces, to the fullName variable

Example 4

```
Dim userEntry As String = String.Empty
userEntry = InputBox("Number:", "Entry").Trim("$"c, " "c, "%"c)
```
assigns the user's entry, excluding any leading and trailing dollar signs, spaces, and percent signs, to the userEntry variable

Figure 7-20: How to use the TrimStart, TrimEnd, and Trim methods

Study the four examples shown in Figure 7-20. When processing the fullName = nameTextBox.Text.TrimStart statement in Example 1, the computer first makes a temporary copy of the string stored in the nameTextBox's Text property. It then removes any leading spaces from the temporary copy of the string and assigns the resulting string to the fullName variable. If the user enters the string " Karen" (two spaces followed by the name Karen) in the nameTextBox, the statement assigns the name "Karen" to the fullName variable; however, the nameTextBox's Text property still contains " Karen" (two spaces followed by the name Karen). After the statement is processed, the computer removes the temporary copy of the string from its internal memory. Notice that the TrimStart method in Example 1 does not remove the leading spaces from the nameTextBox's Text property. To remove the leading spaces from the Text property, you use the statement nameTextBox.Text = nameTextBox.Text.TrimStart. The Decimal.TryParse(rateTextBox.Text.TrimEnd("%"c), rate) statement in Example 2 converts the contents of the rateTextBox (excluding any trailing percent signs) to Decimal and then assigns the result to the rate variable. The letter c that appears after the string in the *trimChars* argument is one of the literal type characters in Visual Basic. As you learned in Chapter 3, a literal type character forces a literal constant to assume a data type other than the one its form indicates. In this case, the letter c forces the "%" string to assume the Char (character) data type. The fullName = nameTextBox.Text.Trim statement in Example 3 assigns the contents of the nameTextBox, excluding any leading and trailing spaces, to the fullName variable. Lastly, the userEntry = InputBox("Number:", "Entry").Trim("$"c, " "c, "%"c) statement in Example 4 assigns the user's entry (excluding any leading and trailing dollar signs, spaces, and percent signs) to the userEntry variable.

THE REMOVE METHOD

Besides using the TrimStart, TrimEnd, and Trim methods, you also can use the Remove method to remove characters from a string. However, the **Remove method** allows you to remove one or more characters located anywhere in a string, not just at the beginning and/or end of the string. The Remove method returns a string with the appropriate characters removed. The Remove method's syntax is shown in Figure 7-21. Notice that the method has two arguments: *startIndex* and *count*. The *startIndex* argument is the index of the first character you want removed from the string. A character's index is a number that indicates the character's position in the string. The first character in a string has an index of zero, the second character has an index of one, and so on. The *count* argument is the number of characters you want removed. To remove only the first character from a string, you use the number 0 as the *startIndex*, and the number 1 as the *count*. To remove the fourth through eighth characters, you use the number 3 as the *startIndex*, and the number 5 as the *count*. When processing the Remove method, the computer makes a temporary copy of the *string* in memory, and then removes the characters from the copy only. Like the TrimStart, TrimEnd, and Trim methods, the Remove method does not remove any characters from the original *string*. Figure 7-21 includes examples of using the Remove method. (The Remove method is used in the Social Security Number application, which is contained in the VbReloaded2008\Chap07\String\Social Security Solution-Remove folder.)

»HOW TO . . .

USE THE REMOVE METHOD

Syntax	Purpose
string.**Remove**(*startIndex*, *count*)	removes characters from anywhere in a string

Example 1

Dim fullName As String = "John Cober"
nameTextBox.Text = fullName.Remove(0, 5)

assigns the string "Cober" to the nameTextBox's Text property

Example 2

Dim fullName As String = "John"
nameTextBox.Text = fullName.Remove(2, 1)

assigns the string "Jon" to the nameTextBox's Text property

Figure 7-21: How to use the Remove method

REPLACING CHARACTERS IN A STRING

You can use the **Replace method** to replace a sequence of characters in a string with another sequence of characters, such as replacing area code "800" with area code "877" in a phone number. Or, you can use it to replace the dashes in a Social Security number with the empty string. Figure 7-22 shows the syntax of the Replace method and includes examples of using the method. In the syntax, *oldValue* is the sequence of characters that you want to replace in the *string*, and *newValue* is the replacement characters. When processing the Replace method, the computer makes a temporary copy of the *string* in memory, and then replaces the characters in the copy only. The Replace method returns a string with *all* occurrences of *oldValue* replaced with *newValue*. (The Replace method is used in the Social Security Number application, which is contained in the VbReloaded2008\Chap07\String\Social Security Solution-Replace folder.)

USE THE REPLACE METHOD

Syntax	Purpose
string.**Replace**(oldValue, newValue)	replaces all occurrences of a sequence of characters in a string with another sequence of characters

Example 1

```
Dim socialNum As String = "000-11-9999"
socialNum = socialNum.Replace("-", "")
```
assigns the string "000119999" to the socialNum variable

Example 2

```
Dim word As String = "latter"
word = word.Replace("t", "d")
```
assigns the string "ladder" to the word variable

Figure 7-22: How to use the Replace method

THE MID STATEMENT

You can use the **Mid statement** to replace a specified number of characters in a string with characters from another string. Figure 7-23 shows the syntax of the Mid statement and includes examples of using the statement. In the syntax, *targetString* is the string in which you want characters replaced, and *replacementString* contains the replacement characters. *Start* is the character position of the first character you want replaced in the *targetString*. The first character in the *targetString* is in character position one, the second is in character position two, and so on. Notice that the character position is not the same as the index, which begins with zero. The optional *count* argument specifies the number of characters to replace in the *targetString*. If *count* is omitted, the Mid statement replaces the lesser of either the number of characters in the *replacementString* or the number of characters in the *targetString* from position *start* through the end of the *targetString*. (The Mid statement is used in the Area Code application, which is contained in the VbReloaded2008\Chap07\String\Area Code Solution folder.)

USE THE MID STATEMENT

Syntax	Purpose
Mid(targetString, start [, count]**)** = replacementString	replaces a specific number of characters in a string with characters from another string

Example 1

Dim fullName As String = "Rob Smith"
Mid(fullName, 7, 1) = "y"
changes the contents of the fullName variable to "Rob Smyth"

Example 2

Dim fullName As String = "Ann Johnson"
Mid(fullName, 5) = "Carl"
changes the contents of the fullName variable to "Ann Carlson"

Example 3

Dim fullName As String = "Earl Cho"
Mid(fullName, 6) = "Liverpool"
changes the contents of the fullName variable to "Earl Liv"

Figure 7-23: How to use the Mid statement

INSERTING CHARACTERS IN A STRING

In addition to removing and replacing characters in a string, you also can insert characters in a string. To insert characters at either the beginning or end of a string, you can use the PadLeft and PadRight methods, respectively. Both methods pad the string with a character until the string is a specified length, then they return the padded string. The **PadLeft method** pads the string on the left. In other words, it inserts the padded characters at the beginning of the string, which right-aligns the characters within the string. The **PadRight method**, on the other hand, pads the string on the right, which inserts the padded characters at the end of the string and left-aligns the characters within the string. Figure 7-24 shows the syntax of the PadLeft and PadRight methods. In each syntax, *length* is an integer that represents the desired length of the *string*. In other words, *length* represents the total number of characters you want the *string* to contain. The *character* argument is the character that each method uses to pad the *string* until it reaches the desired *length*. The *character* argument is optional in each syntax; if omitted, the default *character* is the space character. When processing the PadLeft and PadRight methods, the computer makes a temporary copy of the *string* in memory, and then inserts the characters in the copy only. Examples of using the methods are shown in Figure 7-24. Notice that two methods appear in the expression in Example 2: ToString and PadLeft. When an expression contains more than one method, the computer processes the methods from left to right. In this case, the computer will process the ToString method before processing the PadLeft method. (The PadLeft method is used in the Item Prices application, which is contained in the VbReloaded2008\Chap07\String\Item Prices Solution folder.)

»HOW TO . . .

USE THE PADLEFT AND PADRIGHT METHODS

Syntax	Purpose
string.**PadLeft**(*length*[, *character*])	pads the beginning of a string with a character until the string is a specified length
string.**PadRight**(*length*[, *character*])	pads the end of a string with a character until the string is a specified length

Example 1

```
Dim outputNumber As String = "42"
outputNumber = outputNumber.PadLeft(5)
```
assigns "   42" (three spaces and the string "42") to the outputNumber variable

Example 2

```
Dim netPay As Double = 767.89
Dim formattedNetPay As String
formattedNetPay = netPay.ToString("C2").PadLeft(15, "*"c)
```
assigns "********$767.89" to the formattedNetPay variable (Many companies use this type of formatted net pay on their employee paychecks, because it makes it difficult for someone to change the amount.)

Example 3

```
Dim firstName As String = "Sue"
firstName = firstName.PadRight(10)
```
assigns "Sue   " (the string "Sue" and seven spaces) to the firstName variable

Figure 7-24: How to use the PadLeft and PadRight methods

THE INSERT METHOD

The PadLeft and PadRight methods can be used to insert characters only at the beginning and end, respectively, of a string. To insert characters within a string, you use the **Insert method**. Possible uses for the method include inserting an employee's middle initial within his or her name, and inserting parentheses around the area code in a phone number. Figure 7-25 shows the syntax of the Insert method and includes two examples of using the method. In the syntax, *startIndex* specifies where in the string you want the *value* inserted. To insert the *value* at the beginning of the string, you use the number 0 as the *startIndex*. To insert the *value* as the second character in the string, you use the number 1 as the *startIndex*, and so on. When processing the Insert method, the computer makes a temporary copy of the *string* in memory, and then inserts the characters in the copy only. The Insert method returns a string with the appropriate characters inserted. (The Insert method is used in the Date application, which is contained in the VbReloaded2008\Chap07\String\Date Solution folder.)

»HOW TO . . .

USE THE INSERT METHOD

Syntax	Purpose
string.**Insert(***startIndex***,** *value***)**	inserts characters within a string

Example 1

Dim name As String = "Rob Smith"
Dim fullName As String = String.Empty
fullName = name.Insert(4, "T. ")

assigns the string "Rob T. Smith" to the fullName variable

Example 2

Dim phone As String = "3120501111"
phone = phone.Insert(0, "(")
phone = phone.Insert(4, ")")
phone = phone.Insert(8, "-")

changes the contents of the phone variable to "(312)050-1111"

Figure 7-25: How to use the Insert method

SEARCHING A STRING

In some applications, you might need to determine whether a string begins or ends with a specific character or characters. For instance, you may need to determine whether a phone number entered by the user begins with area code "312", which indicates that the customer lives in Chicago. Or, you may need to determine whether a tax rate entered by the user ends with a percent sign, because the percent sign will need to be removed before the tax rate can be used in a calculation. In Visual Basic, you can use the **StartsWith method** to determine whether a specific sequence of characters occurs at the beginning of a string, and the **EndsWith method** to determine whether it occurs at the end of a string. Figure 7-26 shows the syntax of the StartsWith and EndsWith methods along with examples of using each method. In the syntax for both methods, *subString* is a string that represents the sequence of characters you want to search for either at the beginning or end of the *string*. The StartsWith method returns the Boolean value True when the *subString* is located at the beginning of the *string*; otherwise, it returns the Boolean value False. Similarly, the EndsWith method returns the Boolean value True when the *subString* is located at the end of *string*; otherwise, it returns the Boolean value False. Both methods perform a case-sensitive search, which means that the case of the *subString* must match the case of the *string* for the methods to return the True value. (The EndsWith method is used in the Sales Tax Calculator application, which is contained in the VbReloaded2008\Chap07\String\Sales Tax Solution folder.)

»HOW TO . . .

USE THE STARTSWITH AND ENDSWITH METHODS

Syntax	Purpose
string.**StartsWith**(*subString*)	determines whether a specific sequence of characters occurs at the beginning of a string
string.**EndsWith**(*subString*)	determines whether a specific sequence of characters occurs at the end of a string

Example 1

```
Dim phone As String = String.Empty
phone = InputBox("10-digit phone number", "Phone")
Do While phone.StartsWith("312")
    phoneListBox.Items.Add(phone)
    phone = InputBox("10-digit phone number", "Phone")
Loop
```

determines whether the string stored in the phone variable begins with "312"; if it does, the contents of the phone variable are added to the phoneListBox and the user is prompted to enter another phone number (You also can write the Do clause in this example as Do While phone. StartsWith("312") = True.)

Figure 7-26: How to use the StartsWith and EndsWith methods (*continued on next page*)

Example 2
```
Dim cityState As String = String.Empty
cityState = cityStateTextBox.Text.ToUpper
If cityState.EndsWith("CA") Then
    stateLabel.Text = "California customer"
End If
```
determines whether the string stored in the cityState variable ends with "CA"; if it does, the string "California customer" is assigned to the stateLabel's Text property (You also can write the If clause in this example as If cityState.EndsWith("CA") = True Then.)

Figure 7-26: How to use the StartsWith and EndsWith methods (*continued from previous page*)

The StartsWith and EndsWith methods can be used only to determine whether a string begins or ends with a specific sequence of characters. To determine whether one or more characters appear anywhere in a string, you can use either the Contains method or the IndexOf method. You learn about the Contains method first.

THE CONTAINS METHOD

You can use the **Contains method** to search a string to determine whether it contains a specific sequence of characters. For example, you can use the method to determine whether the area code "(312)" appears in a phone number, or whether the street name "Elm Street" appears in an address. Figure 7-27 shows the syntax of the Contains method and includes examples of using the method. In the syntax, *subString* is a string that represents the sequence of characters for which you are searching within the *string*. The Contains method returns the Boolean value True when the *subString* is contained anywhere within the string; otherwise, it returns the Boolean value False. Like the StartsWith and EndsWith methods, the Contains method performs a case-sensitive search. (The Contains method is used in the Part Numbers application, which is contained in the VbReloaded2008\Chap07\String\Part Number Solution folder.)

USE THE CONTAINS METHOD

Syntax	Purpose
string.**Contains(***subString***)**	searches a string to determine whether it contains a specific sequence of characters, and then returns a Boolean value that indicates whether the characters appear within the string

Example 1

```
Dim address As String = "345 Main Street, Glendale, CA"
Dim isContained As Boolean
isContained = address.ToUpper.Contains("MAIN STREET")
```
assigns the Boolean value True to the isContained variable, because "MAIN STREET" appears in the address variable when its contents are temporarily converted to uppercase

Example 2

```
Dim phone As String = "(312) 999-9999"
If phone.Contains("(312)") Then
```
the If...Then...Else statement's *condition* evaluates to True, because "(312)" appears in the phone variable

---

Figure 7-27: How to use the Contains method

THE INDEXOF METHOD

In addition to using the Contains method to search for a *subString* anywhere within a *string*, you also can use the **IndexOf method**. Unlike the Contains method, which returns a Boolean value that indicates whether the *string* contains the *subString*, the IndexOf method returns an integer that represents the location of the *subString* within the *string*. Figure 7-28 shows the syntax of the IndexOf method and includes examples of using the method. In the syntax, *subString* is the sequence of characters for which you are searching in the *string*, and *startIndex* is the index of the character at which the search should begin. In other words, *startIndex* specifies the starting position for the search. Recall that the first character in a string has an index of zero, the second character has an index of one, and so on. The *startIndex* argument is optional in the IndexOf method's syntax; if omitted, the method begins the search with the first character in the *string*. The IndexOf method searches for the *subString* within the *string*, beginning with the character whose index is *startIndex*. If the IndexOf method does not find the *subString*, it returns the number -1. Otherwise, it returns the index of the starting position of the *subString* within the *string*. Like the Contains method, the IndexOf method performs a case-sensitive search. (The IndexOf method is used in the Count application, which is contained in the VbReloaded2008\Chap07\String\Count Solution folder.)

»HOW TO . . .

USE THE INDEXOF METHOD

<u>Syntax</u>

string.**IndexOf(***subString*[**,** *startIndex*]**)**

<u>Purpose</u>

searches a string to determine whether it contains a specific sequence of characters, and then returns an integer that indicates the starting position of the characters within the string

<u>Example 1</u>

```
Dim message As String = "Have a nice day"
Dim indexNum As Integer
indexNum = message.ToUpper.IndexOf("NICE")
```
assigns the number 7 to the indexNum variable

<u>Example 2</u>

```
Dim message As String = "Have a nice day"
Dim indexNum As Integer
indexNum = message.IndexOf("v", 5)
```
assigns the number -1 to the indexNum variable

Figure 7-28: How to use the IndexOf method

ACCESSING CHARACTERS CONTAINED IN A STRING

In some applications, it is necessary to access one or more characters contained in a string. For instance, you may need to determine whether a specific letter appears as the third character in a string, because the letter identifies the department in which an employee works. Or, you may need to display only the string's first five characters, which identify an item's location in the warehouse. Visual Basic provides the **Substring method** for accessing any number of characters contained in a string. Figure 7-29 shows the syntax of the Substring method, which contains two arguments: *startIndex* and *count*. *StartIndex* is the index of the first character you want to access in the *string*. As you learned earlier, the first character in a string has an index of zero; the second character has an index of one, and so on. The optional *count* argument specifies the number of characters you want to access. The Substring method returns a string that contains *count* number of characters, beginning with the character whose index is *startIndex*. If you omit the *count* argument, the Substring method returns all characters from the *startIndex* position through the end of the string. Examples of using the method are included in Figure 7-29. (The Substring method is used in the Names application, which is contained in the VbReloaded2008\Chap07\String\Names Solution folder.)

»HOW TO . . .

USE THE SUBSTRING METHOD

Syntax   Purpose

string.**Substring(***startIndex*[**,** *count*]**)**   accesses one or more characters
                                                   contained in a string

Example 1

Dim fullName As String = "Peggy Ryan"
firstName = fullName.Substring(0, 5)
lastName = fullName.Substring(6)
assigns "Peggy" to the firstName variable, and assigns "Ryan" to the lastName variable

Example 2

Dim employeeNum As String = "56P34"
Dim department As String = String.Empty
department = employeeNum.Substring(2, 1)
assigns the letter P to the department variable

Figure 7-29: How to use the Substring method

COMPARING STRINGS

In addition to using the comparison operators to compare two strings, you also can use the **String.Compare method**. Figure 7-30 shows the method's syntax. The *string1* and *string2* arguments in the syntax represent the two strings you want compared. The optional *ignoreCase* argument is a Boolean value that indicates whether you want to perform a case-insensitive (True) or a case-sensitive (False) comparison of both strings. The default *ignoreCase* value is False. The method returns an integer that indicates the result of comparing *string1* with *string2*. When both strings are equal, the method returns the number 0. When *string1* is greater than *string2*, the method returns the number 1. When *string1* is less than *string2*, the method returns the number –1. The String.Compare method uses rules called **word sort rules** when comparing the strings. Following these rules, numbers are considered less than lowercase letters, which are considered less than uppercase letters. Figure 7-30 shows examples of using the method. (The String.Compare method is used in the Alphabet application, which is contained in the VbReloaded2008\Chap07\String\Alphabet Solution-Compare folder.)

»HOW TO ...

USE THE STRING.COMPARE METHOD

Syntax   Purpose

String.Compare(_string1_**,** _string2_[**,** _ignoreCase_]**)**   compares two strings

Example 1

Dim result As Integer
result = String.Compare("Dallas", "DALLAS")
assigns the number –1 to the result variable, because the second character in _string1_ (a) is less than the second character in _string2_ (A)

Example 2

Dim result As Integer
result = String.Compare("Dallas", "DALLAS", True)
assigns the number 0 to the result variable, because both strings are equal

Example 3

Dim result As Integer
result = String.Compare("Dallas", "Boston")
assigns the number 1 to the result variable, because the first character in _string1_ (D) is greater than the first character in _string2_ (B)

Figure 7-30: How to use the String.Compare method

THE LIKE OPERATOR

You also can use the Like operator to compare strings. Unlike the String.Compare method, the **Like operator** allows you to use pattern-matching characters to determine whether one string is equal to another string. Figure 7-31 shows the Like operator's syntax. In the syntax, both _string_ and _pattern_ must be String expressions; however, _pattern_ can contain one or more of the pattern-matching characters listed in the figure. The last two pattern-matching characters contain a _charList_, which stands for _character list_ and is simply a listing of characters. "[A9M]" is a _charList_ that contains three characters: A, 9, and M. You also can include a range of values in a _charList_; you do this using a hyphen. For example, to include all lowercase letters in a _charList_, you use "[a-z]". To include both uppercase and lowercase letters, you use "[a-zA-Z]" as the _charList_. The Like operator evaluates to True when the _string_ matches the _pattern_; otherwise it evaluates to False. Figure 7-31 includes examples of using the Like operator. (The Like operator is used in the Alphabet application, which is contained in the VbReloaded2008\Chap07\String\Alphabet Solution-Like folder.)

»HOW TO . . .

USE THE LIKE OPERATOR

Syntax	Purpose
string **Like** *pattern*	compares two strings using pattern-matching characters

Pattern-matching characters	Matches in *string*
?	any single character
*	zero or more characters
#	any single digit (0-9)
[*charList*]	any single character in the *charList* (for example, "[AMT]" matches A, M, or T, whereas "[a-z]" matches any lowercase letter)
[!*charList*]	any single character not in the *charList* (for example, "[!a-z]" matches any character that is not a lowercase letter)

Example 1

isEqual = firstName.ToUpper Like "B?LL"

Assigns the Boolean value True to the isEqual variable when the string stored in the firstName variable begins with the letter B followed by one character and then the two letters LL; otherwise, assigns the Boolean value False to the isEqual variable. Examples of *strings* that would make the expression evaluate to True include "Bill", "Ball", "bell", and "bull". Examples of *strings* for which the expression would evaluate to False include "BPL", "BLL", and "billy".

Example 2

If state Like "K*" Then

The condition evaluates to True when the string stored in the state variable begins with the letter K followed by zero or more characters; otherwise, it evaluates to False. Examples of *strings* that would make the condition evaluate to True include "KANSAS", "Ky", and "Kentucky". Examples of *strings* for which the condition would evaluate to False include "kansas" and "ky".

Figure 7-31: How to use the Like operator (*continued on next page*)

Example 3

Do While id Like "###*"

The condition evaluates to True when the string stored in the id variable begins with three digits followed by zero or more characters; otherwise, it evaluates to False. Examples of *strings* that would make the condition evaluate to True include "178" and "983Ab". Examples of *strings* for which the condition would evaluate to False include "X34" and "34Z5".

Example 4

If firstName.ToUpper Like "T[OI]M" Then

The condition evaluates to True when the string stored in the firstName variable is either "Tom" or "Tim" (entered in any case). When the firstName variable does not contain "Tom" or "Tim"—for example, when it contains "Tam" or "Tommy"—the expression evaluates to False.

Example 5

isLowercase = letter Like "[a-z]"

Assigns the Boolean value True to the isLowercase variable when the string stored in the letter variable is a lowercase letter; otherwise, it evaluates to False. You use a hyphen (-) to specify a range of values in a *charList*.

Example 6

```
For indexNum As Integer = 0 to userEntry.Length - 1
    If userEntry.Substring(indexNum, 1) Like "[!a-zA-Z]" Then
        nonLetter = nonLetter + 1
    End If
Next indexNum
```

compares each character contained in the userEntry variable with the lowercase and uppercase letters of the alphabet, and counts the number of characters that are not letters

Figure 7-31: How to use the Like operator (*continued from previous page*)

The string manipulation techniques covered in this chapter are summarized in the Quick Review section. You have completed the concepts section of Chapter 7.

PROGRAMMING TUTORIAL

CREATING THE HANGMAN GAME

Mr. Mitchell teaches second grade at Hinsbrook School. On days when the weather is bad and the students cannot go outside to play, he spends recess time playing a simplified version of the Hangman game with his class. The game requires two people to play. First, Mr. Mitchell thinks of a word that has five letters. He then draws five dashes on the chalkboard—one for each letter in the word. One student then is chosen to guess the word, letter by letter. When the student guesses a correct letter, Mr. Mitchell replaces the appropriate dash or dashes with the letter. For example, if the original word is *moose* and the student guesses the letter *o*, Mr. Mitchell changes the fives dashes on the chalkboard to -oo--. If the student's letter does not appear in the word, Mr. Mitchell begins drawing the Hangman image, which contains nine lines and one circle. The game is over when the student guesses all of the letters in the word, or when he or she makes 10 incorrect guesses, whichever comes first. Figures 7-32 and 7-33 show the application's TOE chart and user interface.

Task	Object	Event
1. Hide the 10 picture boxes 2. Get a 5-letter word from player 1 3. Determine whether the word contains exactly 5 letters 4. Display five dashes in the wordLabel 5. Clear the incorrectLabel 6. Get a letter from player 2 7. Search the word for the letter 8. If the letter is contained in the word, replace any appropriate dashes 9. If the letter is not contained in the word, display the letter in the incorrectLabel, add 1 to the number of incorrect guesses, and show the appropriate picture box 10. If all of the dashes have been replaced, the game is over, so display the message "Great guessing!" in a message box 11. If the user makes 10 incorrect guesses, the game is over, so display an appropriate message and the word in a message box	playButton	Click

Figure 7-32: TOE Chart (*continued on next page*)

Task	Object	Event
End the application	exitButton	Click
Display the Hangman images	bottomPictureBox, postPictureBox, topPictureBox, ropePictureBox, headPictureBox, bodyPictureBox, rightArmPictureBox, leftArmPictureBox, rightLegPictureBox, leftLegPictureBox	None
Display dashes and letters (from playButton)	wordLabel	None
Display the incorrect letters (from playButton)	incorrectLabel	None

Figure 7-32: TOE Chart (*continued from previous page*)

Figure 7-33: User interface

CODING THE HANGMAN GAME

According to the application's TOE chart, the Click event procedures for the exitButton and playButton need to be coded.

To open the Hangman Game application:

1. Start Visual Studio. If necessary, close the Start Page window. Open the **Hangman Game Solution** (**Hangman Game Solution.sln**) file, which is contained in the VbReloaded2008\Chap07\Hangman Game Solution folder.

2. Open the Code Editor window, which already contains the appropriate comments and Option statements. It also contains the code for the exitButton's Click event procedure.

The only procedure you need to code is the playButton's Click event procedure. The procedure's pseudocode is shown in Figure 7-34.

---

playButton Click Event Procedure

1. hide the 10 picture boxes
2. get a 5-letter word from player 1 and convert it to uppercase
3. if the word does not contain exactly 5 characters
      assign False to isWordValid variable
  else
      if the word does not contain only letters
          assign False to isWordValid variable
      end if
  end if
4. if the isWordValid variable contains False
      display an appropriate message
  else
      display 5 dashes in the wordLabel
      clear the incorrectLabel

      get a letter from player 2 and convert it to uppercase
      repeat while the user entered a letter and the game is not over
          repeat for each letter in the word
              if the current letter is the same as the letter entered by player 2
                 replace the appropriate dash in the wordLabel
                 assign True to isDashReplaced variable
             end if
         end repeat

         if the isDashReplaced variable contains True
           if the wordLabel does not contain any dashes
              assign True to the isGameOver variable
              display the "Great guessing!" message
           else
              assign False to the isDashReplaced variable
           end if
         else
           display the incorrect letter in the incorrectLabel
           add 1 to the number of incorrect guesses counter

Figure 7-34: Pseudocode for the playButton's Click event procedure (*continued on next page*)

```
                    value of the number of incorrect guesses counter:
                        1 show the bottomPictureBox
                        2 show the postPictureBox
                        3 show the topPictureBox
                        4 show the ropePictureBox
                        5 show the headPictureBox
                        6 show the bodyPictureBox
                        7 show the rightArmPictureBox
                        8 show the leftArmPictureBox
                        9 show the rightLegPictureBox
                       10 show the leftLegPictureBox
                          assign True to the isGameOver variable
                          display the "Sorry, the word is" message and the word
                end if

                if the isGameOver variable contains False
                    get another letter from the user
                end if
        end repeat
end if
```

Figure 7-34: Pseudocode for the playButton's Click event procedure (*continued from previous page*)

To code the playButton's Click event procedure:

1. Open the code template for the playButton's Click event procedure. Type **' simulates the Hangman game** and press **Enter** twice.

2. The procedure will use six procedure-level variables: two String variables, three Boolean variables, and one Integer variable. The two String variables, word and letter, will store the word entered by player 1 and the letter entered by player 2. The Boolean isWordValid variable will store a Boolean value that indicates whether the word entered by player 1 is valid; to be valid, the word must contain exactly 5 letters. The Boolean isDashReplaced variable will keep track of whether a dash was replaced in the word, and the Boolean isGameOver variable will indicate whether the game is over. (As you learned in Chapter 3, Boolean variables are automatically initialized to False.) The Integer incorrectCounter variable will keep track of the number of incorrect guesses made by player 2. Enter the following Dim statements. Press **Enter** twice after typing the last Dim statement.

```
Dim word As String = String.Empty

Dim letter As String = String.Empty

Dim isWordValid As Boolean

Dim isDashReplaced As Boolean

Dim isGameOver As Boolean

Dim incorrectCounter As Integer
```

3. The first step in the pseudocode is to hide the 10 picture boxes. Enter the following comment and assignment statements. Press **Enter** twice after typing the last assignment statement.

```
' hide the picture boxes

bottomPictureBox.Visible = False

postPictureBox.Visible = False

topPictureBox.Visible = False

ropePictureBox.Visible = False

headPictureBox.Visible = False

bodyPictureBox.Visible = False

rightArmPictureBox.Visible = False

leftArmPictureBox.Visible = False

rightLegPictureBox.Visible = False

leftLegPictureBox.Visible = False
```

4. The next step is to get a 5-letter word from player 1 and convert it to uppercase. Type **' get a 5-letter word from player 1, convert to uppercase** and press **Enter**. Type **word = inputbox("Enter a 5-letter word:", _** and press **Enter**, then type **"Hangman Game").toupper** and press **Enter** twice.

5. Now you need to verify that the word contains exactly 5 letters. Type the comments and code indicated in Figure 7-35, then position the insertion point as shown in the figure. (Be sure to include the exclamation point in the "[!A-Z]" *charList*.)

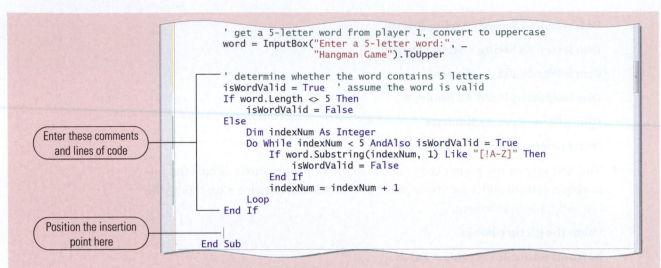

```
          ' get a 5-letter word from player 1, convert to uppercase
          word = InputBox("Enter a 5-letter word:", _
                          "Hangman Game").ToUpper

          ' determine whether the word contains 5 letters
          isWordValid = True    ' assume the word is valid
          If word.Length <> 5 Then
              isWordValid = False
          Else
              Dim indexNum As Integer
              Do While indexNum < 5 AndAlso isWordValid = True
                  If word.Substring(indexNum, 1) Like "[!A-Z]" Then
                      isWordValid = False
                  End If
                  indexNum = indexNum + 1
              Loop
          End If

      End Sub
```

Enter these comments and lines of code

Position the insertion point here

Figure 7-35: Additional comments and code entered in the procedure

6. If the word does not have exactly 5 letters, the isWordValid variable will contain False. In that case, you should display an appropriate message. Type the comment and code indicated in Figure 7-36, then position the insertion point as shown in the figure.

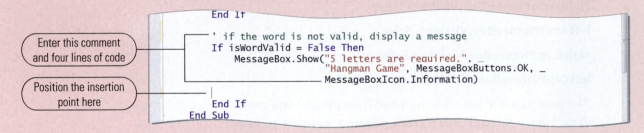

```
          End If
          ' if the word is not valid, display a message
          If isWordValid = False Then
              MessageBox.Show("5 letters are required.", _
                             "Hangman Game", MessageBoxButtons.OK, _
                             MessageBoxIcon.Information)

          End If
      End Sub
```

Enter this comment and four lines of code

Position the insertion point here

Figure 7-36: Comment and selection structure's true path

7. However, if the word has exactly 5 letters, you should display 5 dashes in the wordLabel and then clear the incorrectLabel. Type **else** and press **Enter**, then enter the following comments and assignment statements. (The first assignment statement assigns 5 hyphens to the wordLabel.) Press **Enter** twice after typing the last assignment statement.

' display five dashes in the wordLabel

' and clear the incorrectLabel

wordLabel.Text = "-----"

incorrectLabel.Text = String.Empty

8. Now get a letter from player 2 and convert it to uppercase. Enter the following comment and InputBox function. Press **Enter** twice after typing the last line of code.

' get a letter from player 2, convert to uppercase

letter = InputBox("Enter a letter:", _

"Letter", "", 820, 590).ToUpper

9. The next task in the pseudocode is a pretest loop that repeats its instructions as long as both of the following conditions are true: player 2 entered a letter and the game is not over. Enter the following comments and Do...Loop statement. Press **Enter** twice after typing the Do clause.

' verify that player 2 entered a letter

' and that the game is not over

Do While letter <> String.Empty AndAlso isGameOver = False

10. If the user entered a letter and the game is not over, you need to determine whether the letter appears in the word. You can accomplish this using a For loop that compares the letter with each character in the word, character by character. Type **' search the word for the letter** and press **Enter**, then type **for indexNum as integer = 0 To 4** and press **Enter**. Change the Next clause to **Next indexNum**.

11. The For loop contains a selection structure that compares the current letter in the word with the letter entered by player 2. If both letters are the same, the selection structure's true path replaces the appropriate dash in the wordLabel. It also assigns the Boolean value True to the isDashReplaced variable to indicate that a dash was replaced in the label. Type the comments and selection structure shown in Figure 7-37, then position the insertion point as shown in the figure.

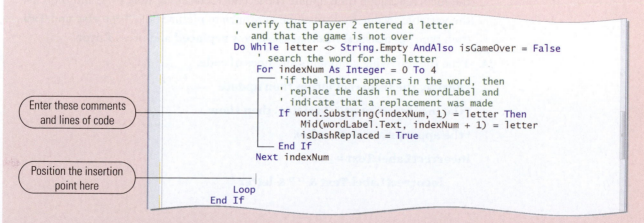

```
' verify that player 2 entered a letter
' and that the game is not over
Do While letter <> String.Empty AndAlso isGameOver = False
    ' search the word for the letter
    For indexNum As Integer = 0 To 4
        'if the letter appears in the word, then
        ' replace the dash in the wordLabel and
        ' indicate that a replacement was made
        If word.Substring(indexNum, 1) = letter Then
            Mid(wordLabel.Text, indexNum + 1) = letter
            isDashReplaced = True
        End If
    Next indexNum

Loop
End If
```

Enter these comments and lines of code

Position the insertion point here

Figure 7-37: Comments and selection structure entered in the procedure

12. If a dash was replaced in the wordLabel, you need to determine whether the wordLabel contains any more dashes. If there are no more dashes in the wordLabel, it means that the user has guessed the word and the game is over. In that case, you should assign True to the isGameOver variable and display the "Great guessing!" message. However, if the wordLabel contains at least one dash, you should reset the IsDashReplaced variable's value to False. Enter the comments and selection structure shown in Figure 7-38, then position the insertion point as shown in the figure.

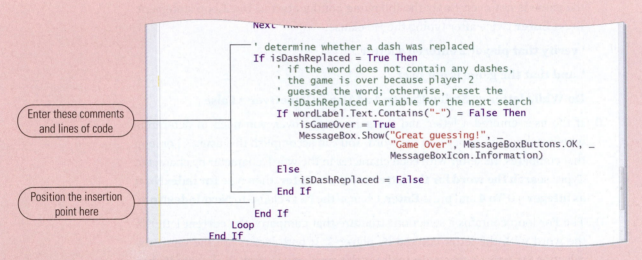

Enter these comments and lines of code

Position the insertion point here

```
Next

        ' determine whether a dash was replaced
        If isDashReplaced = True Then
            ' if the word does not contain any dashes,
            ' the game is over because player 2
            ' guessed the word; otherwise, reset the
            ' isDashReplaced variable for the next search
            If wordLabel.Text.Contains("-") = False Then
                isGameOver = True
                MessageBox.Show("Great guessing!", _
                            "Game Over", MessageBoxButtons.OK, _
                            MessageBoxIcon.Information)
            Else
                isDashReplaced = False
            End If
        End If
    Loop
End If
```

Figure 7-38: Additional comments and selection structures entered in the procedure

13. On the other hand, if no dash was replaced, it means that player 2's letter does not appear in the word. Therefore, you should display the incorrect letter in the incorrectLabel, then update the incorrectCounter variable by 1, and then use the variable's value to display the appropriate picture box. Type **else** and **Tab**, then type **' processed when no dash was replaced** and press **Enter**.

14. Type the following comments and lines of code.

' display the incorrect letter, then update

' the incorrectCounter variable, then show

' the appropriate picture box

incorrectLabel.Text = _

    incorrectLabel.Text & " " & letter

```
incorrectCounter = incorrectCounter + 1
Select Case incorrectCounter
    Case 1
        bottomPictureBox.Visible = True
    Case 2
        postPictureBox.Visible = True
    Case 3
        topPictureBox.Visible = True
    Case 4
        ropePictureBox.Visible = True
    Case 5
        headPictureBox.Visible = True
    Case 6
        bodyPictureBox.Visible = True
    Case 7
        rightArmPictureBox.Visible = True
    Case 8
        leftArmPictureBox.Visible = True
    Case 9
        rightLegPictureBox.Visible = True
    Case 10
        leftLegPictureBox.Visible = True
        isGameOver = True
        MessageBox.Show("Sorry, the word is " _
                        & word & ".", "Game Over", _
                        MessageBoxButtons.OK, _
                        MessageBoxIcon.Information)
End Select
```

15. The last task in the pseudocode determines whether you need to get another letter from the user. As the pseudocode indicates, another letter is necessary only when the game is not over. Insert two blank lines above the Loop clause, then enter the comment and selection structure shown in Figure 7-39.

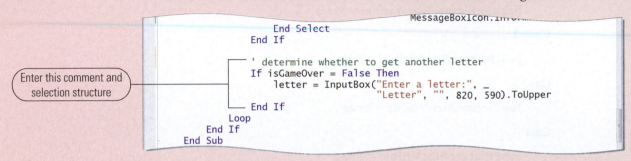

```
                        End Select
                   End If

                   ' determine whether to get another letter
                   If isGameOver = False Then
                       letter = InputBox("Enter a letter:", _
                                         "Letter", "", 820, 590).ToUpper
                   End If
              Loop
          End If
     End Sub
```

Enter this comment and selection structure

Figure 7-39: Final comment and selection structure entered in the procedure

16. Before testing the application, compare the code you entered in the playButton's Click event procedure with the code shown in Figure 7-40. Make any needed corrections.

```
Private Sub playButton_Click(ByVal sender As Object, _
    ByVal e As System.EventArgs) Handles playButton.Click
    ' simulates the Hangman game

    Dim word As String = String.Empty
    Dim letter As String = String.Empty
    Dim isWordValid As Boolean
    Dim isDashReplaced As Boolean
    Dim isGameOver As Boolean
    Dim incorrectCounter As Integer

    ' hide the picture boxes
    bottomPictureBox.Visible = False
    postPictureBox.Visible = False
    topPictureBox.Visible = False
    ropePictureBox.Visible = False
    headPictureBox.Visible = False
    bodyPictureBox.Visible = False
    rightArmPictureBox.Visible = False
    leftArmPictureBox.Visible = False
    rightLegPictureBox.Visible = False
    leftLegPictureBox.Visible = False
```

Figure 7-40: The playButton's Click event procedure (*continued on next page*)

```vb
' get a 5-letter word from player 1, convert to uppercase
word = InputBox("Enter a 5-letter word:", _
                "Hangman Game").ToUpper

' determine whether the word contains 5 letters
isWordValid = True  ' assume the word is valid
If word.Length <> 5 Then
    isWordValid = False
Else
    Dim indexNum As Integer
    Do While indexNum < 5 AndAlso isWordValid = True
        If word.Substring(indexNum, 1) Like "[!A-Z]" Then
            isWordValid = False
        End If
        indexNum = indexNum + 1
    Loop
End If

' if the word is not valid, display a message
If isWordValid = False Then
    MessageBox.Show("5 letters are required.", _
                    "Hangman Game", MessageBoxButtons.OK, _
                    MessageBoxIcon.Information)
Else
    ' display five dashes in the wordLabel
    ' and clear the incorrectLabel
    wordLabel.Text = "-----"
    incorrectLabel.Text = String.Empty


    ' get a letter from player 2, convert to uppercase
    letter = InputBox("Enter a letter:" , _
                    "Letter", "", 820, 590).ToUpper

    ' verify that player 2 entered a letter
    ' and that the game is not over
    Do While letter <> String.Empty AndAlso isGameOver = False
        ' search the word for the letter
        For indexNum As Integer = 0 To 4
            ' if the letter appears in the word, then
            ' replace the dash in the wordLabel and
            ' indicate that a replacement was made
```

Figure 7-40: The playButton's Click event procedure (*continued from previous page and on next page*)

```
                         If word.Substring(indexNum, 1) = letter Then
                             Mid(wordLabel.Text, indexNum + 1) = letter
                             isDashReplaced = True
                         End If
                 Next indexNum

                 ' determine whether a dash was replaced
                 If isDashReplaced = True Then
                     ' if the word does not contain any dashes,
                     ' the game is over because player 2
                     ' guessed the word; otherwise, reset the
                     ' isDashReplaced variable for the next search
                     If wordLabel.Text.Contains("-") = False Then
                         isGameOver = True
                         MessageBox.Show("Great guessing!", _
                                         "Game Over", MessageBoxButtons.OK, _
                                         MessageBoxIcon.Information)
                     Else
                         isDashReplaced = False
                     End If
                 Else    ' processed when no dash was replaced
                     ' display the incorrect letter, then update
                     ' the incorrectCounter variable, then show
                     ' the appropriate picture box
                     incorrectLabel.Text = _
                         incorrectLabel.Text & " " & letter
                     incorrectCounter = incorrectCounter + 1
                     Select Case incorrectCounter
                         Case 1
                             bottomPictureBox.Visible = True
                         Case 2
                             postPictureBox.Visible = True
                         Case 3
                             topPictureBox.Visible = True
                         Case 4
                             ropePictureBox.Visible = True
                         Case 5
                             headPictureBox.Visible = True
                         Case 6
                             bodyPictureBox.Visible = True
                         Case 7
                             rightArmPictureBox.Visible = True
```

Figure 7-40: The playButton's Click event procedure (*continued from previous page and on next page*)

```
        Case 8
            leftArmPictureBox.Visible = True
        Case 9
            rightLegPictureBox.Visible = True
        Case 10
            leftLegPictureBox.Visible = True
            isGameOver = True
            MessageBox.Show("Sorry, the word is " _
                            & word & ".", "Game Over", _
                            MessageBoxButtons.OK, _
                            MessageBoxIcon.Information)
        End Select
    End If

    ' determine whether to get another letter
    If isGameOver = False Then
        letter = InputBox("Enter a letter:", _
                          "Letter", "", 820, 590).ToUpper
    End If
    Loop
    End If
End Sub
```

Figure 7-40: The playButton's Click event procedure (*continued from previous page*)

Now that you have finished coding the application, you will test it to verify that it is working correctly.

To test the Hangman Game application:

1. Save the solution, then start the application. Click the **Play the Game** button. The Hangman Game dialog box opens and prompts you to enter a 5-letter word. Type **cat** in the dialog box, then press **Enter** to select the OK button. Because the word does not contain five characters, a message box opens and informs you that five letters are required. Press **Enter** to close the message box.

2. Click the **Play the Game** button again. Type **cats4** in the dialog box and press **Enter**. Because the word contains a character that is not a letter, a message box opens and informs you that five letters are required. Press **Enter** to close the message box.

3. Click the **Play the Game** button again. Type **puppy** and press **Enter**. The Letter dialog box opens and prompts you to enter a letter. Type **p** in the dialog box and press **Enter**. The playButton's Click event procedure replaces, with the letter P, three of the dashes in the wordLabel, as shown in Figure 7-41.

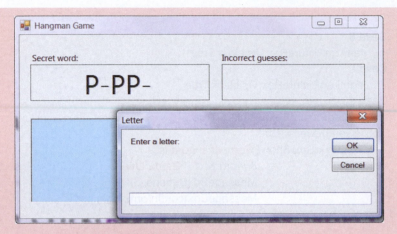

Figure 7-41: Dashes replaced with the letter P

4. Type **a** in the Letter dialog box and press **Enter**. The playButton's Click event procedure displays the letter A in the incorrectLabel and also makes the bottomPictureBox visible, as shown in Figure 7-42.

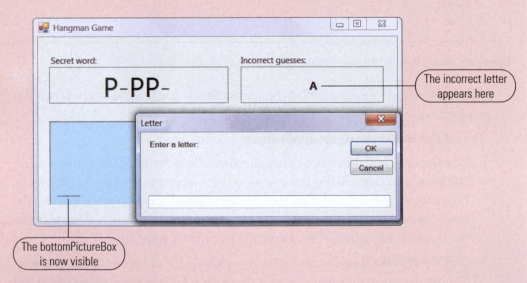

The incorrect letter appears here

The bottomPictureBox is now visible

Figure 7-42: Result of entering the first incorrect letter

5. Type **b** in the Letter dialog box and press **Enter**. The playButton's Click event procedure adds the letter B to the contents of the incorrectLabel and also makes the postPictureBox visible.

6. Type **u** in the Letter dialog box and press **Enter**, then type **y** in the dialog box and press **Enter**. The playButton's Click event procedure displays the "Great guessing!" message in a message box. Drag the message box down and to the right until you can see the entire contents of the wordLabel and incorrectLabel controls. See Figure 7-43.

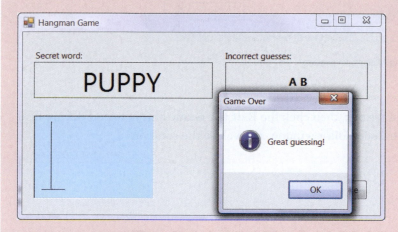

Figure 7-43: Result of guessing the word

7. Click the **OK** button to close the message box.

8. Now you will observe what happens when you make 10 incorrect guesses. Click the **Play the Game** button. Type **basic** and press **Enter**. Now type the following 12 letters, pressing **Enter** after typing each letter: **d, c, e, f, g, h, a, j, k, x, y, z**. The playButton's Click event procedure displays the 10 incorrect letters, the 10 picture boxes, and a message box. Drag the message box to the location shown in Figure 7-44.

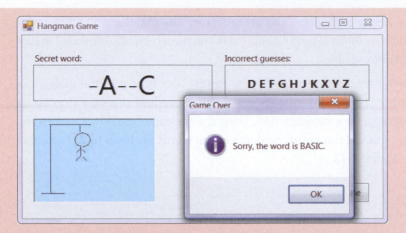

Figure 7-44: Result of making 10 incorrect guesses

9. Close the message box, then click the **Exit the Game** button to end the application. Close the Code Editor window, then close the solution.

PROGRAMMING EXAMPLE

PRINCIPAL AND INTEREST CALCULATOR

Create a Visual Basic application that displays a monthly payment on a loan of $3000 for 1 year at 7% interest. The application also should display the amount applied to the loan's principal each month, and the amount that represents interest. Name the solution, project, and form file Principal and Interest Solution, Principal and Interest Project, and Main Form.vb, respectively. Save the application in the VbReloaded2008\Chap07 folder. The application will use the Financial.Pmt method, which you learned about in the chapter, to calculate the monthly payment. It also will use the Financial.PPmt method to calculate the portion of the payment applied to the principal each month. The method's syntax is **Financial.PPmt(**Rate**,** Per**,** NPer**,** PV**)**, where Rate is the interest rate, NPer is the number of payment periods, and PV is the present value of the loan. The Per argument is the payment period in which you are interested and must be from 1 through NPer. See Figures 7-45 through 7-49.

Task	Object	Event
1. Calculate the monthly payment 2. Calculate the amount applied to the principal 3. Calculate the amount that represents interest 4. Display the monthly payment in the paymentLabel 5. Display the amount applied to the principal and the amount that represents interest in the tableTextBox	displayButton	Click
End the application	exitButton	Click
Display the monthly payment (from displayButton)	paymentLabel	None
Display the amount applied to the principal and the amount that represents interest (from displayButton)	tableTextBox	None

Figure 7-45: TOE chart

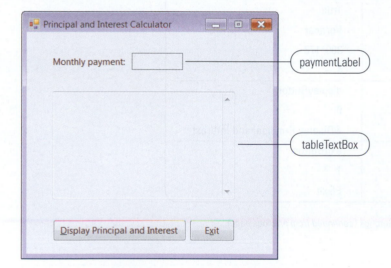

Figure 7-46: User interface

Object	Property	Setting
Form1	Name	MainForm
	Font	Segoe UI, 9 point
	MaximizeBox	False
	StartPosition	CenterScreen
	Text	Principal and Interest Calculator

Figure 7-47: Objects, Properties, and Settings (*continued on next page*)

Object	Property	Setting
Label1	TabIndex	2
	Text	Monthly payment:
Label2	Name	paymentLabel
	AutoSize	False
	BorderStyle	FixedSingle
	TabIndex	3
	Text	(empty)
	TextAlign	MiddleCenter
TextBox1	Name	tableTextBox
	Font	Courier New, 9 pt
	Multiline	True
	ReadOnly	True
	ScrollBars	Vertical
	Size	300, 178
	TabIndex	4
Button1	Name	displayButton
	TabIndex	0
	Text	&Display Principal and Interest
Button2	Name	exitButton
	TabIndex	1
	Text	E&xit

Figure 7-47: Objects, Properties, and Settings (*continued from previous page*)

---

exitButton Click Event Procedure
1. close the application

displayButton Click Event Procedure
1. calculate the monthly payment on a $3000 loan for 1 year at 7% interest
2. display the monthly payment in the paymentLabel
3. repeat for each of the 12 months in a year
    calculate the amount of the monthly payment applied to the principal for the current month
    calculate the interest by subtracting the amount applied to the principal from the monthly payment
    display the amount of the monthly payment applied to the principal, as well as the interest
        amount, in the tableTextBox
  end repeat

Figure 7-48: Pseudocode

```
' Project name:        Principal And Interest Project
' Project purpose:     Display a monthly payment and a
'                      table showing principal and interest
' Created/revised by:  <your name> on <current date>

Option Explicit On
Option Strict On
Option Infer Off

Public Class MainForm

    Private Sub exitButton_Click(ByVal sender As Object, _
        ByVal e As System.EventArgs) Handles exitButton.Click
        Me.Close()
    End Sub

    Private Sub displayButton_Click(ByVal sender As Object, _
        ByVal e As System.EventArgs) Handles displayButton.Click
        ' displays the amount of a monthly payment and
        ' the amount applied to principal and interest

        Dim payment As Decimal
        Dim toPrincipal As Decimal
        Dim toInterest As Decimal

        ' calculate and display the monthly payment
        payment = Convert.ToDecimal(-Financial.Pmt(0.07 / 12, 12, 3000))
        paymentLabel.Text = payment.ToString("C2")

        ' display column headings in the table
        tableTextBox.Text = "Principal      Interest" & ControlChars.NewLine

        ' calculate and display the amount applied to principal
        ' and the amount of interest
        For period As Integer = 1 To 12
            toPrincipal = _
                Convert.ToDecimal(-Financial.PPmt(0.07 / 12, period, 12, 3000))
            toInterest = payment - toPrincipal

            tableTextBox.Text = _
                tableTextBox.Text & toPrincipal.ToString("N2").PadLeft(8)
            tableTextBox.Text = _
                tableTextBox.Text & toInterest.ToString("N2").PadLeft(15) _
                & ControlChars.NewLine
        Next period
    End Sub
End Class
```

Figure 7-49: Code

QUICK REVIEW

» You can use the For...Next statement to code a pretest loop whose instructions you want processed a precise number of times.

» A variable declared in a For clause has block scope and can be used only within the For...Next loop.

» Many programmers use a hexagon in a flowchart to represent a repetition structure that is coded using the For...Next statement.

» You can use the Financial.Pmt method to calculate a periodic payment on a loan.

» It is customary in Windows applications to highlight, or select, the existing text in a text box when the text box receives the focus. You can do this by entering the SelectAll method in the text box's Enter event procedure.

» When either the user or the application's code changes the text contained in a control, the control's TextChanged event occurs.

» Combo boxes are similar to list boxes in that they allow the user to select from a list of choices. However, combo boxes also have a text field that the user may or may not edit.

» Three styles of combo boxes are available. The style is specified in a combo box's DropDownStyle property. You can use a combo box to save space in an interface.

» You use the Items collection's Add method to add an item to a combo box.

» You can use the SelectedIndex, SelectedItem, or Text property to select the default item in a combo box.

» Use a label control to provide keyboard access to a combo box. Set the label's TabIndex property to a value that is one number less than the combo box's TabIndex value.

» The value stored in a combo box's Items.Count property indicates the number of items listed in the combo box.

» You can use the Sorted property to sort the items listed in a combo box.

» A combo box's SelectedItem property contains the value of the item selected in the list portion of the combo box. A combo box's Text property contains the value that appears in the text portion of the combo box.

» A combo box's TextChanged event occurs when the user either selects an item in the list portion or types a value in the text portion.

» Figure 7-50 summarizes the string manipulation techniques covered in the chapter. (It also includes the comparison operators, which you learned about in Chapter 4.)

Technique	Syntax	Purpose
Length property	*string*.**Length**	stores the number of characters contained in a string
Trim method	*string*.**Trim**[(*trimChars*)]	removes characters from both the beginning and end of a string
TrimStart method	*string*.**TrimStart**[(*trimChars*)]	removes characters from the beginning of a string
TrimEnd method	*string*.**TrimEnd**[(*trimChars*)]	removes characters from the end of a string
Remove method	*string*.**Remove**(*startIndex, count*)	removes characters from anywhere in a string
Replace method	*string*.**Replace**(*oldValue, newValue*)	replaces all occurrences of a sequence of characters in a string with another sequence of characters
Mid statement	**Mid**(*targetString, start* [, *count*]) = *replacementString*	replaces a specific number of characters in a string with characters from another string
PadLeft method	*string*.**PadLeft**(*length*[, *character*])	pads the beginning of a string with a character until the string is a specified length
PadRight method	*string*.**PadRight**(*length*[, *character*])	pads the end of a string with a character until the string is a specified length
Insert method	*string*.**Insert**(*startIndex, value*)	inserts characters within a string
StartsWith method	*string*.**StartsWith**(*subString*)	determines whether a string begins with a specific sequence of characters
EndsWith method	*string*.**EndsWith**(*subString*)	determines whether a string ends with a specific sequence of characters
Contains method	*string*.**Contains**(*subString*)	determines whether a string contains a specific sequence of characters; returns a Boolean value
IndexOf method	*string*.**IndexOf**(*subString*[, *startIndex*])	determines whether a string contains a specific sequence of characters; returns an integer that indicates the starting position of the characters
Substring method	*string*.**Substring**(*startIndex*[, *count*])	accesses one or more characters contained in a string
String.Compare method	**String.Compare**(*string1, string2*[, *ignoreCase*])	compares two strings
Like operator	*string* **Like** *pattern*	compares two strings using pattern-matching characters
=, <>, <, <=, >, >=	*string1 operator string2*	compares two strings

Figure 7-50: String manipulation techniques

KEY TERMS

Combo box—a control that allows the user to select from a list of choices; also has a text field that may or may not be editable

Enter event—occurs when a control receives the focus

Financial.Pmt method—used to calculate a periodic payment on a loan

For...Next statement—provides a convenient way of coding a pretest loop whose instructions you want processed a precise number of times

SelectAll method—used to select all of the text contained in a text box

String manipulation—refers to the processing of strings; the string manipulation techniques are listed in Figure 7-50

TextChanged event—occurs when a change is made to the contents of a control's Text property

SELF-CHECK QUESTIONS AND ANSWERS

1. A For...Next statement contains the following For clause: For temp As Integer = 5 To 11 Step 2. What value is stored in the temp variable when the For...Next statement ends?

    a. 11   b. 12

    c. 13   d. None of the above.

2. Which of the following calculates the monthly payment on a loan of $5,000 for two years at 4% interest? Payments should be expressed as a positive number.

    a. -Financial.Pmt(.04/12, 24, 5000)   b. -Financial.Pmt(24, .04/12, 5000)

    c. -Financial.Pmt(5000, .04/12, 24)   d. None of the above.

3. You use the _____ method to add items to a combo box.

    a. AddItem   b. AddList

    c. ItemAdd   d. None of the above.

4. If the word variable contains the string "Irene Turner", the word.Contains("r") method returns _____.

    a. True   b. False

    c. 1   d. 2

5. When a user tabs to a text box, the text box's _____ event occurs.

    a. Access   b. Enter

    c. TabOrder   d. None of the above.

Answers: 1) c, 2) a, 3) d, 4) a, 5) b

REVIEW QUESTIONS

1. How many times will the MessageBox.Show method in the following code be processed?

```
For counter As Integer = 4 To 11 Step 2
    MessageBox.Show("Hello")
Next counter
```

    a. 3   b. 4

    c. 5   d. 8

2. What is the value stored in the counter variable when the loop in Question 1 stops?

    a. 10   b. 11

    c. 12   d. 13

3. Which of the following calculates an annual payment on a $50,000 loan? The term is 10 years and the interest rate is 3%.

    a. -Financial.Pmt(.03 / 12, 10, 50000)

    b. -Financial.Pmt(.03/12, 10 * 12, 50000)

    c. -Financial.Pmt(.03, 10, 50000)

    d. -Financial.Pmt(.03, 10 * 12, 50000)

4. Which of the following selects the "Cat" item, which appears third in the animalComboBox?

    a. animalComboBox.SelectedIndex = 2

    b. animalComboBox.SelectedItem = "Cat"

    c. animalComboBox.Text = "Cat"

    d. All of the above.

5. The _____ property stores the item that the user enters in the text portion of a combo box.

    a. SelectedItem   b. SelectedValue

    c. Text   d. TextItem

6. Which of the following removes the leading and trailing spaces from the addressTextBox?

   a. addressTextBox.Text = addressTextBox.Text.Trim

   b. addressTextBox.Text = addressTextBox.Text.TrimAll

   c. addressTextBox.Text = addressTextBox.Trim

   d. None of the above.

7. Which of the following changes the name "Mary Smyth" to "Mark Smyth"? The name is stored in the fullName variable.

   a. fullName = fullName.Change("y", "k")

   b. fullName =fullName.Replace("y", "k")

   c. Mid(fullName, 4) = "k"

   d. Both b and c.

8. You can use the _____ method to right-align a string within a control.

   a. Align   b. PadLeft

   c. StartsWith   d. None of the above.

9. Which of the following changes the name "Mary Smyth" to "Mary"? The name is stored in the fullName variable.

   a. fullName = fullName.Replace(" Smyth", "")

   b. fullName = fullName.Remove("Smyth")

   c. fullName = fullName.TrimEnd(" Smyth")

   d. All of the above.

10. Which of the following methods will return the Boolean value True when the petName variable contains the string "Micki"?

   a. petName.StartsWith("M")   b. petName.Contains("k")

   c. petName Like "M*"   d. All of the above.

11. Which of the following expressions evaluates to True when the partNum variable contains the string "123X45"?

   a. partNum Like "999[A-Z]99"   b. partNum Like "######"

   c. partNum Like "###[A-Z]##"   d. None of the above.

12. What will the address.IndexOf("Main") method return when the address variable contains "34 Main Street"?

    a. 3   b. 4

    c. True   d. None of the above.

13. Which of the following can be used to determine whether the item variable contains either the word "shirt" or the word "skirt"? The item variable contains uppercase letters only.

    a. If item = "SHIRT" AndAlso item = "SKIRT" Then

    b. If item = "S[HK]IRT" Then

    c. If item Like "S[HK]IRT" Then

    d. If item Like "S[H-K]IRT" Then

14. Which of the following assigns the contents of the message variable followed by four exclamation points (!) to the newMessage variable? The message variable contains the string "Great job".

    a. newMessage = message.PadLeft(4, "!"c)

    b. newMessage = message.PadLeft(13, "!")

    c. newMessage = message.PadRight(4, "!")

    d. newMessage = message.PadRight(13, "!"c)

REVIEW EXERCISES— SHORT ANSWER

1. When processing the For...Next statement, the computer performs three tasks, as shown below. Put these tasks in their proper order by placing the numbers 1 through 3 on the line to the left of the task.

    » _____ Adds the *stepvalue* to the *counter*.

    » _____ Initializes the *counter* to the *startvalue*.

    » _____ Checks whether the value in the *counter* is greater (less) than the *endvalue*.

2. Create a chart (similar to the one shown earlier in Figure 7-3) that lists the processing steps for the code shown in Example 2 in Figure 7-1.

3. Write the Visual Basic code to calculate the quarterly payment on a loan of $6,000 for three years at 9% interest. Payments should be expressed as a negative number.

4. Write three different statements that you can use to select the first item in a combo box named deptComboBox. The first item is "Accounting."

5. Write the statement to select the existing text in the itemTextBox.

6. Write the statement to display (in the sizeLabel) the number of characters contained in the message variable.

7. Write the statement to remove the leading spaces from the city variable.

8. Write the statement to remove the leading and trailing spaces from a String variable named number.

9. Write the statement to remove any trailing spaces, commas, and periods from a String variable named amount.

10. Write the statement that uses the Remove method to remove the first two characters from the fullName variable.

11. Write the Visual Basic code that uses the EndsWith method to determine whether the string stored in the inputRate variable ends with the percent sign. If it does, the code should use the TrimEnd method to remove the percent sign from the variable's contents.

12. The partNum variable contains the string "ABCD34G". Write the statement to assign the number 34 in the variable to the code variable.

13. The amount variable contains the string "3,123,560". Write the statement to assign the contents of the variable, excluding the commas, to the amount variable.

14. Write the Mid statement that changes the contents of the word variable from "mouse" to "mouth".

15. Write the statement that uses the Insert method to change the contents of the word variable from "mend" to "amend".

16. Write the statement that uses the IndexOf method to determine whether the address variable contains the street name "Elm Street" (entered in uppercase, lowercase, or a combination of uppercase and lowercase). Begin the search with the first character in the variable, and assign the method's return value to the indexNum variable.

17. Write the statement that uses the Contains method to determine whether the address variable contains the street name "Elm Street" (entered in uppercase, lowercase, or a combination of uppercase and lowercase). Assign the method's return value to a Boolean variable named isContained.

18. Write the statement that uses the String.Compare method to determine whether the string stored in the item variable is equal to the string stored in the itemOrdered variable. Assign the method's return value to an Integer variable named result.

19. Write an If clause that uses the Like operator to determine whether the string stored in the state variable is equal to any of the following state names: "New York", "New Jersey", or "New Mexico".

20. Write the statement to change the contents of the pay variable from "235.67" to "****235.67".

21. What will the newPhone = phone.Replace("800", "877") statement assign to the newPhone variable when the phone variable contains the string "1-800-999-9980"? What will it assign when the phone variable contains the string "1-800-999-8006"?

22. If the inventoryNum variable contains the string "ABX34", the inventoryNum = inventoryNum.Replace("X", "Z") statement changes the contents of the variable to "ABZ34". Rather than replace the letter X with the letter Z, you can remove the letter X and then insert the letter Z. Write the statements to accomplish the remove and insert operations.

23. Write the statement to compare the string stored in the departmentName variable with the string "Accounting". Ignore the case of the string when performing the comparison. Store the result of the comparison in an Integer variable named result.

24. Write the statement to search for the period in a string named price. Assign the location of the period to an Integer variable named location.

COMPUTER EXERCISES

1. In this exercise, you modify the Hangman Game application from this chapter's Programming Tutorial.

   a. Use Windows to make a copy of the Hangman Game Solution folder, which is contained in the VbReloaded2008\Chap07 folder. Rename the copy Modified Hangman Game Solution.

   b. Open the Hangman Game Solution (Hangman Game Solution.sln) file contained in the VbReloaded2008\Chap07\Modified Hangman Game Solution folder. Modify the application to allow player 1 to enter a word that contains any number of characters.

   c. Save the solution, then start and test the application. End the application, then close the solution.

2. In this exercise, you modify the Principal and Interest application from this chapter's Programming Example.

   a. If necessary, create the Principal and Interest application shown in this chapter's Programming Example. Use Windows to make a copy of the Principal and Interest Solution folder, which is contained in the VbReloaded2008\Chap07 folder. Rename the copy Modified Principal and Interest Solution.

   b. Open the Principal and Interest Solution (Principal and Interest Solution.sln) file contained in the VbReloaded2008\Chap07\Modified Principal and Interest Solution folder. Modify the application to display the total of the principal amounts and the total of the interest amounts listed in the text box. Display the totals at the end of the list in the text box.

   c. Save the solution, then start and test the application. End the application, then close the solution.

3. In this exercise, you code an application that displays the squares of the even integers from 2 through 12 in a label control.

   a. Open the Even Squares Solution (Even Squares Solution.sln) file, which is contained in the VbReloaded2008\Chap07\Even Squares Solution folder.

   b. Code the Display button's Click event procedure so that it displays the squares of the even integers from 2 through 12 in the squaresLabel control. Display each square on a separate line in the control. Use the For...Next statement.

   c. Save the solution. Start and then test the application. End the application, then close the solution.

4. In this exercise, you code an application that allows the user to enter two integers. The application then displays all of the odd numbers between both integers and all of the even numbers between both integers.

   a. Open the OddEven Solution (OddEven Solution.sln) file, which is contained in the VbReloaded2008\Chap07\OddEven Solution folder. Code the application. Use the For...Next statement.

   b. Save the solution, then start the application. Test the application using the following integers: 6 and 25. The application should display the following odd numbers: 7, 9, 11, 13, 15, 17, 19, 21, and 23. It also should display the following even numbers: 8, 10, 12, 14, 16, 18, 20, 22, and 24. Now test it again using the following integers: 10 and 3.

   c. End the application, then close the solution.

5. In this exercise, you code an application that displays a shipping charge based on the state name either selected or entered in a combo box.

   a. Open the Gentry Supplies Solution (Gentry Supplies Solution.sln) file, which is contained in the VbReloaded2008\Chap07\Gentry Supplies Solution folder. Add the following state names to the combo box: Alabama, Georgia, Louisiana, and North Carolina.

b. Code the combo box's TextChanged event procedure, which should display the following message in the label control: "The shipping charge for *state* is *charge*.", where *state* is the name of the state either selected or entered in the combo box, and *charge* is the shipping charge. The shipping charges are listed below.

State name	Shipping charge
Alabama	$20
Georgia	$35
Louisiana	$30
North Carolina	$28
All other entries	$15

c. Save the solution, then start and test the application. End the application, then close the solution.

6. In this exercise, you code an application that displays a multiplication table similar to the one shown in Figure 7-51, where *x* is a number entered by the user and *y* is the result of multiplying *x* by the numbers 1 through 9.

Multiplication table:

$x * 1 = y$
$x * 2 = y$
$x * 3 = y$
$x * 4 = y$
$x * 5 = y$
$x * 6 = y$
$x * 7 = y$
$x * 8 = y$
$x * 9 = y$

Figure 7-51

a. Open the Multiplication Solution (Multiplication Solution.sln) file, which is contained in the VbReloaded2008\Chap07\Multiplication Solution folder. Code the application.

b. Save the solution, then start and test the application. End the application, then close the solution.

7. In this exercise, you complete an application that displays a shipping charge based on the ZIP code entered by the user.

   a. Open the Zip Solution (Zip Solution.sln) file, which is contained in the VbReloaded2008\Chap07\Zip Solution folder.

   b. The Display Shipping Charge button's Click event procedure should display the appropriate shipping charge based on the ZIP code entered by the user. To be valid, the ZIP code must contain exactly five digits, and the first three digits must be either "605" or "606". All ZIP codes beginning with "605" have a $25 shipping charge. All ZIP codes beginning with "606" have a $30 shipping charge. All other ZIP codes are invalid and the procedure should display an appropriate message. Code the procedure.

   c. Save the solution, then start the application. Test the application using the following ZIP codes: 60677, 60511, 60344, and 7130. End the application, then close the solution.

8. In this exercise, you code an application that displays the color of an item.

   a. Open the Color Solution (Color Solution.sln) file, which is contained in the VbReloaded2008\Chap07\Color Solution folder.

   b. The Display Color button's Click event procedure should display the color of the item whose item number is entered by the user. All item numbers contain exactly five characters. All items are available in four colors: blue, green, red, and white. The third character in the item number indicates the item's

Character	Color
B or b	Blue
G or g	Green
R or r	Red
W or w	White

   color, as indicated in the chart shown here. For example, if the user enters 12b45, the procedure should display the word "Blue" in the colorLabel. If the item number does not contain exactly five characters, or if the third character is not one of the characters listed in the chart, the procedure should display an appropriate message in a message box.

   c. Save the solution, then start the application. Test the application using the following item numbers: 12x, 12b45, 99G44, abr55, 78w99, and 23abc. End the application, then close the solution.

9. In this exercise, you code an application that allows the user to enter a name (the first name followed by a space and the last name). The application then displays the name (the last name followed by a comma, a space, and the first name).

   a. Open the Reverse Name Solution (Reverse Name Solution.sln) file, which is contained in the VbReloaded2008\Chap07\Reverse Name Solution folder. Code the application.

   b. Save the solution, then start the application. Test the application using the following names: Carol Smith, Jose Martinez, Sven Miller, and Susan. End the application, then close the solution.

10. In this exercise, you modify the application that you coded in Computer Exercise 9 so that it displays the names using proper case.

    a. Use Windows to make a copy of the Reverse Name Solution folder, which is contained in the VbReloaded2008\Chap07 folder. Rename the folder Proper Case Solution.

    b. Open the Reverse Name Solution (Reverse Name Solution.sln) file contained in the Proper Case Solution folder. Modify the application to display the first and last names in the proper case. In other words, the first and last names should begin with an uppercase letter, and the remaining letters should be lowercase.

    c. Save the solution, then start the application. Test the application using jAke millEr as the name. The application should display Miller, Jake. End the application, then close the solution.

11. In this exercise, you code an application that allows the user to enter a phone number. The application then removes any hyphens, spaces, and parentheses from the phone number before displaying the phone number.

    a. Open the Phone Solution (Phone Solution.sln) file, which is contained in the VbReloaded2008\Chap07\Phone Solution folder.

    b. Code the application. Save the solution, then start the application. Test the application using the following phone numbers: (555) 111-1111, 555-5555, and 123-456-1111. End the application, then close the solution.

12. In this exercise, you code an application that displays a message indicating whether a portion of a string begins with another string.

    a. Open the String Solution (String Solution.sln) file, which is contained in the VbReloaded2008\Chap07\String Solution folder.

    b. The application allows the user to enter a name (first name followed by a space and the last name) and the search text. If the last name (entered in any case) begins with the search text (entered in any case), the Display Message button's Click event procedure should display the message "The last name begins with" followed by a space and the search text. If the characters in the last name come before the search text (using word sort rules), display the message "The last name comes before" followed by a space and the search text. Finally, if the characters in the last name come after the search text (using word sort rules), display the message "The last name comes after" followed by a space and the search text.

    c. Save the solution, then start the application. To test the application, enter Helga Swanson as the name, then use the following strings for the search text: g, ab, he, s, SY, sw, swan, and wan. End the application, then close the solution.

13. In this exercise, you learn how to use the Financial.Pmt method to calculate a periodic payment on an investment (rather than on a loan).

    a. Open the Investment Solution (Investment Solution.sln) file, which is contained in the VbReloaded2008\Chap07\Investment Solution folder. The application should calculate the amount you need to save each month to accumulate $40,000 at the end of 20 years, assuming a 6% interest rate. You can calculate this amount using the syntax **Financial.Pmt(*Rate*, *NPer*, *PV*, *FV*)**. The *Rate* argument is the interest rate per period, and the *NPer* argument is the total number of payment periods. The *PV* argument is the present value of the investment, which is 0 (zero). The *FV* argument is the future value of the investment. The future value is the amount you want to accumulate.

    b. Open the Code Editor window and code the application. Display the monthly amount as a positive number.

    c. Save the solution, then start and test the application. (The answer should be $86.57.) End the application.

    d. Modify the application to allow you to enter any future value. Save the solution, then start and test the application. End the application, then close the solution.

14. In this exercise, you practice debugging an application.

    a. Open the Debug Solution (Debug Solution.sln) file, which is contained in the VbReloaded2008\Chap07\Debug Solution folder. Open the Code Editor window and review the existing code.

    b. Start the application. Test the application by entering Tampa, Florida in the Address text box, then click the Display City button. The button displays the letter T in a message box, which is incorrect; it should display the word Tampa. Close the dialog box, then end the application.

    c. Correct the application's code. Save the solution, then start and test the application. Close the dialog box. End the application, then close the solution.

CASE PROJECTS

GEORGETOWN CREDIT

Credit card companies typically assign a special digit, called a check digit, to the end of each customer's credit card number. Many methods for creating the check digit have been developed. One simple method is to multiply every other number in the credit card number by two, then add the products to the remaining numbers to get the total.

You then take the last digit in the total and append it to the end of the number, as illustrated in Figure 7-52. Create an application that allows the user to enter a five-digit credit card number, with the fifth digit being the check digit. The application should use the method illustrated in Figure 7-52 to verify that the credit card number is valid. Display appropriate messages indicating whether the credit card is valid or invalid. Name the solution, project, and form file Georgetown Solution, Georgetown Project, and Main Form.vb, respectively. Save the solution in the VbReloaded2008\Chap07 folder. You can either create your own interface or create the one shown in Figure 7-53.

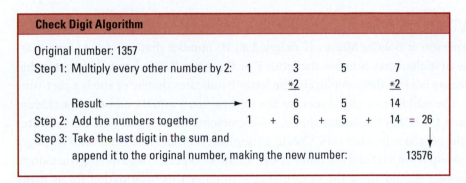

Figure 7-52: Illustration of a check digit algorithm

Figure 7-53: Sample interface for Georgetown Credit

JACOBSON FINANCE

Create an application that allows the user to enter a password that contains five, six, or seven characters. The application should create and display a new password using the following three rules. First, replace all vowels (A, E, I, O, and U) with the letter X. Second, replace all numbers with the letter Z. Third, reverse the characters in the password. Name the solution, project, and form file Jacobson Solution, Jacobson Project, and Main Form.vb, respectively. Save the solution in the VbReloaded2008\ Chap07 folder. You can either create your own interface or create the one shown in Figure 7-54.

Figure 7-54: Sample interface for Jacobson Finance

BOBCAT MOTORS

Each salesperson at BobCat Motors is assigned an ID number that consists of four characters. The first character is either the letter F or the letter P. The letter F indicates that the salesperson is a full-time employee. The letter P indicates that he or she is a part-time employee. The middle two characters are the salesperson's initials, and the last character is either a 1 or a 2. A 1 indicates that the salesperson sells new cars, and a 2 indicates that the salesperson sells used cars. Create an application that allows the sales manager to enter a salesperson's ID and the number of cars the salesperson sold during the month. The application should allow the sales manager to enter this information for as many salespeople as needed. The application should calculate and display the total number of cars sold by each of the following four categories of employees: full-time employees, part-time employees, employees selling new cars, and employees selling used cars. Name the solution, project, and form file BobCat Motors Solution, BobCat Motors Project, and Main Form.vb, respectively. Save the solution in the VbReloaded2008\Chap07 folder.

PIG LATIN

Create an application that allows the user to enter a word. The application should display the word in pig latin form. The rules for converting a word into pig latin form are shown below. Name the solution, project, and form file Pig Latin Solution, Pig Latin Project, and Main Form.vb, respectively. Save the solution in the VbReloaded2008\Chap07 folder.

» If the word begins with a vowel (A, E, I, O, or U), then add the string "-way" (a dash followed by the letters w, a, and y) to the end of the word. For example, the pig latin form of the word "ant" is "ant-way".

» If the word does not begin with a vowel, first add a dash to the end of the word. Then continue moving the first character in the word to the end of the word until the first character is the letter A, E, I, O, U, or Y. Then add the string "ay" to the end of the word. For example, the pig latin form of the word "Chair" is "air-Chay".

» If the word does not contain the letter A, E, I, O, U, or Y, then add the string "-way" to the end of the word. For example, the pig latin form of "56" is "56-way".

8

SUB AND FUNCTION PROCEDURES

After studying Chapter 8, you should be able to:

Explain the difference between a Sub procedure and
    a Function procedure

Create a Sub procedure and a Function procedure

Create a procedure that receives information passed to it

Explain the difference between passing data *by value* and
    passing data *by reference*

Explain the purpose of the sender and e parameters

Associate a procedure with more than one object and event

Utilize a timer control

Convert an Object variable to a different type using the
    TryCast operator

PROCEDURES

A **procedure** is a block of program code that performs a specific task. Most procedures in Visual Basic are either Sub procedures or Function procedures. The difference between both types of procedures is that a **Function procedure** returns a value after performing its assigned task, whereas a **Sub procedure** does not return a value. Although you have been using Sub procedures since Chapter 1, this chapter provides a more in-depth look into their creation and use. After exploring the topic of Sub procedures, you then learn how to create and use Function procedures.

SUB PROCEDURES

There are two types of Sub procedures in Visual Basic: event procedures and independent Sub procedures. The procedures you coded in previous chapters were event procedures. An event procedure is a Sub procedure that is associated with a specific object and event, such as a button's Click event or a text box's TextChanged event. Recall that the computer automatically processes an event procedure when the event occurs. An **independent Sub procedure**, on the other hand, is a procedure that is independent of any object and event. An independent Sub procedure is processed only when called (invoked) from code. Programmers use independent Sub procedures for two reasons. First, they allow the programmer to avoid duplicating code in different parts of a program. If a program needs to perform the same task several times, it is more efficient to enter the appropriate code once, in a procedure, and then call the procedure to perform its task when needed. Second, procedures allow large and complex applications, which typically are written by a team of programmers, to be broken into small and manageable tasks. Each member of the team is assigned one or more tasks to code as a procedure. When each programmer completes his or her procedure, all of the procedures are gathered together into one application. Figure 8-1 shows the syntax you use to create an independent Sub procedure. It also includes an example of an independent Sub procedure, as well as the steps you follow to enter an independent Sub procedure in the Code Editor window.

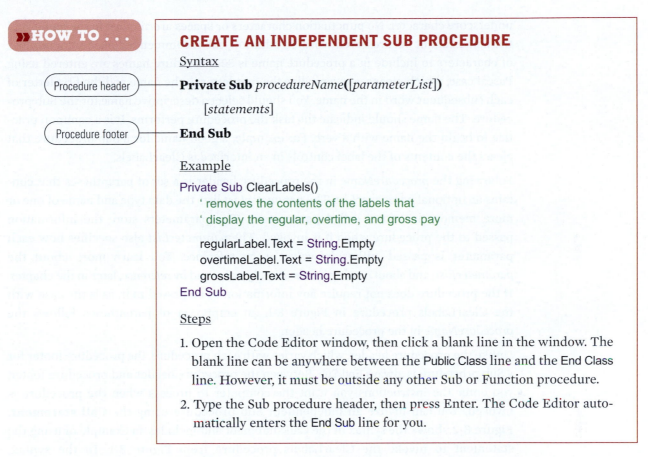

»HOW TO . . .

CREATE AN INDEPENDENT SUB PROCEDURE

<u>Syntax</u>

Procedure header — **Private Sub** *procedureName*(*[parameterList]*)

    [statements]

Procedure footer — **End Sub**

<u>Example</u>

```
Private Sub ClearLabels()
    ' removes the contents of the labels that
    ' display the regular, overtime, and gross pay

    regularLabel.Text = String.Empty
    overtimeLabel.Text = String.Empty
    grossLabel.Text = String.Empty
End Sub
```

<u>Steps</u>

1. Open the Code Editor window, then click a blank line in the window. The blank line can be anywhere between the Public Class line and the End Class line. However, it must be outside any other Sub or Function procedure.

2. Type the Sub procedure header, then press Enter. The Code Editor automatically enters the End Sub line for you.

Figure 8-1: How to create an independent Sub procedure

As do all procedures, independent Sub procedures have both a procedure header and procedure footer. In most cases, the procedure header begins with the keyword Private, which indicates that the procedure can be used only by the other procedures in the current form. Following the Private keyword in the procedure header is the keyword Sub, which identifies the procedure as a Sub procedure. After the Sub keyword is the *procedureName*. The rules for naming an independent Sub procedure are the same as those for naming variables and constants. Recall that the rules state that the name must begin with a letter or an underscore and can contain only letters, numbers, and the underscore character. No punctuation characters or spaces are allowed in the name, and the name cannot be a reserved word. In addition, the recommended maximum number of characters to include in a procedure name is 32. Procedure names are entered using Pascal case, which means you capitalize the first letter in the name and the first letter of each subsequent word in the name. You should select a descriptive name for the Sub procedure. The name should indicate the task the procedure performs. It is a common practice to begin the name with a verb. For example, a good name for a Sub procedure that clears the contents of the label controls in an interface is ClearLabels.

Following the *procedureName* in the procedure header is a set of parentheses that contains an optional *parameterList*. The *parameterList* lists the data type and name of one or more memory locations, called **parameters**. The parameters store the information passed to the procedure when it is invoked. The *parameterList* also specifies how each parameter is passed—either *by value* or *by reference*. You learn more about the *parameterList*, and about passing information *by value* and *by reference*, later in the chapter. If the procedure does not require any information to be passed to it, as is the case with the ClearLabels procedure in Figure 8-1, an empty set of parentheses follows the *procedureName* in the procedure header.

Unlike the procedure header, which varies with each procedure, the procedure footer for a Sub procedure is always End Sub. Between the procedure header and procedure footer, you enter the instructions you want the computer to process when the procedure is invoked. You can invoke an independent Sub procedure using the **Call statement**. Figure 8-2 shows the syntax of the Call statement and includes an example of using the statement to invoke the ClearLabels procedure from Figure 8-1. In the syntax, *procedureName* is the name of the procedure you are calling (invoking), and *argumentList* (which is optional) is a comma-separated list of arguments you want passed to the procedure. If you have no information to pass to the procedure that you are calling, as is the case with the ClearLabels procedure, you include an empty set of parentheses after the *procedureName* in the Call statement. The ClearLabels procedure is used in the Gadis Antiques application, which you view in the next section.

» HOW TO . . .

CALL AN INDEPENDENT SUB PROCEDURE

Syntax

Call *procedureName*(**[***argumentList***]**)

Example

Call ClearLabels()

Figure 8-2: How to call an independent Sub procedure

THE GADIS ANTIQUES APPLICATION

The manager at Gadis Antiques wants an application that calculates an employee's regular pay, overtime pay, and gross pay. Employees are paid on an hourly basis and receive time and one-half for the hours worked over 40. Figure 8-3 shows a sample run of the Gadis Antiques application, and Figure 8-4 shows a portion of the application's code. Notice that the ClearLabels procedure is entered above the event procedures in the code. It is a good programming practice to enter the procedures you create either above the first event procedure or below the last event procedure. By organizing the code in this manner, you can more easily locate the independent Sub and Function procedures in the Code Editor window. As Figure 8-4 indicates, three event procedures need to clear the contents of the three label controls: the Clear button's Click event procedure, the hoursComboBox's TextChanged event procedure, and the rateComboBox's TextChanged event procedure. You can accomplish the task by entering the appropriate assignment statements in each of the three event procedures. Or, you can enter the assignment statements in an independent Sub procedure, and then call the Sub procedure from each of the three event procedures, as shown in Figure 8-4. Entering the code in an independent Sub procedure saves you from having to enter the same statements more than once. In addition, if the application is modified—for example, if the user prefers to assign the string "0.00" rather than the empty string to the labels—you need to make the change in only one place in the code.

TIP

When you enter a procedure below the last event procedure in the Code Editor window, be sure to enter it above the End Class line.

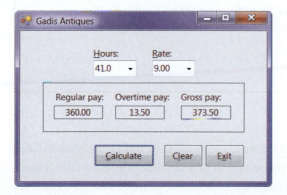

Figure 8-3: Sample run of the Gadis Antiques application

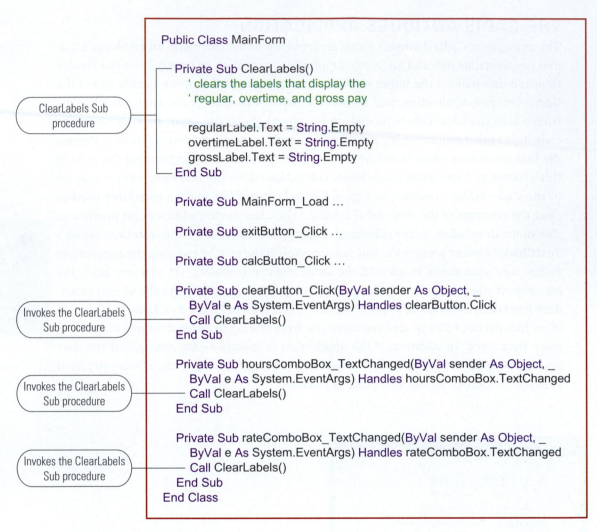

Figure 8-4: Partial code for the Gadis Antiques application

When the computer processes the Call ClearLabels() statement in the clearButton's Click event procedure, it temporarily leaves the procedure to process the code in the ClearLabels procedure. The assignment statements in the ClearLabels procedure remove the contents of three label controls in the interface. After processing the assignment statements, the computer processes the ClearLabels procedure's End Sub statement, which ends the procedure. The computer then returns to the clearButton's Click event procedure and processes the line of code located immediately below the Call statement. The line below the Call statement is End Sub, which ends the clearButton's Click event procedure.

Now study the code in the TextChanged event procedures for the two combo boxes. As you learned in Chapter 7, a combo box's TextChanged event occurs when the user either selects an item from the list portion of the combo box or types a value in the text portion. In this case, the computer processes the Call ClearLabels() statement when the TextChanged event for either combo box occurs. As before, when processing the statement, the computer temporarily leaves the current event procedure to process the code contained in the ClearLabels procedure. When the ClearLabels procedure ends, the computer returns to the current event procedure and processes the code immediately below the Call statement.

INCLUDING PARAMETERS IN AN INDEPENDENT SUB PROCEDURE

» TIP

Visual Basic allows you to specify that an argument in the Call statement is optional. To learn more about optional arguments, complete Computer Exercise 16 at the end of the chapter.

As mentioned earlier, an independent Sub procedure can contain one or more parameters in its procedure header. Each parameter stores data that is passed to the procedure when the procedure is invoked by the Call statement. The Call statement passes the information in its optional *argumentList*. The number of arguments listed in the Call statement's *argumentList* should agree with the number of parameters listed in the *parameterList* in the procedure header. If the *argumentList* includes one argument, then the procedure header should have one parameter in its *parameterList*. Similarly, a procedure that is passed three arguments when called requires three parameters in its *parameterList*. (Refer to the first TIP on this page for an exception to this general rule.) In addition to having the same number of parameters as arguments, the data type and position of each parameter in the *parameterList* should agree with the data type and position of its corresponding argument in the *argumentList*. If the argument is an integer, then the parameter that will store the integer should have a data type of Integer, Short, or Long, depending on the size of the integer. Likewise, if two arguments are passed to a procedure—the first one a String variable and the second one a Decimal variable—the first parameter should have a data type of String and the second parameter should have a data type of Decimal. You can pass a literal constant, named constant, keyword, or variable to an independent Sub procedure; in most cases, you will pass a variable.

PASSING VARIABLES

» TIP

The internal memory of a computer is like a large post office, where each memory cell, like each post office box, has a unique address.

Each variable you declare in an application has both a value and a unique address that represents the location of the variable in the computer's internal memory. Visual Basic allows you to pass either the variable's value or its address to the receiving procedure. Passing a variable's value is referred to as **passing by value**. Passing a variable's address is referred to as **passing by reference**. The method you choose—*by value* or *by reference*—depends on whether you want the receiving procedure to have access to the variable in memory. In other words, it depends on whether you want to allow the receiving procedure to change the contents of the variable. Although the idea of passing information *by value* and *by reference* may sound confusing at first, it is a concept with which you already are familiar.

To illustrate, assume you have a savings account at a local bank. During a conversation with a friend, you mention the amount of money you have in the account. Telling someone the amount of money in your account is similar to passing a variable *by value*. Knowing the balance in your account does not give your friend access to your bank account. It merely gives your friend some information that he or she can use—perhaps to compare to the amount of money he or she has saved. The savings account example also provides an illustration of passing information *by reference*. To deposit money to or withdraw money from your account, you must provide the bank teller with your account number. The account number represents the location of your account at the bank and allows the teller to change the account balance. Giving the teller your bank account number is similar to passing a variable *by reference*. The account number allows the teller to change the contents of your bank account, similar to the way the variable's address allows the receiving procedure to change the contents of the variable passed to the procedure.

PASSING VARIABLES BY VALUE

To pass a variable *by value* in Visual Basic, you include the keyword ByVal (which stands for "by value") before the variable's corresponding parameter in the receiving procedure's *parameterList*. When you pass a variable *by value*, the computer passes only the contents of the variable to the receiving procedure. When only the contents are passed, the receiving procedure is not given access to the variable in memory; therefore, it cannot change the value stored inside the variable. You pass a variable *by value* when the receiving procedure needs to *know* the variable's contents, but the receiving procedure does not need to *change* the contents. Unless specified otherwise, variables are passed *by value* in Visual Basic. Figure 8-5 shows a sample run of the Pet Information application, and Figure 8-6 shows a portion of the application's code. The Call statement in the code passes two String variables *by value* to an independent Sub procedure named DisplayMessage. Notice that the number, data type, and sequence of the arguments in the Call statement match the number, data type, and sequence of the corresponding parameters in the procedure header. Also notice that the names of the parameters do not need to be identical to the names of the corresponding arguments. In fact, to avoid confusion, it usually is better to use different names for the arguments and parameters.

Figure 8-5: Sample run of the Pet Information application

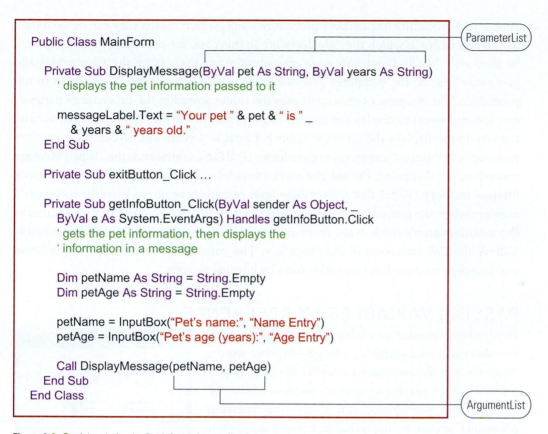

```
Public Class MainForm                                              ParameterList

    Private Sub DisplayMessage(ByVal pet As String, ByVal years As String)
        ' displays the pet information passed to it

        messageLabel.Text = "Your pet " & pet & " is " _
            & years & " years old."
    End Sub

    Private Sub exitButton_Click …

    Private Sub getInfoButton_Click(ByVal sender As Object, _
        ByVal e As System.EventArgs) Handles getInfoButton.Click
        ' gets the pet information, then displays the
        ' information in a message

        Dim petName As String = String.Empty
        Dim petAge As String = String.Empty

        petName = InputBox("Pet's name:", "Name Entry")
        petAge = InputBox("Pet's age (years):", "Age Entry")

        Call DisplayMessage(petName, petAge)
    End Sub
End Class                                                          ArgumentList
```

Figure 8-6: Partial code for the Pet Information application

The getInfoButton's Click event procedure prompts the user to enter the name and age (in years) of her pet. If the user enters "Spot" as the name and "4" as the age, the computer stores the string "Spot" in the petName variable and stores the string "4" in the petAge variable. The Call DisplayMessage(petName, petAge) statement calls the DisplayMessage procedure, passing it the petName and petAge variables *by value*, which means that only the contents of the variables—in this case, "Spot" and "4"—are passed to the procedure. You can tell that the variables are passed *by value* because the keyword ByVal appears before each variable's corresponding parameter in the DisplayMessage procedure header. At this point, the computer temporarily leaves the getInfoButton's Click event procedure to process the code contained in the DisplayMessage procedure. The first instruction processed in the DisplayMessage procedure is the procedure header. When processing the procedure header, the computer creates the variables listed in the *parameterList*, and stores the information passed to the procedure in those variables. In this case, the computer creates the pet and years variables, storing the string "Spot" in the pet variable and the string "4" in the years variable. The variables that

> **» TIP**
> You cannot determine by looking at the Call statement whether a variable is being passed *by value* or *by reference*. You must look at the procedure header to make the determination.

appear in a procedure header have procedure scope, which means they can be used only by the procedure in which they are declared. In this case, the pet and years variables can be used only by the DisplayMessage procedure. After processing the DisplayMessage procedure header, the computer processes the assignment statement contained in the procedure. The assignment statement uses the values stored in the procedure's parameters (pet and years) to display the appropriate message in the messageLabel. In this case, the statement displays the message "Your pet Spot is 4 years old." Next, the computer processes the DisplayMessage procedure footer (End Sub), which ends the DisplayMessage procedure. At this point, the pet and years variables are removed from the computer's internal memory. (Recall that a procedure-level variable is removed from the computer's memory when the procedure in which it is declared ends.) The computer then returns to the getInfoButton's Click event procedure to process the End Sub, which immediately follows the Call statement in the procedure. The computer then removes the petName and petAge procedure-level variables from its internal memory.

PASSING VARIABLES BY REFERENCE

In addition to passing a variable's value to a procedure, you also can pass a variable's address—in other words, its location in the computer's internal memory. As you learned earlier, passing a variable's address is referred to as passing *by reference*, and it gives the receiving procedure access to the variable being passed. You pass a variable *by reference* when you want the receiving procedure to change the contents of the variable. To pass a variable *by reference* in Visual Basic, you include the keyword ByRef (which stands for "by reference") before the variable's corresponding parameter in the receiving procedure's header. The ByRef keyword tells the computer to pass the variable's address

Figure 8-7: Sample run of the Gross Pay application

rather than its contents. Figure 8-7 shows a sample run of the Gross Pay application, and Figure 8-8 shows a portion of the application's code. The calcButton's Click event procedure passes three variables to the CalcGrossPay procedure: two *by value* and one *by reference*. Notice that the number, data type, and sequence of the arguments in the Call statement match the number, data type, and sequence of the corresponding parameters in the procedure header. Here again, notice that the names of the parameters do not need to be identical to the names of the arguments to which they correspond.

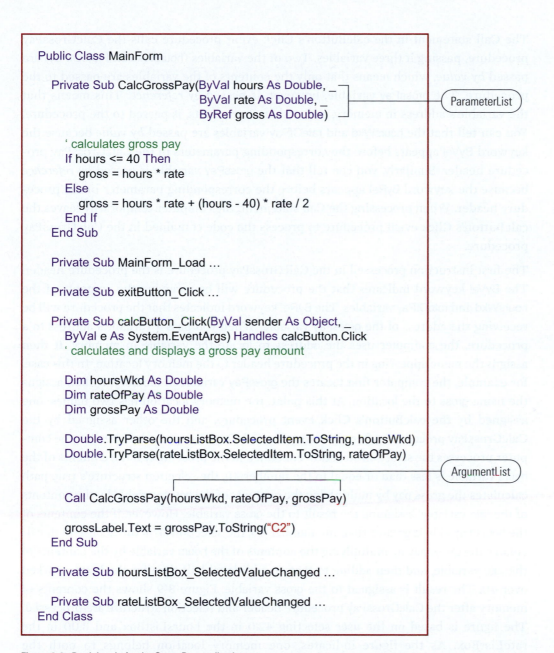

```
Public Class MainForm

    Private Sub CalcGrossPay(ByVal hours As Double, _
                             ByVal rate As Double, _
                             ByRef gross As Double)

        ' calculates gross pay
        If hours <= 40 Then
            gross = hours * rate
        Else
            gross = hours * rate + (hours - 40) * rate / 2
        End If
    End Sub

    Private Sub MainForm_Load …

    Private Sub exitButton_Click …

    Private Sub calcButton_Click(ByVal sender As Object, _
        ByVal e As System.EventArgs) Handles calcButton.Click
        ' calculates and displays a gross pay amount

        Dim hoursWkd As Double
        Dim rateOfPay As Double
        Dim grossPay As Double

        Double.TryParse(hoursListBox.SelectedItem.ToString, hoursWkd)
        Double.TryParse(rateListBox.SelectedItem.ToString, rateOfPay)


        Call CalcGrossPay(hoursWkd, rateOfPay, grossPay)

        grossLabel.Text = grossPay.ToString("C2")
    End Sub

    Private Sub hoursListBox_SelectedValueChanged …

    Private Sub rateListBox_SelectedValueChanged …
End Class
```

ParameterList

ArgumentList

Figure 8-8: Partial code for the Gross Pay application

The Call statement in the calcButton's Click event procedure calls the CalcGrossPay procedure, passing it three variables. Two of the variables (hoursWkd and rateOfPay) are passed *by value*, which means that only the contents of the variables are passed to the procedure. The grossPay variable, however, is passed *by reference*. This means that the variable's address in memory, rather than its contents, is passed to the procedure. You can tell that the hoursWkd and rateOfPay variables are passed *by value* because the keyword ByVal appears before the corresponding parameters in the CalcGrossPay procedure header. Similarly, you can tell that the grossPay variable is passed *by reference* because the keyword ByRef appears before the corresponding parameter in the procedure header. When processing the Call statement, the computer temporarily leaves the calcButton's Click event procedure to process the code contained in the CalcGrossPay procedure.

The first instruction processed in the CalcGrossPay procedure is the procedure header. The ByVal keyword indicates that the procedure will be receiving the contents of the hoursWkd and rateOfPay variables. The ByRef keyword indicates that the procedure will be receiving the address of the grossPay variable. When you pass a variable's address to a procedure, the computer uses the address to locate the variable in memory. It then assigns the name appearing in the procedure header to the memory location. In this case, for example, the computer first locates the grossPay variable in memory. It then assigns the name gross to the location. At this point, the memory location has two names: one assigned by the calcButton's Click event procedure, and the other assigned by the CalcGrossPay procedure. After processing the CalcGrossPay procedure header, the computer processes the selection structure contained in the procedure. If the contents of the hours variable is less than or equal to the number 40, the selection structure's true path calculates the gross pay by multiplying the contents of the hours variable by the contents of the rate variable, assigning the result to the gross variable. However, if the contents of the hours variable is greater than the number 40, the selection structure's false path calculates the gross pay by multiplying the contents of the hours variable by the contents of the rate variable, and then adding to that an additional half-time for the hours worked over 40. The result is assigned to the gross variable. Figure 8-9 shows the contents of memory after the CalcGrossPay procedure header and selection structure are processed. The figure is based on the user selecting 42.0 in the hoursListBox and 8.00 in the rateListBox. As the figure indicates, one memory location belongs to both the calcButton's Click event procedure and the CalcGrossPay procedure. Although both procedures can access the memory location, each procedure uses a different name to do so. The calcButton's Click event procedure uses the name grossPay to refer to the memory location, whereas the CalcGrossPay procedure uses the name gross. Because the names refer to the same location in memory, changing the contents of the gross variable also changes the contents of the grossPay variable.

≫ TIP

Although the grossPay and gross variables refer to the same location in memory, the grossPay variable is recognized only within the calcButton's Click event procedure. Similarly, the gross variable is recognized only within the CalcGrossPay procedure.

Memory locations known only to the calcButton's Click event procedure	
hoursWkd	rateOfPay
42.0	8.00

Memory locations known only to the CalcGrossPay procedure	
hours	rate
42.0	8.00

Memory location known to both procedures
grossPay (calcButton's Click event procedure)
gross (CalcGrossPay procedure)
344.00

Figure 8-9: Contents of memory after the CalcGrossPay procedure header and selection structure are processed

The End Sub line in the CalcGrossPay procedure is processed next and ends the procedure. At this point, the computer removes the memory locations that belong only to the CalcGrossPay procedure: hours and rate. In addition, it removes the name gross, which is assigned to the memory location that belongs to both procedures. Figure 8-10 shows the contents of memory after the hours and rate variables, as well as the gross variable name, are removed from memory. Notice that the grossPay memory location now has only one name: the name assigned to it by the calcButton's Click event procedure.

Memory locations known only to the calcButton's Click event procedure		
hoursWkd	rateOfPay	grossPay
42.0	8.00	344.00

Figure 8-10: Contents of memory after the appropriate variables and variable name are removed

The computer then returns to the statement located immediately below the Call statement in the calcButton's Click event procedure. The statement displays the gross pay in the grossLabel, as shown earlier in Figure 8-7. Next, the computer processes the End Sub statement in the calcButton's Click event procedure, which ends the procedure. The computer then removes the hoursWkd, rateOfPay, and grossPay variables from its internal memory.

ASSOCIATING A PROCEDURE WITH DIFFERENT OBJECTS AND EVENTS

As you learned in Chapter 1, the Handles keyword appears in an event procedure's header and indicates the object and event associated with the procedure. The Handles clearButton.Click clause in the code in Figure 8-11 indicates that the clearButton_Click procedure is associated with the Click event of the clearButton. As a result, the procedure will be processed when the clearButton's Click event occurs. Although the name of an event procedure includes the object name and event name, both of which appear after the Handles keyword, that is not a requirement. You can change the name of an event procedure to any name that follows the naming rules for procedures. For example, you can change the name clearButton_Click to Clear and the procedure will still work correctly. This is because the Handles clause, rather than the event procedure's name, determines when the procedure is invoked.

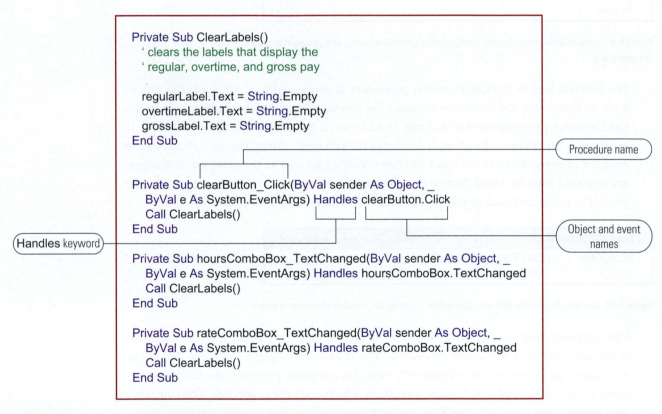

```
Private Sub ClearLabels()
    ' clears the labels that display the
    ' regular, overtime, and gross pay

    regularLabel.Text = String.Empty
    overtimeLabel.Text = String.Empty
    grossLabel.Text = String.Empty
End Sub

Private Sub clearButton_Click(ByVal sender As Object, _
    ByVal e As System.EventArgs) Handles clearButton.Click
    Call ClearLabels()
End Sub

Private Sub hoursComboBox_TextChanged(ByVal sender As Object, _
    ByVal e As System.EventArgs) Handles hoursComboBox.TextChanged
    Call ClearLabels()
End Sub

Private Sub rateComboBox_TextChanged(ByVal sender As Object, _
    ByVal e As System.EventArgs) Handles rateComboBox.TextChanged
    Call ClearLabels()
End Sub
```

Procedure name

Object and event names

Handles keyword

Figure 8-11: Some of the Gadis Antiques application's code from Figure 8-4

You also can associate a procedure with more than one object and event, as long as each event contains the same parameters in its procedure header. For example, in the code shown in Figure 8-11, you can associate the ClearLabels procedure with the clearButton's Click event, the hoursComboBox's TextChanged event, and the rateComboBox's TextChanged event, because the three event procedures have the same parameters in their procedure header. In this case, the three event procedures contain the ByVal sender As Object and ByVal e As System.EventArgs parameters. You may have noticed that all event procedures contain a sender parameter and an e parameter. The sender parameter contains the memory address of the object that raised the event. For example, when the clearButton's Click event occurs, the button's address in memory is stored in the sender parameter. Similarly, when either of the combo box's TextChanged event occurs, the corresponding combo box's memory address is stored in the sender parameter. The e parameter in an event procedure contains additional information provided by the object that raised the event. For instance, the e parameter in a text box's KeyPress event procedure contains information regarding the key that the user pressed on the keyboard. You can determine the items of information contained in an event procedure's e parameter by viewing its properties. You do this by displaying the event procedure's code template in the Code Editor window, and then typing the letter e followed by a period. The Code Editor displays a list that includes the properties.

To associate a procedure with more than one object and event, you list each parameter in the procedure's *parameterList*, and list each object and event in the Handles clause, as shown in Figure 8-12. You use commas to separate each parameter, as well as to separate each object and event. The Handles clause in the ClearLabels procedure tells the computer to invoke the procedure when any of the following occurs: the clearButton's Click event, the hoursComboBox's TextChanged event, or the rateComboBox's TextChanged event.

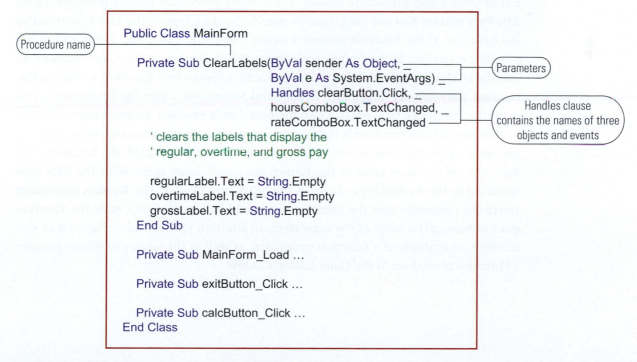

```
Public Class MainForm

    Private Sub ClearLabels(ByVal sender As Object, _
                            ByVal e As System.EventArgs) _
                            Handles clearButton.Click, _
                            hoursComboBox.TextChanged, _
                            rateComboBox.TextChanged
        ' clears the labels that display the
        ' regular, overtime, and gross pay

        regularLabel.Text = String.Empty
        overtimeLabel.Text = String.Empty
        grossLabel.Text = String.Empty
    End Sub

    Private Sub MainForm_Load …

    Private Sub exitButton_Click …

    Private Sub calcButton_Click …
End Class
```

Procedure name

Parameters

Handles clause contains the names of three objects and events

Figure 8-12: A different version of the code for the Gadis Antiques application

FUNCTION PROCEDURES

Like a Sub procedure, a Function procedure, referred to more simply as a **function**, is a block of code that performs a specific task. However, unlike a Sub procedure, a function returns a value after completing its task. Visual Basic provides many built-in functions that you can use, such as the InputBox function covered in Chapter 6. You also can create your own functions in Visual Basic, and you can pass (send) information to the functions either *by value* or *by reference*. After creating a function, you then can invoke it from one or more places in an application. You invoke a function that you create in exactly the same way as you invoke a built-in function: by including the function's name along with any arguments in a statement. Usually the statement will display the function's return value, use the return value in a calculation, or assign the return value to a variable. For example, the newPrice = CalcNew(oldPrice) statement invokes a function named CalcNew and assigns the function's return value to the newPrice variable.

Figure 8-13 shows the syntax you use to create a Function procedure. The procedure header for a function is almost identical to the procedure header for a Sub procedure, except it includes the Function keyword rather than the Sub keyword. Also different from a Sub procedure header, a function's procedure header includes the As *dataType* clause. You use the clause to specify the data type of the value returned by the function. If the function returns a string, you include As String at the end of the procedure header. If the function returns a Decimal type number, you include As Decimal in the procedure header. The procedure footer in a function is always End Function. Between the procedure header and footer, you enter the instructions you want the computer to process when the function is invoked. In most cases, the last statement within a function is Return *expression*, where *expression* represents the one and only value that will be returned to the statement that called the function. The data type of the *expression* in the Return statement must agree with the data type specified in the As *dataType* clause in the procedure header. The **Return statement** alerts the computer that the function has completed its task and ends the function after returning the value of the *expression*. In addition to the syntax, Figure 8-13 also includes an example of a Function procedure, as well as the steps you follow to enter a Function procedure in the Code Editor window.

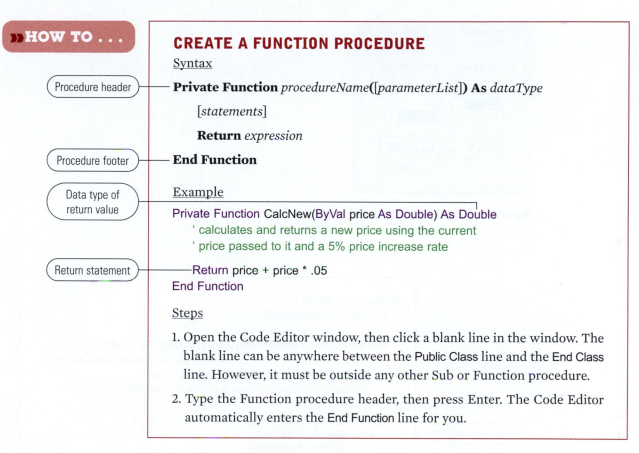

Figure 8-13: How to create a Function procedure

THE PINE LODGE APPLICATION

In this section, you view an application that creates and uses a function. The owner of the Pine Lodge wants an application that calculates an employee's new hourly pay, given the employee's current hourly pay and raise rate. Figure 8-14 shows a sample run of the Pine Lodge application, and Figure 8-15 shows a portion of the application's code.

Figure 8-14: Sample run of the Pine Lodge application

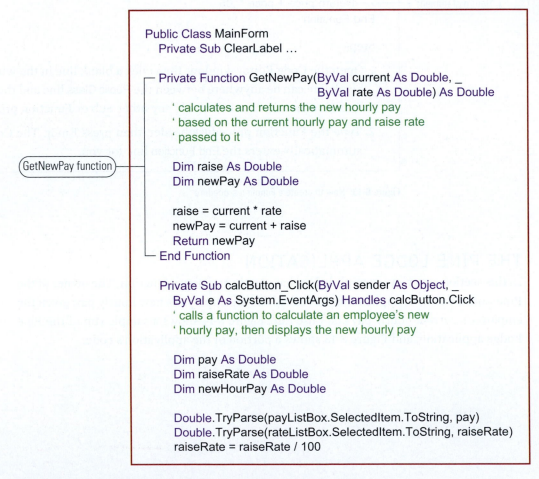

```
Public Class MainForm
    Private Sub ClearLabel ...

    Private Function GetNewPay(ByVal current As Double, _
                              ByVal rate As Double) As Double
        ' calculates and returns the new hourly pay
        ' based on the current hourly pay and raise rate
        ' passed to it

        Dim raise As Double
        Dim newPay As Double

        raise = current * rate
        newPay = current + raise
        Return newPay
    End Function

    Private Sub calcButton_Click(ByVal sender As Object, _
        ByVal e As System.EventArgs) Handles calcButton.Click
        ' calls a function to calculate an employee's new
        ' hourly pay, then displays the new hourly pay

        Dim pay As Double
        Dim raiseRate As Double
        Dim newHourPay As Double

        Double.TryParse(payListBox.SelectedItem.ToString, pay)
        Double.TryParse(rateListBox.SelectedItem.ToString, raiseRate)
        raiseRate = raiseRate / 100
```

GetNewPay function

Figure 8-15: Partial code for the Pine Lodge application (*continued on next page*)

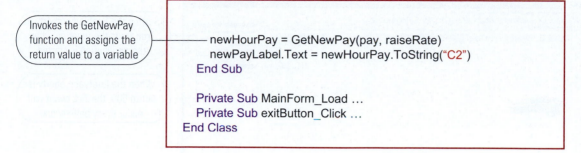

Invokes the GetNewPay function and assigns the return value to a variable

```
newHourPay = GetNewPay(pay, raiseRate)
newPayLabel.Text = newHourPay.ToString("C2")
End Sub

Private Sub MainForm_Load ...
Private Sub exitButton_Click ...
End Class
```

Figure 8-15: Partial code for the Pine Lodge application (*continued from previous page*)

The newHourPay = GetNewPay(pay, raiseRate) statement in the calcButton's Click event procedure calls the GetNewPay function, passing it the values stored in the pay and raiseRate variables. The computer stores the values in the current and rate variables that appear in the GetNewPay function's header. After processing the header, the computer processes the statements contained in the function. The assignment statements calculate the employee's raise and new pay amounts. The Return newPay statement then returns the contents of the newPay variable to the statement that called the function, which is the newHourPay = GetNewPay(pay, raiseRate) statement in the calcButton's Click event procedure. After the Return statement is processed, the GetNewPay function ends and the computer removes the current, rate, raise, and newPay variables from its internal memory. When the newHourPay = GetNewPay(pay, raiseRate) statement receives the value returned by the GetNewPay function, it assigns the value to the newHourPay variable. The newPayLabel.Text = newHourPay.ToString("C2") statement then displays the new hourly pay in the interface, as shown earlier in Figure 8-14. Finally, the computer processes the End Sub statement in the calcButton's Click event procedure, which ends the procedure. The computer then removes the pay, raiseRate, and newHourPay variables from its internal memory.

THE TIMER CONTROL

The game you will create in the Programming Tutorial requires you to use a timer control. You add a timer control to an interface using the Timer tool, which is located in the Components section of the toolbox. When you add a timer to a form, it does not appear on the form in the designer window. Instead, it is placed in a special area in the IDE, called the component tray, as shown in Figure 8-16. The component tray stores all controls that do not appear in the user interface when the application is running. In other words, the user will not see the timer control when the form appears on the screen.

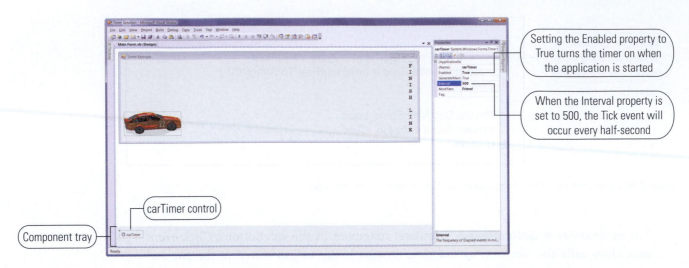

Figure 8-16: Timer shown in the Component tray

The purpose of a **timer control** is to process code at one or more regular intervals. The length of each interval is specified in milliseconds and entered in the timer's Interval property. A millisecond is 1/1000 of a second. In other words, there are 1000 milliseconds in a second. A timer's Enabled property indicates the timer's state, which can be either running (Enabled=True) or stopped (Enabled=False). If the timer is running, its Tick event occurs each time an interval has elapsed, and the code entered in its Tick event procedure is processed. If the timer is stopped, the Tick event does not occur; therefore, the Tick event procedure's code is not processed. Figure 8-17 shows the code entered in the carTimer's Tick event procedure. The code moves the car from the left side of the form to the right side, stopping when the car reaches the finish line.

```
Private Sub carTimer_Tick(ByVal sender As System.Object, _
    ByVal e As System.EventArgs) Handles carTimer.Tick
    ' moves the car across the form

    If carPictureBox.Left < 950 Then
        carPictureBox.Left = carPictureBox.Left + 10
    Else
        carTimer.Enabled = False
        MessageBox.Show("Race Over!", "Car Race", _
            MessageBoxButtons.OK, MessageBoxIcon.Information)
    End If
End Sub
```

Turns the timer off

Figure 8-17: The carTimer's Click event procedure

You have completed the concepts section of Chapter 8.

PROGRAMMING TUTORIAL

CODING THE CONCENTRATION GAME APPLICATION

In this tutorial, you code an application that simulates a game called Concentration. The game board contains 16 labels. Scattered among the labels are eight pairs of matching words that are hidden from view. The user begins by clicking one of the labels to reveal a word. He then clicks another label to reveal another word. If the two words match, the words remain on the screen. However, if the words do not match, they are hidden once again. The game is over when all of the matching words are revealed. The user can start a new game by clicking the New Game button in the interface. In each game, the words will appear in different locations on the game board. This is accomplished using an independent Sub procedure that generates random numbers. Figures 8-18 and 8-19 show the application's TOE chart and user interface.

Task	Object	Event
1. Fill the list box with 8 pairs of matching words 2. Call a procedure to shuffle the words in the list box	MainForm	Load
End the application	exitButton	Click
1. Clear the label controls, then enable them 2. Reset the counter to 0 3. Call a procedure to shuffle the words in the list box	newButton	Click
1. Enable the boardTableLayoutPanel 2. Disable the matchTimer	matchTimer	Tick
1. Clear the words from the chosen labels 2. Enable the boardTableLayoutPanel 3. Disable the noMatchTimer	noMatchTimer	Tick
1. Use a counter to keep track of whether this is the first or second label clicked 2. If this is the first label clicked, display a word from the list box in the label 3. If this is the second label clicked, disable the boardTableLayoutPanel, display a word from the list box in the label, and then compare both words 4. If both words match, disable both labels, then turn on the matchTimer 5. If both words do not match, turn on the noMatchTimer 6. Reset the counter to 0	16 Label controls	Click
Store the 16 words	wordListBox	None
Display the game board	boardTableLayoutPanel	None

Figure 8-18: TOE Chart

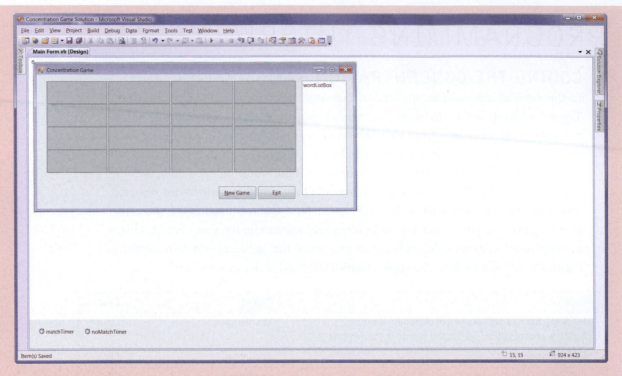

Figure 8-19: User interface

CODING THE CONCENTRATION GAME

According to the application's TOE chart, the MainForm's Load event procedure and the Click event procedures for the exitButton, newButton, and 16 labels need to be coded. You also need to code the Tick event procedures for the two timers.

To begin coding the Concentration Game application:

1. Start Visual Studio. If necessary, close the Start Page window. Open the **Concentration Game Solution** (**Concentration Game Solution.sln**) file, which is contained in the VbReloaded2008\Chap08\Concentration Game Solution folder. The interface contains a table layout panel, 16 labels, two buttons, two timers, and a list box.

2. Open the Code Editor window, which contains some of the application's code.

First, you will complete the MainForm's Load event procedure, which is responsible for filling the wordListBox with eight pairs of matching words, and then reordering the words. The list box provides the words that will appear on the game board. The procedure's pseudocode is shown in Figure 8-20.

> **MainForm Load Event Procedure**
> 1. fill the wordListBox with 8 pairs of matching words
> 2. call the ShuffleWords procedure to rearrange the words in the list box

Figure 8-20: Pseudocode for the MainForm's Load event procedure

To complete the MainForm's Load event procedure:

1. Scroll down the Code Editor window to view the code already entered in the MainForm's Load event procedure. Notice that the first eight statements in the procedure add eight unique words to the wordListBox control, and the last eight statements duplicate the words in the control.

2. Save the solution, then run the application. The Load event procedure adds the 16 words to the list box, as shown in Figure 8-21. The words appear in the order in which they are added in the Load event procedure.

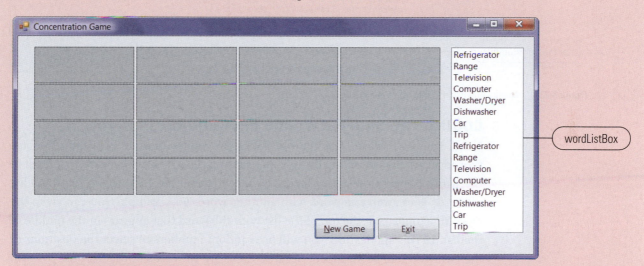

Figure 8-21: Sixteen words added to the list box

3. Click the **Exit** button to end the application.

4. To complete the Load event procedure, you just need to enter a statement to call a procedure named ShuffleWords. The ShuffleWords procedure will reorder (or shuffle) the words in the list box. If you do not shuffle the words, they will appear in the exact same location on the game board each time the application is started. Shuffling the words makes the game more challenging, because the user will never be sure exactly where each word will appear on the game board. The ShuffleWords procedure will be a Sub procedure, because it will not need to return

a value. Click the **blank line** above End Sub. Type the Call statement shown in Figure 8-22, then click the **blank line** above the statement. Do not be concerned about the jagged line that appears below the ShuffleWords procedure name in the Code Editor window. The line will disappear when you create the procedure.

```
(MainForm Events)                                      Load
    Private Sub MainForm_Load(ByVal sender As Object, ByVal e As System.EventArgs
        ' fills the list box with 8 pairs of matching words,
        ' then calls a procedure to shuffle the words

        wordListBox.Items.Add("Refrigerator")
        wordListBox.Items.Add("Range")
        wordListBox.Items.Add("Television")
        wordListBox.Items.Add("Computer")
        wordListBox.Items.Add("Washer/Dryer")
        wordListBox.Items.Add("Dishwasher")
        wordListBox.Items.Add("Car")
        wordListBox.Items.Add("Trip")
        wordListBox.Items.Add("Refrigerator")
        wordListBox.Items.Add("Range")
        wordListBox.Items.Add("Television")
        wordListBox.Items.Add("Computer")
        wordListBox.Items.Add("Washer/Dryer")
        wordListBox.Items.Add("Dishwasher")
        wordListBox.Items.Add("Car")
        wordListBox.Items.Add("Trip")

        Call ShuffleWords()
    End Sub
```

Enter the Call statement

Figure 8-22: Completed MainForm's Load event procedure

CODING THE SHUFFLEWORDS PROCEDURE

Next, you will create the ShuffleWords procedure, which is responsible for reordering the words in the list box. Reordering the words will ensure that most of the words appear in different locations in each game. An easy way to reorder a list of words is to swap one word with another word. For example, you can swap the word that appears at the top of the list with the word that appears in the middle of the list. In this application, you will use random numbers to select the positions of the two words to be swapped. Because there are 16 words in the list box, you will perform the swap 16 times to ensure that the words are sufficiently reordered. The pseudocode for the ShuffleWords procedure is shown in Figure 8-23.

ShuffleWords Procedure
1. repeat 16 times
       generate two random numbers from 0 through 15, inclusive
       use the random numbers to swap the words in the list box
    end repeat

Figure 8-23: Pseudocode for the ShuffleWords procedure

To code the ShuffleWords procedure, then test the procedure:

1. Click the **blank line** immediately above the MainForm's Load event procedure. Type **private sub ShuffleWords()** and press **Enter**. The Code Editor enters the procedure footer (End Sub) for you. Notice that the jagged line no longer appears below the ShuffleWords name in the Load event procedure. Type **' shuffles the words in the list box** and press **Enter** twice.

2. The ShuffleWords procedure will use four variables named randomGenerator, index1, index2, and temp. The randomGenerator variable will represent Visual Basic's pseudo-random number generator in the procedure. The index1 and index2 variables will store two random integers from 0 through 15, inclusive. Each integer corresponds to the index of a word in the wordListBox. The temp variable will be used during the swapping process. Enter the following Dim statements. Press **Enter** twice after typing the last Dim statement.

   Dim randomGenerator As New Random

   Dim index1 As Integer

   Dim index2 As Integer

   Dim temp As String = String.Empty

3. The first step in the pseudocode is a repetition structure that repeats its instructions 16 times. Type **for counter as integer = 1 to 16** and press **Enter**.

4. The first task in the repetition structure is to generate two random numbers from 0 through 15, inclusive. The random numbers will represent the indexes of the words to be swapped in the list box. Recall that the first item in a list box has an index of 0; the second has an index of 1, and so on. Therefore, although the list box contains 16 words, you use indexes of 0 through 15 to access the words. Type **'generate two random numbers** and press **Enter**. Type **index1 = randomGenerator.next(0, 16)** and press **Enter**, then type **index2 = randomGenerator.next(0, 16)** and press **Enter**.

5. The second task in the repetition structure is to use the random numbers to swap the words in the list box. You learned how to swap the contents of two variables in Chapter 4. You can use a similar process to swap two words in the wordListBox. You begin by storing the first word, temporarily, in a variable. The index1 variable contains the index of the first word you want to swap. Type **' swap the two words** and press **Enter**, then type **temp = wordListBox.items(index1).tostring** and press **Enter**.

6. Next, you replace the word located in the index1 position in the list box with the word located in the index2 position. Type **wordListBox.items(index1) = wordListBox.items(index2)** and press **Enter**.

7. Finally, you replace the word located in the index2 position in the list box with the word stored in the temp variable. Type **wordListBox.items(index2) = temp**.

8. Change the Next clause in the procedure to **Next counter**. Figure 8-24 shows the completed ShuffleWords procedure.

```
Private Sub ShuffleWords()
    ' shuffles the words in the list box

    Dim randomGenerator As New Random
    Dim index1 As Integer
    Dim index2 As Integer
    Dim temp As String = String.Empty

    For counter As Integer = 1 To 16
        ' generate two random numbers
        index1 = randomGenerator.Next(0, 16)
        index2 = randomGenerator.Next(0, 16)
        ' swap the two words
        temp = wordListBox.Items(index1).ToString
        wordListBox.Items(index1) = wordListBox.Items(index2)
        wordListBox.Items(index2) = temp
    Next counter
End Sub
```

Figure 8-24: Completed ShuffleWords procedure

9. Save the solution, then start the application. The 16 words appear in the wordListBox. This time, however, they do not appear in the order in which they are entered in the Load event procedure. Instead, they appear in a random order. Click the **Exit** button to end the application.

CODING THE LABELS' CLICK EVENT PROCEDURES

Next, you will code the Click event procedures for the 16 labels in the interface. Each label is associated with a word in the list box. The first label is associated with the first word; the second label with the second word, and so on. When the user clicks a label, the label's Click event procedure will access the appropriate word in the list box, and then display the word in the label. For example, if the user clicks the first label on the game board, the Click event procedure will assign the first word in the list box to the label's Text property. After the user selects two labels, the procedure will determine whether the labels contain matching words. If the words match, they will remain visible in their respective labels. If the words do not match, the user will be given a short amount of time to memorize the location of the words before the words are hidden again. The pseudocode for the labels' Click event procedures is shown in Figure 8-25.

Label Controls' Click Event Procedures

1. add 1 to the selection counter, which keeps track of whether this is the first or second label selected on the game board
2. if this is the first label selected

  extract the number from the label's name and assign it to the labelNum variable

  subtract 1 from the labelNum variable and assign the result to the index1 variable

  use the index1 variable to access the appropriate word in the list box, and display the word in the label

 else (which means it is the second label selected)

  disable the game board to prevent the user from making another selection

  extract the number from the label's name and assign it to the labelNum variable

  subtract 1 from the labelNum variable and assign the result to the index2 variable

  use the index2 variable to access the appropriate word in the list box, and display the word in the label

  if both labels contain the same word

   disable both labels on the game board

   turn the matchTimer on

  else

   turn the noMatchTimer on

  end if

  reset the selection counter to 0

end if

Figure 8-25: Pseudocode for the Click event procedures of the 16 label controls

To begin coding the Click event procedures for the 16 label controls:

1. Scroll down the Code Editor window to view the TestForMatch procedure. The Handles clause indicates that the procedure will be processed when the Click event occurs for any of the 16 label controls.

2. The TestForMatch procedure will use a String variable named labelNum and two Integer variables named index1 and index2. When the user clicks a label on the game board, the procedure will assign the number portion of the label's name to the labelNum variable. For example, if the user clicks the Label1 control, the number 1 will be assigned to the variable. Similarly, if the user clicks the Label12 control, the number 12 will be assigned to the variable. Recall that the Label1 control is associated with the first word in the list box; that word has an index of 0. Likewise, the Label12 control is associated with the word whose index is 11. Notice that the label's number (1 and 12) is always one number more than the word's index (0 and 11). Therefore, you can determine the index of the word associated with a label by subtracting the number 1 from the contents of the labelNum variable. The procedure will use the other two variables, index1 and index2, to

store the indexes of the words. Click the **blank line** above End Sub, then enter the following Dim statements. Press **Enter** twice after typing the last Dim statement.

Dim labelNum As String = String.Empty

Dim index1 As Integer

Dim index2 As Integer

3. The procedure also will use three module-level variables named selectionCounter, firstLabel, and secondLabel. The variables need to be module-level variables because they will be used by more than one procedure in the application. The selectionCounter variable will keep track of whether the user has clicked one or two labels. The firstLabel and secondLabel variables will keep track of the labels the user clicked. Click the **blank line** below Public Class MainForm, then press **Enter** to insert another blank line. Enter the following Private statements in the MainForm's Declarations section. (Be sure to press Enter after typing the last Private statement.)

Private firstLabel As Label

Private secondLabel As Label

Private selectionCounter As Integer

4. The first step in the pseudocode is to add the number one to the selection counter. Click the **blank line** above End Sub in the TestForMatch procedure. Type **' update the selection counter** and press **Enter**, then type **selectionCounter = selectionCounter + 1** and press **Enter** twice.

5. The next step is a selection structure that determines whether this is the first label control selected. Type **' determine whether this is the first or second selection** and press **Enter**. Type **if selectionCounter = 1 then** and press **Enter**.

6. If this is the first of two labels selected on the game board, you should extract the number from the label's name and assign it to the labelNum variable. At this point, you may be wondering how you will know which label name to use, because the TestForMatch procedure will be processed when any of the 16 labels are clicked. You can use the sender parameter to determine the appropriate name. Recall that the sender parameter contains the address of the object that raised the event. In this case, it will contain the address of the label that was clicked. Therefore, you should be able to access the label's name using the syntax sender.Name. Type **sender.** (be sure to type the period). As Figure 8-26 shows, the Name property does not appear in the list of choices. This is because the sender parameter in the procedure header is declared using the Object data type, and Object variables do not have a Name property.

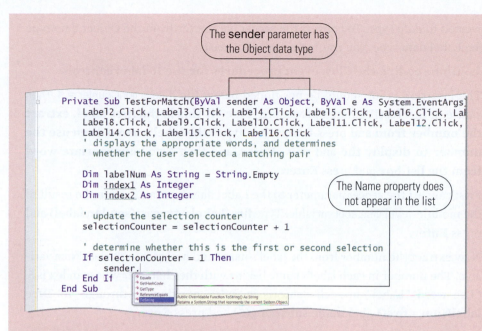

```
Private Sub TestForMatch(ByVal sender As Object, ByVal e As System.EventArgs)
    Label2.Click, Label3.Click, Label4.Click, Label5.Click, Label6.Click, Lal
    Label8.Click, Label9.Click, Label10.Click, Label11.Click, Label12.Click,
    Label14.Click, Label15.Click, Label16.Click
    ' displays the appropriate words, and determines
    ' whether the user selected a matching pair

    Dim labelNum As String = String.Empty
    Dim index1 As Integer
    Dim index2 As Integer

    ' update the selection counter
    selectionCounter = selectionCounter + 1

    ' determine whether this is the first or second selection
    If selectionCounter = 1 Then
        sender.
    End If
End Sub
```

The **sender** parameter has the Object data type

The Name property does not appear in the list

Figure 8-26: List of choices for the **sender** parameter

7. Before you can continue coding the procedure, you need to learn how to convert an Object variable to a different data type. Press the **Backspace** key seven times to delete the sender. text, then save the solution.

CONVERTING OBJECT VARIABLES

The ByVal sender As Object text that appears in a procedure header creates a variable named sender and assigns the Object data type to it. An Object variable can store many different types of data, and it also can freely change the type of stored data while the application is running. You can store the number 40 in an Object variable at the beginning of the application and then, later on in the application, store the text "John Smith" in the same variable. You also can store the address of an object in an Object variable, such as the address of a label, text box, or button. The computer cannot determine the type of data stored in an Object variable until the application is run. Unlike variables declared using the String and numeric data types, variables declared using the Object data type do not have a set of properties. This is because there are no common attributes for all of the different types of data that can be stored in an Object variable. To access the properties of the object whose address is stored in the sender parameter, you must convert the object to the appropriate data type. You can do this using the **TryCast operator**. The operator's syntax is **TryCast(*object*, *dataType*)**, where *object* is the name of the object you want converted to *dataType*. To convert the sender parameter from the Object data type to the Label data type, you use TryCast(sender, Label).

To continue coding the Click event procedures for the 16 label controls:

1. The insertion point should be positioned below the If selectionCounter = 1 Then clause in the TestForMatch procedure. Type **' if this is the first label, extract the number from** and press **Enter**, then type **' the label's name, then use the number to display the** and press **Enter**, and then type **' appropriate word from the list box** and press **Enter**.

2. First convert the sender parameter to the Label data type, and assign the result to the module-level firstLabel variable. Type **firstLabel = trycast(sender, label)** and press **Enter**.

3. Now extract the number from the label's name and assign it to the labelNum variable. The number in each label's name begins with the character whose index is 5. (The word "Label" in each name is in index positions 0 through 4.) Type **labelNum = firstLabel.name.substring(5)** and press **Enter**.

4. Next, convert the contents of the labelNum variable from String to Integer and assign the result to the index1 variable; then subtract the number one from the variable. (Recall that the label's number is one number more than the word's index.) Type **integer.tryparse(labelNum, index1)** and press **Enter**, then type **index1 = index1 - 1** and press **Enter**.

5. Now use the number stored in the index1 variable to access the appropriate word in the list box. Display the word in the label whose address is stored in the firstLabel variable. Type **firstLabel.text = wordListBox.items(index1).tostring** and press **Enter**.

6. Type **else** and press **Enter**.

7. If this is the second label the user clicked, the procedure will need to compare the contents of both labels before the user makes the next selection. Therefore, you will disable the game board, temporarily. Type **' this is the second label, so disable the game board** and press **Enter**. Type **' then extract the number from the label's name and** and press **Enter**. Type **' use the number to display the appropriate word from** and press **Enter**, then type **' the list box** and press **Enter**. Type **boardTableLayoutPanel.enabled = false** and press **Enter**.

8. Now convert the sender parameter to the Label data type and assign the result to the module-level secondLabel variable. Then extract the number from the label's name. Type **secondLabel = trycast(sender, label)** and press **Enter**. Type **labelNum = secondLabel.name.substring(5)** and press **Enter**.

9. Now calculate the index, then use the index to display the appropriate word. Type **integer.tryparse(labelNum, index2)** and press **Enter**, then type **index2 = index2 - 1** and press **Enter**. Type **secondLabel.text = wordListBox.items(index2).tostring** and press **Enter** twice.

10. The next task in the pseudocode (shown earlier in Figure 8-25) is to compare the contents of both labels. If both labels contain the same word, you will disable the labels to prevent them from responding if the user inadvertently clicks them again. You also will turn on the matchTimer. If the labels do not contain the same word, you will turn on the noMatchTimer. Type the following comments and selection structure.

    ' if both words match, disable the corresponding

    ' label controls, then turn on the matchTimer;

    ' otherwise, turn on the noMatchTimer

    If firstLabel.Text = secondLabel.Text Then

    **   firstLabel.Enabled = False**

    **   secondLabel.Enabled = False**

    **   matchTimer.Enabled = True**

    Else

    **   noMatchTimer.Enabled = True**

    End If

11. Click **immediately after the letter f** in the first End If line, then press **Enter** twice.

12. The last task in the pseudocode is to reset the selection counter to zero. Recall that the selection counter keeps track of whether the user has clicked one or two labels. Type **' reset the selection counter** and press **Enter**, then type **selectionCounter = 0**.

13. Save the solution. Figure 8-27 shows the code for the TestForMatch procedure, which is processed when any of the 16 label controls are clicked.

```vbnet
Private Sub TestForMatch(ByVal sender As Object, _
    ByVal e As System.EventArgs) Handles Label1.Click, _
    Label2.Click, Label3.Click, Label4.Click, Label5.Click, _
    Label6.Click, Label7.Click, Label8.Click, Label9.Click, _
    Label10.Click, Label11.Click, Label12.Click, Label13.Click, _
    Label14.Click, Label15.Click, Label16.Click
    ' displays the appropriate words, and determines
    ' whether the user selected a matching pair

    Dim labelNum As String = String.Empty
    Dim index1 As Integer
    Dim index2 As Integer

    ' update the selection counter
    selectionCounter = selectionCounter + 1

    ' determine whether this is the first or second selection
    If selectionCounter = 1 Then
        ' if this is the first label, extract the number from
        ' the label's name, then use the number to display the
        ' appropriate word from the list box
        firstLabel = TryCast (sender, Label)
        labelNum = firstLabel.Name.Substring(5)
        Integer.TryParse(labelNum, index1)
        index1 = index1 - 1
        firstLabel.Text = wordListBox.Items(index1).ToString
    Else
        ' this is the second label, so disable the game board
        ' then extract the number from the label's name and
        ' use the number to display the appropriate word from
        ' the list box
        boardTableLayoutPanel.Enabled = False
        secondLabel = TryCast (sender, Label)
        labelNum = secondLabel.Name.Substring(5)
        Integer.TryParse(labelNum, index2)
        index2 = index2 - 1
        secondLabel.Text = wordListBox.Items(index2).ToString
```

Figure 8-27: Completed TestForMatch procedure (*continued on next page*)

```
         ' if both words match, disable the corresponding
         ' label controls, then turn on the matchTimer;
         ' otherwise, turn on the noMatchTimer
         If firstLabel.Text = secondLabel.Text Then
             firstLabel.Enabled = False
             secondLabel.Enabled = False
             matchTimer.Enabled = True
         Else
             noMatchTimer.Enabled = True
         End If

         ' reset the selection counter
         selectionCounter = 0
     End If
End Sub
```

Figure 8-27: Completed TestForMatch procedure (*continued from previous page*)

CODING THE TIMERS' TICK EVENT PROCEDURES

Figure 8-28 shows the pseudocode for the matchTimer's Tick event procedure, which performs two tasks. First, it enables the game board so the user can make another selection. Second, it turns off the matchTimer. Turning off the timer stops the timer's Tick event and prevents its code from being processed again. The matchTimer's Tick event procedure will not be processed again until the timer is turned back on, which happens when the user locates a matching pair of words on the game board.

---

matchTimer Tick Event Procedure
1. enable the game board
2. turn the matchTimer off

Figure 8-28: Pseudocode for the matchTimer's Tick event procedure

To code the matchTimer's Tick event procedure:

1. Locate the matchTimer's Tick event procedure in the Code Editor window.

2. Click the **blank line** above End Sub. Type **boardTableLayoutPanel.enabled = true** and press **Enter**, then type **matchTimer.enabled = false**.

Figure 8-29 shows the pseudocode for the noMatchTimer's Tick event procedure, which performs three tasks. The first task clears the contents of the labels whose addresses are stored in the firstLabel and secondLabel variables. The second task enables the game board so the user can make another selection. The last task turns off the noMatchTimer to prevent the timer's Tick event from occurring and its code being processed. The noMatchTimer's Tick event procedure will not be processed again until the timer is turned back on, which happens when the two labels selected by the user contain different words.

---

noMatchTimer Tick Event Procedure
1. clear the contents of the firstLabel and secondLabel
2. enable the game board
3. turn the noMatchTimer off

Figure 8-29: Pseudocode for the noMatchTimer's Tick event procedure

To code the noMatchTimer's Tick event procedure:

1. Locate the noMatchTimer's Tick event procedure in the Code Editor window.

2. Click the **blank line** above End Sub, then enter the following four assignment statements.

   firstLabel.Text = String.Empty

   secondLabel.Text = String.Empty

   boardTableLayoutPanel.Enabled = True

   noMatchTimer.Enabled = False

3. Save the solution.

CODING THE NEWBUTTON'S CLICK EVENT PROCEDURE

Figure 8-30 shows the pseudocode for the newButton's Click event procedure. The first two steps have already been coded for you in the Code Editor window.

---

newButton Click Event Procedure
1. clear the contents of the 16 labels
2. enable the 16 labels
3. reset the selection counter to zero
4. call the ShuffleWords procedure to rearrange the words in the list box

---

Figure 8-30: Pseudocode for the newButton's Click event procedure

To complete the newButton's Click event procedure:

1. Locate the newButton's Click event procedure in the Code Editor window. Click the **blank line** above End Sub, then enter the following two lines of code.

   selectionCounter = 0

   Call ShuffleWords( )

2. Save the solution.

Before testing the Concentration Game application, compare the code you entered in the Code Editor window with the code shown in Figure 8-31. Make any needed corrections.

```
' Project name:        Concentration Game Project
' Project purpose:     Simulates the Concentration game,
'                      where a player tries to find
'                      matching pairs of words
' Created/revised by:  <your name> on <current date>

Option Explicit On
Option Strict On
Option Infer Off

Public Class MainForm

    Private firstLabel As Label
    Private secondLabel As Label
    Private selectionCounter As Integer

    Private Sub ShuffleWords()
        ' shuffles the words in the list box

        Dim randomGenerator As New Random
        Dim index1 As Integer
        Dim index2 As Integer
        Dim temp As String = String.Empty

        For counter As Integer = 1 To 16
            ' generate two random numbers
            index1 = randomGenerator.Next(0, 16)
            index2 = randomGenerator.Next(0, 16)
```

Figure 8-31: Code for the Concentration Game application (*continued on next page*)

```vb
          ' swap the two words
          temp = wordListBox.Items(index1).ToString
          wordListBox.Items(index1) = wordListBox.Items(index2)
          wordListBox.Items(index2) = temp
      Next counter
End Sub

Private Sub MainForm_Load(ByVal sender As Object, _
      ByVal e As System.EventArgs) Handles Me.Load
      ' fills the list box with 8 pairs of matching words,
      ' then calls a procedure to shuffle the words

      wordListBox.Items.Add("Refrigerator")
      wordListBox.Items.Add("Range")
      wordListBox.Items.Add("Television")
      wordListBox.Items.Add("Computer")
      wordListBox.Items.Add("Washer/Dryer")
      wordListBox.Items.Add("Dishwasher")
      wordListBox.Items.Add("Car")
      wordListBox.Items.Add("Trip")
      wordListBox.Items.Add("Refrigerator")
      wordListBox.Items.Add("Range")
      wordListBox.Items.Add("Television")
      wordListBox.Items.Add("Computer")
      wordListBox.Items.Add("Washer/Dryer")
      wordListBox.Items.Add("Dishwasher")
      wordListBox.Items.Add("Car")
      wordListBox.Items.Add("Trip")

      Call ShuffleWords()
End Sub

Private Sub exitButton_Click(ByVal sender As Object, _
      ByVal e As System.EventArgs) Handles exitButton.Click
      Me.Close()
End Sub

Private Sub newButton_Click(ByVal sender As Object, _
      ByVal e As System.EventArgs) Handles newButton.Click
      ' removes any words from the label controls, then
      ' enables the label controls, then resets the
      ' selection counter, and then calls a procedure
      ' to shuffle the words
```

Figure 8-31: Code for the Concentration Game application (*continued from previous page and on next page*)

```
        Label1.Text = String.Empty
        Label2.Text = String.Empty
        Label3.Text = String.Empty
        Label4.Text = String.Empty
        Label5.Text = String.Empty
        Label6.Text = String.Empty
        Label7.Text = String.Empty
        Label8.Text = String.Empty
        Label9.Text = String.Empty
        Label10.Text = String.Empty
        Label11.Text = String.Empty
        Label12.Text = String.Empty
        Label13.Text = String.Empty
        Label14.Text = String.Empty
        Label15.Text = String.Empty
        Label16.Text = String.Empty

        Label1.Enabled = True
        Label2.Enabled = True
        Label3.Enabled = True
        Label4.Enabled = True
        Label5.Enabled = True
        Label6.Enabled = True
        Label7.Enabled = True
        Label8.Enabled = True
        Label9.Enabled = True
        Label10.Enabled = True
        Label11.Enabled = True
        Label12.Enabled = True
        Label13.Enabled = True
        Label14.Enabled = True
        Label15.Enabled = True
        Label16.Enabled = True

        selectionCounter = 0
        Call ShuffleWords()
    End Sub
```

Figure 8-31: Code for the Concentration Game application (*continued from previous page and on next page*)

```vb
Private Sub TestForMatch(ByVal sender As Object, _
    ByVal e As System.EventArgs) Handles Label1.Click, _
    Label2.Click, Label3.Click, Label4.Click, Label5.Click, _
    Label6.Click, Label7.Click, Label8.Click, Label9.Click, _
    Label10.Click, Label11.Click, Label12.Click, Label13.Click, _
    Label14.Click, Label15.Cllck, Label16.Click
    ' displays the appropriate words, and determines
    ' whether the user selected a matching pair

    Dim labelNum As String = String.Empty
    Dim index1 As Integer
    Dim index2 As Integer

    ' update the selection counter
    selectionCounter = selectionCounter + 1

    ' determine whether this is the first or second selection
    If selectionCounter = 1 Then
        ' if this is the first label, extract the number from
        ' the label's name, then use the number to display the
        ' appropriate word from the list box
        firstLabel = TryCast(sender, Label)
        labelNum = firstLabel.Name.Substring(5)
        Integer.TryParse(labelNum, index1)
        index1 = index1 - 1
        firstLabel.Text = wordListBox.Items(index1).ToString
    Else
        ' this is the second label, so disable the game board
        ' then extract the number from the label's name and
        ' use the number to display the appropriate word from
        ' the list box
        boardTableLayoutPanel.Enabled = False
        secondLabel = TryCast(sender, Label)
        labelNum = secondLabel.Name.Substring(5)
        Integer.TryParse(labelNum, index2)
        index2 = index2 - 1
        secondLabel.Text = wordListBox.Items(index2).ToString

        ' if both words match, disable the corresponding
        ' label controls, then turn on the matchTimer;
        ' otherwise, turn on the noMatchTimer
```

Figure 8-31: Code for the Concentration Game application (*continued from previous page and on next page*)

```
        If firstLabel.Text = secondLabel.Text Then
            firstLabel.Enabled = False
            secondLabel.Enabled = False
            matchTimer.Enabled = True
        Else
            noMatchTimer.Enabled = True
        End If

        ' reset the selection counter
        selectionCounter = 0
    End If
End Sub

Private Sub matchTimer_Tick(ByVal sender As Object, _
    ByVal e As System.EventArgs) Handles matchTimer.Tick
    ' when the two words match, the game board is enabled
    ' and the timer is turned off

    boardTableLayoutPanel.Enabled = True
    matchTimer.Enabled = False
End Sub

Private Sub noMatchTimer_Tick(ByVal sender As Object, _
    ByVal e As System.EventArgs) Handles noMatchTimer.Tick
    ' when the words do not match, the words are
    ' removed from the labels, the game board is enabled,
    ' and the timer is turned off

    firstLabel.Text = String.Empty
    secondLabel.Text = String.Empty
    boardTableLayoutPanel.Enabled = True
    noMatchTimer.Enabled = False
End Sub
End Class
```

Figure 8-31: Code for the Concentration Game application (*continued from previous page*)

Now that you have finished coding the application, you will test it to verify that it is working correctly.

To test the Concentration Game application:

1. Save the solution, then start the application. Click the **label in the upper-left corner of the game board**. The TestForMatch procedure assigns the first word in the wordListBox to the label's Text property. See Figure 8-32. Recall that the ShuffleWords procedure uses random numbers to reorder the list of words in the list box. Therefore, the first word in your list box, and therefore the word that appears in the Label1 control, might be different from the one shown in the figure.

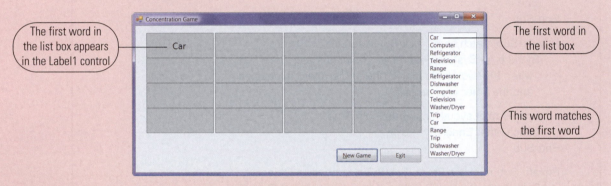

Figure 8-32: First word appears in the label on the game board

2. First, test the code that handles two matching words. To do this, you will need to find the word in the list box that matches the first word, and then click its associated label. Count down the list of words in the list box, stopping when you reach the word that matches the first word in your list box. In Figure 8-32, the word that matches the first word (Car) is the twelfth word in the list box.

3. Now count each label control, from left to right, beginning with the first row on the game board. Stop counting when you reach the label control whose number is the same as in the previous step. In Figure 8-32, for example, you would stop counting when you reached the twelfth label control, which is located in the fourth column of the third row. Click the **label control associated with the matching word**. See Figure 8-33.

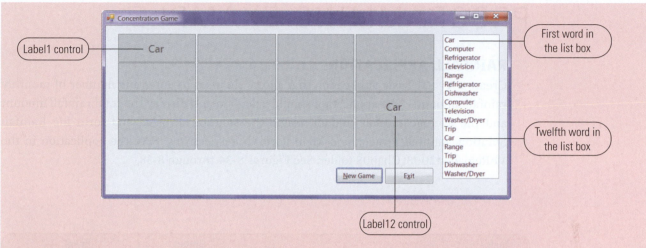

Figure 8-33: Both labels contain the same word

4. Click the **Label1 control** again. Nothing happens because the TestForMatch procedure disables the label when the matching word is found.

5. Now test the code that handles two words that do not match. Click a **blank label control on the game board**, then **click another blank label control**. However, be sure that the second label's word is not the same as the first label's word. Because both words are not the same, they are hidden after a short time.

6. Finally, verify that the code entered in the newButton's Click event procedure works correctly. Click the **New Game** button. The button's Click event procedure clears the contents of the label controls and also enables them. In addition, it resets the selection counter to zero and calls the ShuffleWords procedure to reorder the words in the list box.

7. On your own, test the application several more times. When you are finished, click the **Exit** button to end the application.

8. Now that you know that the application works correctly, you can hide the list box and resize the form. Close the Code Editor window. Set the wordListBox's Visible property to **False**. Unlock the controls on the form, then drag the form's right border so that it covers most of the list box. (Or change the form's Size property to approximately **790, 423**.) Lock the controls on the form.

9. Save the solution, then start the application to verify that the list box is no longer visible in the interface. Click the **Exit** button, then close the solution.

PROGRAMMING EXAMPLE

RAINFALL APPLICATION

Create a Visual Basic application that allows the user to enter any number of monthly rainfall amounts. The application should calculate and display the total rainfall amount and the average rainfall amount. Name the solution, project, and form file Rainfall Solution, Rainfall Project, and Main Form.vb, respectively. Save the application in the VbReloaded2008\Chap08 folder. See Figures 8-34 through 8-38.

Task	Object	Event
1. Call the CalcTotalAndAverage procedure to calculate the total and average rainfall amounts 2. Display the total rainfall amount and average rainfall amount in totalLabel and averageLabel 3. Send the focus to the monthlyTextBox 4. Select the monthlyTextBox's existing text	calcButton	Click
End the application	exitButton	Click
Display the total rainfall amount (from calcButton)	totalLabel	None
Display the average rainfall amount (from calcButton)	averageLabel	None
Get and display the monthly rainfall amounts	monthlyTextBox	None
Select the existing text		Enter
Clear the totalLabel and averageLabel		TextChanged

Figure 8-34: TOE chart

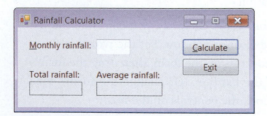

Figure 8-35: User interface

Object	Property	Setting
Form1	Name	MainForm
	AcceptButton	calcButton
	Font	Segoe UI, 9 point
	MaximizeBox	False
	StartPosition	CenterScreen
	Text	Rainfall Calculator
Label1	TabIndex	0
	Text	&Monthly rainfall:
Label2	TabIndex	4
	Text	Total rainfall:
Label3	TabIndex	5
	Text	Average rainfall:
Label4	Name	totalLabel
	AutoSize	False
	BorderStyle	FixedSingle
	TabIndex	6
	Text	(empty)
	TextAlign	MiddleCenter
Label5	Name	averageLabel
	AutoSize	False
	BorderStyle	FixedSingle
	TabIndex	7
	Text	(empty)
	TextAlign	MiddleCenter
TextBox1	Name	monthlyTextBox
	TabIndex	1
Button1	Name	calcButton
	TabIndex	2
	Text	&Calculate
Button2	Name	exitButton
	TabIndex	3
	Text	E&xit

Figure 8-36: Objects, Properties, and Settings

exitButton Click Event Procedure
1. close the application

monthlyTextBox Enter Event Procedure
1. select the existing text

monthlyTextBox TextChanged Event Procedure
1. remove the contents of the totalLabel and averageLabel

calcButton Click Event Procedure
1. call the CalcTotalAndAverage procedure to calculate the total and average rainfall amounts
2. display the total and average rainfall amounts in the totalLabel and averageLabel
3. send the focus to the monthlyTextBox
4. select the existing text in the monthlyTextBox

CalcTotalAndAverage Procedure
1. assign the rainfall amount to a variable
2. add 1 to the rainfall counter
3. add the rainfall amount to the rainfall accumulator
4. calculate the average rainfall by dividing the rainfall accumulator by the rainfall counter

Figure 8-37: Pseudocode

```
' Project name:      Rainfall Project
' Project purpose:   Displays the total and average
'                    rainfall amounts
' Created/revised by: <your name> on <current date>

Option Explicit On
Option Strict On
Option Infer Off

Public Class MainForm

    Private Sub CalcTotalAndAverage(ByRef counter As Integer, _
                                    ByRef accumulator As Decimal, _
                                    ByRef avg As Decimal)
        ' calculates the total and average rainfall amount

        Dim monthRain As Decimal

        Decimal.TryParse(monthlyTextBox.Text, monthRain)
```

Figure 8-38: Code (*continued on next page*)

```
        ' update the counter and accumulator, then calculate the
        ' average rainfall
        counter = counter + 1
        accumulator = accumulator + monthRain

        avg = accumulator / (Convert.ToDecimal(counter))
    End Sub

    Private Sub exitButton_Click(ByVal sender As Object, _
        ByVal e As System.EventArgs) Handles exitButton.Click
        Me.Close()
    End Sub

    Private Sub calcButton_Click(ByVal sender As Object, _
        ByVal e As System.EventArgs) Handles calcButton.Click
        ' calls a procedure to calculate the total and average
        ' rainfall amounts, then displays both amounts

        Static rainCounter As Integer
        Static rainAccum As Decimal
        Dim avgRain As Decimal

        Call CalcTotalAndAverage(rainCounter, rainAccum, avgRain)

        totalLabel.Text = rainAccum.ToString("N2")
        averageLabel.Text = avgRain.ToString("N2")

        monthlyTextBox.Focus()
        monthlyTextBox.SelectAll()
    End Sub

    Private Sub monthlyTextBox_Enter(ByVal sender As Object, _
        ByVal e As System.EventArgs) Handles monthlyTextBox.Enter
        monthlyTextBox.SelectAll()
    End Sub

    Private Sub monthlyTextBox_TextChanged(ByVal sender As Object, _
        ByVal e As System.EventArgs) Handles monthlyTextBox.TextChanged
        totalLabel.Text = String.Empty
        averageLabel.Text = String.Empty
    End Sub
End Class
```

Figure 8-38: Code (*continued from previous page*)

QUICK REVIEW

» The difference between a Sub procedure and a Function procedure is that a Function procedure returns a value, whereas a Sub procedure does not return a value.

» An event procedure is a Sub procedure that is associated with one or more objects and events.

» Independent Sub procedures and Function procedures are not associated with any specific object or event. The names of independent Sub procedures and Function procedures typically begin with a verb.

» Procedures allow programmers to avoid duplicating code in different parts of a program. They also allow a team of programmers to work on large and complex programs.

» You can use the Call statement to invoke an independent Sub procedure. The Call statement allows you to pass arguments to the Sub procedure.

» You invoke a Function procedure by including its name and any arguments in a statement.

» When calling a procedure, the number of arguments listed in the *argumentList* should agree with the number of parameters listed in the *parameterList* in the procedure header. Also, the data type and position of each parameter in the *parameterList* should agree with the data type and position of its corresponding argument in the *argumentList*.

» You can pass information to a Sub or Function procedure either *by value* or *by reference*. To pass a variable *by value*, you precede the variable's corresponding parameter with the keyword ByVal. To pass a variable *by reference*, you precede the variable's corresponding parameter with the keyword ByRef. The procedure header indicates whether a variable is being passed *by value* or *by reference*.

» When you pass a variable *by value*, only the contents of the variable are passed. When you pass a variable *by reference*, the variable's address is passed.

» Variables that appear in the *parameterList* in a procedure header have procedure scope, which means they can be used only by the procedure.

» The purpose of a timer control is to process code at one or more specified intervals. You start a timer by setting its Enabled property to True. You stop a timer by setting its Enabled property to False. You use a timer's Interval property to specify the number of milliseconds that must elapse before the timer's Tick event occurs.

» You can use the TryCast operator to convert an Object variable to a different data type.

KEY TERMS

Call statement—the Visual Basic statement used to invoke an independent Sub procedure in a program

Function—another term for a Function procedure

Function procedure—a procedure that returns a value after performing its assigned task

Independent Sub procedure—a procedure that is not associated with any specific object or event and is processed only when invoked (called) from code

Parameters—the memory locations listed in a procedure header

Passing by reference—the process of passing a variable's address to a procedure

Passing by value—the process of passing a variable's contents to a procedure

Procedure—a block of program code that performs a specific task

Return statement—the Visual Basic statement that returns a function's value to the statement that invoked the function

Sub procedure—a procedure that does not return a value after performing its assigned task

Timer control—the control used to process code at one or more regular intervals

TryCast operator—used to convert an Object variable to a different data type

SELF-CHECK QUESTIONS AND ANSWERS

1. The items listed in the Call statement are referred to as _____.

   a. arguments   b. parameters

   c. passers   d. None of the above.

2. Which of the following is a valid procedure header for a procedure that receives the contents of two String variables?

   a. Private Sub Display(ByRef x As String, ByRef y As String)

   b. Private Sub Display(ByVal x As String, ByVal y As String)

   c. Private Sub Display(ByValue x As String, ByValue y As String)

   d. None of the above.

3. Which of the following is a valid procedure header for a procedure that returns a Decimal number?

   a. Private Function Calculate() As Decimal

   b. Private Sub Calculate() As Decimal

   c. Private Sub Calculate(Decimal)

   d. Both a and b.

4. Which of the following statements invokes a Sub procedure named Display, passing it the contents of a String variable named empName?

   a. Call Display(empName As String)

   b. Call Display(String empName)

   c. Call Display(empName)

   d. None of the above.

5. A function procedure can return _____.

   a. one value only   b. one or more values

   c. zero or more values

Answers: 1) a, 2) b, 3) a, 4) c, 5) a

REVIEW QUESTIONS

1. To determine whether a variable is being passed to a procedure either *by value* or *by reference,* you will need to examine _____.

   a. the Call statement

   b. the procedure header

   c. the statements entered in the procedure

   d. Either a or b.

2. Which of the following statements can be used to call the CalcArea Sub procedure, passing it two variables *by value*?

   a. Call CalcArea(length, width)

   b. Call CalcArea(ByVal length, ByVal width)

   c. Call CalcArea ByVal(length, width)

   d. Call ByVal CalcArea(length, width)

3. Which of the following is a valid procedure header for a procedure that receives an integer followed by a number with a decimal place?

   a. Private Sub CalcFee(base As Integer, rate As Decimal)

   b. Private Sub CalcFee(ByRef base As Integer, ByRef rate As Decimal)

   c. Private Sub CalcFee(ByVal base As Integer, ByVal rate As Decimal)

   d. None of the above.

4. Which of the following indicates that the procedure should be processed when the user clicks either the firstCheckBox or the secondCheckBox?

   a. Private Sub Clear(ByVal sender As Object, ByVal e As System.EventArgs) Handles firstCheckBox.Click, secondCheckBox.Click

   b. Private Sub Clear(ByVal sender As Object, ByVal e As System.EventArgs) Handles firstCheckBox_Click, secondCheckBox_Click

   c. Private Sub Clear_Click(ByVal sender As Object, ByVal e As System.EventArgs) Handles firstCheckBox, secondCheckBox

   d. Private Sub Clear(ByVal sender As Object, ByVal e As System.EventArgs) Handles firstCheckBox.Click and secondCheckBox.Click

5. Which of the following is false?

   a. In most cases, the number of arguments should agree with the number of parameters.

   b. The data type of each argument should match the data type of its corresponding parameter.

   c. The name of each argument should be identical to the name of its corresponding parameter.

   d. When you pass information to a procedure *by value*, the procedure stores the value of each item it receives in a separate memory location.

6. Which of the following instructs a function to return the contents of the stateTax variable to the statement that called the function?

   a. Return stateTax

   b. Return stateTax ByVal

   c. Return ByVal stateTax

   d. Return ByRef stateTax

7. Which of the following is a valid procedure header for a procedure that receives the value stored in an Integer variable first, and the address of a Decimal variable second?

   a. Private Sub CalcFee(ByVal base As Integer, ByAdd rate As Decimal)

   b. Private Sub CalcFee(base As Integer, rate As Decimal)

   c. Private Sub CalcFee(ByVal base As Integer, ByRef rate As Decimal)

   d. None of the above.

8. Which of the following is false?

   a. When you pass a variable *by reference*, the receiving procedure can change its contents.

   b. When you pass a variable *by value*, the receiving procedure creates a procedure-level variable that it uses to store the value passed to it.

   c. Unless specified otherwise, all variables in Visual Basic are passed *by value*.

   d. To pass a variable *by reference* in Visual Basic, you include the keyword ByRef before the variable's name in the Call statement.

9. A Sub procedure named CalcEndingInventory is passed four Integer variables named begin, sales, purchases, and ending. The procedure's task is to calculate the ending inventory, based on the beginning inventory, sales, and purchase amounts passed to the procedure. The procedure should store the result in the ending memory location. Which of the following procedure headers is correct?

   a. Private Sub CalcEndingInventory(ByVal b As Integer, ByVal s As Integer, ByVal p As Integer, ByRef final As Integer)

   b. Private Sub CalcEndingInventory(ByVal b As Integer, ByVal s As Integer, ByVal p As Integer, ByVal final As Integer)

   c. Private Sub CalcEndingInventory(ByRef b As Integer, ByRef s As Integer, ByRef p As Integer, ByVal final As Integer)

   d. Private Sub CalcEndingInventory(ByRef b As Integer, ByRef s As Integer, ByRef p As Integer, ByRef final As Integer)

10. Which of the following statements should you use to call the CalcEndingInventory procedure described in Question 9?

   a. Call CalcEndingInventory(begin, sales, purchases, ending)

   b. Call CalcEndingInventory(ByVal begin, ByVal sales, ByVal purchases, ByRef ending)

   c. Call CalcEndingInventory(ByRef begin, ByRef sales, ByRef purchases, ByRef ending)

   d. Call CalcEndingInventory(ByVal begin, ByVal sales, ByVal purchases, ByVal ending)

REVIEW EXERCISES—SHORT ANSWER

1. Explain the difference between a Sub procedure and a Function procedure.

2. Explain the difference between passing a variable *by value* and passing it *by reference*.

3. Write the Visual Basic code for a Sub procedure that receives an integer passed to it. The HalveNumber procedure should divide the integer by 2 and then display the result in the numLabel.

4. Write an appropriate statement to invoke the HalveNumber procedure created in Review Exercise 3. Pass the integer 87 to the procedure.

5. Write the Visual Basic code for a Sub procedure that prompts the user to enter the name of a city, and then stores the user's response in the String variable whose address is passed to the procedure. Name the procedure GetCity.

6. Write an appropriate statement to invoke the GetCity procedure created in Review Exercise 5. Pass a String variable named city.

7. Write the Visual Basic code for a Sub procedure that receives four Integer variables: the first two *by value* and the last two *by reference*. The procedure should calculate the sum of and the difference between the two variables passed *by value*, and then store the results in the variables passed *by reference*. (When calculating the difference, subtract the contents of the second variable from the contents of the first variable.) Name the procedure CalcSumAndDiff.

8. Write an appropriate statement to invoke the CalcSumAndDiff procedure created in Review Exercise 7. Pass the Integer variables named firstNum, secondNum, sum, and difference.

9. Write the Visual Basic code for a Sub procedure that receives three Decimal variables: the first two *by value* and the last one *by reference*. The procedure should divide the first variable by the second variable, and then store the result in the third variable. Name the procedure CalcQuotient.

10. Write the Visual Basic code for a Function procedure that receives the value stored in an Integer variable. Name the procedure DivideNumber. The procedure should divide the integer by 2 and then return the result (which may contain a decimal place).

11. Write an appropriate statement to call the DivideNumber function created in Review Exercise 10. The name of the Integer variable passed to the function is number. Assign the value returned by the function to the answer variable.

12. Write the Visual Basic code for a Function procedure that prompts the user to enter the name of a state, and then returns the user's response to the calling procedure. Name the procedure GetState.

13. Write an appropriate statement to invoke the GetState function created in Review Exercise 12. Display the function's return value in a message box.

14. Write the Visual Basic code for a Function procedure that receives the contents of four Integer variables. The procedure should calculate the average of the four integers and then return the result (which may contain a decimal place). Name the procedure CalcAverage.

15. Write an appropriate statement to invoke the CalcAverage function created in Review Exercise 14. The Integer variables passed to the function are named num1, num2, num3, and num4. Assign the function's return value to a Decimal variable named average.

16. Write the Visual Basic code for a Function procedure that receives two numbers that both have a decimal place. The procedure should divide the first number by the second number and then return the result. Name the procedure CalcQuotient.

17. Write the procedure header for a Sub procedure named CalculateTax. The procedure should be invoked when any of the following occurs: the rate1Button's Click event, the rate2Button's Click event, and the salesListBox's SelectedValueChanged event.

18. Write the statement to convert the sender parameter to a radio button. Assign the result to a RadioButton variable named currentRadioButton.

COMPUTER EXERCISES

1. In this exercise, you complete an application that calculates an employee's regular pay, overtime pay, and gross pay.

   a. Open the Gadis Antiques Solution (Gadis Antiques Solution.sln) file, which is contained in the VbReloaded2008\Chap08\Gadis Antiques Solution folder.

   b. Finish coding the application, using Figure 8-4 as a guide. Save the solution, then start and test the application. End the application, then close the solution.

2. In this exercise, you modify the application from Computer Exercise 1. The modified application will process the ClearLabels procedure in response to any one of three different events.

   a. Use Windows to make a copy of the Gadis Antiques Solution folder, which is contained in the VbReloaded2008\Chap08 folder. Rename the copy Gadis Antiques Solution-Modified.

b. Open the Gadis Antiques Solution (Gadis Antiques Solution.sln) file contained in the Gadis Antiques Solution—Modified folder. Use the information from Figure 8-12 to modify the application's code. Save the solution, then start and test the application. End the application, then close the solution.

3. In this exercise, you complete an application that displays a message containing a pet's name and age.

   a. Open the Pet Information Solution (Pet Information Solution.sln) file, which is contained in the VbReloaded2008\Chap08\Pet Information Solution folder.

   b. Code the application, using Figure 8-6 as a guide. Save the solution, then start and test the application. End the application, then close the solution.

4. In this exercise, you code an application that calculates a 10% bonus amount.

   a. Open the Bonus Calculator Solution (Bonus Calculator Solution.sln) file, which is contained in the VbReloaded2008\Chap08\Bonus Calculator Solution folder.

   b. Code the application, using an independent Sub procedure to both calculate and display the bonus amount. Also use a Sub procedure named ClearLabel to clear the contents of the bonusLabel when the TextChanged event occurs for either text box. In addition, code each text box's Enter event procedure.

   c. Save the solution, then start and test the application. End the application, then close the solution.

5. In this exercise, you complete an application that calculates gross pay.

   a. Open the Gross Pay Solution (Gross Pay Solution.sln) file, which is contained in the VbReloaded2008\Chap08\Gross Pay Solution folder.

   b. Finish coding the application, using Figure 8-8 as a guide. Save the solution, then start and test the application. End the application.

   c. Modify the application so that it uses one procedure to clear the contents of the grossLabel when the SelectedValueChanged event occurs for either list box. Save the solution, then start and test the application. End the application, then close the solution.

6. In this exercise, you complete an application that calculates an employee's new pay.

   a. Open the Pine Lodge Solution (Pine Lodge Solution.sln) file, which is contained in the VbReloaded2008\Chap08\Pine Lodge Solution folder.

   b. Finish coding the application, using Figure 8-15 as a guide. Save the solution, then start and test the application. End the application, then close the solution.

7. In this exercise, you code an application that uses a timer.

   a. Open the Timer Solution (Timer Solution.sln) file, which is contained in the VbReloaded2008\Chap08\Timer Solution folder. Add a timer control to the interface. Change the timer's Name property to carTimer. Change its Enabled property to True and its Interval property to 500.

   b. In the timer's Tick event procedure, enter the code shown in Figure 8-17. Save the solution, then start and test the application. End the application, then close the solution.

8. In this exercise, you modify the application completed in Computer Exercise 5.

   a. Use Windows to make a copy of the Gross Pay Solution folder, which is contained in the VbReloaded2008\Chap08 folder. Rename the copy Gross Pay Solution-Modified.

   b. Open the Gross Pay Solution (Gross Pay Solution.sln) file contained in the VbReloaded2008\Chap08\Gross Pay Solution-Modified folder.

   c. Modify the code so that it uses a Function procedure (rather than a Sub procedure) to calculate and return the gross pay amount. Save the solution, then start and test the application. End the application, then close the solution.

9. In this exercise, you modify the application completed in Computer Exercise 6.

   a. Use Windows to make a copy of the Pine Lodge Solution folder, which is contained in the VbReloaded2008\Chap08 folder. Rename the copy Pine Lodge Solution-Modified.

   b. Open the Pine Lodge Solution (Pine Lodge Solution.sln) file contained in the VbReloaded2008\Chap08\Pine Lodge Solution-Modified folder.

   c. Modify the code so that it uses a Sub procedure (rather than a Function procedure) to calculate the new pay amount. Save the solution, then start and test the application. End the application, then close the solution.

10. In this exercise, you modify the Concentration Game application you created in the chapter's Programming Tutorial.

   a. Use Windows to make a copy of the Concentration Game Solution folder, which is contained in the VbReloaded2008\Chap08 folder. Rename the copy Concentration Game Solution-Color.

   b. Open the Concentration Game Solution (Concentration Game Solution.sln) file contained in the VbReloaded2008\Chap08\Concentration Game Solution-Color folder.

   c. When the user finds a matching pair of words, change the BackColor property of the corresponding labels to a different color. Be sure to return the labels to their original color when the user clicks the New Game button.

d. Also modify the application so that it displays the message "Game Over" when the user has located all of the matching pairs.

e. Save the solution, then start and test the application. End the application, then close the solution.

11. In this exercise, you modify the Concentration Game application you created in the chapter's Programming Tutorial.

a. Use Windows to make a copy of the Concentration Game Solution folder, which is contained in the VbReloaded2008\Chap08 folder. Rename the copy Concentration Game Solution-Wild.

b. Open the Concentration Game Solution (Concentration Game Solution.sln) file contained in the VbReloaded2008\Chap08\Concentration Game Solution-Wild folder.

c. Replace the Washer/Dryer values in the list box with two Wild Card values. A Wild Card value matches any other value on the board. Modify the code appropriately.

d. Save the solution, then start and test the application. The game is over when all of the words are revealed, or when two unmatched words remain on the board. End the application, then close the solution.

12. In this exercise, you modify the Rainfall application you created in the chapter's Programming Example.

a. Create the Rainfall application shown in the chapter's Programming Example. Save the application in the VbReloaded2008\Chap08 folder.

b. Modify the application so that it uses two function procedures rather than a Sub procedure to calculate the total and average rainfall amounts.

c. Add a Start Over button to the interface. The button should clear the contents of the counter and accumulator variables so that the user can enter a new set of rainfall amounts. Also clear the totalLabel and averageLabel, and send the focus to the text box.

d. Save the solution, then start and test the application. End the application, then close the solution.

13. In this exercise, you code an application that uses two independent Sub procedures: one to convert a temperature from Fahrenheit to Celsius, and the other to convert a temperature from Celsius to Fahrenheit.

a. Build an appropriate interface. Name the solution, project, and form file Temperature Solution, Temperature Project, and Main Form.vb, respectively. Save the application in the VbReloaded2008\Chap08 folder.

b. Code the application. Save the solution, then start and test the application. End the application, then close the solution.

14. In this exercise, you modify the application that you created in Computer Exercise 13 so that it uses two functions rather than two Sub procedures.

   a. Use Windows to make a copy of the Temperature Solution folder, which is contained in the VbReloaded2008\Chap08 folder. Rename the copy Temperature Solution-Modified.

   b. Open the Temperature Solution (Temperature Solution.sln) file contained in the VbReloaded2008\Chap08\Temperature Solution-Modified folder. Modify the code so that it uses two functions (rather than two Sub procedures) to convert the temperatures.

   c. Save the solution, then start and test the application. End the application, then close the solution.

15. In this exercise, you modify the Concentration Game application you created in the chapter's Programming Tutorial.

   a. Use Windows to make a copy of the Concentration Game Solution folder, which is contained in the VbReloaded2008\Chap08 folder. Rename the copy Concentration Game Solution-Counters.

   b. Open the Concentration Game Solution (Concentration Game Solution.sln) file contained in the VbReloaded2008\Chap08\Concentration Game Solution-Counters folder.

   c. Modify the application so that it displays (in two labels) the number of times the user selects a matching pair of words, and the number of times the user does not select a matching pair of words.

   d. Save the solution, then start and test the application. End the application, then close the solution.

16. In this exercise, you learn how to specify that one or more arguments are optional in a Call statement.

   a. Open the Optional Solution (Optional Solution.sln) file, which is contained in the VbReloaded2008\Chap08\Optional Solution folder.

   b. Study the application's existing code. The calcButton's Click event procedure contains two Call statements. The first Call statement passes three variables to the GetBonus procedure. The second Call statement passes only two variables to the procedure; the rate variable is omitted from this statement. (Do not be concerned about the jagged line that appears below the second Call statement.) You indicate that the rate variable is optional in the Call statement by including the keyword Optional before the variable's corresponding parameter in the procedure header. You enter the Optional keyword before the ByVal keyword. You also assign a default value that the procedure will use for the missing parameter when the procedure is called. You assign the default value by entering the assignment operator (=) followed by the default value after the parameter in the procedure header. In this case, you will assign the number .1D as the default value for the rate variable. (Optional parameters must be listed at the end of the procedure header.)

c. Change the ByVal bonusRate As Decimal in the procedure header appropriately.

d. Save the solution, then start the application. Calculate the bonus for a salesperson with an "A" code, $1000 in sales, and a rate of .05. The Call GetBonus(sales, bonus, rate) statement calls the GetBonus procedure, passing it the number 1000, the address of the bonus variable, and the number .05. The GetBonus procedure stores the number 1000 in the totalSales variable. It also assigns the name bonusAmount to the bonus variable, and stores the number .05 in the bonusRate variable. The procedure then multiplies the contents of the totalSales variable (1000) by the contents of the bonusRate variable (.05), and assigns the result (50) to the bonusAmount variable. The bonusLabel.Text = bonus.ToString("C2") statement then displays the number $50.00 in the bonusLabel.

e. Now calculate the bonus for a salesperson with a code of "B" and a sales amount of $2000. The Call GetBonus(sales, bonus) statement calls the GetBonus procedure, passing it the number 2000 and the address of the bonus variable. The GetBonus procedure stores the number 2000 in the totalSales variable, and assigns the name bonusAmount to the bonus variable. Because the Call statement did not supply a value for the bonusRate variable, the default value (.1) is assigned to the variable. The procedure then multiplies the contents of the totalSales variable (2000) by the contents of the bonusRate variable (.1), and assigns the result (200) to the bonusAmount variable. The bonusLabel.Text = bonus.ToString("C2") statement then displays the number $200.00 in the bonusLabel.

f. End the application, then close the solution.

17. In this exercise, you modify the Bonus Calculator application that you coded in Computer Exercise 4.

a. Use Windows to make a copy of the Bonus Calculator Solution folder, which is contained in the VbReloaded2008\Chap08 folder. Rename the copy Bonus Calculator Solution-Modified.

b. Open the Bonus Calculator Solution (Bonus Calculator Solution.sln) file contained in the VbReloaded2008\Chap08\Bonus Calculator Solution-Modified folder.

c. Modify the code so that it uses one procedure (rather than two) to select the existing text in the text box. The procedure should be processed when the Enter event of either text box occurs.

d. Save the solution, then start and test the application. End the application, then close the solution.

18. In this exercise, you find and correct an error in an application. The process of finding and correcting errors is called debugging.

a. Open the Debug Solution (Debug Solution.sln) file, which is contained in the VbReloaded2008\Chap08\Debug Solution folder.

b. Open the Code Editor window. Review the existing code, which should display the name entered by the user. Start the application. Click the Display Name button. When prompted to enter a name, type your name and press Enter. Notice that your name did not appear in the nameLabel. End the application.

c. Correct the application's code. Save the solution, then start and test the application. End the application, then close the solution.

CASE PROJECTS

CAR SHOPPERS INC.

In an effort to boost sales, Car Shoppers Inc. is offering buyers a choice of either a large cash rebate or an extremely low financing rate, much lower than the rate most buyers would pay by financing the car through their local bank. Jake Miller, the manager of Car Shoppers Inc., wants you to create an application that helps buyers decide whether to take the lower financing rate from his dealership, or take the rebate and then finance the car through their local bank. Be sure to use one or more independent Sub or Function procedures in the application. (*Hint*: Use the Financial.Pmt method, which you learned about in Chapter 7, to calculate the payments.) You can either create your own interface or create the one shown in Figure 8-39. Name the solution, project, and form file Car Shoppers Solution, Car Shoppers Project, and Main Form.vb, respectively. Save the application in the VbReloaded2008\Chap08 folder.

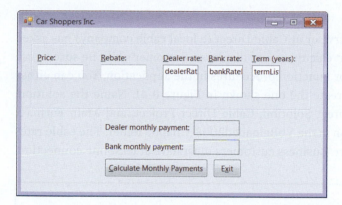

Figure 8-39: Sample interface for Car Shoppers Inc.

WALLPAPER WAREHOUSE

Last year, Johanna Liu opened a new wallpaper store named Wallpaper Warehouse. Business is booming at the store, and Johanna and her salesclerks are always busy. Recently, however, Johanna has received several complaints from customers about the store's slow service, and she has decided to ask her salesclerks for suggestions on improving the service. The overwhelming response from the salesclerks is that they need a more convenient way to calculate the number of single rolls of wallpaper required to cover a room. Currently, the salesclerks perform this calculation manually, using pencil and paper. Doing this for so many customers, however, takes a great deal of time, and service has begun to suffer. Johanna has asked for your assistance in this matter. She would like you to create an application that the salesclerks can use to quickly calculate and display the required number of rolls. Be sure to use one or more independent Sub or Function procedures in the application. You can either create your own interface or create the one shown in Figure 8-40. Name the solution, project, and form file Wallpaper Warehouse Solution, Wallpaper Warehouse Project, and Main Form.vb, respectively. Save the application in the VbReloaded2008\Chap08 folder.

Figure 8-40: Sample interface for the Wallpaper Warehouse

CABLE DIRECT

Sharon Barrow, the billing supervisor at Cable Direct (a local cable company) has asked you to create an application that calculates and displays a customer's bill. Be sure to use one or more independent Sub or Function procedures in the application. You can either create your own interface or create the one shown in Figure 8-41. Name the solution, project, and form file Cable Direct Solution, Cable Direct Project, and Main Form.vb, respectively. Save the application in the VbReloaded2008\Chap08 folder. The cable rates are shown in the following chart. Business customers must have at least one connection.

Residential customers:
        Processing fee: $4.50
        Basic service fee: $30
        Premium channels: $5 per channel

Business customers:
        Processing fee: $16.50
        Basic service fee: $80 for first 10 connections; $4 for each additional connection
        Premium channels: $50 per channel for any number of connections

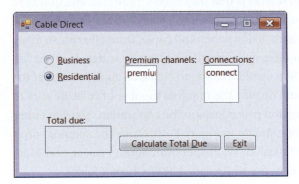

Figure 8-41: Sample interface for Cable Direct

HARVEY INDUSTRIES

Khalid Patel, the payroll manager at Harvey Industries, manually calculates each employee's weekly gross pay, Social Security and Medicare (FICA) tax, federal withholding tax (FWT), and net pay—a very time-consuming process and one that is prone to mathematical errors. Mr. Patel has asked you to create an application that performs the payroll calculations both efficiently and accurately. Name the solution, project, and form file Harvey Industries Solution, Harvey Industries Project, and Main Form.vb, respectively. Save the application in the VbReloaded2008\Chap08 folder. Employees at Harvey Industries are paid every Friday. All employees are paid on an hourly basis, with time and one-half paid for the hours worked over 40. The amount of FICA tax to deduct from an employee's weekly gross pay is calculated by multiplying the gross pay amount by 7.65%. The amount of FWT to deduct from an employee's weekly gross pay is based on the employee's filing status—either single (including head of household) or married—and his or her weekly taxable wages. You calculate the weekly taxable wages by first multiplying the number of withholding allowances by $63.46 (the value of a withholding allowance), and then subtracting the result from the weekly gross pay. For example, if your weekly gross pay is $400 and you have two withholding allowances, your weekly taxable wages are $273.08. You use the weekly taxable wages, along with the filing status and the appropriate weekly Federal Withholding Tax table, to determine the amount of FWT to withhold. The weekly tax tables for the year 2006 are shown in Figure 8-42. Be sure to use one or more independent Sub or Function procedures in the application.

FWT Tables – Weekly Payroll Period				
Single person (including head of household)				
If the taxable wages are:	The amount of income tax to withhold is			
Over	**But not over**	**Base amount**	**Percentage**	**Of excess over**
	$ 51	0		
$ 51	$ 192	0	10%	$ 51
$ 192	$ 620	$ 14.10 plus	15%	$ 192
$ 620	$1,409	$ 78.30 plus	25%	$ 620
$1,409	$3,013	$ 275.55 plus	28%	$1,409
$3,013	$6,508	$ 724.67 plus	33%	$3,013
$6,508		$1,878.02 plus	35%	$6,508
Married person				
If the taxable wages are:	The amount of income tax to withhold is			
Over	**But not over**	**Base amount**	**Percentage**	**Of excess over**
	$ 154	0		
$ 154	$ 440	0	10%	$ 154
$ 440	$1,308	$ 28.60 plus	15%	$ 440
$1,308	$2,440	$ 158.80 plus	25%	$1,308
$2,440	$3,759	$ 441.80 plus	28%	$2,440
$3,759	$6,607	$ 811.12 plus	33%	$3,759
$6,607		$1,750.96 plus	35%	$6,607

Figure 8-42: Weekly FWT tables

9

ARRAYS

After studying Chapter 9, you should be able to:

Declare and initialize a one-dimensional array

Store data in a one-dimensional array

Display the contents of a one-dimensional array

Code a loop using the For Each...Next statement

Access an element in a one-dimensional array

Search a one-dimensional array

Compute the average of a one-dimensional array's contents

Find the highest entry in a one-dimensional array

Update the contents of a one-dimensional array

Sort a one-dimensional array

Create and manipulate parallel one-dimensional arrays

Create and initialize a two-dimensional array

Store data in a two-dimensional array

Search a two-dimensional array

USING ARRAYS

All of the variables you have used so far have been simple variables. A **simple variable**, also called a **scalar variable**, is one that is unrelated to any other variable in memory. In many applications, however, you may need to reserve a block of related variables, referred to as an array. An **array** is a group of variables that have the same name and data type and are related in some way. Each variable in the array might contain an inventory quantity, a state name, or an employee record (name, Social Security number, pay rate, and so on). It may be helpful to picture an array as a group of small, adjacent boxes inside the computer's memory. You can write information to the boxes and you can read information from the boxes; you just cannot *see* the boxes. Programmers use arrays to temporarily store related data in the internal memory of the computer. Examples of data stored in an array would include the federal withholding tax tables in a payroll program and a price list in an order entry program. Storing data in an array increases the efficiency of a program, because data can be both written to and read from internal memory much faster than it can be written to and read from a file on a disk. After data is entered into an array, which typically is done at the beginning of the program, the program can use the data as many times as desired. A payroll program, for example, can use the federal withholding tax tables stored in an array to calculate the amount of each employee's federal withholding tax. The most commonly used arrays are one-dimensional and two-dimensional.

ONE-DIMENSIONAL ARRAYS

You can visualize a **one-dimensional array** as a column of variables. A unique number called a **subscript** identifies each variable in a one-dimensional array. The computer assigns the subscripts to the array variables when the array is created. The subscript indicates the variable's position in the array. The first variable in a one-dimensional array has a subscript of 0, the second a subscript of 1, and so on. You refer to each variable in an array by the array's name and the variable's subscript, which is specified in a set of parentheses immediately following the array name. To refer to the first variable in a one-dimensional array named states, you use states(0)—read "states sub zero." Similarly, to refer to the third variable in the states array, you use states(2). Figure 9-1 illustrates this naming convention.

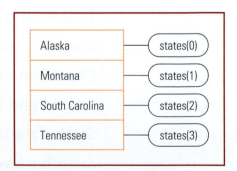

Figure 9-1: Names of the variables in a one-dimensional array named states

Before you can use an array, you first must declare (create) it. Figure 9-2 shows two versions of the syntax you use to declare a one-dimensional array in Visual Basic. The {Dim | Private} portion in each version indicates that you can select only one of the keywords appearing within the braces. The appropriate keyword depends on whether you are creating a procedure-level array (Dim) or a module-level array (Private). *ArrayName* is the name of the array, and *dataType* is the type of data the array variables, referred to as elements, will store. In Version 1 of the syntax, *highestSubscript* is an integer that specifies the highest subscript in the array. When the array is created, it will contain one element more than the number specified in the *highestSubscript* argument; this is because the first element in a one-dimensional array has a subscript of 0. Also included in Figure 9-2 are examples of using both versions of the syntax.

»HOW TO . . .

DECLARE A ONE-DIMENSIONAL ARRAY

Syntax—Version 1

{**Dim** | **Private**} *arrayName*(*highestSubscript*)**As** *dataType*

Syntax—Version 2

{**Dim** | **Private**} *arrayName*() **As** *dataType* = {*initialValues*}

Example 1

Dim cities(3) As String

declares a four-element procedure-level array named cities; each element is automatically initialized using the keyword Nothing

Example 2

Private numbers(5) As Integer

declares a six-element module-level array named numbers; each element is automatically initialized to the number 0

Example 3

Dim sales() As Decimal = {75.33D, 9.65D, 23.55D, 6.89D}

declares and initializes a four-element procedure-level array named sales

Figure 9-2: How to declare a one-dimensional array

»TIP

Module-level arrays are declared in the form's Declarations section, which begins with the Public Class line and ends with the End Class line.

When you use Version 1 of the syntax, the computer automatically initializes each element in the array when the array is created. If the array's data type is String, each element in the array is initialized using the keyword Nothing. As you learned in Chapter 3, variables initialized to Nothing do not actually contain the word "Nothing"; rather, they contain no data at all. Elements in a numeric array are initialized to the number 0, and elements in a Boolean array are initialized to the Boolean value False. Date array elements are initialized to 12:00 AM January 1, 0001. Rather than having the computer use a default value to initialize each array element, you can use Version 2 of the syntax to specify each element's initial value when the array is declared. Assigning initial values to an array is often referred to as **populating the array**. You list the initial values in the *initialValues* section of the syntax, using commas to separate the values, and you enclose the list of values in braces ({}). Notice that Version 2's syntax does not include the *highestSubscript* argument; instead, an empty set of parentheses follows the array name. The computer automatically calculates the highest subscript based on the number of values listed in the *initialValues* section. Because the first subscript in a one-dimensional array is the number 0, the highest subscript is always one number less than the number of values listed in the *initialValues* section. The Dim sales() As Decimal = {75.33D, 9.65D, 23.55D, 6.89D} statement in Example 3 in Figure 9-2, for instance, creates a four-element array with subscripts of 0, 1, 2, and 3. The computer assigns the number 75.33 to the sales(0) element, 9.65 to the sales(1) element, 23.55 to the sales(2) element, and 6.89 to the sales(3) element.

After an array is declared, you can use an assignment statement to store a different value in an array element. Figure 9-3 shows the syntax and examples of such an assignment statement. In the syntax, *arrayName*(*subscript*) is the name and subscript of the element to which you want the value assigned.

»HOW TO . . .

STORE DATA IN A ONE-DIMENSIONAL ARRAY

Syntax

arrayName(*subscript*) = *value*

Example 1

cities(0) = "Madrid"
assigns the string "Madrid" to the first element in the cities array

Example 2

For x As Integer = 1 To 6
    numbers(x − 1) = x * x
Next x
assigns the squares of the numbers from 1 through 6 to the numbers array

Example 3

Decimal.TryParse(salesTextBox.Text, sales(2))
assigns either the value entered in the salesTextBox (converted to Decimal) or the number 0 to the third element in the sales array

Figure 9-3: How to store data in a one-dimensional array

MANIPULATING ONE-DIMENSIONAL ARRAYS

The variables (elements) in an array can be used just like any other variables. You can assign values to them, use them in calculations, display their contents, and so on. In the next several sections, you view sample procedures that demonstrate how one-dimensional arrays are used in an application. More specifically, the procedures will show you how to perform the following tasks using a one-dimensional array:

1. Display the contents of an array.

2. Access an array element using its subscript.

3. Search the array.

4. Calculate the average of the data stored in a numeric array.

5. Find the highest value stored in an array.

6. Update the array elements.

7. Sort the array elements.

In most applications, the values stored in an array come from a file on the computer's disk and are assigned to the array after it is declared. However, so that you can follow the code and its results more easily, most of the procedures you view in this chapter use the Dim statement to store the appropriate values in the array. The first procedure you view displays the contents of a one-dimensional array.

DISPLAYING THE CONTENTS OF A ONE-DIMENSIONAL ARRAY

Figure 9-4 shows a sample run of the Months application, which assigns to a label control the item selected in a list box. Figure 9-5 shows the pseudocode for the MainForm's Load event procedure contained in the application, and Figure 9-6 shows the corresponding Visual Basic code. The Load event procedure demonstrates how you can use the For...Next loop to display the contents of an array in a list box. The first time the loop is processed, the subscript variable contains the number 0, and the monthListBox.Items.Add(months(subscript)) statement adds the contents of the months(0) element—JAN—to the monthListBox. The Next subscript line then adds the number 1 to the value stored in the subscript variable, giving 1. When the loop is processed the second time, the monthListBox.Items.Add(months(subscript)) statement adds the contents of the months(1) element—FEB—to the monthListBox, and so on. The computer repeats the loop instructions for each element in the months array, beginning with the element whose subscript is 0 (JAN) and ending with the element whose subscript is 11 (DEC). The computer stops processing the loop when the value contained in the subscript variable is 12, which is one number more than the highest subscript in the array.

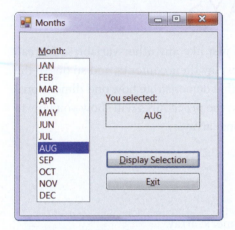

Figure 9-4: Sample run of the Months application

MainForm Load Event Procedure
1. declare and initialize a String array named months
2. repeat for each element in the months array
    add the current array element to the monthListBox
  end repeat
3. select the first item in the monthListBox

Figure 9-5: Pseudocode for the MainForm's Load event procedure

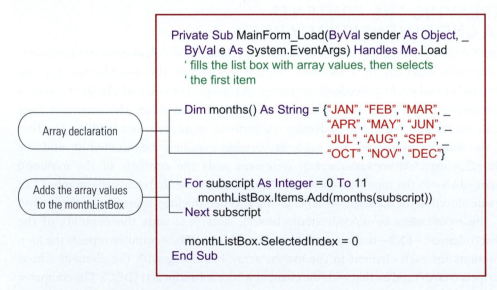

```
Private Sub MainForm_Load(ByVal sender As Object, _
    ByVal e As System.EventArgs) Handles Me.Load
    ' fills the list box with array values, then selects
    ' the first item

    Dim months() As String = {"JAN", "FEB", "MAR", _
                              "APR", "MAY", "JUN", _
                              "JUL", "AUG", "SEP", _
                              "OCT", "NOV", "DEC"}

    For subscript As Integer = 0 To 11
        monthListBox.Items.Add(months(subscript))
    Next subscript

    monthListBox.SelectedIndex = 0
End Sub
```

Array declaration

Adds the array values to the monthListBox

Figure 9-6: MainForm's Load event procedure

As you learned in Chapter 6, you can code a repetition structure (loop) in Visual Basic using the For...Next, Do...Loop, or For Each...Next statement. The Load event procedure in Figure 9-6 uses the For...Next statement to display each array element in the list box. You also could use the Do...Loop statement (which you learned about in Chapter 6) or the For Each...Next statement (which you learn about next).

THE FOR EACH...NEXT STATEMENT

You can use the **For Each...Next statement** to code a loop whose instructions you want processed for each element in a group, such as for each variable in an array. Figure 9-7 shows the syntax of the For Each...Next statement. It also shows two ways of using the statement to code the loop from Figure 9-6. As the syntax indicates, the For Each...Next statement begins with the For Each clause and ends with the Next clause. Between the two clauses, you enter the instructions you want the loop to repeat for each *element* in the *group*. When using the statement to process an array, *element* is the name of a variable that the computer can use to keep track of each array element, and *group* is the name of the array. You can use the **As** *dataType* portion of the For Each clause to declare the *element* variable, as shown in the first example in Figure 9-7. When you declare a variable in the For Each clause, the variable has block scope and can be used only by instructions within the For Each...Next loop. Alternatively, you can declare the *element* variable in a Dim statement, as shown in the last example in Figure 9-7. When a variable is declared in a Dim statement at the beginning of a procedure, it has procedure scope and can be used by the entire procedure. The data type of the *element* variable must match the data type of the *group*. If the *group* is an Integer array, then the *element*'s data type must be Integer. Likewise, if the *group* is a String array, then the *element*'s data type must be String. In the examples shown in Figure 9-7, *group* is a String array named months, and *element* is a String variable named monthName. The monthListBox.Items.Add(monthName) statement in both examples adds the current array element to the monthListBox and will be processed for each element in the months array. The code shown in both examples will display the same result as shown earlier in Figure 9-4.

> **» TIP**
>
> You can use the Exit For statement to exit the For Each...Next statement prematurely, which means exit it before it has finished processing. You may need to do this if the loop encounters an error when processing its instructions.

> **» TIP**
>
> You can nest For Each...Next statements.

» HOW TO . . .

USE THE FOR EACH...NEXT STATEMENT

<u>Syntax</u>

For Each *element* [**As** *dataType*] **In** *group*

    [*statements*]

Next *element*

Figure 9-7: How to use the For Each...Next statement (*continued on next page*)

Example 1

```
For Each monthName As String In months
    monthListBox.Items.Add(monthName)
Next monthName
```
displays the contents of the months array in the monthListBox

Example 2

```
Dim monthName As String = String.Empty
For Each monthName In months
    monthListBox.Items.Add(monthName)
Next monthName
```
same as Example 1

Figure 9-7: How to use the For Each...Next statement (*continued from previous page*)

Next, you view a procedure that uses the array subscript to access the appropriate element in an array.

USING THE SUBSCRIPT TO ACCESS AN ELEMENT IN A ONE-DIMENSIONAL ARRAY

XYZ Corporation pays its managers based on six different salary codes, 1 through 6. Each code corresponds to a different salary amount. Figure 9-8 shows a sample run of the Salary Code application, which displays the salary amount associated with the salary code. Figure 9-9 shows the pseudocode for the displayButton's Click event procedure contained in the application, and Figure 9-10 shows the corresponding Visual Basic code. The Click event procedure uses an array element's subscript to access the element in the array. Before accessing an array element, a procedure always should verify that the subscript is valid—in other words, that it is in range. If the procedure uses a subscript that is not in range, Visual Basic displays an error message and the procedure ends abruptly. Notice that, to access the correct element in the salaries array, the number 1 must be subtracted from the contents of the code variable. This is because the salary code is one number more than the subscript of its associated salary amount in the array. As Figure 9-8 indicates, the procedure displays $70,000 when the user enters the number 4 as the salary code.

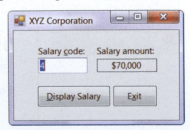

Figure 9-8: Sample run of the Salary Code application

478

> **displayButton's Click Event Procedure**
> 1. declare and initialize an Integer array named salaries
> 2. assign the salary code to a variable
> 3. if the salary code is from 1 through 6
>   calculate the array element's subscript by subtracting 1 from the salary code, then display the salary amount stored in the element
> else
>   display the message "Enter a code from 1 through 6." in a message box
> end if
> 4. send the focus to the codeTextBox

Figure 9-9: Pseudocode for the displayButton's Click event procedure

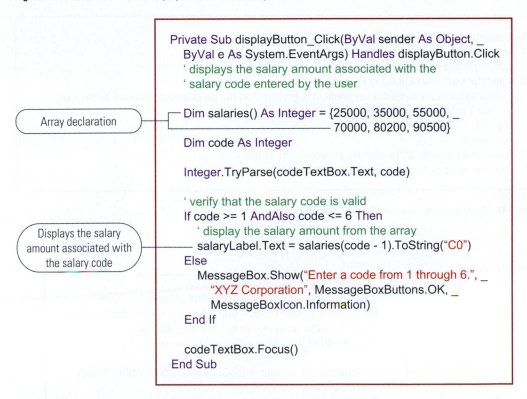

```
Private Sub displayButton_Click(ByVal sender As Object, _
    ByVal e As System.EventArgs) Handles displayButton.Click
    ' displays the salary amount associated with the
    ' salary code entered by the user

    Dim salaries() As Integer = {25000, 35000, 55000, _
                                 70000, 80200, 90500}
    Dim code As Integer

    Integer.TryParse(codeTextBox.Text, code)

    ' verify that the salary code is valid
    If code >= 1 AndAlso code <= 6 Then
        ' display the salary amount from the array
        salaryLabel.Text = salaries(code - 1).ToString("C0")
    Else
        MessageBox.Show("Enter a code from 1 through 6.", _
            "XYZ Corporation", MessageBoxButtons.OK, _
            MessageBoxIcon.Information)
    End If

    codeTextBox.Focus()
End Sub
```

Array declaration

Displays the salary amount associated with the salary code

Figure 9-10: The displayButton's Click event procedure

SEARCHING A ONE-DIMENSIONAL ARRAY

The sales manager at Jacobsen Motors wants an application that determines the number of salespeople selling above an amount specified by the sales manager. To accomplish this task, the application will search an array that contains the amount sold by each salesperson. The application will look for array values that are greater than the amount provided by the sales manager. A counter will be used to keep track of the number of values that meet this specification. Figure 9-11 shows a sample run of the Sales application. Figure 9-12 shows the pseudocode for the searchButton's Click event procedure contained in the application, and Figure 9-13 shows the corresponding Visual Basic code. As Figure 9-11 indicates, the procedure displays the number 3 when the sales manager enters 4000 as the sales amount.

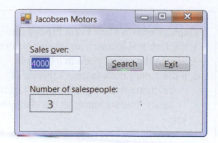

Figure 9-11: Sample run of the Sales application

searchButton's Click Event Procedure
1. declare and initialize an Integer array named sales
2. assign the sales amount to a variable
3. repeat for each element in the sales array
    if the value in the current array element is greater than the sales amount entered by the user
      add 1 to the counter variable
    end if
  end repeat
4. display the contents of the counter variable in the countLabel
5. send the focus to the salesTextBox

Figure 9-12: Pseudocode for the searchButton's Click event procedure

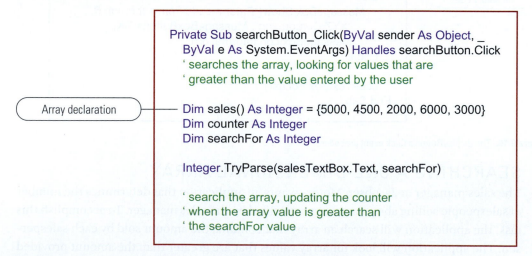

Array declaration

```
Private Sub searchButton_Click(ByVal sender As Object, _
    ByVal e As System.EventArgs) Handles searchButton.Click
    ' searches the array, looking for values that are
    ' greater than the value entered by the user

    Dim sales() As Integer = {5000, 4500, 2000, 6000, 3000}
    Dim counter As Integer
    Dim searchFor As Integer

    Integer.TryParse(salesTextBox.Text, searchFor)

    ' search the array, updating the counter
    ' when the array value is greater than
    ' the searchFor value
```

Figure 9-13: The searchButton's Click event procedure (*continued on next page*)

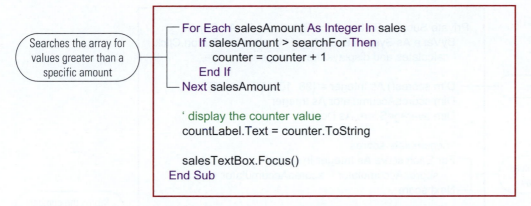

Searches the array for values greater than a specific amount

```
For Each salesAmount As Integer In sales
    If salesAmount > searchFor Then
        counter = counter + 1
    End If
Next salesAmount

' display the counter value
countLabel.Text = counter.ToString

salesTextBox.Focus()
End Sub
```

Figure 9-13: The searchButton's Click event procedure (*continued from previous page*)

CALCULATING THE AVERAGE AMOUNT STORED IN A ONE-DIMENSIONAL NUMERIC ARRAY

Professor Jeremiah wants an application that displays the average test score earned by his students on the final exam. To accomplish this task, the application will add together the test scores stored in an array, and then divide the sum by the number of array elements. Figure 9-14 shows a sample run of the Average application. Figure 9-15 shows the pseudocode for the calcButton's Click event procedure contained in the application, and Figure 9-16 shows the corresponding Visual Basic code. The averageScore = scoresAccumulator / scores.Length instruction in the code calculates the average score by dividing the contents of the scoresAccumulator variable by the contents of the array's Length property. The Length property, whose syntax is *arrayName*.**Length**, contains an integer that represents the number of elements in the array; in this case, the Length property contains the number 5. As Figure 9-14 shows, the average score is 72.6.

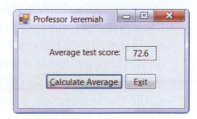

Figure 9-14: Sample run of the Average application

---

calcButton's Click Event Procedure
1. declare and initialize an Integer array named scores
2. repeat for each element in the scores array
   add the contents of the current array element to an accumulator variable
   end repeat
3. calculate the average score by dividing the contents of the accumulator variable by the number of array elements
4. display the average score in the averageLabel

Figure 9-15: Pseudocode for the calcButton's Click event procedure

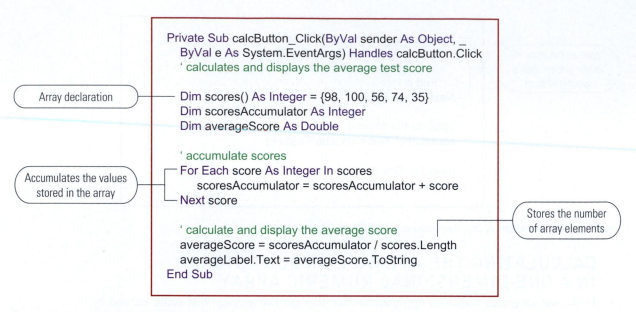

```
Private Sub calcButton_Click(ByVal sender As Object, _
    ByVal e As System.EventArgs) Handles calcButton.Click
    ' calculates and displays the average test score

    Dim scores() As Integer = {98, 100, 56, 74, 35}
    Dim scoresAccumulator As Integer
    Dim averageScore As Double

    ' accumulate scores
    For Each score As Integer In scores
        scoresAccumulator = scoresAccumulator + score
    Next score

    ' calculate and display the average score
    averageScore = scoresAccumulator / scores.Length
    averageLabel.Text = averageScore.ToString
End Sub
```

Array declaration

Accumulates the values stored in the array

Stores the number of array elements

Figure 9-16: The calcButton's Click event procedure

DETERMINING THE HIGHEST VALUE STORED IN A ONE-DIMENSIONAL ARRAY

Sharon Johnson keeps track of the amount of money she earns each week. She wants an application that displays the highest amount earned in a week. The application will store the weekly pay amounts in a one-dimensional array. Similar to the Sales application (shown earlier in Figures 9-11 through 9-13), the Pay application will need to search the array. However, rather than searching for values greater than a specific amount, the Pay application will look for the highest amount in the array. Figure 9-17 shows a sample run of the Pay application. Figure 9-18 shows the pseudocode for the displayHighButton's Click event procedure contained in the application, and Figure 9-19 shows the corresponding Visual Basic code. Notice that the loop searches the second through the last element in the pays array. The first element is not included in the search because its value is assigned to the highestPay variable when the variable is created. The first time the loop is processed, the selection structure within the loop compares the value stored in the second array element—pays(1)—with the value stored in the highestPay variable. At this point, the highestPay variable contains the same value as the first array element. If the value stored in the second array element is greater than the value stored in the highestPay variable, then the highestPay = pays (subscript) statement assigns the array element value to the highestPay variable. The Next subscript clause then adds the number 1 to the subscript variable, giving 2. The next time the loop is processed, the selection structure

Figure 9-17: Sample run of the Pay application

compares the value stored in the third array element—pays(2)—with the value stored in the highestPay variable, and so on. When the loop ends, which is when the subscript variable contains the number 5, the procedure displays the contents of the highestPay variable in the highestLabel. As Figure 9-17 indicates, the procedure displays $50.00.

---

displayHighButton's Click Event Procedure
1. declare and initialize a Decimal array named pays
2. declare a Decimal variable named highestPay, and initialize the variable using the contents of the first element in the pays array
3. repeat for the second through the last array element
    if the value in the current array element is greater than the value in the highestPay variable
      assign the value in the current array element to the highestPay variable
    end if
  end repeat
4. display the contents of the highestPay variable in the highestLabel

---

Figure 9-18: Pseudocode for the displayHighButton's Click event procedure

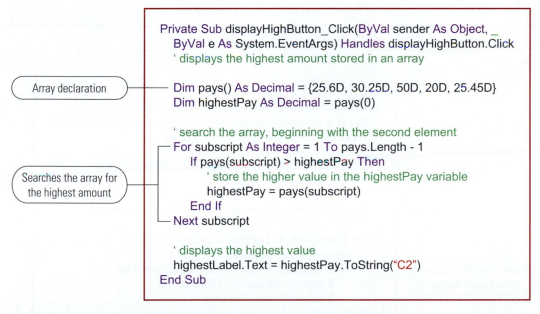

```
Private Sub displayHighButton_Click(ByVal sender As Object, _
    ByVal e As System.EventArgs) Handles displayHighButton.Click
    ' displays the highest amount stored in an array

    Dim pays() As Decimal = {25.6D, 30.25D, 50D, 20D, 25.45D}
    Dim highestPay As Decimal = pays(0)

    ' search the array, beginning with the second element
    For subscript As Integer = 1 To pays.Length - 1
        If pays(subscript) > highestPay Then
            ' store the higher value in the highestPay variable
            highestPay = pays(subscript)
        End If
    Next subscript

    ' displays the highest value
    highestLabel.Text = highestPay.ToString("C2")
End Sub
```

Array declaration

Searches the array for the highest amount

Figure 9-19: The displayHighButton's Click event procedure

UPDATING THE VALUES STORED IN A ONE-DIMENSIONAL ARRAY

The sales manager at Jillian Company wants an application that increases the price of each item the company sells. The application will store the prices in a one-dimensional array, and then increase the value contained in each array element. In addition, the sales manager wants the application to display each item's new price. Figure 9-20 shows a sample run of the Prices application when the user enters the number 5 in the Increase box. Notice that each new price is $5 more than its corresponding original price in the prices array (see Figure 9-22). Figure 9-21 shows the pseudocode for the updateButton's Click event procedure, and Figure 9-22 shows the corresponding Visual Basic code.

Figure 9-20: Sample run of the Prices application

updateButton's Click Event Procedure
1. declare a Decimal array named prices
2. assign the increase amount to a variable
3. repeat for each element in the prices array
      add the increase amount to the value stored in the current array element
      display the contents of the current array element in the newPricesLabel
   end repeat
4. send the focus to the increaseTextBox

Figure 9-21: Pseudocode for the updateButton's Click event procedure

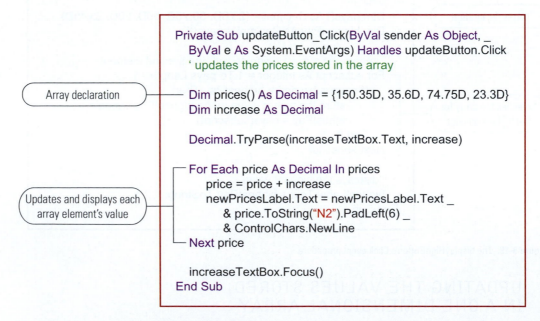

```
Private Sub updateButton_Click(ByVal sender As Object, _
    ByVal e As System.EventArgs) Handles updateButton.Click
    ' updates the prices stored in the array

    Dim prices() As Decimal = {150.35D, 35.6D, 74.75D, 23.3D}
    Dim increase As Decimal

    Decimal.TryParse(increaseTextBox.Text, increase)

    For Each price As Decimal In prices
        price = price + increase
        newPricesLabel.Text = newPricesLabel.Text _
            & price.ToString("N2").PadLeft(6) _
            & ControlChars.NewLine
    Next price

    increaseTextBox.Focus()
End Sub
```

Array declaration

Updates and displays each array element's value

Figure 9-22: The updateButton's Click event procedure

SORTING THE DATA STORED IN A ONE-DIMENSIONAL ARRAY

In some applications, you might need to arrange the contents of an array in either ascending or descending order. Arranging data in a specific order is called **sorting**. When an array is sorted in ascending order, the first element in the array contains the smallest value and the last element contains the largest value. When an array is sorted in descending order, on the other hand, the first element contains the largest value and the last element contains the smallest value. You can use the **Array.Sort method** to sort the elements in a one-dimensional array in ascending order. The method's syntax is **Array.Sort(***arrayName***)**, where *arrayName* is the name of the one-dimensional array to be sorted. To sort a one-dimensional array in descending order, you first use the Array.Sort method to sort the array in ascending order, and then use the **Array.Reverse method** to reverse the array elements. The syntax of the Array.Reverse method is **Array.Reverse(***arrayName***)**, where *arrayName* is the name of the one-dimensional array whose elements you want reversed. The State application that you view in this section uses both the Array.Sort and Array.Reverse methods. The application allows the user to enter the names of five states. It stores the state names in a module-level one-dimensional String array named stateNames. You typically use a module-level array when you need more than one procedure in the same form to use the same array. In this application, the stateNames array will be used by the Click event procedures for the enterButton, sortAscendButton, and sortDescendButton. After entering the state names, the user can choose to display the names in either ascending or descending order. Figure 9-23 shows a sample run of the State application when the user enters the following state names and then clicks the Descending Sort button: Illinois, Texas, Alaska, New York, and Idaho. Figure 9-24 shows most of the Visual Basic code for the State application.

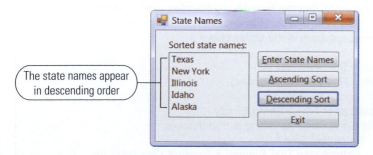

The state names appear in descending order

Figure 9-23: Sample run of the State application

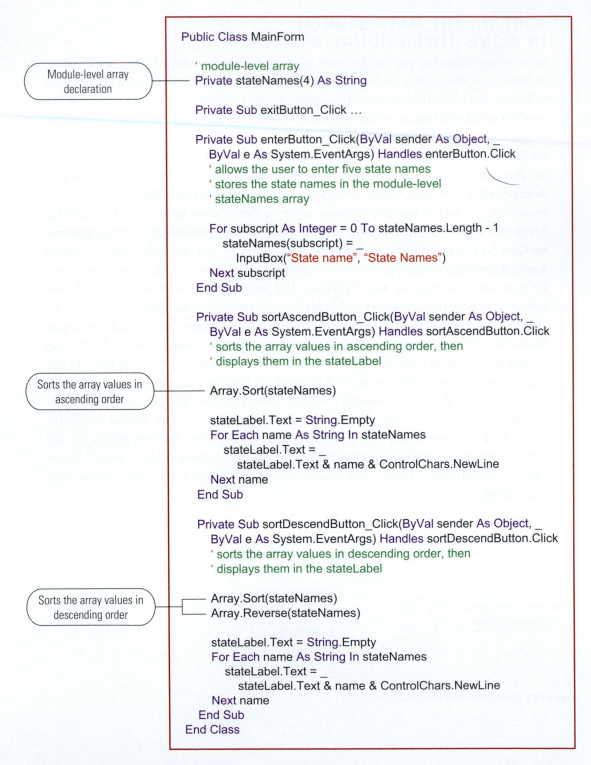

```
Public Class MainForm

    ' module-level array
    Private stateNames(4) As String          ◄── Module-level array
                                                  declaration

    Private Sub exitButton_Click …

    Private Sub enterButton_Click(ByVal sender As Object, _
        ByVal e As System.EventArgs) Handles enterButton.Click
        ' allows the user to enter five state names
        ' stores the state names in the module-level
        ' stateNames array

        For subscript As Integer = 0 To stateNames.Length - 1
            stateNames(subscript) = _
                InputBox("State name", "State Names")
        Next subscript
    End Sub

    Private Sub sortAscendButton_Click(ByVal sender As Object, _
        ByVal e As System.EventArgs) Handles sortAscendButton.Click
        ' sorts the array values in ascending order, then
        ' displays them in the stateLabel

        Array.Sort(stateNames)          ◄── Sorts the array values in
                                             ascending order

        stateLabel.Text = String.Empty
        For Each name As String In stateNames
            stateLabel.Text = _
                stateLabel.Text & name & ControlChars.NewLine
        Next name
    End Sub

    Private Sub sortDescendButton_Click(ByVal sender As Object, _
        ByVal e As System.EventArgs) Handles sortDescendButton.Click
        ' sorts the array values in descending order, then
        ' displays them in the stateLabel

        Array.Sort(stateNames)          ◄── Sorts the array values in
        Array.Reverse(stateNames)            descending order

        stateLabel.Text = String.Empty
        For Each name As String In stateNames
            stateLabel.Text = _
                stateLabel.Text & name & ControlChars.NewLine
        Next name
    End Sub
End Class
```

Figure 9-24: Partial code for the State application

PARALLEL ONE-DIMENSIONAL ARRAYS

Takoda Tapahe owns a small gift shop named Treasures. She wants an application that displays the price of the item whose product ID she enters. Figure 9-25 shows a portion of the gift shop's price list.

Product ID	Price
BX35	13
CR20	10
FE15	12
KW10	24
MM67	4

Figure 9-25: A portion of the gift shop's price list

Recall that all of the variables in an array have the same data type. So how can you store a price list, which includes a string (the product ID) and a number (the price), in an array? One solution is to use two one-dimensional arrays: a String array to store the product IDs and an Integer array to store the prices. Both arrays, referred to as parallel arrays, are illustrated in Figure 9-26. **Parallel arrays** are two or more arrays whose elements are related by their position in the arrays; in other words, they are related by their subscript. The ids and prices arrays are parallel because each element in the ids array corresponds to the element located in the same position in the prices array. For example, the item whose product ID is BX35 [ids(0)] has a price of $13 [prices(0)]. Likewise, the item whose product ID is CR20 [ids(1)] has a price of $10 [prices(1)]. The same relationship is true for the remaining elements in both arrays. To determine an item's price, you locate the item's ID in the ids array and then view its corresponding element in the prices array.

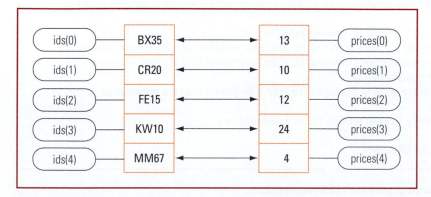

Figure 9-26: Illustration of a price list stored in two one-dimensional arrays

Figure 9-27 shows a sample run of the Price List application. Figure 9-28 shows the pseudocode for the displayButton's Click event procedure contained in the application, and Figure 9-29 shows the corresponding code. Notice that each product ID is stored in the ids array, while its price is stored in the corresponding location in the prices array. The loop in the procedure searches for the product ID in each element in the ids array. The loop stops either when there are no more array elements to search or when the product ID is located in the array. After the loop completes its processing, the selection structure in the procedure compares the number stored in the subscript variable with the value stored in the ids array's Length property (5). If the subscript variable contains a number that is less than 5, it indicates that the loop stopped processing because the product ID was located in the array. In that case, the procedure displays the price located in the same position in the prices array. However, if the subscript variable's value is not less than 5, it indicates that the loop stopped processing because it reached the end of the array without finding the product ID. In that case, the procedure displays the "Invalid product ID." message. As Figure 9-27 shows, the procedure displays a price of $10 when the user enters CR20 as the product ID.

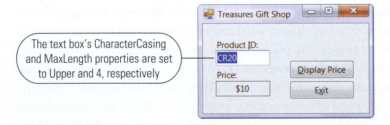

Figure 9-27: Sample run of the Price List application

displayButton's Click Event Procedure
1. declare and initialize two parallel arrays: a String array named ids and an Integer array named prices
2. assign the product ID to a variable named searchFor
3. search the ids array for the value stored in the searchFor variable; stop the search either when there are no more array elements to search or when the product ID is located in the array
4. if the product ID is in the ids array
   use its location in the array to display the corresponding price from the prices array
   else
   display the message "Invalid product ID." in a message box
   end if
5. send the focus to the idTextBox

Figure 9-28: Pseudocode for the displayButton's Click event procedure

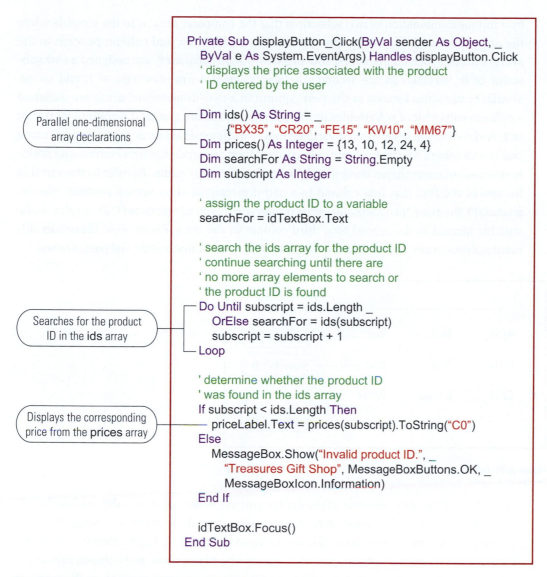

```
Private Sub displayButton_Click(ByVal sender As Object, _
    ByVal e As System.EventArgs) Handles displayButton.Click
    ' displays the price associated with the product
    ' ID entered by the user

    Dim ids() As String = _
        {"BX35", "CR20", "FE15", "KW10", "MM67"}
    Dim prices() As Integer = {13, 10, 12, 24, 4}
    Dim searchFor As String = String.Empty
    Dim subscript As Integer

    ' assign the product ID to a variable
    searchFor = idTextBox.Text

    ' search the ids array for the product ID
    ' continue searching until there are
    ' no more array elements to search or
    ' the product ID is found
    Do Until subscript = ids.Length _
        OrElse searchFor = ids(subscript)
        subscript = subscript + 1
    Loop

    ' determine whether the product ID
    ' was found in the ids array
    If subscript < ids.Length Then
        priceLabel.Text = prices(subscript).ToString("C0")
    Else
        MessageBox.Show("Invalid product ID.", _
            "Treasures Gift Shop", MessageBoxButtons.OK, _
            MessageBoxIcon.Information)
    End If

    idTextBox.Focus()
End Sub
```

Parallel one-dimensional array declarations

Searches for the product ID in the **ids** array

Displays the corresponding price from the **prices** array

Figure 9-29: The displayButton's Click event procedure using parallel one-dimensional arrays

USING TWO-DIMENSIONAL ARRAYS

As mentioned earlier, you can visualize a one-dimensional array as a column of variables. A **two-dimensional array**, on the other hand, resembles a table in that the variables (elements) are in rows and columns. Each variable in a two-dimensional array is identified by a unique combination of two subscripts that the computer assigns to the variable when the array is created. The subscripts specify the variable's row and column position in the array. Variables located in the first row in a two-dimensional array are assigned a row subscript of 0. Variables in the second row are assigned a row subscript of 1, and so on. Similarly, variables located in the first column in a two-dimensional array are assigned a column subscript of 0. Variables in the second column are assigned a column subscript of 1, and so on. You refer to each variable in a two-dimensional array by the array's name and the variable's row and column subscripts, which are separated by a comma and specified in a set of parentheses immediately following the array name. To refer to the variable located in the first row, first column in a two-dimensional array named products, you use products(0, 0)—read "products sub zero comma zero." You use products(1, 2) to refer to the variable located in the second row, third column in the array. Figure 9-30 illustrates this naming convention. Notice that the row subscript is listed first within the parentheses.

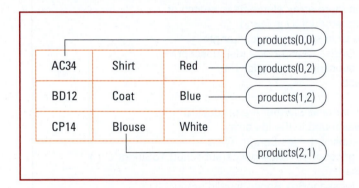

Figure 9-30: Names of some of the variable's contained in the products array

Figure 9-31 shows two versions of the syntax you use to declare a two-dimensional array in Visual Basic. In each version, *arrayName* is the name of the array and *dataType* is the type of data the array variables will store. In Version 1's syntax, *highestRowSubscript* and *highestColumnSubscript* are integers that specify the highest row and column subscripts in the array. When the array is created, it will contain one row more than the number specified in the *highestRowSubscript* argument, and one column more than the number specified in the *highestColumnSubscript* argument. This is because the first row subscript in a two-dimensional array is 0, and so is the first column subscript. When you declare a two-dimensional array using the syntax shown in Version 1, the computer automatically initializes each element in the array when the array is created. Now compare Version 1's syntax with Version 2's syntax. Notice that a comma appears within the parentheses that follow the array name in Version 2. The comma indicates that the array is a two-dimensional array. (Recall that a comma is used to separate the row subscript from the column subscript in a two-dimensional array.) You can use Version 2's syntax to specify each variable's initial value when the array is created. You do this by including a separate *initialValues* section, enclosed in braces, for each row in the array. If the array has two rows, then the statement that declares and initializes the array should have two *initialValues* sections. If the array has five rows, then the declaration statement should have five *initialValues* sections. Within the individual *initialValues* sections, you enter one or more values separated by commas. The number of values to enter corresponds to the number of columns in the array. If the array contains 10 columns, then each individual *initialValues* section should contain 10 values. In addition to the set of braces enclosing each individual *initialValues* section, Version 2's syntax also requires all of the *initialValues* sections to be enclosed in a set of braces. Figure 9-31 shows examples of using both syntax versions.

»HOW TO . . .

DECLARE A TWO-DIMENSIONAL ARRAY

Syntax—Version 1

{**Dim** | **Private**} *arrayName*(*highestRowSubscript*, *highestColumnSubscript*) **As** *dataType*

Syntax—Version 2

{**Dim** | **Private**} *arrayName*(,) **As** *dataType* = {{*initialValues*},... {*initialValues*}}

Example 1

Dim cities(5, 3) As String
declares a six-row, four-column array named cities; each element is automatically initialized using the keyword Nothing

Example 2

Dim scores(,) As Integer = {{75, 90}, {9, 25}, {23, 56}, {6, 12}}
declares and initializes a four-row, two-column array named scores; initializes the scores(0, 0) element to 75, scores(0, 1) to 90, scores(1, 0) to 9, scores(1, 1) to 25, scores(2, 0) to 23, scores(2, 1) to 56, scores(3, 0) to 6, and scores(3, 1) to 12

Figure 9-31: How to declare a two-dimensional array

As with one-dimensional arrays, you generally use an assignment statement to enter data into a two-dimensional array. Figure 9-32 shows the syntax and examples of such an assignment statement. In the syntax, *arrayName*(*rowSubscript*, *columnSubscript*) is the name and subscripts of the element to which you want the value assigned.

»HOW TO . . .

STORE DATA IN A TWO-DIMENSIONAL ARRAY

Syntax

arrayName(*rowSubscript*, *columnSubscript*) = *value*

Example 1

cities(0, 1) = "Paris"

assigns the string "Paris" to the variable located in the first row, second column in the cities array

Example 2

```
For row As Integer = 0 To 3
    For column As Integer = 0 To 1
        scores(row, column) = 0
    Next column
Next row
```

assigns the number 0 to each variable in the scores array

Figure 9-32: How to store data in a two-dimensional array

SEARCHING A TWO-DIMENSIONAL ARRAY

In the *Parallel One-Dimensional Arrays* section of this chapter, you viewed an application created for the Treasures Gift Shop. The application stores the gift shop's price list in two one-dimensional arrays. It then displays the price of the item corresponding to the product ID entered by the user. Instead of using two one-dimensional arrays for the price list, you can use a two-dimensional array. Figure 9-33 shows a sample run of the modified Price List application. Figure 9-34 shows the modified pseudocode for the displayButton's Click event procedure, and Figure 9-35 shows the corresponding Visual Basic code. To store the price list in a two-dimensional array, you will need to treat the product IDs and prices as Strings. This is because all of the variables in an array must have the same data type. Notice (in Figure 9-35) that each product ID is stored in the first column of the products array, and its price is stored in the corresponding row in the second column. The loop in the procedure searches for the product ID in the first column in the array. The loop stops either when there are no more array elements to search in the first column or when the product ID is located in the array. After the loop completes its processing, the selection structure in the procedure compares the number stored in the row variable with the number 5, which is the number of rows contained in the array. If the row variable contains a number that is less than 5, it indicates that the loop stopped processing because the product ID was located in the array. In that case, the procedure displays the price located in the same row as the product ID, but in the second column of the array. However, if the row variable's value is not less than 5, it indicates that the loop stopped processing because it reached the end of the array's first column without finding the product ID. In that case, the message "Invalid product ID." is displayed in a message box. As Figure 9-33 indicates, the procedure displays a price of $12 when the user enters FE15 as the product ID.

> **TIP**
> You can use an array's GetUpperBound method to determine the highest row subscript and highest column subscript in a two-dimensional array. To learn more about the method, complete Computer Exercise 16 at the end of the chapter.

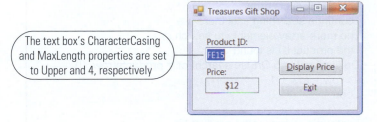

The text box's CharacterCasing and MaxLength properties are set to Upper and 4, respectively

Figure 9-33: Sample run of the modified Price List application

---

displayButton's Click Event Procedure
1. declare and initialize a two-dimensional String array named products
2. assign the product ID to a variable named searchFor
3. search the first column in the products array for the value stored in the searchFor variable; stop the search either when there are no more array elements to search in the first column or when the product ID is located in the array
4. if the product ID is in the first column of the products array
     use its location in the array to display the corresponding price from the second column in the array
   else
     display the message "Invalid product ID." in a message box
   end if
5. send the focus to the idTextBox

Figure 9-34: Modified pseudocode for the displayButton's Click event procedure

---

Two-dimensional array declaration

Searches for the product ID in the first column of the array

Displays the corresponding price from the second column of the array

```
Private Sub displayButton_Click(ByVal sender As Object, _
    ByVal e As System.EventArgs) Handles displayButton.Click
    ' displays the price associated with the product
    ' ID entered by the user

    Dim products(,) As String = {{"BX35", "13"}, _
                                 {"CR20", "10"}, _
                                 {"FE15", "12"}, _
                                 {"KW10", "24"}, _
                                 {"MM67", "4"}}
    Dim searchFor As String = String.Empty
    Dim row As Integer

    ' assign the product ID to a variable
    searchFor = idTextBox.Text

    ' search for the product ID in the first column
    ' of the products array
    ' continue searching until there are
    ' no more array elements to search or
    ' the product ID is found
    Do Until row = 5 OrElse searchFor = products(row, 0)
        row = row + 1
    Loop

    ' determine whether the product ID
    ' was found in the products array
    If row < 5 Then
        priceLabel.Text = "$" & products(row, 1)
    Else
        MessageBox.Show("Invalid product ID.", _
            "Treasures Gift Shop", MessageBoxButtons.OK, _
            MessageBoxIcon.Information)
    End If

    idTextBox.Focus()
End Sub
```

Figure 9-35: The displayButton's Click event procedure using a two-dimensional array

You have completed the concepts section of Chapter 9.

PROGRAMMING TUTORIAL

LOTTERY GAME APPLICATION

In this tutorial, you code an application that generates and displays six unique random numbers for a Lottery Game. Each number can range from 1 through 54 only. Figures 9-36 and 9-37 show the application's TOE chart and user interface.

Task	Object	Event
1. Generate random numbers from 1 through 54 2. Store six unique random numbers in a one-dimensional array 3. Display the contents of the array in the lotteryLabel	displayButton	Click
End the application	exitButton	Click
Show the six unique lottery numbers	lotteryLabel	None

Figure 9-36: TOE Chart

Figure 9-37: User interface

CODING THE LOTTERY GAME APPLICATION

According to the TOE chart, the Click event procedures for the displayButton and exitButton need to be coded. The exitButton has already been coded for you, so you just need to code the displayButton. Figure 9-38 shows the pseudocode for the displayButton's Click event procedure.

```
displayButton's Click Event Procedure
1. generate a random number from 1 through 54 and store it in the first array element
2. repeat the following until all of the remaining array elements contain a unique random number:
      generate a random number from 1 through 54
      search the array elements that contain numbers
      if the random number is not already in the array
         store the random number in the current array element, then continue with the next array element
      end if
   end repeat
3. display the contents of the array in the lotteryLabel
```

Figure 9-38: Pseudocode for the displayButton's Click event procedure

To code the displayButton's Click event procedure:

1. Start Visual Studio. If necessary, close the Start Page window. Open the **Lottery Game Solution** (**Lottery Game Solution.sln**) file, which is contained in the VbReloaded2008\Chap09\Lottery Game Solution folder. The interface contains two labels and two buttons.

2. Open the Code Editor window, then open the code template for the displayButton's Click event procedure. The procedure will store six unique random numbers in a six-element one-dimensional array named numbers. Enter **' generates and displays six unique random** and press **Enter**, then type **' numbers from 1 through 54** and press **Enter** twice. Type **dim numbers(5) as integer** and press **Enter**.

3. While the procedure is populating the array, it will use an Integer variable to keep track of the array subscripts. Type **dim subscript as integer** and press **Enter**.

4. The procedure will use an Integer variable to keep track of the array subscripts while it searches the array for the random number. Type **dim searchSubscript as integer** and press **Enter**.

5. The procedure will use an Integer variable to store the random number after it is generated, but before it is added to the array. Type **dim randomNum as integer** and press **Enter**.

6. The procedure will use a Random object to represent Visual Basic's pseudo-random number generator. Type **dim randomGenerator as new random** and press **Enter**.

7. The procedure will use a Boolean variable to indicate whether the random number is already contained in the array. Type **dim isFound as boolean** and press **Enter** twice.

8. The first step in the procedure's pseudocode is to generate a random number from 1 through 54 and store it in the first array element. Enter the following comments and assignment statement. Press **Enter** twice after typing the assignment statement.

    ' generate the first random number, and

    ' store it in the first array element

    numbers(0) = randomGenerator.next(1, 55)

9. Next, the procedure should fill the remaining array elements with unique random numbers. The remaining elements have subscripts of 1 through 5. Enter the following comments and lines of code. Press **Enter** twice after typing the last assignment statement.

    ' fill remaining array elements with

    ' unique random numbers

    subscript = 1

    do while subscript < numbers.length

        randomNum = randomGenerator. next(1, 55)

10. Now the procedure needs to search the array to verify that it does not contain the random number stored in the randomNum variable. Only the array elements that already contain numbers need to be searched. Those elements have subscripts starting with 0 and ending with the subscript that is one less than the current subscript. In other words, if the current subscript is 1, you need to search only the numbers(0) element, because that is the only element that contains a number. Similarly, if the current subscript is 5, you need to search only the numbers(0), numbers(1), numbers(2), numbers(3), and numbers(4) elements. Type the following comments. Press **Enter** after typing each comment.

    ' search the array to determine whether it

    ' already contains the random number

    ' stop the search when there are no more array

    ' elements or when the random number is found

11. Type **searchSubscript = 0** and press **Enter**. This will start the search with the first array element.

12. Before the search begins, the procedure will assume that the random number is not contained in the array. Type **isFound = false** and press **Enter**.

13. The procedure should continue searching as long as there are array elements to search and, at the same time, the random number has not been found in the array. Type **do while searchSubscript < subscript _** and press **Enter**. Press **Tab**, then type **andalso isFound = false** and press **Enter**.

14. Type the following comments. Press **Enter** after typing each comment.

    ' if the random number is in the current array

    ' element, assign True to isFound

    ' otherwise, search the next element

15. Type **if numbers(searchSubscript) = randomNum then** and press **Enter**, then type **isFound = true** and press **Enter**. Type **else** and press **Enter**, then type **searchSubscript = searchSubscript + 1**.

16. If the random number is not in the array, the procedure should assign the random number to the current array element, and then prepare to fill the next element. Type the comments and selection structure shown in Figure 9-39, then position the insertion point as shown in the figure.

```
displayButton                                    Click
            ' if the random number is in the current array
            ' element, assign True to isFound
            ' otherwise, search the next element
            If numbers(searchSubscript) = randomNum Then
                isFound = True
            Else
                searchSubscript = searchSubscript + 1
            End If
        Loop

            ' if the random number is not in the array
            ' assign the random number to the current array
            ' element, then move to the next element
            If isFound = False Then
                numbers(subscript) = randomNum
                subscript = subscript + 1
            End If
        Loop

        End Sub
    End Class
```

Enter these comments and lines of code

Position the insertion point here

Figure 9-39: Additional comments and selection structure shown in the procedure

17. The last step in the procedure's pseudocode is to display in the lotteryLabel the contents of the numbers array, which now contains the six lottery numbers. Type the following comment and code. Press **Enter** after typing each line.

    ' display the contents of the array

    lotteryLabel.text = String.Empty

    For Each num As Integer In numbers

18. Type **lotteryLabel.text = lotteryLabel.text & " "** _ (be sure to include two spaces between the quotation marks, as well as a space before the line continuation character) and press **Enter**. Press **Tab**, then type **& num.tostring**.

19. Change the Next clause to **Next num**, then save the solution.

Before testing the Lottery Game application, compare the code you entered in the Code Editor window with the code shown in Figure 9-40. Make any needed corrections.

```
' Project name:         Lottery Game Project
' Project purpose:      Displays six unique random
'                       numbers from 1 through 54
' Created/revised by:   <your name> on <current date>

Option Explicit On
Option Strict On
Option Infer Off

Public Class MainForm

    Private Sub exitButton_Click(ByVal sender As Object, _
    ByVal e As System.EventArgs) Handles exitButton.Click
        Me.Close()
    End Sub

    Private Sub displayButton_Click(ByVal sender As Object, _
    ByVal e As System.EventArgs) Handles displayButton.Click
        ' generates and displays six unique random
        ' numbers from 1 through 54

        Dim numbers(5) As Integer
        Dim subscript As Integer
        Dim searchSubscript As Integer
        Dim randomNum As Integer
        Dim randomGenerator As New Random
        Dim isFound As Boolean

        ' generate the first random number, and
        ' store it in the first array element
        numbers(0) = randomGenerator.Next(1, 55)

        ' fill remaining array elements with
        ' unique random numbers
        subscript = 1
```

Figure 9-40: Code for the Lottery Game application (*continued on next page*)

```
            Do While subscript < numbers.Length
                randomNum = randomGenerator.Next(1, 55)

                ' search the array to determine whether it
                ' already contains the random number
                ' stop the search when there are no more array
                ' elements or when the random number is found
                searchSubscript = 0
                isFound = False
                Do While searchSubscript < subscript _
                    AndAlso isFound = False
                    ' if the random number is in the current array
                    ' element, assign True to isFound
                    ' otherwise, search the next element
                    If numbers(searchSubscript) = randomNum Then
                        isFound = True
                    Else
                        searchSubscript = searchSubscript + 1
                    End If
                Loop

                ' if the random number is not in the array
                ' assign the random number to the current array
                ' element, then move to the next element
                If isFound = False Then
                    numbers(subscript) = randomNum
                    subscript = subscript + 1
                End If
            Loop

            ' display the contents of the array
            lotteryLabel.Text = String.Empty
            For Each num As Integer In numbers
                lotteryLabel.Text = lotteryLabel.Text & " " _
                    & num.ToString
            Next num
        End Sub
End Class
```

Figure 9-40: Code for the Lottery Game application (*continued from previous page*)

To test the Lottery Game application:

1. Save the solution, if necessary, then start the application. Click the **Display Lottery Numbers** button. Six unique numbers appear in the interface, as shown in Figure 9-41. Because the numbers are random, your numbers might be different from those shown in the figure.

Figure 9-41: Lottery numbers in the interface

2. Click the **Display Lottery Numbers** button several more times. When you are finished testing the application, click the **Exit** button to end the application.

3. Close the Code Editor window, then close the solution.

PROGRAMMING EXAMPLE

PERRYTOWN GENERAL STORE APPLICATION

Stanley Habeggar is the owner and manager of the Perrytown General Store. Every Friday afternoon, Mr. Habeggar calculates the weekly pay for his six employees. The most time-consuming part of this task, and the one prone to the most errors, is the calculation of the federal withholding tax (FWT). The appropriate tax amount is based on the employee's taxable wages and marital status, as indicated in the FWT tables shown in Figure 9-42. Both tables contain five columns of information. The first two columns list the various ranges, called brackets, of taxable wage amounts. The first column (Over) lists the amount that a taxable wage in that bracket must be over, and the second column (But not over) lists the maximum amount included in the bracket. The remaining three columns (Base amount, Percentage, and Of excess over) indicate how the tax for each bracket is calculated. For example, assume that you are married and your weekly taxable wages are $280. Before you can calculate the amount of your tax, you need to locate your taxable wages in the first two columns of the Married table. In this case, your taxable wages fall within the $154 through $453 bracket. After locating the bracket that contains your taxable wages, you then use the remaining three columns in the table to calculate your tax. According to the Married table, taxable wages in the $154 through $453 bracket have a tax of 10% of the amount over $154; therefore, your tax is $12.60.

FWT Tables – Weekly Payroll Period				
Single person (including head of household)				
If the taxable wages are:	The amount of income tax to withhold is			
Over	**But not over**	**Base amount**	**Percentage**	**Of excess over**
	$ 51	0		
$ 51	$ 198	0	10%	$ 51
$ 198	$ 653	$ 14.70 plus	15%	$ 198
$ 653	$1,533	$ 82.95 plus	25%	$ 653
$1,533	$3,202	$ 302.95 plus	28%	$1,533
$3,202	$6,916	$ 770.27 plus	33%	$3,202
$6,916		$1,995.89 plus	35%	$6,916
Married person				
If the taxable wages are:	The amount of income tax to withhold is			
Over	**But not over**	**Base amount**	**Percentage**	**Of excess over**
	$ 154	0		
$ 154	$ 453	0	10%	$ 154
$ 453	$1,388	$ 29.90 plus	15%	$ 453
$1,388	$2,651	$ 170.15 plus	25%	$1,388
$2,651	$3,994	$ 485.90 plus	28%	$2,651
$3,994	$7,021	$ 861.94 plus	33%	$3,994
$7,021		$1,860.85 plus	35%	$7,021

Figure 9-42: Weekly federal withholding tax tables

Create an application that calculates the FWT. Name the solution, project, and form file Perrytown Solution, Perrytown Project, and Main Form.vb, respectively. Save the application in the VbReloaded2008\Chap09 folder. See Figures 9-43 through 9-47.

Task	Object	Event
1. Calculate the FWT 2. Display the FWT in the fwtLabel	calcButton	Click
End the application	exitButton	Click
Display the FWT (from calcButton)	fwtLabel	None
Get and display the taxable wages	taxableTextBox	None
Select existing text		Enter
Remove contents of fwtLabel		TextChanged
Get the marital status	singleRadioButton, marriedRadioButton	None
Remove contents of fwtLabel		Click

Figure 9-43: TOE chart

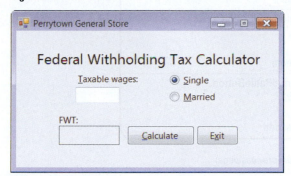

Figure 9-44: User interface

Object	Property	Setting
Form1	Name Font MaximizeBox StartPosition Text	MainForm Segoe UI, 9 point False CenterScreen Perrytown General Store
Label1	Font TabIndex Text	Segoe UI, 14 point 6 Federal Withholding Tax Calculator
Label2	TabIndex Text	0 &Taxable wages:
Label3	TabIndex Text	7 FWT:

Figure 9-45: Objects, Properties, and Settings (*continued on next page*)

Object	Property	Setting
Label4	Name	fwtLabel
	AutoSize	False
	BorderStyle	FixedSingle
	TabIndex	8
	Text	(empty)
	TextAlign	MiddleCenter
TextBox1	Name	taxableTextBox
	TabIndex	1
Button1	Name	calcButton
	TabIndex	4
	Text	&Calculate
Button2	Name	exitButton
	TabIndex	5
	Text	E&xit
RadioButton1	Name	singleRadioButton
	Checked	True
	TabIndex	2
	Text	&Single
RadioButton2	Name	marriedRadioButton
	Checked	False
	TabIndex	3
	Text	&Married

Figure 9-45: Objects, Properties, and Settings (*continued from previous page*)

MainForm Declarations Section
1. store the Single tax table in a two-dimensional array
2. store the Married tax table in a two-dimensional array

exitButton Click Event Procedure
1. close the application

taxableTextBox Enter Event Procedure
1. select the existing text

taxableTextBox TextChanged, singleRadioButton Click, marriedRadioButton Click Event Procedures
1. remove the contents of the fwtLabel

calcButton Click Event Procedure
1. assign the taxable wages to a variable
2. if the singleRadioButton is selected
    use the Single tax table array
  else
    use the Married tax table array
  end if

Figure 9-46: Pseudocode (*continued on next page*)

3. repeat while there are still rows in the tax table array to search and the taxable wages have not been found
    if the taxable wages are less than or equal to the value stored in the first column of the current row in the tax table
        calculate the federal withholding tax using the information stored in the second, third, and fourth columns in the tax table
        indicate that the taxable wages were found
    else
        continue the search in the next row in the tax table
    end if
    end repeat
4. display the federal withholding tax in the fwtLabel
5. send the focus to the taxableTextBox

Figure 9-46: Pseudocode (*continued from previous page*)

```
' Project name:          Perrytown Project
' Project purpose:       Displays the Federal Withholding
'                        Tax (FWT)
' Created/revised by:    <your name> on <current date>

Option Explicit On
Option Strict On
Option Infer Off

Public Class MainForm

    Private singleTable(,)As Double = {{51, 0, 0, 0}, _
                                {198, 0, 0.10, 51}, _
                                {653, 14.7, 0.15, 198}, _
                                {1533, 82.95, 0.25, 653}, _
                                {3202, 302.95, 0.28, 1533}, _
                                {6916, 770.27, 0.33, 3202}, _
                                {99999, 1995.89, 0.35, 6916}}

    Private marriedTable(,)As Double = {{154, 0, 0, 0}, _
                                {453, 0, 0.1, 154}, _
                                {1388, 29.9, 0.15, 453}, _
                                {2651, 170.15, 0.25, 1388}, _
                                {3994, 485.9, 0.28, 2651}, _
                                {7021, 861.94, 0.33, 3994}, _
                                {99999, 1860.85, 0.35, 7021}}
```

Figure 9-47: Code (*continued on next page*)

```
Private Sub exitButton_Click(ByVal sender As Object, _
    ByVal e As System.EventArgs) Handles exitButton.Click
    Me.Close()
End Sub

Private Sub taxableTextBox_Enter(ByVal sender As Object, _
    ByVal e As System.EventArgs) Handles taxableTextBox.Enter
    taxableTextBox.SelectAll()
End Sub

Private Sub ClearLabel(ByVal sender As Object, _
    ByVal e As System.EventArgs) Handles taxableTextBox.TextChanged, _
    singleRadioButton.Click, marriedRadioButton.Click
    fwtLabel.Text = String.Empty
End Sub

Private Sub calcButton_Click(ByVal sender As Object, _
    ByVal e As System.EventArgs) Handles calcButton.Click
    ' calculates and displays the FWT

    Dim taxTable(5, 3) As Double
    Dim taxableWages As Double
    Dim fwt As Double
    Dim row As Integer
    Dim isFound As Boolean

    Double.TryParse(taxableTextBox.Text, taxableWages)

    ' determine the appropriate tax table
    If singleRadioButton.Checked Then
        taxTable = singleTable
    Else
        taxTable = marriedTable
    End If

    ' search for the taxable wages in the first column
    ' in the array
    Do Until row = 6 OrElse isFound
        If taxableWages <= taxTable(row, 0) Then
            ' calculate the FWT
            fwt = taxTable(row, 1) + taxTable(row, 2) _
                * (taxableWages - taxTable(row, 3))
            isFound = True
```

Figure 9-47: Code (*continued from previous page and on next page*)

```
        Else
            ' continue searching for the taxable wages
            row = row + 1
        End If
    Loop

    ' display the FWT
    fwtLabel.Text = fwt.ToString("C2")

    taxableTextBox.Focus()
End Sub
End Class
```

Figure 9-47: Code (*continued from previous page*)

QUICK REVIEW

» Programmers use arrays to temporarily store related data in the internal memory of the computer.

» All of the variables in an array have the same name and data type.

» Each element in a one-dimensional array is identified by a unique subscript that appears in parentheses after the array's name. The first subscript in a one-dimensional array is 0.

» Each element in a two-dimensional array is identified by a unique combination of two subscripts: a row subscript and a column subscript. The subscripts appear in parentheses after the array's name. You list the row subscript first, followed by a comma and the column subscript. The first row subscript in a two-dimensional array is 0. Likewise, the first column subscript also is 0.

» When declaring a one-dimensional array, you provide either the highest subscript or the initial values.

» When declaring a two-dimensional array, you provide either the highest row and column subscripts or the initial values.

» The number of elements in a one-dimensional array is one number more than its highest subscript.

» The number of rows in a two-dimensional array is one number more than its highest row subscript. Likewise, the number of columns is one number more than its highest column subscript.

» You usually use an assignment statement to store data in an array.

» You refer to an element in a one-dimensional array using the array's name followed by the element's subscript.

» You refer to an element in a two-dimensional array using the array's name followed by the element's row and column subscripts, which are separated by a comma.

» You can use the For Each...Next statement to code a loop whose instructions you want processed for each element in an array. You also can use the For...Next statement or the Do...Loop statement.

» A one-dimensional array's Length property contains an integer that represents the number of elements in the array.

» The Array.Sort method sorts the elements in a one-dimensional array in ascending order.

» The Array.Reverse method reverses the order of the elements in a one-dimensional array.

» The elements in parallel arrays are related by their subscript (or position) in the arrays.

KEY TERMS

Array—a group of variables that have the same name and data type and are related in some way

Array.Reverse method—reverses the order of the elements in a one-dimensional array

Array.Sort method—sorts the elements in a one-dimensional array in ascending order

For Each...Next statement—the Visual Basic statement used to code a loop whose instructions you want processed for each element in a group

One-dimensional array—an array whose elements are identified by a unique number (subscript)

Parallel arrays—two or more arrays whose elements are related by their subscript (position) in the arrays

Populating the array—refers to the process of assigning the initial values to an array

Scalar variable—another term for a simple variable

Simple variable—a variable that is unrelated to any other variable in the computer's internal memory; also called a scalar variable

Sorting—arranging data in a specific order

Subscript—an integer that indicates the position of an element in an array

Two-dimensional array—an array whose elements are identified by a unique combination of two numbers: a row subscript and a column subscript

SELF-CHECK QUESTIONS AND ANSWERS

1. Which of the following declares a one-dimensional, four-element String array named letters?

   a. Dim letters(3) As String

   b. Dim letters() As String = "A", "B", "C", "D"

   c. Dim letters(4) As String = {"A", "B", "C", "D"}

   d. All of the above.

2. Which of the following declares a two-dimensional String array named letters that contains four rows and two columns?

   a. Dim letters(3, 1) As String

   b. Private letters(3, 1) As String

   c. Dim letters(,) = {{"A", "B"}, {"C", "D"}, _
   {"E", "F"}, {"G", "H"}}

   d. All of the above.

3. Which of the following statements assigns to the countLabel the number of elements contained in a one-dimensional array named items?

   a. countLabel.Text = items.Len.ToString

   b. countLabel.Text = items.Length.ToString

   c. countLabel.Text = Length(items).ToString

   d. None of the above.

4. Which of the following statements assigns the string "Scottsburg" to the fifth element in a one-dimensional array named cities?

   a. cities(4) = "Scottsburg"   b. cities[4] = "Scottsburg"

   c. cities(5) = "Scottsburg"   d. None of the above.

5. Which of the following statements assigns the Boolean value True to the element located in the third row, first column of a two-dimensional Boolean array named testAnswers?

   a. testAnswers(0, 2) = True   b. testAnswers(1, 3) = True

   c. testAnswers(3, 1) = True   d. None of the above.

Answers: 1) a, 2) d, 3) b, 4) a, 5) d

REVIEW QUESTIONS

1. Which of the following statements declares a five-element, one-dimensional array named prices?

    a. Dim prices(4) As Decimal

    b. Dim prices(5) As Decimal

    c. Dim prices(4) As Decimal = {3.55D, 6.7D, 8D, 4D, 2.34D}

    d. Both a and c.

2. The items array is declared using the Dim items(20) As String statement. The x variable keeps track of the array subscripts and is initialized to 0. Which of the following Do clauses will process the loop instructions for each element in the array?

    a. Do While x > 20

    b. Do While x < 20

    c. Do While x >= 20

    d. Do While x <= 20

    Use the sales array to answer Questions 3 through 6. The array was declared using the following statement: Dim sales() As Integer = {10000, 12000, 900, 500, 20000}.

3. The statement sales(3) = sales(3) + 10 will _____.

    a. replace the 500 amount with 10

    b. replace the 500 amount with 510

    c. replace the 900 amount with 10

    d. replace the 900 amount with 910

4. Which of the following If clauses can be used to verify that the array subscript, named x, is valid for the sales array?

    a. If sales(x) >= 0 AndAlso sales(x) < 4 Then

    b. If sales(x) >= 0 AndAlso sales(x) <= 4 Then

    c. If x >= 0 AndAlso x < 4 Then

    d. If x >= 0 AndAlso x <= 4 Then

5. Which of the following loops will correctly add 100 to each element in the sales array? The x variable was declared as an Integer variable and initialized to 0.

a. Do While x <= 4

    x = x + 100

Loop

b. Do While x <= 4

    sales = sales + 100

Loop

c. Do While sales < 5

    sales(x) = sales(x) + 100

Loop

d. Do While x < 5

    sales(x) = sales(x) + 100

    x = x + 1

Loop

6. Which of the following statements sorts the sales array in ascending order?

a. Array.Sort(sales)

b. sales.Sort()

c. Sort(sales)

d. SortArray(sales)

Use the numbers array to answer Questions 7 through 12. The array was declared using the following statement: Dim numbers() As Integer = {10, 5, 7, 2}. The total and x variables were declared as Integer variables and initialized to 0. The avg variable was declared as a Decimal variable and initialized to 0.

7. Which of the following will correctly calculate the average of the elements included in the numbers array?

a. Do While x < 4

    numbers(x) = total + total

    x = x + 1

Loop

avg = Convert.ToDecimal(total / x)

b. Do While x < 4

 total = total + numbers(x)

 x = x + 1

Loop

avg = Convert.ToDecimal(total / x)

c. Do While x < 4

 total = total + numbers(x)

 x = x + 1

Loop

avg = Convert.ToDecimal(total / x – 1)

d. Do While x < 4

 total = total + numbers(x)

 x = x + 1

Loop

avg = Convert.ToDecimal(total / (x - 1))

8. What will the code in Question 7's answer a assign to the avg variable?

 a. 0   b. 5

 c. 6   d. 8

9. What will the code in Question 7's answer b assign to the avg variable?

 a. 0   b. 5

 c. 6   d. 8

10. What will the code in Question 7's answer c assign to the avg variable?

 a. 0   b. 5

 c. 6   d. 8

11. What will the code in Question 7's answer d assign to the avg variable?

 a. 0   b. 5

 c. 6   d. 8

12. Which of the following statements assigns to the elements variable the number of elements included in the numbers array?

 a. elements = Len(numbers)   b. elements = Length(numbers)

 c. elements = numbers.Len   d. elements = numbers.Length

13. Which of the following statements creates a two-dimensional array that contains three rows and four columns?

    a. Dim temps(2, 3) As Decimal

    b. Dim temps(3, 4) As Decimal

    c. Dim temps(3, 2) As Decimal

    d. Dim temps(4, 3) As Decimal

Use the sales array to answer Questions 14 through 16. The array was declared using the following statement: Dim sales(,) As Decimal = {{1000, 1200, 900, 500, 2000}, _

{350, 600, 700, 800, 100}}

14. The sales(1, 3) = sales(1, 3) + 10 statement will _____.

    a. replace the 900 amount with 910

    b. replace the 500 amount with 510

    c. replace the 700 amount with 710

    d. replace the 800 amount with 810

15. The sales(0, 4) = sales(0, 4 - 2) statement will _____.

    a. replace the 500 amount with 1200

    b. replace the 2000 amount with 900

    c. replace the 2000 amount with 1998

    d. result in an error

16. Which of the following If clauses can be used to verify that the row and col array subscripts are valid for the sales array?

    a. If sales(row, col) >= 0 AndAlso sales(row, col) < 5 Then

    b. If sales(row, col) >= 0 AndAlso sales(row, col) <= 5 Then

    c. If row >= 0 AndAlso row < 3 AndAlso col >= 0 AndAlso col < 6 Then

    d. If row >= 0 AndAlso row < 2 AndAlso col >= 0 AndAlso col < 5 Then

17. Which of the following statements assigns the string "California" to the variable located in the third column, fifth row of a two-dimensional array named states?

    a. states(3, 5) = "California"   b. states(5, 3) = "California"

    c. states(2, 4) = "California"   d. states(4, 2) = "California"

18. Which of the following assigns the number 1 to each element in a five-element, one-dimensional Integer array named counters?

    a. For row As Integer = 0 To 4

          counters(row) = 1

       Next row

    b. Dim row As Integer

       Do While row < 5

          counters(row) = 1

          row = row + 1

       Loop

    c. For row As Integer = 1 To 5

          counters(row − 1) = 1

       Next row

    d. All of the above.

19. Which of the following assigns the number 0 to each element in a two-dimensional Integer array named sums? The array contains two rows and four columns.

    a. For row As Integer = 0 To 1

          For column As Integer = 0 To 3

             sums(row, column) = 0

          Next column

       Next row

    b. Dim row As Integer

       Dim column As Integer

       Do While row < 2

          column = 0

          Do While column < 4

             sums(row, column) = 0

             column = column + 1

          Loop

          row = row + 1

       Loop

c. For x As Integer = 1 To 2

    For y As Integer = 1 To 4

        sums(x – 1, y – 1) = 0

    Next y

  Next x

d. All of the above.

20. If the elements in two arrays are related by their subscripts, the arrays are called _____ arrays.

    a. associated   b. coupled

    c. matching   d. parallel

REVIEW EXERCISES— SHORT ANSWER

1. Write the statement to declare a procedure-level one-dimensional array named numbers. The array should be able to store 20 integers. Then write the statement to store the number 7 in the second element.

2. Write the statement to declare a module-level one-dimensional array named products. The array should be able to store 10 strings. Then write the statement to store the string "Paper" in the third element.

3. Write the statement to declare and initialize a procedure-level one-dimensional array named rates that has five elements. Use the following numbers to initialize the array: 6.5, 8.3, 4, 2, 10.5.

4. Write the code to display the contents of the rates array from Review Exercise 3 in the ratesLabel. Use the For...Next statement.

5. Rewrite the code from Review Exercise 4 using the Do...Loop statement.

6. Rewrite the code from Review Exercise 4 using the For Each...Next statement.

7. Write the statement to sort the rates array in ascending order.

8. Write the statement to reverse the contents of the rates array.

9. Write the code to calculate the average of the elements stored in the rates array from Review Exercise 3. Display the average in the averageLabel. Use the For...Next statement.

10. Rewrite the code from Review Exercise 9 using the Do...Loop statement.

11. Rewrite the code from Review Exercise 9 using the For Each...Next statement.

12. Write the code to display (in the smallestLabel) the smallest number stored in the rates array from Review Exercise 3. Use the Do...Loop statement.

13. Rewrite the code from Review Exercise 12 using the For...Next statement.

14. Rewrite the code from Review Exercise 12 using the For Each...Next statement.

15. Write the code to subtract the number 1 from each element in the rates array from Review Exercise 3. Use the Do...Loop statement.

16. Rewrite the code from Review Exercise 15 using the For...Next statement.

17. Rewrite the code from Review Exercise 15 using the For Each...Next statement.

18. Write the code to multiply by 2 the number stored in the first element of a one-dimensional array named numbers. Store the result in the doubleNum variable.

19. Write the code to add together the numbers stored in the first and second elements of a one-dimensional array named numbers. Display the sum in the sumLabel.

20. Write the statement to declare a two-dimensional Decimal array named balances. The array should have four rows and six columns.

21. Write a loop that stores the number 10 in each element in the balances array from Review Exercise 20. Use the For...Next statement.

22. Rewrite the code from Review Exercise 21 using a Do...Loop statement.

COMPUTER EXERCISES

1. In this exercise, you modify the Lottery Game application you created in the chapter's Programming Tutorial.

   a. Use Windows to make a copy of the Lottery Game Solution folder, which is contained in the VbReloaded2008\Chap09 folder. Rename the folder Modified Lottery Game Solution.

   b. Open the Lottery Game Solution (Lottery Game Solution.sln) file contained in the VbReloaded2008\Chap09\Modified Lottery Game Solution folder. Open the Code Editor window. Change both Do While clauses to Do Until clauses.

   c. Save the solution, then start and test the application. End the application, then close the solution.

2. In this exercise, you modify the Perrytown General Store application created in the chapter's Programming Example.

   a. Create the Perrytown General Store application shown in the chapter's Programming Example. Save the application in the VbReloaded2008\Chap09 folder.

   b. Open the Code Editor window. Remove the Dim taxTable(5,3) As Double statement from the calcButton's Click event procedure. Modify the selection structure so that it passes the taxable wages and the appropriate array (either the singleTable or marriedTable array) to a function named CalculateFwt.

   c. Create a function named CalculateFwt. The function will need to accept the taxable wages and the array passed to it. Move the code that calculates the federal withholding tax from the calcButton's Click event procedure to the CalculateFwt function.

   d. Save the solution, then start the application. Use the application to display the tax for a married employee with taxable wages of $675.34. The application should display $63.25 as the tax. Now use the application to display the tax for a single employee with taxable wages of $600. The application should display $75.00 as the tax. End the application, then close the solution.

3. In this exercise, you code the Salary Code application that you viewed in the chapter.

   a. Open the Salary Code Solution (Salary Code Solution.sln) file, which is contained in the VbReloaded2008\Chap09\Salary Code Solution folder.

   b. Open the Code Editor window, then enter the code shown in Figure 9-10. Save the solution, then start and test the application. End the application, then close the solution.

4. In this exercise, you modify the Salary Code application you coded in Computer Exercise 3. The modified application will allow the user to enter the salary code by selecting it from a list box.

   a. Use Windows to make a copy of the Salary Code Solution folder. Rename the folder Salary Code Solution-ListBox.

   b. Open the Salary Code Solution (Salary Code Solution.sln) file contained in the VbReloaded2008\Chap09\Salary Code Solution-ListBox folder. Modify the application's interface so that it uses a list box to display the salary codes. Also make the appropriate modifications to the application's code.

   c. Save the solution, then start and test the application. End the application, then close the solution.

5. In this exercise, you code an application that displays the number of days in a month.

   a. Open the NumDays Solution (NumDays Solution.sln) file, which is contained in the VbReloaded2008\Chap09\NumDays Solution folder.

   b. Open the Display Days button's Click event procedure. Declare a 12-element, one-dimensional array named days. Use the number of days in each month to initialize the array. (Usc 28 for February.)

   c. Code the displayButton's Click event procedure so that it displays (in the daysLabel) the number of days in the month whose month number is entered in the monthTextBox. For example, if the monthTextBox contains the number 1, the procedure should display 31 in the daysLabel, because there are 31 days in January. The procedure should display an appropriate message in a message box when the user enters an invalid number in the monthTextBox.

   d. Save the solution, then start the application. Enter the number 20 in the monthTextBox, then click the Display Days button. An appropriate message should appear in a message box. Close the message box.

   e. Now test the application by entering numbers from 1 through 12 in the monthTextBox. Click the Display Days button after entering each number.

   f. End the application, then close the solution.

6. In this exercise, you code an application that displays the lowest value stored in an array.

   a. Open the Lowest Solution (Lowest Solution.sln) file, which is contained in the VbReloaded2008\Chap09\Lowest Solution folder.

   b. Locate the Display Lowest button's Click event procedure. The procedure declares and initializes a 20-element, one-dimensional Integer array named scores. Code the procedure so that it displays (in the lowestLabel) the lowest score stored in the array.

   c. Save the solution, then start the application. Click the Display Lowest button. The number 13, which is the lowest score in the array, should appear in the lowestLabel. End the application, then close the solution.

7. In this exercise, you code an application that updates each value stored in an array.

   a. Open the Update Prices Solution (Update Prices Solution.sln) file, which is contained in the VbReloaded2008\Chap09\Update Prices Solution folder.

   b. Open the Increase button's Click event procedure. Declare a one-dimensional Decimal array named prices. The array should contain 10 elements and be initialized using the following prices: 6.75, 12.50, 33.50, 10, 9.50, 25.50, 7.65, 8.35, 9.75, 3.50. The procedure should ask the user for a percentage amount by which each price should be increased. It then should increase each price by that amount and display the increased prices in the interface.

   c. Save the solution, then start the application. Click the Increase button. Increase each price by 5%. End the application, then close the solution.

8. In this exercise, you modify the application from Computer Exercise 7. The modified application allows the user to update a specific price.

   a. Use Windows to make a copy of the Update Prices Solution folder, which is contained in the VbReloaded2008\Chap09 folder. Rename the copy Modified Update Prices Solution.

   b. Open the Update Prices Solution (Update Prices Solution.sln) file contained in the VbReloaded2008\Chap09\Modified Update Prices Solution folder. Modify the Increase button's Click event procedure so that it also asks the user to enter a number from 1 through 10. If the user enters the number 1, the procedure should update the first price in the array. If the user enters the number 2, the procedure should update the second price in the array, and so on.

   c. Save the solution, then start the application. Click the Increase button. Increase the second price by 10%. Click the Increase button again. This time, increase the tenth price by 2%. (The second price in the list box should still reflect the 10% increase.) End the application, then close the solution.

9. In this exercise, you code an application that displays the number of students earning a specific score.

   a. Open the Scores Solution (Scores Solution.sln) file, which is contained in the VbReloaded2008\Chap09\Scores Solution folder.

   b. Open the Display button's Click event procedure. Declare a 20-element, one-dimensional Integer array named scores. Assign the following numbers to the array: 88, 72, 99, 20, 66, 95, 99, 100, 72, 88, 78, 45, 57, 89, 85, 78, 75, 88, 72, 88.

   c. Code the displayButton's Click event procedure so that it prompts the user to enter a score from 0 through 100. The procedure then should display (in a message box) the number of students who earned that score.

   d. Save the solution, then start the application. Use the application to answer the following questions: How many students earned a score of 72? How many students earned a score of 88? How many students earned a score of 20? How many students earned a score of 99? End the application, then close the solution.

10. In this exercise, you modify the application that you coded in Computer Exercise 9. The modified application allows the user to display the number of students earning a score within a specific range.

    a. Use Windows to make a copy of the Scores Solution folder, which is contained in the VbReloaded2008\Chap09 folder. Rename the copy Modified Scores Solution.

    b. Open the Scores Solution (Scores Solution.sln) file contained in the VbReloaded2008\Chap09\Modified Scores Solution folder. Modify the Display button's Click event procedure so that it prompts the user to enter a minimum score and a maximum score. The procedure then should display (in a message box) the number of students who earned a score within that range.

    c. Save the solution, then start the application. Use the application to answer the following questions: How many students earned a score from 70 through 79, inclusive? How many students earned a score from 65 through 85, inclusive? How many students earned a score from 0 through 50, inclusive? End the application, then close the solution.

11. In this exercise, you code an application that allows Professor Carver to display a grade based on the number of points he enters. The grading scale is shown in Figure 9-48.

Minimum points	Maximum points	Grade
0	299	F
300	349	D
350	399	C
400	449	B
450	No maximum	A

Figure 9-48

    a. Open the Carver Solution (Carver Solution.sln) file, which is contained in the VbReloaded2008\Chap09\Carver Solution folder.

    b. Store the minimum points in a five-element, one-dimensional Integer array named points. Store the grades in a five-element, one-dimensional String array named grades. The arrays should be parallel arrays.

    c. Code the Display Grade button's Click event procedure so that it declares both arrays. It also should search the points array for the number of points entered by the user, and then display the corresponding grade from the grades array.

    d. Save the solution, then start the application. Enter 455 in the Points text box, then click the Display Grade button. A grade of A appears in the interface. Enter 210 in the Points text box, then click the Display Grade button. A grade of F appears in the interface. End the application, then close the solution.

12. In this exercise, you modify the application that you coded in Computer Exercise 11. The modified application allows the user to change the grading scale when the application is started.

   a. Use Windows to make a copy of the Carver Solution folder, which is contained in the VbReloaded2008\Chap09 folder. Rename the copy Modified Carver Solution.

   b. Open the Carver Solution (Carver Solution.sln) file contained in the VbReloaded2008\Chap09\Modified Carver Solution folder. When the form is loaded into the computer's memory, the Load event procedure should use the InputBox function to prompt the user to enter the total number of possible points—in other words, the total number of points a student can earn in the course. Modify the application's code to perform this task.

   c. Modify the application's code so that it uses the grading scale shown in Figure 9-49. For example, if the user enters the number 500 in response to the InputBox function, the code should enter 450 (90% of 500) as the minimum number of points for an A. If the user enters the number 300, the code should enter 270 (90% of 300) as the minimum number of points for an A.

Minimum points	Grade
0	F
60% of the possible points	D
70% of the possible points	C
80% of the possible points	B
90% of the possible points	A

Figure 9-49

   d. Save the solution, then start the application. Enter 300 as the number of possible points, then enter 185 in the Points text box. Click the Display Grade button. A grade of D appears in the interface. End the application.

   e. Start the application again. Enter 500 as the number of possible points, then enter 363 in the Points text box. Click the Display Grade button. A grade of C appears in the interface. End the application, then close the solution.

13. In this exercise, you code an application that sums the values contained in a two-dimensional array.

   a. Open the Inventory Solution (Inventory Solution.sln) file, which is contained in the VbReloaded2008\Chap09\Inventory Solution folder. Code the Display Total button's Click event procedure so that it adds together the values stored in the inventory array. Display the sum in the totalLabel.

   b. Save the solution, then start the application. Click the Display Total button to display the sum of the array values. End the application, then close the solution.

14. In this exercise, you code an application that displays the highest score earned on the midterm exam and the highest score earned on the final exam.

   a. Open the Highest Solution (Highest Solution.sln) file, which is contained in the VbReloaded2008\Chap09\Highest Solution folder. Code the Display Highest button's Click event procedure so that it displays (in the appropriate label controls) the highest score earned on the midterm exam and the highest score earned on the final exam.

   b. Save the solution, then start the application. Click the Display Highest button to display the highest scores. End the application, then close the solution.

15. In this exercise, you learn about the ReDim statement.

   a. Research the Visual Basic ReDim statement. What is the purpose of the statement? What is the purpose of the Preserve keyword?

   b. Open the ReDim Solution (ReDim Solution.sln) file, which is contained in the VbReloaded2008\Chap09\ReDim Solution folder. Open the Code Editor window and view the displayButton's Click event procedure. Study the existing code, then modify the procedure so that it stores any number of sales amounts in the sales array.

   c. Save the solution, then start the application. Click the Display Sales button, then enter the following sales amounts: 700, 550, and 800. Click the Cancel button. The displayButton's Click event procedure should display each sales amount in a separate message box.

   d. Click the Display Sales button again, then enter the following sales amounts: 5, 9, 45, 67, 8, and 0. Click the Cancel button. The displayButton's Click event procedure should display each sales amount in a separate message box. End the application, then close the solution.

16. In this exercise, you learn about the Array.GetUpperBound method.

   a. Research the Visual Basic Array.GetUpperBound method. What is the purpose of the method?

   b. Open the Price List Solution (Price List Solution.sln) file, which is contained in the VbReloaded2008\Chap09\Price List Solution folder. Open the Code Editor window, then enter the code shown earlier in Figure 9-35. Save the solution, then start and test the application. End the application.

   c. Modify the code so that it uses the Array.GetUpperBound method rather than the number 5. Save the solution, then start and test the application. End the application, then close the solution.

17. In this exercise, you find and correct an error in an application. The process of finding and correcting errors is called debugging.

    a. Open the Debug Solution (Debug Solution.sln) file, which is contained in the VbReloaded2008\Chap09\Debug Solution folder.

    b. Open the Code Editor window. Review the existing code. Notice that the names array contains five rows and two columns. Column one contains five first names, and column two contains five last names. The displayButton's Click event procedure should display the first and last names in the firstLabel and lastLabel, respectively.

    c. Notice that a jagged line appears below some of the lines of code in the Code Editor window. Correct the code to remove the jagged lines.

    d. Save the solution, then start the application. Click the Display button. If an error occurs, click Debug on the menu bar, then click Stop Debugging. Correct the errors in the application's code. Save the solution, then start and test the application. When the application is working correctly, end the application, then close the solution.

CASE PROJECTS

JM SALES

JM Sales employs 10 salespeople. The sales made by the salespeople during the months of January, February, and March are shown in Figure 9-50. The sales manager wants an application that allows him to enter the current bonus rate. The application should display each salesperson's number (1 through 10), total sales amount, and total bonus amount. It also should display the total bonus paid to all salespeople. Be sure to use one or more arrays in the application. You can either create your own interface or create the one shown in Figure 9-51. (The text box in the figure has its BorderStyle property set to Fixed3D, its Font property set to Courier New 10 point, its MultiLine property set to True, its ReadOnly property set to True, and its ScrollBars property set to Vertical.) Name the solution, project, and form file JM Sales Solution, JM Sales Project, and Main Form.vb, respectively. Save the application in the VbReloaded2008\ Chap09 folder.

Salesperson	January	February	March
1	2400	3500	2000
2	1500	7000	1000
3	600	450	2100
4	790	240	500
5	1000	1000	1000
6	6300	7000	8000
7	1300	450	700
8	2700	5500	6000
9	4700	4800	4900
10	1200	1300	400

Figure 9-50: Sales figures

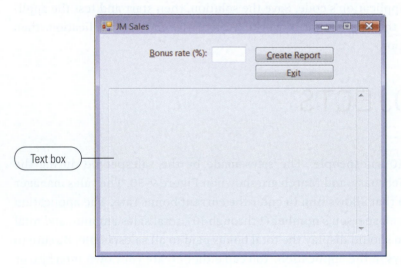

Figure 9-51: Sample interface for JM Sales

WATERGLEN HORSE FARMS

Each year, Sabrina Cantrell, the owner of Waterglen Horse Farms, enters four of her horses in five local horse races. She uses the table shown in Figure 9-52 to keep track of her horses' performances in each race. In the table, a 1 indicates that the horse won the race, a 2 indicates second place, and a 3 indicates third place. A 0 indicates that the horse did not finish in the top three places. Sabrina wants an application that displays a summary of each horse's individual performance, as well as the performances of all the horses. For example, using the table shown in Figure 9-52, horse 1 won one race, finished second in one race, finished third in one race, and didn't finish in the top three in two races. Overall, Sabrina's horses won 4 races, finished second in 3 races, finished third in 3 races, and didn't finish in the top three in 10 races. Be sure to use one or more arrays in the application. You can either create your own interface or create the one shown in Figure 9-53. Name the solution, project, and form file Waterglen Solution, Waterglen Project, and Main Form.vb, respectively. Save the application in the VbReloaded2008\ Chap09 folder.

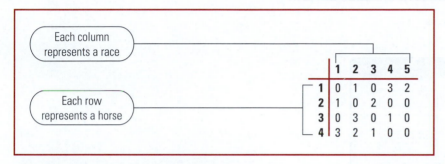

Figure 9-52: Table for keeping track of each horse race

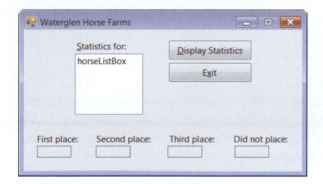

Figure 9-53: Sample interface for Waterglen Horse Farms

CONWAY ENTERPRISES

Conway Enterprises has both domestic and international sales operations. The company's sales manager wants an application that she can use to display the total domestic, total international, and total company sales made during a six-month period. The sales amounts are shown in Figure 9-54. Be sure to use one or more arrays in the application. You can either create your own interface or create the one shown in Figure 9-55. Name the solution, project, and form file Conway Solution, Conway Project, and Main Form.vb, respectively. Save the application in the VbReloaded2008\Chap09 folder.

Month	Domestic	International
1	100,000	150,000
2	90,000	120,000
3	75,000	210,000
4	88,000	50,000
5	125,000	220,000
6	63,000	80,000

Figure 9-54: Sales amounts

Figure 9-55: Sample interface for Conway Enterprises

TIC-TAC-TOE

Create an application that simulates the Tic-Tac-Toe game, which requires two players. Be sure to use one or more arrays in the application. Name the solution, project, and form file TicTacToe Solution, TicTacToe Project, and Main Form.vb, respectively. Save the application in the VbReloaded2008\Chap09 folder.

10

STRUCTURES AND SEQUENTIAL ACCESS FILES

After studying Chapter 10, you should be able to:

Create a structure

Declare and use a structure variable

Create an array of structure variables

Write information to a sequential access file

Align the text written to a sequential access file

Read information from a sequential access file

Determine whether a file exists

Delete a file while an application is running

Code the FormClosing event

Prevent a form from closing

STRUCTURES

In previous chapters, you used only the data types built into Visual Basic, such as the Integer and Decimal data types. You also can create your own data types in Visual Basic using the **Structure statement**. Data types created using the Structure statement are referred to as **user-defined data types** or **structures**. Figure 10-1 shows the syntax of the Structure statement and includes an example of using the statement to create a structure (user-defined data type) named Employee. The Structure statement begins with the Structure clause and ends with the End Structure clause. Between the clauses, you define the members included in the structure. The members can be variables, constants, or procedures. However, in most cases, the members will be variables; such variables are referred to as **member variables**. Each member variable's definition contains the keyword Public followed by the name of the variable, the keyword As, and the variable's *dataType*. The *dataType* identifies the type of data the member variable will store and can be any of the standard data types available in Visual Basic; it also can be another structure (user-defined data type). The Employee structure shown in Figure 10-1 contains four member variables: three String variables and one Decimal variable.

»HOW TO . . .

»TIP

Most programmers use the Class statement, rather than the Structure statement, to create data types that contain procedures. You learn about the Class statement in Chapter 11.

»TIP

The Structure statement merely defines the structure. In other words, it is a pattern from which variables can be created.

CREATE A STRUCTURE (USER-DEFINED DATA TYPE)

Syntax

Structure *structureName*

    Public *memberVariableName1* **As** *dataType*

    [**Public** *memberVariableNameN* **As** *dataType*]

End Structure

Example

```
Structure Employee
    Public number As String
    Public firstName As String
    Public lastName As String
    Public salary As Double
End Structure
```

Figure 10-1: How to create a structure (user-defined data type)

In most applications, you enter the Structure statement in the form's Declarations section in the Code Editor window. Recall that the form's Declarations section begins with the Public Class line and ends with the End Class line. After entering the Structure statement, you then can use the structure to declare a variable.

DECLARING A STRUCTURE VARIABLE

As you can with the standard data types built into Visual Basic, you can declare a variable using a structure (user-defined data type). Variables declared using a structure are often referred to as **structure variables**. Figure 10-2 shows the syntax for creating a structure variable. The figure also includes examples of declaring structure variables using the Employee structure from Figure 10-1.

»HOW TO . . .

DECLARE A STRUCTURE VARIABLE

Syntax

{**Dim** | **Private**} *structureVariableName* **As** *structureName*

Example 1

Dim manager As Employee
declares a procedure-level Employee structure variable named manager

Example 2

Private salaried As Employee
declares a module-level Employee structure variable named salaried

Figure 10-2: How to declare a structure variable

Similar to the way the Dim age As Integer instruction declares an Integer variable named age, the Dim manager As Employee instruction in Example 1 declares an Employee variable named manager. However, unlike the age variable, the manager variable contains four member variables. In code, you refer to the entire structure variable by its name—in this case, manager. You refer to a member variable by preceding its name with the name of the structure variable in which it is defined. You use the dot member access operator (a period) to separate the structure variable's name from the member variable's name. For instance, to refer to the member variables within the manager structure variable, you use manager.number, manager.firstName, manager.lastName, and manager.salary. The Private salaried As Employee instruction in Example 2 in Figure 10-2 declares a module-level Employee variable named salaried. The names of the member variables within the salaried variable are salaried.number, salaried.firstName, salaried.lastName, and salaried.salary.

The member variables contained in a structure variable can be used just like any other variables. You can assign values to them, use them in calculations, display their contents, and so on. Figure 10-3 shows various ways of using the member variables created by the statements shown in Figure 10-2.

»TIP

The dot member access operator indicates that number, firstName, lastName, and salary are members of the manager and salaried variables.

»HOW TO . . .

USE A MEMBER VARIABLE

<u>Example 1</u>

manager.lastName = "Lopenski"

assigns the string "Lopenski" to the manager.lastName member variable

<u>Example 2</u>

manager.salary = manager.salary * 1.05

multiplies the contents of the manager.salary member variable by 1.05, and then assigns the result to the member variable

<u>Example 3</u>

salaryLabel.Text = salaried.salary.ToString("C2")

formats the value contained in the salaried.salary member variable to Currency with two decimal places, and then displays the result in the salaryLabel

Figure 10-3: How to use a member variable

Programmers use structures to group related items into one unit. The advantages of doing this will become more apparent as you read through the next two sections.

PASSING A STRUCTURE VARIABLE TO A PROCEDURE

The sales manager at Willow Pools wants an application that determines the amount of water required to fill a rectangular pool. To perform this task, the application will need to calculate the volume of the pool. You calculate the volume by first multiplying the pool's length by its width, and then multiplying the result by the pool's depth. Figure 10-4 shows a sample run of the Willow Pools application, and Figure 10-5 shows one way of coding the application without using a structure. Notice that the calcButton's Click event procedure calls the CalcVolume function, passing it three variables *by value*. The CalcVolume function determines whether the three values passed to it are greater than zero. If they are, the function uses the values to calculate the volume of the pool; otherwise, it assigns the number 0 as the pool's volume. The function returns the volume as a Decimal number to the calcButton's Click event procedure, which assigns the value to the poolVolume variable.

Figure 10-4: Sample run of the Willow Pools application

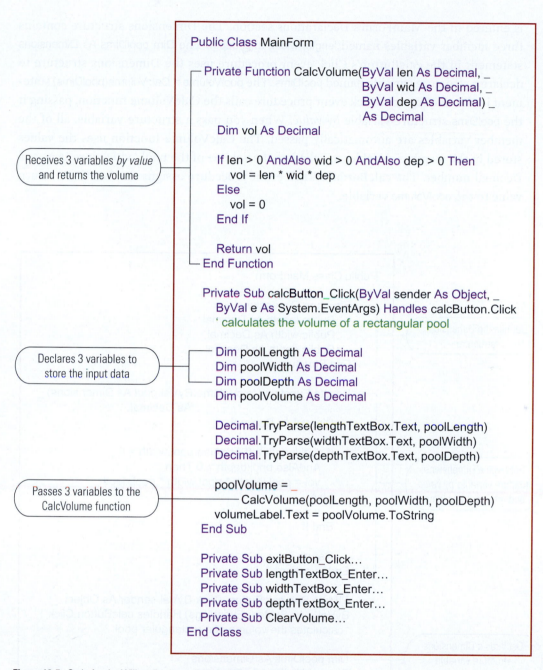

```
Public Class MainForm

    Private Function CalcVolume(ByVal len As Decimal, _
                               ByVal wid As Decimal, _
                               ByVal dep As Decimal) _
                               As Decimal
        Dim vol As Decimal

        If len > 0 AndAlso wid > 0 AndAlso dep > 0 Then
            vol = len * wid * dep
        Else
            vol = 0
        End If

        Return vol
    End Function

    Private Sub calcButton_Click(ByVal sender As Object, _
        ByVal e As System.EventArgs) Handles calcButton.Click
        ' calculates the volume of a rectangular pool

        Dim poolLength As Decimal
        Dim poolWidth As Decimal
        Dim poolDepth As Decimal
        Dim poolVolume As Decimal

        Decimal.TryParse(lengthTextBox.Text, poolLength)
        Decimal.TryParse(widthTextBox.Text, poolWidth)
        Decimal.TryParse(depthTextBox.Text, poolDepth)

        poolVolume = _
                CalcVolume(poolLength, poolWidth, poolDepth)
        volumeLabel.Text = poolVolume.ToString
    End Sub

    Private Sub exitButton_Click...
    Private Sub lengthTextBox_Enter...
    Private Sub widthTextBox_Enter...
    Private Sub depthTextBox_Enter...
    Private Sub ClearVolume...
End Class
```

Receives 3 variables *by value* and returns the volume

Declares 3 variables to store the input data

Passes 3 variables to the CalcVolume function

Figure 10-5: Code for the Willow Pools application (without a structure)

Figure 10-6 shows a more convenient way of writing the code for the Willow Pools application. In this version of the code, a structure named Dimensions is used to group together the input data. The Structure statement that defines the Dimensions structure is entered in the MainForm's Declarations section. The Dimensions structure contains three member variables named length, width, and depth. The Dim poolDims As Dimensions statement in the calcButton's Click event procedure uses the Dimensions structure to declare a structure variable named poolDims. The poolVolume = CalcVolume(poolDims) statement in the calcButton's Click event procedure calls the CalcVolume function, passing it the poolDims structure variable *by value*. When you pass a structure variable, all of the member variables are automatically passed. The CalcVolume function uses the values stored in the member variables to calculate the volume of the pool, which it returns as a Decimal number. The calcButton's Click event procedure assigns the function's return value to the poolVolume variable.

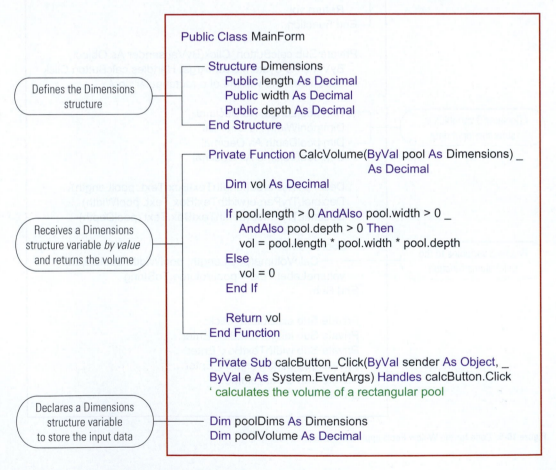

Defines the Dimensions structure

Receives a Dimensions structure variable *by value* and returns the volume

Declares a Dimensions structure variable to store the input data

```
Public Class MainForm

    Structure Dimensions
        Public length As Decimal
        Public width As Decimal
        Public depth As Decimal
    End Structure

    Private Function CalcVolume(ByVal pool As Dimensions) _
                                        As Decimal
        Dim vol As Decimal

        If pool.length > 0 AndAlso pool.width > 0 _
            AndAlso pool.depth > 0 Then
            vol = pool.length * pool.width * pool.depth
        Else
            vol = 0
        End If

        Return vol
    End Function

    Private Sub calcButton_Click(ByVal sender As Object, _
    ByVal e As System.EventArgs) Handles calcButton.Click
    ' calculates the volume of a rectangular pool

        Dim poolDims As Dimensions
        Dim poolVolume As Decimal
```

Figure 10-6: Code for the Willow Pools application (with a structure) (*continued on next page*)

```
            Decimal.TryParse(lengthTextBox.Text, poolDims.length)
            Decimal.TryParse(widthTextBox.Text, poolDims.width)
            Decimal.TryParse(depthTextBox.Text, poolDims.depth)

            poolVolume = CalcVolume(poolDims)
            volumeLabel.Text = poolVolume.ToString
        End Sub

        Private Sub exitButton_Click…
        Private Sub lengthTextBox_Enter…
        Private Sub widthTextBox_Enter…
        Private Sub depthTextBox_Enter…
        Private Sub ClearVolume…
    End Class
```

Passes the Dimensions structure variable to the CalcVolume function

Figure 10-6: Code for the Willow Pools application (with a structure) (*continued from previous page*)

Compare the calcButton's Click event procedure in Figure 10-6 with the same procedure shown earlier in Figure 10-5. Notice that the procedure in Figure 10-5 uses three scalar variables to store the input data, while the procedure in Figure 10-6 uses only one structure variable for this purpose. The procedure in Figure 10-5 also passes three scalar variables (rather than one structure variable) to the CalcVolume function, which uses three scalar variables (rather than one structure variable) to accept the data. Imagine if the input data consisted of 20 items rather than just three items! Passing a structure variable would be much easier than passing 20 individual scalar variables. As you will learn in the next section, another advantage of grouping related data into one unit is that the unit then can be stored in an array.

> **» TIP**
> Recall from Chapter 9 that a scalar variable (also called a simple variable) is one that is unrelated to any other variable in memory.

CREATING AN ARRAY OF STRUCTURE VARIABLES

In Chapter 9, you learned how to use two parallel one-dimensional arrays to store a price list for the Treasures gift shop. You also learned how to store the price list in a two-dimensional String array. Rather than using parallel one-dimensional arrays or a two-dimensional array, you also can use a one-dimensional array of structure variables. (Notice that there are many different ways of solving the same problem.) Figure 10-7 shows a sample run of the Price List application, and Figure 10-8 shows the application's code using an array of structure variables. Notice that the displayButton's Click event procedure declares a five-element one-dimensional array named gifts, using the Item structure defined in the MainForm's Declarations section as the array's data type.

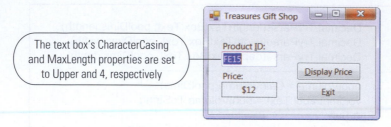

The text box's CharacterCasing and MaxLength properties are set to Upper and 4, respectively

Figure 10-7: Sample run of the Price List application

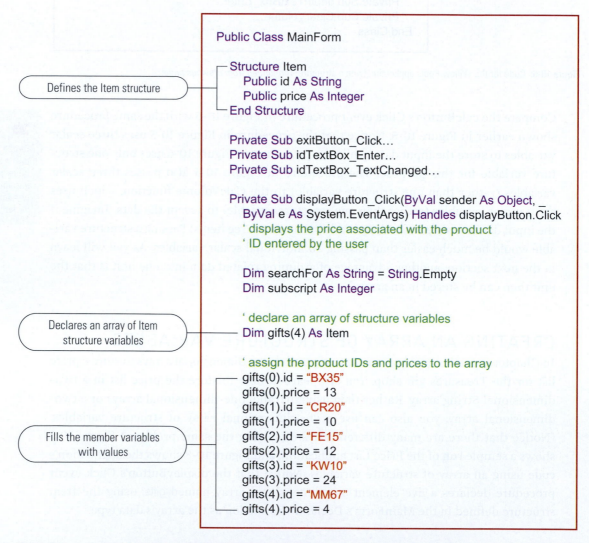

Defines the Item structure

Declares an array of Item structure variables

Fills the member variables with values

```
Public Class MainForm

    Structure Item
        Public id As String
        Public price As Integer
    End Structure

    Private Sub exitButton_Click…
    Private Sub idTextBox_Enter…
    Private Sub idTextBox_TextChanged…

    Private Sub displayButton_Click(ByVal sender As Object, _
        ByVal e As System.EventArgs) Handles displayButton.Click
        ' displays the price associated with the product
        ' ID entered by the user

        Dim searchFor As String = String.Empty
        Dim subscript As Integer

        ' declare an array of structure variables
        Dim gifts(4) As Item

        ' assign the product IDs and prices to the array
        gifts(0).id = "BX35"
        gifts(0).price = 13
        gifts(1).id = "CR20"
        gifts(1).price = 10
        gifts(2).id = "FE15"
        gifts(2).price = 12
        gifts(3).id = "KW10"
        gifts(3).price = 24
        gifts(4).id = "MM67"
        gifts(4).price = 4
```

Figure 10-8: Code for the Price List application using an array of structure variables (*continued on next page*)

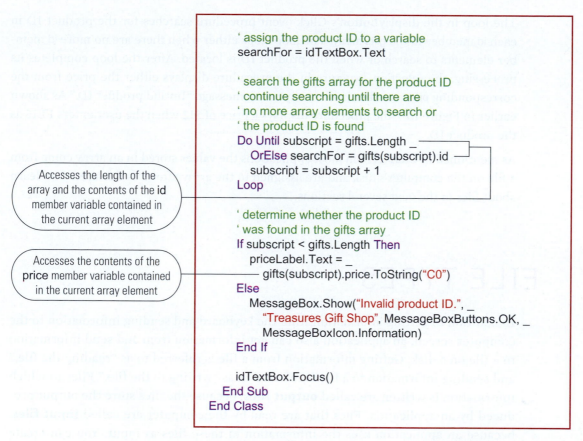

```
' assign the product ID to a variable
searchFor = idTextBox.Text

' search the gifts array for the product ID
' continue searching until there are
' no more array elements to search or
' the product ID is found
Do Until subscript = gifts.Length _
    OrElse searchFor = gifts(subscript).id
    subscript = subscript + 1
Loop

' determine whether the product ID
' was found in the gifts array
If subscript < gifts.Length Then
    priceLabel.Text = _
        gifts(subscript).price.ToString("C0")
Else
    MessageBox.Show("Invalid product ID.", _
        "Treasures Gift Shop", MessageBoxButtons.OK, _
        MessageBoxIcon.Information)
End If

idTextBox.Focus()
End Sub
End Class
```

Accesses the length of the array and the contents of the **id** member variable contained in the current array element

Accesses the contents of the **price** member variable contained in the current array element

Figure 10-8: Code for the Price List application using an array of structure variables (*continued from previous page*)

Each element in the gifts array is a structure variable that contains two member variables: a String variable named id and an Integer variable named price. After declaring the array, the procedure populates the array by assigning the appropriate IDs and prices to it. You refer to a member variable in an array element using the syntax *arrayName*(*subscript*).*memberVariableName*. For example, gifts(0).price refers to the price member contained in the first element in the gifts array. Likewise, gifts(4).id refers to the id member contained in the last element in the gifts array. Figure 10-9 illustrates this naming convention.

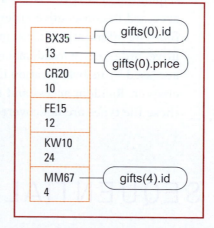

Figure 10-9: Names of some of the member variables in the gifts array

The loop in the displayButton's Click event procedure searches for the product ID in each id member in the gifts array. The loop stops either when there are no more id member elements to search or when the product ID is located. After the loop completes its processing, the selection structure in the procedure displays either the price from the corresponding price member in the array or the message "Invalid product ID." As shown earlier in Figure 10-7, the procedure displays a price of $12 when the user enters FE15 as the product ID.

As mentioned in Chapter 9, in most applications the values stored in an array come from a file on the computer's disk and are assigned to the array after it is declared. You learn about files in the next several sections.

FILE TYPES

In addition to getting information from the keyboard and sending information to the computer screen, an application also can get information from and send information to a file on a disk. Getting information from a file is referred to as "reading the file," and sending information to a file is referred to as "writing to the file." Files to which information is written are called **output files**, because the files store the output produced by an application. Files that are read by the computer are called **input files**, because an application uses the information in these files as input. You can create three different types of files in Visual Basic: sequential, random, and binary. The file type refers to how the information in the file is accessed. The information in a sequential access file is always accessed sequentially. In other words, it is always accessed in consecutive order from the beginning of the file through the end of the file. The information stored in a random access file can be accessed either in consecutive order or in random order. The information in a binary access file can be accessed by its byte location in the file. You learn about sequential access files in this chapter. Random access and binary access files are used less often in programs, so these file types are not covered in this book.

SEQUENTIAL ACCESS FILES

A **sequential access file** is often referred to as a **text file**, because it is composed of lines of text. The text might represent an employee list, as shown in Example 1 in Figure 10-10. Or, it might be a memo or a report, as shown in Examples 2 and 3 in the figure.

Example 1—employee list
Bonnel, Jacob
Carlisle, Donald
Eberg, Jack
Hou, Chang

Example 2—memo
To all employees: Effective January 1, 2010, the cost of dependent coverage will increase from $35 to $38.50 per month.

Jefferson Williams
Insurance Manager

Example 3—report
ABC Industries Sales Report

State	Sales
California	15000
Montana	10000
Wyoming	7000
Total sales:	$32000

Figure 10-10: Examples of text stored in a sequential access file

Sequential access files are similar to cassette tapes in that each line in the file, like each song on a cassette tape, is both stored and retrieved in consecutive order (sequentially). In other words, before you can record (store) the fourth song on a cassette tape, you first must record songs one through three. Likewise, before you can write (store) the fourth line in a sequential access file, you first must write lines one through three. The same is true for retrieving a song from a cassette tape and a line of text from a sequential access file. To listen to the fourth song on a cassette tape, you must play (or fast-forward through) the first three songs. Likewise, to read the fourth line in a sequential access file, you first must read the three lines that precede it.

WRITING TO A SEQUENTIAL ACCESS FILE

You can use the **WriteAllText method** to write information to a sequential access file. Figure 10-11 shows the method's syntax and includes examples of using the method. The "My" in the syntax refers to Visual Basic's **My feature**—a feature that exposes a set of commonly used objects to the programmer. One of the objects exposed by the My feature is the My.Computer object. You can use the My.Computer object to access other objects that allow you to manipulate files, such as the **FileSystem object**. The WriteAllText method is one of the methods provided by the FileSystem object. The *file* argument in the method's syntax is a string that contains the name of the sequential access file to which you want to write information. The *file* argument can contain an optional folder path. If the folder path is not specified, the computer looks for the file in the current project's bin\Debug folder. If the current project is stored in the VbReloaded2008\Chap10\Payroll Solution\Payroll Project folder, the computer will look for the file in the VbReloaded2008\Chap10\Payroll Solution\Payroll Project\bin\Debug folder. If the file whose name is specified in the *file* argument does not exist, the computer creates the file before writing the information to it. The information to write is specified in the *text* argument. Like the *file* argument, the *text* argument must be a string. The *append* argument in the syntax is a Boolean value, either True or False. If *append* is True, the information contained in the *text* argument is added to the end of any existing information in the file. If *append* is False, the existing information in the file is erased before the information in the *text* argument is written to the file.

»HOW TO . . .

WRITE TO A SEQUENTIAL ACCESS FILE

Syntax

My.Computer.FileSystem.WriteAllText(file, text, append)

Example 1

My.Computer.FileSystem.WriteAllText("msg.txt", "Hi", False)

Result

Hi|

Example 2

My.Computer.FileSystem.WriteAllText("msg.txt", _
    "Hi" & ControlChars.NewLine, False)

Result

Hi
|

Example 3

Const File As String = "top.txt"
Const Line As String = "The top salesperson is "
Dim name As String = nameTextBox.Text

Figure 10-11: How to write to a sequential access file (*continued on next page*)

```
My.Computer.FileSystem.WriteAllText(File, Line, False)
My.Computer.FileSystem.WriteAllText(File, name & ".", True)
My.Computer.FileSystem.WriteAllText(File, _
    ControlChars.NewLine & ControlChars.NewLine, True)
My.Computer.FileSystem.WriteAllText(File, "ABC Sales", True)
```

Result (when the user enters Carolyn in the nameTextBox)

The top salesperson is Carolyn.

ABC Sales|

Example 4

```
Const File As String = "F:\VbReloaded2008\Chap10\report.txt"
Dim price As Double = 5.6
My.Computer.FileSystem.WriteAllText(File, _
    "Total price: ", False)
My.Computer.FileSystem.WriteAllText(File, _
    price.ToString("C2") & ControlChars.NewLine, True)
```

Result

Total price: $5.60
|

Example 5

```
Dim file As String = fileTextBox.Text
My.Computer.FileSystem.WriteAllText(file, _
    Strings.Space(10) & "A" & Strings.Space(5) & "B", False)
```

Result

    A   B|

Figure 10-11: How to write to a sequential access file (*continued from previous page*)

›› TIP

Although it is not a requirement, the "txt" (short for "text") filename extension typically is used when naming sequential access files. This is because sequential access files are text files.

The My.Computer.FileSystem.WriteAllText("msg.txt", "Hi", False) statement in Example 1 tells the computer to write the string "Hi" to a file named msg.txt. If the msg.txt file does not exist, the computer creates it before writing the string to it. However, if the msg.txt file exists, the *append* argument's False value tells the computer to erase the file's contents before writing the string to the file. The computer uses a file pointer to keep track of the next character to either write to or read from a file. After processing the statement in Example 1, the computer positions the file pointer immediately after the last letter in the string "Hi", as indicated by the | symbol in the example. To position the file pointer on the next line in the file, you concatenate the ControlChars.NewLine constant with the *text* argument, as shown in Example 2. The first WriteAllText method in Example 3 tells the computer to write the string "The top salesperson is " to the top.txt file. After processing the statement, the computer positions the file pointer after the last character in the string (in this case, after the space character). The second WriteAllText method tells the computer to concatenate the contents of the name variable with a period, and then write the result to the top.txt file. The *append* argument's True value tells the computer to append (add) the concatenated string to the file. In this case, the concatenated string will be written on the same line as the previous string, immediately after the last space character in the string. The third WriteAllText method in Example 3 writes two new line characters to the file, which positions the file pointer two lines below the previously written text in the file. The last WriteAllText method in Example 3 writes the string "ABC Sales" to the file. After the statement is processed, the file pointer is located after the last character in the string, as indicated in the example. The WriteAllText methods in Example 4 write the string "Total price: " and the contents of the price variable (formatted with a dollar sign and two decimal places) on the same line in the file. The file pointer is then positioned at the beginning of the next line in the file. Example 5 shows how you can use the **Strings.Space method** to write a specific number of spaces to a file. The method's syntax is **Strings.Space(***number***)**, where *number* represents the number of spaces to write. The WriteAllText method in Example 5 writes 10 spaces, the letter "A", 5 spaces, and the letter "B" to the file. It then positions the file pointer immediately after the letter B in the file.

ALIGNING COLUMNS OF INFORMATION IN A SEQUENTIAL ACCESS FILE

In Chapter 7, you learned how to use the PadLeft and PadRight methods to pad a string with a character until the string is a specified length. Recall that the syntax of the PadLeft method is *string*.**PadLeft(***length*[, *character*]**)**, and the syntax of the PadRight method is *string*.**PadRight(***length*[, *character*]**)**. In each syntax, *length* is an integer that represents the desired length of the *string*, and *character* (which is optional) is the character that each method uses to pad the *string* until it reaches the desired length. If the *character* argument is omitted, the default *character* is the space character. Figure 10-12 shows examples of using the PadLeft and PadRight methods to align columns of information written to a sequential access file. Example 1 aligns a column of numbers by the decimal point. Notice that you first format each number in the column to ensure that each has the same number of digits to the right of the decimal point. You then use the PadLeft method to insert spaces at the beginning of the number; this right-aligns the number within the column. Because each number has the same number of digits to the right of the decimal point, aligning each number on the right will align each by its decimal point. Example 2 shows how you can align the second column of information when the first column contains strings with varying lengths. First, you use either the PadRight or PadLeft method to ensure that each string in the first column contains the same number of characters. You then concatenate the padded string to the information in the second column before writing the concatenated string to the file. The code in Example 2, for instance, uses the PadRight method to ensure that each name in the first column contains exactly 15 characters. It then concatenates the 15 characters with the age stored in the age variable, and then writes the concatenated string to the file. Because each name has 15 characters, each age will automatically appear beginning in character position 16 in the file.

»HOW TO . . .

ALIGN COLUMNS OF INFORMATION IN A SEQUENTIAL ACCESS FILE

Example 1

```
Dim formatPrice As String = String.Empty
For price As Double = 1 To 3 Step 0.5
    formatPrice = price.ToString("N2")
    My.Computer.FileSystem.WriteAllText("prices.txt", _
        formatPrice.PadLeft(4), True)
    My.Computer.FileSystem.WriteAllText("prices.txt", _
        ControlChars.NewLine, True)
Next price
```

Result

```
1.00
1.50
2.00
2.50
3.00
```

Example 2

```
Dim heading As String = "Name" & Strings.Space(11) & "Age"
Dim name As String = String.Empty
Dim age As String = String.Empty
My.Computer.FileSystem.WriteAllText("info.txt", _
    heading & ControlChars.NewLine, True)
name = InputBox("Enter name:", "Name")
```

Figure 10-12: How to align columns of information in a sequential access file (*continued on next page*)

```
Do While name <> String.Empty
    age = InputBox("Enter age:", "Age")
    My.Computer.FileSystem.WriteAllText("info.txt", _
        name.PadRight(15) & age _
        & ControlChars.NewLine, True)
    name = InputBox("Enter name:", "Name")
Loop
```

Result (when the user enters the following names and ages: Janice, 23, Sue, 67)

Name	Age
Janice	23
Sue	67

Figure 10-12: How to align columns of information in a sequential access file (*continued from previous page*)

READING FROM A SEQUENTIAL ACCESS FILE

You can use the FileObject's **ReadAllText method** to read the text contained in a sequential access file. Figure 10-13 shows the method's syntax and includes examples of using the method. The *file* argument in the syntax is a string that contains the name of the sequential access file. The *file* argument can contain an optional folder path. If the folder path is not specified, the computer looks for the file in the current project's bin\Debug folder. If the file does not exist, an error occurs and your application will end abruptly. You will learn one way of handling this situation in the next section.

» HOW TO . . .

READ FROM A SEQUENTIAL ACCESS FILE

Syntax

My.Computer.FileSystem.ReadAllText(*file*)

Example 1

```
Dim contents As String
contents = My.Computer.FileSystem.ReadAllText("prices.txt")
```
reads the text from the prices.txt file and assigns the text to the contents variable

Figure 10-13: How to read from a sequential access file (*continued on next page*)

Example 2

```
Const Path As String = "F:\VbReloaded2008\Chap10\"
reportTextBox.Text = _
     My.Computer.FileSystem.ReadAllText(Path & "info.txt")
```

reads the text from the info.txt file and displays the text in the reportTextBox

Figure 10-13: How to read from a sequential access file (*continued from previous page*)

The assignment statement in Example 1 reads the text contained in the prices.txt file and assigns the text to a String variable named contents. Because the *file* argument does not specify a folder path, the computer will look for the prices.txt file in the current project's bin\Debug folder. The assignment statement in Example 2 reads the text contained in the info.txt file and assigns the text to the reportTextBox's Text property. In this case, the computer will look for the info.txt file in the F:\VbReloaded2008\Chap10 folder.

DETERMINING WHETHER A FILE EXISTS

As mentioned earlier, an error occurs when the computer attempts to read a sequential access file that does not exist. To prevent the error from occurring, you should determine whether a file exists before you attempt to read it. The FileSystem object provides the **FileExists method** for determining whether a file exists. Figure 10-14 shows the method's syntax and includes examples of using the method. The *file* argument in the syntax represents the file's name. If you do not include a folder path in the *file* argument, the computer searches for the file in the current project's bin\Debug folder. The FileExists method returns the Boolean value True when the file exists; otherwise, it returns the Boolean value False.

»HOW TO . . .

DETERMINE WHETHER A FILE EXISTS

Syntax

My.Computer.FileSystem.FileExists(*file*)

Example 1

```
If My.Computer.FileSystem.FileExists("prices.txt") Then
    pricesLabel.Text = _
         My.Computer.FileSystem.ReadAllText("prices.txt")
```

Figure 10-14: How to determine whether a file exists (*continued on next page*)

```
    Else
        MessageBox.Show("File does not exist", "Prices", _
            MessageBoxButtons.OK, MessageBoxIcon.Information)
    End If
```

reads the prices.txt file if the file exists; otherwise, displays the "File does not exist" message in a message box

Example 2

```
Dim answer As DialogResult
If My.Computer.FileSystem.FileExists("info.txt") Then
    answer = MessageBox.Show("Erase the file?", _
        "Information", MessageBoxButtons.YesNo, _
        MessageBoxIcon.Exclamation, _
        MessageBoxDefaultButton.Button2)
    If answer = Windows.Forms.DialogResult.Yes Then
        My.Computer.FileSystem.WriteAllText("info.txt", _
        String.Empty, False)
    End If
End If
```

if the info.txt file exists, displays the "Erase the file?" message in a message box; the file is erased when the user clicks the Yes button in the message box

Figure 10-14: How to determine whether a file exists (*continued from previous page*)

The selection structure in Example 1 determines whether the prices.txt file exists. If the file exists, the assignment statement assigns the contents of the file to the pricesLabel. If the file does not exist, an appropriate message is displayed in a message box. The first selection structure in Example 2 determines whether the info.txt file exists. If the file exists, the message "Erase the file?" is displayed in a message box along with Yes and No buttons. If the user clicks the Yes button in the message box, the WriteAllText method erases the contents of the file by writing the empty string to it.

DELETING A FILE WHILE AN APPLICATION IS RUNNING

At times, you may need to delete a file while an application is running. You do this using the FileSystem object's **DeleteFile method**. Figure 10-15 shows the method's syntax and includes an example of using the method. The *file* argument in the syntax is the name of the file you are deleting.

DELETE A FILE WHILE AN APPLICATION IS RUNNING

Syntax

My.Computer.FileSystem.DeleteFile(*file*)

Example

My.Computer.FileSystem.DeleteFile("prices.txt")
deletes the prices.txt file

Figure 10-15: How to delete a file while an application is running

Before viewing a complete application that uses a sequential access file, you learn about a form's FormClosing event. You often will enter code related to files in the FormClosing event procedure.

THE FORMCLOSING EVENT

A form's **FormClosing event** occurs when a form is about to be closed. In most cases, this happens when the computer processes the Me.Close() statement in the form's code. However, it also occurs when the user clicks the Close button on the form's title bar. Figure 10-16 shows examples of code you might enter in the FormClosing event procedure. Example 1 writes the contents of the dateLabel to the date.txt file. Example 2 displays the "Do you want to exit?" message in a message box, along with Yes and No buttons. If the user clicks the No button in the message box, it indicates that she does not want to exit the application. In that case, the FormClosing event procedure should stop the computer from closing the MainForm. You prevent the computer from closing a form by setting the **Cancel property** of the FormClosing procedure's e parameter to True.

USE THE FORMCLOSING EVENT PROCEDURE

Example 1—writes information to a sequential access file

```
Private Sub MainForm_FormClosing(ByVal sender As Object, _
    ByVal e As System.Windows.Forms.FormClosingEventArgs) _
    Handles Me.FormClosing
    My.Computer.FileSystem.WriteAllText("date.txt", _
        dateLabel.Text, True)
End Sub
```

Figure 10-16: How to use the FormClosing event procedure (*continued on next page*)

Example 2—verifies that the user wants to exit the application

```
Private Sub MainForm_FormClosing(ByVal sender As Object, _
    ByVal e As System.Windows.Forms.FormClosingEventArgs) _
    Handles Me.FormClosing
    Dim button As DialogResult
    button = MessageBox.Show("Do you want to exit?", "Payroll", _
        MessageBoxButtons.YesNo, _
        MessageBoxIcon.Exclamation, _
        MessageBoxDefaultButton.Button2)
    If button = Windows.Forms.DialogResult.No Then
        ' stop the form from closing
        e.Cancel = True
    End If
End Sub
```

Figure 10-16: How to use the FormClosing event procedure (*continued from previous page*)

Next, you view an application that demonstrates what you have learned about sequential access files and the FormClosing event procedure.

THE FRIENDS APPLICATION

Figure 10-17 shows a sample run of the Friends application, which allows you to both add names to and remove names from a list box. When you exit the application, it saves the contents of the list box in a sequential access file. Figure 10-18 shows the application's code.

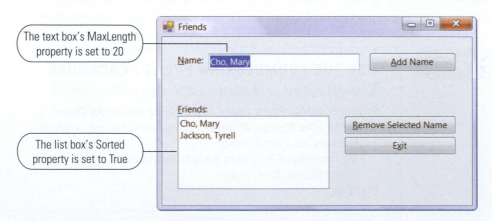

The text box's MaxLength property is set to 20

The list box's Sorted property is set to True

Figure 10-17: Sample run of the Friends application

```
Public Class MainForm

    Private Sub exitButton_Click...
    Private Sub nameTextBox_Enter...

    Private Sub addButton_Click(ByVal sender As Object, _
        ByVal e As System.EventArgs) Handles addButton.Click
        ' adds a name to the list box

        Dim name As String = nameTextBox.Text.Trim
        If name <> String.Empty Then
            friendListBox.Items.Add(name)
        End If
        nameTextBox.Focus()
    End Sub

    Private Sub removeButton_Click(ByVal sender As Object, _
        ByVal e As System.EventArgs) Handles removeButton.Click
        ' removes a name from the list box

        If friendListBox.SelectedIndex > -1 Then
            friendListBox.Items.RemoveAt(friendListBox.SelectedIndex)
        End If
    End Sub

    Private Sub MainForm_FormClosing(ByVal sender As Object, _
        ByVal e As System.Windows.Forms.FormClosingEventArgs) _
        Handles Me.FormClosing
        ' writes the contents of the list box to a sequential access file

        If My.Computer.FileSystem.FileExists("friends.txt") Then
            My.Computer.FileSystem.DeleteFile("friends.txt")
        End If

        For Each item As String In friendListBox.Items
            My.Computer.FileSystem.WriteAllText("friends.txt", _
                item.PadRight(20) & ControlChars.NewLine, True)
        Next item
    End Sub

    Private Sub MainForm_Load(ByVal sender As Object, _
        ByVal e As System.EventArgs) Handles Me.Load
        ' reads names from a sequential access file and displays
        ' the names in a list box
```

Figure 10-18: Code for the Friends application (*continued on next page*)

```
        Dim fileContents As String = String.Empty
        Dim name As String = String.Empty
        Dim numChars As Integer
        Dim startIndex As Integer

        ' clear the contents of the list box
        friendListBox.Items.Clear()

        If My.Computer.FileSystem.FileExists("friends.txt") Then
            ' if the file exists, assign its contents to a variable
            fileContents = My.Computer.FileSystem.ReadAllText("friends.txt")
            ' determine the length of the string contained in the variable
            numChars = fileContents.Length
            ' parse the entire string
            Do While startIndex < numChars
                ' the name begins with the character located in
                ' the startIndex position; its length is 20 characters
                name = fileContents.Substring(startIndex, 20)
                friendListBox.Items.Add(name)
                ' start the next search immediately after the
                ' newline character
                startIndex = startIndex + 20 + ControlChars.NewLine.Length
            Loop
        End If
    End Sub
End Class
```

»TIP
You learned about a string's Length property and its Trim and Substring methods in Chapter 7.

Figure 10-18: Code for the Friends application (*continued from previous page*)

When the user clicks the Add Name button in the interface, the addButton's Click event procedure assigns the contents of the nameTextBox, excluding any leading and trailing spaces, to the name variable. The procedure then verifies that the name variable contains a value; if it does, the procedure adds the value to the friendListBox. When the user clicks the Remove Selected Name button, the removeButton's Click event procedure verifies that an item is selected in the list box. As you learned in Chapter 6, a list box's SelectedIndex property contains the number -1 when no item is selected. If an item is selected, the procedure uses the RemoveAt method to remove the selected item from the list. The RemoveAt method's syntax is *object*.**Items.RemoveAt**(*index*), where *object* is the list box's name and *index* is the item's index. When the user clicks the Exit button in the interface, the computer processes the Me.Close() statement, which triggers the MainForm's FormClosing event. (The FormClosing event also is triggered when the user clicks the Close button on the MainForm's title bar.) The FormClosing event procedure determines whether the friends.txt file exists in the project's bin\Debug folder. If the file exists, the FileObject's DeleteFile method deletes the file. The procedure then uses the For Each...Next statement and the WriteAllText method to write the contents of the list box, one name at a time, to the friends.txt file. The item.PadRight(20) portion of the WriteAllText method pads each name on the right with spaces so that each contains exactly 20 characters. The & ControlChars.NewLine portion appends the newline character to the end of each name before the name is written to the file. Appending the newline character to the end of the name ensures that each name appears on a separate line in the file, as shown in Figure 10-19. The first name is highlighted in the figure to show the spaces and newline character appended to the end of the name. Although not obvious in the figure (or file), the newline character is composed of two characters: a carriage return and a line feed.

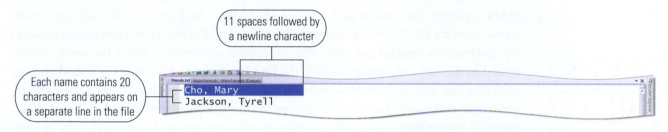

Figure 10-19: Contents of the friends.txt file

Each time the application is started, the computer processes the MainForm's Load event procedure (shown in Figure 10-18). The procedure begins by declaring four variables. It then uses the **Clear method**, whose syntax is *object*.**Items.Clear()**, to clear the contents of the friendListBox. Next, the selection structure determines whether the friends.txt file exists. If the file exists, the procedure reads the contents of the file and assigns the contents to a String variable named fileContents. At this point, the variable contains a string composed of letters, spaces, and newline characters, as illustrated in Figure 10-20. The figure also shows the index of each character in the string. Notice that the newline character, which is composed of a carriage return (CR) and a line feed (LF), takes up two index positions.

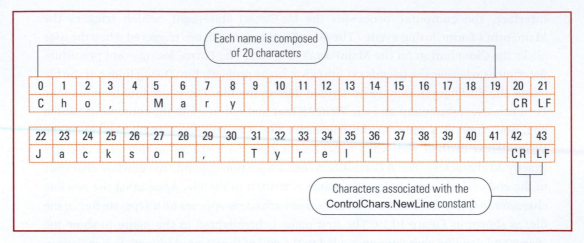

Figure 10-20: Index of each character stored in the fileContents variable

The names contained in the fileContents variable should be added to the friendListBox. To accomplish this task, the Load event procedure must **parse** (or separate) the variable's contents into names and newline characters. As Figure 10-20 indicates, each name contains 20 characters, and each is followed by the two characters that represent the ControlChars.NewLine constant. The procedure will need to parse the entire string stored in the variable, beginning with the first character (whose index is 0) and ending with the last character (whose index is 43). First, the numChars = fileContents.Length statement assigns the length of the string (44) to the numChars variable. The Do While startIndex < numChars clause tells the computer to process the loop instructions as long as the startIndex variable contains a value that is less than the value stored in the numChars variable. The startIndex variable, whose initial value is 0, keeps track of the position of the first character in each name. The first instruction in the loop, name = fileContents.Substring(startIndex, 20), assigns to the name variable the first 20 characters in the string, beginning with the character whose index is 0. The first 20 characters have indexes of 0 through 19 and represent the first name in the string. The next instruction in the loop adds the name to the friendListBox. The last instruction in the loop, startIndex = startIndex + 20 + ControlChars.NewLine.Length, updates the index stored in the startIndex variable. The next name will begin after the current name and its newline character, so you update the index by adding two values to it: the number 20 (which represents the length of the name) and the length of the newline character. Although you could use the number 2 to represent the newline character's length, using ControlChars.NewLine.Length makes the code more meaningful. You have completed the concepts section of Chapter 10.

PROGRAMMING TUTORIAL

MODIFIED CONCENTRATION GAME APPLICATION

In this tutorial, you modify the Concentration Game application from Chapter 8's Programming Tutorial. The modified application will use the words contained in one of four different sequential access files, which will be chosen randomly when the application is started. Three of the files are contained in the VbReloaded2008\Chap10\Concentration Game Solution\Concentration Game Project\bin\Debug folder and are named Words1.txt, Words2.txt, and Words3.txt. Figures 10-21 through 10-23 show the contents of each file. (To open a file in the IDE, click File on the menu bar and then click Open File.) You will create the Words4.txt file in this tutorial.

Figure 10-21: Contents of the Words1.txt file

Figure 10-22: Contents of the Words2.txt file

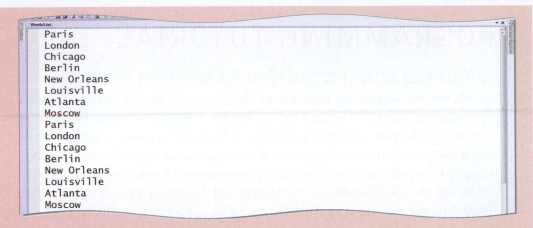

Figure 10-23: Contents of the Words3.txt file

CREATING THE WORDS4.TXT FILE

In this first set of steps, you will create the Words4.txt file shown in Figure 10-24.

Figure 10-24: Contents of the Words4.txt file

To create the Words4.txt file:

1. Start Visual Studio. If necessary, close the Start Page window. Open the **Concentration Game Solution** (**Concentration Game Solution.sln**) file, which is contained in the VbReloaded2008\Chap10\Concentration Game Solution folder.

2. Rather than using the WriteAllText method to create a text file, you also can use the New File option on the File menu. Click **File** on the menu bar, then click **New File** to open the New File dialog box. If necessary, click **General** in the Categories list and click **Text File** in the Templates list. See Figure 10-25.

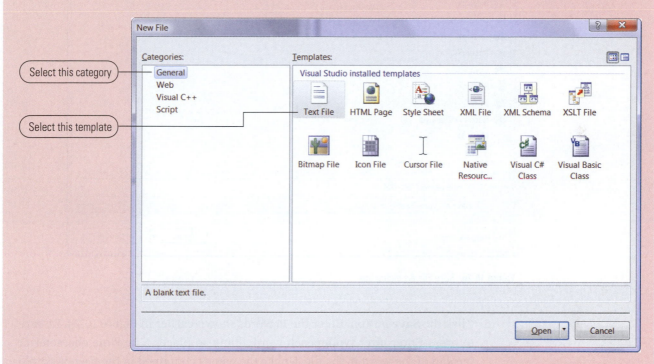

Figure 10-25: New File dialog box

3. Click the **Open** button. The TextFile1.txt window opens in the IDE.

4. Click **File**, then click **Save TextFile1.txt As** to open the Save File As dialog box. If necessary, click the **Browse Folders** button. Open the Concentration Game Solution\Concentration Game Project\bin\Debug folder. Type **Words4** in the File name box. See Figure 10-26. (If you are using Windows XP, the instructions you use to save the file, as well as your Save File As dialog box, may be different.)

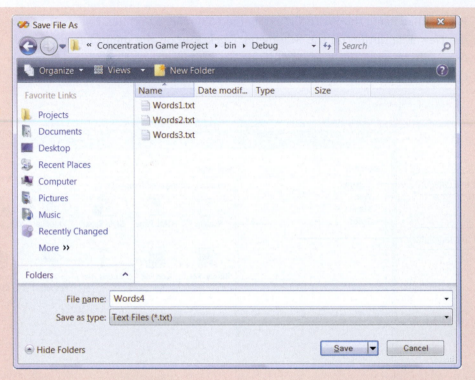

Figure 10-26: Save File As dialog box

5. Click the **Save** button. Enter the 16 words shown earlier in Figure 10-24. Be sure to press Enter after typing each word; doing so places a newline character at the end of the word in the file. Unlike the names contained in the friends.txt file (see Figures 10-19 and 10-20), which each contain 20 characters, the words in the Words4.txt file are of varying lengths. The same is true for the words contained in the Words1.txt, Words2.txt, and Words3.txt files.

6. Save the Words4.txt file, then close the Words4.txt window.

MODIFYING THE CONCENTRATION GAME APPLICATION

Figure 10-27 shows the code entered in the MainForm's Load event procedure in Chapter 8. (The complete code is shown in Figure 8-31 in Chapter 8.) You will need to modify only the code entered in this procedure.

```
Private Sub MainForm_Load(ByVal sender As Object, _
    ByVal e As System.EventArgs) Handles Me.Load
    ' fills the list box with 8 pairs of matching words,
    ' then calls a procedure to shuffle the words

    wordListBox.Items.Add("Refrigerator")
    wordListBox.Items.Add("Range")
    wordListBox.Items.Add("Television")
    wordListBox.Items.Add("Computer")
    wordListBox.Items.Add("Washer/Dryer")
    wordListBox.Items.Add("Dishwasher")
    wordListBox.Items.Add("Car")
    wordListBox.Items.Add("Trip")
    wordListBox.Items.Add("Refrigerator")
    wordListBox.Items.Add("Range")
    wordListBox.Items.Add("Television")
    wordListBox.Items.Add("Computer")
    wordListBox.Items.Add("Washer/Dryer")
    wordListBox.Items.Add("Dishwasher")
    wordListBox.Items.Add("Car")
    wordListBox.Items.Add("Trip")

    Call ShuffleWords()
End Sub
```

Figure 10-27: MainForm's Load event procedure from Chapter 8

First you will modify the procedure so that it uses the Words4.txt file to fill the list box with data.

To begin modifying the Load event procedure:

1. Open the Code Editor window, then locate the MainForm's Load event procedure. The procedure will use a String variable to store the name of one of the four text files. For now, you will initialize the variable to "Words4.txt". Click the **blank line above the first Add method**, then press **Enter** to insert another blank line. Type **dim file as string = "Words4.txt"** and press **Enter**.

2. When the procedure reads the Words4.txt file, it will store the file's contents in a String variable named fileContents. Type **dim fileContents as string = string.empty** and press **Enter**.

3. The procedure will need to separate (parse) the string contained in the fileContents variable into words and newline characters. While parsing the string, the procedure will use three variables named word, newLineIndex, and startPos. The word variable will store each word, one at a time. The newLineIndex variable will keep track of each newline character's index in the string. Recall that each newline character marks the end of a word. The startPos variable will keep track of where each word begins in the string. Type **dim word as string = string.empty** and press **Enter**. Type **dim newLineIndex as integer** and press **Enter**, then type **dim startPos as integer** and press **Enter** twice.

4. Before opening the text file, the procedure should test whether the file exists. Type **if my.computer.FileSystem.FileExists(file) then** and press **Enter**.

5. If the file exists, the selection structure's true path should open the file and assign its contents to the fileContents variable. Type **fileContents = _** and press **Enter**. Press **Tab**, then type **my.computer.FileSystem.ReadAllText(file)** and press **Enter**.

6. The next instruction in the true path should search the fileContents variable for the newline character, beginning with the first character in the variable. You can perform the search using the IndexOf method from Chapter 7. The method's syntax is *string*.**IndexOf**(*subString*[**,** *startIndex*]). Recall that *subString* is the sequence of characters for which you are searching in the *string*, and the optional *startIndex* specifies the starting position for the search. If *startIndex* is omitted, the search begins with the first character in the string. The IndexOf method returns the number –1 when the *subString* cannot be located in the *string*. Otherwise, it returns the index of the starting position of the *subString* within the *string*. In this case, *substring* is the ControlChars.NewLine constant, and *string* is the fileContents variable. The search should begin with the first character in the variable, so you can either use the number 0 as the *startIndex* or simply omit the *startIndex*. You will assign the method's return value to the newLineIndex variable, because the value indicates the location (index) of the first newline character in the string. Type **newLineIndex = fileContents.IndexOf(ControlChars.NewLine)** and press **Enter**.

7. The next instruction in the true path is a loop that repeats its instructions until the newLineIndex variable contains the number –1, which indicates that the IndexOf method did not locate a ControlChars.NewLine constant. Type **do until newLineIndex = –1** and press **Enter**.

8. Save the solution. Figure 10-28 shows the code entered in the Load event procedure.

```
(MainForm Events)                                    ▼  Load

    Private Sub MainForm_Load(ByVal sender As Object, ByVal e As System.Event
        ' fills the list box with 8 pairs of matching words,
        ' then calls a procedure to shuffle the words

        Dim file As String = "Words4.txt"
        Dim fileContents As String = String.Empty
        Dim word As String = String.Empty
        Dim newLineIndex As Integer
        Dim startPos As Integer

        If My.Computer.FileSystem.FileExists(file) Then
            fileContents = _
                My.Computer.FileSystem.ReadAllText(file)
            newLineIndex = fileContents.IndexOf(ControlChars.NewLine)
            Do Until newLineIndex = -1

            Loop
        End If
        wordListBox.Items.Add("Refrigerator")
        wordListBox.Items.Add("Range")
        wordListBox.Items.Add("Television")
        wordListBox.Items.Add("Computer")
```

Figure 10-28: Code entered in the Load event procedure

The first instruction in the loop will extract a word from the variable. But how do you know the number of characters to extract when the lengths of the words vary? The illustration shown in Figure 10-29 should help you answer this question. The figure shows the first three words from the fileContents variable, along with the index of each character in the words. You can calculate the number of characters in a word by subtracting the index of the first character in the word from the index of the carriage return (CR) that follows the word. For example, the word "Apple" contains 5 characters, which is the difference between the letter A's index (0) and the index of the carriage return at the end of the word (5). Similarly, the word "Banana" has 6 letters, which is calculated by subtracting the letter B's index (7) from the index of the carriage return that follows the word (13). You can use this information, along with the Substring method from Chapter 7, to access each word stored in the fileContents variable.

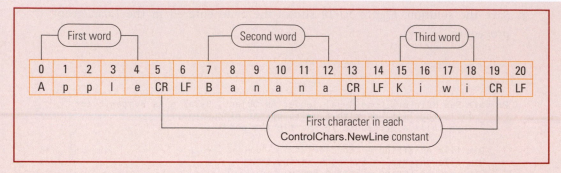

Figure 10-29: Index of each character in the first three words stored in the fileContents variable

To continue modifying the Load event procedure:

1. Recall that the Substring method's syntax is *string*.**Substring(***startIndex* [, *count*]**)**. The *startIndex* argument is the index of the first character you want to access in the *string*. In this case, you will use the startPos variable as the *startIndex* argument. As mentioned earlier, the startPos variable will keep track of where each word begins in the string. The variable's initial value is 0. For the *count* argument, which specifies the number of characters to access, you will use the expression newLineIndex – startPos. The expression subtracts the index of the first character in the word from the index of the first character in the ControlChars.NewLine constant; the result is the number of characters in the word. You will assign the Substring method's return value to the word variable. Type **word = _** and press **Enter**. Press **Tab**, then type **fileContents.Substring(startPos, newLineIndex – startPos)** and press **Enter**.

2. Now add the word to the wordListBox. Type **wordListBox.items.add(word)** and press **Enter**.

3. The loop now needs to locate the next ControlChars.NewLine constant in the fileContents variable. You should begin the search with the character located immediately after the previous ControlChars.NewLine constant. If you don't, the Load event procedure will not work correctly because the IndexOf method will continue to find the same constant. Type **startPos = newLineIndex + ControlChars.NewLine.Length** and press **Enter**. Type **newLineIndex = _** and press **Enter**. Press **Tab**, then type **fileContents.IndexOf(ControlChars. NewLine, startPos)**.

4. If the Words4.txt file does not exist, the procedure will display a message and then use the 16 Add methods to fill the list box with words. Click **immediately after the letter p** in the word Loop, then press **Enter** to insert a blank line. Type **else** and press **Enter**.

5. Type **messagebox.show("Can't find " & file, "Missing File", _** and press **Enter**, then type **messageboxbuttons.ok, messageboxicon.information)**.

6. Cut the End If clause from its current location and paste it in the blank line above the Call ShuffleWords() statement, then press **Enter**.

7. Save the solution, then start the application. Keep playing the game until all of the words appear on the game board, then click the **Exit** button.

8. Now test the application using a file name that does not exist. Change the "Words4.txt" string in the first Dim statement to **"Words5.txt"**. Save the solution, then start the application. The "Can't find Words5.txt" message appears in a message box. Click the **OK** button. The Load event procedure uses the 16 Add methods to fill the list box with words. Keep playing the game until all of the words appear on the game board, then click the **Exit** button.

You are not yet finished modifying the application. As mentioned at the beginning of the Programming Tutorial section, the application should use the words contained in one of four different sequential access files, which should be chosen randomly when the application is started. The Load event procedure will accomplish this task by assigning the names of the four files to an array, and then using the random number generator to select one of the file names.

To complete the modifications to the Concentration Game application:

1. Click **the blank line above the first Dim statement**, then press **Enter** to insert another blank line. Type **dim fileList() as string = {"Words1.txt", _** and press **Enter**, then type **"Words2.txt", _** and press **Enter**. Type **"Words3.txt", _** and press **Enter**, then type **"Words4.txt"}** and press **Enter**.

2. Type **dim randomGenerator as new random** and press **Enter**.

3. Change the Dim file As String = "Words5.txt" statement to **Dim file As String = fileList(randomGenerator.next(0, 4))**.

4. Save the solution.

Before testing the Concentration Game application, compare the code you entered in the Load event procedure with the code shown in Figure 10-30. Make any needed corrections.

```vb
Private Sub MainForm_Load(ByVal sender As Object, _
    ByVal e As System.EventArgs) Handles Me.Load
    ' fills the list box with 8 pairs of matching words,
    ' then calls a procedure to shuffle the words

    Dim fileList() As String = {"Words1.txt", _
                                "Words2.txt", _
                                "Words3.txt", _
                                "Words4.txt"}
    Dim randomGenerator As New Random

    Dim file As String = fileList(randomGenerator.Next(0, 4))
    Dim fileContents As String = String.Empty
    Dim word As String = String.Empty
    Dim newLineIndex As Integer
    Dim startPos As Integer

    If My.Computer.FileSystem.FileExists(file) Then
        fileContents = _
            My.Computer.FileSystem.ReadAllText(file)
        newLineIndex = fileContents.IndexOf(ControlChars.NewLine)
        Do Until newLineIndex = -1
            word = _
                fileContents.Substring(startPos, newLineIndex - startPos)
            wordListBox.Items.Add(word)
            startPos = newLineIndex + ControlChars.NewLine.Length
            newLineIndex = _
                fileContents.IndexOf(ControlChars.NewLine, startPos)
        Loop
    Else
        MessageBox.Show("Can't find " & file, "Missing File", _
            MessageBoxButtons.OK, MessageBoxIcon.Information)

    wordListBox.Items.Add("Refrigerator")
    wordListBox.Items.Add("Range")
    wordListBox.Items.Add("Television")
    wordListBox.Items.Add("Computer")
    wordListBox.Items.Add("Washer/Dryer")
    wordListBox.Items.Add("Dishwasher")
    wordListBox.Items.Add("Car")
    wordListBox.Items.Add("Trip")
    wordListBox.Items.Add("Refrigerator")
    wordListBox.Items.Add("Range")
```

Figure 10-30: Load event procedure for the Concentration Game application (*continued on next page*)

```
        wordListBox.Items.Add("Television")
        wordListBox.Items.Add("Computer")
        wordListBox.Items.Add("Washer/Dryer")
        wordListBox.Items.Add("Dishwasher")
        wordListBox.Items.Add("Car")
        wordListBox.Items.Add("Trip")
    End If

    Call ShuffleWords()
End Sub
```

Figure 10-30: Load event procedure for the Concentration Game application (*continued from previous page*)

To test the completed Concentration Game application:

1. Save the solution, if necessary, then start the application. Play the game until all of the words appear on the game board, then click the **Exit** button.

2. Start the application again. Continue testing the application until each of the four files has been used. When you are finished testing the application, close the Code Editor window, then close the solution.

PROGRAMMING EXAMPLE

GLOVERS APPLICATION

Glovers Industries stores the item numbers and prices of its products in a sequential access file named itemInfo.txt. The company's sales manager wants an application that displays the price of an item whose number she selects in a list box. Name the solution, project, and form file Glovers Solution, Glovers Project, and Main Form.vb, respectively. Save the application in the VbReloaded2008\Chap10 folder. You also will need to create the itemInfo.txt file. Save the file in the project's bin\Debug folder. See Figures 10-31 through 10-36.

Task	Object	Event
1. Fill the items array with the item numbers and prices stored in the itemInfo.txt file 2. Fill the numbersListBox with the item numbers 3. Select the first item in the numbersListBox	MainForm	Load
Display the price of the item whose number is selected in the numbersListBox	numbersListBox	SelectedIndexChanged
End the application	exitButton	Click

Figure 10-31: TOE chart

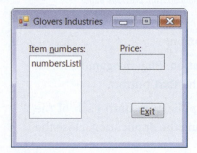

Figure 10-32: User interface

Object	Property	Setting
Form1	Name	MainForm
	Font	Segoe UI, 9 point
	MaximizeBox	False
	StartPosition	CenterScreen
	Text	Glovers Industries
Label1	TabIndex	0
	Text	Item &numbers:
Label2	TabIndex	3
	Text	Price:

Figure 10-33: Objects, Properties, and Settings (*continued on next page*)

Object	Property	Setting
Label3	Name	priceLabel
	AutoSize	False
	BorderStyle	FixedSingle
	TabIndex	4
	Text	(empty)
	TextAlign	MiddleCenter
ListBox1	Name	numbersListBox
	TabIndex	1
Button1	Name	exitButton
	TabIndex	2
	Text	E&xit

Figure 10-33: Objects, Properties, and Settings (*continued from previous page*)

```
12AVX,5
23ABC,8.97
23TWT,4.69
34ZAB,12.5
91BAN,34.67
```

Figure 10-34: The itemInfo.txt file

---

exitButton Click Event Procedure
1. close the application

MainForm Load Event Procedure
1. if the itemInfo.txt file exists
    assign the file's contents to the fileContents variable
    repeat for each element in the module-level items array
        locate the newline character in the fileContents variable

        assign the item number and price from the fileContents variable to the numAndPrice variable

        locate the comma in the numAndPrice variable

        assign the item number (which appears to the left of the comma in the numAndPrice variable) to the current array element's number member

        assign the price (which appears to the right of the comma in the numAndPrice variable) to the current array element's price member

---

Figure 10-35: Pseudocode (*continued on next page*)

```
            add the item number to the list box

            update the index that keeps track of the next item number's position in the fileContents
            variable
      end repeat
      select the first item in the list box
end if
```

numbersListBox SelectedIndexChanged Event Procedure
1. display the price associated with the item number selected in the list box

Figure 10-35: Pseudocode (*continued from previous page*)

```vb
' Project name:        Glovers Project
' Project purpose:     Display the price of an item
' Created/revised by:  <your name> on <current date>

Option Explicit On
Option Strict On
Option Infer Off

Public Class MainForm

    ' define the Product structure
    Structure Product
        Public number As String
        Public price As Decimal
    End Structure

    ' declare module-level array
    Private items(4) As Product

    Private Sub MainForm_Load(ByVal sender As Object, _
        ByVal e As System.EventArgs) Handles Me.Load
        ' fills the items array and numbersListBox
        ' with the data stored in a sequential access file

        Dim fileContents As String
        Dim newLineIndex As Integer
        Dim numIndex As Integer
        Dim numAndPrice As String
        Dim commaIndex As Integer

        If My.Computer.FileSystem.FileExists("itemInfo.txt") Then
            ' if the file exists, assign its contents to a variable
            fileContents = My.Computer.FileSystem.ReadAllText("itemInfo.txt")
```

Figure 10-36: Code (*continued on next page*)

```
            For subscript As Integer = 0 To 4
                ' locate the newline character in the fileContents variable
                newLineIndex = _
                    fileContents.IndexOf(ControlChars.NewLine, numIndex)

                ' assign the number and price from the fileContents
                ' variable to the numAndPrice variable
                numAndPrice = _
                    fileContents.Substring(numIndex, newLineIndex - numIndex)

                ' locate the comma in the numAndPrice variable
                commaIndex = numAndPrice.IndexOf(",", 0)

                ' assign the item number and price to the array
                items(subscript).number = numAndPrice.Substring(0, commaIndex)
                items(subscript).price = _
                    Convert.ToDecimal(numAndPrice.Substring(commaIndex + 1))

                ' add the item number to the list box
                numbersListBox.Items.Add(items(subscript).number)

                ' update the numIndex variable
                numIndex = newLineIndex + ControlChars.NewLine.Length
            Next subscript

            ' select the first item in the list box
            numbersListBox.SelectedIndex = 0
        End If
    End Sub

    Private Sub numbersListBox_SelectedIndexChanged_
        (ByVal sender As Object, ByVal e As System.EventArgs) _
        Handles numbersListBox.SelectedIndexChanged
        ' displays the price corresponding to the item selected
        ' in the list box

        priceLabel.Text = _
            items(numbersListBox.SelectedIndex).price.ToString("N2")
    End Sub

    Private Sub exitButton_Click(ByVal sender As Object, _
        ByVal e As System.EventArgs) Handles exitButton.Click
        Me.Close()
    End Sub
End Class
```

Figure 10-36: Code (*continued from previous page*)

QUICK REVIEW

» You can use the Structure statement to define a user-defined data type (or structure) in Visual Basic. You typically enter the Structure statement in the form's Declarations section in the Code Editor window.

» After defining a structure, you can use the structure to declare a structure variable. A structure variable contains one or more member variables. You access a member variable using the structure variable's name, followed by the dot member access operator and the member variable's name.

» The member variables contained in a structure variable can be used just like any other variables.

» A structure variable can be passed to a procedure.

» You can create a one-dimensional array of structure variables. You access a member variable in an array element using the array's name, followed by the element's subscript enclosed in parentheses, the dot member access operator, and the member variable's name.

» An application can write information to a file (called an output file) and also read information from a file (called an input file).

» The information in a sequential access file (referred to as a text file) is always accessed in consecutive order (sequentially) from the beginning of the file through the end of the file.

» In Visual Basic, you can use the FileSystem object's WriteAllText method to write text to a sequential access file, and its ReadAllText method to read the text contained in a sequential access file.

» You can use the Strings.Space method to write a specific number of spaces to a file.

» You can use the PadLeft and PadRight methods to align the text stored in a sequential access file.

» You should use the FileExists method to determine whether a file exists before attempting to read the file, because an error occurs when the computer tries to read a non-existent file. The method returns the Boolean value True if the file exists; otherwise, it returns the Boolean value False.

» You can use the FileSystem object's DeleteFile method to delete a file while an application is running.

» The FormClosing event occurs when a form is about to be closed.

» You can prevent a form from being closed by setting the Cancel property of the e parameter in the FormClosing event procedure to True.

» You can use the Clear method to remove the items from a list box.

KEY TERMS

Cancel property—a property of the e parameter in the FormClosing event procedure; when set to True, it prevents the form from closing

Clear method—a method of the Items collection; can be used to clear the contents of a list box

DeleteFile method—a method of the FileSystem object; deletes a file while an application is running

FileExists method—a method of the FileSystem object; determines whether a file exists

FileSystem object—an object used to manipulate files in Visual Basic

FormClosing event—occurs when a form is about to be closed, which can happen as a result of the computer processing the Me.Close() statement or the user clicking the Close button on the form's title bar

Input files—files from which applications read information

Member variables—the variables contained in a structure

My feature—a Visual Basic feature that exposes a set of commonly used objects to the programmer

Output files—files to which applications write information

Parse—the process of separating something into its component parts

ReadAllText method—a method of the FileSystem object; reads the text contained in a sequential access file

Sequential access file—a file composed of lines of text that are both stored and retrieved sequentially; also called a text file

Strings.Space method—can be used to write a specific number of spaces to a file

Structure statement—the statement used to create user-defined data types (structures) in Visual Basic

Structure variables—variables declared using a structure (user-defined data type)

Structures—user-defined data types created using the Structure statement

Text file—another term for a sequential access file

User-defined data types—the data types created using the Structure statement; also called structures

WriteAllText method—a method of the FileSystem object; writes text to a sequential access file

SELF-CHECK QUESTIONS AND ANSWERS

1. In most applications, the code to define a user-defined data type is entered in the form's _____

   a. Declarations section   b. Definition section

   c. Load event procedure   d. User-defined section

2. Which of the following statements assigns the string "Maple" to the street member variable within a structure variable named address?

   a. address&street = "Maple"   b. address.street = "Maple"

   c. street.address = "Maple"   d. None of the above.

3. An array is declared using the statement Dim inventory(4) As Product. Which of the following statements assigns the number 100 to the quantity member variable contained in the last array element?

   a. inventory.quantity(4) = 100

   b. inventory(4).Product.quantity = 100

   c. inventory(3).quantity = 100

   d. inventory(4).quantity = 100

4. Which of the following statements writes the contents of the addressTextBox to a sequential access file named address.txt, replacing the file's existing text?

   a. My.Computer.FileSystem.WriteAll("address.txt", addressTextBox.Text, False)

   b. My.Computer.FileSystem.WriteAllText("address.txt", addressTextBox.Text, False)

   c. My.Computer.FileSystem.WriteAllText("address.txt", addressTextBox.Text, True)

   d. My.Computer.FileSystem.WriteText("address.txt", addressTextBox.Text, Replace)

5. Which of the following statements reads the contents of a sequential access file named address.txt and assigns the contents to a String variable named fileContents?

   a. fileContents = My.Computer.File.Read("address.txt")

   b. fileContents = My.Computer.File.ReadAll("address.txt")

   c. fileContents = My.Computer.FileSystem.ReadAll("address.txt")

   d. fileContents = My.Computer.FileSystem.ReadAllText("address.txt")

Answers: 1) a, 2) b, 3) d, 4) b, 5) d

REVIEW QUESTIONS

1. Which of the following statements declares a Country variable named spain?

   a. Private spain As Country

   c. Dim Country As spain

   b. Dim spain As Country

   d. Both a and b.

2. Which of the following statements assigns the string "Madrid" to the city member of a Country variable named spain?

   a. city.spain = "Madrid"

   c. Country.spain.city = "Madrid"

   b. Country.city = "Madrid"

   d. spain.city = "Madrid"

3. An application uses a structure named Employee. Which of the following statements creates a five-element one-dimensional array of Employee structure variables?

   a. Dim workers(4) As Employee

   c. Dim workers As Employee(4)

   b. Dim workers(5) As Employee

   d. Dim workers As Employee(5)

4. Each structure variable in the items array contains two members: a String variable named number and an Integer variable named quantity. Which of the following statements assigns the inventory number "123XY" to the first element in the array?

   a. items(0).number = "123XY"

   c. items.number(0) = "123XY"

   b. items(1).number = "123XY"

   d. items.number(1) = "123XY"

5. If the specified file does not exist, the _____ method results in an error when the computer processes it.

   a. AppendText

   c. WriteAllText

   b. ReadAllText

   d. FileExists

6. Which of the following writes the string "Your pay is $56" to a sequential access file? The file's name is stored in the file variable. The pay variable contains the number 56.

   a. My.Computer.FileSystem.WriteAllText(file, "Your pay is $", False)

      My.Computer.FileSystem.WriteAllText(file, pay.ToString, True)

   b. My.Computer.FileSystem.WriteAllText(file, "Your pay is $" & pay.ToString, False)

   c. My.Computer.FileSystem.WriteAllText(file, "Your ", False)

      My.Computer.FileSystem.WriteAllText(file, "pay is ", True)

      My.Computer.FileSystem.WriteAllText(file, pay.ToString("C0"), True)

   d. All of the above.

7. The _____ event occurs when the computer processes the Me.Close() statement or when the user clicks the Close button on the form's title bar.

   a. FormClosing   b. FormFinish

   c. Finish   d. None of the above.

8. Which of the following reads the text from a sequential access file, and assigns the text to the fileContents variable? The file's name is stored in the file variable.

   a. My.Computer.FileSystem.ReadText(file, fileContents)

   b. My.Computer.FileSystem.ReadAllText(file, fileContents)

   c. fileContents = My.Computer.FileSystem.ReadText(file)

   d. fileContents = My.Computer.FileSystem.ReadAllText(file)

9. Which of the following clauses determines whether the employ.txt file exists?

   a. If FileExists("employ.txt") Then

   b. If My.FileExists("employ.txt") Then

   c. If My.Computer.FileSystem.FileExists("employ.txt") Then

   d. None of the above.

10. When entered in the FormClosing event procedure, which of the following statements keeps the form open?

   a. e.Cancel = True   b. e.Cancel = False

   c. e.Open = True   d. e.Open = False

REVIEW EXERCISES— SHORT ANSWER

1. Write a Structure statement that defines a structure named Book. The structure contains two String member variables named title and author, and a Decimal member variable named cost. Then write a Private statement that declares a Book variable named fiction.

2. Write a Structure statement that defines a structure named Tape. The structure contains three String member variables named name, artist, and songLength, and an Integer member variable named songNum. Then write a Dim statement that declares a Tape variable named blues.

3. An application contains the following Structure statement:

```
Structure Computer
     Public model As String
     Public cost As Decimal
End Structure
```

   a. Write a Dim statement that declares a Computer variable named homeUse.

   b. Write an assignment statement that assigns the string "IB-50" to the model member variable.

   c. Write an assignment statement that assigns the number 2400 to the cost member variable.

4. An application contains the following Structure statement:

```
Structure Friend
     Public last As String
     Public first As String
End Structure
```

   a. Write a Dim statement that declares a Friend variable named school.

   b. Write an assignment statement that assigns the value in the firstTextBox to the first member variable.

   c. Write an assignment statement that assigns the value in the lastTextBox to the last member variable.

   d. Write an assignment statement that assigns the value in the last member variable to the lastLabel.

   e. Write an assignment statement that assigns the value in the first member variable to the firstLabel.

5. An application contains the following Structure statement:

```
Structure Computer
     Public model As String
     Public cost As Decimal
End Structure
```

   a. Write a Private statement that declares a 10-element one-dimensional array of Computer variables. Name the array business.

   b. Write an assignment statement that assigns the string "HPP405" to the model member variable contained in the first array element.

   c. Write an assignment statement that assigns the number 3600 to the cost member variable contained in the first array element.

6. An application contains the following Structure statement:

```
Structure Friend
    Public last As String
    Public first As String
End Structure
```

   a. Write a Private statement that declares a 5-element one-dimensional array of Friend variables. Name the array home.

   b. Write an assignment statement that assigns the value in the firstTextBox to the first member variable contained in the last array element.

   c. Write an assignment statement that assigns the value in the lastTextBox to the last member variable contained in the last array element.

7. Write the string "Employee" and the string "Name" to a sequential access file named report.txt. Each string should appear on a separate line in the file.

8. Write the contents of a String variable named capital, followed by 20 spaces, the contents of a String variable named state, and the ControlChars.NewLine constant to a sequential access file named geography.txt.

9. Write the statement to assign the contents of the report.txt file to a String variable named fileContents.

10. Write the statement to assign the contents of the report.txt file to the reportTextBox.

11. Write the code to determine whether the janSales.txt file exists. If it does, the code should display the string "File exists" in the messageLabel; otherwise, it should display the string "File does not exist" in the messageLabel.

COMPUTER EXERCISES

1. In this exercise, you code an application that uses a structure.

   a. Open the Pool Solution (Pool Solution.sln) file, which is contained in the VbReloaded2008\Chap10\Pool Solution folder. Open the Code Editor window. The window contains the code shown in Figure 10-5 in the chapter.

   b. Use Figure 10-6 in the chapter to modify the application's code so that it uses a structure. Save the solution, then start and test the application. End the application, then close the solution.

2. In this exercise, you code an application that uses an array of structure variables.

   a. Open the Price List Solution (Price List Solution.sln) file, which is contained in the VbReloaded2008\Chap10\Price List Solution folder.

b. Use Figure 10-8 in the chapter to finish coding the application. Save the solution, then start and test the application. End the application, then close the solution.

3. In this exercise, you code an application that writes information to a sequential access file.

   a. Open the Employee List Solution (Employee List Solution.sln) file, which is contained in the VbReloaded2008\Chap10\Employee List Solution folder.

   b. The Write button should write the contents of the nameTextBox to a sequential access file named names.txt. Each name should appear on a separate line in the file. Save the file in the project's bin\Debug folder.

   c. Save the solution, then start the application. Test the application by writing five names to the file. End the application.

   d. Open the names.txt file to verify that it contains five names. Close the names.txt window, then close the solution.

4. In this exercise, you code an application that writes information to a sequential access file.

   a. Open the Memo Solution (Memo Solution.sln) file, which is contained in the VbReloaded2008\Chap10\Memo Solution folder.

   b. The Write button should write the contents of the memoTextBox to a sequential access file named memo.txt. Save the file in the project's bin\Debug folder.

   c. Save the solution, then start the application. Test the application by writing the following memo to the file, then end the application.

   To all employees:

   The annual picnic will be held at Rogers Park on Saturday, July 13. Bring your family for a day full of fun!

   Carolyn Meyer
   Personnel Manager

   d. Open the memo.txt file to verify that it contains the memo. Close the memo.txt window, then close the solution.

5. In this exercise, you code an application that writes information to a sequential access file.

   a. Open the Report Solution (Report Solution.sln) file, which is contained in the VbReloaded2008\Chap10\Report Solution folder.

   b. Open the Code Editor window. The application uses an array to store three state names and their corresponding sales. Code the application so that it creates the report shown in Example 3 in Figure 10-10 in the chapter. Use hyphens for the underline. Use an accumulator to total the sales amounts. Save the report in a sequential access file named report.txt. Save the file in the project's bin\Debug folder.

c. Save the solution, then start and test the application. End the application.

d. Open the report.txt file to verify that it contains the report. Close the report.txt window, then close the solution.

6. In this exercise, you code an application that writes information to and reads information from a sequential access file.

a. Create the Friends interface shown in Figure 10-17 in the chapter. Name the solution, project, and form file Friends Solution, Friends Project, and Main Form.vb, respectively. Save the application in the VbReloaded2008\Chap10 folder.

b. Use the code shown in Figure 10-18 in the chapter to code the application.

c. Save the solution, then start the application. Test the application by entering six names, then removing the second name. End the application.

d. Open the friends.txt file to verify that it contains five names. The file is contained in the project's bin\Debug folder. Close the friends.txt window, then close the solution.

7. In this exercise, you modify the application from Computer Exercise 3. The modified application allows the user to either create a new file or append information to the end of an existing file.

a. Use Windows to make a copy of the Employee List Solution folder, which is contained in the VbReloaded2008\Chap10 folder. Rename the copy Modified Employee List Solution.

b. Use Windows to delete the names.txt file from the project's bin\Debug folder.

c. Open the Employee List Solution (Employee List Solution.sln) file contained in the VbReloaded2008\Chap10\Modified Employee List Solution folder.

d. When the writeButton's Click event procedure is processed the first time, the procedure should determine whether the names.txt file exists. If the file exists, the procedure should use the MessageBox.Show method to ask the user whether he wants to replace the existing file. Include Yes and No buttons in the message box. If the user clicks the Yes button, replace the existing file; otherwise, append to the existing file.

e. Save the solution, then start the application. Type Helen in the Name text box, then click the Write button. End the application.

f. Start the application again. Type Ginger in the Name text box, then click the Write button. The application should ask if you want to replace the existing file. Click the No button, then end the application.

g. Open the names.txt file, which is contained in the project's bin\Debug folder. The file should contain two names: Helen and Ginger. Close the names.txt window.

h. Start the application again. Type George in the Name text box, then click the Write button. The application should ask if you want to replace the existing file. Click the Yes button, then end the application.

i. Open the names.txt file. The file should contain one name: George. Close the names.txt window, then close the solution.

8. In this exercise, you modify the application from Computer Exercise 2. The modified application will display both the name and price of the product ID entered by the user.

a. Use Windows to make a copy of the Price List Solution folder, which is contained in the VbReloaded2008\Chap10 folder. Rename the copy Modified Price List Solution.

b. Open the Price List Solution (Price List Solution.sln) file contained in the VbReloaded2008\Chap10\Modified Price List Solution folder. Modify the interface and code so that the application displays the product ID's name and price. The names of the products are shown Figure 10-37.

Product ID	Name
BX35	Necklace
CR20	Bracelet
FE15	Jewelry box
KW10	Doll
MM67	Ring

Figure 10-37

c. Save the solution, then start and test the application. End the application, then close the solution.

9. In this exercise, you code an application that displays a grade based on the number of points a student earns. The grading scale is shown in Figure 10-38.

Minimum points	Maximum points	Grade
0	299	F
300	349	D
350	399	C
400	449	B
450	Unlimited	A

Figure 10-38

a. Open the Carver Solution (Carver Solution.sln) file, which is contained in the VbReloaded2008\Chap10\Carver Solution folder.

b. Create a structure that contains two fields: an Integer field for the minimum points and a String field for the grades. Code the Display Grade button's Click event procedure so that it uses the structure to declare a five-element one-dimensional array named gradeScale. Store the minimum points and grades in the array.

c. The Display Grade button should search the array for the number of points earned, and then display the appropriate grade from the array.

d. Save the solution, then start and test the application. End the application, then close the solution.

10. In this exercise, you modify the Concentration Game application from the chapter's Programming Tutorial.

a. Use Windows to make a copy of the Concentration Game Solution folder, which is contained in the VbReloaded2008\Chap10 folder. Rename the copy Modified Concentration Game Solution.

b. Open the Concentration Game Solution (Concentration Game Solution.sln) file contained in the VbReloaded2008\Chap10\Modified Concentration Game Solution folder. Modify the interface and code so that the application allows the user to select the file name (Words1.txt, Words2.txt, Words3.txt, or Words4.txt) from a list box while the application is running. The selected file should be used when the New Game button is clicked.

c. Save the solution, then start and test the application. End the application, then close the solution.

11. In this exercise, you update the contents of a sequential access file.

a. Open the Pay Solution (Pay Solution.sln) file, which is contained in the VbReloaded2008\Chap10\Pay Solution folder.

b. Open the payrates.txt file, which is contained in the project's bin\Debug folder. View the file's contents, then close the payrates.txt window.

c. Code the Increase button's Click event procedure so that it increases each pay rate by 10%. Save the increased prices in a sequential access file named updated.txt. Save the file in the project's bin\Debug folder.

d. Save the solution, then start the application. Click the Increase Pay Rates button to update the pay rates, then end the application.

e. Open the payrates.txt file. Also open the updated.txt file. The pay rates contained in the updated.txt file should be 10% more than the pay rates contained in the payrates.txt file. Close the updated.txt and payrates.txt windows, then close the solution.

12. In this exercise, you practice debugging an application.

   a. Open the Debug Solution (Debug Solution.sln) file, which is contained in the VbReloaded2008\Chap10\Debug Solution folder. Open the Code Editor window and review the existing code.

   b. Start and test the application. Notice that the application is not working correctly. Correct the application's code.

   c. Save the solution, then start and test the application. When the application is working correctly, close the solution.

CASE PROJECTS

WARREN HIGH SCHOOL

This year, three students are running for senior class president: Mark Stone, Sheima Patel, and Sam Perez. Create an application that keeps track of the voting. Save the voting information in a sequential access file. The application also should display the number of votes per candidate. You can either create your own interface or create the one shown in Figure 10-39. Name the solution, project, and form file Warren Solution, Warren Project, and Main Form.vb, respectively. Save the application in the VbReloaded2008\Chap10 folder.

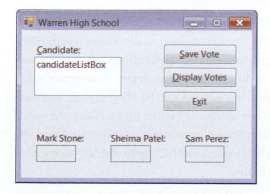

Figure 10-39: Sample interface for Warren High School

WKRK-RADIO

Each year, WKRK-Radio polls its audience to determine which Super Bowl commercial was the best. The choices are as follows: Budweiser, FedEx, E*Trade, and Pepsi. The station manager has asked you to create an application that allows him to enter a caller's choice. The choice should be saved in a sequential access file. The application also should display the number of votes for each commercial. You can either create your own interface or create the one shown in Figure 10-40. Name the solution, project, and form file WKRK Solution, WKRK Project, and Main Form.vb, respectively. Save the application in the VbReloaded2008\Chap10 folder.

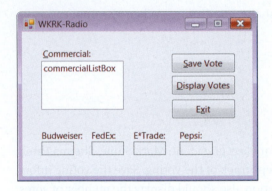

Figure 10-40: Sample interface for WKRK-Radio

SHOE CIRCUS

Shoe Circus sells 10 styles of children's shoes. The style numbers and prices are stored in a sequential access file named shoeInfo.txt. The file is contained in the VbReloaded2008\ Chap10 folder. The store manager has asked you to create an application that she can use to enter a style number and then display the style's price. Use an array of structure variables to store the style number and price information for the 10 shoe styles. You can either create your own interface or create the one shown in Figure 10-41. Name the solution, project, and form file Shoe Circus Solution, Shoe Circus Project, and Main Form.vb, respectively. Save the application in the VbReloaded2008\Chap10 folder. Copy the shoeInfo.txt file to your project's bin\Debug folder.

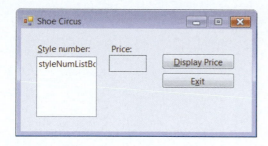

Figure 10-41: Sample interface for Shoe Circus

REVELLOS

Revellos has stores located in several states. The sales manager has asked you to create an application that he can use to enter the following information for each store: the store number, the state in which the store is located, and the store manager's name. The application should save the information in a sequential access file. Each store's information should appear on a separate line in the file. In other words, the first store's number, state name, and manager name should appear on the first line in the file. The application also should allow the sales manager to enter a store number, and then display both the state in which the store is located and the store manager's name. Use the information shown in Figure 10-42. Name the solution, project, and form file Revellos Solution, Revellos Project, and Main Form.vb, respectively. Save the application in the VbReloaded2008\ Chap10 folder.

Number	State	Manager
1004	Texas	Jeffrey Jefferson
1005	Texas	Paula Hendricks
1007	Arizona	Jake Johansen
1010	Arizona	Henry Abernathy
1011	California	Barbara Millerton
1013	California	Inez Baily
1015	California	Sung Lee
1016	California	Lou Chan
1017	California	Homer Gomez
1019	New Mexico	Ingrid Nadkarni

Figure 10-42: Revellos information

11

CREATING CLASSES AND OBJECTS

After studying Chapter 11, you should be able to:

Define a class

Instantiate an object from a class that you define

Add Property procedures to a class

Include data validation in a class

Create default and parameterized constructors

Include methods in a class

Overload the methods in a class

Create a derived class using inheritance

Override a method in the base class

Refer to the base class using the MyBase keyword

CLASSES AND OBJECTS

As you learned in Chapter 1, Visual Basic 2008 is an object-oriented programming language, which is a language that allows the programmer to use objects to accomplish a program's goal. Recall that an object is anything that can be seen, touched, or used; in other words, an object is nearly any *thing*. The objects used in an object-oriented program can take on many different forms. The text boxes, list boxes, and buttons included in most Windows programs are objects. An object also can represent something found in real life, such as a wristwatch or a car. Every object is created from a **class**, which is a pattern or blueprint that the computer follows when creating the object. Using object-oriented programming (**OOP**) terminology, objects are **instantiated** (created) from a class, and each object is referred to as an **instance** of the class. A button control, for example, is an instance of the Button class, which is the class from which a button is instantiated. A text box, on the other hand, is an instance of the TextBox class.

Every object has **attributes**, which are the characteristics that describe the object. Attributes are also called properties. Included in the attributes of buttons and text boxes are the Name and Text properties. List boxes have a Name property as well as a Sorted property. In addition to attributes, every object also has behaviors. An object's **behaviors** include methods and events. **Methods** are the operations (actions) that the object is capable of performing. For example, a button control can use its Focus method to send the focus to another control in the interface. **Events** are the actions to which an object can respond. A button control's Click event, for instance, allows it to respond to a mouse click. A class contains—or, in OOP terms, it **encapsulates**—all of the attributes and behaviors of the object it instantiates.

In previous chapters, you instantiated objects using classes that are built into Visual Basic, such as the TextBox and Label classes. You used the instantiated objects in a variety of ways in many different applications. In some applications, you used a text box to enter a name, while in other applications you used it to enter a sales tax rate. Similarly, you used label controls to identify text boxes and also to display the result of calculations. The ability to use an object for more than one purpose saves programming time and money—an advantage that contributes to the popularity of object-oriented programming.

DEFINING A CLASS

In addition to using the classes built into Visual Basic, you also can define your own classes and then create instances (objects) from those classes. The classes you define can represent something encountered in real life, such as a credit card receipt, a check, or an employee. Like the Visual Basic classes, your classes must specify the attributes and behaviors of the objects they create. You use the **Class statement** to define the class. Figure 11-1 shows the statement's syntax, which begins with the Public Class clause and

> **TIP**
> The class itself is not an object. Only an instance of the class is an object.

> **TIP**
> The term "encapsulate" means "to enclose in a capsule." In the context of OOP, the "capsule" is a class.

> **TIP**
> Each tool in the toolbox represents a class. When you drag a tool from the toolbox to the form, the computer uses the class to instantiate the appropriate object.

> **TIP**
> Although you can create a class in a matter of minutes, the objects produced by such a class probably will not be of much use. The creation of a good class—one whose objects can be used in a variety of ways by many different applications—requires a lot of planning.

ends with the End Class clause. Although it is not required by the syntax, the convention is to use Pascal case for the class name. Recall that Pascal case means you capitalize the first letter in the name and the first letter in any subsequent words in the name. The names of Visual Basic classes (for example, String and TextBox) also follow this naming convention. Within the Class statement, you define the attributes and behaviors of the objects the class will create. The attributes are represented by variables and Property procedures. The behaviors are represented by Sub and Function procedures, more commonly referred to as methods. Also included in Figure 11-1 is an example of using the Class statement to create a class named TimeCard.

»TIP

You also can include Event procedures in a Class statement; however, that topic is beyond the scope of this book.

»HOW TO . . .

DEFINE A CLASS

Syntax

Public Class *className*

attributes section

behaviors section

End Class

Example

Public Class TimeCard

variables and Property procedures appear in the attributes section

Sub and Function procedures appear in the behaviors section

End Class

Figure 11-1: How to define a class

You enter the Class statement in a class file. Figure 11-2 lists the steps you follow to add a class file to an open project, and Figure 11-3 shows a completed Add New Item - *projectName* dialog box.

»HOW TO . . .

ADD A CLASS FILE TO AN OPEN PROJECT

1. Click Project on the menu bar, then click Add Class. The Add New Item - *projectName* dialog box opens with Class selected in the Visual Studio installed templates box.
2. Type the name of the class followed by a period and the letters vb in the Name box, then click the Add button.

Figure 11-2: How to add a class file to an open project

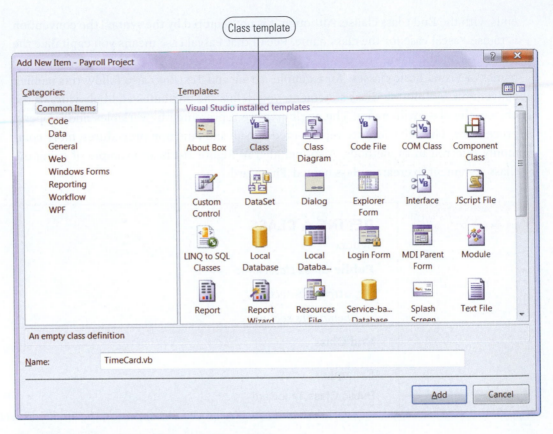

Figure 11-3: Completed Add New Item - *projectName* dialog box

When you click the Add button in the Add New Item - *projectName* dialog box shown in Figure 11-3, the computer adds a file named TimeCard.vb to the Payroll project. As you learned in Chapter 1, the .vb on a filename indicates that the file is a "Visual Basic" source file, which is a file that contains program instructions. The Code Editor also opens the TimeCard.vb file in the Code Editor window, and automatically enters the Class statement in the file, as shown in Figure 11-4. Within the Class statement, you enter the attributes and behaviors of the class's objects.

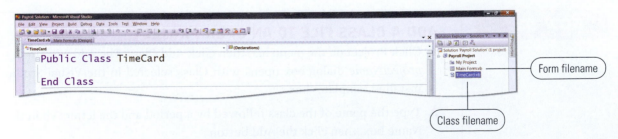

Figure 11-4: TimeCard.vb file opened in the Code Editor window

After you define the class, it then can be used to instantiate one or more objects. Figure 11-5 shows two versions of the syntax that instantiates an object from a class. In both versions, *class* is the name of the class and *variableName* is the name of a variable that will store the object's address. The difference between both versions relates to when the object is actually created. The computer creates the object only when it processes the statement containing the New keyword. Also included in Figure 11-5 is an example of using each version of the syntax. In Example 1, the Private employeeTimeCard As TimeCard instruction creates a module-level variable named employeeTimeCard that can store the address of a TimeCard object; however, it does not create the object. The object isn't created until the computer processes the employeeTimeCard = New TimeCard statement, which uses the TimeCard class to instantiate a TimeCard object. The statement assigns the object's address to the employeeTimeCard variable. In Example 2, the Dim employeeTimeCard As New TimeCard instruction creates a procedure-level variable named employeeTimeCard. It also instantiates a TimeCard object and assigns its address to the variable.

»HOW TO . . .

INSTANTIATE AN OBJECT FROM A CLASS

<u>Syntax - Version 1</u>

{**Dim** | **Private**} *variableName* **As** *class*

variableName = **New** *class*

<u>Syntax - Version 2</u>

{**Dim** | **Private**} *variableName* **As New** *class*

<u>Example 1 (syntax version 1)</u>

Private employeeTimeCard As TimeCard
employeeTimeCard = New TimeCard
the first instruction creates a TimeCard variable named employeeTimeCard; the second instruction instantiates a TimeCard object and assigns its address to the variable

<u>Example 2 (syntax version 2)</u>

Dim employeeTimeCard As New TimeCard
the instruction creates a TimeCard variable named employeeTimeCard and also instantiates a TimeCard object; it assigns the object's address to the variable

Figure 11-5: How to instantiate an object from a class

One way to learn about classes and objects is to view examples of class definitions, as well as examples of code in which objects are instantiated and used. You will begin with a simple example of a class that contains attributes only. In the example, each of the attributes is represented by a Public variable.

EXAMPLE 1—USING A CLASS THAT CONTAINS PUBLIC VARIABLES ONLY

The sales manager at Sweets Unlimited wants an application that allows him to save each salesperson's name, sales amount, and bonus amount in a sequential access file named sales.txt. Each salesperson is associated with three items of information: a name, a sales amount, and a bonus amount. In the context of OOP, each salesperson can be treated as an object having three attributes. By including the attributes in a Class statement, you can create a pattern that any application can use to instantiate a salesperson object. In this case, the Sweets Unlimited application will use the Class statement to create a class named Salesperson. It then will use the Salesperson class to instantiate a salesperson object, which will be used to store each salesperson's information before the information is written to the sequential access file. Figure 11-6 shows the Salesperson class defined in a class file named Salesperson.vb. The class contains three attributes, each represented by a Public variable. When a variable in a class is declared using the Public keyword, it can be accessed by any application that contains an instance of the class. In this case, the variables included in the Salesperson class can be used by any application that instantiates a Salesperson object. Unlike most variable names, the variable names in the Salesperson class are not entered using camel case. This is because the convention is to use Pascal case for the names of the Public variables in a class. Notice that the class file contains the three Option statements typically entered in the form file. As is true when coding a form, it is a good programming practice to enter the Option statements when coding a class. The Option statements have the same meaning in a class file as they have in a form file.

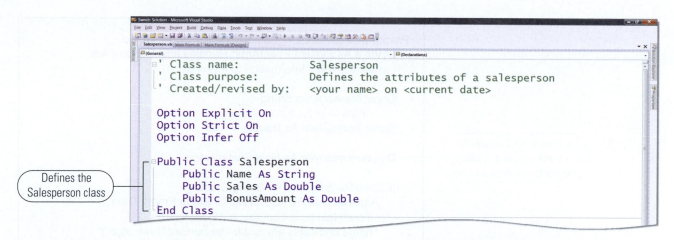

Figure 11-6: Salesperson class defined in the Salesperson.vb file

Figure 11-7 shows the interface for the Sweets Unlimited application, and Figure 11-8 shows a sample of the sequential access file created by the application. Figure 11-9 shows the code for the saveButton's Click event procedure.

Figure 11-7: Interface for the Sweets Unlimited application

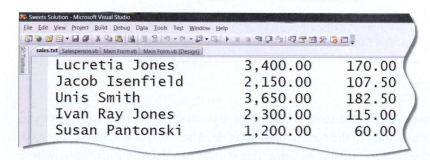

Figure 11-8: Sample sequential access file created by the application

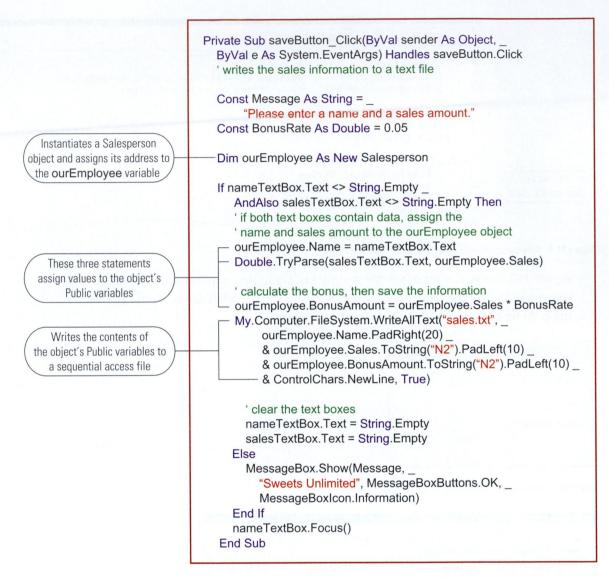

Figure 11-9: The saveButton's Click event procedure

The Dim ourEmployee As New Salesperson statement instantiates a Salesperson object and assigns the object's address to the ourEmployee variable. After the statement is processed, you can access the object's attributes using the syntax *variableName.attribute*, where *variableName* is the name of the variable containing the object's address. In this case, you would use ourEmployee.Name, ourEmployee.Sales, and ourEmployee.BonusAmount. The ourEmployee.Name = nameTextBox.Text statement in Figure 11-9 assigns the contents of the nameTextBox to the Salesperson object's Name attribute. Similarly, the ourEmployee.BonusAmount = ourEmployee.Sales * BonusRate statement multiplies the contents of the object's Sales attribute by 5%, and then stores the result in the object's BonusAmount attribute. The object's Sales attribute receives its value from the Double.TryParse(salesTextBox.Text, ourEmployee.Sales) statement in the procedure. The saveButton's Click event procedure uses the WriteAllText method (which you learned about in Chapter 10) to write the contents of the object's three attributes to the sales.txt file.

Although you can define a class that contains only attributes represented by Public variables—like the Salesperson class shown in Figure 11-6—that is rarely done. The disadvantage of using Public variables in a class is that a class cannot control the values assigned to its Public variables. As a result, the class cannot validate the values to ensure they are appropriate for the variables. Furthermore, most classes contain not only attributes, but behaviors as well. This is because the purpose of a class in OOP is to encapsulate the properties that describe an object, the methods that allow the object to perform tasks, and the events that allow the object to respond to actions. The next example will show you how to include data validation code and methods in a class. (The creation of class events is beyond the scope of this book.)

EXAMPLE 2—USING A CLASS THAT CONTAINS A PRIVATE VARIABLE, A PROPERTY PROCEDURE, AND TWO METHODS

In this example, you view the code for a class named Square. The Square class can be used to instantiate a Square object. Square objects have one attribute: the length of a side. Square objects also have two behaviors: they can initialize their side measurement when they are created, and they can calculate their area. Figure 11-10 shows the Square class defined in the Square.vb file. The Private _side As Integer instruction declares a Private variable named _side. When naming the Private variables in a class, many programmers use the underscore as the first character and then camel case for the remainder of the name. The Private keyword indicates that the _side variable can be used only within the class in which it is defined; in this case, it can be used only by the code entered in the Square class. The code uses the variable to store the side measurement of the square whose area is to be calculated.

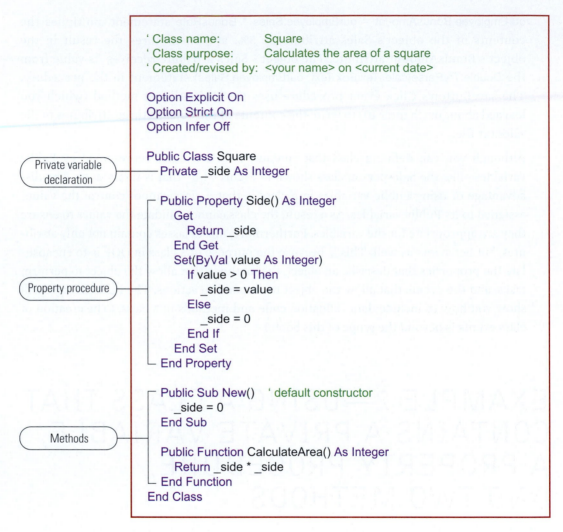

```
' Class name:          Square
' Class purpose:       Calculates the area of a square
' Created/revised by:  <your name> on <current date>

Option Explicit On
Option Strict On
Option Infer Off

Public Class Square
    Private _side As Integer

    Public Property Side() As Integer
        Get
            Return _side
        End Get
        Set(ByVal value As Integer)
            If value > 0 Then
                _side = value
            Else
                _side = 0
            End If
        End Set
    End Property

    Public Sub New()       ' default constructor
        _side = 0
    End Sub

    Public Function CalculateArea() As Integer
        Return _side * _side
    End Function
End Class
```

Private variable declaration

Property procedure

Methods

Figure 11-10: Square class defined in the Square.vb file

When an application instantiates an object, only the Public members of the object's class are made available to the application; the application cannot access the Private members of the class. Using OOP terminology, the Public members are exposed to the application, whereas the Private members are hidden from the application. For an application to assign data to or retrieve data from a Private variable in a class, it must use a Public property. In other words, an application cannot directly refer to a Private variable in a class. Rather, it must refer to the variable indirectly, through the use of a Public property. You create a Public property using a **Property procedure**. Figure 11-11 shows the syntax of a Property procedure and includes examples of Property procedures.

»HOW TO . . .

CREATE A PROPERTY PROCEDURE

Syntax

Property procedure header

Public [ReadOnly | WriteOnly] Property *propertyName***() As** *dataType*

   Get

      [*instructions*]

      Return *privateVariable*

   End Get

   Set(ByVal value As *dataType***)**

      [*instructions*]

      privateVariable = {**value** | *defaultValue*}

   End Set

Property procedure footer

End Property

Example 1—an application can both retrieve and set the Side property's value

```
Public Property Side() As Integer
    Get
        Return _side
    End Get
    Set(ByVal value As Integer)
        If value > 0 Then
            _side = value
        Else
            _side = 0
        End If
    End Set
End Property
```

Example 2—an application can retrieve the Bonus property's value, but not set it

```
Public ReadOnly Property Bonus() As Decimal
    Get
        Return _bonus
    End Get
End Property
```

Figure 11-11: How to create a property procedure (*continued on next page*)

Example 3—an application can set the AnnualSale property's value, but not retrieve it

```
Public WriteOnly Property AnnualSale() As Integer
    Set(ByVal value As Integer)
        _annualSale = value
    End Set
End Property
```

Figure 11-11: How to create a property procedure (*continued from previous page*)

In most cases, a Property procedure header begins with the keywords Public Property. However, as the syntax indicates, the header also can include either the keyword ReadOnly or the keyword WriteOnly. The ReadOnly keyword indicates that the property's value can be retrieved (read) by an application, but the application cannot set (write to) the property. The property would get its value from the class itself rather than from the application. The WriteOnly keyword indicates that an application can set the property's value, but it cannot retrieve the value. In this case, the value would be set by the application for use within the class. Following the Property keyword in the header is the name of the property. You should use nouns and adjectives to name a property and enter the name using Pascal case, as in Side, Bonus, and AnnualSale. Following the property name is a set of parentheses, the keyword As, and the property's *dataType*. The *dataType* must match the data type of the Private variable associated with the Property procedure. A Public Property procedure creates a property that is visible to any application that contains an instance of the class.

»TIP

A string's Length property, which you learned about in Chapter 7, is an example of a ReadOnly property.

A Property procedure ends with the procedure footer, which contains the keywords End Property. Between the procedure header and procedure footer, you include a Get block of code, a Set block of code, or both Get and Set blocks of code. The appropriate block or blocks of code to include depends on the keywords contained in the procedure header. If the header contains the ReadOnly keyword, you include only a Get block of code in the Property procedure. The code contained in the **Get block** allows an application to retrieve the contents of the Private variable associated with the property. In the Property procedure shown in Example 2 in Figure 11-11, the ReadOnly keyword indicates that an application can retrieve the contents of the Bonus property, but it cannot set the property's value. If the header contains the WriteOnly keyword, you include only a Set block of code in the procedure. The code in the **Set block** allows an application to assign a value to the Private variable associated with the property. In the Property procedure shown in Example 3 in Figure 11-11, the WriteOnly keyword indicates that an application can assign a value to the AnnualSale property, but it cannot retrieve the property's contents. If the Property procedure header does not contain the ReadOnly or WriteOnly keywords, you include both a Get block of code and a Set block of code in the procedure, as shown in Example 1 in Figure 11-11. In this case, an application can both retrieve and set the Side property's value.

The Get block uses the **Get statement**, which begins with the keyword Get and ends with the keywords End Get. Most times, you will enter only the Return *privateVariable* instruction within the Get statement. The instruction directs the computer to return the contents of the Private variable associated with the property. In Example 1 in Figure 11-11, the Return _side statement tells the computer to return the contents of the _side variable, which is the Private variable associated with the Side property. Similarly, the Return _bonus statement in Example 2 tells the computer to return the contents of the _bonus variable, which is the Private variable associated with the Bonus property. Example 3 in Figure 11-11 does not contain a Get statement, because the AnnualSale property is designated as a WriteOnly property.

The Set block uses the **Set statement**, which begins with the keyword Set and ends with the keywords End Set. The Set keyword is followed by a parameter enclosed in parentheses. The parameter begins with the keywords ByVal value As. The keywords are followed by a *dataType*, which must match the data type of the Private variable associated with the Property procedure. The value parameter temporarily stores the value that is passed to the property by the application. You can enter one or more instructions within the Set statement. One of the instructions should assign the contents of the value parameter to the Private variable associated with the property. In Example 3 in Figure 11-11, the _annualSale = value statement assigns the contents of the procedure's value parameter to the Private _annualSale variable.

In the Set statement, you often will include instructions to validate the value received from the application before assigning it to the Private variable. The Set statement shown in Example 1 in Figure 11-11 includes a selection structure that determines whether the side measurement received from the application is valid. In this case, a valid side measurement is an integer that is greater than zero. If the side measurement is valid, the _side = value instruction assigns the integer stored in the value parameter to the Private _side variable; otherwise, the _side = 0 instruction assigns a default value (in this case, 0) to the variable. The Property procedure in Example 2 does not contain a Set statement, because the Bonus property is designated as a ReadOnly property.

In addition to the Side property, the Square class shown earlier in Figure 11-10 also contains two methods named New and CalculateArea. The New method is the default constructor for the class. You learn about constructors next.

CONSTRUCTORS

A **constructor** is a class method whose instructions the computer automatically processes each time an object is instantiated from the class. The sole purpose of a constructor is to initialize the class's Private variables. As Figure 11-12 shows, a constructor's syntax begins with the keywords Public Sub New followed by a set of parentheses that contains an optional *parameterList*; it ends with the keywords End Sub. Constructors never return a value, so they are always Sub procedures (rather than Function procedures). Within the constructor you enter the code to initialize the class's Private variables. The initialization occurs each time an object is instantiated from the class. A class can have more than one constructor. Each constructor will have the same name, New, but its parameters (if any) must be different from any other constructor in the class. A constructor that has no parameters is called the **default constructor**. A class can have only one default constructor. Figure 11-12 shows the default constructor for the Square class (shown earlier in Figure 11-10). The default constructor initializes the Square class's Private _side variable to the number 0. The computer automatically processes the default constructor when you instantiate a Square object. Examples of statements that will instantiate a Square object include Dim mySquare As New Square and mySquare = New Square.

»HOW TO . . .

CREATE A CONSTRUCTOR

Syntax

Public Sub New([*parameterList*]**)**

    instructions to initialize the class's Private variables

End Sub

Example

Public Sub New()   ' default constructor
   _side = 0
End Sub

Figure 11-12: How to create a constructor

METHODS OTHER THAN CONSTRUCTORS

A class also can contain methods other than constructors. Except for constructors, which must be Sub procedures, the methods included in a class can be either Sub procedures or Function procedures. Recall from Chapter 8 that the difference between both types of procedures is that a Function procedure returns a value after performing its assigned task, whereas a Sub procedure does not return a value. Figure 11-13 shows the syntax of a method that is not a constructor. The {Sub | Function} in the syntax indicates that you can select only one of the keywords appearing within the braces. Method names, like property names, should be entered using Pascal case. However, unlike property names, the first word in a method name should be a verb, and any subsequent words should be nouns and adjectives; the name CalculateArea follows this naming convention. Figure 11-13 also includes the CalculateArea method from the Square class (shown earlier in Figure 11-10). The CalculateArea method is represented by a Function procedure. The Return _side * _side statement within the procedure uses the contents of the class's Private _side variable to calculate the area of a square. The statement then returns the area to the application that called the procedure.

»HOW TO . . .

CREATE A METHOD THAT IS NOT A CONSTRUCTOR

Syntax

Public {Sub | Function} *methodName*(*[parameterList]*) **As** *dataType*

    instructions

End {Sub | Function}

Example

Public Function CalculateArea() As Integer
    Return _side * _side
End Function

Figure 11-13: How to create a method that is not a constructor

The Area application uses the Square class to first instantiate and then manipulate a Square object. Figure 11-14 shows a sample run of the application, and Figure 11-15 shows the calcButton's Click event procedure. The Dim mySquare As New Square statement instantiates a Square object, assigning the object's address to the mySquare variable. When creating the Square object, the computer uses the class's default constructor to initialize the class's Private _side variable to 0. The TryParse method converts the contents of the sideTextBox to Integer and stores the result in the Square object's Side property. Next, the area = mySquare.CalculateArea() statement uses the Square object's CalculateArea method to calculate and return the area; the return value is assigned to the area variable. The procedure then displays the contents of the area variable in the areaLabel.

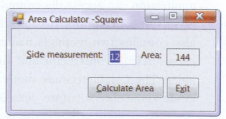

Figure 11-14: Sample run of the Area application

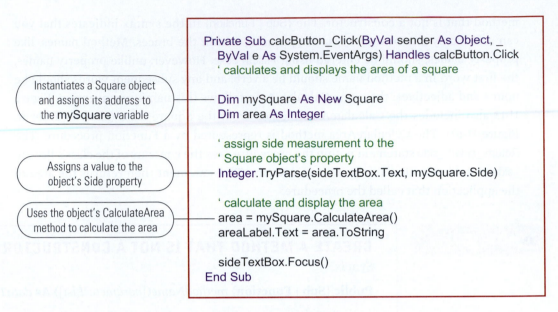

```
Private Sub calcButton_Click(ByVal sender As Object, _
    ByVal e As System.EventArgs) Handles calcButton.Click
    ' calculates and displays the area of a square

    Dim mySquare As New Square
    Dim area As Integer

    ' assign side measurement to the
    ' Square object's property
    Integer.TryParse(sideTextBox.Text, mySquare.Side)

    ' calculate and display the area
    area = mySquare.CalculateArea()
    areaLabel.Text = area.ToString

    sideTextBox.Focus()
End Sub
```

Instantiates a Square object and assigns its address to the **mySquare** variable

Assigns a value to the object's Side property

Uses the object's CalculateArea method to calculate the area

Figure 11-15: The calcButton's Click event procedure in the Area application

EXAMPLE 3—USING A CLASS THAT CONTAINS A READONLY PROPERTY

In this example, you use a class named CourseGrade to instantiate an object. CourseGrade objects have three attributes: two test scores and a letter grade. They also have two behaviors: they can initialize their attributes and calculate their letter grade. Figure 11-16 shows the CourseGrade class defined in the CourseGrade.vb file. The class contains three Private variables named _score1, _score2, and _letterGrade. It also contains three Property procedures named Score1, Score2, and LetterGrade. Notice that the LetterGrade property is designated as a ReadOnly property. As you learned earlier, an application can access the contents of a ReadOnly property, but it cannot set the property's value. In addition to the variables and Property procedures, the CourseGrade class also contains two methods named New and CalculateGrade. The New method is the class's default constructor and simply assigns initial values to the class's Private variables. The CalculateGrade method is responsible for assigning the appropriate letter grade to the class's Private _letterGrade variable.

```
' Class name:        CourseGrade
' Class purpose:     Calculates a grade
' Created/revised:   <your name> on <current date>

Option Explicit On
Option Strict On
Option Infer Off

Public Class CourseGrade
    Private _score1 As Integer
    Private _score2 As Integer
    Private _letterGrade As String

    Public Property Score1() As Integer
      Get
         Return _score1
      End Get
      Set(ByVal value As Integer)
         _score1 = value
      End Set
    End Property

    Public Property Score2() As Integer
      Get
         Return _score2
      End Get
      Set(ByVal value As Integer)
         _score2 = value
      End Set
    End Property

    Public ReadOnly Property LetterGrade() As String    ◄── ReadOnly property
      Get
         Return _letterGrade
      End Get
    End Property

    Public Sub New()
      _score1 = 0
      _score2 = 0
      _letterGrade = "?"
    End Sub
```

Figure 11-16: CourseGrade class defined in the CourseGrade.vb file (*continued on next page*)

```
Public Sub CalculateGrade()
    Dim total As Integer
    total = _score1 + _score2

    Select Case total
        Case Is >= 180
            _letterGrade = "A"
        Case Is >= 160
            _letterGrade = "B"
        Case Is >= 140
            _letterGrade = "C"
        Case Is >= 120
            _letterGrade = "D"
        Case Else
            _letterGrade = "F"
    End Select
End Sub
End Class
```

Figure 11-16: CourseGrade class defined in the CourseGrade.vb file (*continued from previous page*)

The CourseGrade class is used in the Grade application. Figure 11-17 shows a sample run of the application, and Figure 11-18 shows the displayButton's Click event procedure. The Dim grade As New CourseGrade instruction instantiates a CourseGrade object and assigns the object's address to the grade variable. When creating the CourseGrade object, the computer uses the class's default constructor to initialize the three Private variables. The next two statements in the procedure assign the selected list box items to the CourseGrade object's Score1 and Score2 properties. The Call grade.CalculateGrade() statement invokes the CourseGrade object's CalculateGrade method, which assigns the appropriate grade to the _letterGrade variable. The gradeLabel.Text = grade.LetterGrade statement uses the CourseGrade object's LetterGrade property to access the contents of the _letterGrade variable, displaying the contents in the gradeLabel.

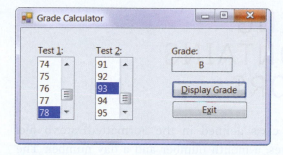

Figure 11-17: Sample run of the Grade application

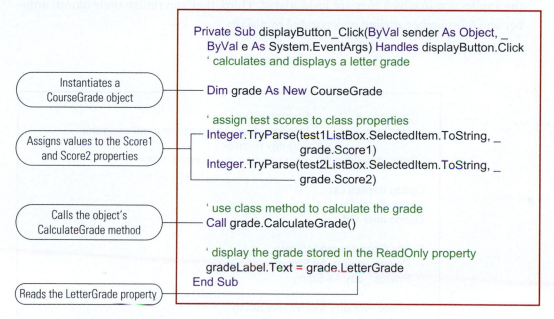

Instantiates a
CourseGrade object

Assigns values to the Score1
and Score2 properties

Calls the object's
CalculateGrade method

Reads the LetterGrade property

```
Private Sub displayButton_Click(ByVal sender As Object, _
    ByVal e As System.EventArgs) Handles displayButton.Click
    ' calculates and displays a letter grade

    Dim grade As New CourseGrade

    ' assign test scores to class properties
    Integer.TryParse(test1ListBox.SelectedItem.ToString, _
        grade.Score1)
    Integer.TryParse(test2ListBox.SelectedItem.ToString, _
        grade.Score2)

    ' use class method to calculate the grade
    Call grade.CalculateGrade()

    ' display the grade stored in the ReadOnly property
    gradeLabel.Text = grade.LetterGrade
End Sub
```

Figure 11-18: The displayButton's Click event procedure

EXAMPLE 4—USING A CLASS THAT CONTAINS TWO CONSTRUCTORS

Figure 11-19 shows the FormattedDate class defined in the FormattedDate.vb file. FormattedDate objects have two attributes: a month number and a day number. The objects also have three behaviors. First, they can initialize their attributes using values provided by the class. Second, they can initialize their attributes using values provided by the application in which they are instantiated. Third, they can return their month number and day number attributes, separated by a slash.

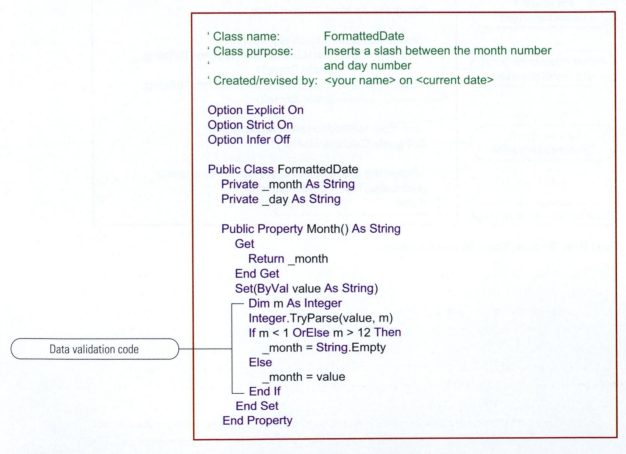

```
' Class name:         FormattedDate
' Class purpose:      Inserts a slash between the month number
'                     and day number
' Created/revised by: <your name> on <current date>

Option Explicit On
Option Strict On
Option Infer Off

Public Class FormattedDate
    Private _month As String
    Private _day As String

    Public Property Month() As String
        Get
            Return _month
        End Get
        Set(ByVal value As String)
            Dim m As Integer
            Integer.TryParse(value, m)
            If m < 1 OrElse m > 12 Then
                _month = String.Empty
            Else
                _month = value
            End If
        End Set
    End Property
```

Data validation code

Figure 11-19: FormattedDate class defined in the FormattedDate.vb file (*continued on next page*)

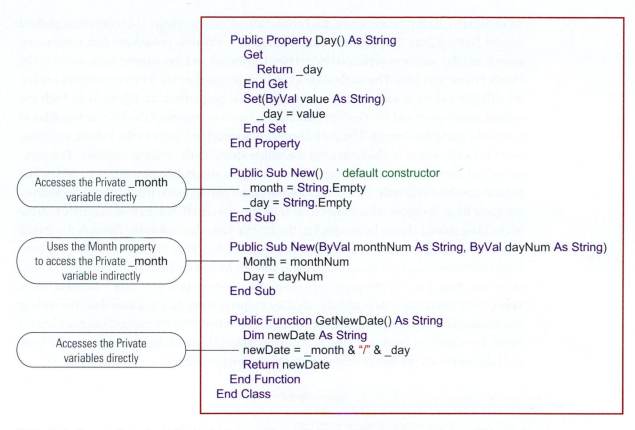

```
                    Public Property Day() As String
                        Get
                            Return _day
                        End Get
                        Set(ByVal value As String)
                            _day = value
                        End Set
                    End Property

                    Public Sub New()    ' default constructor
                        _month = String.Empty
                        _day = String.Empty
                    End Sub

                    Public Sub New(ByVal monthNum As String, ByVal dayNum As String)
                        Month = monthNum
                        Day = dayNum
                    End Sub

                    Public Function GetNewDate() As String
                        Dim newDate As String
                        newDate = _month & "/" & _day
                        Return newDate
                    End Function
                End Class
```

Accesses the Private _month variable directly

Uses the Month property to access the Private _month variable indirectly

Accesses the Private variables directly

Figure 11-19: FormattedDate class defined in the FormattedDate.vb file (*continued from previous page*)

As mentioned earlier, a class can have more than one constructor, although only one can be the default constructor. The FormattedDate class shown in Figure 11-19 contains two constructors. The first constructor is the default constructor, because it does not have any parameters. The computer processes the default constructor when you use either of the following statements to instantiate an object: Dim payDate As New FormattedDate or payDate = New FormattedDate. The second constructor allows you to specify the initial values for a FormattedDate object when the object is created. In this case, the initial values must be strings, because the constructor's *parameterList* contains two String variables. You include the initial values, enclosed in a set of parentheses, in the statement that instantiates the object, like this: Dim payDate As New FormattedDate(numMonth, numDay). The computer determines which class constructor to use by matching the number, data type, and position of the arguments with the number, data type, and position of the parameters listed in each constructor's *parameterList*. In this case, the computer will use the second constructor in the FormattedDate class, because it contains two String variables in its *parameterList*. Constructors that contain parameters are called **parameterized constructors**. The method name combined with its optional *parameterList* is called the method's **signature**.

In addition to the two constructors, the FormattedDate class in Figure 11-19 contains a method named GetNewDate. The GetNewDate method is a function procedure that returns the month and day numbers, separated by a slash. The month and day numbers are stored in the class's Private variables. The methods in a class can access the class's Private variables either directly (by name) or indirectly (through the Public properties). In Figure 11-19, both the default constructor and the GetNewDate method use the names of the Private variables to access the variables directly. The default constructor assigns values to the Private variables, and the GetNewDate method retrieves the values stored in the Private variables. The parameterized New constructor, on the other hand, uses the Public properties to access the Private variables indirectly. This is because the values passed to the parameterized constructor come from the application rather than from the class itself. Values that originate outside of the class should always be assigned to the Private variables indirectly, through the Public properties. Doing this ensures that the Property procedure's Set block, which typically contains validation code, is processed. Currently, only the Month Property procedure validates its incoming data; the Day Property procedure does not contain any data validation code. However, if validation code is added to the Day Property procedure at a later date, the code in the parameterized constructor will not need to be modified. The FormattedDate class is used in the Personnel application. Figure 11-20 shows a sample run of the application, and Figure 11-21 shows the Click event procedures for the parameterizedButton and defaultButton.

Figure 11-20: Sample run of the Personnel application

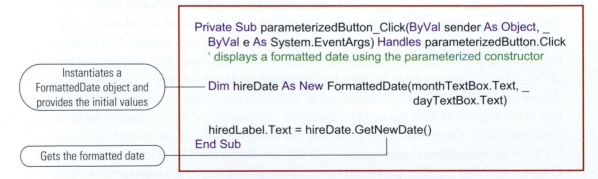

```
Private Sub parameterizedButton_Click(ByVal sender As Object, _
    ByVal e As System.EventArgs) Handles parameterizedButton.Click
    ' displays a formatted date using the parameterized constructor

    Dim hireDate As New FormattedDate(monthTextBox.Text, _
                            dayTextBox.Text)

    hiredLabel.Text = hireDate.GetNewDate()
End Sub
```

Instantiates a FormattedDate object and provides the initial values

Gets the formatted date

Figure 11-21: Click event procedures for the parameterizedButton and defaultButton (*continued on next page*)

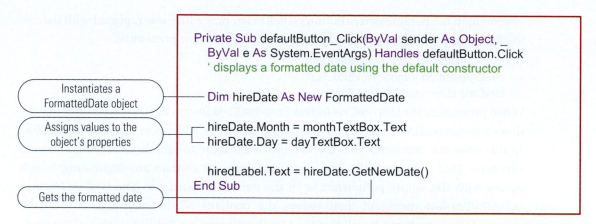

Figure 11-21: Click event procedures for the parameterizedButton and defaultButton (*continued from previous page*)

First, study the code contained in the parameterizedButton's Click event procedure. The Dim hireDate As New FormattedDate(monthTextBox.Text, dayTextBox.Text) statement instantiates a FormattedDate object and assigns its address to the hireDate variable. The computer will use the parameterized constructor to initialize the object. This is because the Dim statement contains two String arguments, which agrees with the *parameterList* in the second constructor. The computer passes the two String arguments (*by value*) to the parameterized constructor. The constructor receives the values and stores them in the monthNum and dayNum parameters listed in its procedure header. The Month = monthNum instruction in the parameterized constructor assigns the value stored in the monthNum variable to the Month property. When you assign a value to a property, the computer passes the value to the property's Set statement, where it is stored in the Set statement's value parameter. In this case, the selection structure in the Set statement (shown earlier in Figure 11-19) determines whether the value parameter contains a valid value. If the value is not valid, the selection structure's true path assigns the empty string to the Private _month variable; otherwise, it assigns the value parameter's value to the variable. Next, the Day = dayNum instruction in the parameterized constructor assigns the value stored in the dayNum variable to the Day property. The computer passes the value to the Day property's Set statement, where it is stored in the statement's value parameter. The _day = value instruction in the Set statement assigns the contents of the value parameter to the Private _day variable. Finally, the hiredLabel.Text = hireDate.GetNewDate() statement uses the FormattedDate object's GetNewDate method to return the month and day numbers, separated by a slash. The statement displays the formatted date in the hiredLabel.

Compare the code contained in the parameterizedButton's Click event procedure with the code contained in the defaultButton's Click event procedure (also shown in Figure 11-21). Notice that the Dim hireDate As New FormattedDate(monthTextBox.Text, dayTextBox.Text) statement in the parameterizedButton's Click event procedure was replaced with the following three lines of code in the defaultButton's Click event procedure:

```
Dim hireDate As New FormattedDate
hireDate.Month = monthTextBox.Text
hireDate.Day = dayTextBox.Text
```

When processing the Dim hireDate As New FormattedDate instruction, the computer instantiates a FormattedDate object, and it assigns the object's address to the hireDate variable. In this case, the computer uses the default constructor to initialize the class's Private variables. This is because the Dim statement does not contain any arguments, which agrees with the empty *parameterList* in the default constructor. The hireDate.Month = monthTextBox.Text statement then assigns the contents of the monthTextBox to the object's Month property. Recall that the Month property is a Public member of the class, and all Public members are exposed to any application that uses an instance of the class. Similarly, the hireDate.Day = dayTextBox.Text statement assigns the contents of the dayTextBox to the object's Public Day property. Finally, the hiredLabel.Text = hireDate.GetNewDate() statement gets the formatted date and displays it in the hiredLabel.

EXAMPLE 5—USING A CLASS THAT CONTAINS OVERLOADED METHODS

In this example, you use the Employee class to instantiate an object. Employee objects have two attributes: an employee number and an employee name. Employee objects also have the following four behaviors:

1. They can initialize their attributes using values provided by the class.

2. They can initialize their attributes using values provided by the application in which they are instantiated.

3. They can calculate and return the gross pay for salaried employees. The gross pay is calculated by dividing the salaried employee's annual salary by 24, because the salaried employees are paid twice per month.

4. They can calculate and return the gross pay for hourly employees. The gross pay is calculated by multiplying the number of hours the employee worked during the week by his or her pay rate.

Figure 11-22 shows the Employee class defined in the Employee.vb file. The class contains two Private variables named _number and _empName, along with their associated Number and EmpName Property procedures. It also contains four methods. The two New methods are the class's constructors. The first New method is the default constructor and the second is a parameterized constructor. When two or more methods have the same name but different parameters, the methods are referred to as **overloaded methods**. The two constructors are overloaded methods, because each is named New and each has a different *parameterList*. You can overload any of the methods contained in a class, not just constructors. The two CalculateGross methods in the Employee class also are overloaded methods, because they have the same name but a different *parameterList*. If the methods being overloaded are not constructors, you must use the Overloads keyword in the procedure header, as shown in both CalculateGross methods in Figure 11-22. The Overloads keyword is not used when overloading constructors.

> **»TIP**
> The New methods in the FormattedDate class in Figure 11-19 also are overloaded methods.

```
' Class name:      Employee
' Class purpose:   Calculates the gross pay for salaried
'                  and hourly employees
' Created/revised: <your name> on <current date>

Option Explicit On
Option Strict On
Option Infer Off

Public Class Employee
    Private _number As String
    Private _empName As String

    Public Property Number() As String
        Get
            Return _number
        End Get
        Set(ByVal value As String)
            _number = value
        End Set
    End Property
```

Figure 11-22: Employee class defined in the Employee.vb file (*continued on next page*)

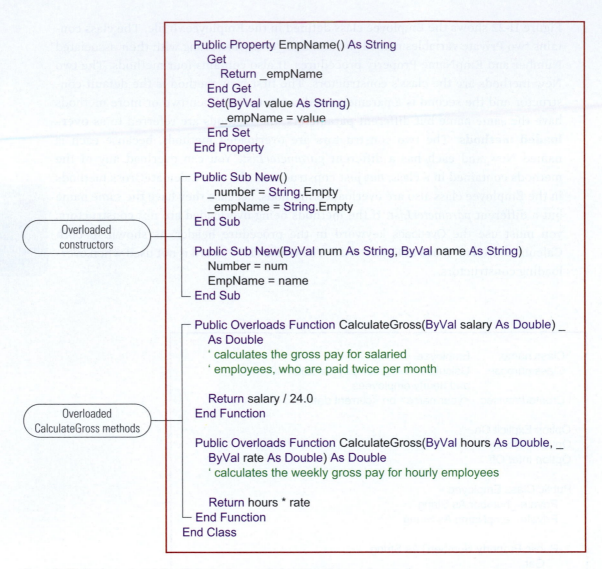

```
                    Public Property EmpName() As String
                        Get
                            Return _empName
                        End Get
                        Set(ByVal value As String)
                            _empName = value
                        End Set
                    End Property

                    Public Sub New()
                        _number = String.Empty
                        _empName = String.Empty
                    End Sub

                    Public Sub New(ByVal num As String, ByVal name As String)
                        Number = num
                        EmpName = name
                    End Sub

                    Public Overloads Function CalculateGross(ByVal salary As Double) _
                        As Double
                        ' calculates the gross pay for salaried
                        ' employees, who are paid twice per month

                        Return salary / 24.0
                    End Function

                    Public Overloads Function CalculateGross(ByVal hours As Double, _
                        ByVal rate As Double) As Double
                        ' calculates the weekly gross pay for hourly employees

                        Return hours * rate
                    End Function
                End Class
```

Overloaded constructors

Overloaded CalculateGross methods

Figure 11-22: Employee class defined in the Employee.vb file (*continued from previous page*)

You already are familiar with overloaded methods, as you have used several of the overloaded methods built into Visual Basic. Examples of such methods include ToString, TryParse, Convert.ToDecimal, and MessageBox.Show. The IntelliSense feature in the Code Editor window displays a box that allows you to view a method's signatures, one signature at a time. The box shown in Figure 11-23 displays the second of the ToString method's four signatures. You use the up and down arrows in the box to display the other signatures. The IntelliSense feature also will display the signatures of the overloaded methods contained in the classes you create.

```
' display the gross pay, then set the focus
grossLabel.Text = grossPay.ToString(|
numTextBox.Focus()   ●2 of 4●  ToString (format As String) As String
                     format: A numeric format string.
```
Signature

Figure 11-23: Box displaying one signature of the ToString method

Overloading is useful when two or more methods require different parameters to perform essentially the same task. Both overloaded constructors in the Employee class initialize the class's Private variables. However, the default constructor does not need to be passed any information to perform the task, while the parameterized constructor requires two items of information (the employee number and name). Similarly, both CalculateGross methods in the Employee class calculate and return a gross pay amount. However, the first CalculateGross method performs its task for salaried employees and requires an application to pass it one item of information: the employee's annual salary. The second CalculateGross method performs its task for hourly employees and requires two items of information: the number of hours the employee worked and his or her rate of pay. Rather than using two overloaded CalculateGross methods, you could have used two methods having different names, such as CalcSalariedGross and CalcHourlyGross. However, by overloading the CalculateGross method, you need to remember the name of only one method. The ABC Company application uses the Employee class to instantiate an object. Figures 11-24 and 11-25 show sample runs of the application, and Figure 11-26 shows the calcButton's Click event procedure.

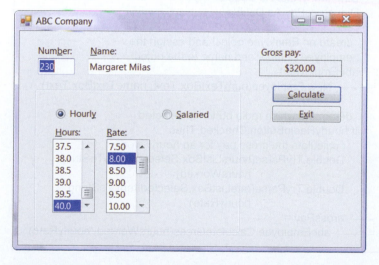

Figure 11-24: Sample run showing the gross pay for an hourly worker

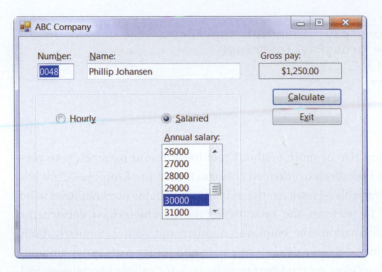

Figure 11-25: Sample run showing the gross pay for a salaried worker

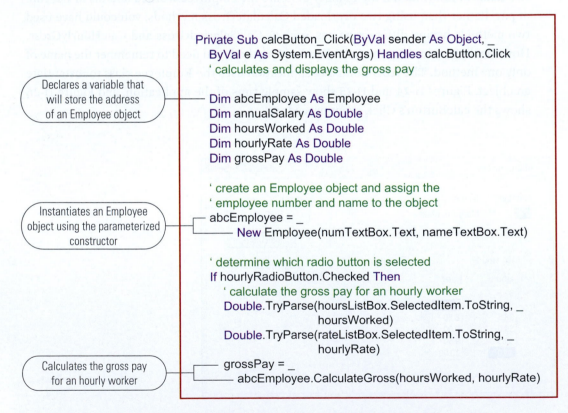

```
Private Sub calcButton_Click(ByVal sender As Object, _
    ByVal e As System.EventArgs) Handles calcButton.Click
    ' calculates and displays the gross pay

    Dim abcEmployee As Employee
    Dim annualSalary As Double
    Dim hoursWorked As Double
    Dim hourlyRate As Double
    Dim grossPay As Double

    ' create an Employee object and assign the
    ' employee number and name to the object
    abcEmployee = _
        New Employee(numTextBox.Text, nameTextBox.Text)

    ' determine which radio button is selected
    If hourlyRadioButton.Checked Then
        ' calculate the gross pay for an hourly worker
        Double.TryParse(hoursListBox.SelectedItem.ToString, _
            hoursWorked)
        Double.TryParse(rateListBox.SelectedItem.ToString, _
            hourlyRate)
        grossPay = _
            abcEmployee.CalculateGross(hoursWorked, hourlyRate)
```

Declares a variable that will store the address of an Employee object

Instantiates an Employee object using the parameterized constructor

Calculates the gross pay for an hourly worker

Figure 11-26: The calcButton's Click event procedure in the ABC Company application (*continued on next page*)

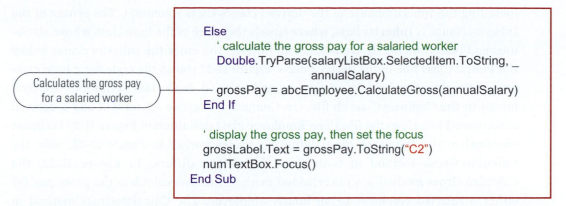

```
          Else
              ' calculate the gross pay for a salaried worker
              Double.TryParse(salaryListBox.SelectedItem.ToString, _
                          annualSalary)
              grossPay = abcEmployee.CalculateGross(annualSalary)
          End If

          ' display the gross pay, then set the focus
          grossLabel.Text = grossPay.ToString("C2")
          numTextBox.Focus()
      End Sub
```

Calculates the gross pay for a salaried worker

Figure 11-26: The calcButton's Click event procedure in the ABC Company application (*continued from previous page*)

The Dim abcEmployee As Employee statement in the procedure declares a variable that will store the address of an Employee object when the object is created. The Employee object is instantiated using the abcEmployee = New Employee(numTextBox.Text, nameTextBox.Text) statement. When instantiating the object, the computer will use the class's parameterized constructor to initialize the object's Private variables. Notice that the CalculateGross method is invoked by two statements in the procedure. The computer uses the signature of the method in each statement to determine which of the class's CalculateGross methods to process. The grossPay = abcEmployee.CalculateGross(hoursWorked, hourlyRate) statement tells the computer to use the CalculateGross method that contains two parameters, and then assign the return value to the grossPay variable. In the Employee class, the CalculateGross method that contains two parameters calculates and returns the gross pay amount for an hourly worker. The grossPay = abcEmployee.CalculateGross(annualSalary) statement, on the other hand, tells the computer to process the CalculateGross method that contains one parameter, and then assign the return value to the grossPay variable. In the Employee class, the CalculateGross method that contains one parameter calculates and returns the gross pay amount for a salaried worker. The calcButton's Click event procedure displays the contents of the grossPay variable, formatted with a dollar sign and two decimal places, in the grossLabel.

EXAMPLE 6—USING A BASE CLASS AND A DERIVED CLASS

You can create one class from another class. In OOP, this is referred to as **inheritance**. The new class is called the **derived class** and it inherits the attributes and behaviors of the original class, called the **base class**. You indicate that a class is a derived class by including the Inherits clause in the derived class's Class statement. The syntax of the Inherits clause is **Inherits** *base*, where *base* is the name of the base class whose attributes and behaviors the derived class will inherit. You enter the Inherits clause below the Public Class line in the derived class. Figure 11-27 shows the code for a base class named Employee and a derived class named Salaried. Both class definitions are contained in the CompanyClass.vb file. (In Computer Exercise 9, you will add a derived class named Hourly to the file.) The Employee class definition in Figure 11-27 is almost identical to the Employee class definition shown earlier in Figure 11-22; only the CalculateGross method in both class definitions differs. In Figure 11-22, the CalculateGross method is an overloaded method that can calculate the gross pay for either a salaried employee or an hourly employee. The CalculateGross method in Figure 11-27, on the other hand, does not perform any calculations; it doesn't even contain any code. In addition, its procedure header contains the Overridable keyword, which indicates that the method can be overridden by any class that is derived from the Employee class. In other words, classes derived from the Employee class will provide their own CalculateGross method.

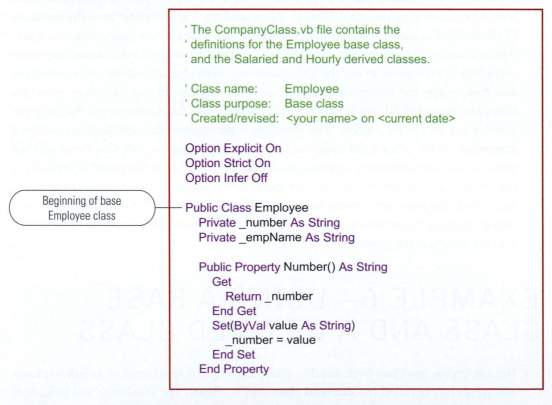

```
' The CompanyClass.vb file contains the
' definitions for the Employee base class,
' and the Salaried and Hourly derived classes.

' Class name:       Employee
' Class purpose:    Base class
' Created/revised:  <your name> on <current date>

Option Explicit On
Option Strict On
Option Infer Off

Public Class Employee
    Private _number As String
    Private _empName As String

    Public Property Number() As String
      Get
         Return _number
      End Get
      Set(ByVal value As String)
         _number = value
      End Set
    End Property
End Property
```

Beginning of base Employee class

Figure 11-27: Base Employee class and derived Salaried class defined in the CompanyClass.vb file (*continued on next page*)

```
        Public Property EmpName() As String
          Get
              Return _empName
          End Get
          Set(ByVal value As String)
              _empName = value
          End Set
        End Property

        Public Sub New()
          _number = String.Empty
          _empName = String.Empty
        End Sub

        Public Sub New(ByVal num As String, ByVal name As String)
          Number = num
          EmpName = name
        End Sub
```

Indicates that the method can be overridden in the derived class

```
        Public Overridable Function CalculateGross() As Double
              ' will be overridden in the derived classes
        End Function
      End Class


      ' Class name:      Salaried
      ' Class purpose:   Derived class that calculates
      '                  the gross pay for salaried employees
      ' Created/revised: <your name> on <current date>
```

Beginning of the derived Salaried class

```
      Public Class Salaried
        Inherits Employee
```

The derived class inherits the base class's attributes and behaviors

```
        Private _salary As Double

        Public Property Salary() As Double
          Get
              Return _salary
          End Get
          Set(ByVal value As Double)
              _salary = value
          End Set
        End Property

        Public Sub New()
          MyBase.New()
          _salary = 0
        End Sub
```

Calls the base class's default constructor

Figure 11-27: Base Employee class and derived Salaried class defined in the CompanyClass.vb file (*continued from previous page and on next page*)

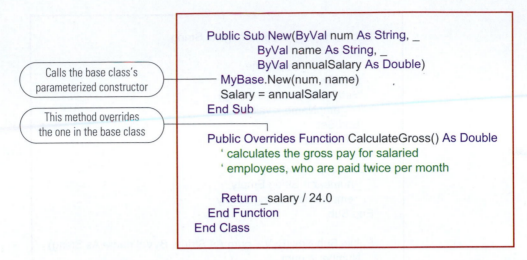

Calls the base class's parameterized constructor

This method overrides the one in the base class

```
Public Sub New(ByVal num As String, _
          ByVal name As String, _
          ByVal annualSalary As Double)
     MyBase.New(num, name)
     Salary = annualSalary
End Sub

Public Overrides Function CalculateGross() As Double
     ' calculates the gross pay for salaried
     ' employees, who are paid twice per month

     Return _salary / 24.0
End Function
End Class
```

Figure 11-27: Base Employee class and derived Salaried class defined in the CompanyClass.vb file (*continued from previous page*)

Study the code contained in the Salaried class. The Inherits Employee clause that appears below the Public Class Salaried line indicates that the Salaried class is derived from the Employee class. This means that the Salaried class includes all of the attributes and behaviors of the Employee class. The Salaried class also contains an attribute of its own: salary. The salary attribute is represented by the Private _salary variable and the Public Salary property. The salary attribute belongs to the Salaried class only. Both constructors in the Salaried class contain the statement **MyBase.New(**[*parameterList*]**)**. The statement tells the computer to process the code contained in the appropriate constructor in the base class. You refer to the base class using the MyBase keyword. The MyBase.New() statement in the default constructor tells the computer to process the code contained in the base class's default constructor. The MyBase.New(num, name) statement in the parameterized constructor indicates that the code in the base class's parameterized constructor should be processed. The CalculateGross method in the Salaried class calculates the gross pay for a salaried employee. The method's header contains the Overrides keyword, which indicates that the method overrides (replaces) the CalculateGross method contained in the base Employee class.

Earlier, you viewed the code for the calcButton's Click event procedure in the ABC Company application. The procedure used the overloaded methods from the Employee class. (The code for the procedure and class appear in Figures 11-26 and 11-22, respectively.) Figure 11-28 shows a different version of the procedure. In this version, the procedure uses the derived Salaried class shown in Figure 11-27. The code pertaining to the Salaried

▶▶TIP

Sample runs of the ABC Company application appear in Figures 11-24 and 11-25.

class is shaded in the figure. (You will complete the calcButton's Click event procedure in Computer Exercise 9 at the end of the chapter.)

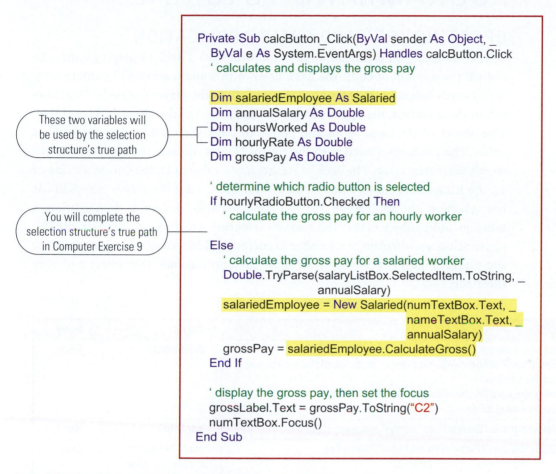

```
Private Sub calcButton_Click(ByVal sender As Object, _
    ByVal e As System.EventArgs) Handles calcButton.Click
    ' calculates and displays the gross pay

    Dim salariedEmployee As Salaried
    Dim annualSalary As Double
    Dim hoursWorked As Double
    Dim hourlyRate As Double
    Dim grossPay As Double

    ' determine which radio button is selected
    If hourlyRadioButton.Checked Then
        ' calculate the gross pay for an hourly worker

    Else
        ' calculate the gross pay for a salaried worker
        Double.TryParse(salaryListBox.SelectedItem.ToString, _
            annualSalary)
        salariedEmployee = New Salaried(numTextBox.Text, _
                                        nameTextBox.Text, _
                                        annualSalary)
        grossPay = salariedEmployee.CalculateGross()
    End If

    ' display the gross pay, then set the focus
    grossLabel.Text = grossPay.ToString("C2")
    numTextBox.Focus()
End Sub
```

These two variables will be used by the selection structure's true path

You will complete the selection structure's true path in Computer Exercise 9

Figure 11-28: Salaried class used in the calcButton's Click event procedure

The Dim salariedEmployee As Salaried instruction declares a variable that can store the address of a Salaried object. The salariedEmployee = New Salaried(numTextBox.Text, nameTextBox.Text, annualSalary) statement instantiates a Salaried object and assigns the object's address to the salariedEmployee variable. The statement passes three items of information to the Salaried class's parameterized constructor, which uses the items to initialize the newly created object. The grossPay = salariedEmployee.CalculateGross() statement uses the Salaried class's CalculateGross method to calculate and return the gross pay, which the statement assigns to the grossPay variable. You have completed the concepts section of Chapter 11.

PROGRAMMING TUTORIAL

CREATING THE CARD GAME APPLICATION

In this tutorial, you create an application that uses a deck of playing cards. To reduce the amount of code, the deck used in this application will contain only the 13 cards belonging to the suit of Hearts. When the player clicks the Deal button in the interface, the application will display two of the 13 cards, face-down. The object of the game is for the player to click the card having the highest value. The cards associated with the two of Hearts through the 10 of Hearts are worth their face value. The Jack of Hearts has a value of 11, the Queen a value of 12, the King a value of 13, and the Ace a value of 14. After the player makes his or her selection, the application displays the two cards face-up. It then displays a message indicating whether the player's selection was correct or incorrect. The application also displays the number of correct and incorrect selections made by the player. Figures 11-29 and 11-30 show the application's TOE chart and user interface.

Task	Object	Event
1. Shuffle the cards 2. Display the first two cards, face-down, in the card1PictureBox and card2PictureBox 3. Enable the card1PictureBox and card2PictureBox 4. Clear the msgLabel	dealButton	Click
Display either the "Correct!" or "Sorry!" message	msgLabel	None
1. Disable the card1PictureBox and card2PictureBox 2. Display the first two cards, face-up 3. Convert the face values of the two cards to numbers 4. Determine the highest card 5. Determine whether the player selected the highest card 6. Display appropriate message in the msgLabel 7. Update either the correct or incorrect counter 8. Display the counter values in the correctLabel and incorrectLabel	card1PictureBox, card2PictureBox	Click
End the application	exitButton	Click
Display the number of correct selections	correctLabel	None
Display the number of incorrect selections	incorrectLabel	None

Figure 11-29: TOE Chart

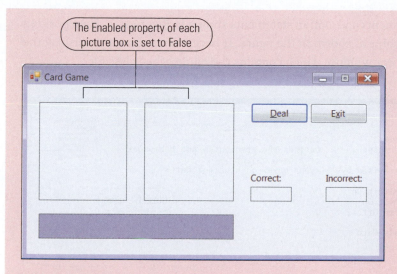

The Enabled property of each picture box is set to False

Figure 11-30: User interface

OPENING THE CARD GAME APPLICATION

Before you can begin coding the Card Game application, you need to open the Card Game Solution file.

To open the Card Game Solution file:

1. Start Visual Studio. If necessary, close the Start Page window.

2. Open the **Card Game Solution** (**Card Game Solution.sln**) file, which is contained in the VbReloaded2008\Chap11\Card Game Solution folder.

CREATING THE CARD CLASS

First you will define a class named Card. Card objects have four attributes: the face-up picture (which appears on the front of the card), the face-down picture (which appears on the back of the card), the card's face value, and the card's suit. Card objects also have two behaviors: they can initialize their attributes using values provided by the class, and they can initialize their attributes using values provided by the application.

To code the Card class:

1. First, you will need to add a class file to the project. Click **Project** on the menu bar, then click **Add Class**. The Add New Item - Card Game Project dialog box opens with Class selected in the Visual Studio installed templates list. Change the filename in the Name box to **Card.vb**, then click the **Add** button.

2. Enter the comments and Option statements shown in Figure 11-31, then position the insertion point as shown in the figure. If necessary, temporarily display the Solution Explorer window, which contains the name of the class file.

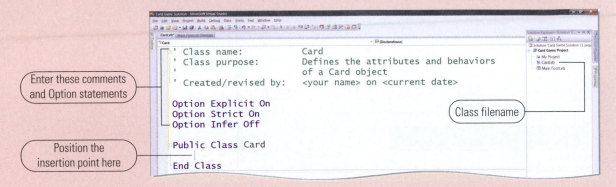

Enter these comments and Option statements

Position the insertion point here

Class filename

Figure 11-31: Comments and Option statements entered in the Card.vb class file

3. Now create Private variables for the four attributes. Enter the following Private statements. Press **Enter** twice after typing the last statement:

   Private _front As String

   Private _back As String

   Private _faceValue As String

   Private _suit As String

4. Next, you will create a Public property for each Private variable in the class. A Public property allows an application indirect access to its associated Private variable. (Recall that an application cannot directly access a Private variable in a class.) Type **Public Property Front As String** and press **Enter**. Notice that the Code Editor inserts a set of parentheses after the property name. Also notice that it enters the Get and Set statements for you, and positions the insertion point within the Get statement.

5. Recall that the Get block in a Property procedure simply returns the contents of the procedure's Private variable. Type **Return _front**.

6. The Set block in the Property procedure should assign the contents of the property's value parameter to the Private variable. Position the insertion point within the Set statement, then type **_front = value**. Figure 11-32 shows the completed Front Property procedure.

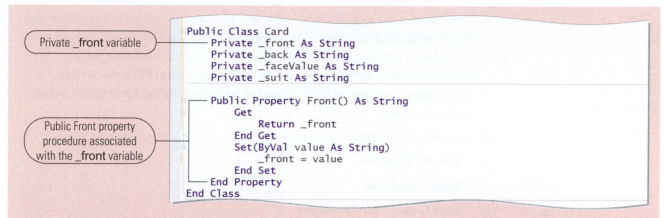

Private **_front** variable

Public Front property procedure associated with the **_front** variable

```
Public Class Card
    Private _front As String
    Private _back As String
    Private _faceValue As String
    Private _suit As String

    Public Property Front() As String
        Get
            Return _front
        End Get
        Set(ByVal value As String)
            _front = value
        End Set
    End Property
End Class
```

Figure 11-32: Completed Front Property procedure

7. Insert two blank lines below the End Property line. Now enter the Property procedure for the _back Private variable. Type **Public Property Back As String** and press **Enter**. Within the Get statement, type **Return _back**. Within the Set statement, type **_back = value**.

8. Insert two blank lines below the Back property's End Property line. Now enter the Property procedure for the _faceValue Private variable. Type **Public Property FaceValue As String** and press **Enter**. Within the Get statement, type **Return _facevalue**. Within the Set statement, type **_facevalue = value**.

9. Insert two blank lines below the FaceValue property's End Property line. Now enter the Property procedure for the _suit Private variable. Type **Public Property Suit As String** and press **Enter**. Within the Get statement, type **Return _suit**. Within the Set statement, type **_suit = value**.

10. Now you can enter the class's behaviors. You will enter the default constructor first. Insert two blank lines below the Suit property's End Property line, then enter the following code:

    Public Sub new()

    _front = String.Empty

    _back = String.Empty

    _faceValue = String.Empty

    _suit = String.Empty

    End Sub

11. The parameterized constructor is next. The parameterized constructor will allow an application to provide the initial values for the class's Private variables. Insert two blank lines below the default constructor's End Sub line. Type **Public Sub New(ByVal frontFile As String, ByVal backFile As String, _** and press **Enter**. Type **ByVal faceCharacter As String, ByVal faceSuit As String)** and press **Enter**.

12. Complete the parameterized constructor by entering the following code:

> **Front = frontFile**
>
> **Back = backFile**
>
> **FaceValue = faceCharacter**
>
> **Suit = faceSuit**

13. Save the solution. Before continuing, compare your code with the code shown in Figure 11-33. Make any needed corrections, then save the solution.

```
' Class name:          Card
' Class purpose:       Defines the attributes and behaviors
'                      of a Card object
' Created/revised by:  <your name> on <current date>

Option Explicit On
Option Strict On
Option Infer Off

Public Class Card
    Private _front As String
    Private _back As String
    Private _faceValue As String
    Private _suit As String

    Public Property Front() As String
        Get
            Return _front
        End Get
        Set(ByVal value As String)
            _front = value
        End Set
    End Property
```

Figure 11-33: Code entered in the Card class (*continued on next page*)

```vbnet
    Public Property Back() As String
        Get
            Return _back
        End Get
        Set(ByVal value As String)
            _back = value
        End Set
    End Property

    Public Property FaceValue() As String
        Get
            Return _faceValue
        End Get
        Set(ByVal value As String)
            _faceValue = value
        End Set
    End Property

    Public Property Suit() As String
        Get
            Return _suit
        End Get
        Set(ByVal value As String)
            _suit = value
        End Set
    End Property

    Public Sub New()
        _front = String.Empty
        _back = String.Empty
        _faceValue = String.Empty
        _suit = String.Empty
    End Sub

    Public Sub New(ByVal frontFile As String, ByVal backFile As String, _
                ByVal faceCharacter As String, ByVal faceSuit As String)
        Front = frontFile
        Back = backFile
        FaceValue = faceCharacter
        Suit = faceSuit
    End Sub
End Class
```

Figure 11-33: Code entered in the Card class (*continued from previous page*)

CREATING THE DECKOFCARDS CLASS

Next, you will define a class named DeckOfCards. In this application, a DeckOfCards object is composed of 13 Card objects. Each Card object represents a playing card from the suit of Hearts. DeckOfCards objects have two behaviors: they can initialize their attributes using values provided by the class, and they can shuffle themselves.

To code the DeckOfCards class:

1. First add another class file to the project. Click **Project** on the menu bar, then click **Add Class**. Change the filename in the Name box to **DeckOfCards.vb**, then click the **Add** button.

2. Enter the comments and Option statements shown in Figure 11-34, then position the insertion point as shown in the figure. If necessary, temporarily display the Solution Explorer window, which contains the names of the class files.

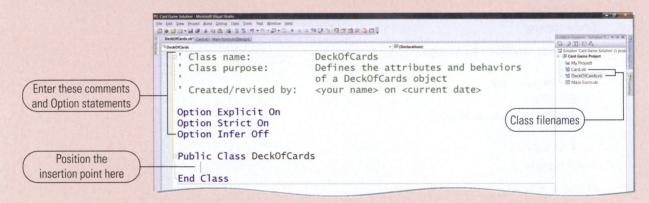

Figure 11-34: Comments and Option statements entered in the DeckOfCards.vb class file

3. As mentioned earlier, a DeckOfCards object is composed of 13 Card objects. You will store the Card objects in an array. Type **Private _cards(12) As Card** and press **Enter** twice. Notice that you can use the Card class to define an attribute of another class.

4. Next, you will create a Public property that will allow an application to access a Card object in the Private _cards array. The property should be ReadOnly, because the application will not need to set the object's attributes; the attributes will be set by the DeckOfCards class itself. To access a specific Card object in the _cards array, the application will need to pass the object's subscript to the Public property. Type **Public ReadOnly Property Cards(ByVal subscript As Integer) As Card** and press **Enter**. Notice that the Code Editor enters only the Get statement in the Property procedure. Type **Return _cards(subscript)**.

5. Now enter the default constructor, which should initialize the attribute of a DeckOfCards object. To do this, the default constructor will need to initialize each Card object's attributes. Recall that Card objects have four attributes: the face-up picture, the face-down picture, the card's value, and the card's suit. The face-up and face-down pictures of each card are stored in image files in the project's bin\Debug folder. For example, the face-up picture of the Ace of Hearts card is stored in an image file named AH.tif. (The A stands for *Ace* and the H stands for *Hearts*.) The face-down picture of each card is stored in the CardBack.tif file. Insert two blank lines below the Cards property's End Property line, then enter the following code. The code initializes each Card object in a DeckOfCards by invoking the Card class's parameterized constructor (shown earlier in Figure 11-33). The first argument is the face-up picture, the second is the face-down picture, the third is the card's face value, and the fourth is the card's suit.

```
Public Sub New()

    _cards(0) = New Card("AH.tif", "cardback.tif", "A", "H")

    _cards(1) = New Card("KH.tif", "cardback.tif", "K", "H")

    _cards(2) = New Card("QH.tif", "cardback.tif", "Q", "H")

    _cards(3) = New Card("JH.tif", "cardback.tif", "J", "H")

    _cards(4) = New Card("10H.tif", "cardback.tif", "10", "H")

    _cards(5) = New Card("9H.tif", "cardback.tif", "9", "H")

    _cards(6) = New Card("8H.tif", "cardback.tif", "8", "H")

    _cards(7) = New Card("7II.tif", "cardback.tif", "7", "H")

    _cards(8) = New Card("6H.tif", "cardback.tif", "6", "H")

    _cards(9) = New Card("5H.tif", "cardback.tif", "5", "H")

    _cards(10) = New Card("4H.tif", "cardback.tif", "4", "H")

    _cards(11) = New Card("3H.tif", "cardback.tif", "3", "H")

    _cards(12) = New Card("2H.tif", "cardback.tif", "2", "H")

End Sub
```

6. Finally, you will enter a method that can shuffle the 13 cards contained in a DeckOfCards object. Insert two blank lines below the default constructor's End Sub line. Type **Public Sub ShuffleCards()** and press **Enter**.

7. As you learned when you coded the Concentration Game application in Chapter 8, an easy way to reorder items is to swap one item with another item. In this case, you will swap one card in the _cards array with another card in the array. You can use random numbers to select the subscripts of the two cards to be swapped. To ensure that the cards are shuffled sufficiently, the ShuffleCards method will perform 25 swaps. Enter the following lines of code:

```
Dim randomGenerator As New Random
Dim randNum1 As Integer
Dim randNum2 As Integer
Dim temp As New Card

For x As Integer = 1 To 25
    randNum1 = randomGenerator.Next(0, 13)
    randNum2 = randomGenerator.Next(0, 13)
    temp = _cards(randNum1)
    _cards(randNum1) = _cards(randNum2)
    _cards(randNum2) = temp
Next x
```

8. Save the solution. Before continuing, compare the code you entered with the code shown in Figure 11-35. Make any needed corrections, then save the solution.

```
' Class name:          DeckOfCards
' Class purpose:       Defines the attributes and behaviors
'                      of a DeckOfCards object
' Created/revised by:  <your name> on <current date>

Option Explicit On
Option Strict On
Option Infer Off

Public Class DeckOfCards
    Private _cards(12) As Card

    Public ReadOnly Property Cards(ByVal subscript As Integer) As Card
        Get
            Return _cards(subscript)
        End Get
    End Property
```

Figure 11-35: Code entered in the DeckOfCards class (*continued on next page*)

```
    Public Sub New()
        _cards(0) = New Card("AH.tif", "cardback.tif", "A", "H")
        _cards(1) = New Card("KH.tif", "cardback.tif", "K", "H")
        _cards(2) = New Card("QH.tif", "cardback.tif", "Q", "H")
        _cards(3) = New Card("JH.tif", "cardback.tif", "J", "H")
        _cards(4) = New Card("10H.tif", "cardback.tif", "10", "H")
        _cards(5) = New Card("9H.tif", "cardback.tif", "9", "H")
        _cards(6) = New Card("8H.tif", "cardback.tif", "8", "H")
        _cards(7) = New Card("7H.tif", "cardback.tif", "7", "H")
        _cards(8) = New Card("6H.tif", "cardback.tif", "6", "H")
        _cards(9) = New Card("5H.tif", "cardback.tif", "5", "H")
        _cards(10) = New Card("4H.tif", "cardback.tif", "4", "H")
        _cards(11) = New Card("3H.tif", "cardback.tif", "3", "H")
        _cards(12) = New Card("2H.tif", "cardback.tif", "2", "H")
    End Sub

    Public Sub ShuffleCards()
        Dim randomGenerator As New Random
        Dim randNum1 As Integer
        Dim randNum2 As Integer
        Dim temp As New Card

        For x As Integer = 1 To 25
            randNum1 = randomGenerator.Next(0, 13)
            randNum2 = randomGenerator.Next(0, 13)
            temp = _cards(randNum1)
            _cards(randNum1) = _cards(randNum2)
            _cards(randNum2) = temp
        Next x
    End Sub
End Class
```

Figure 11-35: Code entered in the DeckOfCards class (*continued from previous page*)

CODING THE CARD GAME APPLICATION

Now that you have finished defining the Card and DeckOfCards classes, you can begin coding the Card Game application. According to the TOE chart shown earlier in Figure 11-29, four event procedures need to be coded.

To open the Code Editor window:

1. Close the DeckOfCards.vb window, then close the Card.vb window.

2. Right-click the **form**, then click **View Code** to open the Code Editor window.

Notice that the Code Editor window contains a function named GetNumber. The GetNumber function receives a String value that represents the card's face value. Examples of values that will be passed to the function include "5", "Q" (for Queen), and "A" (for Ace). The function returns the Integer value associated with the String value. When the String value is "5", the function returns the number 5. Similarly, the function returns the number 12 when the String value is "Q", and returns the number 14 when the String value is "A". The Code Editor window also contains the code for the exitButton's Click event procedure.

To begin coding the application:

1. First declare a module-level variable that can store the address of a DeckOfCards object. Click the **blank line below the Public Class line**, then press **Enter**. Type **Private cardDeck As New DeckOfCards** and press **Enter**.

2. The first procedure you will code is the dealButton's Click event procedure. According to the TOE chart, the procedure should perform four tasks: shuffle the cards, display the first two cards face-down in the picture boxes, enable the picture boxes, and clear the msgLabel. Open the code template for the dealButton's Click event procedure, then type **' shuffles the cards, then displays two cards** and press **Enter** twice.

3. You can use the DeckOfCards object's ShuffleCards method to shuffle the cards. Type **cardDeck.shufflecards()** and press **Enter** twice.

4. Now display the first two cards from the DeckOfCards object, face-down. You can access an individual Card object using the DeckOfCards object's Cards property. Recall that the Cards property is a Public ReadOnly property. To access the first Card object, for example, you use cardDeck.Cards(0). To refer to the Public Back property of the first Card object, you use cardDeck.Cards(0).Back. Because the Back property of each Card object contains the name of a file (in this case, it contains cardback.tif), you need to use the **Image.FromFile method** to retrieve the file. The Image.FromFile method's syntax is **Image.FromFile(*string*)**, where *string* is the name of the file you want to retrieve. Enter the following comment and assignment statements. Press **Enter** twice after typing the last assignment statement. As you are typing the assignment statements, notice that the list displayed by the IntelliSense feature includes the names of your classes and Public properties.

   ' display the back of the first two cards

   card1PictureBox.Image = _

   Image.FromFile(cardDeck.Cards(0).Back)

```
    card2PictureBox.Image = _

        Image.FromFile(cardDeck.Cards(1).Back)
```

5. Next, enable the picture boxes. Enter the following comment and assignment statements. Press **Enter** twice after typing the last assignment statement.

   ' enable the picture boxes

   card1PictureBox.Enabled = True

   card2PictureBox.Enabled = True

6. Finally, clear the contents of the msgLabel. Type **' clear the msgLabel** and press **Enter**, then type **msgLabel.Text = String.Empty**.

You will code the Click event procedures for the card1PictureBox and card2PictureBox next. According to the TOE chart, both procedures should perform the same tasks. Rather than entering the same code in both procedures, you will enter the code in an independent Sub procedure named DetermineHighest. When a picture box is clicked, its Click event procedure will call the Sub procedure to perform the necessary tasks. The event procedure will pass the DetermineHighest procedure a string that indicates the picture box that was clicked.

To code the Click event procedures for the two picture boxes:

1. Open the code template for the card1PictureBox's Click event procedure. Type **Call DetermineHighest("card1")**.

2. Open the code template for the card2PictureBox's Click event procedure. Type **Call DetermineHighest("card2")**.

3. Save the solution.

The last procedure you need to code is the independent DetermineHighest Sub procedure. The procedure's pseudocode is shown in Figure 11-36.

DetermineHighest Procedure
1. declare two static Integer variables for the correct and incorrect counters
2. declare two Integer variables to store the numeric face value of both cards displayed in the picture boxes
3. declare a String variable (named highest) to keep track of the highest card displayed in the picture boxes
4. disable the picture boxes so they don't respond when the user clicks them
5. display in the picture boxes the first two cards stored in the array; display the cards face-up
6. call the GetNumber function to return the numeric equivalents of both cards' face values

---

Figure 11-36: Pseudocode (*continued on next page*)

7. if the first card's numeric face value is greater than the second card's numeric face value
    assign "card1" to the highest variable
else
    assign "card2" to the highest variable
end if
8. if the user selected the highest card
    display the "Correct!" message in the msgLabel
    add 1 to the correct counter
else
    display the "Sorry!" message in the msgLabel
    add 1 to the incorrect counter
end if
9. display the correct and incorrect counter values in the correctLabel and incorrectLabel

Figure 11-36: Pseudocode (*continued from previous page*)

To code the DetermineHighest procedure:

1. Click the **blank line above the Private Function GetNumber line**, then press **Enter**. Type **Private Sub DetermineHighest(ByVal selection As String)** and press **Enter**.

2. Enter the comments and variable declaration statements indicated in Figure 11-37, then position the insertion point as shown in the figure.

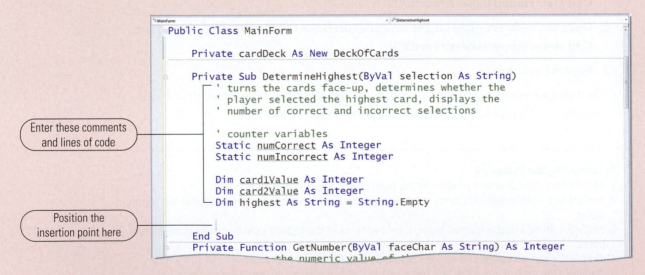

Figure 11-37: Comments and code entered in the DetermineHighest procedure

3. Step 4 in the pseudocode is to disable the picture boxes. Enter the following comment and assignment statements. Press **Enter** twice after typing the last assignment statement.

> **' disable the picture boxes**
>
> **card1PictureBox.Enabled = False**
>
> **card2PictureBox.Enabled = False**

4. Step 5 is to display the first two cards, face-up. Enter the following comment and assignment statements. Press **Enter** twice after typing the last assignment statement.

> **' display cards face-up**
>
> **card1PictureBox.Image = _**
>
> > **Image.FromFile(cardDeck.Cards(0).Front)**
>
> **card2PictureBox.Image = _**
>
> > **Image.FromFile(cardDeck.Cards(1).Front)**

5. Step 6 in the pseudocode is to call the GetNumber function to convert each card's face value to a number. You will need to call the function twice, once for each card. You will store the function's return values in the card1Value and card2Value variables. Enter the following comment and assignment statements. Press **Enter** twice after typing the last assignment statement.

> **' convert the face values to numbers**
>
> **card1Value = GetNumber(cardDeck.Cards(0).FaceValue)**
>
> **card2Value = GetNumber(cardDeck.Cards(1).FaceValue)**

6. Step 7 is a selection structure that determines the highest card. Enter the following comment and selection structure.

> **' determine the highest card**
>
> **If card1Value > card2Value Then**
>
> > **highest = "card1"**
>
> **Else**
>
> > **highest = "card2"**
>
> **End If**

7. Step 8 in the pseudocode is a selection structure that determines whether the user chose the highest card. It then displays the appropriate message and updates the appropriate counter variable. Insert two blank lines below the End If line, then type the following comment and selection structure.

' determine whether the player's choice is correct

If selection = highest Then

    msgLabel.Text = "Correct!"

    numCorrect = numCorrect + 1

Else

    msgLabel.Text = "Sorry!"

    numIncorrect = numIncorrect + 1

End If

8. The last step in the pseudocode is to display the counter values in the label controls. Insert two blank lines below the End If line from Step 7, then enter the following comment and assignment statements.

' display the counters

correctLabel.Text = numCorrect.ToString

incorrectLabel.Text = numIncorrect.ToString

9. Save the solution. Before continuing, compare your code with the code shown in Figure 11-38. Make any needed corrections, then save the solution.

```
' Project name:        Card Game Project
' Project purpose:     The project displays two cards
'                      and allows the player to guess
'                      the card with the highest value
' Created/revised by:  <your name> on <current date>

Option Explicit On
Option Strict On
Option Infer Off

Public Class MainForm

    Private cardDeck As New DeckOfCards
```

Figure 11-38: Code entered in the Main Form.vb file (*continued on next page*)

```vb
Private Sub DetermineHighest(ByVal selection As String)
    ' turns the cards face-up, determines whether the
    ' player selected the highest card, displays the
    ' number of correct and incorrect selections

    ' counter variables
    Static numCorrect As Integer
    Static numIncorrect As Integer

    Dim card1Value As Integer
    Dim card2Value As Integer
    Dim highest As String = String.Empty

    ' disable the picture boxes
    card1PictureBox.Enabled = False
    card2PictureBox.Enabled = False

    ' display cards face-up
    card1PictureBox.Image = _
        Image.FromFile(cardDeck.Cards(0).Front)
    card2PictureBox.Image = _
        Image.FromFile(cardDeck.Cards(1).Front)

    ' convert the face values to numbers
    card1Value = GetNumber(cardDeck.Cards(0).FaceValue)
    card2Value = GetNumber(cardDeck.Cards(1).FaceValue)

    ' determine the highest card
    If card1Value > card2Value Then
        highest = "card1"
    Else
        highest = "card2"
    End If

    ' determine whether the player's choice is correct
    If selection = highest Then
        msgLabel.Text = "Correct!"
        numCorrect = numCorrect + 1
    Else
        msgLabel.Text = "Sorry!"
        numIncorrect = numIncorrect + 1
    End If
```

Figure 11-38: Code entered in the Main Form.vb file (*continued from previous page and on next page*)

```vbnet
        ' display the counters
        correctLabel.Text = numCorrect.ToString
        incorrectLabel.Text = numIncorrect.ToString
End Sub

Private Function GetNumber(ByVal faceChar As String) As Integer
        ' returns the numeric value of the Card object

        Dim number As Integer

        Select Case faceChar
            Case "2", "3", "4", "5", "6", "7", "8", "9", "10"
                Integer.TryParse(faceChar, number)
            Case "J"
                number = 11
            Case "Q"
                number = 12
            Case "K"
                number = 13
            Case "A"
                number = 14
        End Select

        Return number
End Function

Private Sub exitButton_Click(ByVal sender As Object, _
        ByVal e As System.EventArgs) Handles exitButton.Click
        Me.Close()
End Sub

Private Sub dealButton_Click(ByVal sender As Object, _
        ByVal e As System.EventArgs) Handles dealButton.Click
        ' shuffles the cards, then displays two cards

        cardDeck.ShuffleCards()

        ' display the back of the first two cards
        card1PictureBox.Image = _
            Image.FromFile(cardDeck.Cards(0).Back)
        card2PictureBox.Image = _
            Image.FromFile(cardDeck.Cards(1).Back)

        ' enable the picture boxes
        card1PictureBox.Enabled = True
        card2PictureBox.Enabled = True
```

Figure 11-38: Code entered in the Main Form.vb file (*continued from previous page and on next page*)

```
      ' clear the msgLabel
      msgLabel.Text = String.Empty
   End Sub

   Private Sub card1PictureBox_Click(ByVal sender As Object, _
      ByVal e As System.EventArgs) Handles card1PictureBox.Click
      Call DetermineHighest("card1")
   End Sub

   Private Sub card2PictureBox_Click(ByVal sender As Object, _
      ByVal e As System.EventArgs) Handles card2PictureBox.Click
      Call DetermineHighest("card2")
   End Sub
End Class
```

Figure 11-38: Code entered in the Main Form.vb file (*continued from previous page*)

To test the completed Card Game application:

1. Save the solution, if necessary, then start the application. Press **Enter** to select the Deal button, which is the form's default button. Two cards appear face-down in the interface, as shown in Figure 11-39.

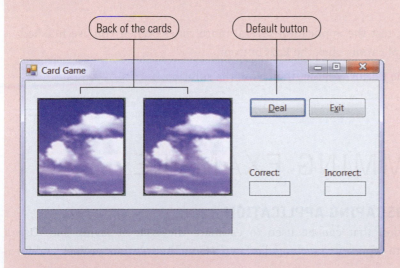

Figure 11-39: Cards are dealt face-down

---

2. Click one of the cards in the interface. The application displays the cards face-up and the appropriate message (either "Correct!" or "Sorry!") in the msgLabel. See Figure 11-40. Because the application uses random numbers to shuffle the cards, your cards and message might be different. The numbers in the correctLabel and incorrectLabel also might be different.

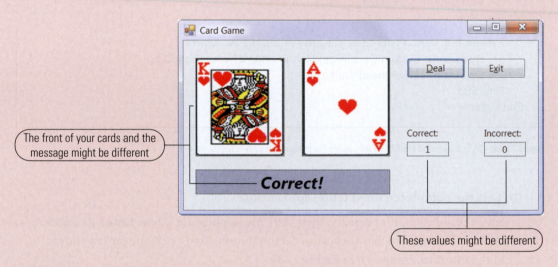

The front of your cards and the message might be different

These values might be different

Figure 11-40: The front of the cards and a message appear in the interface

3. On your own, test the application several more times. When you are finished testing the application, click the **Exit** button.

4. Close the Code Editor window, then close the solution.

PROGRAMMING EXAMPLE

KESSLER LANDSCAPING APPLICATION

Create an application that can be used to estimate the cost of laying sod. Use a MyRectangle class to represent a rectangular lawn. Name the solution, project, and form file Kessler Solution, Kessler Project, and Main Form.vb, respectively. Name the class file MyRectangle.vb. Save the application in the VbReloaded2008\Chap11 folder. See Figures 11-41 through 11-45.

Task	Object	Event
1. Calculate the area of the rectangle 2. Calculate the total price 3. Display the total price in the totalPriceLabel	calcButton	Click
End the application	exitButton	Click
Display the total price (from calcButton)	totalPriceLabel	None
Get the length in feet	lengthTextBox	None
Get the width in feet	widthTextBox	None
Get the price of the sod per square yard	priceTextBox	None
Clear the contents of the totalPriceLabel	lengthTextBox, widthTextBox, priceTextBox	TextChanged
Select the existing text		Enter

Figure 11-41: TOE chart

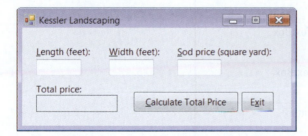

Figure 11-42: User interface

Object	Property	Setting
Form1	Name	MainForm
	Font	Segoe UI, 9 point
	MaximizeBox	False
	StartPosition	CenterScreen
	Text	Kessler Landscaping
Label1	TabIndex	0
	Text	&Length (feet):
Label2	TabIndex	2
	Text	&Width (feet):
Label3	TabIndex	4
	Text	&Sod price (square yard):
Label4	TabIndex	8
	Text	Total price:
Label5	Name	totalPriceLabel
	AutoSize	False
	BorderStyle	FixedSingle
	TabIndex	9
	Text	(empty)
	TextAlign	MiddleCenter
TextBox1	Name	lengthTextBox
	TabIndex	1
TextBox2	Name	widthTextBox
	TabIndex	3
TextBox3	Name	priceTextBox
	TabIndex	5
Button1	Name	calcButton
	TabIndex	6
	Text	&Calculate Total Price
Button2	Name	exitButton
	TabIndex	7
	Text	E&xit

Figure 11-43: Objects, Properties, and Settings

exitButton Click Event Procedure
1. close the application

calcButton Click Event Procedure
1. declare a MyRectangle object
2. assign the length and width to the MyRectangle object's Public properties
3. assign the sod price to a variable
4. calculate the area of the rectangle
5. calculate the total price of the sod
6. display the total price of the sod in the totalPriceLabel

lengthTextBox, widthTextBox, and priceTextBox TextChanged Event Procedures
1. clear the contents of the totalPriceLabel

lengthTextBox, widthTextBox, and priceTextBox Enter Event Procedures
1. select the existing text

Figure 11-44: Pseudocode

```
' Class name:          MyRectangle
' Class purpose:       Calculates the area of a rectangle.                Code entered in the
' Created/revised by:  <your name> on <current date>                     MyRectangle.vb file

Option Explicit On
Option Strict On
Option Infer Off

Public Class MyRectangle
    Private _length As Decimal
    Private _width As Decimal

    Public Property Length() As Decimal
        Get
            Return _length
        End Get
        Set(ByVal value As Decimal)
            _length = Value
        End Set
    End Property

    Public Property Width() As Decimal
        Get
            Return _width
        End Get
```

Figure 11-45: Code (*continued on next page*)

```vb
            Set(ByVal value As Decimal)
                _width = value
            End Set
        End Property

        Public Sub New()      'default constructor
            _length = 0D
            _width = 0D
        End Sub

        Public Sub New(ByVal len As Decimal, ByVal wid As Decimal)
            Length = len
            Width = wid
        End Sub

        Public Function CalculateArea() As Decimal
            Return _length * _width
        End Function
    End Class

    'Project name:        Kessler Project
    'Project purpose:     Displays the cost of laying sod
    'Created/revised by:  <your name> on <current date>

    Option Explicit On
    Option Strict On
    Option Infer Off

    Public Class MainForm

        Private Sub SelectText(ByVal sender As Object, _
            ByVal e As System.EventArgs) _
            Handles lengthTextBox.Enter, widthTextBox.Enter, priceTextBox.Enter
            ' selects the existing text
            Dim current As TextBox
            current = TryCast(sender, TextBox)
            current.SelectAll()
        End Sub

        Private Sub ClearLabel(ByVal sender As Object, _
            ByVal e As System.EventArgs) _
            Handles lengthTextBox.TextChanged, widthTextBox.TextChanged, _
            priceTextBox.TextChanged
            ' clears the total price label
            totalPriceLabel.Text = String.Empty
        End Sub
```

(Code entered in the Main Form.vb file)

Figure 11-45: Code (*continued from previous page and on next page*)

```
    Private Sub exitButton_Click(ByVal sender As Object, _
        ByVal e As System.EventArgs) Handles exitButton.Click
        Me.Close()
    End Sub

    Private Sub calcButton_Click(ByVal sender As Object, _
        ByVal e As System.EventArgs) Handles calcButton.Click
        ' calculates the cost of laying sod

        Dim lawn As New MyRectangle
        Dim sodPrice As Decimal
        Dim area As Decimal
        Dim totalPrice As Decimal

        Decimal.TryParse(lengthTextBox.Text, lawn.Length)
        Decimal.TryParse(widthTextBox.Text, lawn.Width)
        Decimal.TryParse(priceTextBox.Text, sodPrice)

        ' calculate the area (in square yards)
        area = lawn.CalculateArea / 9D

        ' calculate and display the total price
        totalPrice = area * sodPrice
        totalPriceLabel.Text = totalPrice.ToString("C2")
    End Sub
End Class
```

Figure 11-45: Code (*continued from previous page*)

QUICK REVIEW

» The objects used in an object-oriented program are instantiated (created) from classes.

» A class encapsulates (contains) the attributes that describe the object it creates, and the behaviors that allow the object to perform tasks and respond to actions.

» In Visual Basic, you use the Class statement to define a class. Class names are entered using Pascal case. You enter the class definition in a class file, which you can add to the current project using the Project menu.

» It is a good programming practice to enter the Option Explicit On, Option Strict On, and Option Infer Off statements in the form file and in any class files.

» The names of the Public variables in a class are entered using Pascal case. Variables declared using the Public keyword in a class definition can be accessed by any application that uses an object created from the class. A class cannot control the values assigned to its Public variables.

» Most classes contain properties and methods.

» When naming the Private variables in a class, many programmers begin the name with the underscore character. Subsequent characters in the name should be entered using camel case.

» When an object is instantiated in an application, the Public members of the class are exposed to the application; the Private members are hidden from the application.

» When an application needs to assign data to or retrieve data from a Private variable in a class, it must use a Public property to do so. You create a Public property using a Property procedure.

» You use the ReadOnly keyword in a Property procedure header to create a property whose value can be retrieved (read), but not set.

» You use the WriteOnly keyword in a Property procedure header to create a property whose value can be set, but not retrieved.

» The names of the properties in a class should be entered using Pascal case. You should use nouns and adjectives in the name.

» The Get block in a Property procedure allows an application to access the contents of the Private variable associated with the property.

» The Set block in a Property procedure allows an application to assign a value to the Private variable associated with the property.

» A class can have one or more constructors. All constructors are Sub procedures that are named New. Each constructor must have a different *parameterList* (if any).

» A constructor that has no parameters is the default constructor. A class can contain only one default constructor. Constructors that contain parameters are called parameterized constructors.

» The computer processes the constructor whose parameters match (in number, data type, and position) the arguments contained in the statement that instantiates the object.

» The names of the methods in a class should be entered using Pascal case. You should use a verb for the first word in the name, and nouns and adjectives for any subsequent words in the name.

» Values that originate outside the class should always be assigned to the Private variables indirectly, through the Public properties.

» You use the Overridable keyword to indicate that a method in the base class can be overridden (replaced) in the derived class.

» You use the Overrides keyword to indicate that a method in the derived class overrides (replaces) a method in the base class.

» You use the Inherits clause to create a derived class.

» The MyBase keyword refers to the base class.

» While an application is running, you can use the Image.FromFile method to retrieve an image file from a computer disk.

KEY TERMS

Attributes—the characteristics that describe an object

Base class—the original class from which another class is derived

Behaviors—includes an object's methods and events

Class—a pattern (or blueprint) that the computer follows when creating (instantiating) an object

Class statement—the statement used to define a class in Visual Basic

Constructor—a method whose instructions are automatically processed each time the class instantiates an object; its purpose is to initialize the class's variables

Default constructor—a constructor that has no parameters

Derived class—a class that inherits the attributes and behaviors of a base class

Encapsulates—an OOP term that means "contains"

Events—the actions to which an object can respond

Get block—the section of a Property procedure that contains the Get statement

Get statement—appears in a Get block in a Property procedure; contains the code that allows an application to retrieve the contents of the Private variable associated with the property

Image.FromFile method—retrieves an image file from a computer disk while an application is running

Inheritance—the ability to create one class from another class

Instance—an object created from a class

Instantiated—the process of creating an object from a class

Methods—the actions that an object is capable of performing

OOP—an acronym for Object-Oriented Programming

Overloaded methods—methods that have the same name but different *parameterLists*

Parameterized constructors—constructors that contain parameters

Property procedure—creates a Public property that can be used to access a Private variable in a class

Set block—the section of a Property procedure that contains the Set statement

Set statement—appears in a Set block in a Property procedure; contains the code that allows an application to assign a value to the Private variable associated with the property

Signature—a method name combined with its *parameterList*

SELF-CHECK QUESTIONS AND ANSWERS

1. In Visual Basic, you enter the Class statement in a class file whose filename ends with

   _____.

   a. .cla

   b. .cls

   c. .vb

   d. None of the above.

2. When two methods have the same name but different *parameterLists*, the methods are referred to as _____ methods.

   a. loaded

   b. overloaded

   c. parallel

   d. None of the above.

3. Some constructors return a value.

   a. True

   b. False

4. The Product class contains a Private variable named _price that is associated with a Public property named Price. The class also contains a Public method named CalculateNewPrice; the method is a Function procedure. An application instantiates a Product object and assigns its address to a variable named item. Which of the following statements can the application use to assign the number 45 to the _price variable?

   a. _price = 45

   b. Price = 45

   c. _price.item = 45

   d. None of the above.

5. Which of the following statements can be used by the application in Question 4 to call the CalculateNewPrice method?

   a. newPrice = Call CalculateNewPrice()

   b. newPrice = Price.CalculateNewPrice()

   c. newPrice = item.CalculateNewPrice()

   d. newPrice = item.CalculateNewPrice(_price)

Answers: 1) c, 2) b, 3) b, 4) d, 5) c

REVIEW QUESTIONS

1. Which of the following statements is false?

   a. An example of an attribute is the _minutes variable in a Time class.

   b. An example of a behavior is the SetTime method in a Time class.

   c. An object created from a class is referred to as an instance of the class.

   d. A class is considered an object.

2. A Private variable in a class can be accessed directly by a Public method in the same class.

   a. True   b. False

3. An application can access the Private variables in a class _____.

   a. directly

   b. using properties created by Property procedures

   c. through Private procedures contained in the class

   d. None of the above.

4. To expose a variable or method contained in a class, you declare the variable or method using the keyword _____.

   a. Exposed   b. Private

   c. Public   d. Viewed

5. The name of the default constructor for a class named Animal is _____.

   a. Animal

   b. AnimalConstructor

   c. Constructor

   d. None of the above.

6. An overloaded method that is not a constructor must contain the keyword _____ in its procedure header.

    a. Loaded   b. Overload

    c. Overloaded   d. None of the above.

7. The method name combined with the method's optional *parameterList* is called the method's _____.

    a. autograph   b. inscription

    c. signature   d. None of the above.

8. A constructor is _____.

    a. a Function procedure   b. a Property procedure

    c. a Sub procedure   d. either a Function procedure or a Sub procedure

9. Which of the following creates an Animal object and assigns the object's address to the dog variable?

    a. Dim dog As Animal

    b. Dim dog As New Animal

    c. Dim dog As Animal

       dog = New Animal

    d. Both b and c.

10. An application creates an Animal object and assigns its address to the dog variable. Which of the following calls the DisplayBreed method contained in the Animal class?

    a. Call Animal.DisplayBreed()   b. Call DisplayBreed.Animal()

    c. Call DisplayBreed().Dog   d. Call dog.DisplayBreed()

11. If you need to validate a value before assigning it to a Private variable, you enter the validation code in the _____ block in a Property procedure.

    a. Assign   b. Get

    c. Set   d. Validate

12. An application creates a Date object and assigns its address to the payDate variable. The Date class contains a Public Month property that is associated with a Private String variable named _month. Which of the following assigns the number 12 to the Month property?

    a. payDate.Month = "12"   b. payDate.Month._month = "12"

    c. payDate._month = "12"   d. Date.Month = "12"

13. The Return statement is entered in the _____ block in a Property procedure.

    a. Get   b. Set

14. Which of the following statements retrieves the image stored in the "Dog.gif" file and displays the image in the animalPictureBox?

    a. animalPictureBox.Image = Image.FromFile("Dog.gif")

    b. animalPictureBox.Image.FromFile("Dog.gif")

    c. animalPictureBox.FileImage("Dog.gif")

    d. animalPictureBox.Image = ImageFile("Dog.gif")

15. Which of the following clauses allows a derived class named Dog to have the same attributes and behaviors as its base class, which is named Animal?

    a. Inherits Animal   b. Inherits Dog

    c. Overloads Animal   d. Overloads Dog

16. A base class contains a method named CalcBonus. Which of the following procedure headers can be used in the base class to indicate that a derived class can provide its own code for the method?

    a. Public Inherits Sub CalcBonus()

    b. Public Overloads Sub CalcBonus()

    c. Public Overridable Sub CalcBonus()

    d. Public Overrides Sub CalcBonus()

17. A base class contains a method named CalcBonus. Which of the following procedure headers can be used in the derived class to indicate that it is providing its own code for the method?

    a. Public Inherits Sub CalcBonus()

    b. Public Overloads Sub CalcBonus()

    c. Public Overridable Sub CalcBonus()

    d. Public Overrides Sub CalcBonus()

18. A class contains a Private variable named _location that is associated with a Public property named Location. Which of the following is the correct way for the default constructor to assign the value "Unknown" to the variable?

    a. _location = "Unknown"

    b. _location.Location = "Unknown"

    c. Location._location = "Unknown"

    d. None of the above.

19. A class contains a Private variable named _capital that is associated with a Public property named Capital. Which of the following is the best way for a parameterized constructor to assign the value stored in its capName parameter to the variable?

    a. _capital - capName

    b. Capital = capName

    c. _capital.Capital = capName

    d. None of the above.

20. A class can contain only one constructor.

    a. True   b. False

REVIEW EXERCISES— SHORT ANSWER

1. Write a Class statement that defines a class named Book. The class contains three Public variables named Title, Author, and Cost. The Title and Author variables are String variables. The Cost variable is a Decimal variable. Then use the syntax shown in Version 1 in Figure 11-5 to declare a variable that can store the address of a Book object; name the variable fiction. Create the Book object and assign its address to the fiction variable.

2. Write a Class statement that defines a class named Tape. The class contains four Public String variables named Name, Artist, SongNumber, and Length. Then use the syntax shown in Version 2 in Figure 11-5 to create a Tape object, assigning its address to a variable named blues.

3. An application contains the class definition shown in Figure 11-46.

```
Public Class Computer
    Private _model As String
    Private _cost As Decimal

    Public Property Model() As String
        Get
            Return _model
        End Get
        Set(ByVal value As String)
            _model = value
        End Set
    End Property
```

Figure 11-46 (continued on next page)

```
    Public Property Cost() As Decimal
        Get
            Return _cost
        End Get
        Set(ByVal value As Decimal)
            _cost = value
        End Set
    End Property

    Public Sub New()
        _model = String.Empty
        _cost = 0D
    End Sub

    Public Sub New(ByVal comType As String, ByVal price As Decimal)
        Model = comType
        Cost = price
    End Sub

    Public Function IncreasePrice() As Decimal
        Return _cost * 1.2D
    End Function
End Class
```

Figure 11-46 (*continued from previous page*)

a. Write a Dim statement that creates a Computer object and initializes it using the default constructor. Assign the object's address to a variable named homeUse.

b. Write an assignment statement that uses the Computer object created in Step a to assign the string "IB-50" to the Model property.

c. Write an assignment statement that uses the Computer object created in Step a to assign the number 2400 to the Cost property.

d. Write an assignment statement that uses the Computer object created in Step a to call the IncreasePrice function. Assign the function's return value to a variable named newPrice.

e. Write a Dim statement that creates a Computer object and initializes it using the parameterized constructor. Assign the object's address to a variable named companyUse. Use the following values to initialize the object: "IBM" and 1236.99.

4. Write the class definition for a class named Employee. The class should include Private variables and Property procedures for an Employee object's name and salary. The salary may contain a decimal place. The class also should contain two constructors: the default constructor and a constructor that allows an application to assign values to the Private variables.

5. Add the CalculateNewSalary method to the Employee class you defined in Review Exercise 4. The method should calculate and return an Employee object's new salary, which is based on a raise percentage provided by the application using the object. Before calculating the new salary, the method should verify that the raise percentage is greater than or equal to zero. If the raise percentage is less than zero, the method should assign the number 0 as the new salary.

6. Write the Property procedure for a ReadOnly property named BonusRate. The property's data type is Decimal.

7. What are overloaded methods and why are they used?

COMPUTER EXERCISES

1. In this exercise, you create an application that uses a class.

   a. Create the Sweets Unlimited interface shown in Figure 11-7. Name the solution Sweets Solution. Name the project Sweets Project. Name the form file Main Form.vb. Save the application in the VbReloaded2008\Chap11 folder.

   b. Add a class file to the project. Name the class file Salesperson.vb. Use the code shown in Figure 11-6 to define the class. Close the Salesperson.vb window.

   c. Use the code shown in Figure 11-9 to code the saveButton's Click event procedure. Also code both text boxes' Enter event procedure; both procedures should select the existing text.

   d. Save the solution, then start the application. Test the application using the data shown in Figure 11-8. End the application.

   e. Open the sales.txt file to verify its contents, then close the sales.txt window. Close the Code Editor window, then close the solution.

2. In this exercise, you modify the Sweets Unlimited application from Computer Exercise 1.

   a. Use Windows to make a copy of the Sweets Solution folder, which is contained in the VbReloaded2008\Chap11 folder. Rename the folder Modified Sweets Solution.

   b. Use Windows to delete the sales.txt file contained in the VbReloaded2008\Chap11\Modified Sweets Solution\Sweets Project\bin\Debug folder.

   c. Open the Sweets Solution (Sweets Solution.sln) file contained in the VbReloaded2008\Chap11\Modified Sweets Solution folder.

d. Modify the Salesperson class so that it uses Private variables and Public Property procedures rather than Public variables for the name and sales. Remove the bonus amount from the class. Include two constructors in the class: the default constructor and a parameterized constructor. Include a method that calculates and returns the bonus amount, using the bonus rate provided by the application.

e. Make the necessary modifications to the Sweets Unlimited application's code.

f. Save the solution, then start the application. Test the application using the data shown in Figure 11-8. End the application.

g. Open the sales.txt file to verify its contents, then close the sales.txt window. Close the Code Editor window, then close the solution.

3. In this exercise, you code an application that uses a class.

a. Open the Area Solution (Area Solution.sln) file, which is contained in the VbReloaded2008\Chap11\Area Solution folder.

b. Add a class file to the project. Name the class file Square.vb. Use the code shown in Figure 11-10 to define the class. Close the Square.vb window.

c. Use the code shown in Figure 11-15 to code the calcButton's Click event procedure. Also code the text box's Enter and TextChanged event procedures. The Enter event procedure should select the existing text. The TextChanged event procedure should clear the contents of the areaLabel.

d. Save the solution, then start and test the application. End the application. Close the Code Editor window, then close the solution.

4. In this exercise, you modify the application from Computer Exercise 3.

a. Use Windows to make a copy of the Area Solution folder, which is contained in the VbReloaded2008\Chap11 folder. Rename the folder Modified Area Solution.

b. Open the Area Solution (Area Solution.sln) file contained in the VbReloaded2008\Chap11\Modified Area Solution folder.

c. Make the following modifications to the Square class:

1) Add a Private variable named _area.

2) Associate the _area variable with a Property procedure named Area.

3) Change the CalculateArea method to a Sub procedure. The method should calculate the area and then assign the result to the _area variable.

4) Include a parameterized constructor in the class. The constructor should accept one argument: the side measurement. After using the Public property to initialize the Private variable, the constructor should automatically call the CalculateArea method.

d. Modify the calcButton's Click event procedure so that it uses the parameterized constructor to instantiate the Square object. The parameterized constructor will automatically calculate the area of the square; therefore, you can delete the line of code that calls the CalculateArea method in the event procedure.

e. Save the solution, then start and test the application. End the application. Close the Code Editor windows, then close the solution.

5. In this exercise, you code an application that uses a class.

a. Open the Grade Solution (Grade Solution.sln) file, which is contained in the VbReloaded2008\Chap11\Grade Solution folder.

b. Add a class file to the project. Name the class file CourseGrade.vb. Use the code shown in Figure 11-16 to define the class. Close the CourseGrade.vb window.

c. Use the code shown in Figure 11-18 to code the displayButton's Click event procedure.

d. Save the solution, then start and test the application. End the application. Close the Code Editor window, then close the solution.

6. In this exercise, you code an application that uses a class.

a. Open the Personnel Solution (Personnel Solution.sln) file, which is contained in the VbReloaded2008\Chap11\Personnel Solution folder.

b. Add a class file to the project. Name the class file FormattedDate.vb. Use the code shown in Figure 11-19 to define the class. Close the FormattedDate.vb window.

c. Use the code shown in Figure 11-21 to code the Click event procedures for the parameterizedButton and defaultButton.

d. Save the solution, then start and test the application. End the application. Close the Code Editor window, then close the solution.

7. In this exercise, you modify the application from Computer Exercise 6.

a. Use Windows to make a copy of the Personnel Solution folder, which is contained in the VbReloaded2008\Chap11 folder. Rename the folder Modified Personnel Solution.

b. Open the Personnel Solution (Personnel Solution.sln) file contained in the VbReloaded2008\Chap11\Modified Personnel Solution folder.

c. Modify the interface to allow the user to enter the year number.

d. The FormattedDate class should create an object that returns a month number, followed by a slash, a day number, a slash, and a year number. Modify the class appropriately.

e. Modify the FormattedDate class to validate the day number, which should be from 1 through 31.

    f. Make the necessary modifications to the Personnel application's code.

    g. Save the solution, then start and test the application. End the application. Close the Code Editor windows, then close the solution.

8. In this exercise, you code an application that uses a class.

    a. Open the ABC Solution (ABC Solution.sln) file, which is contained in the VbReloaded2008\Chap11\ABC Solution folder.

    b. Open the Employee.vb class file in the Code Editor window. Use the code shown in Figure 11-22 to code the class.

    c. Use the code shown in Figure 11-26 to code the calcButton's Click event procedure.

    d. Save the solution, then start and test the application, using Figures 11-24 and 11-25 as a guide. End the application. Close the Code Editor windows, then close the solution.

9. In this exercise, you modify the application from Computer Exercise 8. The modified application uses a base class and a derived class.

    a. Use Windows to make a copy of the ABC Solution folder, which is contained in the VbReloaded2008\Chap11 folder. Rename the folder Modified ABC Solution.

    b. Open the ABC Solution (ABC Solution.sln) file contained in the VbReloaded2008\Chap11\Modified ABC Solution folder.

    c. In the Solution Explorer, change the name of the Employee.vb file to CompanyClass.vb.

    d. Right-click CompanyClass.vb in the Solution Explorer window, then click View Code. Use the code shown in Figure 11-27 to modify the file's contents.

    e. Right-click the form, then click View Code. Use the code shown in Figure 11-28 to modify the calcButton's Click event procedure.

    f. Save the solution, then start and test the application, using Figure 11-25 as a guide. End the application.

    g. Include another class definition in the CompanyClass.vb file. Name the class Hourly. The Hourly class should contain a CalculateGross method that calculates the gross pay for an hourly employee. Calculate the gross pay by multiplying the hours worked by the pay rate.

    h. Use the Hourly class to instantiate an object in the calcButton's Click event procedure, then complete the selection structure's true path.

    i. Save the solution, then start and test the application, using Figures 11-24 and 11-25 as a guide. End the application. Close the Code Editor windows, then close the solution.

10. In this exercise, you use the Employee class from Review Exercise 5.

   a. Open the Salary Solution (Salary Solution.sln) file, which is contained in the VbReloaded2008\Chap11\Salary Solution folder.

   b. Open the Employee.vb class file in the Code Editor window, then enter the class definition that you created in Review Exercise 5.

   c. Open the Main Form.vb file in the Code Editor window. Use the comments that appear in the code to enter the missing instructions.

   d. Save the solution, then start the application. Test the application by entering your name, a current salary amount of 54000, and a raise percentage of 10 (for 10%). The application should display the number $59,400. End the application. Close the Code Editor windows, then close the solution.

11. In this exercise, you modify the MyRectangle class from the chapter's Programming Example. You then use the class in a different application.

   a. Jack Sysmanski, the owner of All-Around Fence Company, wants an application that calculates the cost of installing a fence. Create an interface that allows the user to enter the length and width (both in feet) of a rectangle, as well as the fence cost per linear foot. Name the solution, project, and form file Fence Solution, Fence Project, and Main Form.vb, respectively. Save the application in the VbReloaded2008\Chap11 folder.

   b. Use Windows to copy the MyRectangle.vb file from the VbReloaded2008\Chap11\Kessler Solution\Kessler Project folder to the VbReloaded2008\Chap11\Fence Solution\Fence Project folder.

   c. Use the Project menu to add the existing MyRectangle.vb class file to the Fence project.

   d. Modify the MyRectangle class so that it calculates and returns the perimeter of a rectangle. To calculate the perimeter, the class will need to add together the length and width measurements, and then multiply the sum by 2.

   e. Code the Fence application so that it displays the cost of installing the fence.

   f. Save the solution, then start the application. Test the application using 120 as the length, 75 as the width, and 10 as the cost per linear foot. The application should display $3,900.00 as the installation cost. End the application. Close the Code Editor windows, then close the solution.

12. In this exercise, you modify the MyRectangle class from the chapter's Programming Example. You then use the class in a different application.

   a. The manager of Pool-Time, which sells in-ground pools, wants an application that determines the number of gallons of water required for filling an in-ground pool—

a question commonly asked by customers. (*Hint*: To calculate the number of gallons, you need to find the volume of the pool. You can do this using the formula *length * width * depth.*) Create an appropriate interface. Name the solution, project, and form file Pool Solution, Pool Project, and Main Form.vb, respectively. Save the application in the VbReloaded2008\Chap11 folder.

b. Use Windows to copy the MyRectangle.vb file from the VbReloaded2008\ Chap11\Kessler Solution\Kessler Project folder to the VbReloaded2008\Chap11\ Pool Solution\Pool Project folder.

c. Use the Project menu to add the existing MyRectangle.vb class file to the Pool project.

d. Modify the MyRectangle class so that it also calculates and returns the volume.

e. Code the Pool application so that it displays the number of gallons. To calculate the number of gallons, you divide the volume by .13368.

f. Save the solution, then start the application. Test the application using 25 feet as the length, 15 as the width, and 6.5 feet as the depth. The application should display 18,233.84 as the number of gallons. End the application. Close the Code Editor windows, then close the solution.

13. In this exercise, you define a Triangle class. You also create an application that uses the Triangle class to create a Triangle object.

a. Create an interface that allows the user to display either the area of a triangle or the perimeter of a triangle. (*Hint*: The formula for calculating the area of a triangle is 1/2 * *base * height*. The formula for calculating the perimeter of a triangle is $a + b + c$, where *a*, *b*, and *c* are the lengths of the sides.) Name the solution, project, and form file Math Solution, Math Project, and Main Form.vb, respectively. Save the application in the VbReloaded2008\Chap11 folder.

b. Add a class file to the project. Name the class file Triangle.vb. The Triangle class should verify that the dimensions are greater than zero before assigning the values to the Private variables. The class also should include a method to calculate the area of a triangle and a method to calculate the perimeter of a triangle.

c. Save the solution, then start and test the application. End the application. Close the Code Editor windows, then close the solution.

14. In this exercise, you modify the Card Game application from the chapter's Programming Tutorial.

a. Use Windows to make a copy of the Card Game Solution folder, which is contained in the VbReloaded2008\Chap11 folder. Rename the copy Modified Card Game Solution.

b. Open the Card Game Solution (Card Game Solution.sln) file contained in the VbReloaded2008\Chap11\Modified Card Game Solution folder.

c. Currently, the application shuffles the cards each time the user clicks the Deal button. It also displays only the first two cards from the array. Modify the application so that it displays the first two cards when the Deal button is clicked the first time, the next two cards when the Deal button is clicked the second time, and so on. Shuffle the cards only after the first 12 cards have been displayed.

d. Save the solution, then start and test the application. End the application. Close the Code Editor windows, then close the solution.

15. In this exercise, you modify the Card Game application from Computer Exercise 14.

a. Use Windows to make a copy of the Modified Card Game Solution folder, which is contained in the VbReloaded2008\Chap11 folder. Rename the copy Modified Card Game Solution-Disc1.

b. Open the Card Game Solution (Card Game Solution.sln) file contained in the VbReloaded2008\Chap11\Modified Card Game Solution-Disc1 folder.

c. Modify the application so that it uses the 52 cards found in a typical deck of playing cards. The face-up pictures of each card are stored in image files contained in the project's bin\Debug folder. The application should shuffle the cards only after each of the 52 cards has been displayed.

d. If the two cards in the interface have the same face value, use the following rules to determine the higher card: Hearts are the highest, followed by Diamonds, then Clubs, and then Spades. For example, if the two cards are the 10 of Diamonds and the 10 of Clubs, the 10 of Diamonds is the higher card.

e. Save the solution, then start and test the application. End the application. Close the Code Editor windows, then close the solution.

16. In this exercise, you modify the Card Game application from the chapter's Programming Tutorial.

a. Use Windows to make a copy of the Card Game Solution folder, which is contained in the VbReloaded2008\Chap11 folder. Rename the copy Modified Card Game Solution-Disc2.

b. Open the Card Game Solution (Card Game Solution.sln) file contained in the VbReloaded2008\Chap11\Modified Card Game Solution-Disc2 folder.

c. Modify the application so that it displays three cards rather than two cards.

d. Save the solution, then start and test the application. End the application. Close the Code Editor windows, then close the solution.

17. In this exercise, you practice debugging an application.

   a. Open the Debug Solution (Debug Solution.sln) file, which is contained in the VbReloaded2008\Chap11\Debug Solution folder.

   b. Open the Code Editor window. Review the existing code in the Main Form.vb and Computer.vb files. Notice that a jagged line appears below some of the lines of code in the Main Form.vb window. Correct the code to remove the jagged lines.

   c. Save the solution, then start the application. Correct the errors in the application's code, then save the solution and start the application again. Test the application.

   d. End the application, then close the solution.

CASE PROJECTS

GLASGOW HEALTH CLUB

Each member of Glasgow Health Club must pay monthly dues that consist of a basic fee and one or more optional charges. The basic monthly fee for a single membership is $50; for a family membership, it is $90. If the member has a single membership, the additional monthly charges are $30 for tennis, $25 for golf, and $20 for racquetball. If the member has a family membership, the additional monthly charges are $50 for tennis, $35 for golf, and $30 for racquetball. The application should display the member's basic fee, additional charges, and monthly dues. Name the solution, project, and form file Glasgow Health Solution, Glasgow Health Project, and Main Form.vb, respectively. Save the application in the VbReloaded2008\Chap11 folder. Be sure to use a class in the application. You can either create your own interface or create the one shown in Figure 11-47.

Figure 11-47: Sample interface for Glasgow Health Club

FRANKLIN CALENDARS

Jeremiah Carter, the manager of the Accounts Payable department at Franklin Calendars, wants an application that keeps track of the checks written by his department. More specifically, he wants to record (in a sequential access file) the check number, date, payee, and amount of each check. Name the solution, project, and form file Franklin Calendars Solution, Franklin Calendars Project, and Main Form.vb, respectively. Save the application in the VbReloaded2008\Chap11 folder. Be sure to use a class in the application. You can either create your own interface or create the one shown in Figure 11-48.

Figure 11-48: Sample interface for Franklin Calendars

BINGO GAME

Create an application that simulates the game of Bingo. Name the solution, project, and form file Bingo Game Solution, Bingo Game Project, and Main Form.vb, respectively. Save the application in the VbReloaded2008\Chap11 folder. Be sure to use a class in the application. You can either create your own interface or create the one shown in Figure 11-49.

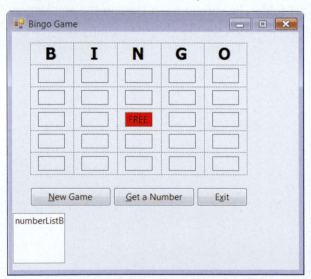

Figure 11-49: Sample interface for the Bingo Game application

PENNINGTON BOOK STORE

Shelly Jones, the manager of Pennington Book Store, wants an application that she can use to calculate and display the total amount a customer owes. Name the solution, project, and form file Pennington Solution, Pennington Project, and Main Form.vb, respectively. Create the interface shown in Figure 11-50. Assume that a customer can purchase one or more books at either the same price or different prices. The application should keep a running total of the amount the customer owes, and display the total in the Total due box. For example, a customer might purchase two books at $6 and three books at $10. To calculate the total due, Shelly will need to enter 2 in the Quantity box and 6 in the Price box, and then click the Add to Sale button. The Total due box should display $12.00. To complete the order, Shelly will need to enter 3 in the Quantity box and 10 in the Price box, and then click the Add to Sale button. The Total due box should display $42.00. Before calculating the next customer's order, Shelly will need to click the New Order button. Be sure to use a class in the application.

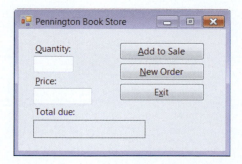

Figure 11-50: Interface for the Pennington Book Store

CHAPTER TWELVE

12

WORKING WITH ACCESS DATABASES AND LINQ

After studying Chapter 12, you should be able to:

Define the terms used when talking about databases

Connect an application to a Microsoft Access database

Bind table and field objects to controls

Explain the purpose of the DataSet, BindingSource,

TableAdapter, TableAdapterManager, and

BindingNavigator objects

Customize a DataGridView control

Handle errors using the Try...Catch statement

Position the record pointer in a dataset

Query a dataset using LINQ

Use the LINQ aggregate methods

DATABASE TERMINOLOGY

In order to maintain accurate records, most businesses store information about their employees, customers, and inventory in computer databases. A **computer database** is an electronic file that contains an organized collection of related information. Many products exist for creating computer databases; such products are called database management systems (or DBMS). Some of the most popular database management systems are Microsoft Access, Microsoft SQL Server, and Oracle. You can use Visual Basic to access the data stored in databases created by these database management systems. This allows a company to create a standard interface in Visual Basic that employees can use to access information stored in a variety of database formats. Instead of learning each DBMS's user interface, the employee needs to know only one interface. The actual format of the database is unimportant and will be transparent to the user.

In this chapter, you learn how to access the data stored in Microsoft Access databases. Databases created using Microsoft Access are relational databases. A **relational database** is one that stores information in tables composed of columns and rows, similar to the format used in a spreadsheet. Each column in a table represents a field, and each row represents a record. A **field** is a single item of information about a person, place, or thing—such as a name, a salary amount, a Social Security number, or a price. A **record** is a group of related fields that contain all of the necessary data about a specific person, place, or thing. The college you are attending keeps a student record on you. Examples of fields contained in your student record include your Social Security number, name, address, phone number, credits earned, and grades earned. The place where you are employed also keeps a record on you. Your employee record contains your Social Security number, name, address, phone number, starting date, salary or hourly wage, and so on. A group of related records is called a **table**. Each record in a table pertains to the same topic, and each contains the same type of information. In other words, each record in a table contains the same fields.

A relational database can contain one or more tables. A one-table database would be a good choice for storing information about the college courses you have taken. An example of such a table is shown in Figure 12-1. Each record in the table contains four fields: an ID field that indicates the department name and course number, a course title field, a number of credit hours field, and a grade field. In most tables, one of the fields uniquely identifies each record and is called the **primary key**. In the table shown in Figure 12-1, you could use either the ID field or the Title field as the primary key, because the data in those fields will be unique for each record.

ID	Title	Hours	Grade
CIS100	Intro to Computers	3	A
ENG100	English Composition	3	B
PHIL105	Philosophy Seminar	2	C
CIS201	Visual Basic 2008	3	A

Figure 12-1: Example of a one-table relational database

You might use a two-table database to store information about a CD (compact disc) collection. You would store the general information about each CD (such as the CD's name and the artist's name) in one table, and store the information about the songs on each CD (such as their title and track number) in the other table. You then would use a common field—for example, a CD number—to relate the records contained in both tables. Figure 12-2 shows an example of a two-table database that stores CD information. The first table is referred to as the **parent table**, and the second table is referred to as the **child table**. The CD_Number field is the primary key in the parent table, because it uniquely identifies each record in the table. The CD_Number field in the child table is used solely to link the song title and track information to the appropriate CD in the parent table. In the child table, the CD_Number field is called the **foreign key**.

> **» TIP**
>
> Parent and child tables also are referred to as master and detail tables, respectively.

CD_Number	Name	Artist
01	Western Way	Dolly Draton
02	Midnight Blue	Paul Elliot

The two tables are related by the CD_Number field

CD_Number	Song_Title	Track
01	Country	1
01	Night on the Road	2
01	Old Times	3
02	Lovely Nights	1
02	Colors	2
02	Heavens	3

Figure 12-2: Example of a two-table relational database

Storing data in a relational database offers many advantages. The computer can retrieve data stored in a relational format both quickly and easily, and the data can be displayed in any order. The information in the CD database, for example, can be arranged by artist name, song title, and so on. You also can control the amount of information you want to view from a relational database. You can view all of the information in the CD database, or you can view only the information pertaining to a certain artist, or only the names of the songs contained on a specific CD.

CONNECTING AN APPLICATION TO A MICROSOFT ACCESS DATABASE

The concepts portion of this chapter uses a Microsoft Access database named Employees. The Employees database is stored in the Employees.accdb file, which is located in the VbReloaded2008\Chap12\Access Databases folder. The .accdb filename extension stands for Access Database and indicates that the database was created using Microsoft Access 2007. The Employees database contains one table, which is named tblEmploy. Figure 12-3 shows the table data displayed in a window in the IDE. The table contains seven fields and 12 records. The Emp_Number field is the primary key, because it uniquely identifies each record in the table. The Status field contains the employment status, which is either the letter F (for full-time) or the letter P (for part-time). The Code field identifies the employee's department: 1 for Accounting, 2 for Advertising, 3 for Personnel, and 4 for Inventory.

»TIP

To open a database table in the IDE, first connect the database to an application, then right-click the table's name in the Server Explorer window, and then click Retrieve Data.

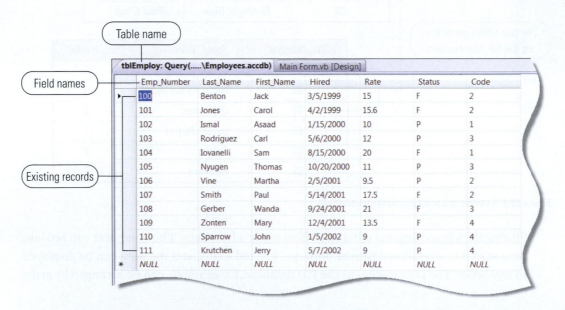

tblEmploy: Query(.....\Employees.accdb) | Main Form.vb [Design]

Emp_Number	Last_Name	First_Name	Hired	Rate	Status	Code
100	Benton	Jack	3/5/1999	15	F	2
101	Jones	Carol	4/2/1999	15.6	F	2
102	Ismal	Asaad	1/15/2000	10	P	1
103	Rodriguez	Carl	5/6/2000	12	P	3
104	Iovanelli	Sam	8/15/2000	20	F	1
105	Nyugen	Thomas	10/20/2000	11	P	3
106	Vine	Martha	2/5/2001	9.5	P	2
107	Smith	Paul	5/14/2001	17.5	F	2
108	Gerber	Wanda	9/24/2001	21	F	3
109	Zonten	Mary	12/4/2001	13.5	F	4
110	Sparrow	John	1/5/2002	9	P	4
111	Krutchen	Jerry	5/7/2002	9	P	4
NULL	*NULL*	*NULL*	*NULL*	*NULL*	*NULL*	*NULL*

Table name · Field names · Existing records

Figure 12-3: Data contained in the tblEmploy table

Before an application can access the data stored in a database, you need to connect the application to the database. You can make the connection using the Data Source Configuration Wizard. Figure 12-4 shows the general procedure for using the wizard. Detailed steps can be found in the Programming Tutorial section in this chapter.

»HOW TO . . .

CONNECT AN APPLICATION TO A MICROSOFT ACCESS DATABASE

1. Open the application's solution file. Click View on the menu bar, then click Server Explorer to open the Server Explorer window, which lists the available connections.

2. Click Data on the menu bar, then click Show Data Sources to open the Data Sources window.

3. Click the Add New Data Source link in the Data Sources window. This opens the Data Source Configuration Wizard dialog box and displays the Choose a Data Source Type screen. If necessary, click Database. See Figure 12-5.

4. Click the Next button, then continue using the wizard to specify the data source and the name of the database file. The data source for a Microsoft Access database is Microsoft Access Database File (OLE DB).

Figure 12-4: How to connect an application to a Microsoft Access database

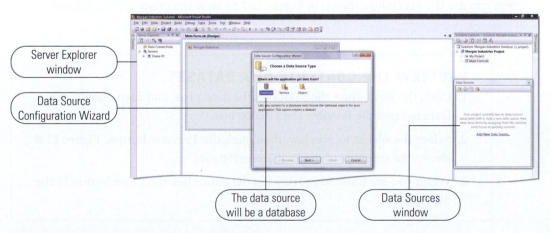

Server Explorer window

Data Source Configuration Wizard

The data source will be a database

Data Sources window

Figure 12-5: Data Source Configuration Wizard dialog box

After connecting the application to the database, the Data Source Configuration Wizard adds several files to the project; the filenames appear in the Solution Explorer window. The Wizard also lists a connection to the database file in the Server Explorer window and adds a dataset's name to the Data Sources window. A **dataset** is a copy of the data (fields and records) the application can access from the database. The dataset is stored in the computer's internal memory. Figure 12-6 shows the result of connecting the Morgan Industries application to the Employees database. The EmployeesDataSet contains one table object and seven field objects. The table object is the tblEmploy table contained in the Employees database, and the seven field objects correspond to the seven fields in the table.

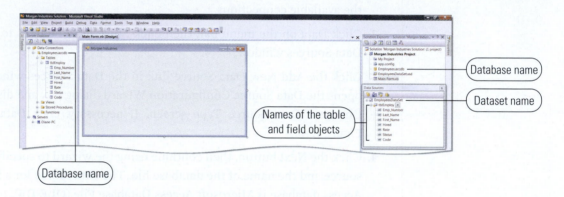

Figure 12-6: Result of running the Data Source Configuration Wizard

PREVIEWING THE CONTENTS OF A DATASET

You can use the procedure shown in Figure 12-7 to view the contents of a dataset.

» HOW TO . . .

PREVIEW THE CONTENTS OF A DATASET

1. Click the form, then click Data on the menu bar, and then click Preview Data to open the Preview Data dialog box.

2. Select the object to preview, then click the Preview button. Figure 12-8 shows the contents of the EmployeesDataSet.

3. When you are finished previewing the data, click the Close button in the dialog box.

Figure 12-7: How to preview the contents of a dataset

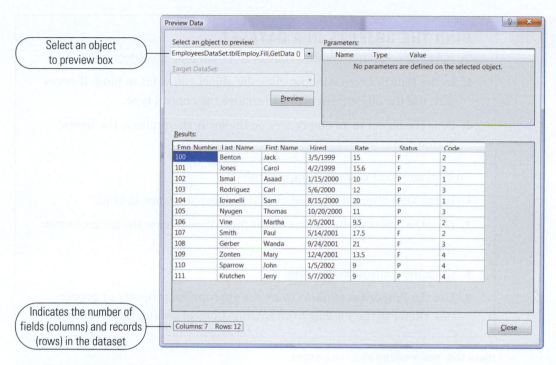

Select an object to preview box

Indicates the number of fields (columns) and records (rows) in the dataset

Figure 12-8: Preview Data dialog box

Notice that EmployeesDataSet.tblEmploy.Fill, GetData() appears in the Select an object to preview box in Figure 12-8. EmployeesDataSet is the name of the dataset in the application, and tblEmploy is the name of the table included in the dataset. Fill and GetData are methods. The Fill method populates an existing table with data, while the GetData method creates a new table and populates it with data.

BINDING THE OBJECTS IN A DATASET

For the user to view the contents of a dataset while an application is running, you need to connect one or more objects in the dataset to one or more controls in the interface. Connecting an object to a control is called **binding**, and the connected controls are called **bound controls**. Figure 12-9 shows various ways of binding the objects in a dataset. You can bind an object to a control that the computer creates for you; or, you can bind it to an existing control in the interface.

»TIP
Bound controls also are referred to as data-aware controls.

»HOW TO . . .

BIND THE OBJECTS IN A DATASET

To have the computer create a control and then bind an object to it:

1. In the Data Sources window, click the object you want to bind. If necessary, use the object's list arrow to change the control type.

2. Drag the object to an empty area on the form, then release the mouse button.

To bind an object to an existing control:

1. In the Data Sources window, click the object you want to bind.

2. Drag the object to the control on the form, then release the mouse button.

   OR

1. Click the control on the form.

2. Use the Properties window to set the appropriate property or properties. (Refer to the *Binding to an Existing Control* section in this chapter.)

Figure 12-9: How to bind the objects in a dataset

HAVING THE COMPUTER CREATE A BOUND CONTROL

As indicated in Figure 12-9, when you drag an object from a dataset to an empty area on the form, the computer creates a control and automatically binds the object to it. The icon that appears before the object's name in the Data Sources window indicates the type of control the computer will create. The 🖳 icon in Figure 12-10 indicates that a DataGridView control will be created when you drag the tblEmploy table object to the form. A **DataGridView control** displays the table data in a row and columnar format, similar to a spreadsheet. Each row in the control represents a record, and each column represents a field. You will learn more about the DataGridView control in the next section. The abl icon, also shown in Figure 12-10, indicates that the computer will create a text box when you drag a field object to the form.

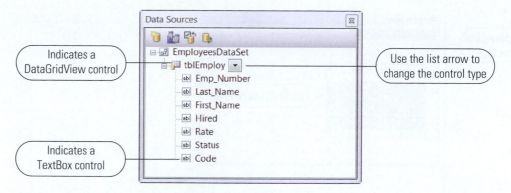

Figure 12-10: Icons in the Data Sources window

You can use the list arrow that appears next to an object's name to change the type of control the computer creates. To display the tblEmploy data in separate text boxes rather than in a DataGridView control, you click tblEmploy in the Data Sources window, then click the tblEmploy list arrow, and then click Details in the list. The Details option tells the computer to create a separate control for each field in the table. Similarly, to display the Last_Name field data in a label control rather than in a text box, you first click Last_Name in the Data Sources window. You then click the field's list arrow, and then click Label in the list.

Figure 12-11 shows the result of dragging the tblEmploy object from the Data Sources window to the MainForm, using the default control type for a table. Besides adding a DataGridView control to the form, the computer also adds a BindingNavigator control. When an application is running, you can use the **BindingNavigator control** to move from one record to the next in the dataset, as well as to add or delete a record and save any changes made to the dataset. The computer also places five objects in the component tray: a DataSet, BindingSource, TableAdapter, TableAdapterManager, and BindingNavigator. As you learned in Chapter 8, the component tray stores objects that do not appear in the user interface when an application is running. An exception to this is the BindingNavigator object, which appears as the BindingNavigator control during both design time and run time.

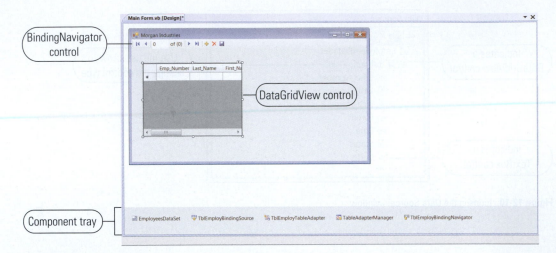

Figure 12-11: Result of dragging the table object to the form

The **TableAdapter object** connects the database to the **DataSet object**, which stores the information you want to access from the database. The TableAdapter is responsible for retrieving the appropriate information from the database and storing it in the DataSet. It also can be used to save to the database any changes made to the data contained in the DataSet. However, in most cases, you will use the **TableAdapterManager object** to save the changes, because it can handle saving data to multiple tables in the DataSet. The **BindingSource object** provides the connection between the DataSet and the bound controls on the form. The TblEmployBindingSource in Figure 12-11 connects the EmployeesDataSet to two bound controls: a DataGridView control and a BindingNavigator control. The TblEmployBindingSource allows the DataGridView control to display the data contained in the EmployeesDataSet. It also allows the BindingNavigator control to access the records stored in the EmployeesDataSet. Figure 12-12 illustrates the relationships among the database, the objects in the component tray, and the bound controls on the form.

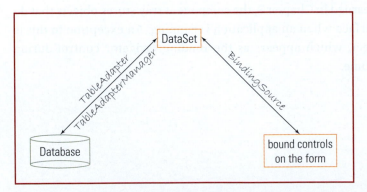

Figure 12-12: Illustration of the relationships among the database, the objects in the component tray, and the bound controls

If a table object's control type is changed from DataGridView to Details, the computer automatically provides the appropriate controls (such as text boxes, labels, and so on) when you drag the table object to the form. It also adds the BindingNavigator control to the form, and adds the five objects to the component tray. The appropriate controls and objects are also automatically included when you drag a field object to an empty area on the form.

THE DATAGRIDVIEW CONTROL

The DataGridView control is one of the most popular controls for displaying table data, because it allows you to view a great deal of information at the same time. The control displays the data in a row and columnar format, similar to a spreadsheet. Each row represents a record, and each column represents a field. Like the PictureBox control, which you learned about in Chapter 1, the DataGridView control has a task list. The task list is shown in Figure 12-13.

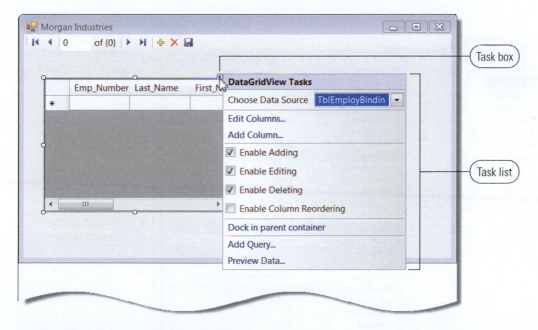

Figure 12-13: Task list for a DataGridView control

Figure 12-14 explains the purpose of each task in the DataGridView's task list, and Figure 12-15 shows the Edit Columns dialog box. The dialog box allows you to add and remove columns from the DataGridView control, as well as reorder the columns. You also can use the dialog box to set the properties of the bound columns. The DefaultCellStyle property, for example, allows you to format a column's data, as well as change the column's width and alignment. You can use the HeaderText property to change a column's heading.

Task	Purpose
Choose Data Source	select a data source
Edit Columns	open the Edit Columns dialog box (See Figure 12-15)
Add Column	add a new column
Enable Adding	allow/disallow the user to add data
Enable Editing	allow/disallow the user to edit data
Enable Deleting	allow/disallow the user to delete data
Enable Column Reordering	allow/disallow the user to reorder the columns
Dock in parent container	bind the borders of the control to the form
Add Query	filter data from a dataset
Preview Data	view the data bound to the control

Figure 12-14: Purpose of each task in the DataGridView's task list

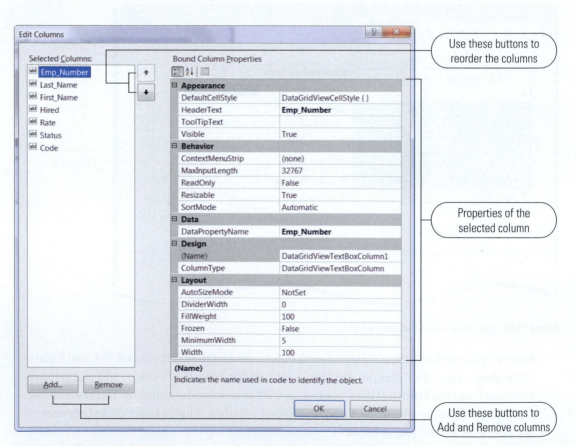

Figure 12-15: Edit Columns dialog box

Many properties of a DataGridView control are listed only in the Properties window. One such property is AutoSizeColumnsMode. The AutoSizeColumnsMode property has seven different settings that control the way the column widths are sized in the DataGridView control. The Fill setting, for example, automatically adjusts the column widths so that all of the columns exactly fill the display area of the control. The ColumnHeader setting automatically adjusts the column widths based on the header text. Figure 12-16 shows the DataGridView control docked in the parent container, which is the MainForm. The Edit Columns dialog box was used to change the header text in several columns, and to both format and align the data in the Pay Rate column. (You won't see the effect of the formatting and aligning until the application is started.) The DataGridView control's AutoSizeColumnsMode property was set to Fill in the Properties window.

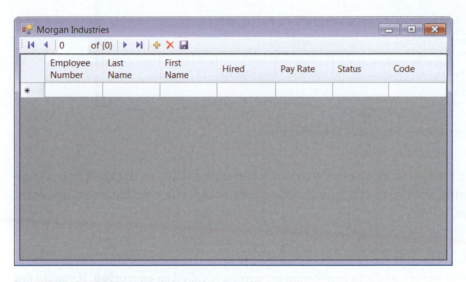

Figure 12-16: DataGridView control after setting some of its properties

VISUAL BASIC CODE

As you learned earlier, when a table or field object is dragged to the form, the computer adds the appropriate controls and objects to the application. It also enters in the Code Editor window the two event procedures shown in Figure 12-17. The Load event procedure uses the TableAdapter object's Fill method to retrieve the data from the database and store it in the DataSet object; in most applications, the code to fill a dataset with data belongs in this procedure. However, as the comments in the Load event procedure indicate, you can either move or delete the code. The TblEmployBindingNavigatorSaveItem_Click procedure is processed when you click the Save Data button on the BindingNavigator control. The procedure's code validates the changes made to the data before saving the data to the database. Two methods are involved in the save operation: the BindingSource object's EndEdit method and the TableAdapterManager's UpdateAll method. The EndEdit method applies any pending changes (such as new records, deleted records, or changed records) to the dataset. The UpdateAll method commits the dataset changes to the database.

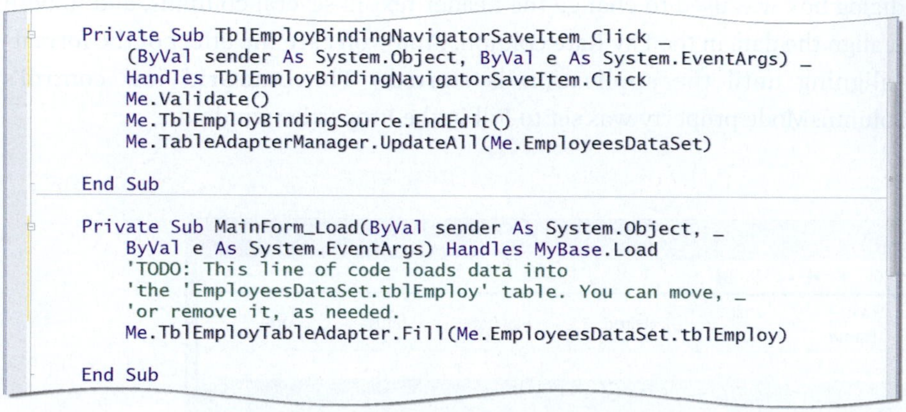

```
Private Sub TblEmployBindingNavigatorSaveItem_Click _
    (ByVal sender As System.Object, ByVal e As System.EventArgs) _
    Handles TblEmployBindingNavigatorSaveItem.Click
    Me.Validate()
    Me.TblEmployBindingSource.EndEdit()
    Me.TableAdapterManager.UpdateAll(Me.EmployeesDataSet)

End Sub

Private Sub MainForm_Load(ByVal sender As System.Object, _
    ByVal e As System.EventArgs) Handles MyBase.Load
    'TODO: This line of code loads data into
    'the 'EmployeesDataSet.tblEmploy' table. You can move, _
    'or remove it, as needed.
    Me.TblEmployTableAdapter.Fill(Me.EmployeesDataSet.tblEmploy)

End Sub
```

Figure 12-17: Code automatically entered in the Code Editor window

Because it is possible for an error to occur when saving data to a database, it is a good programming practice to add error handling code to the Save Data button's Click event procedure.

HANDLING ERRORS IN THE CODE

An error that occurs while an application is running is called an **exception**. If you do not take deliberate steps in your code to handle the exceptions, Visual Basic "handles" them for you. Typically, it does this by displaying an error message and then abruptly terminating the application. You can prevent your application from behaving in such an unfriendly manner by taking control of the exception handling in your code; you can do this using the Try...Catch statement. Figure 12-18 shows the statement's basic syntax and includes examples of using the syntax. The basic syntax contains a Try block and a Catch block. Within the Try block you place the code that could possibly generate an exception. When an exception occurs in the Try block's code, the computer processes the code contained in the Catch block; it then skips to the code following the End Try clause. A description of the exception that occurred is stored in the Message property of the Catch block's ex variable. You can access the description using the code ex.Message, as shown in Example 2 in the figure.

»TIP

When an error occurs in a procedure's code during run time, programmers say that the procedure "threw an exception."

»TIP

The Try...Catch statement also has a Finally block. The code in the Finally block is processed whether or not an exception is thrown within the Try block.

USE THE BASIC SYNTAX OF THE TRY...CATCH STATEMENT

Syntax

Try

   one or more statements that might generate an exception

Catch ex As Exception

   one or more statements to execute when an exception occurs

End Try

Example 1

```
Private Sub displayButton_Click(ByVal sender As System.Object, _
    ByVal e As System.EventArgs) Handles displayButton.Click

    Try
        fileTextBox.Text = My.Computer.FileSystem.ReadAllText("report.txt")
    Catch ex As Exception
        MessageBox.Show("Cannot find the report.txt file.", "File Error", _
            MessageBoxButtons.OK, MessageBoxIcon.Information)
    End Try
End Sub
```

if an exception occurs when processing the ReadAllText method, the code in the Catch block displays an appropriate message before the procedure ends

Example 2

```
Private Sub TblBooksBindingNavigatorSaveItem_Click _
    (ByVal sender As System.Object, ByVal e As System.EventArgs) _
    Handles TblBooksBindingNavigatorSaveItem.Click

    Try
        Me.Validate()
        Me.TblBooksBindingSource.EndEdit()
        Me.TableAdapterManager.UpdateAll(Me.BooksDataSet)
    Catch ex As Exception
        MessageBox.Show(ex.Message, "Book Sellers", _
            MessageBoxButtons.OK, MessageBoxIcon.Information)
    End Try
End Sub
```

if an exception occurs when processing the code in the Try block, the code in the Catch block displays a description of the exception before the procedure ends

Figure 12-18: How to use the basic syntax of the Try...Catch statement

Figure 12-19 shows a Try...Catch statement entered in the Save Data button's Click event procedure in the Morgan Industries application. If the Try block's code does not produce an exception, the MessageBox.Show method in the block displays the "Changes saved" message; otherwise, the MessageBox.Show method in the Catch block displays a description of the exception.

```
Private Sub TblEmployBindingNavigatorSaveItem_Click _
    (ByVal sender As System.Object, ByVal e As System.EventArgs) _
    Handles TblEmployBindingNavigatorSaveItem.Click

    Try
        Me.Validate()
        Me.TblEmployBindingSource.EndEdit()
        Me.TableAdapterManager.UpdateAll(Me.EmployeesDataSet)
        MessageBox.Show("Changes saved.", "Morgan Industries", _
                    MessageBoxButtons.OK, MessageBoxIcon.Information)
    Catch ex As Exception
        MessageBox.Show(ex.Message, "Morgan Industries", _
                    MessageBoxButtons.OK, MessageBoxIcon.Information)
    End Try
End Sub
```

Figure 12-19: Try...Catch statement entered in the Save Data button's Click event procedure

Figure 12-20 shows a sample run of the Morgan Industries application. When the application is started, the statement in the MainForm's Load event procedure retrieves the appropriate data from the Employees database and loads the data into the EmployeesDataSet. The data is displayed in the DataGridView control, which is bound to the tblEmploy table contained in the dataset.

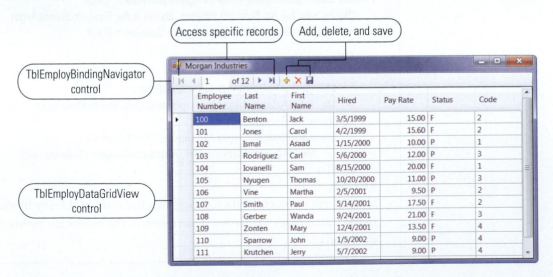

Figure 12-20: Sample run of the Morgan Industries application

You can use the arrow keys on your keyboard to move the highlight to a different cell in the DataGridView control. A **cell** is an intersection of a row and column in the control. When a cell is highlighted, you can modify its existing data by simply typing the new data. The BindingNavigator control provides buttons for accessing the first and last records in the dataset, as well as accessing the previous and next records. You also can use the control to access a record by its record number. The first record in a dataset has a record number of 1; the second has a record number of 2, and so on. The BindingNavigator control also contains buttons for adding a record to the dataset, deleting a record from the dataset, and saving the changes made to the dataset. The way changes are saved to a database is controlled by the database file's Copy to Output Directory property.

THE COPY TO OUTPUT DIRECTORY PROPERTY

When the Data Source Configuration Wizard connects the Morgan Industries application to the Employees database, it adds the database file (Employees.accdb) to the application's project folder. (You can verify this by referring back to Figure 12-6.) A database file contained in a project is referred to as a local database file. The way Visual Basic saves changes to a local database file is determined by the file's **Copy to Output Directory property**. When the property is set to its default setting, Copy always, the file is copied from the project folder to the project folder's bin\Debug folder each time you start the application. In this case, the Employees.accdb file is copied from the Morgan Industries Project folder to the Morgan Industries Project\bin\Debug folder. As a result, the file will appear in two different folders in the solution. When you click the Save Data button on the BindingNavigator control, any changes made in the DataGridView control are recorded only in the file stored in the bin\Debug folder; the file stored in the project folder is not changed. The next time you start the application, the file in the project folder is copied to the bin\Debug folder, overwriting the file that contains the changes. One way to fix this problem is to set the database file's Copy to Output Directory property to "Copy if newer." The "Copy if newer" setting tells the computer to compare the dates on both files to determine which file has the newer (more current) date. If the database file in the project folder has the newer date, then copy it to the bin\Debug folder; otherwise, don't copy it.

BINDING TO AN EXISTING CONTROL

As indicated earlier in Figure 12-9, you can bind an object in a dataset to an existing control on the form. The easiest way to do this is by dragging the object from the Data Sources window to the control. However, you also can click the control and then set one or more properties in the Properties window. The appropriate property (or properties) to set depends on the control you are binding. For example, you use the DataSource property to bind a DataGridView control. However, you use the DataSource and DisplayMember properties to bind a ListBox control. To bind label and text box controls, you use the DataBindings/Text property.

When you drag an object from the Data Sources window to an existing control, the computer does not create a new control; rather, it merely binds the object to the existing control. Because a new control does not need to be created, the computer ignores the control type specified for the object in the Data Sources window. Therefore, it is not necessary to change the control type in the Data Sources window to match the existing control's type. In other words, you can drag an object that is associated with a text box in the Data Sources window to a label control on the form. The computer will bind the object to the label, but it will not change the label to a text box. Figure 12-21 shows the result of dragging four field objects to four existing label controls in the Morgan Industries application. In this case, the computer will bind the Emp_Number, Last_Name, Status, and Code field objects to the numberLabel, lastNameLabel, statusLabel, and codeLabel controls, respectively. In addition to binding the field objects to the controls, the computer also adds DataSet, BindingSource, TableAdapter, and TableAdapterManager objects to the component tray.

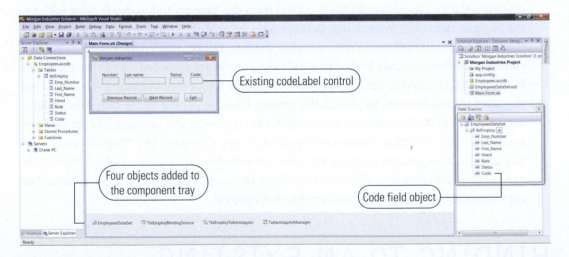

Figure 12-21: Result of dragging field objects to existing label controls

Notice that the computer does not add a BindingNavigator control or a BindingNavigator object to the application when you drag an object from the Data Sources window to an existing control. You can use the BindingNavigator tool in the Toolbox to add a BindingNavigator control to the form; doing this also adds a BindingNavigator object to the component tray. You then must set the BindingNavigator control's DataSource property to the name of the BindingSource object in the application. In this case, for example, you would set the DataSource property to TblEmployBindingSource.

When you drag an object from the Data Sources window to an existing control, the computer enters (in the Code Editor window) the Load event procedure shown earlier in Figure 12-17. Recall that the procedure uses the TableAdapter object's Fill method to retrieve the data from the database and store it in the DataSet object. Figure 12-22 shows a sample run of this version of the Morgan Industries application.

Figure 12-22: Sample run of a different version of the Morgan Industries application

Only the first record in the dataset appears in the interface shown in Figure 12-22. Because the form does not contain a BindingNavigator control, which would allow you to move from one record to the next, you will need to code the Next Record and Previous Record buttons to view the remaining records.

CODING THE NEXT RECORD AND PREVIOUS RECORD BUTTONS

The BindingSource object uses an invisible record pointer to keep track of the current record in the dataset. It stores the position of the record pointer in its **Position property**. The first record is in position 0; the second is in position 1, and so on. Figure 12-23 shows the Position property's syntax and includes examples of using the property.

»HOW TO . . .

USE THE BINDINGSOURCE OBJECT'S POSITION PROPERTY

Syntax

*bindingSourceName.***Position**

Example 1

recordNum = TblEmployBindingSource.Position
assigns the current record's position to the recordNum variable

Figure 12-23: How to use the BindingSource object's Position property (*continued on next page*)

Example 2

TblEmployBindingSource.Position = 4

moves the record pointer to the fifth record in the dataset

Example 3

TblEmployBindingSource.Position = _
    TblEmployBindingSource.Position + 1

moves the record pointer to the next record in the dataset

Figure 12-23: How to use the BindingSource object's Position property (*continued from previous page*)

Rather than using the Position property to position the record pointer in a dataset, you also can use the BindingSource object's Move methods. The Move methods move the record pointer to the first, last, next, and previous record in the dataset. Figure 12-24 shows each Move method's syntax and includes examples of using two of the methods.

»HOW TO . . .

USE THE BINDINGSOURCE OBJECT'S MOVE METHODS

Syntax

bindingSourceName.**MoveFirst()**

bindingSourceName.**MoveLast()**

bindingSourceName.**MoveNext()**

bindingSourceName.**MovePrevious()**

Example 1

TblEmployBindingSource.MoveFirst()
moves the record pointer to the first record in the dataset

Example 2

TblEmployBindingSource.MoveNext()
moves the record pointer to the next record in the dataset

Figure 12-24: How to use the BindingSource object's Move methods

When the user clicks the Next Record button in the Morgan Industries interface, the button's Click event procedure should move the record pointer to the next record in the dataset. Similarly, when the user clicks the Previous Record button, its Click event procedure should move the record pointer to the previous record in the dataset. You can use the TblEmployBindingSource object's MoveNext and MovePrevious methods to code the procedures, as shown in Figure 12-25.

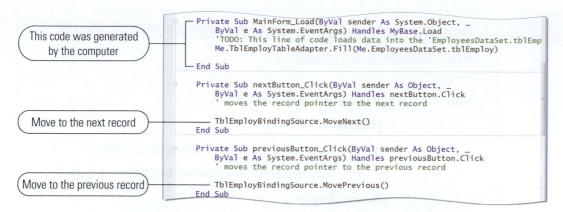

```
        Private Sub MainForm_Load(ByVal sender As System.Object, _
            ByVal e As System.EventArgs) Handles MyBase.Load
            'TODO: This line of code loads data into the 'EmployeesDataSet.tblEmp
        Me.TblEmployTableAdapter.Fill(Me.EmployeesDataSet.tblEmploy)
        End Sub

        Private Sub nextButton_Click(ByVal sender As Object, _
            ByVal e As System.EventArgs) Handles nextButton.Click
            ' moves the record pointer to the next record

        TblEmployBindingSource.MoveNext()
        End Sub

        Private Sub previousButton_Click(ByVal sender As Object, _
            ByVal e As System.EventArgs) Handles previousButton.Click
            ' moves the record pointer to the previous record

        TblEmployBindingSource.MovePrevious()
        End Sub
```

This code was generated by the computer

Move to the next record

Move to the previous record

Figure 12-25: Code entered in the Next Record and Previous Record buttons' Click event procedures

QUERYING A DATASET

You can arrange the records stored in a dataset in any order. The records in the EmployeesDataSet, for example, can be arranged by employee number, pay rate, status, and so on. You also can control the number of records you want to view at any one time. For example, you can view all of the records in the EmployeesDataSet; or you can choose to view only the records for the part-time employees. You use a **query** to specify the records to select in a dataset, as well as the order in which to arrange the records. You can create a query in Visual Basic 2008 using a new language feature called **Language Integrated Query** or, more simply, **LINQ**. Figure 12-26 shows the basic syntax of LINQ when used to select and arrange records in a dataset. The figure also includes examples of using the syntax. In the syntax, *variable* and *element* can be any names you choose, as long as the name follows the naming rules for variables. In other words, there is nothing special about the records and employee names used in the examples. The Where and Order By clauses are optional parts of the syntax. You use the Where clause, which contains a *condition*, to limit the records you want to view. Similar to the *condition* in If...Then...Else and Do...Loop statements, the Where clause *condition* specifies a requirement that must be met for a record to be selected. The Order By clause is used to arrange the records in either ascending (the default) or descending order by one or more fields. Notice that the LINQ syntax does not require you to specify the *variable*'s data type. Instead, the syntax allows the computer to infer the data type from the value being assigned to the *variable*. However, for this inference to take place, you must set Option Infer to On (rather than to Off, as you have been doing). You can do this by entering the Option Infer On statement in the General Declarations section of the Code Editor window.

» TIP

When used to query a dataset, LINQ is referred to more specifically as LINQ to Datasets.

» TIP

As you will learn later in this chapter, you also can use LINQ to Datasets to perform arithmetic calculations (such as a sum or an average) on the data stored in a dataset.

USE THE BASIC LINQ SYNTAX TO SELECT AND ARRANGE RECORDS IN A DATASET

Syntax

Dim *variable* = **From** *element* **In Me.***dataset.table* _

                 [**Where** *condition* _]

                 [**Order By** *element.field1* [**Ascending**|**Descending**] _

                       [, *element.fieldN* [**Ascending**|**Descending**] _]

                 Select *element*

Example 1

```
Dim records = From employee In Me.EmployeesDataSet.tblEmploy _
        Select employee
```

selects all the records contained in the dataset

Example 2

```
Dim records = From employee In Me.EmployeesDataSet.tblEmploy _
        Order By employee.Code _
        Select employee
```

selects all the records contained in the dataset, and arranges the records in ascending order by the Code field

Example 3

```
Dim records = From employee In Me.EmployeesDataSet.tblEmploy _
        Where employee.Status.ToUpper = "P" _
        Select employee
```

selects only the part-time employee records

Example 4

```
Dim records = From employee In Me.EmployeesDataSet.tblEmploy _
        Where employee.Status.ToUpper = "P" _
        Order By employee.Code Descending _
        Select employee
```

selects only the part-time employee records, and arranges the records in descending order by the Code field

Figure 12-26: How to use the basic LINQ syntax to select and arrange records in a dataset

The syntax and examples in Figure 12-26 merely select and/or arrange the appropriate records. To actually view the records, you typically assign the *variable*'s contents to the DataSource property of a BindingSource control. For instance, to view the records selected by Example 1's code, you use Me.TblEmployBindingSource.DataSource = records. As you learned in Chapter 1, Me is a keyword that refers to the current form.

Figure 12-27 provides another example of using LINQ to select records from a dataset. The LINQ code in this example selects records whose Last_Name field begins with one or more letters entered by the user. Notice that the Where clause's *condition* uses the Like operator, along with the asterisk pattern-matching character, to compare the contents of each record's Last_Name field (converted to uppercase) with the user's entry followed by zero or more characters. You learned about the Like operator and the pattern-matching characters in Chapter 7. Figure 12-28 shows a sample run of the application when the user enters the letter s in the InputBox function's dialog box. In this case, two records match the *condition*—the records with last names of Smith and Sparrow. (You can verify that fact by referring back to Figure 12-20.) Only the Smith record appears in the interface. To view the Sparrow record, you would need to click the Next Record button.

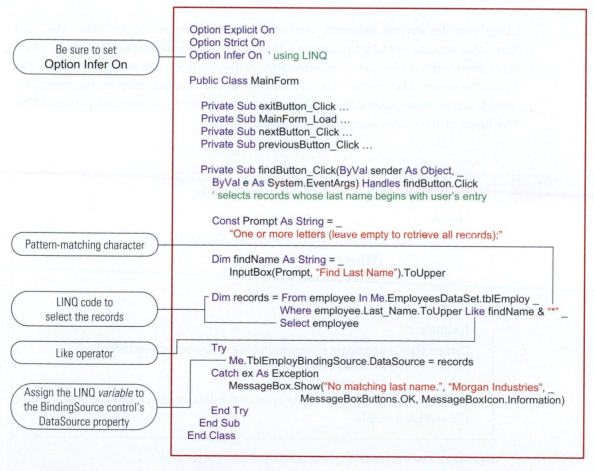

```vb
Option Explicit On
Option Strict On
Option Infer On   ' using LINQ

Public Class MainForm

    Private Sub exitButton_Click …
    Private Sub MainForm_Load …
    Private Sub nextButton_Click …
    Private Sub previousButton_Click …

    Private Sub findButton_Click(ByVal sender As Object, _
        ByVal e As System.EventArgs) Handles findButton.Click
        ' selects records whose last name begins with user's entry

        Const Prompt As String = _
            "One or more letters (leave empty to retrieve all records):"

        Dim findName As String = _
            InputBox(Prompt, "Find Last Name").ToUpper

        Dim records = From employee In Me.EmployeesDataSet.tblEmploy _
                      Where employee.Last_Name.ToUpper Like findName & "*" _
                      Select employee

        Try
            Me.TblEmployBindingSource.DataSource = records
        Catch ex As Exception
            MessageBox.Show("No matching last name.", "Morgan Industries", _
                MessageBoxButtons.OK, MessageBoxIcon.Information)
        End Try
    End Sub
End Class
```

Callouts:
- Be sure to set **Option Infer On**
- Pattern-matching character
- LINQ code to select the records
- Like operator
- Assign the LINQ *variable* to the BindingSource control's DataSource property

Figure 12-27: LINQ code entered in the findButton's Click event procedure

Figure 12-28: Sample run of the Morgan Industries application using LINQ

USING THE LINQ AGGREGATE METHODS

LINQ provides several aggregate methods—namely, Average, Count, Max, Min, and Sum—that you can use when querying a dataset. An **aggregate method** returns a single value from a group of values. The Sum method, for example, returns the sum of the values in the group, whereas the Min method returns the smallest value in the group. You include an aggregate method in a LINQ statement using the syntax shown in Figure 12-29. The figure also includes examples of using the syntax.

»HOW TO . . .

USE THE LINQ AGGREGATE METHODS

Syntax

Dim *variable* = **Aggregate** *element* **In Me.***dataset.table* _
        [**Where** *condition* _]
        Select *element.field* _
        Into *aggregateMethod*()

Example 1

Dim avgRate = Aggregate employee In Me.EmployeesDataSet.tblEmploy _
        Select employee.Rate _
        Into Average()

calculates the average of the pay rates in the dataset and assigns the result to the avgRate variable

Figure 12-29: How to use the LINQ aggregate methods (*continued on next page*)

Example 2

```
Dim maxRate = Aggregate employee In Me.EmployeesDataSet.tblEmploy _
              Where employee.Status.ToUpper = "P" _
              Select employee.Rate _
              Into Max()
```

finds the highest pay rate for a part-time employee and assigns the result to the maxRate variable

Example 3

```
Dim counter = Aggregate employee In Me.EmployeesDataSet.tblEmploy _
              Where employee.Code = 2 _
              Select employee.Emp_Number _
              Into Count()
```

counts the number of employees whose department code is 2 and assigns the result to the counter variable

Figure 12-29: How to use the LINQ aggregate methods (*continued from previous page*)

ADD ITEMS TO THE BINDINGNAVIGATOR CONTROL

As shown earlier in Figure 12-20, the BindingNavigator control contains buttons that allow you to move to a different record in the dataset, as well as to add or delete a record and save any changes made to the dataset. At times, you may want to include additional items—such as another button, a text box, or a drop down button—on the BindingNavigator control. The steps for adding items to the BindingNavigator control are shown in Figure 12-30.

»HOW TO . . .

ADD ITEMS TO A BINDINGNAVIGATOR CONTROL

1. Click an empty area on the BindingNavigator control, then click the control's task box.
2. Click Edit Items in the task list to open the Items Collection Editor dialog box. See Figure 12-31.
3. Select the type of item to add, then click the Add button.

Figure 12-30: How to add items to a BindingNavigator control (*continued on next page*)

4. Make any needed modifications to the item's properties. For example, you may want to set an item's Name, DisplayStyle, Image, or Text property. If the item is a DropDownButton, which displays a list of choices, you will need to set its DropDownItems property.

5. Click the OK button.

Figure 12-30: How to add items to a BindingNavigator control (*continued from previous page*)

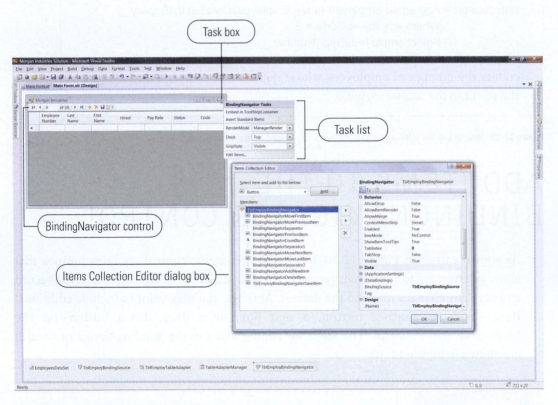

Figure 12-31: Items Collection Editor dialog box

Figure 12-32 shows a DropDownButton on the Morgan Industries BindingNavigator control during design time. The DropDownButton offers a menu that contains three options, called menu items. The menu items allow the user to determine the average pay rate for part-time employees, full-time employees, or all employees. Figure 12-33 shows the code associated with the three menu items, and Figure 12-34 shows a sample run of the Morgan Industries application when the user selects the Part-time Employees menu item.

Figure 12-32: DropDownButton added to the Morgan Industries BindingNavigator control

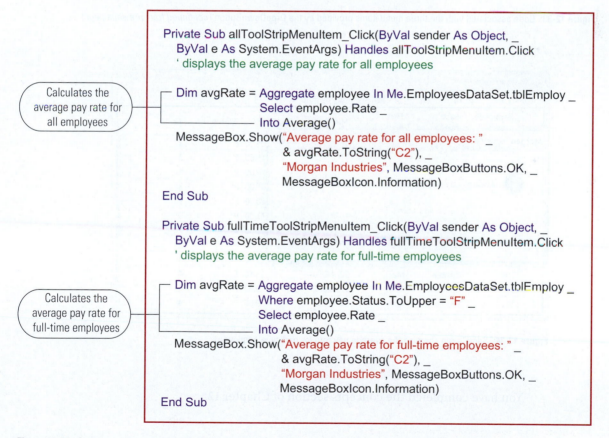

```
Private Sub allToolStripMenuItem_Click(ByVal sender As Object, _
    ByVal e As System.EventArgs) Handles allToolStripMenuItem.Click
    ' displays the average pay rate for all employees

    Dim avgRate = Aggregate employee In Me.EmployeesDataSet.tblEmploy _
                    Select employee.Rate _
                  Into Average()
    MessageBox.Show("Average pay rate for all employees: " _
                    & avgRate.ToString("C2"), _
                    "Morgan Industries", MessageBoxButtons.OK, _
                    MessageBoxIcon.Information)
End Sub

Private Sub fullTimeToolStripMenuItem_Click(ByVal sender As Object, _
    ByVal e As System.EventArgs) Handles fullTimeToolStripMenuItem.Click
    ' displays the average pay rate for full-time employees

    Dim avgRate = Aggregate employee In Me.EmployeesDataSet.tblEmploy _
                    Where employee.Status.ToUpper = "F" _
                    Select employee.Rate _
                  Into Average()
    MessageBox.Show("Average pay rate for full-time employees: " _
                    & avgRate.ToString("C2"), _
                    "Morgan Industries", MessageBoxButtons.OK, _
                    MessageBoxIcon.Information)
End Sub
```

Calculates the average pay rate for all employees

Calculates the average pay rate for full-time employees

Figure 12-33: Code associated with the three menu items provided by the DropDownButton (*continued on next page*)

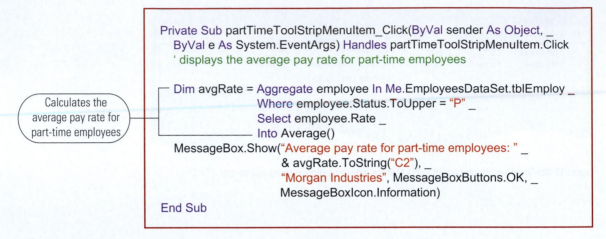

```
Private Sub partTimeToolStripMenuItem_Click(ByVal sender As Object, _
    ByVal e As System.EventArgs) Handles partTimeToolStripMenuItem.Click
    ' displays the average pay rate for part-time employees

    Dim avgRate = Aggregate employee In Me.EmployeesDataSet.tblEmploy _
            Where employee.Status.ToUpper = "P" _
            Select employee.Rate _
        Into Average()
    MessageBox.Show("Average pay rate for part-time employees: " _
            & avgRate.ToString("C2"), _
            "Morgan Industries", MessageBoxButtons.OK, _
            MessageBoxIcon.Information)
End Sub
```

Calculates the average pay rate for part-time employees

Figure 12-33: Code associated with the three menu items provided by the DropDownButton (*continued from previous page*)

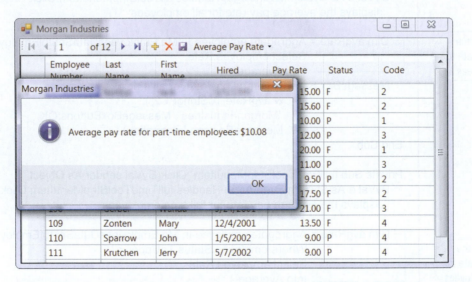

Figure 12-34: Sample run showing the average pay rate for part-time employees

You have completed the concepts section of Chapter 12.

PROGRAMMING TUTORIAL

CREATING THE TRIVIA GAME APPLICATION

In this tutorial, you create an application that displays trivia questions and answers. The questions and answers are stored in a table named tblGame1, which is contained in a Microsoft Access 2007 database named Trivia.accdb. The tblGame1 table contains nine records. Each record contains six fields named Question, AnswerA, AnswerB, AnswerC, AnswerD, and CorrectAnswer. The application allows the user to answer the question. It keeps track of the number of incorrect responses made by the user, and it displays that information after all nine questions have been answered. Figures 12-35 and 12-36 show the application's TOE chart and user interface.

Task	Object	Event
End the application	exitButton	Click
Fill the dataset with data	MainForm	Load
1. Compare the user's answer with the correct answer 2. Keep track of the number of incorrect answers 3. Display the next question and answers from the dataset 4. Display the number of incorrect answers	submitButton	Click
Display questions from the dataset	questionTextBox	None
Display answers from the dataset	aTextBox, bTextBox, cTextBox, dTextBox	None
Get the user's choice	aRadioButton, bRadioButton, cRadioButton, dRadioButton	None

Figure 12-35: TOE Chart

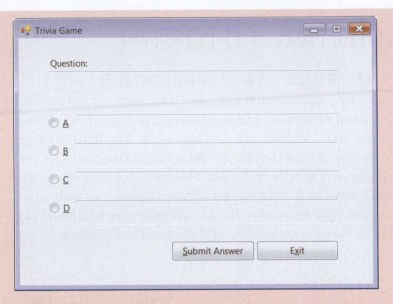

Figure 12-36: User interface

CONNECTING THE TRIVIA GAME APPLICATION
TO THE TRIVIA DATABASE

Before you can connect the Trivia Game application to the Trivia database, you need to open the Trivia Game Solution file.

To open the Trivia Game Solution file, then connect the application to the database:

1. Start Visual Studio. If necessary, close the Start Page window and open the designer window. Open the **Trivia Game Solution** (**Trivia Game Solution.sln**) file, which is contained in the VbReloaded2008\Chap12\Trivia Game Solution folder.

2. Click **View** on the menu bar, then click **Server Explorer** to open the Server Explorer window. Click **Data** on the menu bar, then click **Show Data Sources** to open the Data Sources window.

3. Click **Add New Data Source** in the Data Sources window to start the Data Source Configuration Wizard, which displays the Choose a Data Source Type screen. If necessary, click **Database**. See Figure 12-37.

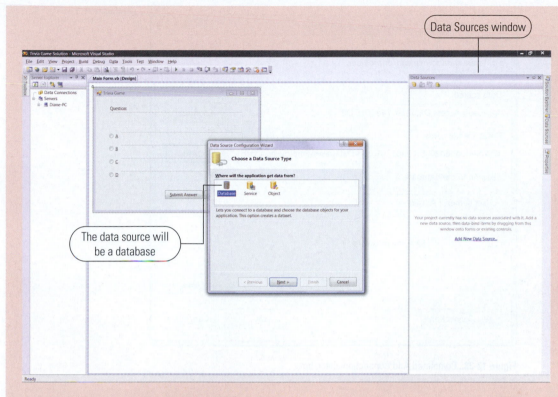

Figure 12-37: Data Source Configuration Wizard dialog box

4. Click the **Next** button to display the Choose Your Data Connection screen. Click the **New Connection** button to open the Add Connection dialog box. (If the Choose Data Source dialog box opens instead, click Microsoft Access Database File, then click the Continue button to open the Add Connection dialog box.) If Microsoft Access Database File (OLE DB) does not appear in the Data source box, click the **Change** button to open the Change Data Source dialog box, then click **Microsoft Access Database File**, and then click the **OK** button to return to the Add Connection dialog box.

5. Click the **Browse** button in the Add Connection dialog box. Open the VbReloaded2008\Chap12\Access Databases folder, then click **Trivia.accdb** in the list of filenames. Click the **Open** button. Figure 12-38 shows the completed Add Connection dialog box. The dialog box in the figure has been widened to show the entire entry in the Database file name box. It is not necessary for you to widen the dialog box.

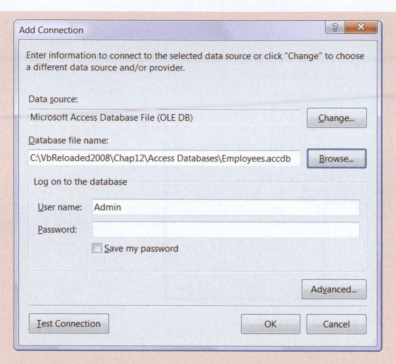

Figure 12-38: Completed Add Connection dialog box

6. Click the **Test Connection** button in the Add Connection dialog box. The "Test connection succeeded." message appears in a message box. Click the **OK** button to close the message box.

7. Click the **OK** button to close the Add Connection dialog box. Trivia.accdb appears in the Choose Your Data Connection screen. Click the **Next** button. A message similar to the one shown in Figure 12-39 appears in a message box. The message asks whether you want to include the database file in the current project. By including the file in the current project, you can more easily copy the application and its database to another computer.

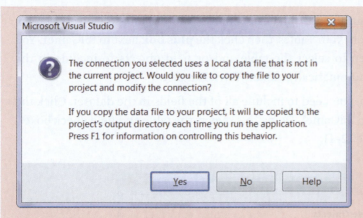

Figure 12-39: Message regarding copying the database file

8. Click the **Yes** button to add the Trivia.accdb file to the current project. The file is added to the application's project folder. The Save the Connection String to the Application Configuration File screen appears next. The name of the connection string, TriviaConnectionString, appears on the screen. See Figure 12-40. If necessary, select the **check box**.

Figure 12-40: Save the Connection String to the Application Configuration File screen

9. Click the **Next** button to display the Choose Your Database Objects screen. Click the **plus box** next to Tables, then click the **plus box** next to tblGame1. You can use this screen to select the table and/or field objects to include in the dataset, which is automatically named TriviaDataSet.

10. In this application, you need to include all of the fields in the dataset. Click the **empty box** next to tblGame1. Doing this selects the table and field check boxes, as shown in Figure 12-41.

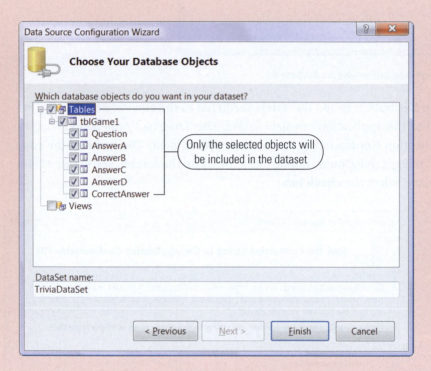

Figure 12-41: Objects selected in the Choose Your Database Objects screen

11. Click the **Finish** button. The computer adds the TriviaDataSet to the Data Sources window. Click the **plus box** next to tblGame1 in the Data Sources window. As Figure 12-42 indicates, the dataset contains one table and six field objects.

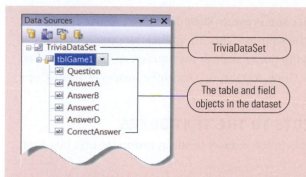

Figure 12-42: TriviaDataSet added to the Data Sources window

12. Now preview the data contained in the dataset. Click the **form**, then click **Data** on the menu bar. Click **Preview Data** to open the Preview Data dialog box, then click the **Preview** button. See Figure 12-43. The TriviaDataSet contains 9 records (rows), each having 6 fields (columns).

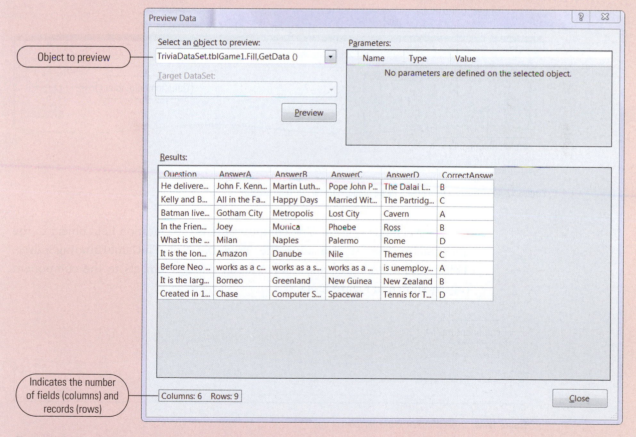

Figure 12-43: Data displayed in the Preview Data dialog box

13. Click the **Close** button to close the Preview Data dialog box. Close the Server Explorer window, then save the solution. (In this application, the user will not be adding, deleting, or modifying the records in the dataset, so you do not need to change the database file's Copy to Output Directory property from Copy always to Copy if newer.)

BINDING THE FIELD OBJECTS TO THE TEXT BOXES

Next, you will bind the field objects in the dataset to the appropriate text boxes on the form.

To bind the field objects to the text boxes, then test the application:

1. If necessary, temporarily display the Data Sources window. Click the **Question** field object in the Data Sources window, then drag the Question field object to the questionTextBox, as shown in Figure 12-44.

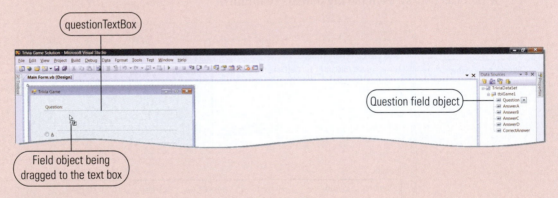

Figure 12-44: Question field object being dragged to the questionTextBox

2. Release the mouse button. The computer binds the Question field object to the questionTextBox. It also adds the TriviaDataSet, TblGame1BindingSource, TblGame1TableAdapter, and TableAdapterManager objects to the component tray, as shown in Figure 12-45.

Figure 12-45: Objects added to the component tray

3. Drag the AnswerA, AnswerB, AnswerC, and AnswerD field objects to the appropriate text boxes.

4. Save the solution, then start the application. The first record in the dataset appears in the interface. See Figure 12-46.

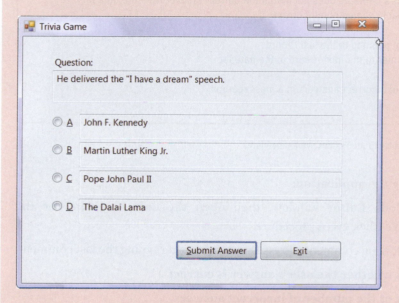

Figure 12-46: First record appears in the interface

5. Click the **Exit** button to end the application, then hide the Data Sources window.

CODING THE TRIVIA GAME APPLICATION

According to the TOE chart (shown earlier in Figure 12-35), only three event procedures need to be coded: the Exit button's Click event procedure, the MainForm's Load event procedure, and the submitButton's Click event procedure. When you open the Code Editor window, you will notice that the exitButton's Click event procedure has already been coded for you. The MainForm's Load event procedure also contains the appropriate code. (Recall that the computer automatically enters the code in the Load event procedure when you drag an object from the Data Sources window to the form.) Therefore, the only procedure you need to code is the submitButton's Click event procedure. Figure 12-47 shows the procedure's pseudocode.

submitButton Click Event Procedure
1. store the position of the record pointer in a variable
2. determine which radio button is selected and assign its Text property (without the ampersand that designates the access key) to a variable named userAnswer
3. if the userAnswer variable's contents does not match the correct answer from the dataset
    add 1 to a counter variable named numIncorrect
end if
4. if the record pointer is not pointing to the last record
    move the record pointer to the next record in the dataset
else
    display the number of incorrect answers in a message box
end if

Figure 12-47: Pseudocode for the submitButton's Click event procedure

To begin coding the application:

1. Open the Code Editor window, then open the code template for the submitButton's Click event procedure.

2. Enter the following comments. Press **Enter** twice after typing the last comment.

   ' determines whether the user's answer is correct

   ' keeps track of the number of incorrect answers

   ' displays the next record or the number of

   ' incorrect answers

3. Type **dim recPtrPos as integer** and press **Enter**, then type **dim userAnswer as string = string.empty** and press **Enter**. The recPtrPos variable will keep track of the position of the record pointer, and the userAnswer variable will store the user's answer (A, B, C, or D) to the question displayed in the questionTextBox.

4. Type **static numIncorrect as integer** and press **Enter** twice. The numIncorrect variable will be the counter that keeps track of the number of incorrect answers made by the user.

5. The first step in the pseudocode is to store the position of the record pointer in a variable. Recall that you can use the BindingSource object's Position property to determine the current position of the record pointer in a dataset. Type **' store position of record pointer** and press **Enter**, then type **recPtrPos = tblgame1bindingsource.position** and press **Enter** twice.

6. Now you will determine which radio button is selected, and then assign its Text property (without the ampersand that designates the access key) to the userAnswer variable. Type the comment and Select Case statement shown in Figure 12-48, then position the insertion point as shown in the figure.

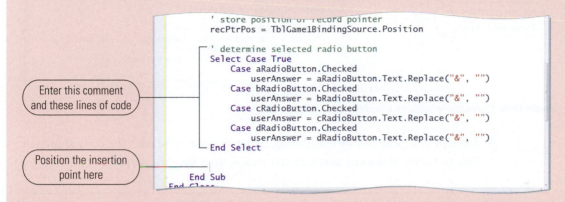

Enter this comment and these lines of code

Position the insertion point here

```
' store position of record pointer
recPtrPos = TblGame1BindingSource.Position

' determine selected radio button
Select Case True
    Case aRadioButton.Checked
        userAnswer = aRadioButton.Text.Replace("&", "")
    Case bRadioButton.Checked
        userAnswer = bRadioButton.Text.Replace("&", "")
    Case cRadioButton.Checked
        userAnswer = cRadioButton.Text.Replace("&", "")
    Case dRadioButton.Checked
        userAnswer = dRadioButton.Text.Replace("&", "")
End Select

        End Sub
End Class
```

Figure 12-48: Comment and Select Case statement entered in the procedure

7. The next step is to compare the contents of the userAnswer variable with the contents of the CorrectAnswer field in the current record. If they are not the same, then you need to increase (by one) the contents of the numIncorrect variable. You can access the value stored in a field in the current record using the syntax *dataSetName.tableName(recordNumber).fieldname*. Type ' **if necessary, update the number of incorrect answers** and press **Enter**. Then type **if userAnswer <> _** and press **Enter**. Press **Tab**, then type **TriviaDataSet.tblGame1 (recPtrPos).CorrectAnswer then** and press **Enter**. Type **numIncorrect = numIncorrect + 1**.

8. The last step in the pseudocode is to determine whether to move to the next record or display a message box indicating the number of incorrect answers. If the record pointer is not pointing to the last record in the dataset, then the procedure should move the record pointer to the next record; doing this will display that record's question and answers. However, if the record pointer is pointing to the last record, it means that there are no more questions and answers to display. In that case, the procedure should display the number of incorrect answers made by the user. Position the insertion point two lines below the End If clause, then type the comment and selection structure shown in Figure 12-49.

```
                      ' if necessary, update the number of incorrect answers
                      If userAnswer <> _
                          TriviaDataSet.tblGame1(recPtrPos).CorrectAnswer Then
                          numIncorrect = numIncorrect + 1
                      End If

                      ' determine position of record pointer
                      If recPtrPos <= 7 Then
                          TblGame1BindingSource.MoveNext()
                      Else
                          MessageBox.Show("Number incorrect: " _
                                          & numIncorrect.ToString, "Trivia Game", _
                                          MessageBoxButtons.OK, _
                                          MessageBoxIcon.Information)
                      End If
                  End Sub
```

Enter this comment and
these lines of code

Figure 12-49: Comment and selection structure entered in the procedure

9. Save the solution. Before continuing, compare your code with the code shown in Figure 12-50. Make any needed corrections, then save the solution.

```
' Project name:        Trivia Game Project
' Project purpose:     Displays trivia questions and
'                      answers from a database
'                      Displays the number of incorrect
'                      answers made by the user
' Created/revised by:  <your name> on <current date>

Option Explicit On
Option Strict On
Option Infer Off

Public Class MainForm

    Private Sub exitButton_Click(ByVal sender As Object,
        ByVal e As System.EventArgs) Handles exitButton.Click
        Me.Close()
    End Sub

    Private Sub MainForm_Load(ByVal sender As System.Object,
        ByVal e As System.EventArgs) Handles MyBase.Load
        'TODO: This line of code loads data into
        'the 'TriviaDataSet.tblGame1' table. You can move,
        'or remove it, as needed.
        Me.TblGame1TableAdapter.Fill(Me.TriviaDataSet.tblGame1)

    End Sub
```

Figure 12-50: Trivia Game application's code (*continued on next page*)

```
Private Sub submitButton_Click(ByVal sender As Object, _
ByVal e As System.EventArgs) Handles submitButton.Click
    ' determines whether the user's answer is correct
    ' keeps track of the number of incorrect answers
    ' displays the next record or the number of
    ' incorrect answers

    Dim recPtrPos As Integer
    Dim userAnswer As String = String.Empty
    Static numIncorrect As Integer

    ' store position of record pointer
    recPtrPos = TblGame1BindingSource.Position

    ' determine selected radio button
    Select Case True
        Case aRadioButton.Checked
            userAnswer = aRadioButton.Text.Replace("&", "")
        Case bRadioButton.Checked
            userAnswer = bRadioButton.Text.Replace("&", "")
        Case cRadioButton.Checked
            userAnswer = cRadioButton.Text.Replace("&", "")
        Case dRadioButton.Checked
            userAnswer = dRadioButton.Text.Replace("&", "")
    End Select

    ' if necessary, update the number of incorrect answers
    If userAnswer <> _
        TriviaDataSet.tblGame1(recPtrPos).CorrectAnswer Then
        numIncorrect = numIncorrect + 1
    End If

    ' determine position of record pointer
    If recPtrPos <= 7 Then
        TblGame1BindingSource.MoveNext()
    Else
        MessageBox.Show("Number incorrect: " _
                        & numIncorrect.ToString, "Trivia Game", _
                        MessageBoxButtons.OK, _
                        MessageBoxIcon.Information)

    End If
End Sub
End Class
```

Figure 12-50: Trivia Game application's code (*continued from previous page*)

To test the completed Trivia Game application:

1. Start the application. Answer the first question correctly. Click the **B** radio button, then click the **Submit Answer** button.

2. Answer the second question incorrectly. Click the **D** radio button, then click the **Submit Answer** button.

3. Answer the remaining seven questions on your own. When you have submitted the answer for the last question, the submitButton's Click event procedure displays the number of incorrect responses in a message box.

4. Click the **OK** button to close the message box, then click the **Exit** button. Close the Code Editor window, then close the solution.

PROGRAMMING EXAMPLE

CARTWRIGHT INDUSTRIES APPLICATION

Carl Simons, the sales manager at Cartwright Industries, records the item number, name, and price of each product the company sells in a database named Items. The Items database is stored in the Items.accdb file, which is contained in the VbReloaded2008\ Chap12\Access Databases folder. The database contains one table, named tblItems. The table contains 10 records, each composed of three fields. The ItemNum and ItemName fields contain text, and the Price field contains numbers. Mr. Simons wants an application that displays the records in a DataGridView control. The application should allow him to sort the records by number, name, or price. Name the solution, project, and form file Cartwright Solution, Cartwright Project, and Main Form.vb, respectively. Save the application in the VbReloaded2008\Chap12 folder. See Figures 12-51 through 12-57.

tblItems: Query(C:\...\Items.accdb)		
ItemNum	ItemName	Price
ABX12	Chair	45
CSR14	Desk	175
JTR23	Table	65
NRE09	End Table	46
OOE68	Bookcase	300
PPR00	Coffee Table	190
PRT45	Lamp	30
REZ04	Love Seat	700
THR98	Side Chair	33
WKP10	Sofa	873
NULL	*NULL*	*NULL*

Figure 12-51: Data contained in the tblItems table

Task	Object	Event
Sort the records	nameToolStripMenuItem, numberToolStripMenuItem, priceToolStripMenuItem	Click
Display the dataset	TblItemsDataGridView	None
1. Move from record to record 2. Save changes to the database	TblItemsBindingNavigator	None Click
Fill the dataset with data	MainForm	Load

Figure 12-52: TOE chart

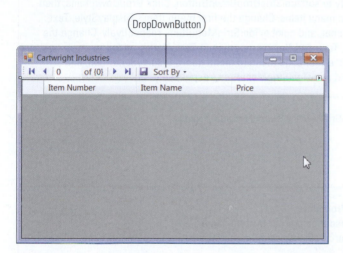

DropDownButton

Figure 12-53: User interface

Object	Property	Setting
Items.accdb file	Copy to Output Directory	Copy if newer
Form1	Name	MainForm
	Font	Segoe UI, 9 point
	MaximizeBox	False
	StartPosition	CenterScreen
	Text	Cartwright Industries
TblItemsDataGridView	AllowUserToAddRows	False
	AllowUserToDeleteRows	False
	AutoSizeColumnsMode	Fill
TblItemsBindingNavigator	Name	TblItemsBindingNavigator

Figure 12-54: Objects, Properties, and Settings

1. Click the TblItemsDataGridView's task box, then click Dock in parent container on the task list. Click Edit Columns in the task list, then do the following:
   a. Change the HeaderText for the ItemNum column to Item Number.
   b. Change the HeaderText for the ItemName column to Item Name.
   c. Change the DefaultCellStyle/Format for the Price column to Numeric with 2 decimal places.

2. Click the TblItemsBindingNavigator's task box. Click Edit Items on the task list, then do the following:
   a. Click BindingNavigatorAddNewItem in the list, then click the *X* button to remove the item from the list. This also will remove the Add new button from the BindingNavigator control.
   b. Click BindingNavigatorDeleteItem in the list, then click the *X* button to remove the item from the list. This also will remove the Delete button from the BindingNavigator control.
   c. Click DropDownButton in the "Select item and add to list below" box, then click the Add button. Change the DropDownButton's DisplayStyle property to Text, then change its Text property to Sort By. Change its Name property to sortToolStripDropDownButton. Click DropDownItems, then click the ellipsis button. Add three menu items. Change the first menu item's DisplayStyle, Text, and Name properties to Text, Number, and numberToolStripMenuItem, respectively. Change the second menu item's DisplayStyle, Text, and Name properties to Text, Name, and nameToolStripMenuItem, respectively. Change the third menu item's DisplayStyle, Text, and Name properties to Text, Price, and priceToolStripMenuItem, respectively.

Figure 12-55: Additional instructions for the DataGridView and BindingNavigator controls

nameToolStripMenuItem Click Event Procedure
1. use LINQ to arrange the records in ascending order by item name
2. assign the records to the BindingSource object's DataSource property

numberToolStripMenuItem Click Event Procedure
1. use LINQ to arrange the records in ascending order by item number
2. assign the records to the BindingSource object's DataSource property

priceToolStripMenuItem Click Event Procedure
1. use LINQ to arrange the records in ascending order by item price
2. assign the records to the BindingSource object's DataSource property

Figure 12-56: Pseudocode

```
' Project name:         Cartwright Project
' Project purpose:      Displays the data contained in a
'                       dataset. Allows the user to sort the records.
' Created/revised by:   <your name> on <current date>

Option Explicit On
Option Strict On
Option Infer On   ' using LINQ

Public Class MainForm

    Private Sub TblItemsBindingNavigatorSaveItem_Click_
        (ByVal sender As System.Object, ByVal e As System.EventArgs) _
        Handles TblItemsBindingNavigatorSaveItem.Click
        Me.Validate()
        Me.TblItemsBindingSource.EndEdit()
        Me.TableAdapterManager.UpdateAll(Me.ItemsDataSet)

    End Sub

    Private Sub MainForm_Load(ByVal sender As System.Object, _
    ByVal e As System.EventArgs) Handles MyBase.Load
        'TODO: This line of code loads data into
        'the 'ItemsDataSet.tblItems' table. You can move, or
        'remove it, as needed.
        Me.TblItemsTableAdapter.Fill(Me.ItemsDataSet.tblItems)

    End Sub

    Private Sub nameToolStripMenuItem_Click(ByVal sender _
        As Object, ByVal e As System.EventArgs) Handles _
        nameToolStripMenuItem.Click
        ' sorts the records in ascending order by item name

        Dim records = From item In Me.ItemsDataSet.tblItems _
                    Order By item.ItemName _
                    Select item
        Me.TblItemsBindingSource.DataSource = records
    End Sub

    Private Sub numberToolStripMenuItem_Click(ByVal sender _
        As Object, ByVal e As System.EventArgs) Handles _
        numberToolStripMenuItem.Click
        ' sorts the records in ascending order by item number
```

Figure 12-57: Code (*continued on next page*)

```
            Dim records = From item In Me.ItemsDataSet.tblItems _
                          Order By item.ItemNum _
                          Select item
            Me.TblItemsBindingSource.DataSource = records
        End Sub

        Private Sub priceToolStripMenuItem_Click(ByVal sender _
            As Object, ByVal e As System.EventArgs) Handles _
            priceToolStripMenuItem.Click
            ' sorts the records in ascending order by item price

            Dim records = From item In Me.ItemsDataSet.tblItems _
                          Order By item.Price _
                          Select item
            Me.TblItemsBindingSource.DataSource = records
        End Sub
End Class
```

Figure 12-57: Code (*continued from previous page*)

QUICK REVIEW

» Companies and individuals use databases to organize information.

» You can use Visual Basic to access the data stored in many different types of databases.

» Databases created by Microsoft Access are relational databases. A relational database can contain one or more tables. Each table contains fields and records.

» Most tables contain a primary key that uniquely identifies each record.

» The data in a relational database can be displayed in any order, and you can control the amount of information you want to view.

» To access the data stored in a database, you first connect the application to the database. Doing this creates a dataset that contains objects, such as table objects and field objects.

» You can display the information contained in a dataset by binding one or more of the objects in the dataset to one or more controls in the application's interface.

» A TableAdapter object connects a database to a DataSet object.

» A BindingSource object connects a DataSet object to the bound controls on a form.

» The DataGridView control displays data in a row and columnar format, similar to a spreadsheet.

» In most applications, the statement to fill a dataset with data is entered in the form's Load event procedure.

» You can use the Try...Catch statement to handle any exceptions that occur while an application is running. A description of the exception is stored in the ex variable's Message property.

» A database file's Copy to Output Directory property determines when and if the file is copied from the project folder to the project folder's bin\Debug folder each time the application is started.

» The BindingSource object uses an invisible record pointer to keep track of the current record. The location of the record pointer in a dataset is stored in the BindingSource object's Position property.

» You can use the BindingSource object's Move methods to move the record pointer in a dataset.

» You can use LINQ to select and arrange the records in a dataset. LINQ also provides the Average, Sum, Count, Min, and Max aggregate methods.

» You can include additional items, such as text boxes and drop down buttons, on a BindingNavigator control. You also can delete items from the control.

KEY TERMS

Aggregate method—a method that returns a single value from a group of values; LINQ provides the Average, Count, Max, Min, and Sum aggregate methods

Binding—the process of connecting an object in a dataset to a control on a form

BindingNavigator control—can be used to move the record pointer from one record to another in a dataset, as well as to add, delete, and save records; also can be customized to include additional functionality

BindingSource object—connects a DataSet object to the bound controls on a form

Bound controls—the controls connected to an object in a dataset

Cell—the intersection of a row and column in a DataGridView control

Child table—a table linked to a parent table

Computer database—an electronic file that contains an organized collection of related information

Copy to Output Directory property—a property of a database file; determines when and if the file is copied from the project folder to the project folder's bin\Debug folder

DataGridView control—displays data in a row and columnar format

Dataset—a copy of the data (database fields and records) that can be accessed by an application

DataSet object—stores the information you want to access from a database

Exception—an error that occurs while an application is running

Field—a single item of information about a person, place, or thing

Foreign key—the field used to link a child table to a parent table

Language Integrated Query—LINQ; the new query language in Visual Basic 2008

LINQ—Language Integrated Query

Parent table—a table linked to a child table

Position property—a property of a BindingSource object; stores the position of the record pointer

Primary key—the field that uniquely identifies each record in a table

Query—specifies the records to select in a dataset, as well as the order in which to arrange the records

Record—a group of related fields that contain all of the necessary data about a specific person, place, or thing

Relational database—a database that stores information in tables composed of columns (fields) and rows (records)

Table—a group of related records

TableAdapter object—connects a database to a DataSet object

TableAdapterManager object—handles saving data to multiple tables in a dataset

SELF-CHECK QUESTIONS AND ANSWERS

1. The _____ object connects a database to a DataSet object.

    a. BindingSource

    b. DataBase

    c. DataGridView

    d. TableAdapter

2. The _____ property stores an integer that represents the location of the record pointer in a dataset.

   a. BindingNavigator object's Position

   b. BindingSource object's Position

   c. TableAdapter object's Position

   d. None of the above.

3. Which of the following will select only records whose LastName field begins with an uppercase letter A?

   a. Dim records = From name In Me.NamesDataSet.tblNames _

           Where name.LastName Like "A" & "*" _

           Select name

   b. Dim records = From Me.NamesDataSet.tblNames _

           Select LastName Like "A" & "*"

   c. Dim records = From tblNames _

           Where tblName.LastName Like "A" & "*" _

           Select name

   d. Dim records = From name In Me.NamesDataSet.tblNames _

           Where tblName.LastName Like "A" & "*" _

           Select name

4. If the record pointer is positioned on record number 5 in a dataset, which of the following BindingSource object methods can be used to move the record pointer to record number 4?

   a. GoPrevious   b. Move(4)

   c. MovePrevious   d. PositionPrevious

5. Which of the following calculates the sum of the values stored in a numeric field named JulySales?

   a. Dim totalSales = From sales In Me.SalesDataSet.tblSales _

           Select sales.JulySales _

           Into Sum()

   b. Dim totalSales = Aggregate sales In Me.SalesDataSet.tblSales _

           Select sales.JulySales _

           Into Sum()

    c. Dim totalSales = From sales In Me.SalesDataSet.tblSales _

            Aggregate sales.JulySales _

            Into Sum()

    d. Dim totalSales = From sales In Me.SalesDataSet.tblSales _

            Sum sales.JulySales

Answers: 1) d, 2) b, 3) a, 4) c, 5) b

REVIEW QUESTIONS

1. A _____ is an organized collection of related information stored in a computer file.

   a. database   b. dataset

   c. field   d. record

2. A _____ database stores information in tables.

   a. columnar   b. relational

   c. sorted   d. tabular

3. The _____ object provides the connection between a DataSet object and a control.

   a. Bound   b. Binding

   c. BindingSource   d. Connecting

4. An application contains DataSet, BindingSource, TableAdapter, TableAdapterManager, and BindingNavigator objects named FriendsDataSet, TblNamesBindingSource, TblNamesTableAdapter, TableAdapterManager, and TblNamesBindingNavigator, respectively. Which of the following statements retrieves data from the Friends database and stores it in the FriendsDataSet?

   a. Me.FriendsDataSet.Fill(Friends.accdb)

   b. Me.TblNamesBindingSource.Fill(Me.FriendsDataSet)

   c. Me.TblNamesBindingNavigator.Fill(Me.FriendsDataSet.tblNames)

   d. Me.TblNamesTableAdapter.Fill(Me.FriendsDataSet.tblNames)

5. Which of the following statements selects all of the records in the tblStates table?

   a. Dim records = From state In Me.StatesDataSet.tblStates _

          Select All state

    b. Dim records = From state In Me.StatesDataSet.tblStates _

        Select state

    c. Dim records = Select state From Me.StatesDataSet.tblStates

    d. Dim records = From Me.StatesDataSet.tblStates _

        Select tblStates.state

6. The tblCities table contains a numeric field named Population. Which of the following statements selects all cities having a population that exceeds 15,000?

    a. Dim records = From city In Me.CitiesDataSet.tblCities _

        Where Population > 15000 _

        Select city

    b. Dim records = From city In Me.CitiesDataSet.tblCities _

        Select city.Population > 15000

    c. Dim records = From city In Me.CitiesDataSet.tblCities _

        Where city.Population > 15000 _

        Select city

    d. Dim records = Select city.Population > 15000 From tblCities

7. The tblCities table contains a numeric field named Population. Which of the following statements calculates the total population of all the cities in the table?

    a. Dim total = Aggregate city In Me.CitiesDataSet.tblCities _

        Select city.Population _

        Into Sum()

    b. Dim total = Sum city In Me.CitiesDataSet.tblCities _

        Select city.Population _

        Into total

    c. Dim total = Aggregate Me.CitiesDataSet.tblCities.city _

        Select city.Population _

        Into Sum()

    d. Dim total = Sum city In Me.CitiesDataSet.tblCities.population

8. In a LINQ statement, the _____ clause limits the records that will be selected.

    a. Limit   b. Order By

    c. Select   d. Where

9. If an application contains the Catch ex As Exception clause, you can use _____ to access the exception's description.

   a. ex.Description
   b. ex.Exception
   c. ex.Message
   d. Exception.Description

10. If the current record is the second record in the dataset, which of the following statements will position the record pointer on the first record?

    a. TblEmployBindingSource.Position = 0
    b. TblEmployBindingSource.Position = TblEmployBindingSource.Position - 1
    c. TblEmployBindingSource.MoveFirst()
    d. All of the above.

REVIEW EXERCISES— SHORT ANSWER

1. The tblMagInfo table contains three fields. The Code and Cost fields are numeric. The Magazine field contains text. Write a LINQ statement that arranges the records in descending order by the Cost field. The dataset's name is MagsDataSet.

2. The tblMagInfo table contains three fields. The Code and Cost fields are numeric. The Magazine field contains text. Write a LINQ statement that selects records having a code of 9. The dataset's name is MagsDataSet.

3. The tblMagInfo table contains three fields. The Code and Cost fields are numeric. The Magazine field contains text. Write a LINQ statement that selects records having a cost of $3 or more. The dataset's name is MagsDataSet.

4. The tblMagInfo table contains three fields. The Code and Cost fields are numeric. The Magazine field contains text. Write a LINQ statement that selects the Daily Food Guide magazine. The dataset's name is MagsDataSet.

5. The tblMagInfo table contains three fields. The Code and Cost fields are numeric. The Magazine field contains text. Write a LINQ statement that selects magazines whose name begins with the letter G (in either uppercase or lowercase). The dataset's name is MagsDataSet.

6. The tblMagInfo table contains three fields. The Code and Cost fields are numeric. The Magazine field contains text. Write a LINQ statement that calculates the average cost of a magazine. The dataset's name is MagsDataSet.

7. Write the statement to assign the location of the record pointer to an Integer variable named recNum. The BindingSource object's name is TblCityBindingSource.

8. Write the statement to move the record pointer to the last record in the dataset. The BindingSource object's name is TblCityBindingSource.

9. How do you remove the Delete button from a BindingNavigator control?

10. Explain the purpose of each of the following objects: DataSet, TableAdapter, TableAdapterManager, and BindingSource.

COMPUTER EXERCISES

1. In this exercise, you use a DataGridView control to display the data stored in a database.

   a. Open the Morgan Industries Solution (Morgan Industries Solution.sln) file, which is contained in the VbReloaded2008\Chap12\Morgan Industries Solution-Ex1 folder.

   b. Connect the application to the Employees.accdb database, which is contained in the VbReloaded2008\Chap12\Access Databases folder.

   c. Drag the table object to the form, then complete the interface so it resembles Figure 12-16.

   d. Add the Try...Catch statement shown in Figure 12-19.

   e. Save the solution, then start the application. The interface should appear as shown in Figure 12-20. Verify that the BindingNavigator control works appropriately.

   f. End the application, then close the solution.

2. In this exercise, you use label controls to display the data stored in a database.

   a. Open the Morgan Industries Solution (Morgan Industries Solution.sln) file, which is contained in the VbReloaded2008\Chap12\Morgan Industries Solution-Ex2 folder.

   b. Connect the application to the Employees.accdb database, which is contained in the VbReloaded2008\Chap12\Access Databases folder.

   c. Drag the field objects to the appropriate label controls.

   d. Code the Previous Record and Next Record buttons. (The code is shown in Figure 12-25.)

   e. Save the solution, then start the application. The interface should appear as shown in Figure 12-22. Test the Next Record and Previous Record buttons to verify that they are working correctly. End the application, then close the solution.

3. In this exercise, you modify the application from Computer Exercise 1. The modified application will allow the user to display the average pay rate for the part-time employees, full-time employees, and all employees.

   a. Use Windows to make a copy of the Morgan Industries Solution-Ex1 folder, which is contained in the VbReloaded2008\Chap12 folder. Rename the copy Morgan Industries Solution-Ex3.

   b. Open the Morgan Industries Solution (Morgan Industries Solution.sln) file contained in the VbReloaded2008\Chap12\Morgan Industries Solution-Ex3 folder.

   c. Add a DropDownButton to the BindingNavigator control. Add three menu items to the control. Use Figure 12-32 as a guide.

   d. Open the Code Editor window. Change Option Infer to On. Code the three menu items, using Figure 12-33 as a guide.

   e. Save the solution, then start the application. Display the average pay rate for the part-time employees. The interface should appear similar to Figure 12-34. Display the average pay rate for the full-time employees, then display the average pay rate for all employees.

   f. End the application, then close the solution.

4. In this exercise, you modify the application from Computer Exercise 1. The modified application will allow the user to display the number of employees in each department.

   a. Use Windows to make a copy of the Morgan Industries Solution-Ex1 folder, which is contained in the VbReloaded2008\Chap12 folder. Rename the copy Morgan Industries Solution-Ex4.

   b. Open the Morgan Industries Solution (Morgan Industries Solution.sln) file contained in the VbReloaded2008\Chap12\Morgan Industries Solution-Ex4 folder.

   c. Add a DropDownButton to the BindingNavigator control. Add four menu items to the control: Accounting, Advertising, Personnel, and Inventory.

   d. Open the Code Editor window. Change Option Infer to On. Code the Click event procedures for the four menu items. Each menu item should display (in a message box) the number of employees in the department. (Code 1 is Accounting, Code 2 is Advertising, Code 3 is Personnel, and Code 4 is Inventory.)

   e. Save the solution, then start the application. Test each menu item. End the application, then close the solution.

5. In this exercise, you modify the application from Computer Exercise 2. The modified application will allow the user to sort the records by employee number, status, or code.

a. Use Windows to make a copy of the Morgan Industries Solution-Ex2 folder, which is contained in the VbReloaded2008\Chap12 folder. Rename the copy Morgan Industries Solution-Ex5.

b. Open the Morgan Industries Solution (Morgan Industries Solution.sln) file contained in the VbReloaded2008\Chap12\Morgan Industries Solution-Ex5 folder.

c. Add three button controls to the form. Use the following captions: Sort by Number, Sort by Status, and Sort by Code.

d. Open the Code Editor window. Change Option Infer to On. Code the Click event procedures for the three buttons. Each button should arrange the records in the appropriate order.

e. Save the solution, then start the application. Test each button. End the application, then close the solution.

6. In this exercise, you modify the application from the chapter's Programming Example.

a. If necessary, create the Cartwright Industries application shown in the chapter's Programming Example. Save the application in the VbReloaded2008\Chap12 folder.

b. Add a Button item to the BindingNavigator control. Code the button's Click event procedure so that it displays the record associated with the item number entered by the user. The code will be similar to the code shown in Figure 12-27; however, you will not need the Try...Catch statement.

c. Save the solution, then start and test the application. End the application, then close the solution.

7. In this exercise, you modify the application from the chapter's Programming Tutorial.

a. Use Windows to make a copy of the Trivia Game Solution folder, which is contained in the VbReloaded2008\Chap12 folder. Rename the copy Modified Trivia Game Solution.

b. Open the Trivia Game Solution (Trivia Game Solution.sln) file contained in the VbReloaded2008\Chap12\Modified Trivia Game Solution folder.

c. Display the question number (from 1 through 9) along with the word "Question" in a label control in the interface.

d. Add another button to the interface. The button should allow the user to start a new game. Allow the user to click the New Game button only after he or she has answered all nine questions.

e. Save the solution, then start and test the application. End the application, then close the solution.

8. In this exercise, you modify the application from the chapter's Programming Tutorial.

   a. Use Windows to make a copy of the Trivia Game Solution folder, which is contained in the VbReloaded2008\Chap12 folder. Rename the copy Discovery Trivia Game Solution.

   b. Open the Trivia Game Solution (Trivia Game Solution.sln) file contained in the VbReloaded2008\Chap12\Discovery Trivia Game Solution folder.

   c. Allow the user to answer the questions in any order, and also to change his or her answers. (You can modify the interface by including additional buttons.) Only display the number of incorrect answers when the user requests that information.

   d. Save the solution, then start and test the application. End the application, then close the solution.

9. In this exercise, you practice debugging an application.

   a. Open the Debug Solution (Debug Solution.sln) file, which is contained in the VbReloaded2008\Chap12\Debug Solution folder.

   b. Open the Code Editor window. Review the existing code. Notice that a jagged line appears below one of the lines of code in the Code Editor window. Correct the code to remove the jagged line.

   c. Save the solution, then start and test the application. Notice that the application is not working correctly. End the application. Correct the errors in the application's code. Save the solution, then start and test the application. When the application is working correctly, end the application, then close the solution.

CASE PROJECTS

ADDISON PLAYHOUSE

In this Case Project, you use a Microsoft Access 2007 database named Play. The Play.accdb database file is located in the VbReloaded2008\Chap12\Access Databases folder. The Play database contains one table named tblReservations. The table contains 20 records, each having three fields: a numeric field named Seat and two text fields named Patron and Phone. Create an application that allows the user to display the contents of the dataset, and also to add, delete, and save records. Name the solution, project, and form file Addison Playhouse Solution, Addison Playhouse Project, and Main Form.vb, respectively. Save the application in the VbReloaded2008\Chap12 folder.

COLLEGE COURSES

In this Case Project, you use a Microsoft Access 2007 database named Courses. The Courses.accdb database file is located in the VbReloaded2008\Chap12\Access Databases folder. The Courses database contains one table named tblCourses. The table contains 10 records, each having four fields: ID, Title, CreditHours, and Grade. The CreditHours field is numeric; the other fields contain text. Create an application that allows the user to display the records for a specific grade (A, B, C, D, or F). The user also should be able to display all of the records. The application should not allow the user to add or delete records. Name the solution, project, and form file College Courses Solution, College Courses Project, and Main Form.vb, respectively. Save the application in the VbReloaded2008\ Chap12 folder.

SPORTS ACTION

In this Case Project, you use a Microsoft Access 2007 database named Sports. The Sports.accdb database file is located in the VbReloaded2008\Chap12\Access Databases folder. The Sports database contains one table named tblScores. The table contains five records, each having five fields that store the following information: a unique number that identifies the game, the date of the game, the name of the opposing team, the home team's score, and the opposing team's score. Create an application that allows a user to view each record, and also to add, delete, and save records. The user also should be able to display the average of the home team's scores. Name the solution, project, and form file Sports Action Solution, Sports Action Project, and Main Form.vb, respectively. Save the application in the VbReloaded2008\Chap12 folder.

THE FICTION BOOKSTORE

Jerry Schmidt, the manager of the Fiction Bookstore, uses a Microsoft Office 2007 database named Books to keep track of the books in his store. The Books.accdb database file is contained in the VbReloaded2008\Chap12\Access Databases folder. The database has one table named tblBooks. The table has five fields. The BookNumber, Price, and QuantityInStock fields are numeric. The Title and Author fields contain text. Mr. Schmidt wants an application that he can use to enter an author's name (or part of a name), and then display only the titles of books written by the author. Display the information in a DataGridView control; however, don't allow the user to add or delete records. (*Hint*: In this application, you need to allow the user to specify the records he or she wants to select while the application is running. One way to accomplish this is to add a text box and a button to the BindingNavigator control.) Mr. Schmidt also wants to display the total value of the books in his store. Name the solution, project, and form file Fiction Bookstore Solution, Fiction Bookstore Project, and Main Form.vb, respectively. Save the application in the VbReloaded2008\Chap12 folder.

HOW TO BOXES

How to	Chapter	Figure
Access an item in a list box	6	6-16
Add a class file to an open project	11	11-2
Add a control to a form	1	1-13
Add a splash screen to a project	2	2-16
Add items to a BindingNavigator control	12	12-30
Add items to a list box	6	6-13
Align columns of information in a sequential access file	10	10-12
Assign a value to a variable	3	3-4
Bind the objects in a dataset	12	12-9
Call an independent Sub procedure	8	8-2
Close a solution	1	1-28
Concatenate strings	4	4-12
Connect an application to a Microsoft Access database	12	12-4
Create a constructor	11	11-12
Create a Function procedure	8	8-13
Create a method that is not a constructor	11	11-13
Create a property procedure	11	11-11
Create a structure (user-defined data type)	10	10-1
Create a Visual Basic 2008 Windows-based application	1	1-4
Create an independent Sub procedure	8	8-1
Declare a named constant	3	3-16

(Table continued on next page)

How to	Chapter	Figure
Declare a one-dimensional array	9	9-2
Declare a structure variable	10	10-2
Declare a two-dimensional array	9	9-31
Declare a variable	3	3-3
Define a class	11	11-1
Delete a file while an application is running	10	10-15
Determine the number of items in a list box	6	6-17
Determine whether a file exists	10	10-14
End an application	1	1-25
Format a number	3	3-32
Generate random numbers	4	4-26
Include arithmetic expressions in assignment statements	3	3-10
Instantiate an object from a class	11	11-5
Manage the windows in the IDE	1	1-7
Manipulate the controls on a form	1	1-14
Name a variable	3	3-1
Open an existing solution	1	1-29
Open the Code Editor window	1	1-16
Plan an application	2	2-1
Preview the contents of a dataset	12	12-7
Print an application's code and user interface	1	1-27
Read from a sequential access file	10	10-13
Save a solution	1	1-20
Select the default list box item	6	6-20
Select the existing text in a text box	7	7-8
Specify the splash screen form	2	2-18
Specify the startup form	1	1-21
Start an application	1	1-23
Start Microsoft Visual Studio 2008	1	1-2
Store data in a one-dimensional array	9	9-3
Store data in a two-dimensional array	9	9-32
Use a member variable	10	10-3
Use the basic LINQ syntax to select and arrange records in a dataset	12	12-26
Use the basic syntax of the Try...Catch statement	12	12-18

(*Table continued from previous page and on next page*)

How to	Chapter	Figure
Use the basic syntax of the TryParse method	3	3-5
Use the BindingSource object's Move methods	12	12-24
Use the BindingSource object's Position property	12	12-23
Use the Contains method	7	7-27
Use the Convert class methods	3	3-6
Use the Do...Loop statement	6	6-1
Use the Financial.Pmt method	7	7-5
Use the For Each...Next statement	9	9-7
Use the For...Next statement	7	7-1
Use the FormClosing event procedure	10	10-16
Use the If...Then...Else statement to code the If and If/Else selection structures	4	4-4
Use the IndexOf method	7	7-28
Use the InputBox function	6	6-8
Use the Insert method	7	7-25
Use the KeyPress event	5	5-18
Use the Length property	7	7-19
Use the Like operator	7	7-31
Use the LINQ aggregate methods	12	12-29
Use the logical operators	4	4-20
Use the MessageBox.Show method	5	5-14
Use the Mid statement	7	7-23
Use the most commonly used comparison operators	4	4-5
Use the PadLeft and PadRight methods	7	7-24
Use the Remove method	7	7-21
Use the Replace method	7	7-22
Use the Select Case statement	5	5-10
Use the SelectedItem and SelectedIndex properties	6	6-19
Use the StartsWith and EndsWith methods	7	7-26
Use the String.Compare method	7	7-30
Use the Substring method	7	7-29
Use the ToUpper and ToLower methods	4	4-17
Use the TrimStart, TrimEnd, and Trim methods	7	7-20
Use the value returned by the MessageBox.Show method	5	5-17
Write to a sequential access file	10	10-11

(*Table continued from previous page*)

MOST COMMONLY USED PROPERTIES OF OBJECTS

Windows Form	
AcceptButton	specify a default button that will be selected when the user presses the Enter key
CancelButton	specify a cancel button that will be selected when the user presses the Esc key
ControlBox	indicate whether the form contains the Control box, as well as the Minimize, Maximize, and Close buttons
Font	specify the font to use for text
FormBorderStyle	specify the appearance and behavior of the form's border
MaximizeBox	specify the state of the Maximize button
MinimizeBox	specify the state of the Minimize button
Name	give the form a meaningful name
StartPosition	indicate the starting position of the form
Text	specify the text that appears in the form's title bar and on the taskbar

(Figure continued on next page)

Button

Enabled	indicate whether the button can respond to the user's actions
Font	specify the font to use for text
Image	specify the image to display on the button's face
ImageAlign	indicate the alignment of the image on the button's face
Name	give the button a meaningful name
TabIndex	indicate the position of the button in the Tab order
Text	specify the text that appears on the button

CheckBox

Checked	indicate whether the check box is selected or unselected
Font	specify the font to use for text
Name	give the check box a meaningful name
TabIndex	indicate the position of the check box in the Tab order
Text	specify the text that appears inside the check box

ComboBox

DropDownStyle	indicate the style of the combo box
Font	specify the font to use for text
Name	give the combo box a meaningful name
SelectedIndex	get or set the index of the selected item
SelectedItem	get or set the value of the selected item
Sorted	specify whether the items in the list portion are sorted
TabIndex	indicate the position of the combo box in the Tab order
Text	get or set the value that appears in the text portion

DataGridView

AutoSizeColumnsMode	control the way the column widths are sized
DataSource	indicate the source of the data to display in the control
Dock	define which borders of the control are bound to its container
Name	give the data grid view control a meaningful name

GroupBox

Name	give the group box a meaningful name
Padding	specify the internal space between the edges of the group box and the edges of the controls contained within the group box
Text	specify the text that appears in the upper-left corner of the group box

Label

AutoSize	enable/disable automatic sizing
BorderStyle	specify the appearance of the label's border
Font	specify the font to use for text
Name	give the label a meaningful name
TabIndex	specify the position of the label in the Tab order
Text	specify the text that appears inside the label
TextAlign	specify the position of the text inside the label

ListBox

Font	specify the font to use for text
Name	give the list box a meaningful name

(*Figure continued from previous page and on next page*)

SelectedIndex	get or set the index of the selected item
SelectedItem	get or set the value of the selected item
SelectionMode	indicate whether the user can select zero choices, one choice, or more than one choice
Sorted	specify whether the items in the list are sorted

PictureBox

Image	specify the image to display
Name	give the picture box a meaningful name
SizeMode	specify how the image should be displayed
Visible	hide/display the picture box

RadioButton

Checked	indicate whether the radio button is selected or unselected
Font	specify the font to use for text
Name	give the radio button a meaningful name
Text	specify the text that appears inside the radio button

TableLayoutPanel

Name	give the table layout panel a meaningful name
CellBorderStyle	specify whether the table cells have a visible border
ColumnCount	indicate the number of columns in the table
Columns	specify the style of each column in the table
Padding	specify the internal space between the edges of the table layout panel and the edges of the controls contained within the table layout panel
RowCount	indicate the number of rows in the table
Rows	specify the style of each row in the table

TextBox

BackColor	indicate the background color of the text box
CharacterCasing	specify whether the text should remain as is or be converted to either uppercase or lowercase
Font	specify the font to use for text
ForeColor	indicate the color of the text inside the text box
Name	give the text box a meaningful name
MaxLength	specify the maximum number of characters the text box will accept
Multiline	control whether the text can span more than one line
PasswordChar	specify the character to display when entering a password
ReadOnly	specify whether the text can be edited
ScrollBars	indicate whether scroll bars appear on a text box (used with a multiline text box)
TabIndex	specify the position of the text box in the Tab order
TabStop	indicate whether the user can use the Tab key to give focus to the text box
Text	get or set the text that appears inside the text box

Timer

Name	give the timer a meaningful name
Enabled	stop/start the timer
Interval	indicate the number of milliseconds between each Tick event

(*Figure continued from previous page*)

VISUAL BASIC CONVERSION FUNCTIONS

This appendix lists the Visual Basic conversion functions. As mentioned in Chapter 3, you can use the conversion functions (rather than the Convert methods) to convert an expression from one data type to another.

Syntax	Return data type	Range for *expression*
CBool(*expression*)	Boolean	Any valid String or numeric expression
CByte(*expression*)	Byte	0 through 255 (unsigned)
CChar(*expression*)	Char	Any valid String expression; value can be 0 through 65535 (unsigned); only the first character is converted
CDate(*expression*)	Date	Any valid representation of a date and time
CDbl(*expression*)	Double	−1.79769313486231570E+308 through −4.94065645841246544E-324 for negative values; 4.94065645841246544E-324 through 1.79769313486231570E+308 for positive values

(*Table continued on next page*)

Syntax	Return data type	Range for *expression*
CDec(*expression*)	Decimal	+/−79,228,162,514,264,337,593,543,950,335 for zero-scaled numbers, that is, numbers with no decimal places. For numbers with 28 decimal places, the range is +/−7.9228162514264337593543950335. The smallest possible non-zero number is 0.0000000000000000000000000001 (+/−1E-28)
CInt(*expression*)	Integer	−2,147,483,648 through 2,147,483,647; fractional parts are rounded
CLng(*expression*)	Long	−9,223,372,036,854,775,808 through 9,223,372,036,854,775,807; fractional parts are rounded
CObj(*expression*)	Object	Any valid expression
CSByte(*expression*)	SByte (signed Byte)	−128 through 127; fractional parts are rounded
CShort(*expression*)	Short	−32,768 through 32,767; fractional parts are rounded
CSng(*expression*)	Single	−3.402823E+38 through −1.401298E-45 for negative values; 1.401298E-45 through 3.402823E+38 for positive values
CStr(*expression*)	String	Depends on the *expression*
CUInt(*expression*)	UInt	0 through 4,294,967,295 (unsigned)
CULng(*expression*)	ULng	0 through 18,446,744,073,709,551,615 (unsigned)
CUShort(*expression*)	UShort	0 through 65,535 (unsigned)

(*Table continued from previous page*)

GUI DESIGN GUIDELINES

FORMBORDERSTYLE, CONTROLBOX, MAXIMIZEBOX, MINIMIZEBOX, AND STARTPOSITION PROPERTIES

» A splash screen should not have Minimize, Maximize, or Close buttons, and its borders should not be sizable. In most cases, a splash screen's FormBorderStyle property is set to FixedSingle. Its StartPosition property is set to CenterScreen.

» A dialog box's FormBorderStyle should be set to FixedDialog. A dialog box should not have Minimize or Maximize buttons; however, it should have a Close button.

» A form that is not a splash screen or a dialog box should always have a Minimize button and a Close button, but you can choose to disable the Maximize button. Typically, the FormBorderStyle property is set to Sizable; however, it also can be set to FixedSingle. Most times, the form's StartPosition property is set to CenterScreen.

LAYOUT AND ORGANIZATION OF THE USER INTERFACE

» Organize the user interface so that the information flows either vertically or horizontally, with the most important information always located in the upper-left corner of the screen.

» When positioning the controls, maintain a consistent margin from the edge of the form.

» Group together related controls using either white (empty) space or one of the tools from the Containers section of the toolbox.

» Use a meaningful caption for each button. Place the caption on one line and use from one to three words only. Use book title capitalization for button captions.

» Use a label to identify each text box in the user interface. Also use a label to identify other label controls that display program output. The label text should be meaningful. It also should be from one to three words only and appear on one line. Left-align the text within the label, and position the label either above or to the left of the control it identifies. Follow the label text with a colon (:) and use sentence capitalization.

» Size the buttons in a group of buttons relative to each other, and place the most commonly used button first in the group.

» Align the borders of the controls wherever possible to minimize the number of different margins used in the interface.

ADDING GRAPHICS

» Include a graphic in an interface only if it is necessary to do so. If the graphic is used solely for aesthetics, use a small graphic and place it in a location that will not distract the user.

SELECTING APPROPRIATE FONT TYPES, STYLES, AND SIZES

» Use only one font type for all of the text in the interface. For applications created for systems running Windows Vista, use the Segoe UI font. For applications created for systems running Windows XP, use the Tahoma font.

» For applications created for systems running Windows Vista, use a 9-point font for the text in an interface. For applications created for systems running Windows XP, use either a 10- or 12-point font for the text in an interface.

» Limit the number of font sizes used to either one or two.

» Avoid using italics and underlining, because these font styles make text difficult to read.

» Limit the use of bold text to titles, headings, and key items that you want to emphasize.

SELECTING APPROPRIATE COLORS

» Build the interface using black, white, and gray first, then add color only if you have a good reason to do so.

» Use white, off-white, or light gray for an application's background, and use black for the text.

» Never use a dark color for the background or a light color for the text. A dark background is hard on the eyes, and light-colored text can appear blurry.

» Limit the number of colors in an interface to three, not including white, black, and gray. The colors you choose should complement each other.

» Never use color as the only means of identification for an element in the user interface.

SETTING THE BORDERSTYLE PROPERTY OF A TEXT BOX AND LABEL

» Leave the BorderStyle property of text boxes at the default value, Fixed3D.

» Leave the BorderStyle property of labels that identify other controls at the default value, None.

» Set to FixedSingle the BorderStyle property of labels that display program output, such as those that display the result of a calculation.

» In Windows applications, a control that contains data that the user is not allowed to edit does not usually appear three-dimensional. Therefore, you should avoid setting a label control's BorderStyle property to Fixed3D.

LOCKING THE CONTROLS

» Lock the controls in place on the form.

RULES FOR ASSIGNING THE DEFAULT BUTTON

» The default button should be the button that is most often selected by the user, except in cases where the tasks performed by the button are both destructive and irreversible. The default button typically is the first button in a group of buttons.

RULES FOR ASSIGNING ACCESS KEYS
AND CONTROLLING THE FOCUS

» Assign a unique access key to each control (in the interface) that can receive user input.

» When assigning an access key to a control, use the first letter of the caption or identifying label, unless another letter provides a more meaningful association. If you can't use the first letter and no other letter provides a more meaningful association, then use a distinctive consonant. Lastly, use a vowel or a number.

» Assign a TabIndex value (begin with 0) to each control in the interface, except for controls that do not have a TabIndex property. The TabIndex values should reflect the order in which the user will want to access the controls.

» To provide keyboard access to a text box, list box, or combo box control, assign an access key to the control's identifying label. Set the identifying label's TabIndex property to a value that is one number less than the value stored in the control's TabIndex property. (In other words, the TabIndex value of the control should be one number greater than the TabIndex value of its identifying label.)

INPUTBOX FUNCTION'S PROMPT AND TITLE

» In the InputBox function, use sentence capitalization for the *prompt,* and book title capitalization for the *title.*

LABELING A GROUP BOX

» Use sentence capitalization for the optional identifying label, which is entered in the group box's Text property.

MESSAGEBOX.SHOW METHOD STANDARDS

» Use sentence capitalization for the *text* argument, but book title capitalization for the *caption* argument. The name of the application typically appears in the *caption* argument.

» Avoid using the words "error," "warning," or "mistake" in the message, as these words imply that the user has done something wrong.

» The default button in the dialog box should be the one that represents the user's most likely action, as long as that action is not destructive.

RADIO BUTTON STANDARDS

» You can use radio buttons to limit the user to one choice from a group of related but mutually exclusive choices.

» The minimum number of radio buttons in a group is two, and the recommended maximum number is seven.

» The text in a radio button's Text property should be entered using sentence capitalization.

» Assign a unique access key to each radio button in an interface.

» Use a container (such as a group box, panel, or table layout panel) to create separate groups of radio buttons.

» Only one radio button in each group of radio buttons can be selected at any one time.

» Designate a default radio button in each group of radio buttons.

CHECK BOX STANDARDS

» You can use check boxes to allow the user to select any number of choices from a group of one or more independent and nonexclusive choices.

» The text in a check box's Text property should be entered using sentence capitalization.

» Assign a unique access key to each check box in an interface.

LIST BOX STANDARDS

» A list box should contain a minimum of three selections.

» A list box should show a minimum of three selections and a maximum of eight selections at a time.

» Use a label control to provide keyboard access to a list box. Set the label's TabIndex property to a value that is one number less than the list box's TabIndex value.

» List box items are either arranged by use (with the most used entries appearing first in the list) or sorted in ascending order.

» If a list box allows the user to make only one selection, then a default item should be selected in the list box when the interface first appears. The default item should be either the most used selection or the first selection in the list. However, if a list box allows more than one selection at a time, you do not select a default item.

COMBO BOX STANDARDS

» Use a label control to provide keyboard access to a combo box. Set the label's TabIndex property to a value that is one number less than the combo box's TabIndex value.

» Combo box items are either arranged by use (with the most used entries appearing first in the list) or sorted in ascending order.

USING LINQ TO SQL

CONNECTING AN APPLICATION TO A SQL SERVER DATABASE

This appendix uses a Microsoft SQL Server database named Employees. The Employees database is stored in the Employees.mdf file, which is located in the VbReloaded2008\ AppE folder. The .mdf filename extension stands for Master Database File and indicates that the file contains a SQL Server database. The Employees database contains one table, which is named tblEmploy. Figure E-1 shows the table data displayed in a window in the IDE. The table contains seven fields and 12 records. The Emp_Number field is the primary key, because it uniquely identifies each record in the table. The Status field contains the employment status, which is either the letter F (for full-time) or the letter P (for part-time). The Code field identifies the employee's department: 1 for Accounting, 2 for Advertising, 3 for Personnel, and 4 for Inventory.

>> TIP

To open a SQL Server database table in the IDE, first connect the database to an application, then right-click the table's name in the Server Explorer window, and then click Show Table Data.

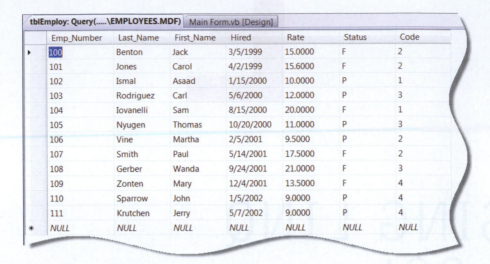

tblEmploy: Query(.....\EMPLOYEES.MDF)	Main Form.vb [Design]					
Emp_Number	Last_Name	First_Name	Hired	Rate	Status	Code
100	Benton	Jack	3/5/1999	15.0000	F	2
101	Jones	Carol	4/2/1999	15.6000	F	2
102	Ismal	Asaad	1/15/2000	10.0000	P	1
103	Rodriguez	Carl	5/6/2000	12.0000	P	3
104	Iovanelli	Sam	8/15/2000	20.0000	F	1
105	Nyugen	Thomas	10/20/2000	11.0000	P	3
106	Vine	Martha	2/5/2001	9.5000	P	2
107	Smith	Paul	5/14/2001	17.5000	F	2
108	Gerber	Wanda	9/24/2001	21.0000	F	3
109	Zonten	Mary	12/4/2001	13.5000	F	4
110	Sparrow	John	1/5/2002	9.0000	P	4
111	Krutchen	Jerry	5/7/2002	9.0000	P	4
* NULL	NULL	NULL	NULL	NULL	NULL	NULL

Figure E-1: Data contained in the tblEmploy table

Before an application can access the data stored in a SQL Server database, you need to create a connection to the database.

To create a connection to the Employees.mdf database:

1. Start Visual Studio. If necessary, close the Start Page window.

2. If necessary, open the Server Explorer window. Right-click **an empty area in the Server Explorer window**, then click **Add Connection**. The Add Connection dialog box opens.

3. If Microsoft SQL Server Database File (SqlClient) does not appear in the Data source box, click the **Change** button to open the Change Data Source dialog box, then click **Microsoft SQL Server Database File**, and then click the **OK** button to return to the Add Connection dialog box.

4. Click the **Browse** button in the Add Connection dialog box. Open the VbReloaded2008\ AppE folder, then click **Employees.mdf** in the list of filenames. Click the **Open** button. Figure E-2 shows the completed Add Connection dialog box.

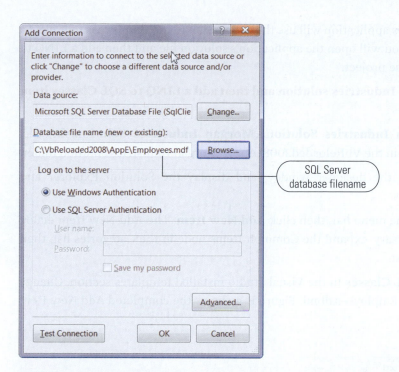

Figure E-2: Completed Add Connection dialog box

5. Click the **Test Connection** button in the Add Connection dialog box. The "Test connection succeeded." message appears in a message box. Click the **OK** button to close the message box.

6. Click the **OK** button to close the Add Connection dialog box. Employees.mdf appears in the Server Explorer window. Expand the Employees.mdf, Tables, and tblEmploy nodes. See Figure E-3.

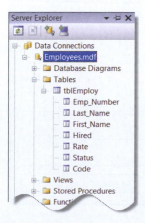

Figure E-3: Server Explorer window

The Morgan Industries application will use the connection to the Employees.mdf file. In the next set of steps, you will open the application's solution file and then add a LINQ to SQL Classes item to the project.

To open the Morgan Industries solution and then add a LINQ to SQL Classes item to the project:

1. Open the **Morgan Industries Solution** (**Morgan Industries Solution.sln**) file, which is contained in the VbReloaded2008\AppE\Morgan Industries Solution folder.

2. If necessary, open the designer window and display the Solution Explorer and Properties windows.

3. Click **Project** on the menu bar, then click **Add New Item**. The Add New Item dialog box opens. If necessary, expand the Common Items node in the Categories list, then click **Data** in the list.

4. Click **LINQ to SQL Classes** in the Visual Studio installed templates section. Change the item's name to Employees.dbml. Figure E-4 shows the completed Add New Item dialog box.

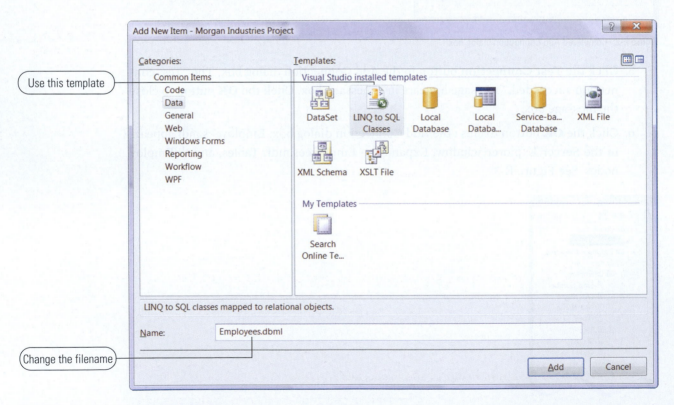

Figure E-4: Completed Add New Item dialog box

5. Click the **Add** button. The Employees.dbml window opens in the IDE, and the Employees.dbml filename is added to the Solution Explorer window. If necessary, close the Error List window. See Figure E-5.

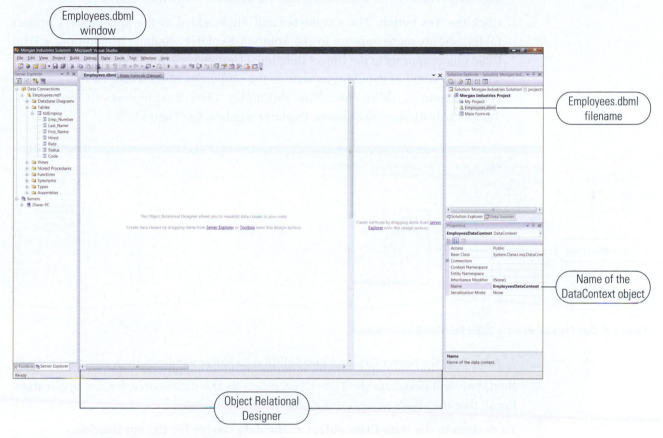

Figure E-5: Result of adding a LINQ to SQL Classes item to the project

As indicated in Figure E-5, the Employees.dbml window contains the Object Relational Designer. The designer allows you to visualize the data classes in your code. You create a data class by dragging an item from the Server Explorer or Toolbox windows to the design surface. When you add a LINQ to SQL Classes item to a project, the computer also creates a DataContext object to handle the connection to the database. The Properties window indicates that the DataContext object's name is EmployeesDataContext.

6. Auto-hide the Solution Explorer and Properties windows.

In the next set of steps, you will drag the table object from the Server Explorer window to the design surface.

To drag the table object to the Object Relational Designer window:

1. Click **tblEmploy** in the Server Explorer window, then drag the table object to the Object Relational Designer window. A message appears in a message box. The message asks whether you want to include the database file in the current project.

2. Click the **Yes** button. The Employees.mdf file is added to the application's project folder, and its name appears in the Solution Explorer window. In addition, a Data Class object appears in the Object Relational Designer window. The Data Class object shows the name of the class, as well as the properties of the class. In this case, the class's name is tblEmploy. The tblEmploy class contains seven properties. Temporarily display the Solution Explorer window. See Figure E-6.

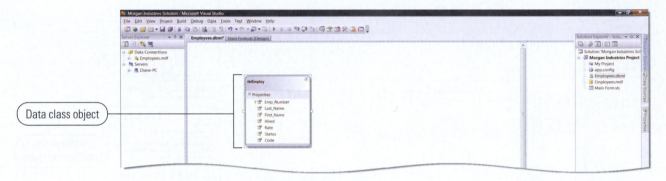

Figure E-6: Data Class object in the Object Relational Designer window

3. Auto-hide the Server Explorer and Solution Explorer windows, then save the solution.

Next, you will designate the Data Class object as the data source for the application. Recall that the class's name is tblEmploy.

To designate the Data Class object as the data source for the application:

1. Click the **Main Form.vb [Design]** tab to make the form the active window.

2. Display the Data Sources window. Click **Add New Data Source** in the Data Sources window. The Choose a Data Source Type screen appears in the Data Source Configuration Wizard dialog box.

3. Click **Object**, then click the **Next** button to display the Select the Object You Wish to Bind to screen. Expand the nodes as shown in Figure E-7, then click **tblEmploy**. (If tblEmploy does not appear in the list, click the Cancel button to close the Configuration Wizard dialog box, then save the solution and repeat Steps 2 and 3.)

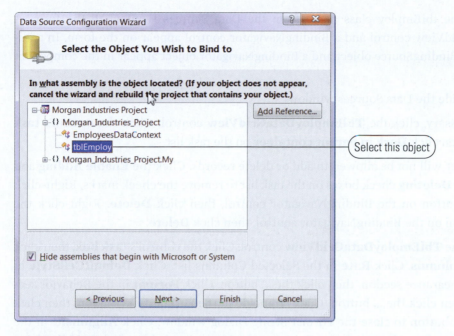

Figure E-7: Select the Object You Wish to Bind to screen

4. Click the **Next** button. The Add Object Data Source screen indicates that the tblEmploy object will be added as a data source.

5. Click the **Finish** button. The class name and the names of its properties appear in the Data Sources window. See Figure E-8.

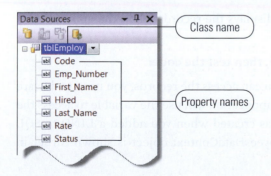

Figure E-8: Data Sources window

6. Drag the tblEmploy class name from the Data Sources window to the form. A DataGridView control and a BindingNavigator control appear on the form. In addition, a BindingSource object and a BindingNavigator object appear in the component tray.

7. Auto-hide the Data Sources window.

8. If necessary, click the **TblEmployDataGridView** control. Click the control's **task box**, then click **Dock in parent container** on the task list.

9. The user will not be allowed to add or delete records. Click the **Enable Adding** and **Enable Deleting** check boxes on the task list to remove the check marks. Right-click the + button on the BindingNavigator control, then click **Delete**. Right-click the **X** button on the BindingNavigator control, then click **Delete**.

10. Click the **TblEmployDataGridView** control. Click the control's **task box**, then click **Edit Columns**. Click **Rate** in the Selected Columns list. Click **DefaultCellStyle** in the Appearance section, then click the **...** button. Click **Format** in the Behavior section, then click the **...** button. Click **Numeric** in the Format type section, then click the **OK** button to close the Format String Dialog window. Click **Alignment** in the Layout section, then click the **down arrow** button, and then click **MiddleRight**. Click the **OK** button to close the CellStyle Builder window.

11. Click **Hired** in the Edit Columns dialog box. Click **DefaultCellStyle** in the Appearance section, then click the **...** button. Click **Alignment** in the Layout section, then click the **down arrow** button, and then click **MiddleRight**. Click the **OK** button to close the CellStyle Builder window, then click the **OK** button to close the Edit Columns dialog box.

12. Save the solution.

Finally, you will code the application so it displays the records when the application is started.

To code the form's Load event procedure, then test the code:

1. Open the Code Editor window. Before you can access the records, you need to declare an EmployeesDataContext variable. The application will use the variable to access the EmployeesDataContext object, which was created when you added a LINQ to SQL Classes item to the project. (The EmployeesDataContext object is shown earlier in Figure E-5.)

2. Click the **blank line** below Public Class MainForm, then press **Enter**. Type **Private db As New EmployeesDataContext** and press **Enter**.

3. Open the code template for the MainForm's Load event procedure. Enter the code indicated in Figure E-9.

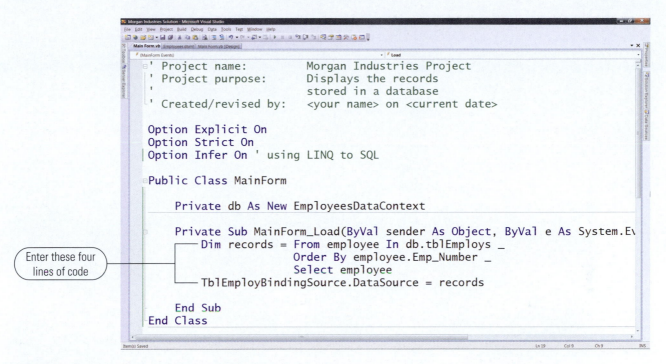

Figure E-9: Code entered in the Load event procedure

4. Save the solution, then start the application. The records appear in the DataGridView control, as shown in Figure E-10.

Emp_Number	Last_Name	First_Name	Hired	Rate	Status	Code
100	Benton	Jack	3/5/1999	15.00	F	2
101	Jones	Carol	4/2/1999	15.60	F	2
102	Ismal	Asaad	1/15/2000	10.00	P	1
103	Rodriguez	Carl	5/6/2000	12.00	P	3
104	Iovanelli	Sam	8/15/2000	20.00	F	1
105	Nyugen	Thomas	10/20/2000	11.00	P	3
106	Vine	Martha	2/5/2001	9.50	P	2
107	Smith	Paul	5/14/2001	17.50	F	2
108	Gerber	Wanda	9/24/2001	21.00	F	3
109	Zonten	Mary	12/4/2001	13.50	F	4
110	Sparrow	John	1/5/2002	9.00	P	4
111	Krutchen	Jerry	5/7/2002	9.00	P	4

Figure E-10: Records shown in the DataGridView control

5. Stop the application. Close the Code Editor window, then close the solution.

You have completed Appendix E.

GLOSSARY

Numbers in parentheses are chapter numbers.

A

Access key—the underlined character in an object's identifying label or caption; allows the user to select the object using the Alt key in combination with the underlined character (2)

Accumulator—a numeric variable used for accumulating (adding together) something (6)

Add method—the Items collection's method used to add items to a list box (6)

Aggregate method—a method that returns a single value from a group of values; LINQ provides the Average, Count, Max, Min, and Sum aggregate methods (12)

Application—another name for a program (1)

Arguments—the items within parentheses following a method's name; represent information that the programmer provides to the method (3)

Array—a group of variables that have the same name and data type and are related in some way (9)

Array.Reverse method—reverses the order of the elements in a one-dimensional array (9)

Array.Sort method—sorts the elements in a one-dimensional array in ascending order (9)

Assignment operator—the equal sign in an assignment statement (1)

Assignment statement—an instruction that assigns a value to something, such as a property of an object (1)

Attributes—the characteristics that describe an object (11)

B

Base class—the original class from which another class is derived (11)

Behaviors—includes an object's methods and events (11)

Binding—the process of connecting an object in a dataset to a control on a form (12)

BindingNavigator control—can be used to move the record pointer from one record to another in a dataset, as well as to add, delete, and save records; also can be customized to include additional functionality (12)

BindingSource object—connects a DataSet object to the bound controls on a form (12)

Block scope—the scope of a variable declared within a statement block; a variable with block scope can be used only within the statement block in which it is declared (4)

Book title capitalization—refers to capitalizing the first letter in each word, except for articles, conjunctions, and prepositions that do not occur at either the beginning or the end of the caption; button captions use this capitalization (2)

Boolean operators—another term for logical operators (4)

Bound controls—the controls connected to an object in a dataset (12)

Bug—an error in a program (3)

Button control—the control used to perform an immediate action when clicked (1)

C

Call statement—the Visual Basic statement used to invoke an independent Sub procedure in a program (8)

Camel case—the practice of lowercasing the first word in an object's name, and then uppercasing the first letter of each subsequent word in the name (1)

Cancel button—the button that can be selected by pressing the Esc key (2)

Cancel property—a property of the e parameter in the FormClosing event procedure; when set to True, it prevents the form from closing (10)

Cell—the intersection of a row and column in a DataGridView control (12)

CharacterCasing property—the text box property that indicates whether the case of the text should remain as typed or be converted to uppercase or lowercase (4)

Child table—a table linked to a parent table (12)

Class—a pattern (or blueprint) that the computer follows when creating (instantiating) an object (1, 11)

Class definition—a block of code that specifies (or defines) the appearance and behaviors of an object (1)

Class Name list box—appears in the Code Editor window and lists the names of the objects included in the user interface (1)

Class statement—the statement used to define a class in Visual Basic (11)

Clear method—a method of the Items collection; can be used to clear the contents of a list box (10)

Code—program instructions (1)

Code Editor window—the window in which you enter your application's code (1)

Collection—a group of one or more individual objects treated as one unit (6)

Combo box—a control that allows the user to select from a list of choices; also has a text field that may or may not be editable (7)

Comments—used to document a program internally; created by placing an apostrophe (') before the text you want to treat as a comment (3)

Comparison operators—operators used to compare values in a selection structure's condition; also called relational operators (4)

Computer database—an electronic file that contains an organized collection of related information (12)

Concatenation operator—the ampersand (&); used to concatenate strings together; must be preceded and followed by a space character (4)

Condition—specifies the decision you are making and must be phrased so that it results in an answer of either True or False only (4)

Const statement—the statement used to create a named constant (3)

Constructor—a method whose instructions are automatically processed each time the class instantiates an object; its purpose is to initialize the class's variables (11)

Control—an object (such as a text box or a button) displayed on a form (1)

ControlChars.NewLine constant—used to advance the insertion point to the next line in a control (4)

Convert class—contains methods that return the result of converting a value to a specified data type (3)

Copy to Output Directory property—a property of a database file; determines when and if the file is copied from the project folder to the project folder's bin\Debug folder (12)

Counter—a numeric variable used for counting something (6)

D

Data type—determines the type of data a memory location can store (3)

Data validation—the process of verifying that a program's input data is within the expected range (4)

DataGridView control—displays data in a row and columnar format (12)

Dataset—a copy of the data (database fields and records) that can be accessed by an application (12)

DataSet object—stores the information you want to access from a database (12)

Debugging—refers to the process of locating and correcting any errors in a program (3)

Default button—the button that can be selected by pressing the Enter key even when it does not have the focus (2)

Default constructor—a constructor that has no parameters (11)

Default radio button—the radio button that is automatically selected when an interface first appears (5)

DeleteFile method—a method of the FileSystem object; deletes a file while an application is running (10)

Demoted—the process of converting a value from one data type to another data type that can store only smaller numbers (3)

Derived class—a class that inherits the attributes and behaviors of a base class (11)

Dialog box—a window that supports and supplements a user's activities in a primary window (2)

Do...Loop statement—a Visual Basic statement that can be used to code both a pretest loop and a posttest loop (6)

Dot member access operator—a period; used to indicate a hierarchy of namespaces (1)

E

Encapsulates—an OOP term that means "contains" (11)

Enter event—occurs when a control receives the focus (7)

Event procedure—a set of Visual Basic instructions that tells an object how to respond to an event (1)

Events—actions to which an object can respond; examples include clicking, double-clicking, and scrolling (1, 11)

Exception—an error that occurs while an application is running (12)

Executable file—a file that can be run outside of the Visual Studio 2008 IDE (1)

Extended selection structures—refers to the If/ElseIf/Else and Case forms of the selection structure, because they have several alternatives from which to choose; also called multiple-path selection structures (5)

F

False path—contains the instructions that are processed when the selection structure's condition evaluates to False (4)

Field—a single item of information about a person, place, or thing (12)

FileExists method—a method of the FileSystem object; determines whether a file exists (10)

FileSystem object—an object used to manipulate files in Visual Basic (10)

Financial.Pmt method—used to calculate a periodic payment on a loan (7)

Flowchart—uses standardized symbols to show the steps a procedure needs to take to accomplish its goal (3)

Flowlines—the lines connecting the symbols in a flowchart (3)

Focus—when a control has the focus, it can accept user input (2)

Focus method—used to move the focus to a control while an application is running (3)

Font—the general shape of the characters used to display text (1)

For Each...Next statement—the Visual Basic statement used to code a loop whose instructions you want processed for each element in a group (9)

For...Next statement—provides a convenient way of coding a pretest loop whose instructions you want processed a precise number of times (7)

Foreign key—the field used to link a child table to a parent table (12)

Form (Windows Form object)—the foundation for the user interface in a Windows-based application (1)

Form file—a file that contains the code associated with a Windows form (1)

Formatting—specifying the number of decimal places and the special characters to display in a number (3)

FormClosing event—occurs when a form is about to be closed, which can happen as a result of the computer processing the Me.Close() statement or the user clicking the Close button on the form's title bar (10)

Function—a procedure that performs a specific task and then returns a value after completing the task; another term for a Function procedure (6, 8)

Function procedure—a procedure that returns a value after performing its assigned task (8)

G

Get block—the section of a Property procedure that contains the Get statement (11)

Get statement—appears in a Get block in a Property procedure; contains the code that allows an application to retrieve the contents of the Private variable associated with the property (11)

Group box control—used to group together related controls (2)

GUI—graphical user interface (1)

H

Handled property—a property of the KeyPress event procedure's e parameter; used to cancel the key pressed by the user (5)

I

IDE—integrated development environment (1)

If selection structure—contains only one set of instructions, which are processed when the selection structure's condition is true (4)

If/Else selection structure—contains two sets of instructions: one set is processed when the selection structure's condition is true and the other set is processed when the condition is false (4)

If...Then...Else statement—used to code the If and If/Else forms of the selection structure in Visual Basic (4)

Image.FromFile method—retrieves an image file from a computer disk while an application is running (11)

Implicit type conversion—the process by which a value is automatically converted to fit the memory location to which it is assigned (3)

Incrementing—another term for updating (6)

Independent Sub procedure—a procedure that is not associated with any specific object or event and is processed only when invoked (called) from code (8)

Index—the unique number that identifies each item in a collection; used to access an item in a list box (6)

Inheritance—the ability to create one class from another class (11)

Initializing—assign a beginning value to a variable, such as a counter variable or an accumulator variable (6)

Input files—files from which applications read information (10)

Input/output symbol—the parallelogram in a flowchart; used to represent input and output tasks (3)

InputBox function—a Visual Basic function that displays a dialog box containing a message, OK and Cancel buttons, and an input area (6)

Instance—an object created from a class (11)

Instantiated—the process of creating an object from a class (11)

Integer division operator—represented by a backslash (\); divides two integers, and then returns the quotient as an integer (3)

Integrated development environment (IDE)—an environment that contains all of the tools and features you need to create, run, and test your programs (1)

Invalid data—data that the application is not expecting the user to enter (3)

Items collection—the collection composed of the items in a list box (6)

K

KeyChar property—a property of the KeyPress event procedure's e parameter; stores the character associated with the key pressed by the user (5)

KeyPress event—occurs each time the user presses a key while the control has the focus (5)

Keyword—a word that has a special meaning in a programming language (1)

L

Label control—the control used to display text that the user is not allowed to edit while the application is running (1)

Language Integrated Query—LINQ; the new query language in Visual Basic 2008 (12)

Lifetime—indicates how long a variable or named constant remains in the computer's internal memory (3)

Line continuation character—the underscore (_); used to break up a long instruction into two or more physical lines in the Code Editor window (3)

LINQ—Language Integrated Query (12)

List box—a control used to display a list of choices from which the user can select zero choices, one choice, or more than one choice (6)

Literal constant—an item of data whose value does not change while an application is running (3)

Literal type character—a character (such as the letter D) appended to a literal constant for the purpose of forcing the literal constant to assume a different data type (such as Decimal) (3)

Load event—the event that occurs when an application is started and the form is displayed the first time (6)

Logic error—occurs when you enter an instruction that is syntactically correct, but does not give you the expected results, or when you neglect to enter an instruction or enter the instructions in the wrong order (3)

Logical operators—the operators used to combine two or more conditions into one compound condition; also called Boolean operators (4)

Loop—another term for the repetition structure (6)

M

MaxLength property—the text box property that specifies the maximum number of characters that can be entered in a text box (4)

Member variables—the variables contained in a structure (10)

MessageBox.Show method—displays a message box that contains text, one or more buttons, and an icon; allows the application to communicate with the user as it is running (5)

Method—a predefined Visual Basic procedure that you can call (or invoke) when needed; performs a task for the class in which it is defined (1, 3)

Method Name list box—appears in the Code Editor window and lists the events to which the selected object is capable of responding (1)

Methods—the actions that an object is capable of performing (11)

Module scope—the scope of a module-level variable; refers to the fact that the variable can be used by any procedure in the form (3)

Module-level variable—a variable that is declared in the form's Declarations section; the variable has module scope (3)

Modulus operator—represented by the keyword Mod; divides two numbers and then returns the remainder (3)

Multiple-path selection structures—another term for extended selection structures (5)

My feature—a Visual Basic feature that exposes a set of commonly used objects to the programmer (10)

N

Named constant—a computer memory location whose contents cannot be changed while the application is running; created using the Const statement (3)

Namespace—a block of memory cells inside the computer; contains the code that defines a group of related classes (1)

Nested selection structure—a selection structure contained in either the true or false path of another selection structure (5)

O

Object—in object-oriented programming, anything that can be seen, touched, or used (1)

Object box—the section of the Properties window that contains the name of the selected object (1)

Object-oriented programming language—a language that allows the programmer to use objects to accomplish a program's goal (1)

One-dimensional array—an array whose elements are identified by a unique number (subscript) (9)

OOP—an acronym for Object-Oriented Programming (11)

Output files—files to which applications write information (10)

Overloaded methods—methods that have the same name but different *parameterLists* (11)

P

Panel control—used to group together related controls (2)

Parallel arrays—two or more arrays whose elements are related by their subscript (position) in the arrays (9)

Parameterized constructors—constructors that contain parameters (11)

Parameters—the memory locations listed in a procedure header (8)

Parent table—a table linked to a child table (12)

Parse—the process of separating something into its component parts (10)

Pascal case—the practice of uppercasing the first letter in a form's name, as well as the first letter of each subsequent word in the name (1)

Passing by reference—the process of passing a variable's address to a procedure (8)

Passing by value—the process of passing a variable's contents to a procedure (8)

Picture box control—the control used to display an image on a form (1)

Point—used to measure font size; 1/72 of an inch (1)

Populating the array—refers to the process of assigning the initial values to an array (9)

Position property—a property of a BindingSource object; stores the position of the record pointer (12)

Posttest loop—a loop whose condition is evaluated *after* the instructions within the loop are processed (6)

Pretest loop—a loop whose condition is evaluated *before* the instructions within the loop are processed (6)

Primary decision—when a selection structure is nested within another selection structure, the primary decision is made by the outer selection structure and determines whether the nested selection structure is processed (5)

Primary key—the field that uniquely identifies each record in a table (12)

Primary window—the window in which the primary viewing and editing of your application's data takes place (2)

Priming read—the input instruction that appears above the loop that it controls; determines whether the loop instructions will be processed the first time (6)

Procedure—a block of program code that performs a specific task (8)

Procedure footer—the last line in a code template (1)

Procedure header—the first line in a code template (1)

Procedure scope—the scope of a procedure-level variable; refers to the fact that the variable can be used only by the procedure in which it is declared (3)

Procedure-level variable—a variable that is declared in a procedure; the variable has procedure scope (3)

Process symbol—the rectangle symbol in a flowchart; used to represent assignment and calculation tasks (3)

Programmers—the people who write programs (1)

Programming languages—the languages that programmers use to communicate with the computer (1)

Programs—the directions given to computers (1)

Project—a container that stores files associated with only a specific piece of a solution (1)

Promoted—the process of converting a value from one data type to another data type that can store larger numbers (3)

Properties—the attributes of an object that control the object's appearance and behavior (1)

Properties list—the section of the Properties window that lists the names of the properties associated with the selected object, as well as each property's value (1)

Properties window—the window that lists an object's attributes (properties) (1)

Property procedure—creates a Public property that can be used to access a Private variable in a class (11)

Pseudocode—uses phrases to describe the steps a procedure needs to take to accomplish its goal (3)

Pseudo-random number generator—used to generate random numbers in Visual Basic (4)

Q

Query—specifies the records to select in a dataset, as well as the order in which to arrange the records (12)

R

Radio button—used in an interface to limit the user to one choice from a group of related but mutually exclusive choices (5)

Random.Next method—used to generate a random integer that is greater than or equal to a minimum value, but less than a maximum value (4)

ReadAllText method—a method of the FileSystem object; reads the text contained in a sequential access file (10)

Record—a group of related fields that contain all of the necessary data about a specific person, place, or thing (12)

Refresh method—used to refresh (redraw) a form (6)

Relational database—a database that stores information in tables composed of columns (fields) and rows (records) (12)

Relational operators—another term for comparison operators (4)

Repetition structure—one of the three programming structures; used to repeatedly process one or more program instructions until some condition is met, at which time the repetition structure ends; also called a loop (6)

Return statement—the Visual Basic statement that returns a function's value to the statement that invoked the function (8)

S

Scalar variable—another term for a simple variable (9)

Scope—indicates where in the application's code a variable or named constant can be used (3)

Secondary decision—when a selection structure is nested within another selection structure, the secondary decision is made by the inner selection structure (5)

Select Case statement—used in Visual Basic to code the Case selection structure (5)

SelectAll method—used to select all of the text contained in a text box (7)

SelectedIndexChanged event—an event that occurs when an item is selected in a list box (6)

SelectedValueChanged event—an event that occurs when an item is selected in a list box (6)

Selection structure—one of the three programming structures; tells the computer to make a decision or comparison, and then select the appropriate path based on the result; also called the decision structure (4)

Selection/repetition symbol—the diamond in a flowchart (4)

Sentence capitalization—refers to capitalizing only the first letter in the first word and in any words that are customarily capitalized; identifying labels use this capitalization (2)

Sequence structure (sequential processing)—refers to the fact that the computer processes a procedure's instructions one after another in the order in which they appear in the procedure (1)

Sequential access file—a file composed of lines of text that are both stored and retrieved sequentially; also called a text file (10)

Sequential processing (sequence structure)—refers to the fact that the computer processes a procedure's instructions one after another in the order in which they appear in the procedure (1)

Set block—the section of a Property procedure that contains the Set statement (11)

Set statement—appears in a Set block in a Property procedure; contains the code that allows an application to assign a value to the Private variable associated with the property (11)

Settings box—the right column of the Properties list; displays the current value (setting) of each of the properties (1)

Short-circuit evaluation—refers to the fact that the AndAlso and OrElse operators do not always evaluate the second condition in a compound condition (4)

Signature—a method name combined with its *parameterList* (11)

Simple variable—a variable that is unrelated to any other variable in the computer's internal memory; also called a scalar variable (9)

Sleep method—used to delay program execution (6)

Solution—a container that stores the projects and files for an entire application (1)

Solution Explorer window—the window that displays a list of the projects contained in the current solution, and the items contained in each project (1)

Sorting—arranging data in a specific order (9)

Source file—a file that contains code (1)

Start/stop symbol—the oval symbol in a flowchart; used to mark the beginning and end of the flowchart (3)

Startup form—the form that appears automatically when an application is started (1)

Statement block—in a selection structure, the set of statements terminated by an Else or End If clause (4)

Static variable—a special type of procedure-level variable that remains in memory and retains its value even when the procedure ends (3)

String—zero or more characters enclosed in quotation marks (1)

String manipulation—refers to the processing of strings; the string manipulation techniques are listed in Figure 7-50 (7)

Strings.Space method—can be used to write a specific number of spaces to a file (10)

Structures—user-defined data types created using the Structure statement (10)

Structure statement—the statement used to create user-defined data types (structures) in Visual Basic (10)

Structure variables—variables declared using a structure (user-defined data type) (10)

Sub procedure—a block of code that performs a specific task; a procedure that does not return a value after performing its assigned task (1, 8)

Subscript—an integer that indicates the position of an element in an array (9)

Syntax—the rules of a programming language (1)

Syntax error—occurs when an instruction violates a programming language's syntax; usually a result of typing errors that occur when entering instructions (3)

T

Table—a group of related records (12)

Table layout panel control—used to group together related controls (2)

TableAdapter object—connects a database to a DataSet object (12)

TableAdapterManager object—handles saving data to multiple tables in a dataset (12)

Text box control—gives the user an area in which to enter data (2)

Text file—another term for a sequential access file (10)

TextChanged event—occurs when a change is made to the contents of a control's Text property (7)

Timer control—the control used to process code at one or more regular intervals (8)

ToLower method—temporarily converts a string to lowercase (4)

Toolbox—Toolbox window (1)

Toolbox window (toolbox)—the window that contains the tools used when creating an interface; each tool represents a class (1)

ToUpper method—temporarily converts a string to uppercase (4)

True path—contains the instructions that are processed when the selection structure's condition evaluates to True (4)

Truth tables—summarize how the computer evaluates the logical operators in an expression (4)

TryCast operator—used to convert an Object variable to a different data type (8)

TryParse method—used to convert a string to a number (3)

Two-dimensional array—an array whose elements are identified by a unique combination of two numbers: a row subscript and a column subscript (9)

U

Unicode—the universal coding scheme that assigns a unique number to each character in the written languages of the world (3)

Updating—adding a number to the value stored in a counter or accumulator variable; also called incrementing (6)

User interface—what you see and interact with when using an application (1)

User-defined data types—the data types created using the Structure statement; also called structures (10)

V

Valid data—data that the application is expecting the user to enter (3)

Variables—computer memory locations where programmers can temporarily store data, and also change the data, while an application is running (3)

W

Web-based application—an application that has a Web user interface and runs on a server (1)

Windows-based application—an application that has a Windows user interface and runs on a desktop computer (1)

Windows Form Designer window—the window in which you create your application's GUI (1)

Windows Form object (**form**)—the foundation for the user interface in a Windows-based application (1)

WriteAllText method—a method of the FileSystem object; writes text to a sequential access file (10)

INDEX